# STATISTICAL INFERENCE
# Testing of Hypotheses

**Manoj Kr. Srivastava**
Associate Professor, Department of Statistics
Institute of Social Sciences
Dr. B.R. Ambedkar University
Agra

**Namita Srivastava**
Associate Professor, Department of Statistics
St. John's College
Agra

AF650976

**PHI Learning Private Limited**
Delhi-110092
2025

*In fond memory of **Shri Asoke K. Ghosh** (October 1942 – February 2024), Founder Chairman and Managing Director of PHI Learning, whose vision endlessly inspires.*

*The Legacy Continues....*

Published by Pushpita Ghosh, PHI Learning Private Limited, Rimjhim House, 111, Patparganj Industrial Estate, Delhi-110092 and Printed by Syndicate Binders, A-20, Hosiery Complex, Noida, Phase-II Extension, Noida-201305 (N.C.R. Delhi).

**₹850.00**

**STATISTICAL INFERENCE: TESTING OF HYPOTHESES**
Manoj Kumar Srivastava and Namita Srivastava

© 2025 by PHI Learning Private Limited, Delhi.

All right reserved. This publication is protected by copyright and may not be reproduced, in whole or in part, in any form or by any electronic, mechanical, or other means, now known or hereafter invented, including photocopying, recording, or any information storage and retrieval system, OR to train artificial intelligence systems without permission in writing from the publisher.

**ISBN-978-81-203-3728-2 (Print Book)**
**ISBN-978-93-5443-785-4 (e-Book)**

The export rights of the book are vested solely with the publisher.

# Contents

# Preface

During our teaching at master's level we realized the need of a book for a core paper on testing of hypotheses, which could cover most of the syllabi of undergraduate and postgraduate courses, and competitive examinations, prescribed by different Universities. We felt that the students require a book which is solely dedicated to testing of hypothesis syllabi, emphasizing on concept building, detailing of proofs to main theorems, their real-life applications, and critical and analytical remarks to explain and develop more insight of the subject. The book has been written to serve these academic requirements of the students.

The text is full semester course on Testing of Hypotheses and non-parametric tests. Chapter 1 of the book assumes knowledge of measure theory and mathematical analysis elaborately.

The questions are framed according to the master's level syllabi of various Indian universities, I.A.S., I.S.S., UGC-NET. The book provides a sufficient number of examples along with the applications of different theorems and results at the end of each chapter. The problems discussed are of varied nature at different levels of difficulty. It is for this reason the book would prove beneficial for those who are preparing for any of the competitive examinations.

Chapter 2 explains the concepts and definitions on decision theoretic setup for hypothesis testing while giving the genesis and proof of Neyman and Pearson lemma. A large number of important application exercises have been given at the end of this chapter.

Chapter 3 deals with treatments given to one-sided problems by Karlin and Rubin (1956) by way of characterizing Polya type-3 family of distributions. Uniformly Most Powerful (UMP) tests, both for Regular and Pitman family, have also been derived with some interesting and critical remarks. A large number of applications are given in support of these theorems.

UMP and UMP unbiased tests were derived for two-sided testing problems in Chapter 4. Further, the class of two-sided tests has been shown to be essentially complete in the decision theoretic setup when a reasonable restriction of unbiasedness was applied to the class of level-$\alpha$ tests that led to the existence of UMP tests.

Multiparameter testing problems have been discussed in Chapter 5 through similar regions having Neyman structure that reduces composite hypotheses involving nuisance parameters to simple and familiar problems. The theory develops through eliminating nuisance parameters from the distribution of complete sufficient statistic $\boldsymbol{T}$ in $k$ parameter exponential family. We have indicated the difficulty arising in calculating the conditional null distribution of the test statistic arrived at for various applications under this approach. To circumvent this problem, unconditional tests in terms of an ancillary statistic- $V$, involving an unconditional distribution, obtained through Basu's theorem, have also been discussed. Every illustration includes conditional and unconditional approaches, giving exposure to the students as to how UMP unbiased test can be calculated in different problems.

Chapter 6 deals with the reduction of testing problems through the principle of invariance enabling the existence of UMP invariant test.

Chapter 7 discusses the time honoured principle of likelihood ratio criteria as an alternative approach towards solving multiparameter testing problems, when the distribution is not among the one type required by Karlin and Rubin, Lehmann and Scheffe among others for the theoretical developments on UMP and UMP unbiased tests. The difficulties in finding out the null distribution of likelihood ratio tests and lack of their small sample statistical properties have also been discussed.

Chapter 8 develops the equivalence of UMP size-$\alpha$ acceptance region to the uniformly most accurate $(1-\alpha)$ level of confidence sets. The chapter also explains that UMP unbiased size-$\alpha$ test gives uniformly most accurate unbiased confidence interval that minimizes the expected length of the unbiased confidence sets. Pratt and Guenther's approach has been followed to this effect.

Chapter 9 discusses the origin and need of non-parametric tests under some general assumptions on the parent population. The criterion of asymptotic relative efficiency for judging the relative performance of a non-parametric test with its counter-part parametric test has also been discussed in detail.

A univariate single sample problem of location has been discussed in Chapter 10. Chi-square and Kolmogorov-Smirnov Test for goodness-of-fit has been discussed along with their large sample properties. One-sided and two-sided sign-test with underlying assumptions has also been discussed and has been shown to be UMP and UMP unbiased, respectively. Case of discontinuous population or tied observations has also been discussed along with necessary modifications on the tests. Rank order statistics discusses Wilcoxon-Signed-Rank Test (1945) as an improvement over sign-test by using distance information between the observations while compromising on additional restriction of symmetry, imposed on the parent population. The chapter also discusses performance criterion for judging the relative performance of these tests with their counterpart parametric tests.

Chapter 11 deals with univariate two-sample problem of location and five standard senses of alternatives. Fraser's (1953, 65) approach of data summarization to the principle of invariance leading to many known two-sample tests (e.g. Wilcoxon-Mann-Whitney Test and $U$-statistic) with their statistical properties and their applications has been discussed. Hoffding-Lehmann and Wold-Wolfovitz central limit theorems have been stated to study large sample properties of these tests. Normal score test and Kolmogorov-Smirnov test have been discussed with their asymptotic properties using Chernoff and Savage (Annals-1958) central limit theorem. The chapter concludes with Mood test for two-sample problem of scale.

Chapter 12 contributes to the study of relationship between the two variables in bivariate population. Kendall's measure of association tau-$\tau$ has been discussed in detail. Chi-square test for independence in contingency table is explained along with its asymptotic properties.

The non-parametric section is largely based on lectures given by our respected teacher late Sri M.P. Gautam at the Institute of Social Sciences, Agra. We are thankful to our teacher Prof. D.D. Joshi, who has always shown us the path of knowledge. We are thankful to Prof. S.V. Pande, Director, Institute of Social Sciences, Agra, for providing us all kinds of support and encouragement during the preparation of this book.

We are equally thankful to Prof. A.H. Khan, Aligarh Muslim University, for critical reading of the manuscript and comments that resulted in many improvements. We also acknowledge the suggestions and comments of Prof. Girdhar Gopal, Lucknow University, and Prof. S.K. Upadhyay, Banaras Hindu University, which helped us to improve our book thoroughly.

**Manoj Kr. Srivastava**
**Namita Srivastava**

# Chapter 1

# Probability Background

## 1.1 INTRODUCTION

The study of statistical inference requires conceptual and foundational background of probability and integration. These concepts have been discussed in this chapter to provide a better understanding of the problems in hypothesis testing. The discussed results are brief in nature.

We shall begin with some basic definitions on measure theory.

**Definition 1.1.1.** (**Field**) A non-empty class $\mathcal{C}$ of subsets of a given non-empty set $\mathcal{L}$ is called a field of subsets of $\mathcal{L}$ if

(a) $\mathcal{C}$ is closed under finite unions, i.e.

$$C_1 \in \mathcal{C}, C_2 \in \mathcal{C} \Rightarrow C_1 \cup C_2 \in \mathcal{C}$$

(b) $\mathcal{C}$ is closed under complementation, i.e.

$$C \in \mathcal{C} \Rightarrow C^c \in \mathcal{C}$$

The intersection of an arbitrary collection of fields of subsets of a given set is again a field.

**Definition 1.1.2.** (**Field Generated by a Class** $\mathcal{A}$) Given a class $\mathcal{A}$ of subsets of a non-empty set $\mathcal{L}$, the smallest field of subsets of $\mathcal{L}$ containing $\mathcal{A}$ is called the field generated by $\mathcal{A}$ and denoted by $\mathcal{C}(\mathcal{A})$.

$\mathcal{C}(\mathcal{A})$ is unique and given $\mathcal{L}$ and a class $\mathcal{A}$ of subsets of $\mathcal{L}$, $\mathcal{C}(\mathcal{A}) = \cap_\alpha \mathcal{C}_\alpha$ where $\{\mathcal{C}_\alpha\}$ is the class of all fields of subsets of $\mathcal{L}$ each containing $\mathcal{A}$.

**Definition 1.1.3.** (**$\sigma$-field**) A field $\mathcal{D}$ of subsets of a given set $\mathcal{L}$ is called a sigma field ( $\sigma$-field) if it is closed under countable unions and complementation, i.e.

(a) $\mathcal{D}$ is a non-empty class.

(b) $\mathcal{D}$ is closed under countable unions, i.e.

$$D_1, D_2, \ldots \in \mathcal{D} \Rightarrow \bigcup_{i=1}^{\infty} D_i \in \mathcal{D}$$

(c) $\mathcal{D}$ is closed under complementation

$$D \in \mathcal{D} \Rightarrow D^c \in \mathcal{D}$$

A $\sigma$-field is a field, but every field is not a $\sigma$-field. Given set $\mathcal{L}$, the smallest $\sigma$-field is $(\phi, \mathcal{L})$, whereas the largest $\sigma$-field is the class of all subsets of $\mathcal{L}$.

**Definition 1.1.4.** (**$\sigma$-field Generated by a Class of Sets $\mathcal{A}$**) Given a non-empty class of sets $\mathcal{A}$, the smallest $\sigma$-field of subsets of $\mathcal{L}$ containing $\mathcal{A}$ is called the $\sigma$-field generated by $\mathcal{A}$ and it is denoted by $\sigma(\mathcal{A})$.

The intersection of an arbitrary collection of $\sigma$-fields is again a $\sigma$-field and that given a non-empty class of sets $\mathcal{A}$, the $\sigma$-field generated by $\mathcal{A}$, $\sigma(\mathcal{A})$, is the intersection of all $\sigma$-fields containing $\mathcal{A}$.

Let us consider $\sigma$-fields in Euclidean spaces, $\mathbb{R}^1$(the real line), $\mathbb{R}^2$(the real plane), and more generally in $\mathbb{R}^n$(the n-dimensional plane). Define a class of half-open intervals $(c,\ d]$ in $\mathbb{R}^1$, denoted by $\mathcal{I}$.

$$\mathcal{I} = \{(c, d] : \ c < d, \ c, \ d \in \mathbb{R}^1\}$$

**Definition 1.1.5.** (**Borel Field**) A $\sigma$-field generated by $\mathcal{I}$ is called a Borel field $\sigma(\mathcal{I})$ in $\mathbb{R}^1$. The sets belong to $\sigma(\mathcal{I})$ are called the Borel sets of $\mathbb{R}^1$.

It is important to note the following:

(a) All single point sets in $\mathbb{R}^1$ are Borel sets.
(b) Open, semi-open and closed intervals of type $(c, d)$, $(c, d]$ and $[c, d]$ are all Borel sets.
(c) Finite sets and countable sets in $\mathbb{R}^1$ are all Borel sets.

The class of all Borel sets in $\mathbb{R}^1$ is a very general class that includes almost all the standard sets in $\mathbb{R}^1$ known to us. These may be finite or infinite intervals, open sets, closed sets, compact sets, sets of rational and irrational numbers and atmost countable sets.

**Definition 1.1.6.** Let $\mathcal{I}^n$ be the class of half-open rectangles in $\mathbb{R}^n$ denoted by

$$\mathcal{I}^n = \{(x_1, x_2, \ldots, x_n) \ : \ x_i \in (a_i, b_i], \ i = 1, \ldots, n\}$$

The $\sigma$-field generated by $\mathcal{I}^n$ is called the Borel field of subsets of $\mathbb{R}^n$, denoted by $\sigma(\mathcal{I}^n)$. Sets belonging to $\sigma(\mathcal{I}^n)$ are called Borel sets of $\mathbb{R}^n$.

**Definition 1.1.7.** (**Set Function**) A mapping $\mu$ on a given non-empty class of sets $\mathcal{A}$ is called a set function if it associates to every set $C$ in $\mathcal{A}$ a unique point $x_0$ in the extended real line $\mathbb{R}^+$. Symbolically, it is denoted by $\mu : \mathcal{A} \rightarrow \mathbb{R}^+$ and $\exists$ a $x_0$ in $\mathbb{R}^+$ s.t. $\mu(C) = x_0$ for every $C \in \mathcal{A}$.

**Definition 1.1.8.** An extended real valued set function $\mu : \mathcal{A} \to \mathbb{R}^+$ is said to be

(a) Non-negative (not necessarily finite) if

$$\mu(A_i) \geq 0 \qquad \forall\ A_i \in \mathcal{A}$$

(b) Finitely additive if, whenever $A_1, A_2 \in \mathcal{A}$, $A_1 \cup A_2 \in \mathcal{A}$ and $A_1 \cap A_2 = 0$ then

$$\mu(A_1 \cup A_2) = \mu(A_1) + \mu(A_2)$$

(c) Countably additive or $\sigma$-additive if, for every finite, disjoint sequence of sets $\{A_i\}$ in $\mathcal{A}$ whose union is also in $\mathcal{A}$ we have

$$\mu(\bigcup_{i=1}^{\infty} A_i) = \sum_{i=1}^{\infty} \mu(A_i)$$

**Definition 1.1.9.** **(Measure Space)** Let $\mathcal{C}$ be a $\sigma$-field of subsets of a given set $\mathcal{L}$. A non-negative countably additive set function $\mu$ defined on $\mathcal{C}$ such that $\mu(\phi) = 0$, is called a measure. The triplet $(\mathcal{L}, \mathcal{C}, \mu)$ is called the measure space, $\mathcal{C}$ is called the power of the measure space $(\mathcal{L}, \mathcal{C}, \mu)$.

**Definition 1.1.10.** A measure $\mu$ on a $\sigma$-field $\mathcal{C}$ of subsets of a given set $\mathcal{L}$ is said to be

(a) *Finite* if $\mu(A) < \infty\ \forall\ A \in \mathcal{C}$ and *totally finite* if $\mu(\mathcal{L}) < \infty$.

(b) *$\sigma$-finite* if for every set $A$ in $\mathcal{C}$, there exists a sequence of sets $\{A_i\}$, in $\mathcal{C}$ such that $A \subset \cup A_i$ and $\mu(A_i) < \infty\ \ \forall\ i$. Further, $\mu$ as *totally $\sigma$-finite* if $A = \cup_{i=1}^{\infty} A_i$.

(c) *Infinite* if $\mu(\mathcal{L}) = \infty$.

(d) *Probability measure* (normed measure) denoted by $P$, if $\mu(\mathcal{L}) = 1$.

### Measure as an extension of a set function

Let a non-negative additive function $\nu$ be defined on some general class of sets $\mathcal{A}$. Consider a class of sets $\mathcal{C}$ that contains $\mathcal{A}$ as its subclass. If one constructs a measure $\mu$ on $\mathcal{C}$ so that it agrees with the initial set function $\nu$ (on $\mathcal{A}$), that is,

$$\mu(A) = \nu(A) \quad \forall\ A \in \mathcal{A}$$

$\mu$ is called extension of a given set function $\nu$. Further, if $\mathcal{C}$ is a $\sigma$-field containing $\mathcal{A}$ and if there exists a measure $\mu$ on $\mathcal{C}$ that agrees with $\nu$ on $\mathcal{A}$, we say that the set function $\nu$ has been extended to a measure $\mu$ on $\mathcal{C}$. And if $\mu$ is the only extension of $\nu$, it is stated that the extension has been determined.

The extension theorem due to Caratheodery is stated as follows:

**Theorem 1.1.1.** *A measure $\nu$ on a field $\mathcal{A}$ can be extended to a measure on $\sigma$-field $\mathcal{C}$ generated by $\mathcal{A}$. Moreover, the extension measure on $\mathcal{C}$ is $\sigma$-finite if the basis measure $\nu$ is $\sigma$-finite.*

**Completion of $\sigma$-field with respect to a measure $\mu$**

**Theorem 1.1.2.** *Consider a $\sigma$-field $\mathcal{C}$ and a measure $\mu$ defined on $\mathcal{C}$. Define a class $\mathcal{C}_\mu$ and a set function $\mu'$ as*

$$\mathcal{C}_\mu = \{C \cup F \,:\, C \in \mathcal{C},\ F \subset N,\ \mu(N) = 0\} \tag{1.1}$$

*and*

$$\mu'(C \cup F) = \mu(C) \tag{1.2}$$

*when $C \in \mathcal{C}$ and $F$ is any arbitrary subset of the $\mu$-null set $N$. Then $\mathcal{C}_\mu$ is a $\sigma$-field and $\mu'$ on $\mathcal{C}_\mu$ is an extension of $\mu$. Here, $\mathcal{C}_\mu$ is called the completion of $\mathcal{C}$ relative to $\mu$ and $\mu'$ a complete measure.*

### 1.1.1 Lebesgue-Stieltjes Measure

Stieltjes and Lebesgue have given generalizations of the classical theory of mathematical analysis known as modern mathematical theory. In their developments they discussed how unique measures are constructed from certain types of point functions namely distribution functions. As a result a well known Lebesgue-Radon correspondence theorem has been stated to show a one-to-one correspondence between the class of distribution functions and the class of Lebesgue-Stieltjes measures. Some main definitions and results have been discussed here to explain the idea.

**Definition 1.1.11.** A point function $F : \mathbb{R}^1 \to \mathbb{R}^1$, non-decreasing and right continuous everywhere, is known as distribution function.

In addition to it if $0 \le F(x) \le 1$ for all real $x$, $F$ is called *probability distribution function.*

**Theorem 1.1.3.** *Consider a distribution function $F$ and a class of intervals*

$$\mathcal{I} = \{(a, b] \,:\, -\infty < a < b < \infty\}$$

*A set function $\nu$ on $\mathcal{I}$, defined as*

$$\nu(a, b] = F(b) - F(a)$$

*can be extended uniquely to a measure $\mu'$ on the Borel field $\mathcal{B}$ of $\mathbb{R}^1$.*

Consider the completion $\mathcal{B}_{\mu'}$ of $\mathcal{B}$ relative to $\mu'$, the increment function $\nu$ defined as above could be extended uniquely to a complete measure $\mu^*$ on the completion $\mathcal{B}_{\mu'}$.

The measure $\mu'$ on the Borel field $\mathcal{B}$ in $\mathbb{R}^1$, which has been obtained as an unique extension of the set function $\nu$, is called the measure induced by the distribution function (d.f.) $F$ and usually referred to as *induced measure.* Given the distribution function $F$ and set function $\nu$ the completion measure $\mu^*$ on the completion $\mathcal{B}_{\mu'}$ is called *Lebesgue-Stieltjes measure* and $\mathcal{B}_{\mu'}$ is called the *Lebesgue-Stieltjes field* in $\mathbb{R}^1$.

**Lebesgue measure in $\mathbb{R}^1$**

If distribution function $F$ is the identity transformation $F(x) = x$, the set function $\nu$, defined in Theorem 1.1.3, becomes

$$\nu(a, b] = b - a$$

which is the length of an interval in $\mathbb{R}^1$ and volume in $\mathbb{R}^n$, the corresponding completion, $\mathcal{B}_{\mu'}$, is called the *Lebesgue field in* $\mathcal{R}^1$ and the complete measure $\mu^*$ is called the *Lebesgue measure.*

**Lebesgue measure in $\mathbb{R}^n$**

If one considers the class of all generalized half-open rectangles of the form

$$R = \{(x_1, x_2, \ldots, x_n) \; : \; x_i \in (a_i, b_i] \; i = 1, 2, \ldots, n\}$$

and a $\sigma$-field generated by $R$, $\sigma(R)$ is called *Borel field* of subsets of $\mathbb{R}^n$ or *Borel field in* $\mathbb{R}^n$, one could easily extend the completion procedure leading to Lebesgue field and Lebesgue measure on the obtained Lebesgue field from $\mathbb{R}^1$ to $\mathbb{R}^n$.

We shall now define a function $f$ on an abstract measure space $(\mathcal{L},\ \mathcal{B},\ \mu)$ into the real line $\mathbb{R}^1$. This extends the original measure space into a new measure space on $\mathbb{R}^1$.

**Definition 1.1.12.** (**Random Variable**) A function $f$ on a given measure space $(\mathcal{L},\ \mathcal{B}, \mu)$ is said to be $\mathcal{B}$*-measurable* if the set $\{L \in \mathcal{L} \text{ s.t. } f(L) < c\} \in \mathcal{B}$ for all $c$ in $\mathbb{R}^1$. If $\mu(\mathcal{L}) = 1$ (if the measure is a normed measure), a $\mathcal{B}$-measurable function on $\mathcal{L}$ will be called a *random variable* written as r.v.

**Definition 1.1.13.** (**Borel Measurable Function**) A function $f : \mathbb{R}^1 \to \mathbb{R}^1$ is called a Borel measurable function (or simply Borel measurable) if $f^{-1}(B)$ is a Borel set for every Borel set $B$ in $\mathbb{R}^1$.

## 1.1.2 Positive and Negative Parts of a Function $f$

The positive and negative parts of a real valued function $f$ on $\mathcal{L}$ [of a measure space $(\mathcal{L},\ \mathcal{C},\ \mu)$] is defined as

$f^+(x) = \max\{f(x), 0\}$ and $f^-(x) = \max\{-f(x), 0\}$. We may express $f$ as

$$f(x) = f^+(x) - f^-(x)$$

It is shown that a real valued function $f$ on the measure space $(\mathcal{L},\ \mathcal{C},\ \mu)$ is measurable if and only if $f^+(x)$ and $f^-(x)$ are measurable.

If $\{f_n\}$ is a sequence of measurable functions on the measure space $(\mathcal{L},\ \mathcal{C},\ \mu)$, then $\sup f_n, \inf f_n, \limsup f_n$ and $\liminf f_n$ are also measurable functions.

**Definition 1.1.14. (Indicator Function)** For a given set $A$ in $\mathcal{L}$, the indicator function $I_A$ of $A$ is defined as

$$I_A(x) = \begin{cases} 1 & \text{if } x \in A \\ 0 & \text{if } x \in A^c \end{cases} \tag{1.3}$$

The set $\mathcal{L}$ is referred to as *reference set*.

**Theorem 1.1.4. (Measurable Indicator Function)** *Indicator function $I_A$ of a set $A \subset \mathcal{L}$, $\mathcal{L}$ from the given measure space $(\mathcal{L}, \mathcal{C}, \mu)$, is measurable if and only if $A \in \mathcal{C}$.*

**Definition 1.1.15. (Simple Function)** A function $f$ defined on a measurable space $\mathcal{L}$, is called *simple function* if there is a finite disjoint class $\{A_1, A_2, \ldots, A_m\}$ of measurable sets and a finite set $\{d_1, d_2, \ldots, d_m\}$ of real numbers such that

$$I_{A_i}(x) = \begin{cases} d_i & \text{if } x \in A_i,\ i = 1, \ldots, n \\ 0 & \text{if } x \notin A_1 \cup \cdots \cup A_n \end{cases} \tag{1.4}$$

i.e.

$$f = \sum_{i=1}^{m} d_i \, I_{A_i}$$

### 1.1.3 Measurable Function as Limit of Simple Function

There is an important result which shows that a measurable function can be expressed as a limit of a convergent sequence of simple functions. This result would be greatly used while defining integral of measurable functions.

**Theorem 1.1.5.** *Given a measure space $(\mathcal{L}, \mathcal{C}, \mu)$, every non-negative measurable function $f$ is a limit of monotonic increasing sequence of simple functions.*

The Lebesgue theory of integration (which would be discussed in Section 1.2) requires the mathematical definition of *measurable functions* on the measure space $(\mathcal{L}, \mathcal{C}, \mu)$.

**Definition 1.1.16. (Measurable Function)** A real valued function on a measure space $(\mathcal{L}, \mathcal{C}, \mu)$ is said to be measurable if it is the limit of a sequence of simple functions.

## 1.2 INTEGRATION

### 1.2.1 Riemann Integral

In classical integral calculus *definite integral* of a real function $f$ of a real variable is defined as the area under the curve. Let $f$ be a real continuous function on an interval $[a, b]$ almost everywhere on the interval. Consider that the interval has been sub-divided into $n$ disjoint intervals so that $\cup_{i=1}^{n}(a_{i-1}, a_i) = (a, b)$, $a_0 = a$, $a_n = b$, $a(= a_0) < a_1 < a_2 \ldots a_{n-1} < b = a_n$; $n$ intervals with length $a_1 - a_0 = l_1$, $a_2 - a_2 = l_2, \ldots a_n - a_{n-1} = l_n$. The vertical strip made at each interval $(a_{i-1}, a_i)$ under the curve of $f$ has width $l_i$ and height $f(a_{i-1})$, the area of the strip is given by $l_i f(a_{i-1})$. The area under the curve on the interval $[a, b]$ is the sum of the areas of strips which are made on the $n$ sub-intervals below the curve, $\sum_{i=1}^{n} l_i f(a_{i-1}) = J_n$. This sum actually underestimates the true area under the curve on the interval $[a, b]$ but converges to the true sum with the increase in the number of sub-intervals. Therefore, the definite integral of $f$ over the interval $[a, b]$ is defined as

$$\int_a^b f(x)\,dx = \lim_{n\to\infty} \sum_{i=1}^{n} l_i f(a_{i-1})$$

This integral is known as *Riemann integral.* The improper integral is defined by

$$\int f(x)\,dx = \lim_{\substack{a\to-\infty \\ b\to+\infty}} \int_a^b f(x)\,dx$$

### 1.2.2 Lebesgue Integral

The generalization of Riemann integral leads to Lebesgue integrals. In such generalization the function $f$, in the classical theory of integration defined on intervals, extends to a measure space $(\mathcal{L}, \mathcal{C}, \mu)$; the continuity of $f$ replaces with $f$ to be measurable (a continuous function over an interval is measurable, but not necessarily every measurable function is continuous); the range of the integral extends from interval to some measurable set; the integration with respect to the length of the interval replaced with a measure of the measurable set at which integral is to be evaluated. The formal definitions of *Lebesque integral* of simple functions, measurable functions and some results on the convergence of integrals have been discussed here.

**Definition 1.2.1.** (**Definite Integral**) The definite integral of a simple function $f = \sum_{i=1}^{m} d_i I_{E_i}$ on a measure space $(\mathcal{L}, \mathcal{C}, \mu)$ on a given set $E \in \mathcal{C}$ is defined as (denoted by $\int_E f d\mu$)

$$\int_E f d\mu = \sum_{i=1}^{m} d_i \mu(E \cap E_i)$$

whenever, $\mu[E \cap \{x : f(x) \neq 0\}] < \infty$. Such a function $f$ is said to be integrable.

If $E \equiv \mathcal{L}$, the integral of a simple function $f$ on the whole space $\mathcal{L}$ is defined as

$$\int_{\mathcal{L}} f d\mu = \sum_{i=1}^{m} d_i \mu(E_i)$$

whenever $\mu(E_i) < \infty$ for every index $i$ for which $d_i \neq 0\,(\,\mu[x : f(x) \neq 0] < \infty)$.

**Definition 1.2.2. (Indefinite Integral)** Consider an integrable simple function $f$ on the measure space $(\mathcal{L}, \mathcal{C}, \mu)$. The set function

$$\nu(E) = \int_E f d\mu \tag{1.5}$$

on $\mathcal{C}$ for every measurable set $E$ is called the *indefinite integral of $f$*.

There is an important result that states that an indefinite integral of a non-negative integrable simple function is a measure, i.e. $\nu$ in Eq. (1.5) is a measure.

**Definition 1.2.3. (Absolute Continuity of a Measure)** A real valued set function $\nu$ on $\mathcal{C}$ of a given measure space $(\mathcal{L}, \mathcal{C}, \mu)$ is said to be *absolutely continuous* with respect to $\mu$ or $\mu$-continuous denoted as $\nu << \mu$, if for every $\epsilon > 0$, there exists a $\delta > 0$ such that $|\nu(E)| < \epsilon$ whenever $\mu(E) < \delta\ \forall\ E \in \mathcal{C}$. In other words, $\nu$ is $\mu$-continuous if and only if $\mu(E) = 0 \Rightarrow \nu(E) = 0\ \forall\ E \in \mathcal{C}$.

**Definition 1.2.4. (Singularity of a Measure)** Given a measure space $(\mathcal{L}, \mathcal{C}, \mu)$, a set function $\phi$ on $\mathcal{C}$ is said to be singular with respect to $\mu$ in or *$\mu$-singular*, denoted by $\phi \perp \mu$, if

$$\phi(F \cap E^c) = 0 \quad \forall \ \ F \in \mathcal{C}$$

where, $E$ is some set in $\mathcal{C}$ for which $\mu(E) = 0$, i.e. $E$ is a $\mu$-null set. In other words, $\phi$ is $\mu$-singular if $\phi$ vanishes outside the $\mu$-null set.

One may note as an important result that the indefinite integral $\nu(E)$ defined in Eq. (1.5) is absolutely continuous with respect to the measure $\mu$ on the measure space $(\mathcal{L}, \mathcal{C}, \mu)$.

We shall now define *Lebesgue integral* of non-negative measurable functions and measurable functions in general.

**Definition 1.2.5. (Lebesgue Integral of Non-negative Measurable Functions)** Let $f$ be a non-negative measurable function on the measure space $(\mathcal{L}, \mathcal{C}, \mu)$. The function $f$ is said to be *integrable over a set $E$* if there exists monotonic increasing sequence of non-negative simple functions $\{f_n\}$, each function is integrable over $E$, converging to $f$ point wise, [i.e. $\lim f_n(x) = f(x)\,\forall\ x \in E$] such that $\lim \int_E f_n d\mu < \infty$. The *definite Lebesgue integral of $f$* over $E$ is defined as

$$\int_E f\, d\mu = \lim \int_E f_n\, d\mu$$

If $E \equiv \mathcal{L}$, we say the $f$ is integrable. We shall now define the Lebesgue integral of a measurable function $f$.

**Definition 1.2.6. (Lebesgue Integral of Measurable Function)** Consider a measurable function $f$ on the measure space $(\mathcal{L}, \mathcal{C}, \mu)$, the function $f$ is said to be integrable over a set $E \in \mathcal{C}$ if both $f^+$ and $f^-$ are integrable over $E \in \mathcal{C}$, i.e. $\int f^+ d\mu < \infty$ and $f^- d\mu < \infty$. The integral of $f$ is defined as

$$\int_E f\, d\mu = \int_E f^+\, d\mu - \int_E f^-\, d\mu$$

Note that $f$ is measurable if and only if both $f^+$ and $f^-$ are measurable.

Let us now define an indefinite integral of a measurable function.

**Definition 1.2.7. (Indefinite Lebesgue Integral of Measurable Function)** Consider a measurable function $f$ on a measure space $(\mathcal{L}, \mathcal{C}, \mu)$. The indefinite integral of $f$ over a set $E \in \mathcal{C}$ is a set function $\nu$ on $\mathcal{C}$ defined as

$$\nu(E) = \int_E f\, d\mu$$

provided $\int_E f d\mu < \infty$.

It is important to note the two results in the sequence, one that the indefinite integral of a non-negative integrable function is a measure on the class of all measurable sets, and second that if $f$ is integrable with respect to a measure $\mu$, and if $E, F$ are measurable sets such that $E \subset F$ and $\mu(F - E) = 0$, then

$$\int_E f\, d\mu = \int_F f\, d\mu$$

### Lebesgue integral as convergence of integrals

We shall now state few results on the convergence of sequence of integrals.

**Theorem 1.2.1. (Monotone Convergence Theorem)** *Consider a monotone increasing sequence $\{f_n\}$ of non-negative measurable functions on a given measure space $(\mathcal{L}, \mathcal{C}, \mu)$, each integrable over a set $E \in \mathcal{C}$. The function $f$ is integrable over the set $E$ if and only if*

$$\lim \int_E f_n\, d\mu < \infty$$

*and the Lebesgue integral of $f$ is obtained as*

$$\int_E f\, d\mu = \lim \int_E f_n\, d\mu$$

In Theorem 1.2.1, the set $E$ has been chosen arbitrarily, therefore, integrability over $E$ may be replaced with $\mathcal{L}$ to obtain the indefinite-integral version of monotone convergence theorem.

Theorem 1.2.2 is a famous result on the convergence of integrals.

**Theorem 1.2.2. (Fatou's Lemma)** *Given a measure space* $(\mathcal{L}, \mathcal{C}, \mu)$, *let* $\{f_n\}$ *be a sequence of integrable functions and* $g, h$ *and* $f$ *are integrable functions,*

(a) $\liminf \int f_n \, d\mu \geq \int \liminf f_n \, d\mu$ *where* $f_n \geq g \ \forall \ n$

(b) $\limsup \int f_n \, d\mu \leq \int \limsup f_n \, d\mu$ *where* $f_n \leq h \ \forall \ n$

(c) $\int f_n \, d\mu \to \int f \, d\mu$ as $n \to \infty$. *when* $f_n \leq h$ *and* $f_n \to f$ *as* $n \to \infty$ *or* $g \leq f_n \leq h$ *and* $f_n \to f$ *as* $n \to \infty$.

Lebesgue later generalized the Fatou's lemma and proved a result which is popularly known as *Lebesgue-dominated Convergence Theorem.*

**Theorem 1.2.3. (Lebesgue-dominated Convergence Theorem)** *Given a measure space* $(\mathcal{L}, \mathcal{C}, \mu)$, *consider a sequence* $\{f_n\}$ *of measurable functions. If*

(a) $f_n \to f$ *as* $n \to \infty$

(b) $|f_n| \leq g \quad \forall n$, *where* $g$ *is some non-negative integrable function, then*

$$\int f_n \, d\mu \to \int f \, d\mu \quad \textit{as} \quad n \to \infty$$

### Lebesgue decomposition and Radon-Nikodym theorem

We shall now state Radon-Nikodym theorem on characterizing the indefinite integrals of some measurable function by a $\mu$-continuous $\sigma$-additive set function. This characterization has become possible on using Lebesgue Decomposition Theorem. For better understanding of Radon-Nikodym theorem, few basic results and definitions are essential, which are given as follows:

(a) Absolute continuity of indefinite integral and $f = g$ except on a $\mu$-null set implies $\int f \, d\mu = \int g \, d\mu$.

(b) A property $\Pi$ is said to hold almost everywhere on a measure space $(\mathcal{L}, \mathcal{C}, \mu)$ with respect to a measure $\mu$ a.e. (almost everywhere). In other words, if the property does not hold on some $E$, it is $\mu$-null set, i.e. $\mu(E) = 0$.

(c) Measurable functions $f$ and $g$ on a measure space $(\mathcal{L}, \mathcal{C}, \mu)$ are said to be $\mu$-equivalent if $f = g$ almost everywhere $\mu$. This implies, $\int f \, d\mu = \int g \, d\mu$.

We shall now state the Lebesgue Decomposition Theorem.

**Theorem 1.2.4. (Lebesque Decomposition Theorem)** *Let* $\mu$ *be a* $\sigma$*-finite measure on the measure space* $(\mathcal{L}, \mathcal{C}, \mu)$ *and* $\nu$ *be a* $\sigma$*-finite,* $\sigma$*-additive set function on* $\mathcal{C}$*. The set function* $\nu$ *decomposes into two* $\sigma$*-additive set functions* $\nu_c$ *a* $\mu$*-continuous set function (as an indefinite integral of a finite measurable function determined up to* $\mu$*-equivalence) and* $\nu_s$ *a* $\mu$*-singular set function*

$$\nu = \nu_c + \nu_s$$

Note in the theorem, the set functions $\nu_c$ and $\nu_s$ on $\mathcal{C}$ have been defined as

$$\nu_c(E) = \int_E f\, d\mu, \quad \nu_s(E) = \nu(E) - \nu_c(E)$$

**Definition 1.2.8. (Radon-Nikodym Derivative)** The integrand $f$ in $\nu(E) = \int_E f d\mu$ defined in $\nu_c$ is called the derivative of $\nu$ with respect $\mu$, and is denoted by $f = d\nu/d\mu$. In this, the finite measurable function $f$ is called the Radon-Nikodym derivative of $\nu$ with respect to $\mu$, and written as $f = d\nu/d\mu$.

We shall now state the famous Radon-Nikodym Theorem.

**Theorem 1.2.5. (Radon-Nikodym Theorem)** *Let us consider the measure space $(\mathcal{L}, \mathcal{C}, \mu)$ with $\mu$ as a $\sigma$-finite measure and $\nu$ a completely additive $\sigma$-finite set function on $\mathcal{C}$. If $\nu$ is $\mu$-continuous then $\nu$ is indefinite integral with respect to $\mu$ of a finite measurable function determined up to $\mu$-equivalence.*

Complete characterization of indefinite integral of a finite measurable function $f$ with respect to a $\sigma$-finite measure $\mu$ on the measure space $(\mathcal{L}, \mathcal{C}, \mu)$ is given in Theorem 1.2.6.

**Theorem 1.2.6.** *Given a measure space $(\mathcal{L}, \mathcal{C}, \mu)$ and a $\sigma$-finite measure $\mu$ on $\mathcal{C}$, a set function $\nu$ on $\mathcal{C}$ is the indefinite integral of a finite measurable function $f$ (determined upto $\mu$-equivalence), if and only if $\nu$ is $\sigma$-finite, $\sigma$-additive and $\mu$-continuous.*

Another important result is given as follows:

**Theorem 1.2.7.** *Let $\mu$ and $\nu$ be two $\sigma$-finite measures on the measure space $(\mathcal{L}, \mathcal{C}, \mu)$ and $\nu$ has been given to be $\mu$-continuous. If $f$ is a measurable function for which $\int f d\mu$ exists almost everywhere on $\mathcal{C}$, then*

$$\int_A f\, d\nu = \int_A (f \cdot \frac{d\nu}{d\mu})\, d\mu$$

### 1.2.3 Lebesgue-Stieltjes Integral

Let us consider a class of intervals on the real line,

$$\mathcal{I} = \{(a, b] \ : \ -\infty < a < b < \infty\}$$

and $F$ as a distribution function defined as $F : \mathbb{R}^1 \to \mathbb{R}^1$. Let $\mathcal{H}$ be a field generated by the class $\mathcal{I}$. Define a set function $\psi$ on $\mathcal{I}$ by

$$\psi(a, b] = F(b) - F(a)$$

Every set $A$ in $\mathcal{H}$ can be expressed as disjoint countable union of intervals in $\mathcal{I}$, $A = \cup_{n=1}^{\infty} E_n$ where $\{E_n\}$ is a disjoint sequence in $\mathcal{I}$. Define a set function $\mu$ on $\mathcal{H}$ by

$$\mu(A) = \sum_{n=1}^{\infty} \psi(E_n)$$

It can easily be seen that $\mu$ is a measure on $\mathcal{H}$ and agrees with $\psi$ (i.e. $\mu = \psi$) on $\mathcal{I}$. By definition of $\psi$, the measure $\mu$, by the extension theorem, could be extended to a unique measure $\mu_0$ on the $\sigma$-field (the Borel field $\mathcal{B}$ in $\mathbb{R}^1$) generated by $\mathcal{H}$. This measure is called induced measure by distribution function $F$. Let the Borel field $\mathcal{B}$ be completed by the measure $\mu_0$, the completion field be denoted by $\mathcal{B}_{\mu_0}$, then $\mathcal{B}_{\mu_0}$ is called *Lebesgue-Stieltjes field in* $\mathbb{R}^1$, and the complete measure on the completion $\mathcal{B}_{\mu_0}$ denoted by $\mu^*$ is called *Lebesgue-Stieltjes measure.* The measure space may now be denoted by $(\mathcal{H},\, \mathcal{B}_{\mu_0},\, \mu^*)$. Consider a measurable function $f$ over sets in $\mathcal{B}_{\mu_0}$. Consider a set $E$ in $\mathcal{B}_{\mu_0}$; $E$ is called as *Lebesgue-Stieltjes set.* Such a set $E$ may be an interval $(a, b)$ with division points $x_1, x_2, \ldots, x_{n-1}$ such that $a < x_1 < x_2 \cdots < x_{n-1} < b$. Define the sum

$$\begin{aligned} J_n &= \sum_{i=1}^{n} f(y_i)\, \mu^*(x_{i-1}, x_i) \\ &= \sum_{i=1}^{n} f(y_i)\, [F(x_i) - F(x_{i-1}] \end{aligned}$$

for any arbitrary point $y_i \in (x_{i-1}, x_i)$, $x_0 = a$, $x_n = b$. If lengths of each subdivision tends to 0 as $n \to \infty$

$$\int_E f\, dF = \lim_{n \to \infty} J_n$$

is called *Lebesgue-Stieltjes integral of f* over a Lebesgue-Stieltjes set $E$ in $\mathcal{B}_{\mu_0}$. The improper integral is defined as

$$\int f\, dF = \lim_{\substack{a \to -\infty, \\ b \to +\infty}} \int_{E \equiv (a,b)} f\, dF$$

### Riemann integral as a special case

We know that the Lebesgue-Stieltjes measure induced by the distribution function $F(x) = x$ is called *Lebesgue measure.* The corresponding measure space is denoted by $(\mathcal{H},\, \mathcal{B}_{\mu_0},\, \mu^*)$, where $\mu^*$ is the complete measure on the completion $\mathcal{B}_{\mu_0}$. Consider a measurable function $f$ which is bounded and continuous almost everywhere with respect to the Lebesgue measure $\mu^*$. Define the sum

$$\begin{aligned} J_n &= \sum_{i=1}^{n} f(y_i)\, \mu^*(x_{i-1}, x_i) \\ &= \sum_{i=1}^{n} f(y_i)\, (x_i - x_{i-1}) \end{aligned}$$

Then $$\int_a^b f(x)\, dx = \lim_{n \to \infty} J_n$$

is called *Riemann integral of a function f*. This integral is, in fact, the Lebesgue-Stieltejes integral of $f$ over the given interval with respect to the Lebesgue measure $F(x) = x$.

The improper integral is given by

$$\int f(x)\,dx = \lim_{\substack{a \to -\infty,\\ b \to +\infty}} \int_a^b f(x)\,dx$$

**Riemann-Stieltjes integral as a special case**

If there exits a function $p(x)$ such that

$$F(x) = \int_{-\infty}^{x} p(x)\,dx$$

The Lebesgue-Stieltejes integral reduces to a Riemann integral

$$\int f(x)\,dF(x) = \int f(x)\,p(x)\,dx$$

This integral is then known as *Riemann-Stieltjes integral.*

## 1.3 PROBABILITY SPACE

An experiment $\xi$, which could be repeated under identical conditions and if all its possible outcomes are known, except that its outcome could not be predicted at any stage, is called an random experiment.

Let $\xi$ be a random experiment and $\mathcal{L}$ be its corresponding set of all possible outcomes; $\mathcal{C}$ be $\sigma$-field of subsets of $\mathcal{L}$. A set function $P$ on $\mathcal{C}$ is called a probability measure if

(a) $0 \le P(A) \le 1 \qquad \forall\ A \in \mathcal{C}$

(b) $P(\mathcal{L}) = 1$

(c) $P(\bigcup_{i=1}^{\infty}) = \sum_{i=1}^{\infty} P(A_i)$ for every disjoint sequence $\{A_i\}$ in $\mathcal{C}$

The triplet $(\mathcal{L}, \mathcal{C}, P)$ is called the probability space (sample space) corresponding to a random experiment $\xi$ where $P$ is called a probability measure, $\mathcal{C}$ is called power of the probability space. Sets in $\mathcal{L}$ are called the elementary events and sets in $\mathcal{C}$ are called simply events.

## 1.4 RANDOM VARIABLE

A real valued function $X$ on a given probability space $(\mathcal{L}, \mathcal{C}, P)$ so that $X : \mathcal{L} \to \mathbb{R}^1$ is called a random variable, written as *r.v.*, if $\{a : X(a) \le x\} \in \mathcal{C}$ for every real number $x$. Generally, random variables are written by capital letters and their values are written by small letters.

We shall now construct the new probability space on the real line equivalent to $(\mathcal{L}, \mathcal{C}, P)$, after defining the random variable on a given probability space.

The *distribution function of a given r.v.* $X$ on a probability space $(\mathcal{L}, \mathcal{C}, P)$ is a point function $F : \mathbb{R}^1 \to \mathbb{R}^1$ defined by

$$F(x) = P\{a : X(a) \leq x\} = P(X^{-1}(-\infty, x])$$

The following theorem states some basic properties of a distribution function of a random variable.

**Theorem 1.4.1.** *A function $F : \mathbb{R}^1 \to \mathbb{R}^1$ is the d.f. of some r.v. $X$ if and only if*

(a) *$F$ is non-decreasing*

(b) $F(-\infty) = 0,\ F(\infty) = 1$ *and* $0 \leq F(x) \leq 1$ *for all real* $x$

(c) *$F$ is right continuous on $\mathbb{R}^1$ (i.e. $F(x^+) = F(x)\ \forall\ x \in \mathbb{R}^1$, $F(x^+)$ denotes the right hand limit of $F$ at $x$ ).*

On a given probability space $(\mathcal{L}, \mathcal{C}, P)$ a random variable $X$ has been defined as a function that maps $\mathcal{L}$ into $\mathbb{R}^1$, $X : \mathcal{L} \to \mathbb{R}^1$. The distribution function of the r.v. $X$ has been defined as $F(x) = P\{X^{-1}(-\infty, x]\}$. Consider now class of intervals of the type $(a, b]$ denoted by $I$ and a Borel field $\mathcal{B}$, a $\sigma$-field generated by $I$. Define a set function $\mu : \mathcal{B} \to \mathbb{R}^1$ so that

$$\mu(a, b] = F(b) - F(a)$$

Note that $\mu$ is non-negative, additive on $I$, $0 \leq \mu(a, b] \leq 1$ for all $a$ and $b \in \mathbb{R}^1$. By the results on extension of measures, $\mu$ can be extended to a unique probability measure $P_F$ on the Borel field $\mathcal{B}$. Thus we have seen that the d.f. of a random variable $X$ on the probability space $(\mathcal{L}, \mathcal{C}, P)$ induces a new probability space $(\mathbb{R}^1, \mathcal{B}, P_F)$ in $\mathbb{R}^1$, equivalent to the original probability space $(\mathcal{L}, \mathcal{C}, P)$. Therefore, assertions regarding the random variable $X$ can be made on the basis of its distribution function $F$ or on the newly induced probability space $(\mathbb{R}^1, \mathcal{B}, P_F)$ and subsequently the original probability space $(\mathcal{L}, \mathcal{C}, P)$ becomes unimportant.

**Some useful remarks are discussed further**

*Remark* 1.4.1. Random variables on $(\mathbb{R}^1, \mathcal{B}, P_F)$ are said to be identically distributed if they have the same distribution function.

*Remark* 1.4.2. For a given distribution function $F$, the saltus of $F$ at $x$ is defined as

$$p(x) = F(x^+) - F(x^-)$$

where, $F(x^+)$ is the right hand limit of $F$ at $x$ and $F(x^-)$ is the left hand limit of $F$ at $x$. The value of $p(x)$ is called the jump of $F$ at $x$ and it is $P(X = x)$, the probability that the r.v. takes on the value $x$ when the r.v. is discrete. If $p(x) > 0$ for some $x$, $x$ is called the discontinuity point of $F$ at $x$ and if $p(x) = 0$ the corresponding $x$ is called the continuity point.

*Remark* 1.4.3. The number of discontinuity points of a distribution function is at most countable.

*Remark* 1.4.4. A random variable $X$ is said to be continuous if and only if its distribution function F is differentiable everywhere. In other words, there exists a non-negative function $f$ such that

$$F(x) = \int_{-\infty}^{x} f(y)\, dy$$

for every real number $x$, where $F$ is the distribution function of the r.v. X.

*Remark* 1.4.5. A function $f$, taking its values from $\mathbb{R}^1$, is the p.d.f. of r.v. $X$ if and only if it satisfies

(a) $f(x) \geq 0, \ \ \forall\, x \in \mathbb{R}^1$
(b) $\lim_{\substack{a \to -\infty \\ b \to +\infty}} f(x)dx = \int_{-\infty}^{\infty} f(x)dx = 1$

## 1.5 INTEGRALS IN HYPOTHESIS TESTING

Statistical decision theory has been defined as a triplet $(\Theta, \mathcal{A}, L)$ and a random quantity $X$ whose distribution is given by $P_\theta$ for some $\theta \in \Theta$; where $\Theta$ is the parameter space from where nature makes her choice; $\mathcal{A}$ the action space available to the statistician, $L$ is a amount of loss incurred to the statistician on account of joint choices of nature and statistician both together. More formally, these terms would be discussed in Chapter 2 where hypothesis testing problems have been shown as special cases of statistical decision problems. Therefore, the foundational framework developed for studying decision problems applies straight way to hypothesis testing problems. The theorems and results which have been developed for statistical decision theory are directly applicable to the theory of hypothesis testing with few minor modifications. For example, a class of behavioural decision rules in decision theory becomes the class of tests in hypothesis testing, which is denoted by $\mathcal{D}$. Given the observation $X = x$, a behavioural decision rule (test) is a probability distribution over the action space (a space of actions available to the statistician where he either accepts or rejects the null-hypothesis). In hypothesis testing one is usually concerned with finding an optimal test from $\mathcal{D}$. The class $\mathcal{D}$ is well defined if risk of every behavioural decision rule (test $\phi$) exists and finite, i.e.

$$\widehat{R}(\theta, \phi) = E_\theta^X L(\theta, \phi(X))$$

so that the expectation exists and is finite, i.e. $\widehat{R}(\theta, \phi) < \infty, \ \forall\, \theta \in \Theta$, where $\theta$ is called the true value of the parameter. Let the random variable $X$ be defined on the measure space $(\mathcal{L}, \mathcal{C}, \mu)$ with its distribution function $F_\theta$; the corresponding induced measure space be given by $(\mathfrak{X}, \mathcal{B}(\mathfrak{X}), \mu_\theta(x))$ where $\mathfrak{X}$ is the sample space, $\mathcal{B}(\mathfrak{X})$ is a $\sigma$-field generated by the subsets of $\mathfrak{X}$ and $\mu_\theta(x)$ is the induced measure on the measure space. It is now important to specify the sense in which the expectation in $\widehat{R}(\theta, \phi)$ be understood. In hypothesis testing problems we would consider this as Lebesgue integral

$$\widehat{R}(\theta,\, \phi) = \int_{\mathfrak{X}} L(\theta,\, \phi(x))\, d\mu_\theta(x)$$

where, for given $X = x$, the loss $L(\theta,\, \phi(x))$ for the randomized action $\phi(x)$ is defined as

$$L(\theta,\, \phi(x)) = E^{Z(x)} L(\theta,\, Z) \tag{1.6}$$

where $Z$ is a random variable defined on the measure space $(\mathcal{A}, \mathcal{B}(\mathcal{A}), \nu_x)$ whose distribution is given by $\phi(x)$, where $\mathcal{A}$ is the action space, $\mathcal{B}(\mathcal{A})$ is the $\sigma$-field generated by the subsets of $\mathcal{A}$, $\nu_x$ is the measure defined on the measure space $(\mathcal{A}, \mathcal{B}(\mathcal{A}), \nu_x)$. Therefore, Eq. (1.6), can be written as

$$L(\theta,\, \phi(x)) = \int_{\mathcal{A}} L(\theta, a)\, d\nu_x(a)$$

where $E^{Z(x)}$ involves a Lebesgue integral. In this, the loss functions, for each field $\theta \in \Theta$, has been assumed to be a Lebesgue integrable function in $a$. This loss function is denoted by $L(\theta, \cdot)$.

Thus, the risk of a behavioural decision rule $\phi$ (a test) is defined in terms of Lebesgue integral by

$$\begin{aligned}\widehat{R}(\theta,\, \phi) &= E_\theta^X E^{Z(X)} L(\theta, Z(X)) \\ &= \int_{\mathfrak{X}} \Big[ \int_{\mathcal{A}} L(\theta,\, a)\, d\nu_x(a) \Big]\, d\mu_\theta(x)\end{aligned}$$

Note that if $\mu$ is generated by a distribution function $F$, the Lebesgue integral converts into Stieltjes-Lebesgue integral.

The main advantage of defining the risk function in terms of Lebesgue integral is that one directly utilizes the results on measure theory in the theoretical developments of testing of hypothesis.

If the measure $\mu_\theta(x)$ is the distribution function $F_\theta(x)$ of the random variable $X$, the Lebesgue integral in the risk function $\widehat{R}(\theta, \phi)$ becomes Lebesgue-Stieltjes integral,

$$\widehat{R}(\theta,\, \phi) = \int_{\mathfrak{X}} L(\theta, \phi(x))\, dF_\theta(x)$$

If the cumulative distribution function $F_\theta(x)$ is absolutely continuous with respect to the probability measure $\mu(x)$ on the probability space $(\mathcal{L},\, \mathcal{C},\, \mu(x))$, by Radon-Nikodym theorem, there exists a function $f_\theta(x)$ so that

$$f_\theta(x) = \frac{d}{d\mu(x)} F_\theta(x)$$

which is called the probability density function of the distribution function $F_\theta(x)$. In this case, the Lebesgue-Stieltjes integral in $\widehat{R}(\theta, \phi)$ is expressed as

$$\widehat{R}(\theta, \phi) = \int_{\mathfrak{X}} L(\theta, \phi(x))\, f_\theta(x)\, d\mu(x)$$

# 1.6 REGULAR AND NON-REGULAR FAMILIES OF DISTRIBUTIONS

In general, statistical models are described by different families of distributions, $F_X(x|\theta)$. We shall usually be interested in such families that would allow great reduction of data through sufficiency principle. The main families of distribution with this property are exponential family of distributions. We would refer these families as *regular* families. The word *regular* stands for the family of distributions that satisfies certain regularity conditions. The other type of families of distributions discussed in this book are *non-regular families*, e.g. the family of uniform distributions. For non-regular families too sufficient statistic exists that allows reduction of data (Ferguson(1967) [54]; Johnson and Kotz(1969)[94, 95]).

## 1.6.1 Regular Families

By regular families we mean exponential families which allow maximum reduction of data. These families are defined by the probability density of the form

$$f_X(x|\boldsymbol{\theta}) = C(\boldsymbol{\theta}) \cdot h(x) \cdot \exp\Big\{\sum_{j=1}^{k} Q_j(\boldsymbol{\theta}) T_j(x)\Big\} \tag{1.7}$$

with respect to a $\sigma$-finite measure $\mu$ on the Euclidean space $(\mathfrak{X}, \sigma(\mathfrak{X}))$, where $\sigma(\mathfrak{X})$ is the $\sigma$-field generated by the subset of $\mathfrak{X}$ and $\boldsymbol{\theta} \subset \Theta$, the parameter space. If we draw a random sample $\mathbf{X} = (X_1, X_2, \ldots, X_n)$ from this family, the joint distribution of sample observations is given by

$$\begin{aligned} f_{\mathbf{X}}(\mathbf{x}|\boldsymbol{\theta}) &= \textstyle\prod_{i=1}^{n} f_{X_i}(x_i|\theta) \\ &= [C(\boldsymbol{\theta})]^n \exp\Big\{\textstyle\sum_{i=1}^{n}\sum_{j=1}^{k} Q_j(\boldsymbol{\theta}) \cdot T_j(x_i)\Big\} \cdot h(x_1, \ldots, x_n) \\ &= [C(\boldsymbol{\theta})]^n \exp\Big\{\textstyle\sum_{j=1}^{k} Q_j(\boldsymbol{\theta})\, (\sum_{i=1}^{n} T_j(x_i))\Big\} \cdot h(x_1, \ldots, x_n) \end{aligned}$$

Note that the distributions like binomial, poisson, normal and gamma are a few members of exponential family (refer Table 1.1).

### Natural parameterization

Usually hypothesis testing involves $Q_j(\theta)$, therefore, we shall re-parameterize $Q_j(\theta)$ as $\theta_j$, and substituting this in Eq. (1.7), we get

$$f_X(x|\boldsymbol{\theta}) = C(\boldsymbol{\theta}) \exp\Big\{\textstyle\sum_{j=1}^{k} \theta_j T_j(x)\Big\} \mu(x)$$

**Table 1.1:** Some Regular Families of Distributions

| *Name* | *Density* | *Parameter Space, Support* |
|---|---|---|
| Bernoulli $b\,(1, p)$ | $p^x q^{1-x}$ | $0 \leq p \leq 1;\ x = 0, 1$ $(q = 1 - p)$ |
| Binomial $b\,(n, p)$ | $\binom{n}{x} p^x (1-p)^{n-x}$ | $0 \leq p \leq 1;\ x = 0, 1, \ldots, n$ $n = 1, 2, \ldots\ (q = 1 - p)$ |
| Poisson $P(\lambda)$ | $\frac{1}{x!} \lambda^x e^{-\lambda}$ | $\lambda > 0;\ x = 0, 1, \ldots$ |
| Negative binomial $Nb(r, p)$ | $\binom{r+x-1}{x} p^r q^x$ | $0 < p \leq 1;\ x = 0, 1, \ldots$ $r > 0\ (q = 1 - p)$ |
| Geometric | $p q^x$ | $0 < p \leq 1;\ x = 0, 1, \ldots$ $(q = 1 - p)$ |
| Normal $N(\mu,\, \sigma^2)$ | $\frac{1}{\sqrt{2\pi}\sigma} \exp\{-\frac{1}{2}(\frac{x-\mu}{\sigma})^2\}$ | $-\infty < \mu < +\infty$ $\sigma^2 > 0,\ -\infty < x < +\infty$ |
| Exponential $E(\lambda)$ | $\lambda \exp\{-\lambda x\}$ | $\lambda > 0,\ 0 < x < \infty$ |
| Gamma $G(\alpha,\, \beta)$ | $\frac{1}{\Gamma\alpha\beta^\alpha} \exp\{-x/\beta\} x^{\alpha-1}$ | $\alpha > 0,\, \beta > 0,\ 0 < x < \infty$ |
| Beta $\mathrm{B}(\alpha,\, \beta)$ | $\frac{\Gamma(\alpha+\beta)}{\Gamma(\alpha)\Gamma(\beta)} x^{\alpha-1}(1-x)^{\beta-1}$ | $\alpha > 0,\, \beta > 0,\ 0 < x < 1$ |
| Lognormal $LN(\mu,\, \sigma^2)$ | $\frac{1}{x\sqrt{2\pi}\sigma} \exp\{-\frac{1}{2}(\frac{log_e x-\mu}{\sigma})^2\}$ | $-\infty < \mu < +\infty;\ \sigma^2 > 0$ $x > 0$ |
| Weibull $W(\alpha,\, \beta)$ | $\alpha\beta x^{\beta-1} \exp\{-\alpha x^\beta\}$ | $\alpha > 0,\ \beta > 0$ $x > 0$ |
| Pareto | $\frac{\theta x_0^\theta}{x^{\theta+1}}$ | $x_0 > 0,\ \theta > 0$ $x_0 < x < +\infty$ |

Since $h(x)$ is the function of $x$ and so is $\mu$, therefore, $h(x)$ is adjusted into $\mu(x)$. The function $C(\boldsymbol{\theta})$ is obtained by the property $\int f_X(x|\boldsymbol{\theta})\, d\mu(x) = 1$, by noting that $f_X(x|\boldsymbol{\theta})$ is the probability density with respect to $\mu(x)$. Unknown $\boldsymbol{\theta} = (\theta_1, \ldots, \theta_k)$ takes values from the parameter space $\Theta$, known as *natural parameter space.*

We shall now discuss some properties of exponential family:

(a) The natural parameter space $\Theta$ of an exponential family is convex. Further, if $\Theta$ lies in a linear space of dimension less then $k$, the term $\sum_{j=1}^{k} \theta_j T_j(x)$ in the exponential density can be written by involving fewer than $k$ components of $\mathbf{T} = (T_1(x), \ldots, T_k(x))$. Therefore, we could assume the dimension of $\Theta$ to be $k$.

(b) (Lehmann, 1986)[130]: Let $X$ be distributed according to the exponential family

$$dF_X(x|\boldsymbol{\theta}, \boldsymbol{\vartheta}) = C(\boldsymbol{\theta}, \boldsymbol{\vartheta}) \exp\{\sum_{i=1}^{r} \theta_i U_i(x) + \sum_{j=1}^{s} \vartheta_j T_j(x)\} \cdot d\mu(x)$$

Then there exist measures $\lambda_{\boldsymbol{\theta}}$ and $\nu_{\mathbf{t}}$ over $s$- and $r$-dimensional Euclidean spaces respectively such that

(i) The distribution of $\mathbf{T} = (T_1, \ldots, T_s)$ is an exponential family of the form
$$dF_{\mathbf{T}}(\mathbf{t}|\boldsymbol{\theta}, \boldsymbol{\vartheta}) = C(\boldsymbol{\theta}, \boldsymbol{\vartheta}) \exp\{\textstyle\sum_{j=1}^{s} \vartheta_j t_j\} \, d\lambda_{\theta}(\mathbf{t})$$

(ii) The conditional distribution of $\mathbf{U} = (U_1, \ldots, U_r)$ given $\mathbf{T} = \mathbf{t}$ is an exponential family of the form

$$dF_{\mathbf{U}|\mathbf{t}}(\mathbf{u}) = C_{\mathbf{t}}(\boldsymbol{\theta}) \exp\{\textstyle\sum_{i=1}^{r} \theta_i u_i\} \, d\nu_{\mathbf{t}}(\mathbf{u})$$

and hence, in particular, the distribution is independent of $\boldsymbol{\vartheta}$.

(c) (Lehmann, 1986)[130] Let $\phi$ be any function on $(\mathfrak{X}, \mathcal{A})$ for which the integral

$$\int \phi(x) \exp\{\sum_{j=1}^{k} \theta_j T_j(x)\} \, d\mu(x)$$

considered as a function of the complex variables $\theta_j = \xi_j + i\eta_j$ $(j = 1, \ldots, k)$ exists for all $(\xi_1, \ldots, \xi_k) \in \Theta$ and is finite. Then

(i) The integral is an *analytic function* of each $\boldsymbol{\theta}$ in the region $R$ of parameter points for which $(\xi_1, \ldots, \xi_k)$ is an interior point of the natural parameter space $\Theta$;

(ii) The derivatives of all orders with respect to each component of $\boldsymbol{\theta}$ in the above integral can be computed under the integral sign.

The results discussed in (a) to (c) are used in different chapters of this book.

Some frequently used distributions belonging to regular families have been listed in Table 1.1 and some other families of distributions in Table 1.2 for their ready reference to the applications of the theory developed on testing of hypotheses.

We shall now discuss the *non-regular families* of distributions which are sometimes referred to as *Pitman family.*

### 1.6.2 Non-regular (Pitman) Families

These families of distributions also allow reduction of data to a great extent, resulting into sufficient statistics of fixed dimension.

**Table 1.2:** Other Distributions

| *Name* | *Density* | *Parameter Space, Support* |
|---|---|---|
| Hypergeometric | $\frac{\binom{k}{x}\binom{M-k}{n-x}}{\binom{M}{n}}$ | $M = 1, 2, \ldots;\ x = 0, 1, \ldots, n$<br>$k = 0, 1, \ldots, M,\ n = 1, 2, \ldots, M$ |
| Double exponential $DE(\alpha,\ \beta)$ | $\frac{1}{2\beta}\exp\{-\frac{\lvert x-\alpha\rvert}{\beta}\}$ | $-\infty < \alpha < \infty,\ \beta > 0$<br>$-\infty < x < \infty$ |
| Cauchy $\mathcal{C}(\alpha,\ \beta)$ | $\frac{\beta}{\pi}\cdot\frac{1}{\beta^2 + (x-\alpha)^2}$ | $-\infty < \alpha < \infty,\ \beta > 0$<br>$-\infty < x < \infty$ |
| Logistic $L(\alpha,\ \beta)$ | $\frac{1}{\beta}\frac{e^{(x-\alpha)/\beta}}{[1 + e^{-(x-\alpha)/\beta}]^2}$ | $-\infty < \alpha < \infty,\ \ \beta > 0$<br>$-\infty < x < \infty$ |
| t-distribution | $\frac{\Gamma(\frac{n+1}{2})}{\Gamma(n/2)}\frac{1}{\sqrt{n\pi}}\frac{1}{(1+x^2/n)^{\frac{n+1}{2}}}$ | $n > 0,\ \ -\infty < x < \infty$ |
| $F$-distribution | $\frac{\Gamma(\frac{m+n}{2})}{\Gamma(m/2)\Gamma(n/2)}(\frac{m}{n})^{m/2}\cdot$<br>$\frac{x^{(m-2)/2}}{[1+(m/n)x]^{(m+n)/2}}$ | $m, n = 1, 2, \ldots;\ x > 0$ |
| $\chi^2$-distribution | $\frac{1}{\Gamma(n/2)}(\frac{1}{2})^{n/2}\cdot$<br>$\chi^{n/2-1}e^{-(1/2)x}$ | $n = 1, 2, \ldots;\ x > 0$ |

Let us consider $u(x)$ as some positive function of $x$ and let $Q_1(\theta)$ and $Q_2(\theta)$ be extended real-valued functions of $\theta$ for which $Q_1(\theta) < Q_2(\theta)$. Let us define a density

$$f_X(x|\theta) = c(\theta)\cdot u(x) \quad \text{for} \quad Q_1(\theta) < x < Q_2(\theta)$$

and

$$[c(\theta)]^{-1} = \int_{Q_1(\theta)}^{Q_2(\theta)} u(x)\,dx < \infty \tag{1.8}$$

Support for this family is given by $S_\theta = \{x|Q_1(\theta) < x < Q_2(\theta)\}$, which depends on $\theta$. Note that for regular families support does not dependent on $\theta$. Support is a range of $x$ on which the density is positive. A family with the density of the type given by Eq. (1.8) is known as *Pitman family.*

If one draws a random sample $X_1, X_2, \ldots, X_n$ from the Pitman family, the joint distribution of the sample observations is given by

$$f_{\mathbf{X}}(\mathbf{x}|\theta) = [c(\theta)]^n\left(\prod_{i=1}^n u(x_i)\right)\mathrm{I}_{(Q_1(\theta),\infty)}(\min x_j)\cdot\mathrm{I}_{(-\infty,\ Q_2(\theta))}(\max x_j)$$

One could easily show that the statistic $(\min X_j,\ \max X_j)$ is sufficient for $\theta$, by using factorization theorem. Therefore, we see that Pitman family allows reduction of data from $n$-dimension to 2, or even to 1 in some cases where one of $Q_1$ or $Q_2$ is infinite.

Table 1.3 lists some commonly distributions that belong to this family.

**Table 1.3:** Some Non-regular Families of Distributions

| *Density* | *Name* | *Parameter space* | *Support* ($S_\theta$) |
|---|---|---|---|
| $\frac{1}{\theta}$ | Uniform $U(0, \theta)$ | $\theta > 0$ | $0 < x < \theta$ |
| $\frac{1}{\theta}$ | Uniform $U(-\theta/2, \theta/2)$ | $\theta > 0$ | $-\theta/2 < x < \theta/2$ |
| 1 | $U(\theta - 1/2, \theta + 1/2)$ | $\theta > 0$ | $\theta - 1/2 < x < \theta + 1/2$ |
| $\frac{1}{N}$ | Uniform | $N \geq 1$ | $x = 1, 2, \ldots, N$ |
| $e^{-(x-\theta)}$ | Family with $\theta$ as location parameter | | $x > \theta$ |
| $c(\theta)2^{-x/\theta}$ $\{(c(\theta) = 2^{1-1/\theta} \cdot (2^{1/\theta} - 1))\}$ | | $\theta > 0$ | $x = \theta,\ \theta + 1, \ldots$ |
| $(1-p)p^{x-\theta}$ | | $0 < p < 1$ | $x = \theta,\ \theta + 1, \ldots;$ $0 < p < 1$ |
| $(2/\theta^2)(\theta - x)$ | | $\theta > 0$ | $0 < x < \theta$ |

# 1.7 SOME RESULTS FROM MATHEMATICAL ANALYSIS

Inner point of a set $M$ is interpreted as a point interior to $M$.

**Definition 1.7.1. (Interior Point)** A point $p$ is called interior point of $M$ if there is a neighbourhood $N$ of $p$ such that $N \subset M$.

**Definition 1.7.2. (Open Set)** A set $M$ is called open if every point of $M$ is an interior point of $M$.

**Definition 1.7.3. (Weak Convergence)** Let $\mathcal{C}$ be a uniformly bounded class of measurable functions. The sequence $\{\phi_n\}$ is said to converge to $\phi$ weakly if

$$\int \phi_n \, p \, d\mu \to \int \phi \, p \, d\mu$$

for all functions $p$ that are $\mu$-integrable.

**Definition 1.7.4. (Compact Space)** A space $\mathcal{F}$ is called compact if every sequence in $\mathcal{F}$ has a convergent subsequence whose limit point is in $\mathcal{F}$. In other words, given any sequence $\{\phi_n\}$, there exists a subsequence $\{\phi_{n_i}\}$ and a function $\phi$ s.t.

$$\lim \int \phi_{n_i} \, p \, d\mu = \int \phi \, p \, d\mu$$

# Chapter 2

# Most Powerful Tests

## 2.1 INTRODUCTION

In the present book the problem of testing of hypothesis has been discussed under the framework of game theory and decision theory. Formally, game theory has been defined by considering three basic elements, $\Theta$: a non-empty set as parameter space; $\mathcal{A}$: a non-empty set of actions available to the statistician; loss function $L(\theta, a)$ : a real valued function defined on $\Theta \times \mathcal{A}$, and is represented by a triplet $(\Theta, \mathcal{A}, L)$. In this, nature chooses a value $\theta$ from $\Theta$ once and for all, statistician chooses an action $a$ from $\mathcal{A}$, without being informed of the choice of the nature. Whereas, statistical decision theory is defined as a game $(\Theta, \mathcal{A}, L)$ with a random variable $X$ whose distribution is given by $P_\theta$, and where $P_\theta$ belongs to a family of distributions $\mathcal{P} = \{P_\theta, \theta \in \Theta\}$. By the rule of the game, statistician is allowed to collect information on the choice of the nature by performing a random experiment $\xi_\theta$, before he makes his choice from action space $\mathcal{A}$. In statistical decision theory nature chooses a value $\theta$ from $\Theta$ without an objective to maximize her winnings, and statistician chooses an action so that he could minimize his losses. Therefore, nature is not a *rational opponent* whereas an statistician is *rational.*

More formally, let $X$ be a random variable taking on its values from sample space $\mathfrak{X}$ which is an Euclidean space; $\mathcal{B}$ be a Borel field generated by all subsets of $\mathfrak{X}$. The probability measure, which $X$ generates over $(\mathfrak{X}, \mathcal{B})$ with respect to a basic measure $\mu$, is denoted by $P_\theta$ or $P_\theta(B)$ for all Borel sets $B \in \mathcal{B}$. For the sets of the type $\{x : x \leq a\}$, $P_\theta(X \leq a)$ is called the cumulative distribution function of $X$ and is denoted by $F_X(x|\theta)$. This $P_\theta$ belongs to a family of distributions $\mathcal{P} = \{P_\theta, \theta \in \Theta\}$. In a statistical decision problem, one is generally interested in characterizing $P_\theta$, on the basis of the information $(X_1, \ldots, X_n)$ collected by the statistician, which the true distribution of the random variable $X$ actually follows in $\mathcal{P}$. Here, the distribution function of $X_1, \ldots, X_n$ induced over $n$-dimensional Euclidean space has been defined by $F_{X_1,\ldots,X_n}(a_1, \ldots, a_n) = P_\theta\{X_1 \leq a_1, \ldots, X_n \leq a_n\}$. In other words, the statistician looks at the random observation $\mathbf{X} = \mathbf{x}$ before making a decision $a$ from $\mathcal{A}$, or mathematically, the statistician defines a mapping from $\mathfrak{X}$ into $\mathcal{A}$. In testing of hypothesis, shown as a special case of statistical decision problem in subsection 2.1.3, the statistician hypothesizes on the parameter $\theta$ with the purpose of knowing whether the hypothesis is true or false. This divides $\mathcal{P}$ into two partitions, one of those for which the hypothesis is true and the other of those for which the hypothesis is false. The statistician then tests, on the basis of observations $X_1, \ldots, X_n$, whether the hypothesis is true or false.

### 2.1.1 Statistical Decision Problem

A decision problem is known as statistical decision problem when the game $(\Theta, \mathcal{A}, L)$ is coupled with an experiment with a random variable $X \sim P_\theta$, $\theta \in \Theta$, where $\theta$ is the true value chosen by nature. For example, if one is to infer about a mean parameter $\theta$ of $N(\theta, 1)$, $\theta \in \mathbb{R}^1$, the statistician would conduct a random experiment and collect information on $X$ by taking a random sample $X_1, X_2, \ldots, X_n$ of size $n$. He then utilizes these observation $\mathbf{X} = \mathbf{x}$ for making an inference about $\theta$.

### 2.1.2 Non-randomized Decision Function

After observing $X = x$, the statistician looks at the data and on the basis of which he decides an action $d(x)$ from $\mathcal{A}$. In other words, statistician defines a mapping from sample space $\mathfrak{X}$ into $\mathcal{A}$. Such an action chosen by the statistician is called non-randomized decision rule so that its risk

$$R(\theta, d) = E_\theta^X L(\theta, d(X)) \tag{2.1}$$

exists and is finite for all $\theta \in \Theta$ [Ferguson, 1967][54]. The class of all non-randomized decision rules is denoted by $D$.

If $D$ consists of those functions $d$ for which $L(\theta, d(x))$, for each fixed $\theta \in \Theta$, is Lebesgue integrable function of $x$, Eq. (2.1) is defined as

$$R(\theta, d) = \int L(\theta, d(x)) \, dP_\theta(x) \tag{2.2}$$

and is known as *Lebesgue integral*. (Refer Chapter 1).

On the other hand, if $D$ contains all such functions $d$ for which $L(\theta, d(x))$, for each fixed $\theta \in \Theta$, is continuous on $x$ under $F_X(x|\theta)$, the expectation is defined as

$$R(\theta, d) = \int L(\theta, d(x)) \, dF_X(x|\theta) \tag{2.3}$$

and is known as *Riemann or Riemann-Stieltjes integral.*

The theoretical developments and mathematical proofs which are discussed in this book would be equally valid for both types of integrals, i.e. Lebesgue and Riemann integrals. Therefore, we would consider the definition of the expectation to be arbitrary unless stated otherwise and would assume $D$ to be well defined.

The decision problem $(\Theta, \mathcal{A}, L)$, after introducing non-randomized decision rules, changes to $(\Theta, D, R)$.

### 2.1.3 Testing Problem as a Special Case of Statistical Decision Problem

Consider a statistical decision problem $(\Theta, \mathcal{A}, L)$ where, $\Theta \subseteq \mathbb{R}^1$ and $\mathcal{A} = \{a_0, a_1\}$ with $X \sim P_\theta$, $\theta \in \Theta$. Let $\Theta_0$ be the subset of $\Theta$ under the null hypothesis $H_0$, which is some hypothesized statement on the parameter $\theta$ and $\Theta_1$ be the subset of $\Theta$ under the alternative hypothesis $H_1$. The null and alternative hypothesis are discussed more formally in Section 2.1.9. Here, $\Theta_0$ and $\Theta_1$ are such that $\Theta_0 \cap \Theta_1 = \{\phi\}$ and $\Theta_0 \cup \Theta_1 = \Theta$. The loss function in hypothesis testing, for some $\theta \in \Theta$, is defined as

$$L(\theta, a_0) = \begin{cases} c_1 & \text{if } \theta \in \Theta_1 \\ 0 & \text{if } \theta \in \Theta_0 \end{cases} \tag{2.4}$$

$$L(\theta, a_1) = \begin{cases} 0 & \text{if } \theta \in \Theta_1 \\ c_2 & \text{if } \theta \in \Theta_0 \end{cases} \tag{2.5}$$

where, $c_1, c_2 > 0$. The loss function in Eqs. (2.4) and (2.5) suggests that the statistician would take action $a_0$ to accept $H_0$ if $\theta \in \Theta_0$ and $a_1$ to reject $H_0$ if $\theta \in \Theta_1$. Such decision problems are called problems of testing of hypothesis. The statistician collects information $X_1, X_2, \ldots, X_n$ on the choices of the nature such that $X \sim P_\theta$, $\theta \in \Theta$; he then utilizes these to take an action $a$ from $\mathcal{A}$. In other words, he deals with a space $D$ of non-randomized decision rules $d$ which map $\mathfrak{X}$ into $\mathcal{A} = \{a_0, a_1\}$. Further, let the probability $P_\theta\{d(x) = a_1\}$ be well defined for all values of $\theta \in \Theta$. Utilizing the loss function given in Eqs. (2.4) and (2.5), the risk of choosing such a decision rule $d$ at some point $\theta \in \Theta$ is given by

$$R(\theta, d) = E_\theta^X L(\theta, d(X)) = \begin{cases} c_1 P_\theta\{d(X) = a_0\} & \text{if } \theta \in \Theta_1 \\ c_2 P_\theta\{d(X) = a_1\} & \text{if } \theta \in \Theta_0 \end{cases} \tag{2.6}$$

### 2.1.4 Probability of Type I and Type II Errors

The risk $R(\theta,\, d)$, as in Eq. (2.6), indicates the amount of loss due to incorrect decision. If $c_1 = c_2 = 1$, the loss function in Eqs. (2.4) and (2.5) is called $0-1$ loss function. In this case, $R(\theta,\, d)$ becomes $P_\theta\{d(X) = a_0\}$ when $\theta \in \Theta_1$, the probability of accepting $H_0$ when it is false, and is known as probability of type II error; and $R(\theta, d)$ becomes $P_\theta\{d(X) = a_1\}$ when $\theta \in \Theta_0$, the probability of rejecting $H_0$ when it is true, and this probability is known as probability of type I error. We shall see in the sections 2.1.12 and 2.2 as to how these error probabilities play a key role in arriving at an optimal decision rule (test) in a well defined class of decision rules for a given hypothesis testing problem.

### 2.1.5 Randomization

Given a decision problem the statistician, sometimes, does not take decision himself, but leaves the choice to some random mechanism. In other words, he defines a probability distribution over a class of decision rules and chooses an action accordingly. Such a probability distribution is known as randomized decision rule.

**Randomized action**

Given a decision problem $(\Theta, \mathcal{A}, L)$, the statistician defines a probability distribution over $\mathcal{A}$. Such a probability distribution is known as randomized action, denoted by $P$. Let $Z$ be a random variable taking values in $\mathcal{A}$, so that $Z$ follows the distribution $P$. The loss of randomized action $P$ has been defined as

$$L(\theta, P) = E^Z L(\theta, Z) \tag{2.7}$$

provided it exists and is finite for every $\theta$. The space of all such randomized actions $P$ is denoted by $\mathcal{A}^*$, and the decision problem is denoted by $(\Theta, \mathcal{A}^*, L)$

**Randomized decision rule**

Given a decision problem $(\Theta, D, R)$, the statistician defines a probability distribution $\delta$ over $D$. This $\delta$ is called a randomized decision rule provided the risk in taking $\delta$

$$R(\theta, \delta) = E^Z R(\theta, Z) \tag{2.8}$$

exists and is finite for all $\theta \in \Theta$. Here, $Z$ is a random variable taking its values from $D$, whose distribution is given by $\delta$. The space of all such randomized decision rules is denoted by $D^*$ and the decision problem is denoted by $(\Theta, D^*, R)$.

### 2.1.6 Behavioural Decision Rule

A mapping $\delta(x)$ from sample space $\mathfrak{X}$ into $\mathcal{A}^*$ is called a behavioural decision rule provided its risk function

$$\widehat{R}(\theta, \delta) = E_\theta^X L(\theta, \delta(X)) \tag{2.9}$$

exists and is finite for all $\theta \in \Theta$. For each $x$ in the sample space, $\delta(x)$ is a probability distribution over $\mathcal{A}$, $\delta(x) \in \mathcal{A}^*$. The class of all such behavioural decision rules is denoted by $\mathcal{D}$ and the decision problem by $(\Theta,\ D, \hat{R})$.

In general, behavioural rules are simpler to use than randomized rules and that $\dim(D) \leq \dim(D^*)$. Further, in quite general situations, the games $(\Theta, D^*, R)$ and $(\Theta, \mathcal{D}, \widehat{R})$ are equivalent in the sense that for any $\delta \in \mathcal{D}^*$ there is a $\hat{\delta}$ in $\mathcal{D}$ for which $R(\theta, \delta) = \widehat{R}(\theta, \hat{\delta})$ for all $\theta$ and conversely. However, in Section 2.1.11, it has been shown that for a given testing problem a behavioural decision rule becomes a test. Therefore, here-after we would confine only to behavioural decision rules while searching for an optimal decision rule for a given testing problem.

### 2.1.7 Comparison of Decision Rules

Rules in some decision space $(D, D^* \text{or} \mathcal{D})$ may be compared on the basis following comparison principle:

**Definition 2.1.1.** A rule $\delta_1$ is said to be *as good as* $\delta_2$ if $R(\theta, \delta_1) \leq R(\theta, \delta_2)$ $\forall\ \theta \in \Theta$; $\delta_1$ is said to be *better* than $\delta_2$ if $R(\theta, \delta_1) \leq R(\theta, \delta_2)$ $\forall\ \theta \in \Theta$, and there exists atleast one $\theta$ in $\Theta$ on which $R(\theta, \delta_1) < R(\theta, \delta_2)$; and $\delta_1$ is said to be equivalent to $\delta_2$ if $R(\theta, \delta_1) = R(\theta, \delta_2)$ $\forall\ \theta \in \Theta$.

The ordering of rules according to Definition 2.1.1 is known as partial order relationship since not every rule could necessarily be compared with other. Following this ordering, an optimal decision rule in some decision space, is defined in Definition 2.1.2.

**Definition 2.1.2. (Admissible Decision Rule)** A rule $\delta$ is said to be admissible if there dose not exist any rule better than $\delta$.

### 2.1.8 Desirable Classes of Rules

**Definition 2.1.3.** A class as a subset of some decision space is said to be *complete* if for any rule outside the class there exists a rule in the class which is better than that. Further, a class is said to be essentially complete if for any rule not in the class there exists a rule which is as good as the considered rule. A class is said to be minimal complete if it is complete and no proper subclass of it is complete. A class is said to be minimal essentially complete if it is essentially complete, and no proper subclass of it is essentially complete.

The advantage of looking for a complete or essentially complete class in a hypothesis testing problem is that the statistician restricts his attention to this class in search for an optimal test, as all optimal tests, are contained in this class. If, for a given testing problem, a minimal complete or minimal essentially complete class exists, it results into maximal reduction of the problem, since this is the smallest class of tests having the nice properties of a complete or essentially complete class. In fact, minimal complete class consists of exactly the admissible tests.

We have shown in subsection 2.1.3 that a testing of hypothesis problem is a special case of statistical decision problem and the tests are behavioral decision rules. Let us, therefore, study the testing problems under a decision theoretic setup. Consequently, all the standard results on decision theory then directly apply to testing of hypothesis with necessary modifications if required.

### 2.1.9 Null Hypothesis

From the introductory course on statistical inference, we notice that a little is known about the values of population parameters that define the probability distributions of the world or some random variable of interest. This is referred to as a statistical model. We often have some prior notion what these parameters might be. Such a guess, which we most often believe to be true, put in a form of a statement about the population parameter, is called the 'null hypothesis' and is denoted by $H_0$. While constructing the null hypothesis the statistician makes a statement of population parameter with a conservative mind and maintains status quo. Sometimes, the null hypothesis is referred to as a statement regarding the population parameter $\theta$, which is tested for its possible rejection. The term hypothesis has been derived from the Greek word *hypotithenai* which means *to put under* or *to suppose*. The complement of the null hypothesis is called the alternative hypothesis and is denoted by $H_1$. However, a research hypothesis is what we want to *prove* and is usually set up as $H_1$. Therefore, we may write $H_0$: the research hypothesis is false.

In order to test the formulated hypothesis some information needs to be collected on the parameter. Therefore, we draw a sample $X_1, X_2, \ldots, X_n$ from the population. On the basis of this observed sample we decide either to accept or reject the null hypothesis. Let us consider a coin for which it is claimed that the probability of coming up head is 0.8 when tossed. The coin is tossed 10 times and turns up head 4 times. The probability of this when the claim is true is $\{n!/(x!\,(n-x)!)\}p^x(1-p)^{n-x} = \{10!/(4!\,6!)\}(0.8)^4(0.2)^6 = 0.005$. This low probability suggests that this outcome serves as an evidence against the claim. If, on the other hand, we get 7 heads in 10 tosses, the probability of the outcome, when the claim is true, is given by $10!/\{7!\,3!\}(0.8)^7(0.2^3) = 0.201$, and we conclude that the data gives us a little reason to doubt the claim. This simple example illustrates the basic idea of testing of hypothesis. Therefore, if what we observe is *unlikely* when the hypothesis is true, we say that the data has evidence against the hypothesis and we doubt the validity of the hypothesis. On the other hand, if what we observe is *not unlikely* when the hypothesis is true then the data does not have sufficient evidence against the hypothesis. At the same time, we cannot take this as an evidence in favour of the hypothesis, since there could be many other competing hypotheses for which the observed outcome has a high probability. We never accept the null hypothesis, but we only state that the data contains no evidence against the null hypothesis, as we do not have enough evidence in favour of $H_0$. Lack of evidence against is not evidence for. If you do not tell somebody that he looks like alien from the other planet, it does not mean that he really is. When we do not have enough evidence against the null hypothesis $H_0$, we do not know whether the null hypothesis is actually true or false within a specified level of significance $\alpha$. Care must be taken when $\hat{\alpha}$($p$-value) (formally discussed in Section 2.2.1) is very large and the sample size is also large, we begin to suspect that $H_0$ is probably true. This may sometimes be a sign that we might have chosen a null hypothesis that was not worth testing. For example, for testing $H_0 : p \leq 1/4$, $p$ being the probability of coming up head, few hundred trials of tossing the coin will probably yield a $p$-value very close to 1. Only under such circumstances one could state that $H_0$ is accepted, otherwise we shall always state that the present sample does not carry enough evidence to reject $H_0$. However, more apt statement would be "we do not have sufficient data to draw a conclusion". On the other hand, rejection of the null hypothesis does not necessarily mean that the alternative is true. We may reject the null hypothesis by chance when it is true, and we were unlucky in our sample (if $\alpha$= 5%), we are unlucky one in twenty. In addition to it, a wrong statistical model might had resulted into rejection of true null hypothesis or a failure to reject a false null hypothesis. As proved rejection of $H_0$ must not be misunderstood with $H_1$. We only say that we accept $H_1$.

### 2.1.10 Simple and Composite Hypothesis

The parametric space, when the null hypothesis is true, denoted by $\Theta_0$ and when the alternative hypothesis is true it is denoted by $\Theta_1$. If $\Theta_0(\Theta_1)$ contains just a single point, we call the hypothesis $H_0 : \theta \in \Theta_0$ $(H_1 : \theta \in \Theta_1)$ as *simple*, otherwise *composite*. In other words, if the distribution $F_\theta(\mathbf{x})$ is completely specified under $\Theta_i$ we call $H_i$ as simple, otherwise composite.

### 2.1.11 A Test Function

Let a random sample $\mathbf{X} = (X_1, X_2, .., X_n)$ be drawn from the population with density function $f_\theta(\mathbf{x})$, $\theta \in \Theta$; and the corresponding sample space be denoted by $\mathfrak{X} \subseteq \mathbb{R}^n$. On the basis of an observation $\mathbf{x}$ the statistician decides whether $a_0$ or $a_1$ is to be chosen, where, $a_0$ corresponds to the acceptance of $H_0$ and $a_1$ corresponds to the rejection of $H_0$. In this way the statistician thinks of a function $d$ that partitions the sample space $\mathfrak{X}$ into two measurable subsets $w$ and $w^c$ such that $w \cup w^c = \mathfrak{X}$. It is then decided to take action $a_1$(to reject $H_0$)when $\mathbf{x}$ falls in $w$ and to take action $a_0$ (to accept $H_0$) when $\mathbf{x}$ falls in $w^c$. This mapping $d$ from sample space into action space, symbolically denoted by $d : \mathfrak{X} \to \mathcal{A}$, is called a *test* or *critical region.*

The consideration of randomized decision rules that involve randomization over all possible measurable subsets $w$ of $\mathfrak{X}$ is difficult to handle. Yet behavioural decision rules are simpler in nature. A behavioural decision rule is a mapping $\phi : \mathfrak{X} \to \mathcal{A}^*$, with the interpretation that, when $X = x$ has been observed, the action $a_1$ (to reject $H_0$) is taken with probability $\phi(x)$ and action $a_0$ (to accept $H_0$) is taken with probability $(1 - \phi(x))$. The function $\phi(x)$, which is the probability of rejecting $H_0$ when $X = x$ has been observed, is known as a *statistical test.* Now, following the notations of behavioural decision rule, a non-randomized decision rule $w$ is expressed as

$$\phi(x) = \begin{cases} 1 & \text{if } x \in w \\ 0 & \text{if } x \in w^c \end{cases} \tag{2.10}$$

### 2.1.12 Power Function of a Test

The risk function of a non-randomized test $w$ is defined as

$$\begin{aligned} R(\theta, w) &= L(\theta, a_0) \cdot (1 - P_\theta\{w\}) + L(\theta, a_1) \cdot P_\theta\{w\} \\ &= L(\theta, a_0) + P_\theta\{w\}(L(\theta, a_1) - L(\theta, a_0)) \end{aligned}$$

where $P_\theta\{w\}$ is the probability of rejecting $H_0$ when $\theta$ is the true state of the nature. Here, $w$ is called a non-randomized test and $P_\theta\{w\}$ is called the *power function of the test* $w$.

Similarly, for any arbitrary behavioural decision rule $\phi$ (or test) the risk function is given by

$$R(\theta, \phi) = L(\theta, a_0) + E_\theta^X[\phi(X)](L(\theta, a_1) - L(\theta, a_0)) \tag{2.11}$$

provided $E_\theta^X\phi(X)$ is well defined and finite for all $\theta \in \Theta$. The term $E_\theta^X\phi(X)$ is called the *power function of the test* $\phi$. If we consider the $0-1$ form of the loss function, the risk of a test $\phi$ becomes

$$R(\theta, \phi) = \begin{cases} E_\theta\phi(X) & \text{if } \theta \in \Theta_0 \\ 1 - E_\theta\phi(X) & \text{if } \theta \in \Theta_1 \end{cases} \tag{2.12}$$

where, the term $E_\theta\phi(X)$ is the probability of rejecting $H_0$ when it is true and is known as the *probability of type I error* whenever $\Theta_0$ is simple, i.e. $\Theta_0 = \{\theta_0\}$. The second term $1 - E_\theta\phi(X)$ is the probability of accepting $H_0$ when it is false, known as the *probability of type II error* denoted by $\beta(\theta)$, whenever $\Theta_1$ is simple, i.e. $\Theta_1 = \{\theta_1\}$. These error probabilities have already been defined in Section 2.1.4, but without referring to power function of a test $\phi$.

The probability of type I error $\alpha$ depends on the choice of the critical region $w$ and on the null hypothesis $H_0$, while probability of type II error $\beta$ depends on both the hypothesis, null and alternative. An increase in $\alpha$ results in decrease in $\beta$ and a decrease in $\alpha$ results in an increase in $\beta$. We would consider few examples to illustrate these and other related concepts when there is only one alternative (Example 2.1.1) and when there is a range of alternatives (Example 2.1.2).

**Example 2.1.1.** *Research and Development department of a pharmaceutical company has recently developed a dietary supplement to reduce cholesterol level. Company applied for license to FDA, a drug regulatory body, to market the drug. The FDA authorities asked the company to administer the supplement on 100 people and check the hypothesis.*

> $H_0$: *The drug does nothing to reduce the cholesterol (p= 0.10)*
> $H_1$: *The drug reduces the cholesterol in 20% people (p= 0.20)*

***Solution:*** FDA knew from the past experience that in about 10% of people cholesterol declines naturally. FDA decided to issue licence for marketing the drug only when the experiment shows strong evidence that the drug reduces cholestrol in 20% of all the people. FDA also supplied the decision rule

$$\phi(\hat{p}) = \begin{cases} 1 & \text{if } \hat{p} > 0.15 \\ 0 & \text{if } \hat{p} \le 0.15 \end{cases} \tag{2.13}$$

where, $\hat{p}$ is observed proportion and $\hat{p} \sim N(p, \frac{pq}{n})$. The standard error of the sample proportion under $H_0$ takes the value 0.03.

We shall discuss here the form of the critical region, the error probabilities, their inter-relationship and the power of the test. Probability of type I error, $\alpha$ is given by

$$\begin{aligned}\alpha &= P(\hat{p} > 0.15 \mid H_0 : p = 0.10)\\ &= P\Big(\frac{\hat{p}-p}{\sqrt{\frac{p(1-p)}{n}}} > \frac{0.15-p}{\sqrt{\frac{p(1-p)}{n}}}\Big| p = 0.10\Big) = P(Z > 1.67)\\ &= 0.0475 \qquad \text{where } Z \text{ is a } N(0,1) \text{ variable.}\end{aligned}$$

Further, $\sigma_{\hat{p}} = \sqrt{\frac{p(1-p)}{n}} = 0.04$ under the alternative hypothesis.

Probability of type II error, $\beta$ is given by

$$\begin{aligned}\beta &= P(\hat{p} \leq 0.15 \mid p = 0.20) = P\Big(Z \leq \frac{0.15-0.20}{0.04}\Big| p = 0.20\Big)\\ &= P(Z \leq -1.25) = 0.1056\end{aligned}$$

The critical region for observed proportions, $\alpha$ and $\beta$ are shown in Figure 2.1.

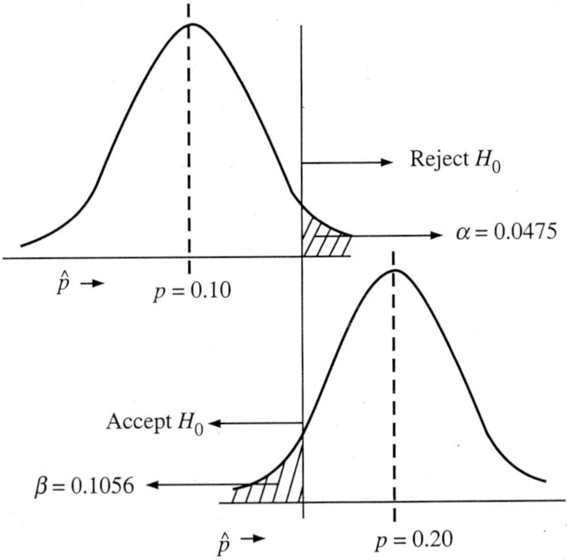


**Figure 2.1:** Error propbabilities and their inter-relationship.

The test has right sided critical region. The region shown on the right side of the vertical line $\hat{p} = 0.15$ is the critical region and region toward left of line $\hat{p} = 0.15$ is the acceptance region. The probability of rejecting $H_0$ when it is true, $\alpha$, is shown by the shaded area in the top panel and the probability of accepting $H_0$ when it is false is shown by the shaded area in bottom panel. From Figure 2.1 it is clear that if we could tolerate more type I error, i.e. more $\alpha$, the critical region shifts toward left, and as a result, area shown in the bottom panel ($\beta$) contracts. Similarly, if $\alpha$ decreases, area in the top panel decreases. Consequently area in the bottom panel expands, i.e. $\beta$ increases. $1-\beta = P(\text{reject } H_0 \mid H_0 \text{ is false})$ is called power of a given test and it measures the ability of the test to differentiate between the null and the true value of the parameter. If we could tolerate more $\alpha$, it would be better as it results into low $\beta$ or high power $1-\beta$ and our test would differentiate between $H_0$ and $H_1$ more clearly. Precisely, probability of type II error ($\beta$) measures the *degree of falseness* of a false null hypothesis. For example, if the null hypothesis is false, but is nearly true such as hypothesizing that $p = 0.10$ when actually it is $p = 0.1005$,

$$\beta = P(\hat{p} \leq 0.15 \mid P = 0.1005) = P\Big(Z \leq \frac{0.15 - 0.1005}{\sqrt{0.000904}}\Big)$$

$$= P(Z \leq 1.65) = 0.9505$$

which is quite large and it is very likely that we accept a false hypothesis, the power $1-\beta$ of such a test 0.0495 is quite low showing the poor ability of the test to differentiate between null and the true parameter value. However, if the null hypothesis is grossly false (such as hypothesizing that $p = 0.10$ when it is actually very high 0.94 say), $\beta$ in this case is very low and we enjoy a higher power. Therefore, we have seen that the power of the test depends on the difference between the hypothesized and the true value of the parameter, true value being unknown, power $1-\beta(\theta)$ is expressed as a function of true value of the parameter $\theta$. The function $\beta(\theta)$ is known as the *operating characteristic (OC) function.*

**Example 2.1.2.** *Staples manufacturing company, Kangaroo, claims that their latest machines put 1000 staples in a box on an average. We doubt its claim and wish to test the company's claim. It is known that the population standard deviation is given by 7. The hypothesis we wish to test is given by*

$$H_0 : \mu = 1000 \quad \text{against} \quad H_1 : \mu < 1000$$

*Let a sample of 81 boxes gives the average number of staples,* $\bar{x} = 997$.
***Solution:*** Let the test for testing the hypothesis be given by

$$\phi(\bar{x}) = \begin{cases} 1 & \text{if } \bar{x} < c \\ 0 & \text{if } \bar{x} \geq c \end{cases} \tag{2.14}$$

where, $c$ is determined so that the size of the test is 0.05. This gives

$$P(\bar{X} < c \mid \mu = 1000) = 0.05$$

$$P\Big(\frac{\bar{X}-\mu}{\sigma/\sqrt{n}} < \frac{c-\mu}{\sigma/\sqrt{n}} \mid \mu = 1000\Big) = 0.05$$

$$P(Z < \frac{c-1000}{7/9}) = 0.05$$

From normal tables, we get $\frac{c-1000}{7/9} = -1.64$ or $c = 998.72$

This gives the critical region $\bar{x} < 998.72$. The observed value of $\bar{x} = 997$ lies in the critical region that leads to rejection of the company's claim. (Refer to Figure 2.2).

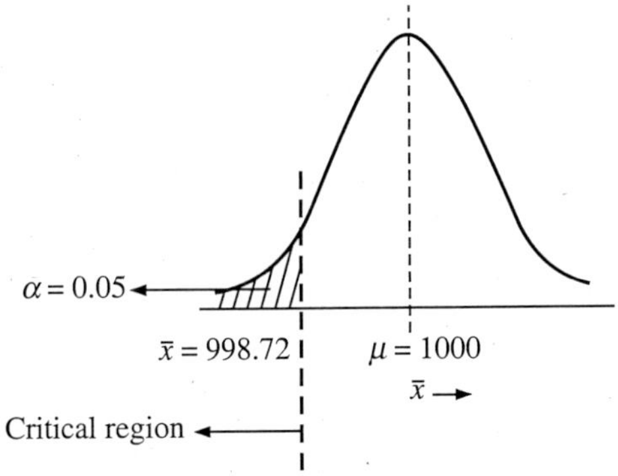


**Figure 2.2:** Critical region (test) at 5% level of significance.

We shall now calculate the power of the test $1-\beta(\mu) = P(\text{rejection of } H_0 \mid \mu)$ at $\mu = 1000$ under $H_0$ and study its behaviour at $\mu$ under $H_1$ when it moves away from $H_0$ as shown in Table 2.1.

**Table 2.1:** Power of test $\phi$ in (2.14) against $\mu$s under $H_1$.

| $\mu$ | 1000 | 999 | 998.5 | 998 | 997 | 996 | $\leq 995$ |
|---|---|---|---|---|---|---|---|
| $1-\beta(\mu)$ | 0.05 | 0.36 | 0.61 | 0.82 | 0.9864 | 0.9989 | 1 |

These values of power function $1-\beta(\mu)$ are plotted in Figure 2.3 by showing $\mu$ on $x$-axis. One could easily note from Figure 2.3 that as true value of $\mu$

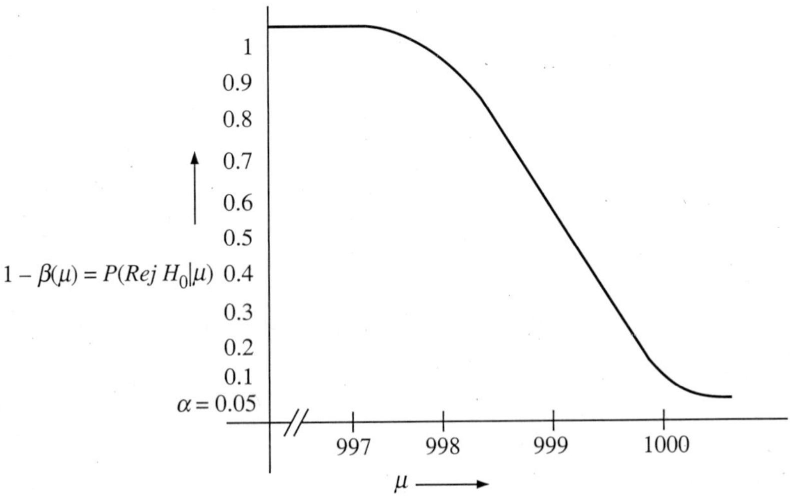


**Figure 2.3:** Power of the test $\phi$ against $\mu$ in $H_1$.

differs increasingly from $H_0$ the power, $P(\text{rejecting } H_0 \mid \mu)$, increases very fast to 1. This shows the strength in the test grows to differentiate between the null and the true value of $\mu$ as $\mu$ moves away from $H_0$.

## 2.2 SIMPLE VERSUS SIMPLE HYPOTHESIS TESTING PROBLEM

Consider the problem $(\Theta, \mathcal{D}, \widehat{R})$ where $\Theta_0 = \{\theta_0\}$(simple null), $\Theta_1 = \{\theta_1\}$ (simple alternative), $\mathcal{A} = \{a_0, a_1\}$, $\Theta = \{\theta_0, \theta_1\}$ and $\mathcal{D}$ is the class of all behavioural decision rules. The risk set of this testing problem, $S \subset \mathbb{E}^2$ is defined as

$$S = \{(R(\theta_0, \phi), R(\theta_1, \phi)) : \phi \in \mathcal{D}\} \tag{2.15}$$

The risk function contains all the pertinent information about a test $\phi$, therefore, we shall consider the risk set $S$ containing all the relevant informations available on the testing problem $(\Theta, \mathcal{D}, \widehat{R})$. Further, if $0-1$ loss function is replaced by a loss function with a reasonable requirement $L(\theta_0, a_0) < L(\theta_0, a_1)$ and $L(\theta_1, a_0) > L(\theta_1, a_1)$, the risk set $S$ takes the shape $S'$ after appropriate origin and scale transformations along both the axes, where

$$S' = \{(\alpha, \beta) : \phi \in \mathcal{D}\} \tag{2.16}$$

with $$\alpha = E_{\theta_0}\phi(X); \quad \beta = E_{\theta_1}(1 - \phi(X)) \tag{2.17}$$

where $\alpha$ is known as the size and $1-\beta$ as power of a test $\phi$. If one considers any two points $\mathbf{x}_1$ and $\mathbf{x}_2$ in $S'$ corresponding to the tests $\phi_1$ and $\phi_2$ in $\mathcal{D}$, one can easily show that the points on the line joining $\mathbf{x}_1$ and $\mathbf{x}_2$, namely, $\alpha\mathbf{x}_1 + (1-\alpha)\mathbf{x}_2$, for $0 < \alpha < 1$, corresponding to the rules $\phi_\alpha = \alpha\phi_1 + (1-\alpha)\phi_2$ in $\mathcal{D}$, belong to $S'$, i.e. the entire line belong to $S'$. This shows that $S'$ is convex. The shape properties of the risk set has been discussed in Remark 2.2.12.

**Definition 2.2.1. (Most Powerful Test)** A test $\phi_0$ is said to be most powerful (best) test for testing $H_0$ against $H_1$ if it is of size $\alpha$ and has maximum power in the class of all level-$\alpha$ tests.

$$\mathcal{C}_\alpha = \{\phi : E_{\theta_0}\phi(X) \leq \alpha, \ \phi \in \mathcal{D}\} \tag{2.18}$$

Neyman and Pearson, (1933) [146] had given a method of finding a best test of size-$\alpha$ in the class $\mathcal{C}_\alpha$ for simple versus simple testing problem, i.e. $H_0 : X \sim f_{\theta_0}$ versus $H_1 : X \sim f_{\theta_1}$, where, $\Theta = \{\theta_0, \theta_1\}$. This method which is known as Neyman-Pearson lemma, is stated in Theorem 2.2.1 under the statistical set up of Section 2.1.

**Theorem 2.2.1.** *Consider the measure space $(\mathfrak{X}, \mathcal{B}, \mu)$, where the distribution of $X$ have densities (mass probabilities) $f(x|\theta_0)$ and $f(x|\theta_1)$ with respect to the probability measure $\mu$.*

(a) *Existence: For testing* $H_0 : X \sim f_{\theta_0}(= f_0)$ *against* $H_1 : X \sim f_{\theta_1}(= f_1)$ *and for every* $0 < \alpha \leq 1$*, there exits a test* $\phi$*,* $k \geq 0$ *and* $\gamma(x) = \gamma$ *such that*

$$E_{\theta_0}\phi(X) = \alpha \tag{2.19}$$

$$\phi(x) = \begin{cases} 1 & \text{if } f_1(x) > kf_0(x) \\ \gamma(x) & \text{if } f_1(x) = kf_0(x) \\ 0 & \text{if } f_1(x) < kf_0(x) \end{cases} \tag{2.20}$$

*And for* $\alpha = 0$ *there exists a test* $\phi$*,* $k = \infty$ *such that*

$$E_{\theta_0}\phi(X) = 0 \tag{2.21}$$

$$\phi(x) = \begin{cases} 1 & \text{if } f_0(x) = 0 \\ 0 & \text{if } f_0(x) > 0 \end{cases} \tag{2.22}$$

(b) *Sufficient condition for most powerful test: If a test satisfies Eqs. (2.19) and (2.20) or Eqs. (2.21) and (2.22) for some* $k \geq 0$ *and* $0 \leq \gamma(x) \leq 1$*, then it is most powerful of its size in* $\mathcal{C}_\alpha$*, where*

$$\mathcal{C}_\alpha = \{\phi | E_{\theta_0}\phi(X) \leq \alpha, \ \phi \in \mathcal{D}\} \tag{2.23}$$

(c) *Necessary condition for a most powerful test (Uniqueness): If* $\phi'$ *is most powerful of its size in* $\mathcal{C}_\alpha$*, then it has the form as given in Eq. (2.20) or Eq. (2.22), except perhaps for a set of* $x$ *with measure* $\mu$ *zero under* $H_0$ *and* $H_1$.

*Proof.* (a) *Existence:* For $\alpha = 0$, we get $k = \infty$, and the test of the Eq. 2.22 exists. For $\alpha = 1$, we get $k = 0$ and the test

$$\phi(x) = \begin{cases} 1 & \text{if } f_0(x) > 0 \\ 0 & \text{if } f_0(x) = 0 \end{cases} \tag{2.24}$$

exists.

We shall now restrict our attention to $0 < \alpha < 1$. Let us consider a random variable $Y = \dfrac{f_1(X)}{f_0(X)}$; we know that the cumulative distribution function of $Y$, $F_Y(y|H_0)$, is non-decreasing and right continuous. If for fixed $\alpha$, $0 < \alpha < 1$, there exists a $k_0$ such that $F_Y(k_0|H_0) = 1-\alpha$ and $F_Y(k_0|H_0)-F_Y(k_0-0|H_0) = P_0(f_1(x) = k_0\, f_0(x)) = 0$; we take $k = k_0, \gamma = 0$ and the test is defined a.e. $\mu$ such that

$$E_{\theta_0}\phi(X) = \alpha$$

$$\phi(x) = \begin{cases} 1 & \text{if } f_1(x) > k_0 f_0(x) \\ 0 & \text{if } f_1(x) < k_0 f_0(x) \end{cases}$$

In other words, randomization on the boundary with probability $\gamma(x) = \gamma$ is not required when the distribution of $Y|H_0$ is continuous. If the above situation is not met (Figure 2.4), i.e.

$$F_Y(k_0 - 0|H_0) \leq 1 - \alpha < F_Y(k_0|H_0)$$

Then we take $k = k_0$ and the test is defined as

$$E_{\theta_0}\phi(X) = \alpha$$

and
$$\phi(x) = \begin{cases} 1 & \text{if } f_1(x) > kf_0(x) \\ \gamma & \text{if } f_1(x) = kf_0(x) \\ 0 & \text{if } f_1(x) < kf_0(x) \end{cases}$$

with
$$\gamma = \frac{F_Y(k_0|H_0) - (1-\alpha)}{F_Y(k_0|H_0) - F_Y(k_0 - 0|H_0)}$$

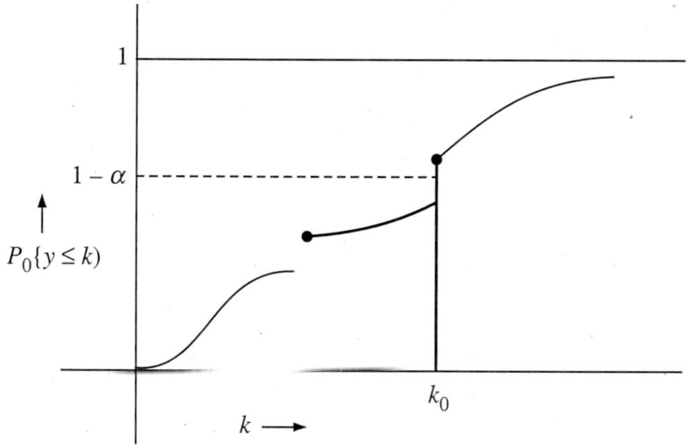


**Figure 2.4:** Discontinuous distribution function.

This test with $\gamma > 0$ is known as a randomized test. Note that the randomization on the boundary is needed when the actual size of a non-randomized test does not reach $\alpha$, and it exceeds $\alpha$ as soon as the point $Y = k_0$ is included in the critical region. This situation may arise when the distribution of $X$ or $(Y)$ is discrete.

Let there be an interval $(k', k'')$ of $Y$ for which every point in $(k', k'')$ satisfies $F_Y(k|H_0) = 1 - \alpha$, and

$$C = \left\{x : f_0(x) > 0, \quad k' < y = \frac{f_1(x)}{f_0(x)} < k''\right\}$$

Then
$$P(C|H_0) = F_Y(k'' - 0|H_0) - F_Y(k'|H_0) = 0$$

Since $f_0(x) > 0 \quad \forall\, x \in C$ and $\mu$ is $\sigma$-finite, then

$$\int_C f_0(x)\, d\mu = 0 \Rightarrow \mu(C) = 0$$

Without loss of generality one can take $\mu = f_0 + f_1$, therefore, $P(C|H_1) = 0$. This implies that $k = k_0$ such that $F_Y(k_0|H_0) = (1-\alpha)$ is unique except perhaps for a set $C$ with $P(C) = 0$ under $H_0$ and $H_1$. Therefore, the points in the sample space, for which there are two different values of $k$ so that $F_Y(k_0|H_0) = 1-\alpha$, could be excluded.

(b) *Sufficient condition for a most powerful test:* Suppose $\phi$ is a test that satisfies Eqs. (2.19) and (2.20) and $\phi'$, $0 \le \phi' \le 1$, be any other test in $\mathcal{C}_\alpha$, where $\alpha > 0$. Let us consider the integral

$$\int_{\mathfrak{X}} (\phi(x) - \phi'(x))(f_1(x) - kf_0(x))\, d\mu(x)$$

Let the sample space $\mathfrak{X}$ be divided into non-overlapping regions $\mathfrak{X}^+$, $\mathfrak{X}^0$ and $\mathfrak{X}^-$ defined as

$$\mathfrak{X}^+ = \{x \in \mathfrak{X}|\ f_1(x) > kf_0(x)\}$$

$$\mathfrak{X}^0 = \{x \in \mathfrak{X}|\ f_1(x) = kf_0(x)\}$$

and

$$\mathfrak{X}^- = \{x \in \mathfrak{X}|\ f_1(x) < kf_0(x)\}$$

so that

$$\mathfrak{X} = \mathfrak{X}^+ \cup \mathfrak{X}^0 \cup \mathfrak{X}^-$$

The above integral can now be written as

$$\int_{\mathfrak{X}^+} (\phi(x) - \phi'(x))(f_1(x) - kf_0(x))\, d\mu + \int_{\mathfrak{X}^0} (\phi(x) - \phi'(x))(f_1(x) - kf_0(x))\, d\mu(x) + \int_{\mathfrak{X}^-} (\phi(x) - \phi'(x))(f_1(x) - kf_0(x))\, d\mu(x)$$

Note that the first term of the integral gives a quantity which is $\ge 0$ since $\phi(x) - \phi'(x) \ge 0, \phi(x)$ being 1 on $\mathfrak{X}^+$ (Refer Eq. 2.19), and $f_1(x) - kf_0(x) > 0$ on $\mathfrak{X}^+$. The second term gives 0 since $f_1(x) - kf_0(x) = 0$ on $\mathfrak{X}^0$ irrespective of the value attained by $(\phi(x) - \phi'(x))$. The third term gives $\ge 0$ since $(\phi(x) - \phi'(x)) \le 0$, $\phi(x)$ being 0 on $\mathfrak{X}^-$, (see Eq. (2.19) and $f_1(x) - kf_0(x)$ being $< 0$ on $\mathfrak{X}^-$). By combining all the three terms the complete integral gives a quantity which is $\ge 0$, and we have

$$\int_{\mathfrak{X}} (\phi(x) - \phi'(x))(f_1(x) - kf_0(x))\, d\mu(x) \ge 0 \tag{2.25}$$

On simplification, we get

$$\int_{\mathfrak{X}} \phi(x) f_1(x)\, d\mu(x) - \int_{\mathfrak{X}} \phi'(x) f_1(x)\, d\mu(x) \ge k\int_{\mathfrak{X}} \phi(x) f_0(x)\, d\mu(x) - k\int_{\mathfrak{X}} \phi'(x) f_0(x)\, d\mu(x)$$

or

$$E_{\theta_1}\phi(X) - E_{\theta_1}\phi'(X) \ge kE_{\theta_0}\phi(X) - kE_{\theta_0}\phi'(X)$$

Since $k \geq 0$ and $E_{\theta_0}\phi'(X) \leq E_{\theta_0}\phi(X)$ ($\phi$ is size $\alpha$ and $\phi'$ in $\mathcal{C}_\alpha$). We get

$$E_{\theta_1}\phi(X) - E_{\theta_1}\phi'(X) \geq 0,$$

i.e. $\phi$ has no smaller power than $\phi'$. Therefore, $\phi$ is the MP size $\alpha$ test in $\mathcal{C}_\alpha$ since $\phi'$ was arbitrarily chosen.

Let us now consider a size 0 test $\phi$ that satisfies Eqs. (2.21) and (2.22) and let $\phi'$, $0 \leq \phi' \leq 1$, be any other test in $C_0$, where

$$\mathcal{C}_0 = \{\phi \in \mathcal{D} \ : \ E_{\theta_0}\phi(X) = 0\}$$

A test $\phi' \in \mathcal{C}_0$ gives $\int \phi'(x) f_0(x)\, d\mu = 0$ which implies that $\phi'(x)$ must be zero almost everywhere on the set $\{x : f_0(x) > 0\}$. Using this and the form of $\phi$ in Eq. (2.22), we get

$$\begin{aligned} E_{\theta_1}\phi(X) - E_{\theta_1}\phi'(X) &= \int_{\{x:\, f_0(x)=0\}} (\phi(x) - \phi'(x)) f_1(x)\ d\mu \\ &\quad + \int_{\{x:\, f_0(x)>0\}} (\phi(x) - \phi'(x)) f_1(x)\ dx \\ &= \int_{\{x:\, f_0(x)=0\}} (1 - \phi'(x)) f_1(x)\ d\mu\ \geq\ 0 \end{aligned}$$

or

$$E_{\theta_1}\phi(X) \geq E_{\theta_1}\phi'(X)$$

This shows that the test $\phi$ in Eq. (2.22) is MP of size 0.

(c) *Necessary condition for a most powerful test(uniqueness):* Let $\phi$ be a test given in Eqs. (2.19) and (2.20), and $\phi'$ be some other MP test of size-$\alpha$ in $\mathcal{C}_\alpha$, $\alpha > 0$, for testing $f_0$ against $f_1$. Consider $\mathfrak{X}^+$, $\mathfrak{X}^0$ and $\mathfrak{X}^-$ with their usual definitions, so that, $\mathfrak{X} = \mathfrak{X}^+ \cup \mathfrak{X}^0 \cup \mathfrak{X}^-$ and assume that the tests $\phi$ and $\phi'$ takes on different values on $\mathfrak{X}^+$ and $\mathfrak{X}^-$. Consider a set

$$S = \mathfrak{X} \cap \{x \ : \ f_1(x) \neq k f_0(x)\} = \{x \ : \ f_1(x) \neq k\ f_0(x)\}$$

Assume $\mu(S) > 0$. Now, consider the integral

$$\begin{aligned} &\int_{\mathfrak{X}} (\phi(x) - \phi'(x))(f_1(x) - k f_0(x))\, d\mu(x) \\ &\quad = \int_S (\phi(x) - \phi'(x))(f_1(x) - k f_0(x))\, d\mu(x) \\ &\qquad + \int_{\mathfrak{X}^0} (\phi(x) - \phi'(x))(f_1(x) - k f_0(x))\, d\mu(x) \end{aligned}$$

The identities $E_{\theta_0}\phi(X) = E_{\theta_0}\phi'(X)$ and $E_{\theta_1}\phi(X) = E_{\theta_1}\phi'(X)$, in the integral gives

$$\int_S (\phi(x) - \phi'(x))(f_1(x) - k f_0(x))\, d\mu(x) = 0$$

$(\phi(x) - \phi'(x))(f_1(x) - kf_0(x)) > 0$ in the integral gives $\mu(S) = 0$. This is a contradiction to the assumption $\mu(S) > 0$. Therefore, $\mu(S) = 0$. Let $\mu$ be such that $\mu = f_0 + f_1$ or $\mu(S) = P(S|H_0) + P(S|H_1)$. Then $\mu(S) = 0$ implies $P(S|H_0)$ and $P(S|H_1)$ are both zero. Thus, the probability measure of the set $S$ on which $\phi$ and $\phi'$ are different, becomes zero under the null and the alternative hypotheses. In other words, we say that $\phi$ and $\phi'$ are of the same form except perhaps on the set $\{x : f_1(x) = kf_0(x)\}$ under $H_0$ and $H_1$. This shows the uniqueness of a most powerful test.

Let $\phi$ be a test given in Eqs. (2.21) and (2.22); and $\phi'$ be a MP size 0 test in $\mathcal{C}_0$. The tests $\phi'$ and $\phi$ differ on the set

$$S = \{x : f_0(x) = 0, f_1(x) > 0\} \cup \{x : f_0(x) > 0, f_1(x) > 0\}$$

Assume $\mu(S) > 0$. Since $(\phi - \phi')f_1(x) > 0$ on $S$ and the integral

$$\int_S (\phi(x) - \phi'(x))f_1(x)\, d\mu$$

becomes 0 since $\phi$ and $\phi'$ are both MP, implies together $\mu(S) = 0$. This is a contradiction, therefore, $\mu(S) = 0$, and $P(S|H_0) = 0$ gives $P(S|H_1) = 0$. This shows that the MP tests $\phi(x)$ and $\phi'(x)$ have the same form as in Eqs. (2.21) and Eqs. (2.22) except perhaps on the set $\{x : f_0(x) > 0\} \sim \{x : f_1(x) > 0\}$ with probability measure zero under $H_0$ and $H_1$. □

### 2.2.1 p-value and Choice Level of Significance

The choice of a level of significance in testing problems is somewhat ad hoc (Lehmann, 1986) [130]. This is so because in many experimental situations one does not know as to how much one could tolerate the first kind of error. During the times of theoretical developments these values were conveniently chosen such as 0.01 or 0.05 in order to reduce the number of tables required to carry out the tests. Later, as a matter of convenience and ready reference, these values became the conventional levels. In fact, the choice of significance level should be such that the power of the test against the alternatives must not be low. One may note from the shape of the risk set (refer Remark 2.2.12), that more power can be achieved if more $\alpha$ is tolerated. But tests with low chance of detecting the effect when it exists (i.e. low probability of rejecting $H_0$ when it is false, or the low power) must be avoided. In a situation where power is very close to 1, one may choose lower $\alpha$ so long as power remains close to 1. Different rules for choosing $\alpha$ in combination with prescribed power have been discussed by Lehman (1958) [122]; Arrow (1960) [2] and Sanathanan (1974), among others.

A pre-experimental motivation of choosing low level of significance $\alpha$ could be when one has strong reason to believe that the null hypothesis is true. In this case one would reject the hypothesis only when one has extremely strong evidence to reject it and therefore, the significance level is set low. This results into a critical region $R$ consisting of the points of $\mathfrak{X}$ whose total probability under the null hypothesis $H_0$ is small. It will be very unlikely, now, that the observation $X = x$ falls in the critical region when $H_0$ were true. More generally, in scientific applications one is not only interested simply in accepting or rejecting the hypothesis but also to assess how strong the data has the evidence to reject $H_0$. In addition to it, to avoid randomization, the experimenter becomes interested in determining the smallest significance level $\hat{\alpha}(\mathbf{x})$ or $p$-value, at which the hypothesis would be rejected for the given observations. For example, for a test statistic $T$ with a critical region of the form $(c, \infty)$ the $p$-value is given by $p = \int_{t_{obs}}^{\infty} f_T(t, \theta_0)\, dt = P(T > t_{obs} \mid \theta = \theta_0)$, where $t_{obs}$ is the observed value of $T$ for a given data $\boldsymbol{X} = \boldsymbol{x}$, $f_T(t, \theta_0)$ is the pdf of $T$ at $\theta = \theta_0$. That means, if a null hypothesis is rejected at $\hat{\alpha}(\mathbf{x})$, it will be rejected at all higher levels, given the data $\boldsymbol{x}$. $p$-value could be defined as probability of a MP-type critical region under the null hypothesis where the points in the CR were included one by one on the basis of MP test rating factor of the type $r(x) = f_1(x)/f_0(x) > C$, till such time the observation $\boldsymbol{x}$ is included in the critical region. This gives us the smallest probability of rejecting the correct $H_0$ given $\boldsymbol{X} = \boldsymbol{x}$. The MP test rejects $H_0$ at level $\hat{\alpha}(\mathbf{x})$ or above. Smaller the value of $\hat{\alpha}(\boldsymbol{x})$, stronger the evidence data has against the null hypothesis. Therefore, $p$-value becomes a measure as to how strongly the null hypothesis $H_0$ is rejected in the given observations. If at a given level of significance $\alpha$, $\hat{\alpha}(\mathbf{x}) < \alpha$, we reject the null hypothesis. Another way to view $\hat{\alpha}$ as the probability that the results obtained were due to chance. Small values of $\hat{\alpha}$ indicates that the results were not due to chance. We, in this case, reject the null hypothesis $H_0$. A large value of $\hat{\alpha}$ would suggest that the difference between the hypothesized value and the recorded value of the parameter was due to chance, and we could accept the null hypothesis $H_0$. It is important to note that $\hat{\alpha}$ becomes smaller and smaller when we increase the sample size. This is because assuming the null hypothesis to be exactly true, a sample statistic deviating from the hypothesized parameter value under $H_0$ is increasing less likely as sample size increases. Sometimes $\hat{\alpha}(\mathbf{x})$ suggests the experimenter as to what level of significance could he fix for his experiment instead always a conventional level 5% or 1% which could result into some bad decision-making consequences. These have been well explored by Sterling (1959)[198] and Greenwald (1975)[75]. In any case the usual choices of $\alpha$ will be 0.05, 0.01 and 0.001 specially in human medical trials.

We shall discuss some useful remarks on this section:

*Remark* 2.2.1. **(Intuitively Appealing Explanation of NP Lemma)** Let the points in sample space $\mathfrak{X} \subseteq \mathbb{R}^n$ be rated on the basis of the ratio, $r(\mathbf{x}) = \dfrac{f_1(\mathbf{x})}{f_0(\mathbf{x})}$, i.e. points in $\mathfrak{X}$ are rated on the basis of the ratio of explanation on $\mathbf{x}$ provided by $H_1$ to the explanation provided by $H_0$. The points with higher values of $r(\mathbf{x})$ enjoys better explanation under $H_1$ as compared to $H_0$. The best critical region, therefore, suggested by Neyman and Pearson takes the form

$$r(\mathbf{x}) > c$$

The constant $c$ is obtained by the condition that the probability of wrongly rejecting the correct $H_0$ is at most $\alpha$ i.e.

$$P_{H_0}\{\mathbf{X} : r(\mathbf{X}) > c\} \leq \alpha$$

*Remark* 2.2.2. The size restriction on the NP lemma test has been defined as $E_{\theta_0}\phi(X) = \alpha$, which implies that the critical region $S$ includes all points $x$ for which $f_1(x)/f_0(x) > C$, where $C$ is determined by the condition

$$P_{H_0}\{X \in S\} = \sum_{\{x : f_1/f_0 > C\}} f_0(x) = \alpha \tag{2.26}$$

Here the $x$ values have been put in the increasing order of the scale $f_1(x)/f_0(x)$ and the points $x$ are included in critical region $S$ so that $f_1(x)/f_0(x) > c$ so that condition given by Eq. (2.27) is satisfied. However, sometimes a difficulty arises in this process of including points in the critical region that at some stage $\sum_{x : f_1/f_0 > c} f_0(x) < \alpha$ and as soon as a next point is included it exceeds $\alpha$ and it never attains $\alpha$ exactly. This problem is avoided by including only a portion of that point by way of allowing randomization. Such tests are known as randomized tests. However, Lehman 1986, [130] has strongly recommended that the experimenter must choose such a $\alpha$ that could be attained exactly without suggesting randomization. This choice of $\alpha$ is known as *exact level of significance* and a test so obtained is known as *non-randomized test.*

*Remark* 2.2.3. If a MP test exists with power 1 at some significance level $\alpha$, it is determined by Eqs. (2.19) and (2.20). Such a MP test may not be unique since there may exist some other test $\phi$, with power 1, at some $\alpha' < \alpha$ (refer the tests on CD in Figure 2.5).

*Remark* 2.2.4. The class of non-randomized test is contained in the class of behavioural decision rules, $D \subset \mathcal{D}$, and also $\dim(\mathrm{D}) \leq \dim(\mathcal{D})$, therefore, it is easier to work with $D$.

*Remark* 2.2.5. It should be noted that the best test of size-$\alpha$ depends on its size and the distribution of $X$ under $H_0$, not on $H_1$ e.g. the best test of size-$\alpha$ when $X \sim N(\theta, 1)$, for every testing problem $H_0 : \theta = 1$ versus $H_1 : \theta = 2$, $H_0 : \theta = 1$ versus $H_1 : \theta = 4$, and $H_0 : \theta = 1$ versus $H_1 : \theta = -1$ is same.

*Remark* 2.2.6. *If $\phi$ is a best test of size $\alpha_0$ and $\phi$ is not admissible, then the probability of second kind of error $\alpha_1 = E_{\theta_1}(1 - \phi(X)) = 0$.*

This situation cannot happen when a better test $\phi'$ exists with $(\alpha_0, \alpha_1(\phi')), \alpha_1(\phi') < \alpha_1$, because then $\phi$ will not be best at size $\alpha_0$. But rather there may exist a test $\phi'$ with $(\alpha_0(\phi'), \alpha_1)$, $\alpha_0(\phi') < \alpha_0$ better than the test $\phi$, which is a contradiction to the fact that $\alpha_1$-curve is convex toward $\alpha_0$-axis. This can only happen when $\alpha_1 = 0$.

*Remark* 2.2.7. *If the family $\{f_\theta, \theta \in \Theta\}$ admits a sufficient statistics $T$, then NP test is a function of $T$.*

Factorization theorem, when applied to best critical region, gives

$$\frac{f_1(x)}{f_0(x)} > k \quad \text{or} \quad \frac{g_{\theta_1}(T(x)) \cdot h(x)}{g_{\theta_0}(T(x)) \cdot h(x)} > k$$

or $g(T) > k$ for some function $g$. This shows that the best critical region is a function of the sufficient statistic $T$ if the later exists. Moreover, the class of level $\alpha$ tests is no different from the class of size-$\alpha$ tests which are the function of sufficient statistic $T$, since $E_{\theta_0}\phi(X) = E^T_{\theta_0}\{E\phi(X)|T\} = E^T_{\theta_0}g(T) \leq \alpha$. Therefore, for simple versus simple hypothesis testing problems, the statistician restricts the search for a best test to a class of tests which are the function of the sufficient statistic $T$ and that their size is at most equal to $\alpha$.

*Remark* 2.2.8. *Let $\phi$ be a best test of size-$\alpha$, $0 < \alpha < 1$ for testing $H_0 : \theta = \theta_0$ against $H_1 : \theta = \theta_1$. Then $E_{\theta_1}\phi(X) > \alpha$ unless $f_{\theta_0} = f_{\theta_1}$. Such a test $\phi$ is also unbiased.*

We consider a class of level $\alpha$ tests, $\mathcal{C}_\alpha$, defined as

$$\mathcal{C}_\alpha = \{\phi \in \mathcal{D} \; : \; E_{\theta_0}\phi(X) \leq \alpha\}$$

The test $\phi(x)$ is given to be the best in $C_\alpha$. Consider a test $\phi'(x) \equiv \alpha$ clearly, it belongs to the class $C_\alpha$ and $E_{\theta_1}\phi(X) \geq E_{\theta_1}\phi'(X)(= \alpha)$. If $E_{\theta_1}\phi(X) = \alpha < 1$, the necessary or the uniqueness part of the NP lemma gives the test $\phi$ and $\phi'$ must take the same form except perhaps on the set $\{x \; : \; f_1(x) = kf_0(x)\}$ since for $0 < \alpha < 1, P_{H_i}\{x : f_1(x) \neq kf_0(x)\} = 0, i = 0, 1$ or $P_{H_i}\{x|f_1(x) = kf_0(x)\} = 1, \quad i = 0, 1$, the most powerful test becomes $\phi(x) = \phi'(x) = \alpha$ on $f_1(x) = kf_0(x)$. On taking integrals on both the sides of $f_1(x) = kf_0(x)$ we get $k = 1$ and the MP test becomes

$$\phi(x) = \phi'(x) = \alpha \qquad \text{on} \qquad f_1(x) = f_0(x)$$

This shows that the null hypothesis $H_0$ is rejected with probability $\alpha$ when $f_1(x) = f_0(x)$, i.e. when both the hypotheses are identical, makes no sense. Therefore, it is concluded that $E_{\theta_1}\phi(X) > \alpha$ unless $f_1(x) = f_0(x)$.

*Alternative proof:* $\phi$ has been given to be best test of size-$\alpha$ in $\mathcal{C}(\alpha)$; $\phi' \equiv \alpha$, belongs to $\mathcal{C}(\alpha)$ and

$$E_{\theta_1}\phi'(X) \leq E_{\theta_1}\phi(X) \;\; \text{or} \;\; \alpha \leq E_{\theta_1}\phi(X)$$

Now, consider a situation when $\alpha = E_{\theta_1}\phi(X)$. Since $\phi$ is best, it would be of the form

$$\phi(x) = \begin{cases} 1 & \text{if } \dfrac{f_1}{f_0} > k \\ 0 & \text{otherwise} \end{cases}$$

where, $k$ is determined by the size condition, i.e.

$$E_{\theta_0}\phi(X) = \alpha \;\; \text{or} \;\; \int_k^\infty \frac{f_1}{f_0} f_0 \, dx = \alpha$$

and the power
$$E_{\theta_1}\phi(X) = \int_k^\infty \frac{f_1}{f_0} f_1 \, dx = \alpha$$

On comparing
$$\int_k^\infty \frac{f_1}{f_0} f_0 \, dx = \int_k^\infty \frac{f_1}{f_0} f_1 \, dx \quad \text{we get } f_0 = f_1 \quad \text{a.e.}$$

Therefore, we conclude that $\alpha < E_{\theta_1}\phi(X)$ unless $f_{\theta_0} = f_{\theta_1}$ almost everywhere. This gives, $E_{\theta_1}\phi(X) > \alpha$ for all $\theta_1 \neq \theta_0$. By the definition of unbiasedness of a test in Section 4.3, the test $\phi$ is unbiased.

*Remark* 2.2.9. Let $\phi$ be a NP test of size-$\alpha$ $(0 < \alpha \leq 1)$ of testing $H_0$ against $H_1$. Denote $k$ for which

$$E_{\theta_0}\phi(X) = P_{H_0}\left[\frac{f_1(X)}{f_0(X)} > k\right] + \gamma P_{H_0}\left[\frac{f_1(X)}{f_0(X)} = k\right] = \alpha$$

or $P_{H_0}[Y \leq k] - \gamma P_{H_0}[Y = k] = 1 - \alpha$ (by letting $Y = \dfrac{f_1(X)}{f_0(X)}$ ) or $k$ for which

$$P_{\theta_0}[Y < k] \leq 1 - \alpha < P_{\theta_0}[Y \leq k]$$

be denoted by $k(\alpha)$. If $\alpha_1 < \alpha_2$ then $1 - \alpha_2 < 1 - \alpha_1$. Therefore, by previous inequality and the fact $P_{\theta_0}[Y \leq k]$ is a non-decreasing function ( $P_{\theta_0}[Y \leq k]$ being the distribution function) implies together that $k(\alpha_2) \leq k(\alpha_1)$.

*Remark* 2.2.10. *The power of NP tests increases with the increase in their sizes.* To show this let us consider a NP test $\phi$ which is obtained by choosing $k$ so that

$$P_{H_0}[Y > k] = \alpha \quad \text{(say)}$$

For $\alpha_1 < \alpha_2$ implies $P_{H_0}(Y > k(\alpha_1)) < P_{H_0}(Y > k(\alpha_2))$, which further implies $k(\alpha_2) \leq k(\alpha_1)$ and we get

$$P_{H_1}(Y > k(\alpha_1)) < P_{H_1}(Y > k(\alpha_2))$$

*Remark* 2.2.11. *Let $\phi$ be the most powerful size-$\alpha$, $0 < \alpha < 1$, test for testing $H_0$ against $H_1$ and power be given by $\beta = E_{H_1}\phi(X) < 1$. Then $1 - \phi$ is the most powerful test of size $1 - \beta$ for testing $H_1$ against $H_0$.* We know that the most powerful test of size-$\alpha$ is

$$\phi(x) = \begin{cases} 1 & \text{if } \dfrac{f_1}{f_0} > k \\ \gamma & \text{if } \dfrac{f_1}{f_0} = k \\ 0 & \text{if } \dfrac{f_1}{f_0} < k \end{cases}$$

where, $k$ and $\gamma$ are determined by

$$E_{H_0}\phi(X) = \alpha$$

Let $f_1/f_0 = Y$, we have

$$P_{H_0}(Y > k) + \gamma P_{H_0}(Y = k) = \alpha$$

Further power is determined by

$$P_{H_1}(Y > k) + \gamma P_{H_1}(Y = k) = \beta < 1$$

Next, consider the dual testing problem $H_1$ against $H_0$ at level $1-\beta$, the most powerful test is

$$\phi'(x) = \begin{cases} 1 & \text{if } \dfrac{f_0}{f_1} > k \\ \gamma & \text{if } \dfrac{f_0}{f_1} \doteq k \\ 0 & \text{if } \dfrac{f_0}{f_1} < k \end{cases}$$

where $k$ and $\gamma$ are determined by

$$P_{H_1}(1/Y > k) + \gamma P_{H_1}(1/Y = k) = 1-\beta$$

$$P_{H_1}\ (Y > 1/k) + (1-\gamma)\ P_{H_1}\ (Y = 1/k) = \beta$$

therefore, the test $\phi'$ is nothing but $1-\phi$.

*Remark* 2.2.12. *The risk set for a simple versus simple testing problem has been defined by*

$$S = \{(\alpha, \beta) : \alpha = E_{\theta_0}\phi(X),\ \beta = E_{\theta_1}(1-\phi(X)) \text{ for some } \phi \in \mathcal{D}\} \quad (2.27)$$

$S$ contains the points (1, 0) and (0, 1) corresponding to the tests $\phi(x) \equiv 1$ and $\phi(x) \equiv 0$ respectively. If $\phi(x)$ in $\mathcal{D}$ corresponds a point $(\alpha,\ \beta)$ in $S$ then $1-\phi(X)$ would also be in $\mathcal{D}$ and the corresponding point $(1-\alpha, 1-\beta)$ would be in $S$. This shows that $S$ is symmetric about the point $(\frac{1}{2},\ \frac{1}{2})$ (Refer Figure 2.5). We would refer tests by points in $S$ since these are their corresponding risk points.

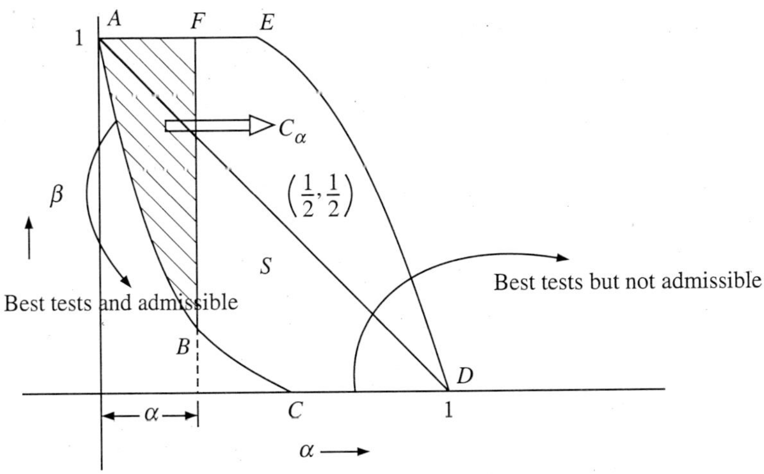


**Figure 2.5:** Shape of the risk set of a hypothesis testing problem

*Remark* 2.2.13. The risk set $S$ in Eq. (2.27) is not only convex (as shown earlier in Section 2.2) but also compact by weak compactness theorem as shown in the generalized Neyman-Pearson lemma. Compactness of the risk set implies that it is bounded from below and closed from below, therefore, by using the results of decision theory the class of best tests forms a complete class. Here, every best test is admissible provided its risk point is a lower boundary point of $S$. Whereas, tests corresponding to the points on CD, excluding the point C, are best but not admissible. This is the case when $\beta = 0$.

Geometrically, a class of level $\alpha$-tests $C_\alpha = \{\phi \in \mathcal{D} | E_{\theta_0}\phi(X) \leq \alpha\}$ for some $\alpha$, $0 < \alpha < 1$, has been shown by the shaded part of the risk set $S$ with abscissa $\leq \alpha$ in the Figure (2.5). The existence of a most powerful test of size $\alpha$ in $C_\alpha$ is ensured since $S$ closed, which corresponds to the lower boundary point of the risk set $S$ with abscissa $\alpha$. This is the only most powerful test in $C_\alpha$ unless there exists a test with its size $\alpha' < \alpha$ and $\beta = 0$ (see tests corresponding to the points on CD in Figure 2.5).

We shall now discuss the extension of Neyman -Pearson lemma to the cases where $f_0$ and $f_1$ may take negative values, not necessarily densities, and there are many side conditions, not just one. We, therefore, discuss the maximization of $\int \phi f d\mu$ for some $\mu$ integrable function $f$ over a class of critical functions $\phi$, satisfying several side conditions. This extension is known as Generalized Neyman-Pearson lemma, which has been discussed in the following section for a measure space $(\mathfrak{X}, \mathcal{B}, \mu)$. Here, $\mathfrak{X}$ has been considered as a Euclidean space, $\mathcal{B}$ as a $\sigma$-field having countable number of generators i.e. there exists a countable number of sets $B_i$ so that $\mathcal{B}$ is a smallest $\sigma$-field containing these $B_i'$s and $\mu$ as a $\sigma$- finite measure over $(\mathfrak{X}, \mathcal{B})$ [Lehmann (1986)][130].

## 2.3 GENERALIZED NP LEMMA

**Theorem 2.3.1:** *Let $f_1, f_2, ..., f_{m+1}$ be real valued $\mu$ integrable functions defined over a measure space $(\mathfrak{X}, \mathcal{B}, \mu)$. Consider a class of critical functions defined as*

$$\mathcal{C} = \{\phi \in \mathcal{D} | \int \phi f_i(x)\, d\mu(x) = a_i, i = 1, 2, ..., m; \quad a_i' s \text{ are given}\}$$

(a) *Existence: There exists a $\phi$ in $\mathcal{C}$ that maximizes $\int \phi f_{m+1} d\mu$.*

(b) *Sufficient condition: A critical function $\phi$ in $\mathcal{C}$ maximizes $\int \phi f_{m+1} d\mu$*

$$\text{if} \quad \phi(x) = \begin{cases} 1 & \text{if } f_{m+1}(x) > \sum_{i=1}^m k_i f_i(x) \\ 0 & \text{if } f_{m+1}(x) < \sum_{i=1}^m k_i f_i(x) \end{cases} \tag{2.28}$$

*where $k_1, k_2, ..., k_m$ are obtained by side conditions in the class $\mathcal{C}$.*

(c) *Necessary condition: If a $\phi$ in $\mathcal{C}$ satisfies Eq. (2.28) with $k_1, \ldots, k_m \geq 0$, then it maximizes $\int \phi f_{m+1} d\mu$ among the critical functions in the class*

$$\mathcal{C}' = \{\phi \in \mathcal{D} | \int \phi f_i(x)\, d\mu(x) \leq a_i, i = 1, 2, \ldots, m\}$$

(d) *The $m$-dimensional risk set $S \subset \mathbb{R}^m$ defined by*

$$\left(\int \phi f_1 d\mu, \ldots, \int \phi f_m d\mu\right)$$

*for some critical function $\phi$ is convex and closed. If $\mathbf{a} = (a_1, \ldots, a_m)'$ is a inner point of $S$, then there exist constants $k_1, \ldots, k_m$ and a critical function $\phi$ in $\mathcal{C}$ satisfying the condition in Eq. (2.28). Further, a necessary condition for a critical function $\phi$ in $\mathcal{C}$ to maximize*

$$\int \phi f_{m+1} d\mu$$

*is that Eq. (2.28) holds a.e. $\mu$.*

*Proof.* (a) The class $\mathcal{C}$ is a class of measurable critical functions satisfying $m$ side conditions. Therefore, the weak compactness theorem holds which states that $\mathcal{C}$ is compact with respect to the weak convergence. If we consider a sequence of critical functions $\{\phi_n\}$ in $\mathcal{C}$ such that

$$\int \phi_n f_{m+1} d\mu \to \sup_{\phi} \int \phi f_{m+1} d\mu$$

The compactness of $\mathcal{C}$ gives that there exists a subsequence $\{\phi_{n_i}\}$ such that

$$\int \phi_{n_i} f_j \, d\mu \to \int \phi f_j \, d\mu \quad j = 1, 2, \ldots, m+1$$

and $\phi$ is in $\mathcal{C}$. This shows that there exists a $\phi$ in $\mathcal{C}$ that maximizes $\int \phi f_{m+1} d\mu$.
(b) Consider a test $\phi$ in $\mathcal{C}$ satisfying Eq. (2.28) and any other critical function $\phi'$ in $\mathcal{C}$. Define subsets of the sample space $\mathfrak{X}$ by $S^+ = \{x \in \mathfrak{X} | (\phi(x) - \phi^*(x)) > 0\}$ and $S^- = \{x \in \mathfrak{X} | (\phi(x) - \phi^*(x)) < 0\}$. The test $\phi$ satisfying Eq. (2.28) must be $> 0$ and $f_{m+1}(x) \geq \sum_{i=1}^m k_i f_i(x)$ on the set $S^+$, must be $< 0$ and $f_{m+1}(x) \leq \sum_{i=1}^m k_i \, f_i(x)$ on the set $S^-$. This gives

$$\begin{aligned}
&\int (\phi(x) - \phi'(x))(f_{m+1}(x) - \sum_{i=1}^m k_i f_i(x)) d\mu \\
&\qquad = \int_{S^+} (\phi(x) - \phi'(x))(f_{m+1}(x) - \sum_{i=1}^m k_i f_i(x)) \, d\mu \\
&\qquad\qquad + \int_{S^-} (\phi(x) - \phi'(x))(f_{m+1}(x) - \sum_{i=1}^m k_i f_i(x)) \, d\mu \geq 0
\end{aligned}$$

or

$$\int (\phi(x) - \phi'(x)) f_{m+1}(x) d\mu \geq \sum_{i=1}^m k_i \int (\phi(x) - \phi'(x)) f_i(x) d\mu$$

Here, $\int (\phi(x) - \phi'(x)) f_i(x)\, d\mu = 0 \ \ \forall\, i$ since $\phi$ and $\phi'$ are in $\mathcal{C}$. This along with arbitrary values of $k_i$s gives $\sum_{i=1}^{m} k_i \int (\phi(x) - \phi'(x)) f_i(x)\, d\mu \geq 0$. Therefore,

$$\int \phi(x) f_{m+1}(x) d\mu \geq \int \phi'(x)) f_{m+1}(x)\, d\mu \geq 0$$

shows that the $\phi$ in $\mathcal{C}$ satisfying Eq. (2.28) maximizes $\int \phi f_{m+1} d\mu$ among all critical functions in $\mathcal{C}$.

(c) By considering $\phi$ in $\mathcal{C}$ satisfying Eq. (2.28) and any other critical function $\phi'$ in $\mathcal{C}'$, result in (b) gives

$$\int (\phi(x) - \phi'(x))(f_{m+1}(x) - \sum_{i=1}^{m} k_i f_i(x))\, d\mu \geq 0$$

or

$$\int (\phi(x) - \phi'(x)) f_{m+1}(x)\, d\mu \geq \sum_{i=1}^{m} k_i \int (\phi(x) - \phi'(x)) f_i(x)\, d\mu$$

The quantity $\sum_{i=1}^{m} k_i \int (\phi(x) - \phi'(x)) f_i(x)\, d\mu$ is $\geq 0$ since $\int (\phi(x) - \phi'(x)) f_i(x)\, d\mu \geq 0$ and $k_1, \ldots, k_m \geq 0$. Therefore

$$\int \phi f_{m+1} d\mu \geq \int \phi' f_{m+1}\, d\mu$$

This proves that $\phi$ in $\mathcal{C}$ satisfying Eq. (2.28) maximizes $\int \phi f_{m+1} d\mu$ among all critical functions in $\mathcal{C}'$.

(d) The risk set $S$ has been defined as

$$S = \{(y_1, y_2, \ldots, y_m) |\ y_j = \int \phi f_j\, d\mu,\ j = 1, \ldots, m \ \text{ for some } \phi \text{ in } \mathcal{D}\}$$

where $\mathcal{D}$ is a class of all critical functions. By weak compactness theorem the risk set $S$ is compact, therefore, closed. The set $S$ is convex. To see this, consider two points in $S$, namely, $(\int \phi_1 f_1\, d\mu, \ \ldots, \ \int \phi_1 f_m d\mu)$ and $(\int \phi_2 f_1\, d\mu, \ \ldots, \ \int \phi_2 f_m d\mu)$ corresponding to the critical functions $\phi_1$ and $\phi_2$ in $\mathcal{D}$. The points on the line joining these points $(\int (\alpha\phi_1 + (1-\alpha)\phi_2) f_1\, d\mu, \ldots, \int (\alpha\phi_1 + (1-\alpha)\phi_2) f_m\, d\mu)$ for $0 < \alpha < 1$ would lie in $S$ since the corresponding critical functions $\phi_\alpha = \alpha\phi_1 + (1-\alpha)\phi_2$ for $0 < \alpha < 1$ belongs to $\mathcal{D}$. We define a set $S_1$ by

$$S_1 = \{(y_1, y_2, \ldots, y_{m+1}) |\ y_j = \int \phi f_j\, d\mu,\ j = 1, \ldots, m+1 \ \text{ for some } \phi \text{ in } \mathcal{D}\}$$

The spaces $S$ and $S_1$ are shown in Figure 2.6. We can show that $N$ is closed and convex by using the above argument. If we fix the first $m$ co-ordinates of a general point $(y_1, \ldots, y_{m+1})$ in $S_1$ at $y_1 = a_1, \ldots, y_m = a_m$, on taking the note that $(a_1, \ldots, a_m)$ is an inner point in $S$ as given in the theorem, we get

$$S_1 = \left\{(a_1, \ldots, a_m, y_{m+1}) | a_0 \leq y_{m+1} \leq a_{00}\right\}$$

as a closed interval.

Let us assume $a_0 < a_{00}$ and denote $\mathbf{a}_0 = (a_1, \ldots, a_m, a_0)'$, $\mathbf{a} = (a_1, \ldots, a_m, a)'$, $a_0 < a < a_{00}$, $\mathbf{a}_{00} = (a_1, \ldots, a_m, a_{00})'$. In this case, there exists a hyperplane $H$, given by $\mathbf{k}'\mathbf{y} = \mathbf{k}'\mathbf{a}_{00}$, passing through the boundary point $\mathbf{a}_{00}$ of $S_1$ such that every point of $S_1$ lies on $H$ or below it. Further, the point $\mathbf{a}$ is an inner point of $S_1$ since $(a_1, \ldots, a_m)$ is an inner point of $S$ and $a_0 < a < a_{00}$. Therefore, there exists a sphere in $S$ with $\mathbf{a}$ as its centre that falls below the hyperplane $H$. This gives that $\mathbf{a}$ is not on the hyperplane $H$, therefore, $k_{m+1} \neq 0$. We may, therefore, take $k_{m+1} = -1$ and state that every point of $S_1$ is on one side of the hyperplane $H$, i.e.

$$\mathbf{k}'\mathbf{y} \leq \mathbf{k}'\mathbf{a}_{00} \quad \text{with} \quad \mathbf{k} = (-k_1, \ldots, -k_m, +1) \ \forall \ \mathbf{y} \in S_1 \tag{2.29}$$

here, co-ordinates in $\mathbf{y}$ are given by $y_j = \int \phi f_j d\mu$, $j = 1, 2 \ldots, m+1$, and the co-ordinates in $\mathbf{a}_{00}$ are given by $a_j = \int \phi_{00} f_j d\mu$, $j = 1, \ldots m$, $a_{00} = \int \phi_{00} f_{m+1} d\mu$. This gives

$$\int \phi \cdot \mathbf{k}'\mathbf{f} \, d\mu \leq \int \phi_{00} \, \mathbf{k}'\mathbf{f} \, d\mu$$

for all $\phi$ corresponding to the points in $S_1$ where, $\mathbf{f} = (f_1, \ldots, f_{m+1})'$. Therefore, there exists a critical function $\phi_{00}$ in $\mathcal{C}$ that maximizes $\int \phi \, \mathbf{k}'\mathbf{f} \, d\mu$, i.e. $\int \phi f_{m+1} d\mu$ since the first $m$-co-ordinates of $S_1$ have been fixed at $a_1, \ldots, a_m$. Such a critical function must satisfy

$$\phi(x) = \begin{cases} 1 & \text{if } \mathbf{k}'\mathbf{f} > 0 \ (f_{m+1} > \sum_{i=1}^{m} k_i f_i) \\ 0 & \text{if } \mathbf{k}'\mathbf{f} < 0 \ (f_{m+1} < \sum_{i=1}^{m} k_i f_i) \end{cases} \tag{2.30}$$

and

$$\int \phi \, f_j d\mu = a_j, \quad j = 1, \ldots, m \tag{2.31}$$

Thus a necessary condition for a member of $\mathcal{C}$ to maximize $\int \phi f_{m+1} d\mu$ is that the conditions of Eqs. (2.30) and (2.31) hold a.e. $\mu$. Further, there exists a $\phi_{00}$ in $\mathcal{C}$ that maximizes $\int \phi f_{m+1} d\mu$ satisfying (2.30) and (2.31).

Consider now the case when $a_0 = a_{00}$ (Figure 2.6). We have seen earlier that $S_1$ is convex and it contains the origin. We will now show that $S_1$ has just one point on the vertical line $y_1 = b_1, \ldots y_m = b_m$, by showing that there exists only one real number $b$ such that the point $(b_1, \ldots, b_m, b)$ is the point of $S_1$ where $(b_1, \ldots, b_m)$ is the point of $S$ other than the inner point $(a_1, \ldots, a_m)$ in $S$. Since $(a_1, \ldots, a_m)$ is an inner point of $S$, we may take a point $(c_1, \ldots, c_m, c)$ in $S_1$ so that the point $(a_1, \ldots, a_m)$ is an interior point of the line joining the points $(b_1, \ldots, b_m)$ and $(c_1, \ldots, c_m)$. Instead of $b$ as just a single real number. □

Corollary 2.3.1 is a generalization of Remark 2.2.8 of this Chapter where one side condition has been replaced by several side conditions [Lehmann(1986)][130].

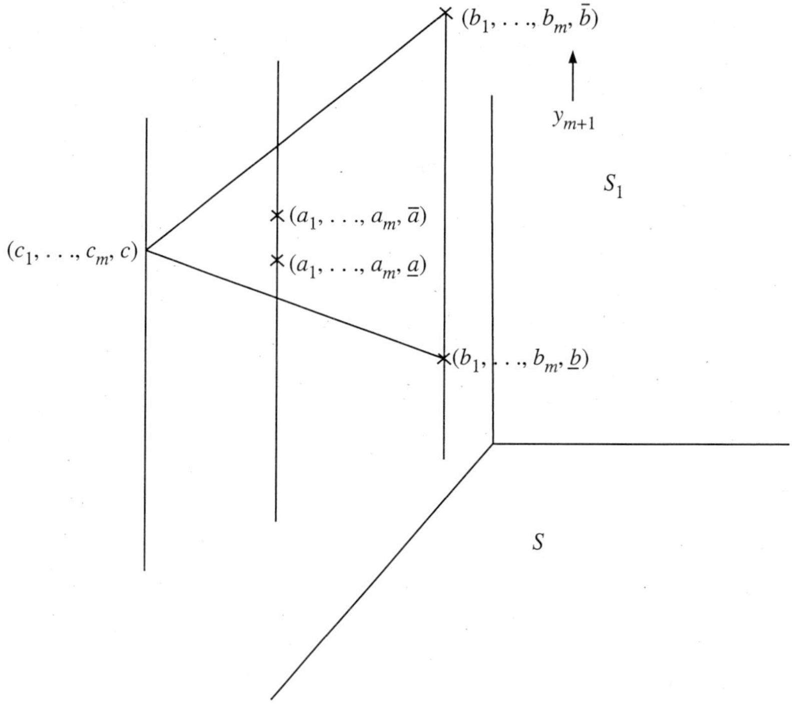


**Figure 2.6:** Spaces of $\mathcal{S}$ and $\mathcal{S}_1$.

**Corollary 2.3.1.** *Let $p_1, p_2, \ldots, p_m, p_{m+1}$ be probability densities with respect to a common measure $\mu$ and let $0 < \alpha < 1$. Then there exists a test $\phi$ such that*

$$E_i\phi(X) = \alpha, \qquad i = 1, 2, \ldots, m$$

*and $E_{m+1}\phi(X) > \alpha$, unless $p_{m+1} = \sum_{i=1}^{m} k_i p_i \qquad$ a.e. $\mu$.*

# 2.4 SOLVED EXAMPLES

**Example 2.4.1.** *State and prove the necessary and sufficient condition for the test to be most powerful for testing a simple hypothesis against a simple alternative. Further, show that such a test always exists. Consider a binomial population with $n = 3$ and $p$ unknown. Obtain a most powerful test for $H_0$ : $p = 0.95$* against $H_1 : p = 0.10$ of size-$\alpha = 0.001$.

***Solution:*** The critical region corresponding to the most powerful test would be $\dfrac{p_{0.10}(x)}{p_{0.95}(x)} > k$, where $X \sim b(3, p)$. This would imply $x < k_1$ since $p_1(= 0.10) < p_0(= 0.95)$. $k_1$ is obtained by $E_{0.95}[\phi(X)] = 0.001$
or

$$P_{0.95}\{X < k_1\} + \gamma\, P_{0.95}\{X = k_1\} = 0.001. \tag{2.32}$$

The constants $k_1$ and $\gamma$ are determined from Eq. (2.32). and by using Binomial tables. Generally these tables are available for $p = 0$ to $0.5$. Note that Eq. (2.32) involves $p = 0.95$, therefore, for the easy reference of Binomial tables, the following relation is used:

$$F_p(r) = P[X \leq r] = \sum_{x=0}^{r} \binom{n}{x} p^x q^{n-x} = \sum_{x=0}^{r} \binom{n}{n-x} q^{n-x} p^x$$

Letting $n - x = y$ we get

$$F_p(r) = \sum_{y=n-r}^{n} \binom{n}{y} q^y p^{n-y}$$

$$= 1 - \sum_{y=0}^{n-r-1} \binom{n}{y} q^y p^{n-y} = 1 - F_{1-p}(n-r-1)$$

We may write (2.32) as

$$F_{0.95}(k_1 - 1) + \gamma[F_{0.95}(k_1) - F_{0.95}(k_1 - 1)] = 0.001$$

or

$$F_{0.05}(n - k_1) - \gamma[F_{0.05}(n - k_1) - F_{0.05}(n - k_1 - 1)] = 0.999$$

From Binomial table we get $3 - k_1 = 2; k_1 = 3 - 2 = 1$, and

$$\gamma = \frac{0.9999 - 0.999}{0.9999 - 0.9928} = \frac{0.0009}{0.0071} = 0.1267$$

Therefore, the most powerful size-$\alpha = 0.001$ test is given by

$$\phi(x) = \begin{cases} 1 & \text{if } x < 1 \\ 0.1267 & \text{if } x = 1 \\ 0 & \text{if } x > 1 \end{cases}$$

**Example 2.4.2.** *Let us consider simple versus simple testing problem $H_0 : \theta = \theta_0$ against $H_1 : \theta = \theta_1$. Consider the prior distribution $\tau$ been defined on $H_0$ and $H_1$ so that it assigns probabilities $\pi$ on $H_0$ and $1 - \pi$ on $H_1$. Find out the Bayes test with respect to the given prior distribution.*

***Solution:*** Let the density of $X$ under $H_0$ be shown by $f_0$ and under $H_1$ by $f_1$. The joint density of random variables $\Theta$ and $X$ be given by

$$h(\Theta, X) = \tau(\Theta) \cdot f_X(x|\Theta)$$

where, $\Theta$ takes on values $\theta_0$ and $\theta_1$. The marginal density of $X$ would be given by

$$m(x) = \pi f_0(x) + (1 - \pi) f_1(x)$$

The posterior probabilities of $H_i$ given $X = x$ are given by

$$\pi(H_0|x) = \frac{\pi f_0(x)}{\pi f_0(x) + (1-\pi) f_1(x)}$$

and

$$\pi(H_1|x) = \frac{(1-\pi) f_1(x)}{\pi f_0(x) + (1-\pi) f_1(x)}$$

The risk of any test $\phi$ is given by

$$R(\theta, \phi) = L(\theta, a_0) + E_\theta \phi(X)[L(\theta, a_1) - L(\theta, a_0)]$$

which takes value at $\theta = \theta_0$

$$R(\theta_0, \phi) = L(\theta_0, a_0) + E_{\theta_0} \phi(X)[L(\theta_0, a_1) - L(\theta_0, a_0)]$$

We know that $L(\theta_0, a_0) = 0 = L(\theta_1, a_1)$ and $L(\theta_0, a_1) = 1 = L(\theta_1, a_0)$ in $0-1$ loss function. This gives

$$R(\theta_0, \phi) = E_{\theta_0} \phi(X)$$

and at $\theta = \theta_1$,

$$\begin{aligned} R(\theta_1, \phi) &= L(\theta_1, a_0) + E_{\theta_1} \phi(X)[L(\theta_1, a_1) - L(\theta_1, a_0)] \\ &= 1 + E_{\theta_1} \phi(X)[0 - 1] = 1 - E_{\theta_1} \phi(X) \end{aligned}$$

The Bayes risk of the decision rule $\phi$, a test, with respect to the given prior $\tau = \{\pi, 1-\pi\}$,

$$r(\tau, \phi) = E^T R(T, \phi)$$

where, $T$ is a random variable taking values $\theta = \theta_0$ with probability $\pi$ and $\theta = \theta_1$ with probability $1 - \pi$. We have

$$\begin{aligned} r(\tau, \phi) &= R(\theta_0, \phi) \cdot P(\theta = \theta_0) + R(\theta_1, \phi) \cdot P(\theta = \theta_1) \\ &= \pi E_{\theta_0} \phi(X) + (1-\pi)(1 - E_{\theta_1} \phi(X)) \\ &= \pi \int_{\mathfrak{X}} \phi(x) f_0(x)\, dx + (1-\pi) \int_{\mathfrak{X}} (1 - \phi(x)) f_1(x)\, dx \\ &= (1-\pi) + \int_{\mathfrak{X}} \phi(x) \{\pi f_0(x) - (1-\pi) f_1(x)\}\, dx \\ &= (1-\pi) + \int_{\mathfrak{X}} \phi(x) \Big\{\pi - (1-\pi) \frac{f_1(x)}{f_0(x)}\Big\} f_0(x)\, dx \end{aligned}$$

By definition, Bayes test $\phi$ is the one that minimizes $r(\tau, \phi)$ with respect to the given prior distribution $\tau$. This is obtained if

$$\phi(x) = \begin{cases} 1 & \text{if } \pi - (1-\pi)\dfrac{f_1(x)}{f_0(x)} < 0 \\ \gamma(x)(0 < \gamma(x) < 1) & \text{if } \pi - (1-\pi)\dfrac{f_1(x)}{f_0(x)} = 0 \\ 0 & \text{if } \pi - (1-\pi)\dfrac{f_1(x)}{f_0(x)} > 0 \end{cases}$$

Denoting $\frac{\pi}{(1-\pi)} = k$, we have

$$\phi(x) = \begin{cases} 1 & \text{if } f_1(x) > kf_0(x) \\ \gamma(x) & \text{if } f_1(x) = kf_1(x) \\ 0 & \text{if } f_1(x) < kf_1(x) \end{cases}$$

This proves NP Lemma best tests are also Bayes.

**Example 2.4.3.** *A sample of two observations $(x_1, x_2)$ is drawn from a normal population. It is required to test the hypothesis that the population mean is zero. Prove that, with equal tails, at 10% level of significance the hypothesis will be rejected if*

$$|x_1 + x_2| > |x_1 - x_2| \tan 81^0$$

***Solution:*** $x_1, x_2$ are drawn from $N(\mu, \sigma^2)$, where both $\mu$ and $\sigma^2$ are unknown, then

$$\bar{X} = \frac{X_1 + X_2}{2} \sim N(\mu, \sigma^2/2)$$

To test $H_0 : \mu = 0$ against $H_1 : \mu \neq 0$, the equal tails test is given by

$$|t_{n-1}| = \left|\frac{\bar{X} - \mu_0}{s/\sqrt{n}}\right| > k, \text{where, } s^2 = \frac{1}{2-1}\sum(x_i - \bar{x})^2$$

and

$$\frac{\bar{X} - \mu_0}{S/\sqrt{n}} \sim t_{n-1}$$

$$t_{n-1} \,|\, H_0 = \frac{\sqrt{2}\,\frac{x_1 + x_2}{2}}{\sqrt{\frac{(x_1 - x_2)^2}{2}}} = \frac{x_1 + x_2}{x_1 - x_2}$$

where, $k$ is obtained by $P\{|t_{n-1}| > k\} = 0.1$ or $P\{t_{n-1} > k\} = \frac{0.1}{2} = .05$ (since $t_{n-1}$ is symmetric about zero) $k = 6.314 = \tan 81^0$. This gives the rejection region

$$|x_1 + x_2| > |x_1 - x_2| \tan 81^0$$

**Example 2.4.4.** *Consider the problem of testing*

$$H_0 : X \sim U(0, 1) \quad \textit{against} \quad H_1 : X \sim U(1/2, 3/2)$$

*Plot risk set $S$ of the above testing problem which is defined by*

$$S = \{(\alpha_0, \alpha_1) | E_{\theta_0}\phi(X) = \alpha_0 \quad \textit{and} \quad 1 - E_{\theta_1}\phi(X) = \alpha_1 \ \textit{for some} \ \phi \in \mathcal{D}\}$$

***Solution:*** NP test is determined by the size condition $\int_k^1 dx = \alpha_0$ which gives $k = 1 - \alpha_0$ and $\alpha_1 = 1 - \int_k^{3/2} dx = 1 - 3/2 + k = 1 - 3/2 + 1 - \alpha_0 = 1/2 - \alpha_0$. Finally the risk set is determined by plotting $(\alpha_0, \alpha_1)$ as follows:

| $\alpha_0$ | 0 | 0.1 | 0.2 | 0.3 | 0.4 | 0.5 |
|---|---|---|---|---|---|---|
| $\alpha_1$ | 0.5 | 0.4 | 0.3 | 0.2 | 0.1 | 0 |

The shape of the risk set has been given in Figure 2.7.

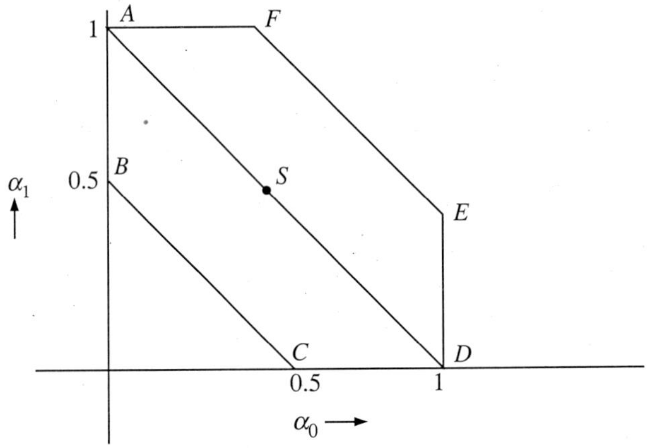


**Figure 2.7:** Risk set.

The tests, which are falling on ABCD are all best of their sizes. Tests on ABC are all admissible, but on $CD \sim \{C\}$ are inadmissible. Note that a test is said to be admissible if there does not exist any test better than that.

**Example 2.4.5.** *Plot the risk set S for testing problem* $H_0 : X \sim B(2, 1/2)$ *against* $H_1 : X \sim B(2, 2/3)$.

***Solution:*** Note that the best critical region would be of the form $x > x_0$ since $f_1/f_0$ is an increasing function of $x$. For given $\alpha_0$, following notations of Example 2.4.1, $x_0$ and $\gamma_0$ are obtained so that

$$F_{0.5}(x_0) - \gamma[F_{0.5}(x_0) - F_{0.5}(x_0 - 1)] = 1 - \alpha_0$$

and $\alpha_1$ is obtained by

$$\begin{aligned}\alpha_1 &= E_{H_1}(1 - \phi(X)) \\ &= F_{2/3}(x_0) - \gamma[F_{2/3}(x_0) - F_{2/3}(x_0 - 1)] \\ &= 1 - F_{1/3}(n - x_0 - 1) - \gamma[F_{1/3}(n - x_0) - F_{1/3}(n - x_0 - 1)]\end{aligned}$$

We get the values as follows:

| $\alpha_0$ | $0,\ x_0 = 2$ $\gamma_0 = 0$ | $0.1,\ x_0 = 2$ $\gamma_0 = .4$ | $0.2,\ x_0 = 2$ $\gamma_0 = .8$ | $0.3, x_0 = 1$ $\gamma_0 = .1$ | $0.4,\ x_0 = 1$ $\gamma_0 = .3$ |
|---|---|---|---|---|---|
| $\alpha_1$ | 1 | 0.8222 | 0.6445 | 0.5112 | 0.4667 |
| $\alpha_0$ | $0.5, x_0 = 1$ $\gamma_0 = .5$ | $0.6, x_0 = 1$ $\gamma_0 = .7$ | $0.7, x_0 = 0$ $\gamma_0 = 0.2$ | $0.9, x_0 = 0$ $\gamma_0 = 0.6$ | $1, x_0 = 0$ $\gamma_0 = 1$ |
| $\alpha_1$ | 0.3334 | 0.2445 | 0.08896 | 0.044487 | 0 |

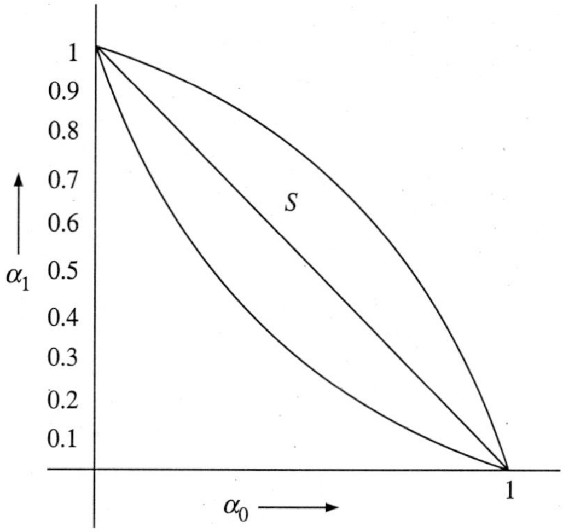


**Figure 2.8:** Risk set.

Based on these values, the shape of the risk set $S$ is shown in Figure 2.8.

**Example 2.4.6.** *Obtain NP test of level $\alpha$ for testing $H_0 : \mu = \mu_0$ against $H_1 : \mu = \mu_1 (\mu_1 > \mu_0)$ based on a random sample of size $n$ from $N(\mu,\ \sigma^2)$, $\sigma^2$: known.* [ If $\sigma^2$ is unknown, the hypothesis will be composite].

***Solution:*** Let $\mathbf{X} = (X_1, X_2, \ldots, X_n)$ be a random sample of size $n$ drawn from $N(\mu, \sigma^2)$. The joint distribution of sample observations is given by

$$\begin{aligned} f(\mathbf{x}|\mu) &= \left(\frac{1}{\sigma\sqrt{2\pi}}\right)^n e^{-\frac{1}{2\sigma^2}\sum_{i=1}^{n}(x_i-\mu)^2} \\ &= \left(\frac{1}{\sigma\sqrt{2\pi}}\right)^n e^{-\frac{n}{2\sigma^2}[s^2+(\bar{x}-\mu)^2]} \end{aligned}$$

NP Lemma most powerful size-$\alpha$ critical region is given as

$$C = \{\mathbf{x} : f_{\mu_1}(\mathbf{x}) \geq k f_{\mu_0}(\mathbf{x})\}$$

where, $k$ is determined by the size condition. Consider

$$\frac{f(\mathbf{x}|\mu_1)}{f(\mathbf{x}|\mu_0)} = \frac{e^{-\frac{n}{2\sigma^2}[s^2+(\bar{x}-\mu_1)^2]}}{e^{-\frac{n}{2\sigma^2}[s^2+(\bar{x}-\mu_0)^2]}} \geq k$$

which gives

$$\exp^{\{-\frac{n}{2\sigma^2}[(\bar{x}-\mu_1)^2-(\bar{x}-\mu_0)^2]\}} \geq k$$

$$-\frac{n}{2\sigma^2}[(\bar{x}-\mu_1)^2-(\bar{x}-\mu_0)^2] \geq \log k$$

or

$$2n\bar{x}(\mu_1 - \mu_0) \geq 2\sigma^2 \log k + n(\mu_1^2 - \mu_0^2)$$

$$\bar{x} \geq \frac{2\sigma^2 \log k + n(\mu_1^2 - \mu_0^2)}{2(\mu_1 - \mu_0)} = k_1$$

(Note this inequality, since $\mu_1 - \mu_0 > 0$). Therefore, one gets the best critical region by

$$\bar{x} \geq k_1$$

where $k_1$ is obtained as

$$P(\bar{X} \geq k_1 | H_0) = \alpha$$

By standardizing the random variable $\bar{X}$ under $H_0$, we get

$$P_{H_0}\left[\frac{\bar{X} - \mu_0}{\sigma/\sqrt{n}} \geq \frac{k_1 - \mu_0}{\sigma/\sqrt{n}}\right] = \alpha$$

$$P_{H_0}\left[N(0,1) \geq \frac{k_1 - \mu_0}{\sigma/\sqrt{n}}\right] = \alpha$$

This shows that, $\frac{k_1 - \mu_0}{\sigma/\sqrt{n}}$ is the upper $\alpha^{\text{th}}$ quantile of $N(0,1)$ distribution. We get

$$\frac{k_1 - \mu_0}{\sigma/\sqrt{n}} = z_\alpha, \quad k_1 = \mu_0 + z_\alpha \cdot \sigma/\sqrt{n}$$

Therefore, NP Lemma best test of size-$\alpha$ is given as

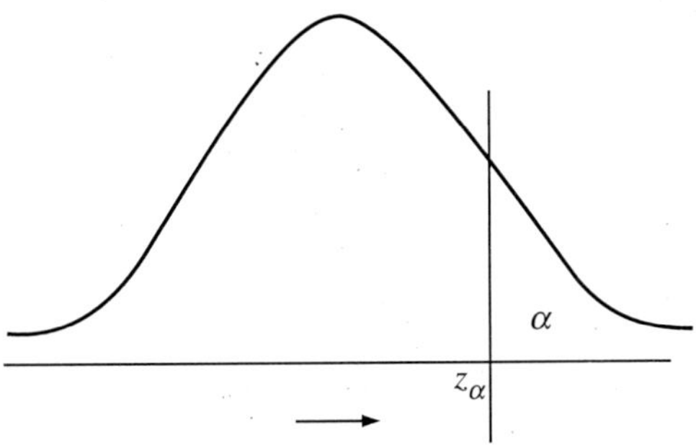


**Figure 2.9:** Critical region.

$$\phi(\mathbf{x}) = \begin{cases} 1 & \text{if } \bar{x} \geq \mu_0 + z_\alpha \cdot \sigma/\sqrt{n} \\ 0 & \text{otherwise} \end{cases}$$

Next, if we consider the alternative hypothesis $H_1 : \mu_1 < \mu_0$, the NP lemma best test becomes

$$\phi(\mathbf{x}) = \begin{cases} 1 & \text{if } \bar{x} \leq k_1 \\ 0 & \text{otherwise} \end{cases}$$

where $k_1$ is obtained by

$$P_{H_0}\{\bar{X} \leq k_1\} = \alpha$$

which gives

$$P_{H_0}\left\{\frac{\bar{X} - \mu_0}{\sigma/\sqrt{n}} \leq \frac{k_1 - \mu_0}{\sigma/\sqrt{n}}\right\} = \alpha$$

Let us denote $P\{Z < -z_\alpha\} = \alpha$ [where $Z \sim N(0, 1)$ and $\alpha$ usually less than 0.5], we get

$$\frac{k_1 - \mu_0}{\sigma/\sqrt{n}} = -z_\alpha, \quad k_1 = \mu_0 - z_\alpha \cdot \sigma/\sqrt{n}$$

Therefore, the best test is given by

$$\phi(\mathbf{x}) = \begin{cases} 1 & \text{if } \bar{x} \leq \mu_0 - z_\alpha \cdot \sigma/\sqrt{n} \\ 0 & \text{otherwise} \end{cases}$$

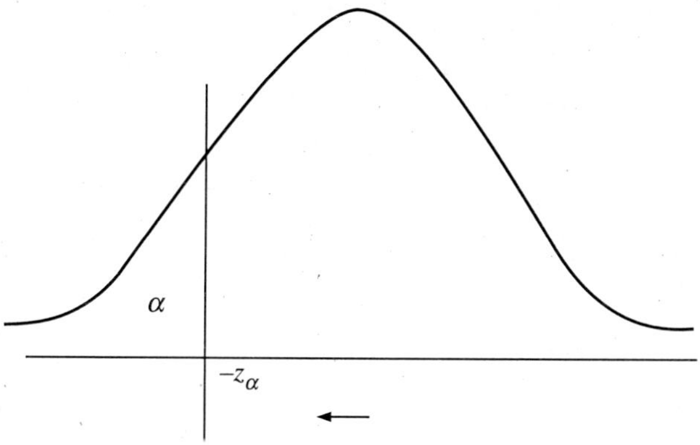


**Figure 2.10:** Critical region.

**Example 2.4.7.** *Let $X$ be normally distributed with $\sigma = 10$ and it is desired to test $H_0 : \mu = 100$ against $H_1 : \mu = 110$, how large should a sample be taken so that*

$$P(\textit{accepting } H_0|H_1 \textit{ is true}) = 0.02$$

*and*

$$P(X \in w|H_0) = 0.05$$

***Solution:*** We have noted from Example 2.4.6 that the best critical region, when $\mu_1 > \mu_0$, is

$$\bar{x} \geq k$$

where

$$k = \mu_0 + z_\alpha . \sigma/\sqrt{n}$$

For $\alpha = 0.05$, we have, $z_\alpha = \dfrac{k-\mu_0}{\sigma/\sqrt{n}} = 1.645$. Also, $\beta = 0.02$, i.e.

$$P_{H_1}\left(\frac{\overline{X}-\mu_1}{\sigma/\sqrt{n}} \le \frac{k-\mu_1}{\sigma/\sqrt{n}}\right) = 0.02$$

From normal table, we get

$$\frac{k-\mu_1}{\sigma/\sqrt{n}} = -2.055$$

Equating $k$ from both the equations, we get

$$\mu_0 + 1.645\ \sigma/\sqrt{n} = \mu_1 - 2.055\ \sigma/\sqrt{n}$$

$$100 + 1.645\ \sigma/\sqrt{n} = 110 - 2.055\ \sigma/\sqrt{n}$$

$$\frac{10}{\sqrt{n}}(1.645 + 2.055) = 10; \quad \sqrt{n} = 3.7 \quad n = 13.69 \cong 14$$

Therefore, the required sample size should at least be 14.

**Example 2.4.8.** *Obtain NP most powerful test of size-$\alpha$ for testing $H_0$ : $\sigma = \sigma_0$ against $H_1 : \sigma = \sigma_1(\sigma_1 > \sigma_0)$ based on a random sample of size $n$ from $N(\mu, \sigma^2)$, where $\mu$ is known.*

***Solution:*** Let $X_1, X_2, \ldots, X_n$ be a random sample from $N(\mu, \sigma^2)$. Here

$$f_{\sigma_1}(\mathbf{x}) = \left(\frac{1}{\sigma_1\sqrt{2\pi}}\right)^n e^{-\frac{1}{2\sigma_1^2}\sum_{i=1}^n (x_i-\mu)^2}$$

$$f_{\sigma_0}(\mathbf{x}) = \left(\frac{1}{\sigma_0\sqrt{2\pi}}\right)^n e^{-\frac{1}{2\sigma_0^2}\sum_{i=1}^n (x_i-\mu)^2}$$

Therefore,

$$\frac{f_{\sigma_1}(\mathbf{x})}{f_{\sigma_0}(\mathbf{x})} = \left(\frac{\sigma_0}{\sigma_1}\right)^n e^{-\frac{1}{2}\sum_{i=1}^n (x_i-\mu)^2[\frac{1}{\sigma_1^2} - \frac{1}{\sigma_0^2}]}$$

$$= e^{-\frac{1}{2}\left(\frac{\sigma_0^2-\sigma_1^2}{\sigma_0^2\sigma_1^2}\right)\sum_{i=1}^n (x_i-\mu)^2} \ge k$$

by assuming $(\frac{\sigma_0}{\sigma_1})^n$ is absorbed in $k$. We now have

$$-\frac{1}{2}\left[\frac{\sigma_0^2-\sigma_1^2}{\sigma_0^2\sigma_1^2}\right]\sum_{i=1}^n (x_i-\mu)^2 \ge \log k$$

We get

$$\sum_{i=1}^n (x_i-\mu)^2 \ge k_1(\text{ since } \sigma_1^2 > \sigma_0^2)$$

where $k_1$ is obtained by

$$P\Big[\sum_{i=1}^{n}\Big(\frac{X_i-\mu}{\sigma_0}\Big)^2 \geq \frac{k_1}{\sigma_0^2}\Big|H_0 \text{ is true}\Big] = \alpha$$

The null distribution of $\sum_{i=1}^{n}\big(\frac{X_i-\mu}{\sigma_0}\big)^2$ is $\chi_n^2$ so that $P[\chi_{(n)}^2 \geq \chi_\alpha^2] = \alpha$. This gives $k_1 = \sigma_0^2 \cdot \chi_\alpha^2$. Therefore, the best test of size-$\alpha$ would be given by

$$\phi(\mathbf{x}) = \begin{cases} 1 & \text{if } \sum_{i=1}^{n}(\frac{x_i-\mu}{\sigma_0})^2 \geq \chi_\alpha^2 \\ 0 & \text{otherwise} \end{cases}$$

**Example 2.4.9.** *Let a random sample be drawn from $f(x)$ with $x$ assuming non-negative integer values. Find out the most powerful size-$\alpha$ test for testing*

$$H_0 : f(x) = \frac{e^{-1}}{x!}\ ; x = 0, 1, 2, \quad \textit{against} \quad H_1 : f(x) = \Big(\frac{1}{2}\Big)^{x+1}\ ; x = 0, 1, 2, \ldots$$

***Solution:*** The most powerful test is given by

$$A(\mathbf{x}) = \frac{f_1(\mathbf{x})}{f_0(\mathbf{x})} = \frac{\prod_{i=1}^{n} x_i!}{(2e^{-1})^n 2^{\sum x_i}} > k \quad \text{or} \quad A(\mathbf{x}) = \frac{\prod_{i=1}^{n} x_i!}{2^{\sum x_i}} > k_1$$

For single observation $n = 1$, the test reduces to

$$A(x) = \frac{x!}{2^x} > k_1$$

The form of the critical region from the shape of $A(x)$ plotted in Figure 2.11 for $k_1 < 1$ is given by $x < x_0$ or $x > x_1$ and for $k_1 \geq 1$ is given by $x > x_2$. For $k_1 = 1$ the critical region is obtained as $C = \{x : x = 3, 4, 5, \ldots\}$ and for $k_2 = 0.8$ it is obtained as $C = \{x : x = 0, 3, 4, 5, \ldots\}$ by noting that $A(0) = 1,\ A(1) = 1/2,\ A(2) = 1/2,\ A(3) = 3/4, A(4) = 3/2, \ldots$. The size of the best test corresponding to $k = 0.8$ would be given by $\alpha = P_{H_0}(X \in C) - 1 - P_{H_0}(X = 1, 2) = 1 - 1/e - 1/2e = 0.448$ and power is given by $P_{H_1}(X \in C) = 1 - (\frac{1}{2})^2 - (\frac{1}{2})^3 = 0.625$

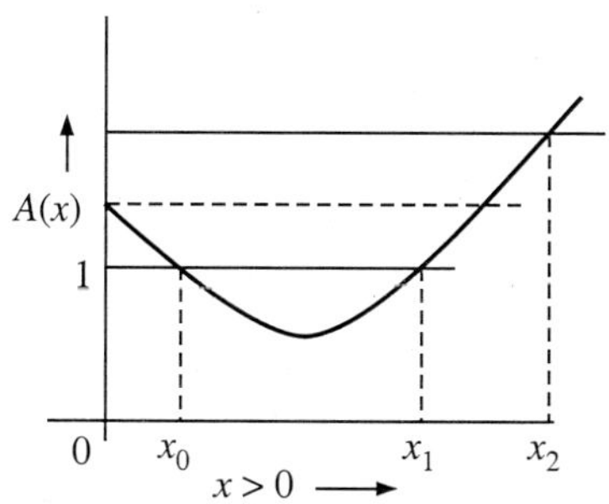


**Figure 2.11:** Graph of $A(x)$ in Example 2.4.9.

**Example 2.4.10.** *Consider the testing* $H_0 : f(x) \sim N(0,1)$ *against* $H_1 : f(x) \sim \mathcal{C}(1,0)$. *Find out the size-*$\alpha$ *most powerful test.*

***Solution:*** Note it is a single observation case. Consider

$$\frac{f_1(x)}{f_0(x)} = \sqrt{2/\pi}\,\frac{e^{x^2/2}}{1+x^2} > k$$

The most powerful test is given as

$$\phi(x) = \begin{cases} 1 & \text{if } \sqrt{2/\pi}\,\dfrac{e^{x^2/2}}{1+x^2} > k \\ 0 & \text{otherwise} \end{cases}$$

We would now study the behaviour of the function $\dfrac{e^{x^2/2}}{1+x^2}$. Setting $y = x^2$, we get

$$h(y) = \frac{e^{y/2}}{1+y}$$

$$h'(y) = \frac{\frac{1}{2}e^{y/2}(1+y) - e^{y/2}}{(1+y)^2} = \frac{e^{y/2}(y-1)}{2(1+y)^2}$$

$$h'(y) = \begin{cases} > 0 & \text{for } y > 1 \\ < 0 & \text{for } y < 1 \end{cases}$$

This suggest the following shape of $h(x) = \dfrac{\exp\{x^2/2\}}{1+x^2}$.

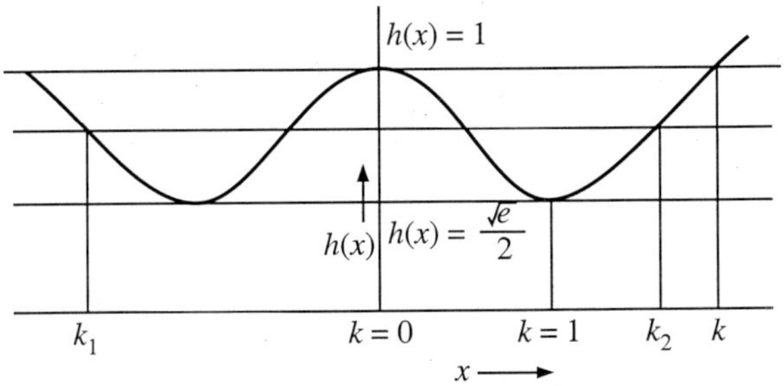


**Figure 2.12:** Graph of $h(x)$ for $x$'s in (i), (ii) and (iii) of Example 2.4.10.

The curve of $h(x)$ cuts at 0 point if $h(x) < \frac{\sqrt{e}}{2}$, at 2 points if $h(x) = \frac{\sqrt{e}}{2}$, 4 points if $h(x) \in (\frac{\sqrt{e}}{2}, 1)$, at 3 points if $h(x) = 1$ and at 2 points if $h(x) > 1$. Therefore, the most powerful critical region $h(x) = \frac{e^{x^2/2}}{1+x^2} > k$ is given by

(i) $-\infty < x < \infty$ if $h(x) < \frac{\sqrt{e}}{2}$

(ii) $|x| < k_1$ or $|x| > k_2$ if $\frac{\sqrt{e}}{2} < h(x) < 1$

(iii) $|x| > k$ if $h(x) > 1$

Usually $\alpha = 0.05$, in this case $h(x) > \frac{\sqrt{e}}{2}$ and the most powerful test is then given by

$$\phi(x) = \begin{cases} 1 & \text{if } |x| > k \\ 0 & \text{otherwise} \end{cases}$$

where, $k$ is obtained by the size condition

$$E_{H_0}\phi(X) = \alpha, \quad \text{or} \quad \int_{-k}^{k} N(0,1)\, dx = 1 - \alpha$$

which gives $k = z_{\alpha/2}$. The power of the test is

$$E_{H_1}\phi(X) = 1 - \int_{-k}^{k} \frac{1}{\pi} \cdot \frac{1}{1+x^2}\, dx = 1 - 2\int_{0}^{k} \frac{1}{\pi} \cdot \frac{1}{1+x^2}\, dx$$

$$= 1 - \frac{2}{\pi}\tan^{-1} k = 1 - \frac{2\tan^{-1} z_{\alpha/2}}{\pi}$$

**Example 2.4.11.** *Consider a testing problem* $H_0 : \theta = \theta_0$ *versus* $H_1 : \theta = \theta_1 (\theta_1 < \theta_0)$ *based on a sample of size one from*

$$f_\theta(x) = \begin{cases} \frac{2}{\theta^2}(\theta - x) & \text{if } 0 < x < \theta \\ 0 & \text{otherwise} \end{cases}$$

*Find out the most powerful test.*

***Solution:*** The most powerful test would be given as

$$A(x) = \frac{f_1(x)}{f_0(x)} = \left(\frac{\theta_0}{\theta_1}\right)^2 \frac{(\theta_1 - x)}{(\theta_0 - x)} \cdot \frac{I_{(0,\theta_1)}(x)}{I_{(0,\theta_0)}(x)} > k$$

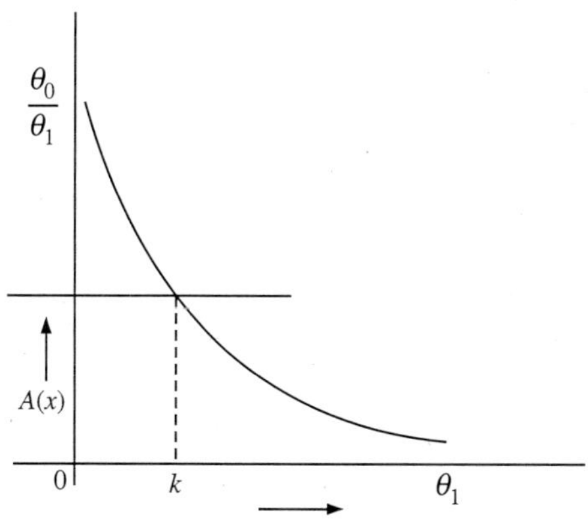


**Figure 2.13:** Graph of $A(x)$ in Example 2.4.10.

Note that $f_1/f_0$ is a decreasing function of $x$, therefore, the best test would be given as

$$\phi(x) = \begin{cases} 1 & \text{if } x < k \\ 0 & \text{otherwise} \end{cases}$$

where, $k$ is obtained by $E_{H_0}\phi(X) = \alpha$ we get, $k = \theta_0 + \theta_0\sqrt{(1-\alpha)}$. The test $\phi$ does not depend on the alternative $\theta_1$, but note the test inverts when $\theta_1 > \theta_0$.

**Example 2.4.12.** *Consider a testing problem* $H_0 : \theta = \theta_0$ *against* $H_1 : \theta = \theta_1 (\theta_0 < \theta_1)$ *on the basis of a single observation being taken from*

$$f_\theta(x) = 2\theta x + 2(1-\theta)(1-x) \quad 0 < x < 1,\ \theta \in [0,1]$$

*Find out the most powerful test.*

***Solution:*** Consider

$$\lambda(x) = f_1/f_0 = \frac{2\theta_1 x + 2(1-\theta_1)(1-x)}{2\theta_0 x + 2(1-\theta_0)(1-x)} > k$$

After some simplifications, we get

$$\lambda(x) = \frac{x[2\theta_1 - 1] + (1-\theta_1)}{x[2\theta_0 - 1] + (1-\theta_0)} > k$$

On differentiating the left side of the inequality and following some simplifications when $\theta_0 < \theta_1$, we get

$$\lambda'(x) = \frac{(\theta_1 - \theta_0)}{[x(2\theta_0 - 1) + (1-\theta_0)]^2} > 0$$

This shows that $\lambda(x)$ is an increasing function of $x$. Hence, the most powerful test will be given by

$$\phi(x) = \begin{cases} 1 & \text{if } x \geq k' \\ 0 & \text{otherwise} \end{cases}$$

where, $k'$ is determined by the size condition

$$E_{\theta_0}\phi(X) = \alpha$$

Densities $f_0$ and $f_1$ are plotted against $x$, as shown in Figure 2.14, on comparing graphs we see that if one gets large value of x it is more likely that it has come from $f_1$, indicating the null hypothesis would be rejected. This falls in agreement to the most powerful critical region $x \geq k'$.

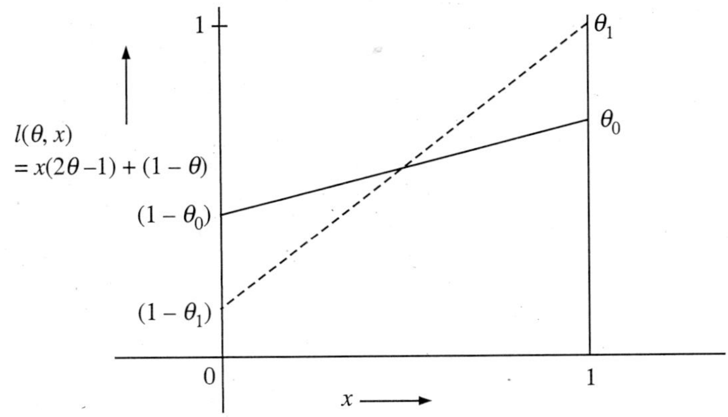


**Figure 2.14:** Plots of the function $l(\theta, x)$, at $\theta_0$ and $\theta_1$, as a function of $x$.

Let

$$B_\phi(\theta) = 2\int_{k'}^{1} (x(2\theta - 1) + (1 - \theta))\,dx$$

$$= (2\theta - 1)(1 - k'^2) + 2(1 - \theta)(1 - k')$$

$B_\phi(\theta_0) = \alpha$ gives

$$-k'^2(2\theta_0 - 1) + (2\theta_0 - 1) - 2(1 - \theta_0)k' + 2(1 - \theta_0) - \alpha = 0$$

$$k'^2(2\theta_0 - 1) + 2(1 - \theta_0)k' + \alpha - 1 = 0$$

$$k' = \frac{-2(1 - \theta_0) \pm \sqrt{4(1 - \theta_0)^2 - 4(2\theta_0 - 1)(\alpha - 1)}}{2(2\theta_0 - 1)}$$

Since $0 \le k' < 1$, we choose

$$k' = \frac{-(1 - \theta_0) + \sqrt{\theta_0^2 - \alpha(2\theta_0 - 1)}}{(2\theta_0 - 1)}$$

But if we put $\theta_0 = 1$ we get $k' = \sqrt{(1 - \alpha)}$. We note that the choice of $k'$ or NP test $\phi(x)$ depends on $\alpha$ and $\theta_0$, but not on $\theta_1$. This suggests the same test $\phi(x)$ is UMP of size-$\alpha$ for testing $H_0 : \theta = \theta_0$ against $H_0 : \theta > \theta_0$; and note that $1 - \phi$ is the UMP size-$\alpha$ test for testing $H_0 : \theta = \theta_0$ against $H_1 : \theta < \theta_0$. The definitions of UMP test will be discussed in Chapter 3.

**Example 2.4.13.** *Let $X \sim Be(\beta, 1)$. We shall find out the NP test of size-$\alpha$ for testing $H_0 : \beta = 1$ against $H_1 : \beta = \beta_1(> 1)$ based on the sample of size 1. Find out the best test.*

***Solution:*** The best rejection region is given as

$$\frac{f_1}{f_0} = \left(\frac{\beta_1}{\beta_0}\right) x^{\beta_1 - \beta_0} > k$$

Since $\beta_1 - \beta_0 > 0$, $f_1/f_0$ is an increasing function of $x$. Therefore, the best test is given as

$$\phi(x) = \begin{cases} 1 & \text{if } x > k \\ 0 & \text{otherwise} \end{cases}$$

where, $k$ is determined as

$$E_{\beta_0 = 1}\phi(X) = \alpha$$

or

$$\int_k^1 \beta x^{\beta-1} dx \Big|_{H_0:\beta=1} = \alpha \text{ gives } k = 1 - \alpha$$

**Example 2.4.14.** *Consider a testing problem*

$$H_0 : X \sim \frac{1}{\sqrt{2\pi}} e^{-x^2/2}, \quad x \in \mathbb{R}^1 \quad \textit{against } H_1 : X \sim \frac{1}{2} e^{-|x|}, x \in \mathbb{R}^1$$

*on the basis of sample of size 1. Find the most powerful test of size-$\alpha$.*

***Solution:*** The most powerful test shall be given as

$$\frac{f_1}{f_0} = \sqrt{\frac{\pi}{2}}\, e^{x^2/2\, -\, |x|} > k$$

On completing the perfect square in the exponent, we get

$$f_1/f_0 = \sqrt{\frac{\pi}{2}}\, e^{1/2((|x|-1)^2 - 1)} > k$$

The equivalent region is given as

$$\big||x| - 1\big| > k \text{ or } |x| \geq k_1 \quad \text{or} \quad |x| \leq k_2$$

This could be seen from Figure 2.15. In this case $H_0$ is likely to be rejected if $x$ is too large or too small. This is in consistence with $f_1$ having high probability near zero and heavy tails for large values of $x$ as compared to $f_0$. The constants $k_1$ and $k_2$ are obtained by

$$E_{H_0}\phi(X) = \alpha \text{ or } \int_{|x| \geq k_1} N(0,1)\, dx + \int_{|x| \leq k_2} N(0,1)\, dx = \alpha$$

$$= 2\{P(Z \geq k_1) + P(0 < Z \leq k_2)\} = \alpha$$

Therefore, no unique pair $(k_1, k_2)$ could be obtained, some rationality criterion need to be adopted. The expression of power could be calculated as

$$\beta_\phi(H_1) = \int_{|x| \geq k_1} \frac{1}{2}\, e^{-|x|}\, dx + \int_{|x| \leq k_2} \frac{1}{2}\, e^{-|x|}\, dx$$

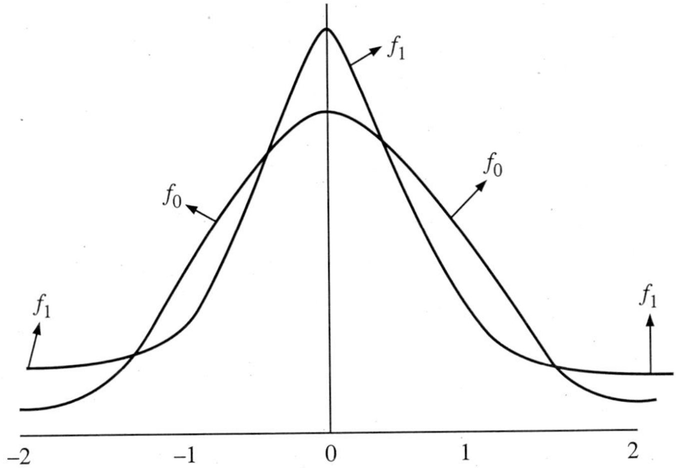


**Figure 2.15:** Plot of null and alternative distributions in Example 2.4.14.

After some simplifications, we get

$$\beta_\phi(H_1) = 1 + e^{-k_1} - e^{-k_2}$$

**Example 2.4.15.** *Let a random sample of size n be drawn from $E(\theta, 1)$, $x \geq \theta$ to test*

$$H_0 : \theta = \theta_0 \text{ against } H_1 : \theta = \theta_1 (\theta_1 > \theta_0)$$

*Find the most powerful size-$\alpha$ test for this testing problem.*

***Solution:*** Note that $(\min x_i, \sum x_i)$ is jointly sufficient for $(a, b)$ in $E(a, b)$. NP test shall be given by

$$\frac{f_1}{f_0} = e^{n(\theta_1 - \theta_0)} \frac{I_{(\theta_1, \infty)}(M_n)}{I_{(\theta_0, \infty)}(M_n)}$$

where, $M_n = \min\{x_i\}$, $f_1/f_0$ is a non-decreasing function of $M_n$, which gives

$$\phi(M_n) = \begin{cases} 1 & \text{if } M_n > k \\ 0 & \text{otherwise} \end{cases}$$

Note that $M_n$ is first order statistic and we require the null distribution of $M_n$ to calculate $k$ by the size condition. The probability density of $r^{\text{th}}$ order statistic is given by

$$g_r(y_r) = \frac{n!}{(r-1)!(n-r)!}[F(y_r)]^{r-1}[1 - F(y_r)]^{n-r} f(y_r)$$

Thus, the distribution of $M_n$ ($m_n$ is the value taken by $M_n$) shall be given as

$$g_1(m_n) = n[1 - F(m_n)]^{n-1} f(m_n)$$

Note that $F(m_n) = 1 - e^{-(m_n-\theta)}$. We get

$$g_1(m_n) = n\big[e^{-(m_n-\theta)}\big]^n, \qquad m_n \geq \theta$$

The constant $k$ is obtained by

$$E_{\theta_0}\phi(M_n) = \alpha$$

$$\int_k^\infty ne^{-n(m_n-\theta_0)}\, dm_n = \alpha$$

This gives $k = \theta_0 - \dfrac{\log\alpha}{n}$

**Example 2.4.16.** *Let a random sample $X_1, \ldots, X_n$ be drawn from $f_\theta(x)$*

$$f_\theta(x) = \theta/x^2 \quad \textit{if} \quad 0 < \theta \leq x < \infty$$

*Find the most powerful size-$\alpha$ test of $H_0 : \theta = \theta_0$ against $H_1 : \theta = \theta_1(\theta_1 \neq \theta_0)$.*

***Solution:*** The NP test of size-$\alpha$ shall be given as

$$\frac{f_1}{f_0} = \left(\frac{\theta_1}{\theta_0}\right)^n \cdot \frac{I_{m_n \geq \theta_1}}{I_{m_n \geq \theta_0}} > k$$

where, $M_n$ is minimum statistic of the sample $X_1, X_2, ..., X_n$, and $m_n$ be the observed value of $M_n$. Now, if we consider $\theta_1 > \theta_0$, $f_1/f_0$ is an increasing function of $M_n$. Then the NP test shall be given by

$$\phi(m_n) = \begin{cases} 1 & \text{if } \; m_n > k \\ 0 & \text{otherwise} \end{cases}$$

The density of $M_n$ under $H_0$ is given by

$$g_1(m_n) = n[1 - F(m_n)]^{n-1} f(m_n)$$

where

$$F(m_n) = \int_\theta^x \theta/x^2 \, dx;\ 0 < \theta \leq x < \infty$$

$$= 1 - \theta/x$$

Therefore,

$$g_1(m_n) = n \cdot \theta^n / m_n^{n+1} \qquad \theta \leq m_n < \infty$$

The constant $k$ is obtained from

$$E_{H_0}\phi(M_n) = \alpha \;\; \text{or} \quad \int_k^\infty n \cdot \theta_0^n \cdot \frac{1}{m_n^{n+1}}\, dm_n = \alpha$$

This gives $k = \theta_0/\alpha^{1/n}$. The same test $\phi$ will be UMP for testing $H_0 : \theta = \theta_0$ against $H_1 : \theta > \theta_0$.

Now, if we consider the testing problem $H_0 : \theta = \theta_0$ against $H_1 : \theta = \theta_1 (\theta_1 < \theta_0)$, the NP test is given by

$$\phi(m_n) = \begin{cases} 1 & \text{if } m_n < k \\ 0 & \text{otherwise} \end{cases}$$

and

$$E_{H_0}\phi(M_n) = \alpha$$

where $k$ is obtained from

$$\int_{\theta_0}^{k} g_1(m_n)\, dm_n = \alpha \text{ which gives } k = \frac{\theta_0}{(1-\alpha)^{\frac{1}{n}}}$$

The above test would be UMP for testing $H_0 : \theta = \theta_0$ against $H_1 : \theta_1 < \theta_0$. Therefore, NP lemma cannot be utilized in this case to get a UMP test for testing $H_0 : \theta = \theta_0$ against $H_1 : \theta \neq \theta_0$.

**Example 2.4.17.** *Consider the distribution*

$$f(x|\theta) = \begin{cases} 1/\theta & \text{if } 0 \le x \le \theta \\ 0 & \text{otherwise} \end{cases}$$

*On the basis of single observation from the above distribution, consider the problem of testing of hypothesis $H_0 : \theta = 1$ against $H_1 : \theta = 2$. Calculate type I and II errors if the intervals* (a) $0.5 \le x$ (b) $1 \le x \le 1.5$ *are taken as critical regions. Also, obtain power function of the test.*

***Solution:*** Let the critical region be given by

(a) $$w = \{x \mid x \ge 0.5\}$$

Here

$$\begin{aligned} \alpha &= P\{X \in w \mid H_0\} \\ &= P\{0.5 \le X \le \theta \mid \theta = 1\} \\ &= \int_{0.5}^{1} f(x|\theta)\,\big|_{\theta=1}\, dx = 0.5 \end{aligned}$$

and

$$\beta = P_{\theta=2}\{X \in w^c\}|\ \theta = 2\} = \int_0^{.5} f(x|\theta)\,\big|_{\theta=2}\, dx = 0.25$$

The power of the test $w$ shall be given by $1 - \beta = 0.75$.

(b) $$w = \{x \mid 1 \le x \le 1.5\}$$

Here

$$\alpha = P_{\theta=1}\{X \in w \mid H_0\} = \int_1^{1.5} f(x|\theta)\big|_{\theta=1}\, dx = 0$$

$$\beta = P_{\theta=2}\{X \in w^c\} = 1 - P_{\theta=2}\{1 \le x \le 1.5\} = 0.75$$

The power shall be given by $1 - \beta = 0.25$.

**Example 2.4.18.** *From the given probability distribution*

$$f(x|\theta) = \begin{cases} 1/\theta & \text{if } 0 \leq x \leq \theta \\ 0 & \text{otherwise} \end{cases}$$

*One observation $x$ is taken to test the hypothesis $H_0 : \theta = 1$ against $H_1 : \theta = 2$. Obtain the probabilities of type I and type II errors for the critical region $x \geq 0.7$.*

***Solution:*** The size of the critical region or probability of type I error is given by

$$\alpha = P(x \geq 0.7 | H_0 : \theta = 1)$$

$$= \int_{0.7}^{1} 1.dx = 1 - 0.7 = 0.3$$

and the probability of type II error is given by

$$\beta = P(x \geq 0.7 | H_1 : \theta = 2)$$

$$= \int_{0.7}^{2} \frac{1}{2} dx = \frac{1}{2}[2 - 0.7] = 0.65$$

**Example 2.4.19.** *Let $X_1, X_2$ be iid observations from*

$$f(x, \theta) = \frac{1}{\theta}\, e^{-x/\theta}; \quad 0 < x < \infty,\ \theta > 0$$

*Consider the acceptance region as $w = \{(x_1, x_2) | x_1 + x_2 < 9.448\}$ for testing $H_0 : \theta = 2$ against $H_1 : \theta = 4$. Determine type I and II errors.*

***Solution:*** For testing $H_0 : \theta = \theta_0$ against $H_1 : \theta = \theta_1 (\theta > \theta_0)$, the best test is of the form $\dfrac{f(\mathbf{x}|\theta_1)}{f(\mathbf{x}|\theta_0)} > k$. $A(\mathbf{x}) = \dfrac{f(\mathbf{x}|\theta_1)}{f(\mathbf{x}|\theta_0)} = \left(\frac{\theta_0}{\theta_1}\right)^n \exp\left\{\left(\frac{1}{\theta_0} - \frac{1}{\theta_1}\right) \sum x_i\right\}$ is increasing in $\sum x_i$ since $(\frac{1}{\theta_0} - \frac{1}{\theta_1}) > 0$. Therefore, the best critical region is of the form $\sum x_i > k_1$.

$$\alpha = P\{X_1 + X_2 \geq 9.448 | \theta = 2\}$$

$$= 1 - P\{X_1 + X_2 < 9.448 | \theta = 2\}$$

$$= 1 - \int_{x_2=0}^{9.448} \int_{x_1=0}^{9.448-x_2} \frac{1}{4}\, e^{-(x_1+x_2)/2}\, dx_1\, dx_2$$

On simplifications, we get $\alpha = 0.05$. Now, consider

$$\beta = P\{(x_1, x_2) \in w^c \mid H_1 : \theta = 4\}$$

$$= \int_0^{9.448} \int_0^{9.448-x_2} \frac{1}{16}\, e^{-(x_1+x_2)/4} dx_1\, dx_2 = 0.39$$

Alternatively, use $Y = X_1 + X_2 \sim G(2, \frac{1}{\theta})$ with density $\frac{1}{\theta^2} y e^{-y/\theta}$ for calculating $\alpha$ and $\beta$.

**Example 2.4.20.** *Let $X_1, X_2$ be a random sample drawn from*

$$f(x, \theta) = \theta\, x^{\theta-1}; \quad 0 < x < 1$$

*If we test $H_0 : \theta = 1$ against $H_1 : \theta = 2$ with the critical region $w = \{(x_1, x_2) \mid x_1.x_2 \geq 3/4\}$, find the size and power of the test.*

***Solution:*** For testing $H_0 : \theta = \theta_0$ against $H_1 : \theta = \theta_1 (\theta > \theta_0)$, the best test is given by $\frac{f(\mathbf{x}|\theta_1)}{f(\mathbf{x}|\theta_0)} > k$. $A(\mathbf{x}) = \frac{f(\mathbf{x}|\theta_1)}{f(\mathbf{x}|\theta_0)} = (\frac{\theta_1}{\theta_0})^n \cdot (\prod x_i)^{\theta_1 - \theta_0}$ is increasing in $\prod x_i$ since $\theta_1 - \theta_0 > 0$. Therefore, the best critical region is of the form $\prod x_i > k_1$.

$$\alpha = P\{(x_1, x_2) \in w \mid H_0\} = P\{x_1 x_2 \geq 3/4 | \theta = 1\}$$

$$= \frac{1}{4} + \frac{3}{4} \log(3/4)$$

$$\beta = P\{x_1 x_2 < 3/4 \mid \theta = 2\} = 1 - P\{x_1 x_2 \geq 3/4 \mid \theta = 2\}$$

$$= 1 - \int_{x_2=3/4}^{1} \int_{x_1=3/4x_2}^{1} 4\, x_1 x_2\, dx_1 dx_2 = 1 - \left[\frac{7}{16} + \frac{9}{16} \log\left(\frac{3}{4}\right)\right]$$

Alternatively, set $x = e^{-y}$ in $f(x, \theta) = \theta x^{\theta-1}$, we get $g(y, \theta) = \theta e^{-y\theta}$ i.e. $Y = -\log X \sim G(1, \theta)$. This gives $\sum Y_i = -\sum \log X_i \sim G(n, \theta)$. Use the density of $\sum Y_i$ for calculating $\alpha$ and $\beta$.

**Example 2.4.21.** *Let a single observation be drawn from $B(4, p)$ to test the hypothesis $H_0 : p = 0.8$ against $H_1 : p = 0.3$. Find the best test of size-$\alpha = 0.01$*

***Solution:*** Note $f_1/f_0 = (28/3)^{-x}(7/2)^4$ is a decreasing function of $x$, therefore, the best test is given as

$$\phi(x) = \begin{cases} 1 & \text{if } \; x < k \\ \gamma & \text{if } \; x = k \\ 0 & \text{if } \; x > k \end{cases}$$

where, $k$ and $\gamma$ are determined by the size condition

$$E_{p=0.8}\phi(X) = 0.01 \quad \text{or,} \quad P_{p=0.8}(X < k) + \gamma P_{\theta_0}(X = k) = 0.01$$

Now, at $k = 1$, we have

$$\gamma = \frac{0.01 - P_{p=0.8}(X < 1)}{P_{p=0.8}(X = 1)} = \frac{0.01 - \binom{4}{0}(0.8)^0(0.2)^{4-0}}{\binom{4}{1}(0.8)^1(0.2)^{4-1}} = 21/64$$

and the best test of size 0.01 shall be given by

$$\phi(x) = \begin{cases} 1 & \text{if } x < 1 \\ 21/64 & \text{if } x = 1 \\ 0 & \text{if } x > 1 \end{cases} \tag{2.33}$$

But at $k = 2$, we get $\gamma = -\frac{172}{1536} \notin [0, 1]$. Hence, there is no best test corresponding to $k = 2$. Similarly, $k$ cannot be equal to 3 or 4.

**Example 2.4.22.** *Let the distribution of $X$ be given by*

| $x$ | *0* | *1* | *2* | *3* |
|---|---|---|---|---|
| $P_\theta(X = x)$ | $\theta$ | $2\theta$ | $0.9 - 2\theta$ | $0.1 - \theta$ |

*where $0 < \theta < 0.1$. For testing $H : \theta = 0.05$ against $H_1 : \theta > 0.05$ at level $\alpha = 0.05$, determine which of the following tests (if any) is UMP:*

(a) $\phi(0) = 1, \quad \phi(1) = \phi(2) = \phi(3) = 0$

(b) $\phi(1) = 0.5, \quad \phi(0) = \phi(2) = \phi(3) = 0$

(c) $\phi(3) = 1, \quad \phi(0) = \phi(1) = \phi(2) = 0$

***Solution:*** We prepare the following table for $f_1/f_0$ for the possible values of $x$:

| $x$ | 0 | 1 | 2 | 3 |
|---|---|---|---|---|
| $f_1/f_0$ | $\theta_1/.05$ | $\theta_1/.05$ | $(0.9 - 2\theta_1)/0.8$ | $(0.1 - \theta_1)/.05$ |

Note that $f_1/f_0$ is nonincreasing in $x$, therefore, the best critical region is given by $x \le x_0$ s.t. $P_{\theta=0.05}\{X \le x_0\} = 0.05$. This gives $x_0 = 0$ and the test does not depend on the alternative $\theta_1$. Therefore, UMP test is given by

$$\phi(0) = 1, \quad \phi(1) = \phi(2) = \phi(3) = 0$$

This shows that the test in (a) is UMP. We, further, note that the test in (b) is of size-$\alpha = 0.05$ and its power $\theta_1$ is same as of the test in (a). So, the test in (b) is also UMP of size-$\alpha = 0.05$.

**Example 2.4.23.** *Let the distribution of a random variable $X$ under $H_0$ and $H_1$ be given as*

| $x$ | 1 | 2 | 3 | 4 | 5 | 6 |
|---|---|---|---|---|---|---|
| $f_0(x)$ | 0.01 | 0.01 | 0.01 | 0.01 | 0.01 | 0.95 |
| $f_1(x)$ | 0.05 | 0.04 | 0.03 | 0.02 | 0.01 | 0.85 |

*Find the best test of size 0.03 and also its power for testing $H_0 : f = f_0$ against $H_1 : f = f_1$.*

| $x$ | 1 | 2 | 3 | 4 | 5 | 6 |
|---|---|---|---|---|---|---|
| $f_1/f_0$ | 5 | 4 | 3 | 2 | 1 | 0.89 |

***Solution:*** From the given data, we obtain
The best test would be given by

$$\phi(x) = \begin{cases} 1 & \text{if} \quad f_1/f_0 \geq k \\ 0 & \text{otherwise} \end{cases}$$

where, $k$ is determined by the condition

$$\begin{aligned} E_{H_0}\phi(X) &\leq 0.03 \\ P_{H_0}[X \leq k] &\leq 0.03 \end{aligned}$$

Since we have seen that $f_1/f_0$ is a decreasing function of $x$, we get $k = 3$ (from the data calculated above). The power of this test becomes

$$P_{H_1}[X \leq 3] = 0.05 + 0.04 + 0.03 = 0.12$$

and

$$P(\text{type II error}) = 1 - 0.12 = 0.88$$

**Example 2.4.24.** *An urn contains 10 balls of which $\theta$ are blue (and the rest of the balls being of red and white colours). We are interested in testing the hypothesis, $H_0 : \theta = 3$ against $H_1 : \theta = 4$.*

*Suppose we take a sample of 3 balls and reject $H_0$ if all the three balls drawn yield blue balls. Compute the error probabilities $\alpha$ and $\beta$, assuming,*

(a) *Sampling was done without replacement.*

(b) *Sampling was done with replacement.*

***Solution:*** (a) *Without replacement*

$$\alpha = P[\text{reject} H_0 | H_0] = P[\text{getting 3 blue balls} | \theta = 3]$$

$$= \frac{\binom{3}{3}\binom{7}{0}}{\binom{10}{3}} = \frac{6}{720} = \frac{1}{120}$$

$$1 - \beta = P[\text{reject} H_0 | H_1] = P[\text{getting 3 blue balls} | \theta = 4]$$

$$= \frac{\binom{4}{3}\binom{6}{0}}{\binom{10}{3}} = \frac{4 \times 3 \times 2}{720} = \frac{24}{720} = \frac{1}{30}; \quad \text{or} \quad \beta = \frac{29}{30}$$

(b) *With replacement*

$$\alpha = P[\text{reject}H_0|H_0] = P[\text{getting 3 blue balls} \mid \theta = 3]$$
$$= \left(\frac{3}{10}\right)^3 = \frac{27}{1000} = 0.027$$
$$1 - \beta = P[\text{reject}H_0|H_1]$$
$$= P[\text{getting 3 blue balls}|\theta = 4] = \left(\frac{4}{10}\right)^3 = 0.064$$

or

$$\beta = 0.936$$

**Example 2.4.25.** *An urn contains 10 marbles of which M are white and 10 − M are black. To test $H_0 : M = 5$ against $H_1 : M = 6$, one draws 3 marbles from the urn without replacement. The null hypothesis is rejected if the sample contains 2 or 3 white marbles; otherwise, it is accepted. Find the size of the test and its power.*

***Solution:*** $H_0 : M = 5$ against $H_1 : M = 6$

$$\alpha = P[\text{reject}H_0|H_0] = P[\text{getting 2 or 3 white marbles}|M = 5]$$
$$= \frac{\binom{5}{2}\binom{5}{1}}{\binom{10}{3}} + \frac{\binom{5}{3}\binom{5}{0}}{\binom{10}{3}} = \frac{300}{720} + \frac{60}{720} = \frac{360}{720} = 0.5$$

and $1 - \beta = P[\text{getting 2 or 3 white marbles}|M = 6]$

$$= \frac{\binom{6}{2}\binom{4}{1}}{\binom{10}{3}} + \frac{\binom{6}{3}\binom{4}{0}}{\binom{10}{3}} = 0.667$$

**Example 2.4.26.** *Let $X \sim \mathcal{C}(\theta, 1)$. Show that the test*

$$\phi(x) = \begin{cases} 1 & \text{if } 1 < x < 3 \\ 0 & \text{otherwise} \end{cases}$$

*is best of its size for testing $H_0 : \theta = 0$ against $H_1 : \theta = 1$. Give a rough plot of the power function as a function of $\theta$.*

***Solution:*** We calculate the size, at which a best of $H_0 : \theta = 0$ against $H_1 : \theta = 0$ is to be obtained, by calculating size of the test $\phi$ given in the example.

$$E_{H_0}\phi(X) = \alpha$$
$$\int_1^3 \mathcal{C}(\theta, 1)|H_0 \, dx = \alpha$$
$$\frac{1}{\pi}\int_1^3 \frac{1}{1 + (x - \theta)^2}\bigg|_{\theta=0} dx = \frac{1}{\pi}\int_1^3 \frac{1}{1 + x^2}\, dx$$
$$= \frac{1}{\pi}\tan^{-1} x\bigg|_1^3 = 0.147584 \text{ (in radian)}$$

The NP test at level $\alpha = 0.1476$ shall be given as

$$f_1/f_0 = \frac{\mathcal{C}(1,1)}{\mathcal{C}(0,1)} = \frac{\frac{1}{\pi} \cdot \frac{1}{1+(x-1)^2}}{\frac{1}{\pi} \cdot \frac{1}{1+x^2}} = \frac{1+x^2}{1+(x-1)^2} > k$$

which implies

$$(k-1)x^2 - 2kx + (2k-1) < 0$$

If $2k > 0$ and $4k^2 - 4(k-1)(2k-1) > 0$, the inequality implies

$$\frac{2k - \sqrt{-4k^2 - 4(k-1)(2k-1)}}{2(k-1)} < x < \frac{2k + \sqrt{-4k^2 - 4(k-1)(2k-1)}}{2(k-1)}$$

or

$$\frac{k - \sqrt{-k^2 + 3k - 1}}{(k-1)} < x < \frac{k + \sqrt{-k^2 + 3k - 1}}{(k-1)}$$

where, $k$ is determined by the size condition

$$\int_{\frac{k-\sqrt{-k^2+3k-1}}{(k-1)}}^{\frac{k+\sqrt{-k^2+3k-1}}{(k-1)}} \frac{1}{1+x^2}\,dx = \frac{1}{\pi}\tan^{-1} x\Big|_{\frac{k-\sqrt{-k^2+3k-1}}{(k-1)}}^{\frac{k+\sqrt{-k^2+3k-1}}{(k-1)}}$$

$$= \frac{1}{\pi}\tan^{-1} x\Big|_1^3$$

$$= \frac{1}{\pi}\tan^{-1}\frac{3-1}{1+3\times 1}$$

$$\frac{\frac{k+\sqrt{-k^2+3k-1}}{(k-1)} - \frac{k+\sqrt{-k^2+3k-1}}{(k-1)}}{1 + \frac{(k+\sqrt{-k^2+3k-1})(k-\sqrt{-k^2+3k-1})}{(k-1)^2}} = \frac{1}{2}$$

$$\frac{2\sqrt{-k^2+3k-1}}{(k-1)} \frac{(k-1)^2}{(k-1)^2 + (2k^2-3k+1)} = \frac{1}{2}$$

or
$$\frac{2(k-1)\sqrt{-k^2+3k-1}}{(k-1)\{(k-1)+(2k-1)\}} = \frac{2\sqrt{-k^2+3k-1}}{(k-1)+(2k-1)} = \frac{1}{2}$$

or
$$16(-k^2+3k-1) = 9k^2 - 12k + 4$$

or
$$(5k-2)(k-2) = 0$$

Corresponding to $k = 2$, we get the critical region as $1 < x < 3$ and to $k = 2/5$, we get $-1 < x < -1/3$.

Now, the power function shall be given as

$$B_\phi(\theta) = \frac{1}{\pi}\int_1^3 \frac{1}{1+(x-\theta)^2}\,dx; \qquad \text{let } y = x-\theta$$

$$B_\phi(\theta) = \frac{1}{\pi}\int_{1-\theta}^{3-\theta} \frac{1}{1+y^2}\,dy = \frac{1}{\pi}\tan^{-1} y\Big|_{1-\theta}^{3-\theta}$$

$$= \frac{1}{\pi}\tan^{-1}\frac{(3-\theta)-(1-\theta)}{1+(3-\theta)(1-\theta)} = \frac{1}{\pi}\tan^{-1}\frac{2}{\theta^2-4\theta+4}$$

The following table gives the values of the power function of the test $\phi$ for different values of $\theta$:

| $\theta$ | $B_\phi(\theta)$ | $\theta$ | $B_\phi(\theta)$ | $\theta$ | $B_\phi(\theta)$ |
|---|---|---|---|---|---|
| –25 | 0.00087 | –5 | 0.012985 | 4 | 0.147584 |
| –20 | 0.001315 | –4 | 0.017666 | 5 | 0.069604 |
| –18 | 0.001592 | –3 | 0.025411 | 6 | 0.039583 |
| –16 | 0.001965 | –2 | 0.039583 | 8 | 0.017666 |
| –14 | 0.002487 | –1 | 0.069604 | 10 | 0.009944 |
| –12 | 0.003248 | 0 | 0.147584 | 12 | 0.006365 |
| –10 | 0.004421 | 1 | 0.352416 | 14 | 0.004421 |
| –8 | 0.006365 | 1.8 | 0.493635 | 16 | 0.003248 |
| –6 | 0.009944 | 3 | 0.352416 | 18 | 0.002487 |

Power function of the test $\phi, B_\theta(\theta)$, at different values of $\theta$ have been plotted in Figure 2.16.

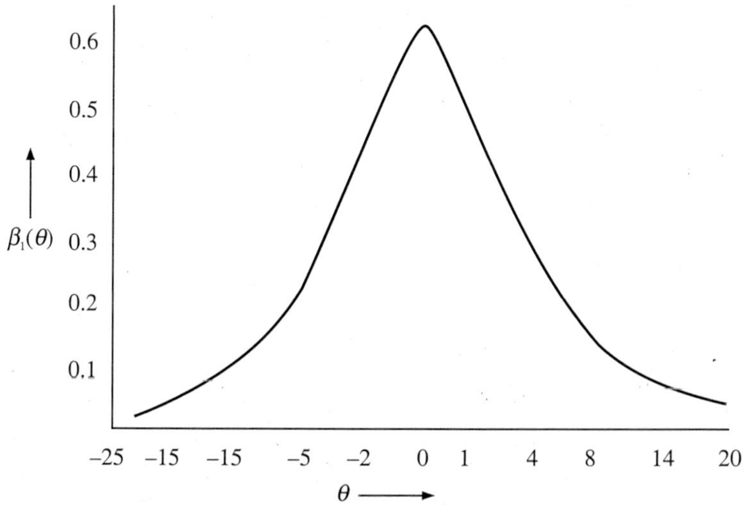


**Figure 2.16:** Plot of the power function.

# *Review Questions*

**2.1** Explain the general decision problem and what is a statistical decision problem? Also show that the problems of estimation and testing of hypothesis are its special cases.

**2.2** Write a brief note on theory of testing of statistical hypotheses with a special emphasis on randomized and non-randomized tests.

**2.3** Show that under certain conditions randomized decision rules and behavioural decision rules are equivalent.

**2.4** Explain the terms power function, best critical region and level of significance. Give an account of the Neyman-Pearson theory of testing a statistical hypothesis, and show how you would obtain a most powerful test for testing a simple null hypothesis against a simple alternative.

**2.5** How is a most powerful randomized test of size-$\alpha$ obtained by Neyman-Pearson lemma? Explaining how to determine the test constants to obtain a test of prescribed size-$\alpha$.

**2.6** Show that the test given by Neyman-Pearson is unique (except on null set).

**2.7** State and prove Neyman-Pearson Lemma in generalized form and bring out its usefulness.

**2.8** If $\phi$ is a best test of size-$\alpha$ and $\phi$ is not admissible, then prove that the probability of type II error is zero .

**2.9** Let $X_1, \ldots, X_n$ be iid Bernoulli b(1, p) random variables. Obtain most powerful size-$\alpha$ test of $H_0 : p = p_0$ against $H_1 : p = p_1 (> p_0)$.

**2.10** Show that the relation between $\alpha$ and $\beta$ for the family of Neyman-Pearson tests is monotone non-decreasing, i.e. larger the $\alpha$, smaller is the $\beta$.

**2.11** Let $X$ have probability distributions $P_0$ and $P_1$ under the null and alternative hypotheses respectively and

$$\mathcal{N} = \{(E_{P_0}\phi(X), E_{P_1}\phi(X)) : 0 \leq \phi(X) \leq 1\}$$

Prove that $\mathcal{N}$ is convex, contains the points (0, 0)and (1, 1) and symmetric about (1/2, 1/2). Find $\mathcal{N}$ when $P_0$ is $U(0,1)$ and $P_1$ is $U(1,2)$. What are the best and the worst points in $\mathcal{N}$ according to you ? Give the tests corresponding to these two points.

**2.12** Find the best test for $H_0 : \mu = 0$ against $H_1 : \mu = 1$ in $N(\mu, 1)$.

**2.13** Use Neyman and Pearson Lemma to test $H_0 : \mu = 2$ against $H_1 : \mu = 4$ on the basis of a random sample $X_1, \ldots, X_n$ of size 10 from $N(\mu, 4)$.

**2.14** If $X_1, X_2, \ldots, X_{16}$ are independent random variables, construct the most powerful test of the hypothesis $H$ that the common distribution of $X$'s is $N(0, 9)$ against the alternative A that it is $N(1, 9)$ at level of significance $\alpha = 0.05$. Also find power of the test.

**2.15** Let the null hypothesis be that $X$ has $N(0,4)$ and the alternative hypothesis be that $X$ has $N(1,4)$. Determine the slope of the curve (in $N$) representing rejection region of the form $\bar{X} > k$ in terms of $k$ and the standard Normal probability density. Hence, find the test which minimizes the sum of the probabilities of the two types of error.

**2.16** A random sample is drawn from a normal universe with zero mean and variance $\sigma^2$. Show how you would test the hypothesis $\sigma = \sigma_0$ against $\sigma = \sigma_1$.

**2.17** State Neyman-Pearson Lemma and apply it to obtain the test for testing $\sigma^2 = 1$ against $\sigma^2 > 1$, when the sample is from $N(0, \sigma^2)$. Is this test UMP? Is it unbiased? Give reasons.

**2.18** Let $X_1, X_2, \ldots, X_{10}$ to be a random sample of size 10 from a normal distribution $N(x, 0, \sigma^2)$.

(a) Find a best critical region of size 0.05 for testing the null hypothesis $H_0 : \sigma^2 = 1$ against the alternative hypothesis $H_1 : \sigma^2 = 2$
(b) Determine whether the critical region found in (a) would be best for testing the same $H_0$ but against $H_1' : \sigma^2 = 4$.
(c) Hence, State whether the critical region found in (a) would be best for testing the same $H_0$ against every alternative hypothesis $\sigma^2 = \sigma_0^2$ where, $\sigma_0^2 > 1$.

**2.19** Let $X_1, \ldots, X_n$ be i.i.d. from $N(\theta, 1)$. The best test of size-$\alpha$ for testing $H_0 : \theta = 0$ against $H_1 : \theta = 1$ shall be given by $\bar{x} > c$ where, $c$ is obtained by $P_{H_0}[\bar{X} > c] = \alpha$. $\bar{X}|H_0 \sim N(0, 1/n)$ for $n = 25$, $\alpha = 5\%$, show that the best test is given by $\bar{x} > 0.329$ with power 0.999 (very high).

**2.20** It is required to test $H_0$ against $H_1$ from a single $X$, where $H_0$ is the hypothesis that the pdf is

$$f(x) = \frac{1}{\sqrt{2\pi}} \, e^{-1/2x^2} \qquad (-\infty < x < \infty)$$

and $H_1$ is the hypothesis that the pdf is

$$f(x) = \frac{2}{\Gamma(\frac{1}{4})} \, e^{-x^4} \qquad (-\infty < x < \infty)$$

Obtain the most powerful test with level of significance $\alpha$ in this case.

**2.21** Let $p$ be the probability of coming up of head in tossing a coin. To test the hypothesis $H_0 : p = \frac{1}{2}$ against $H_1 : p = \frac{3}{4}$, the coin is tossed 5 times and let $H_0$ be rejected if more than 3 heads are obtained. Calculate probabilities of type I and II errors. [$\alpha = 3/16, \beta = 47/128$]

**2.22** Test the hypothesis $H_0 : \theta = 2$ against $H_1 : \theta = 1$ on the basis of a single observation from $f(x/\theta) = \theta e^{-\theta x}$, $0 \le x < \infty$. Let the critical region be given by $w = \{x | x \ge 1\}$. Obtain probabilities of type I and II errors. [$\alpha = e^{-2}$ and $\beta = (e-1)/e$]

**2.23** To test the simple hypothesis that the frequency function of the observed variable is $f_1(x) = 1,\ 0 \le x \le 1$ against the alternative that it is $f_2(x) = 2x,\ 0 \le x \le 1$ on the basis of two independent observation $x_1$ and $x_2$, it is decided to reject the hypothesis if (i) $x_1 + x_2 > 7/4$, (ii) $x_1 x_2 > 8/5$. Calculate the level of significance and power.

[*Hint:* $\alpha = P_{f_1}(X_1 + X_2 > 7/4) = 1 - P_{f_1}(X_1 + X_2 \le 7/4)$

$$= 1 - \int_{x_2=0}^{1} \int_{x_1=0}^{1-x_2} 1 \cdot dx_1 \cdot dx_2 = 0.5$$

$$\beta = 1 - P_{f_2}(X_1 + X_2 \le 7/4)$$

$$= 1 - \int_{x_2=0}^{1} \int_{x_1=0}^{1-x_2} 4\, x_2 x_1\, dx_1\, dx_2 = 0.83]$$

**2.24** Let $(x_1, x_2)$ be the two independent observations from a density

$$f(x|\theta) = \frac{1}{\theta}\, e^{-x/\theta},\quad 0 < x < \infty,\ \theta > 0$$

For testing $H_0 : \theta = 2$, against the alternative $H_1 : \theta = 4$, the $H_0$ is accepted when $x_1 + x_2 < 9.448$. Determine most powerful test.

$$[P(\chi_4^2 \ge 9.448) = 0.05,\ P(\chi_4^2 \ge 0.711) = 0.95]$$

**2.25** Obtain the best critical region of size $\alpha$ to the test $H_0 : \sigma = \sigma_0$ against $H_1 : \sigma = \sigma_1$ when $f(x \mid \sigma) = \sigma e^{-\sigma x},\ x > 0$. State the lemma you use.

**2.26** Obtain the most powerful test for testing $H_0 : \theta = \theta_0$ against $H_1 : \theta = \theta_1$, where $\theta$ is the parameter of the distribution with pdf:

$$f(x \mid \theta) = \theta\, x^{\theta - 1} \quad 0 \le x \le 1,\ \ \theta > 0$$

**2.27** A discrete variate $X$ has the following distribution under the null hypothesis $H_0$ and the alternative hypothesis $H_1$:

| $i$ | 1 | 2 | 3 | 4 | 5 |
|---|---|---|---|---|---|
| $P(X = i \mid H_0)$ | 0.1 | 0.2 | 0.3 | 0.3 | 0.1 |
| $P(X = i \mid H_1)$ | 0.2 | 0.1 | 0.4 | 0.1 | 0.2 |

For $\alpha = 0.5$ find the most powerful test for $H_0$ against $H_1$. Discuss the result in the light of the Neyman-Pearson lemma.

**2.28** Consider the problem of testing $H_0 : \theta = \theta_0$ against $H_1 : \theta = \theta_1$.

(a) Write down the forms of best test of size $\alpha$ $0 \le \alpha \le 1$.

(b) If, $f(x|\theta) = \frac{1}{\pi} \cdot \dfrac{1}{1 + (x - \theta)^2}$, then

$$\phi(x) = \begin{cases} 1 & \text{if } 1 < x < 3 \\ 0 & \text{otherwise} \end{cases}$$

is a best test of its size for testing $H_0 : \theta = 0$ against $H_1 : \theta = 1$. Prove.

**2.29** Prove that Bayes test is a version of Neyman-Pearson test.

**2.30** If $\phi$ were a test for $H_0$ against $H_1$, then show that $1 - \phi$ would be one for $H_1$ against $H_0$.

# Chapter 3

# One-sided Uniformly Most Powerful Tests

## 3.1 INTRODUCTION

In this chapter we shall consider the family of distributions $\{f_\theta,\ \theta \in \Theta\}$, where $\theta$ is a single real valued parameter, $\Theta \subseteq \mathbb{R}^1$, and the testing problems of the type

$$H_0 : \theta \leq \theta_0 \text{ against } H_1 : \theta > \theta_0, \text{ for some } \theta_0 \in \Theta$$

Such testing problems are known as one-sided testing problems. In general, UMP tests do not exist for one-sided testing problems. As a solution towards this, we consider a family of distributions of special type, for which UMP tests do exist for these one sided testing problems.

**Definition 3.1.1. (Composite Hypothesis)** A hypothesis is said to be *composite* if the parameter space when the hypothesis is true contains more than one point. Note that $\Theta_0 = \{\theta : \theta \leq \theta_0\}$ and $\Theta_1 = \{\theta : \theta > \theta_0\}$ are both composite.

**Definition 3.1.2. (Size of a Test)** A test $\phi$ for testing $H_0 : \theta \in \Theta_0$ against $H_1 : \theta \in \Theta_1$, is said to be of size-$\alpha$ if

$$\sup_{\theta \in \Theta_0} E_\theta \phi(X) = \alpha \tag{3.1}$$

**Definition 3.1.3. (Class of Level $\alpha$ Tests)** A class of tests

$$\mathcal{C}_\alpha = \{\phi \in \mathcal{D} | \sup_{\theta \in \Theta_0} E_\theta \phi(X) \leq \alpha\} \tag{3.2}$$

is known as class of level $\alpha$ tests.

**Definition 3.1.4. (Uniformly Most Powerful Tests)** A test $\phi_0$ in $\mathcal{C}_\alpha$ for testing $H_0 : \theta \in \Theta_0$ against $H_1 : \theta \in \Theta_1$ is said to be uniformly most powerful (UMP) test of size-$\alpha$ if it is of size-$\alpha$ and it has no small power than of any other test in $\mathcal{C}_\alpha$ for every $\theta \in \Theta_1$, i.e

$$\text{(a)} \quad \sup_{\theta \in \Theta_0} E_\theta \phi_0(X) = \alpha \quad \text{and}$$

$$\text{(b)} \quad E_\theta \phi_0(X) \geq E_\theta \phi(X) \;\; \forall \;\; \theta \in \Theta_1 \text{ and } \forall \; \phi \; \in \mathcal{C}_\alpha$$

Here, the word the word 'uniformly' stands for 'every $\theta \in \Theta_1$"' for which the test $\phi_0$ has no smaller power as compared to the power of any other test $\phi$ in $\mathcal{C}_\alpha$. The requirement for the existence of a UMP test in $\mathcal{C}_\alpha$ limits us to consider a particular type of family of distributions. We shall, therefore, focus attention to such family of distributions for which a UMP test of size-$\alpha$ exists for a one-sided testing problem.

**Definition 3.1.5. (Family with Monotone Likelihood Ratio)** (Ferguson 1967)[54] A real parameter family of distributions is said to have monotone likelihood ratio in $T(x)$ if the density $f(x|\theta)$ exists such that whenever $\theta_1 < \theta_2$, the likelihood ratio

$$\frac{f(x|\theta_2)}{f(x|\theta_1)}$$

is a non-decreasing function of $T(x)$ in the set of its existence. The set of existence means either or both $f(x|\theta_1)$ and $f(x|\theta_2)$ are positive and further if $f(x|\theta_2) > 0$ and $f(x|\theta_1) = 0$ then the likelihood ratio takes value $+\infty$.

## 3.2 UNIFORMLY MOST POWERFUL TESTS

We shall now discuss a theorem due to Karlin and Rubin (1956)[102] that provides a UMP size-$\alpha$ test for one-sided testing problem $H_0 : \theta \leq \theta_0$ against $H_1 : \theta > \theta_0$ whenever $F_\theta(X \sim F_\theta)$, $\theta \in \Theta$ has monotone likelihood ratio. We shall see that the theorem holds for Regular and Pitman families provided the distributions in them have monotone likelihood ratio in some statistic $T(x)$.

**Theorem 3.2.1.** *(Karlin and Rubin Theorem) Let the family of distributions of* $\boldsymbol{X}$, $\{f_\theta,\ \theta \in \Theta\}$, *have the monotone likelihood ratio in* $T(\mathbf{x})$. *Consider the one-sided testing problem,* $H_0 : \theta \leq \theta_0$ *against* $H_1 : \theta > \theta_0,\quad \theta_0 \in \Theta$. *Any test of the form*

$$\phi(\mathbf{x}) = \begin{cases} 1 & \text{if } T(\mathbf{x}) > t_0 \\ \gamma & \text{if } T(\mathbf{x}) = t_0 \\ 0 & \text{if } T(\mathbf{x}) < t_0 \end{cases} \tag{3.3}$$

*has non-decreasing power function and is UMP of its size provided its size is positive.*

*Further, for every* $\alpha$, $0 \leq \alpha \leq 1$ *and every* $\theta_0 \in \Theta$, *there exist numbers* $-\infty \leq t_0 \leq +\infty$ *and* $0 \leq \gamma_0 \leq 1$ *such that the test in Eq. 3.3 is UMP size-*$\alpha$ *test of* $H_0$ *against* $H_1$.

*Proof.* Let us consider two points $\theta_1,\ \theta_2 \in \Theta$ such that $\theta_1 < \theta_2$. Further, consider the testing problem $H_0 : \theta = \theta_1$ against $H_1 : \theta = \theta_2$. By using NP lemma, one gets the best test of its size

$$\phi(\mathbf{x}) = \begin{cases} 1 & \text{if } \dfrac{f_{\theta_2}(\mathbf{x})}{f_{\theta_1}(\mathbf{x})} > k \\ \gamma(\mathbf{x}) & \text{if } \dfrac{f_{\theta_2}(\mathbf{x})}{f_{\theta_1}(\mathbf{x})} = k \\ 0 & \text{if } \dfrac{f_{\theta_2}(\mathbf{x})}{f_{\theta_1}(\mathbf{x})} < k \end{cases} \tag{3.4}$$

with $0 \leq k < \infty$ and size $E_{\theta_1}\phi(\mathbf{X}) = \alpha > 0$.
And for $k = \infty$, the test

$$\phi(\mathbf{x}) = \begin{cases} 1 & \text{if } f_{\theta_1}(\mathbf{x}) = 0 \\ 0 & \text{if } f_{\theta_1}(\mathbf{x}) > 0 \end{cases} \tag{3.5}$$

is best of size 0.

The critical region of the best test of size $> 0$ has been given by

$$\frac{f_{\theta_2}(\mathbf{x})}{f_{\theta_1}(\mathbf{x})} > k$$

But the family of distributions $\{f_\theta\}$ has monotone likelihood ratio in $T(\mathbf{x})$, i.e. $f_{\theta_2}(\mathbf{x})/f_{\theta_1}(\mathbf{x})$ is a non-decreasing function in $T(\mathbf{x})$, therefore, the best critical region is given by

$$T(\mathbf{x}) > k$$

and the best test given by Eq. (3.5) takes the form as

$$\phi(\mathbf{x}) = \begin{cases} 1 & \text{if } T(\mathbf{x}) > t_0 \\ \gamma(\mathbf{x}) & \text{if } T(\mathbf{x}) = t_0 \\ 0 & \text{if } T(\mathbf{x}) < t_0 \end{cases} \tag{3.6}$$

same as Eq. (3.3) given in the Theorem 3.1.1, provided $\alpha > 0$. We must note that the best test given in Eq. (3.5) cannot be shown to be of the form given by Eq. (3.3) for $\alpha = 0 (k = \infty)$. Therefore, the test $\phi$ in Eq. (3.3) is a best test of size-$\alpha > 0$ for testing $H_0 : \theta = \theta_1$ against $H_1 : \theta = \theta_2$. We shall now show that it has a non-decreasing power function. For this, consider a test $\phi^* \equiv \alpha$, which is a size-$\alpha$ test, and has no larger power at $\theta_2$ as compared to $\phi$ since $\phi$ is given to be best in the Theorem 3.2.1, i.e.

$$E_{\theta_2}\phi(\mathbf{X}) \geq E_{\theta_2}\phi^*(\mathbf{X}) = \alpha = E_{\theta_1}\phi(\mathbf{X}) \tag{3.7}$$

This shows that the power function of the test $\phi$, i.e. $E_\theta\phi(\mathbf{X})$ is non-decreasing function of $\theta$, $\theta_2 > \theta_1$, provided its size $E_{\theta_1}\phi(X) > 0$.

Let us now consider $\theta_1 = \theta_0$ and $\theta_2 > \theta_0$, the testing problem can now be written as

$$H_0 : \theta = \theta_0 \quad \text{against} \quad H_1 : \theta > \theta_0 \tag{3.8}$$

The corresponding class of level $\alpha$ tests becomes

$$\{\phi \in \mathcal{D} \ : \ E_{\theta_0}\phi(\mathbf{X}) \leq \alpha\} \tag{3.9}$$

in which we shall find out a UMP test for the testing problem given by Eq. (3.8). The test $\phi$ in Eq. (3.3) remains best i.e. UMP of size-$\alpha$ in the class Eq. (3.9) since it given by does not depend on what alternative $\theta_2$ has been chosen from $\theta > \theta_0$.

Now, consider the testing problem

$$H_0 : \theta \leq \theta_0 \quad \text{against} H_1 : \theta > \theta_0$$

The reference class of level $\alpha$ tests for this testing problem would be

$$\{\phi \in \mathcal{D} \ : \ \sup_{\theta \leq \theta_0} E_\theta\phi(\mathbf{X}) \leq \alpha\} = \{\phi \in \mathcal{D} \ : \ E_\theta\phi(\mathbf{X}) \leq \alpha \ \forall \ \theta \leq \theta_0\} \tag{3.10}$$

We shall note that the test $\phi$ in Eq. (3.3) belongs to the class given by Eq. (3.10) since its power function is non-decreasing function of $\theta$ and its size-$\alpha > 0$. Further, the class of tests in Eq. (3.10) is contained in Eq. (3.9) because the number of restrictions in Eq. (3.10) is more than of in Eq. (3.9). Therefore, the UMP size-$\alpha$ test $\phi$ in the larger class becomes UMP size-$\alpha$ test in the smaller class since it belongs to the smaller class. Thus, provided $\alpha > 0$, the test in Eq. (3.3) is UMP size-$\alpha$ test for testing one-sided testing problem

$$H_0 : \theta \leq \theta_0 \quad \text{against} \quad H_1 : \theta > \theta_0$$

The proof of the second part of the Theorem 3.2.1 can be obtained on the similar lines as were in the NP lemma. If $\alpha$ is fixed between $[0, 1]$ and $\theta_0 \in \Theta_0$, the size of the test $\phi$ in the Theorem 3.2.1, is given as

$$\sup_{\theta \leq \theta_0} E_\theta\phi(X) = \alpha \quad \text{which implies} \quad E_{\theta_0}\phi(X) = \alpha$$

(since the power of such a test has been shown to be non-decreasing), and

$$E_{\theta_0}\phi(X) = \alpha$$

gives

$$P_{\theta_0}[T > t_0] + \gamma P_{\theta_0}[T = t_0] = \alpha$$

or

$$P_{\theta_0}[T \leq t_0] - \gamma P_{\theta_0}[T = t_0] = 1 - \alpha$$

If one finds a $t_0$ for which $P_{\theta_0}[T \leq t_0] = 1 - \alpha$ then $\gamma$ is set at 0; and if not, there exists a $t_0$ such that

$$P_{\theta_0}[T < t_0] \leq (1 - \alpha) < P_{\theta_0}[T \leq t_0]$$

then we take $t = t_0$ as above and choose $\gamma_0$ by

$$\gamma_0 = \frac{P_{\theta_0}[T \le t_0] - (1-\alpha)}{P_{\theta_0}[T = t_0]}, \quad 0 < \gamma_0 \le 1 \tag{3.11}$$

Let us consider $\alpha = 0$. It is important to note and is not difficult to see that family of distributions $\{f_\theta, \theta \in \Theta\}$ has monotone likelihood ratio if the minimum of the support of $f_\theta$ under $H_0$ is smaller than the minimum of the support of $f_\theta$ under $H_1$. In other words, if we define the support of $f_\theta$ under the null and alternative hypotheses as

$$S_0 = \{x : f(x|\theta_0) > 0\} = \{x|a < x < b\}$$

and

$$S_1 = \{x : f(x|\theta_1) > 0\} = \{x|c < x < d\}$$

then, $a < c$. Without loss, in generality, we may assume that $b \le d$. Let us consider a test $\phi$ of the form as given in Theorem 3.2.1

$$\phi(x) = \begin{cases} 1 & \text{if } T(x) > T(b) \\ 0 & \text{otherwise} \end{cases} \tag{3.12}$$

such that

$$\sup_{\theta \le \theta_0} E_\theta \phi(X) = 0$$

or

$$E_\theta \phi(X) = 0 \ \forall \ \theta \le \theta_0 \ \text{ or, } \ E_{\theta_0}\phi(X) = 0$$

Therefore, the given test satisfies the condition of size 0. Let us consider any other test $\phi'$ of size 0, i.e. $E_{\theta_0}\phi'(X) = 0$ or $\int_{S_0} \phi'(x) f(x|\theta_0)dx = 0$, this gives $\phi'(x) \equiv 0$ on $S_0$. Now, consider the power of the test $\phi$ at any $\theta > \theta_0$

$$E_\theta\phi(X) = \int_{x \ge b} f(x|\,\theta)dx \ge \int_{x \ge b(S_0^c)} \phi'(x) f(x|\,\theta)\,dx$$

$$\text{(since } 0 \le \phi' \le 1\text{)}$$

$$= \int_{S_0} \phi'(x) f(x|\theta)\,dx + \int_{S_0^c} \phi'(x) f(x|\theta)\,dx$$

$$\text{(since } \phi'(x) = 0 \text{ on } S_0\text{)}$$

$$= \int \phi'(x) f(x|\theta)\,dx = E_\theta \phi'(X)$$

which shows that $\phi(x)$ is UMP size 0 test of the form as given in Theorem 3.2.1 with $t_0 = T(b)$ and $\gamma_0 = 0$. □

### 3.2.1 Loss Function for One-sided Testing

In a one-sided testing problem $H_0 : \theta \leq \theta_0$ against $H_1 : \theta \geq \theta_0$, the loss function is construted so that it satisfies

$$L(\theta, a_1) - L(\theta, a_0) \geq 0 \text{ if } \theta < \theta_0$$

and

$$L(\theta, a_1) - L(\theta, a_0) \leq 0 \text{ if } \theta > \theta_0 \tag{3.13}$$

In other words, the loss function should be so defined that it must suggest for accepting $H_0$ whenever $\theta < \theta_0$ and rejecting $H_0$ whenever $\theta > \theta_0$. The class of one-sided tests form an essentially complete class if the loss function satisfies the inequality Eq. (3.13). This result limits the statistician to search for an UMP size-$\alpha$ test for a one-sided testing problem to the class of all one-sided tests Eq. (3.3) since for any test outside this class there exists one test in this class that is as good as the considered test.

### 3.2.2 Forms of UMP Test for One-sided Problems

If the family of distribution $\{f_\theta, \theta \in \Theta\}$ has monotone likelihood ratio in some statistic $T(x)$ so that for $\theta_1 < \theta_2$

I. $A(x) = \dfrac{f(x|\theta_2)}{f(x|\theta_1)}$ is non-decreasing in $T$, UMP size-$\alpha$ test for

(a) $H_0 : \theta \leq \theta_0$ against $H_1 : \theta > \theta_0$ is given by

$$\phi(x) = \begin{cases} 1 & \text{if } T(x) > t_0 \\ \gamma & \text{if } T(x) = t_0 \\ 0 & \text{if } T(x) < t_0 \end{cases}$$

so that $E_{\theta_0}\phi(X) = \alpha$.

(b) $H_0 : \theta \geq \theta_0$ against $H_1 : \theta < \theta_0$ is given by

$$\phi(x) = \begin{cases} 1 & \text{if } T(x) < t_0 \\ \gamma & \text{if } T(x) = t_0 \\ 0 & \text{if } T(x) > t_0 \end{cases}$$

so that $E_{\theta_0}\phi(X) = \alpha$.

II. $A(x)$ is non-decreasing in $T$, UMP size-$\alpha$ test for

(a) $H_0 : \theta \leq \theta_0$ against $H_1 : \theta > \theta_0$ is given by

$$\phi(x) = \begin{cases} 1 & \text{if } T(x) < t_0 \\ \gamma & \text{if } T(x) = t_0 \\ 0 & \text{if } T(x) > t_0 \end{cases}$$

so that $E_{\theta_0}\phi(X) = \alpha$.

(b) $H_0 : \theta \geq \theta_0$ against $H_1 : \theta < \theta_0$ is given by

$$\phi(x) = \begin{cases} 1 & \text{if } T(x) > t_0 \\ \gamma & \text{if } T(x) = t_0 \\ 0 & \text{if } T(x) < t_0 \end{cases}$$

so that $E_{\theta_0}\phi(X) = \alpha$.

### 3.2.3 Testing with p-values

Let the family of distributions $\{f_\theta,\ \theta \in \Theta\}$ have the monotone likelihood ratio in $T$ and the testing problem be $H_0 : \theta \leq \theta_0$ against $H_1 : \theta > \theta_0$. It is not always of interest to test the hypothesis $H_0$, but to know how strongly the null hypothesis $H_0$ is being rejected, in this case, one calculates (in case $T$ is continuous)

$$p\text{-value}(\hat{\alpha})(\text{of UMP test}) = P_{\theta_0}\{T \geq t\}$$

where, $t$ being the observed value of $T$. If $\widehat{\alpha} < \alpha$, $H_0$ is rejected and accepted otherwise. Smaller values of $\hat{\alpha}$ suggest higher strength by which $H_0$ has been rejected. However, if the distribution of $T$ is not continuous, then instead of using a randomized test, one may calculate $\hat{\alpha}$ which, in this case, is known as smallest level of significance at which $H_0$ is rejected.

## 3.3 SOLVED EXAMPLES

**Example 3.3.1.** *Let $X_1, \ldots, X_n$ be a random sample from $f(x|\theta) = \theta\, x^{\theta-1}$, $0 < x < 1$, $\theta > 0$. Find a UMP size-$\alpha$ test of $H_0 : \theta \leq \theta_0$ against $H_1 : \theta > \theta_0$.*

***Solution:*** For $\theta_1 < \theta_2$ consider

$$A(\mathbf{x}) = \frac{f(\mathbf{x}|\theta_2)}{f(\mathbf{x}|\theta_1)} = \frac{\theta_2^n(\prod x_i)^{\theta_2-1}}{\theta_1^n(\prod x_i)^{\theta_1-1}}$$
$$= \left(\frac{\theta_2}{\theta_1}\right)^n \left(\prod x_i\right)^{\theta_2-\theta_1}$$

$A(\mathbf{x})$ is an increasing function of $T(\mathbf{x}) = \prod x_i$. This shows $f(x|\theta)$ has monotone likelihood ratio. Therefore, Karlin and Rubin theorem gives the UMP size-$\alpha$ test for $H_0 : \theta \leq \theta_0$ against $H_0 : \theta > \theta_0$

$$\phi(\mathbf{x}) = \begin{cases} 1 & \text{if } \prod x_i > c \\ 0 & \text{otherwise} \end{cases} \tag{3.14}$$

The critical region $\prod x_i > c$ may be written as $\log \prod x_i > c_1$, or $\sum \log x_i > c_1$ or $U = -\sum_1^n \log x_i < c_2$. The constant $c_2$ is determined by

$$E_{\theta_0}[U < c_2] = \alpha$$

$c_2$ could be obtained by calculating the distribution of $U$ under $H_0$. For this, consider

$$f(x|\theta) = \theta x^{\theta-1}$$

and, the transformation $x = e^{-y}$ or $y = -\log x$. The distribution of $y$ is given by

$$g(y|\theta) = \theta e^{-y(\theta-1)} \cdot |J| = \theta e^{-y(\theta-1)} e^{-y} = \theta e^{-y\theta}$$

$Y \sim G(1, \theta)$, therefore, $U = \sum Y_i = -\sum \log X_i \sim G(n, \theta)$. This gives $c_2$ as upper $(1-\alpha)^{\text{th}}$ quantile of $G(n, \theta)$.

**Example 3.3.2.** *One parameter exponential family has monotone likelihood ratio.*

***Solution:*** The density function of exponential family is given by

$$f(x|\theta) = D(\theta) \cdot S(x) \cdot \exp\{Q(\theta)T(x)\}, \quad \theta \in \Theta \subseteq \mathbb{R}^1$$

If $X_1, \ldots, X_n$ is a sample of size $n$ from this exponential family, then

$$f(x_1, \ldots, x_n|\theta) = [D(\theta)]^n \prod_{j=1}^{n} S(x_j) \cdot \exp\big(Q(\theta) \sum_{j=1}^{n} T(x_j)\big)$$

Consider the likelihood ratio for $\theta_1 < \theta_2$

$$\frac{f(x|\theta_2)}{f(x|\theta_1)} = \left[\frac{D(\theta_2)}{D(\theta_1)}\right]^n \exp\Big[(Q(\theta_2) - Q(\theta_1)) \sum_{j=1}^{n} T(x_j)\Big]$$

which is non-decreasing in $\sum_{j=1}^{n} T(x_j)$ if $Q(\cdot)$ is non-decreasing. Therefore, we see that one parameter exponential family has monotone likelihood ratio in $\sum_{j=1}^{n} T(x_j)$. This family includes Normal, Binomial, Negative Binomial, Poisson, Gamma and Beta distributions (with one parameter fixed). Consider some of these:

(a) *Normal:* Let a random sample of size $n$ has been drawn from $N(\mu, 1)$. For $\mu_1 < \mu_2$

$$\frac{f(\mathbf{x}|\,\mu_2)}{f(\mathbf{x}|\,\mu_1)} = \frac{\exp\{-1/2 \sum (x_i - \mu_2)^2\}}{\exp\{-1/2 \sum (x_i - \mu_1)^2\}}$$

$$= \exp\Big\{(\mu_2 - \mu_1) \sum x_i + \frac{n}{2}(\mu_1^2 - \mu_2^2)\Big\}$$

which is a non-decreasing function in $T(\mathbf{x}) = \sum_{j=1}^{n} x_j$.

Next, consider a sample of size $n$ from $N(0, \sigma^2)$. For $\sigma_1^2 < \sigma_2^2$, we have

$$\frac{f(\mathbf{x}|\sigma_2^2)}{f(\mathbf{x}|\sigma_1^2)} = \frac{(1/2\pi\sigma_2^2)^{n/2} \exp\{-\frac{1}{2\sigma_2^2} \sum x_i^2\}}{(1/2\pi\sigma_1^2)^{n/2} \exp\{-\frac{1}{2\sigma_1^2} \sum x_i^2\}}$$

$$= \left(\frac{\sigma_1}{\sigma_2}\right)^n \exp\Big\{\frac{1}{2}\Big(\frac{1}{\sigma_1^2} - \frac{1}{\sigma_2^2}\Big) \sum x_i^2\Big\}$$

which is non-decreasing in $T(\mathbf{x}) = \sum x_i^2$ since $(\frac{1}{\sigma_1^2} - \frac{1}{\sigma_2^2}) > 0$.
(b) *Bernoulli*: Let a random sample of size $n$ has been drawn from $b(1, p)$, where $p$ is unknown, $p \in [0, 1]$. Let $p_1 < p_2$, then

$$\frac{f(\mathbf{x}|p_2)}{f(\mathbf{x}|p_1)} = \frac{p_2^{\sum x_i}(1-p_2)^{n-\sum x_i}}{p_1^{\sum x_i}(1-p_1)^{n-\sum x_i}}$$
$$= \left(\frac{1-p_2}{1-p_1}\right)^n \left(\frac{p_2}{p_1} \cdot \frac{1-p_1}{1-p_2}\right)^{\sum x_i}$$

$p_2 > p_1$ and $(1-p_1) > (1-p_2)$, imply together $p_2(1-p_1) > p_1(1-p_2)$. Thus, the likelihood ratio $\frac{f(\mathbf{x}|p_2)}{f(\mathbf{x}|p_1)}$ is non-decreasing in $T(\mathbf{x}) = \sum x_i$.
(c)*Poisson*: A random sample of size $n$ has been drawn from $\mathcal{P}(\lambda)$ and $\lambda_1 < \lambda_2$. Consider

$$\frac{f(\mathbf{x}|\lambda_2)}{f(\mathbf{x}|\lambda_1)} = \frac{\lambda_2^{\sum x} \exp\{-n\lambda_2\}/\prod x_i!}{\lambda_1^{\sum x} \exp\{-n\lambda_1\}/\prod x_i!}$$
$$= \exp\{n(\lambda_1 - \lambda_2)\}\left(\frac{\lambda_2}{\lambda_1}\right)^{\sum x_i}$$

which is non-decreasing in $\sum x_i$ since $\frac{\lambda_2}{\lambda_1} > 1$. Therefore, poisson family has monotone likelihood ratio. Note for the one-sided testing problems, in all the above one parameter exponential families, the UMP size-$\alpha$ test due to Karlin and Rubin involve the distribution of sufficient statistic $T(\mathbf{x}) = \sum x_i$ or $\sum x_i^2$ the distribution of these too belong to exponential family.

**Example 3.3.3.** *Let a production be in the process of statistical control where some product is being manufactured and the probability of this product being defective is p. Let this process of manufacturing products be treated as independent trials with constant probability p of being defective. If we define*

$$X_i = \begin{cases} 1 & \textit{if the ith product is defective} \\ 0 & \textit{otherwise} \end{cases}$$

*where,* $X_i \sim b(1, p)$.

*The sufficient statistic* $X = \sum_{i=1}^n X_i$ *follows binomial distribution* $b(n, p)$. *Test the hypothesis*

$$H_0 : p \le p_0 \textit{ against } H_1 : p > p_0$$

***Solution:*** By Karlin Rubin theorem, UMP size-$\alpha$ test for this hypothesis is given by

$$\phi(x) = \begin{cases} 1 & \text{if } x > x_0 \\ \gamma & \text{if } x = x_0 \\ 0 & \text{if } x < x_0 \end{cases}$$

where, $x_0$ is obtained by

$$E_{p_0}\{\phi(X)\} = \alpha$$

or

$$P_{p_0}\{X \leq x_0\} - \gamma P_{p_0}\{X = x_0\} = 1 - \alpha$$

Given the values of $n$ and $p_0$, we obtain $x_0$ and $\gamma = \gamma_0$ from cumulative distribution function table of binomial distribution by choosing $x = x_0$ so that

$$P_{p_0}\{X < x_0\} < (1 - \alpha) \leq P_{p_0}\{X \leq x_0\}$$

If $P_{p_0}\{X \leq x_0\} = 1 - \alpha$, we choose $\gamma_0 = 0$ and if $P_{p_0}\{X \leq x_0\} > 1 - \alpha$, we choose

$$\gamma_0 = \frac{P_{p_0}\{X \leq x_0\} - (1 - \alpha)}{P_{p_0}\{X = x_0\}}$$

The test $\phi$, with these values of $x_0$ and $\gamma_0$, is a randomized UMP size-$\alpha$ test for the testing problems mentioned earlier.

**Example 3.3.4.** *Let $X \sim b(n, p)$. Find out the UMP size-$\alpha$ test for the following testing problem:*

$$H_0 : p \leq p_0 \text{ against } H_1 : p > p_0$$

*Also, find the sample size required by the UMP size-$\alpha$ test to achieve its power atleast 0.9.*

***Solution:*** The UMP size-$\alpha$ test for this testing problem is given by

$$\phi(x) = \begin{cases} 1 & \text{if } x > x_0 \\ \gamma & \text{if } x = x_0 \\ 0 & \text{if } x < x_0 \end{cases} \tag{3.15}$$

where, $x_0$ and $\gamma$ are obtained by

$$E_{p_0}\{\phi(X)\} = \alpha$$

or

$$P_{p_0}\{X \leq x_0\} - \gamma P_{p_0}\{X = x_0\} = 1 - \alpha$$

(a) *Determination of the above test at different $\alpha$* : Consider, $n = 6$, $p_0 = 0.25$. The test $\phi$ at $\alpha = 0.05$ is given as

$$x_0 = 3, \quad \gamma = \frac{0.9624 - 0.95}{0.9624 - 0.8306} = \frac{0.0124}{0.1318} = 0.094$$

The power of this test at $p = p_1$ would be given as

$$\beta_\phi(p_1) = 1 - P_{p_1}[X \leq 3] + 0.094\, P_{p_1}[X = 3]$$

At $p_1 = 0.3$,

$$\beta_\phi(0.3) = 1 - 0.9294 + 0.094\,(0.9294 - 0.7442)$$
$$= 0.0706 + 0.0174088 = 0.088$$

Similarly, readers may find the test at $\alpha = 0.1, 0.2$ and its power at $p_1 = 0.3, 0.4, 0.5, 0.6, 0.7$.

(b) *Determination of sample size for a given power*: Let us consider, $p_0 = 0.2$ and $\alpha = 0.05$ and if we desire for such a test to determine the required sample size to attain the given power at alternative $p_1 = 0.4$.

A non-randomized test is obtained by

$$P_{0.2}\{X > x_0\} \leq \alpha = 0.05$$

or

$$P_{0.2}\{X \leq x_0\} \geq 0.95 \tag{3.16}$$

and the power of the test $\phi$ is atleast 0.9 at $p_1 = 0.4$ gives

$$P_{0.4}\{X > x_0\} \geq 0.9$$

or

$$P_{0.4}\{X \leq x_0\} \leq 1 - 0.9 = 0.1 \tag{3.17}$$

Indeed, one chooses such a sample size so that the conditions given by Eqs. (3.16) and (3.17) are simultaneously satisfied.

In case, we use the normal approximations, the conditions given by Eqs. (3.15) and (3.16) reduce to

$$P_{0.2}\left[\frac{X - 0.2n}{\sqrt{0.16n}} > \frac{x_0 - 0.2n}{\sqrt{0.16n}}\right] \leq 0.05 \tag{3.18}$$

and

$$P_{0.4}\left[\frac{X - 0.4n}{\sqrt{0.24n}} > \frac{x_0 - 0.4n}{\sqrt{0.24n}}\right] \geq 0.9 \tag{3.19}$$

On using the tail probability table of standard normal distribution, we get from Eqs. (3.18) and (3.19)

$$\frac{x_0 - 0.2n}{\sqrt{0.16n}} \geq 1.65$$

and

$$\frac{x_0 - 0.4n}{\sqrt{0.24n}} \leq -1.29$$

or

$$x_0 - 0.2n \geq 0.66\sqrt{n}$$

and

$$x_0 - 0.4n \leq -0.63197\sqrt{n}$$

The first gives

$$x_0 \geq 0.2n + 0.66\sqrt{n}$$

or

$$x_0 - 0.4n \geq -0.2n + 0.66\sqrt{n}$$

but from the second, we get

$$-0.63197\sqrt{n} \geq x_0 - 0.4n \geq -0.2n + 0.66\sqrt{n}$$

or

$$0.2n \geq 1.29197\sqrt{n}$$

or

$$n \geq 41.72 \cong 42$$

Therefore, the required sample size must be at least 42 for an UMP test at 5% level to attain its power atleast 0.9.

Readers may determine the required sample sizes by using normal approximations for $\alpha = 0.05,\ \beta = 0.9,\ p_0 = 0.01$ and $p_1 = 0.02$.

**Example 3.3.5.** (Lehmann, (1986)[130]) *Sometimes one may be interested in a study of the success behaviour of a newly introduced medical treatment. If a patient is cured by this, we call it a success and let its probability be given by p which is unknown. One may be interested in testing the hypothesis, $H_0 : p \leq p_0$ against $H_1 : p > p_0$.*

***Solution:*** Let the experiment be continued till we get $m$ patients cured. Let

$Y_i$ : number of trials required after the $(i-1)th$ patients are cured, but not including the trial on which $ith$ patient being cured.

In this case,

$$P(Y_i = y) = p\,q^y, \quad \text{where,} \quad y = 0, 1, \ldots$$

Therefore, the joint distribution of $Y_1, \ldots, Y_m$ shall be given by

$$p(y_1, \ldots, y_m;\ p) = p^m\ q^{\sum y_i}$$

where

$$y_i = 0, 1, \ldots \ \text{for} \ \ i = 1, 2, \ldots, m.$$

This distribution is a member of the exponential family with sufficient statistic $T(\mathbf{Y}) = \sum_{i=1}^{m} Y_i$. Therefore, UMP size-$\alpha$ test would now be given by

$$\phi(\mathbf{y}) = \begin{cases} 1 & \text{if } \ T(\mathbf{y}) < t_0 \\ \gamma & \text{if } \ T(\mathbf{y}) = t_0 \\ 0 & \text{if } \ T(\mathbf{y}) > t_0 \end{cases}$$

where, $t_0$ and $\gamma$ are obtained by

$$E_{p_0}[\phi(T)] = \alpha$$

Here, $T = \sum_{i=1}^{m} y_i$, the number of trials required in excess of $m$ to get $m$ successes follows negative binomial distribution,

$$p_T(t) = \binom{m+t-1}{m-1} p^m q^t; \qquad t = 0, 1, \ldots.$$

The form of the critical region is $T < t_0$ since $Q(p) = \log(1-p)$ is a decreasing function in the joint distribution of $Y_1, \ldots, Y_m$, which is a member of the exponential family. Small value of $T$ indicates only a few more trials required after $m$ and suggests that the probability of success is high. This leads to rejection of the null hypothesis.

**Example 3.3.6.** *Let $X_1, \ldots, X_n$ be $n$ number of bacterial counts on some given areas of slides or number of $\alpha$-particles produced by a radio active substance in equal time intervals. Let $\lambda$ be the bacterial density or density of $\alpha$-particles. In such cases $X_i$'s are called Poisson variates that follow a Poisson distribution $\mathcal{P}(\lambda)$. Then the joint distribution of random sample $X_1, \ldots, X_n$ be given by*

$$P_\lambda(\mathbf{x}) = \frac{\lambda^{\sum_1^n x_i}}{x_1! \ldots x_n!} e^{-n\lambda}$$

*which is a one parameter exponential family with $T(\mathbf{x}) = \sum x_i$ as sufficient statistic and $Q(\lambda) = \log \lambda$. Find out UMP size-$\alpha$ test for the following one-sided testing problem*

$$H_0 : \lambda \leq \lambda_0 \text{ against } H_1 : \lambda > \lambda_0$$

***Solution:*** Utilizing Karlin Rubin Theorem, the UMP size-$\alpha$ test is given by

$$\phi(T) = \begin{cases} 1 & \text{if } T > t_0 \\ \gamma & \text{if } T = t_0 \\ 0 & \text{if } T < t_0 \end{cases} \tag{3.20}$$

where, $t_0$ and $\gamma$ are obtained by

$$E_{\lambda_0}[\phi(T)] = \alpha$$

where, $T|H_0 \sim \mathcal{P}(\lambda_0)$.

**Example 3.3.7.** ([Lehmann, (1986)][130]) *Let us assume the number of bacterial counts on some given areas of a slide or number of $\alpha$-particles produced by some radio active material in a given time period $\tau$ follows Poisson process. Sometimes we may not be interested in counting the number of bacteria on some given areas of a slide but area over which bacteria are counted is enlarged until we get total count of bacteria as $m$. In the other case, we may* *continue the radio-active experiment till we get a total of* $m$ $\alpha$*-particles. This is known as inverse sampling method. Here, the observations consist of times* $T_1, \ldots, T_m$ *where* $T_1$ *is the time taken for the first occurrence,* $T_2$ *is the time from first to second occurrence and so on.* $T_1, \ldots, T_m$ *are independently distributed, each* $T_i$ *follows exponential distribution with density* $\lambda\, e^{-\lambda t}$ *for* $t \geq 0$. *The joint distribution of* $T_1, \ldots, T_m$ *shall be given by*

$$p(t_1, \ldots, t_m;\ \lambda) = \lambda^m\ e^{-\lambda \sum_1^m t_i}$$

*This density is an exponential density with sufficient statistic* $T(\mathbf{t}) = \sum_1^m t_i$ *with* $Q(\lambda) = -\lambda$. *Find out the UMP size-*$\alpha$ *test for the following testing problem*

$$H_0 : \lambda \leq \lambda_0 \text{ against } H_1 : \lambda > \lambda_0$$

***Solution:*** The UMP size-$\alpha$ test for this hypothesis would be given by

$$\phi(T) = \begin{cases} 1 & \text{if } T \leq t_0 \\ 0 & \text{otherwise} \end{cases}$$

so that $E_{\lambda_0}[\phi(T)] = \alpha$. We know that, each $T_i \sim G(1,\ 1/\lambda)$, therefore, $2\lambda T_i \sim G(1,\ 2)$ or $\chi^2(2)$ i.e. $\chi^2$ with 2 degrees of freedom. This implies that

$$2\lambda T = \sum_1^m 2\lambda\ T_i\ \sim\ \chi^2_{(2m)}$$

We may now write the size condition as

$$P_{\lambda_0}\{2\lambda T \leq 2\lambda t_0\} = \alpha$$

$$\int_0^{2\lambda_0 t_0} \chi^2_{(2m)}\ d\chi^2 = \alpha$$

and we get

$$2\lambda_0 t_0 = \chi^2_{2m,\alpha} \ \text{ or } \ t_0 = \chi^2_{2m,\alpha}/2\lambda_0$$

Therefore, the UMP test is given by

$$\phi(T) = \begin{cases} 1 & \text{if } T \leq \chi^2_{2m,\alpha}/2\lambda_0 \\ 0 & \text{otherwise} \end{cases}$$

**Example 3.3.8.** ([Lehmann, 1986][130]) *Let* $X$ *be the length of life of an electron tube. Generally, this follows exponential distribution with density*

$$f(x|\theta) = \frac{1}{2\theta}\ e^{-x/2\theta} \qquad \textit{for } x \geq 0$$

*Let* $n$ *such tubes be put on test simultaneously, i.e. we draw an independent sample* $X_1, \ldots, X_n$ *from the exponential population. Let* $X'$*s be ordered and denoted by*

$$Y_1 \leq Y_2 \leq \cdots \leq Y_n$$

*where, $Y_1$ be the life of a tube which gets fused first, $Y_2$ be the life of a tube which gets fused next to it and so on. We may decide to continue this experiment till we get $r^{th}$ tube fused. This process is known as inverse sampling. Same model arises in life testing applications where $n$ bulbs are put on testing and this number $n$ is held fixed by replacing each burned-out bulb with a new one and denoting $Y_1$ as the time at which first burn-out bulb is replaced, $Y_2$ as the time at which second bulb is replaced etc., each measured from some fixed time.*

*Find out a UMP size-$\alpha$ test for*

$$H_0 : \theta \geq \theta_0 = 1000 \textit{ against } H_1 : \theta < \theta_0 = 1000$$

*at level $\alpha = 0.05$ on the basis of $Y_1, \ldots, Y_r$.*

***Solution:*** The joint distribution of $Y_1, \ldots, Y_r$ is

$$f(\mathbf{y} \mid \theta) = \frac{1}{(2\theta)^r} \frac{n!}{(n-r)!} \exp\{-\frac{1}{2\theta}\sum_1^r y_i + (n-r)y_r\}$$
$$0 \leq y_1 \leq \ldots \leq y_r$$

which is exponential density with sufficient statistic $\sum_1^r y_i + (n-r)\, y_r$ and parameter $Q(\theta) = -1/2\theta$. Now, define

$$Z_i = \frac{(n-i+1)(Y_i - Y_{(i-1)})}{\theta}$$

On summing over $i$, we get

$$\sum_1^r Z_i = \frac{1}{\theta} \sum_1^r (n-i+1)(Y_i - Y_{i-1}) = \frac{1}{\theta}\{\sum_1^r Y_i + (n-r)Y_r)\}$$

In order to find out the distribution of the sufficient statistic $T(\mathbf{Y}) = \sum_1^r Y_i + (n-r)Y_r = \theta\sum_1^r Z_i = \theta Z$, we shall first find out the distribution of $Z_i$. We have

$$F_X(x) = P(X \leq x) = \frac{1}{2\theta}\int_0^x e^{-x/2\theta} dx = 1 - e^{-x/2\theta}$$

Therefore, the joint pdf of $Y_{i-1}, Y_i$ is given by

$$g_{i-1,i}(y_{i-1},\ y_i) = \frac{n!}{(i-2)!\,0!\,(n-i)!}[F(y_{i-1})]^{i-2}.$$
$$[F(y_i) - F(y_{i-1})]^{i-(i-1)-1} \cdot [1 - F(y_i)]^{n-i} f(y_{i-1}) f(y_i)$$
$$y_{i-1} < y_i$$

$$= \frac{n!}{(i-2)!(n-i)!}\left(1 - e^{-y_{i-1}/2\theta}\right)^{i-2}\left(e^{-y_i/2\theta}\right)^{n-i}.$$
$$\frac{1}{2\theta}\, e^{-y_{i-1}/2\theta} \cdot \frac{1}{2\theta}\, e^{-y_{i-1}/2\theta}$$

We now want to find out the distribution of $U = Y_i - Y_{i-1}$. This will be given by

$$f_U(u) = \int_{-\infty}^{\infty} f(y_{i-1}, u + y_{i-1})\, dy_{i-1}$$

$$= \frac{n!}{(i-2)!(n-i)!} \frac{1}{4\theta^2} \int_{-\infty}^{\infty} \left(1 - e^{-y_{i-1}/2\theta}\right)^{i-2}$$

$$\cdot \left(e^{-(u+y_{i-1})/2\theta}\right)^{n-i} . e^{y_{i-1}/2\theta} \cdot e^{-(u+y_{i-1})/2\theta} dy_{i-1}$$

Let us consider $1 - e^{-y_{i-1}/2\theta} = z,\quad \frac{1}{2\theta} e^{-y_{i-1}/2\theta} = dz$

We get

$$f_U(u) = \frac{n!}{(i-2)!\,(n-i)!} \cdot \frac{1}{4\theta^2} \cdot 2\theta \cdot e^{-(n-i)u/2\theta} \cdot e^{-u/2\theta}.$$

$$\int_{-\infty}^{\infty} z^{(i-1)-1}(1-z)^{(n-i+2)-1}\, dz$$

$$= \frac{n!}{(i-2)!\,(n-i)!} \cdot \frac{1}{2\theta} e^{-(n-i+1)u/2\theta} \cdot \beta(i-1, n-i+2)$$

$$= \frac{n!}{(i-2)!\,(n-1)!} \cdot \frac{(i-2)!\,(n-i+1)!}{n!} \frac{1}{2\theta} e^{-(n-i+1)u/2\theta}$$

$$= \frac{n-i+1}{2\theta} \cdot e^{-(n-i+1)u/2\theta}$$

Consider

$$Z_i = \frac{(n-i+1)u}{\theta}$$

where

$$|J| = \left|\frac{\partial u_i}{\partial z_i}\right| = \frac{\theta}{(n-i+1)}$$

$$f_{Z_i}(z_i) = \frac{1}{2} e^{-z/2} \sim G(2/2, 2) = \chi^2_{(2)}.$$

This shows that the distribution of

$$Z = \sum_1^r Z_i \sim \chi^2_{(2r)} = G(2r/2, 2).$$

But

$$T(Y_1, \ldots, Y_r) = \sum_1^r Y_i + (n-r)Y_r = \theta Z$$

Therefore, the distribution of $T$ would be given by

$$f_T(t|\theta) = \frac{1}{\Gamma(r)2^r} \exp\left\{-\frac{t}{2\theta}\right\} \left(\frac{t}{\theta}\right)^{r-1} |J|,$$

where

$$|J| = \left|\frac{\partial Z}{\partial T}\right| = \frac{1}{\theta}$$

which gives

$$f_T(t|\theta) = \frac{1}{\Gamma(r)\,(2\theta)^r}\exp\left\{-\frac{t}{2\theta}\right\}t^{r-1}$$

and $T \sim G(r,\ 2\theta)$. For $\theta_1 < \theta_2$,

$$A(x) = \frac{f(x|\theta_2)}{f(x|\theta_1)} = \left(\frac{\theta_1}{\theta_2}\right)^r \exp\left\{\frac{t}{2}\left(\frac{1}{\theta_1} - \frac{1}{\theta_2}\right)\right\}$$

is increasing in $t$ since $(\frac{1}{\theta_1} - \frac{1}{\theta_2}) > 0$. Therefore, by Karlin-Rubin theorem, the UMP size-$\alpha$ test based on the sufficient statistic $T(\mathbf{Y}) = \sum_1^r Y_i + (n-r)\,Y_r$ for testing $H_0 : \theta \geq \theta_0$ against $H_1 : \theta < \theta_0$ is given by

$$\phi(T) = \begin{cases} 1 & \text{if } T \leq t_0 \\ 0 & \text{otherwise} \end{cases}$$

where, $t_0$ is obtained by $E_{\theta_0}[\phi(T)] = 1 - \alpha$
or

$$\int_{t_0}^{\infty} \frac{1}{\Gamma(r)(2\theta_0)^r} e^{-t/2\theta_0} \cdot t^{r-1} dt = 1 - \alpha$$

Let us consider $y = t/\theta_0$, we get $dy = dt/\theta_0$

$$\int_{t_0/\theta_0}^{\infty} \frac{1}{\Gamma(r)(2\theta_0)^r} e^{-y/2}(\theta_0 y)^{r-1}\theta_0\, dy = 1 - \alpha$$

or

$$\int_{t_0/\theta_0}^{\infty} \frac{1}{\Gamma(r)2^r} e^{-y/2} \cdot y^{r-1}\, dy = 1 - \alpha$$

$$\int_{t_0/\theta_0}^{\infty} G(2r/2, 2)\, dy = 1 - \alpha$$

or

$$\int_{t_0/\theta_0}^{\infty} \chi^2(2r)\, dy = 1 - \alpha$$

For $\alpha = 0.05$ and $r = 4$, we obtain $t_0$ by the condition

$$\int_{t_0/\theta_0}^{\infty} \chi^2(8)\, dy = 0.95$$

From the table of $\chi^2$-distribution, we get

$$t_0/\theta_0 = 2.733$$

where

$$\theta_0 = 1000$$

or

$$t_0 = 2.733 \times 1000 = 2733$$

The critical region becomes $T \leq 2733$. The power of the test at $\theta_1 = 500$

$$\beta_\phi(500) = 1 - \int_{2733/500}^{\infty} \chi^2(8)\, dy = 1 - \int_{5.466}^{\infty} \chi^2(8)\, dy = 0.3$$

If we desire to obtain $r$ so that $\beta_\phi(500) \geq 0.95$, we have

$$\beta_\phi(500) = 1 - \int_{5.466}^{\infty} \chi^2(2r)\, dy \geq 0.95$$

Let us consider the approximation that $Y = \sqrt{2\chi^2} - \sqrt{2n-1}$ follows $N(0,1)$, where, $n$ is the degrees of freedom. Therefore,

$$P\{2\chi^2(2r) > 2 \times 5.466\} \leq 0.05$$

or

$$P\{\sqrt{2\chi^2(2r)} - \sqrt{2(2r)-1} \geq \sqrt{2 \times 5.466} - \sqrt{2(2r)-1}\} \leq 0.05$$

or

$$P\{N(0,1) \geq \sqrt{2 \times 5.466} - \sqrt{4r-1}\} \leq 0.05$$

From Normal table, we get

$$\sqrt{2 \times 5.466} - \sqrt{2r-1} = 1.65$$

or

$$r = 2$$

**Example 3.3.9.** $X \sim NB(r,\ p)$, $x = 0, 1, 2, \ldots$ *$r$ is the number of successes, $x$ is number of failure that preceed the $r^{\text{th}}$ success, independence of $x+r$ trials, gives*

$$f(x|r,p) = \binom{r+x-1}{x} p^r\, q^x, \quad x = 0, 1, 2 \ldots$$

*Show this family has monotone likelihood ratio.*

***Solution:*** Let $r$ be given and $p_1 < p_2$

$$\frac{p(x|p_2)}{p(x|p_1)} = \left(\frac{p_2}{p_1}\right)^r \left(\frac{q_2}{q_1}\right)^x$$

is non-increasing in $T(x) = x$ since $q_2 < q_1$. As

$$p(x|r,p) = \binom{r+x-1}{x} p^r \exp\{x \log q\}$$

with $D(p) = p^r$; $S(x) = \binom{r+x-1}{x}$, $Q(p) = \log q$, $T(x) = x$ where, $Q(p)$ is non-increasing in $p$, therefore, NB is one parameter exponential family.

Similarly, geometric distribution $NB(1,p)$, i.e.

$$p(x|p) = p\, q^x = p\, \exp\{x \log q\}, \quad x = 0, 1, 2, \ldots$$

has monotone likelihood ratio in $x$ with $Q(p) = \log p$.

**Example 3.3.10.** *Three independent observations $X_1, X_2, X_3$ on a random variable $X$ are available, where*

$$P(X=-1) = P(X=1) = \frac{1}{2}(1-\theta);\ P(X=2)=\theta,\ \ 0<\theta<1.$$

*To test $H_0 : \theta \leq 1/4$ against $H_1 : \theta > 1/4$, it is decided to use the procedure: Reject $H_0$ if and only if $X_1 + X_2 + X_3 > 4$. Compute the size of this test.*

***Solution:*** The test is given as

$$\phi(\sum X_i) = \begin{cases} 1 & \text{if } X_1+X_2+X_3 > 4 \\ 0 & \text{otherwise} \end{cases}$$

The size of this test shall be given by

$$\begin{aligned} E_{\theta_0=1/4}[\phi(\sum X_i)] &= P_{1/4}\{X_1+X_2+X_3>4\} \\ &= \binom{3}{1} P_{1/4}\{X_1=1, X_2=X_3=2\} + P_{1/4}\{X_1=2, X_2=2, X_3=2\} \\ &= 3\cdot\frac{1}{2}(1-\theta_0)\theta_0^2 + \theta_0^3 = \frac{3}{2}\theta_0^2 - \frac{3}{2}\theta_0^3 + \theta_0^3 = \frac{3}{2}\theta_0^2 - \frac{1}{2}\theta_0^3 \\ &= \frac{3}{2}\left(\frac{1}{4}\right)^2 - \frac{1}{2}\left(\frac{1}{4}\right)^3 = \frac{11}{128} = 0.085 \end{aligned}$$

**Example 3.3.11.** *Let $X_1, X_2, \ldots, X_9$ be a random sample from a normal distribution with unknown mean $\theta$ and known variance 16.*

(a) *For testing the null hypothesis $H_0 : \theta = 50$ against the alternative hypothesis $H_1 : \theta = 55$ one uses the critical region $W = \{(x_1, \ldots, x_n) : \sum_1^9 x_i > 473.49\}$. Determine the size and power of the test based on the above critical region.*

(b) *Verify whether the above normal distribution possesses the monotone likelihood ratio property.*

(c) *Construct the UMP critical region for testing $H_0 : \theta = 50$ against $H_1 : \theta > 50$ at level 0.01.*

*The following table contains the upper $\alpha$% points ($x_\alpha$) of the normal deviate for certain values of $\alpha$.*

$$\frac{1}{\sqrt{2\pi}}\int_{x_\alpha}^{\infty} e^{-y^2/2}dy = \alpha$$

| $\alpha$ | 0.05 | 0.0367 | 0.0359 | 0.025 | 0.01 | 0.005 |
|---|---|---|---|---|---|---|
| $x_\alpha$ | 1.645 | 1.79 | 1.80 | 1.96 | 2.326 | 2.576 |

***Solution:*** (a) We know $X_i \sim N(\theta, 16)$, $i = 1, \ldots, 9$. This gives $\bar{X} \sim N(\theta,\ 16/n) = N(\theta,\ 16/9)$. The size of the given test is given by

$$P_{\theta_0=50}(W) = P_{50}\Big\{\sum_1^9 X_i > 473.49\Big\} = P_{50}\Big\{\frac{\bar{X}-50}{4/3} > \frac{473.49/9 - 50}{4/3}\Big\}$$

$$= P_{50}\{N(0,1) > 1.9575\} = 0.025$$

The power of the test $W$ at $\theta = 55$ is given by

$$P_{\theta_1=55}(W) = P_{55}\Big\{\frac{\bar{X}-55}{4/3} > \frac{473.49/9 - 55}{4/3}\Big\} = P_{55}\{N(0,1) > -1.7925\}$$

$$P_{\theta_1=55}(W) = 0.5 - P_{55}\{N(0,1) > 1.7925\}\ +\ 0.5$$

$$= 1 - 0.0367 = 0.9633$$

The critical region and power of the test is shown in Figure 3.1.

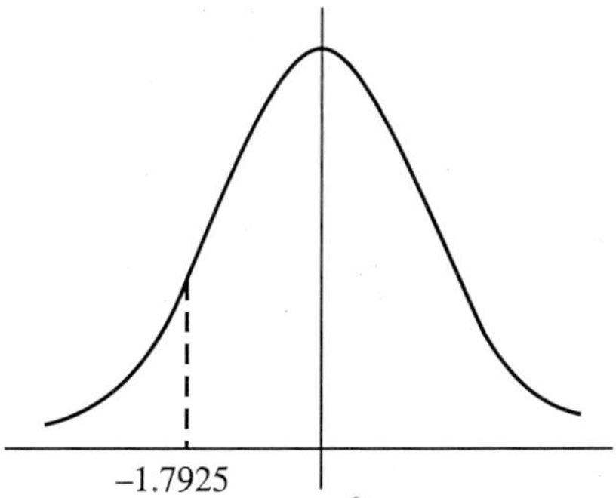


**Figure 3.1:** Critical region.

(b) The joint density of $X_1, \ldots, X_9$ is given by

$$\Big(\frac{1}{32\pi}\Big)^{9/2} \exp\Big\{-\frac{1}{32}\sum_1^9 x_i^2 + \frac{1}{16}\theta\sum_1^9 x_i - \frac{9}{32}\theta^2\Big\}$$

We see this as exponential family with $Q(\theta) = \theta/16$ and $T(\mathbf{x}) = \sum_1^9 x_i$. Thus, the given family has MLR in $\sum x_i$. Alternatively, consider $\theta_1 < \theta_2$ and $A(\mathbf{x}) = \frac{L(\theta_2)}{L(\theta_1)} = \exp\{\frac{1}{16}(\theta_2 - \theta_1)\sum x_i - \frac{9}{32}(\theta_2^2 - \theta_1^2)\}$. $A(\mathbf{x})$ is an increasing function of $\sum x_i$ for $\theta_1 < \theta_2$, therefore, the family $N(\theta, 16)$ has MLR in $\sum x_i$.

(c) Consider a testing problem $H_0 : \theta = 50$ against $H_1 : \theta = \theta_1 (\theta_1 > 50)$. Using NP lemma, the best test is given by

$$\phi(\mathbf{x}) = \begin{cases} 1 & \text{if } \dfrac{f_1(\mathbf{x})}{f_0(\mathbf{x})} > k \\ 0 & \text{otherwise} \end{cases}$$

Note $\phi(\mathbf{x})$ is non-randomized since the distribution of $X$ is continuous. Further, $A(\mathbf{x}) = \frac{f_1(\mathbf{x})}{f_0(\mathbf{x})} = \exp\{\frac{1}{16}(\theta_1 - 50)\sum x_i - \frac{9}{32}(\theta_1^2 - 50^2)\}$ is an increasing function in $\sum x_i$ since $\theta_1 > 50$. Therefore, $f_1(\mathbf{x})/f_0(\mathbf{x}) > k$ given $\sum x_i > k_1$ for some $k_1$ determined by

$$E_{\theta=50}[\phi(\mathbf{X})] = 0.01 \quad \text{or} \quad P_{50}[\sum X_i > k_1] = 0.01$$

or

$$P_{50}\Big\{\frac{\bar{X} - 50}{4/3} > \frac{k_1/9 - 50}{4/3}\Big\} = 0.01$$

Note $\frac{\bar{X}-50}{4/3} \sim N(0,1)$. This gives $\frac{k_1/9-50}{4/3} = 2.326$ or $k_1 \approx 478$

The most powerful test of size 0.01 is given by

$$\phi(\textstyle\sum x_i) = \begin{cases} 1 & \text{if } \sum x_i > 478 \\ 0 & \text{otherwise} \end{cases}$$

Note that this does not depend on $\theta_1$ as long as $\theta_1 > 50$, therefore, it is UMP for testing $H_0 : \theta = 50$ against $H_1 : \theta > 50$.

**Example 3.3.12.** *Consider a random sample $X_1, \ldots, X_n$ drawn from normal distribution $N(\theta,\ 1)$. Derive a UMP test of size-$\alpha$ for testing,*

$$H_0 : \theta = \theta_0 \ \textit{against} \ H_1 : \theta > \theta_0$$

*Calculate the power function and show that it is an increasing function of sample size.*

***Solution:*** Consider the joint distribution of $X_1, \ldots, X_n$

$$f(\mathbf{x}|\theta) = \left(\frac{1}{2\pi}\right)^{n/2} \exp\{-1/2\textstyle\sum x_i^2 + \theta\sum x_i - n/2\,\theta^2\}$$

This family belongs to the exponential family with $Q(\theta) = \theta$ and $T(\mathbf{x}) = \sum x_i$. Therefore, this family has MLR in $T(\mathbf{x}) = \sum x_i$. The UMP size-$\alpha$ test for testing $H_0 : \theta = \theta_0$ aganist $H_1 : \theta > \theta_0$ would be given by

$$\phi(\textstyle\sum x_i) = \begin{cases} 1 & \text{if } \sum x_i > t_0 \\ 0 & \text{if } \sum x_i \le t_0 \end{cases}$$

where, $t_0$ is obtained by the condition

$$P_{\theta_0}\{\textstyle\sum X_i > t_0\} = \alpha$$

or

$$P_{\theta_0}\Big\{\frac{\sum X_i/n - \theta_0}{1/\sqrt{n}} > \frac{t_0/n - \theta_0}{1/\sqrt{n}}\Big\} = \alpha$$

This gives

$$\sqrt{n}(t_0/n - \theta_0) = z_\alpha \quad \text{or} \quad t_0 = \sqrt{n}z_\alpha + n\theta_0$$

The power function of the above test is given by

$$\beta_\phi(\theta; n) = P_\theta\Big\{\frac{\bar{X}-\theta}{1/\sqrt{n}} > \frac{t_0/n-\theta}{1/\sqrt{n}}\Big\} = P_\theta\Big\{N(0,1) > \frac{t_0/n-\theta}{1/\sqrt{n}}\Big\}$$

Consider

$$n_1 < n_2$$

We get

$$t_0/\sqrt{n_1} > t_0/\sqrt{n_2}$$

But

$$\sqrt{n_1}\theta < \sqrt{n_2}\cdot\theta$$

We get

$$t_0/\sqrt{n_1} - \sqrt{n_1}\theta > t_0/\sqrt{n_2} - \sqrt{n_1}\theta > t_0/\sqrt{n_2} - \sqrt{n_2}\theta$$

This gives

$$\beta_\phi(\theta; n_2) > \beta_\phi(\theta; n_1)$$

This proves the power function is an increasing function of sample size.

**Example 3.3.13.** *Let $X_i$ be independently distributed as $N(i\Delta, 1)$, $i = 1, \ldots, n$. Show that there exists a UMP test of $H_0 : \Delta \leq 0$ against $H_1 : \Delta > 0$, and determine it as explicitly as possible.*

***Solution:*** Consider the joint distribution of $X_1, \ldots, X_n$

$$(1/2\pi)^{n/2}\exp\{-\frac{1}{2}\textstyle\sum_i x_i^2 + \Delta\sum_i i\,x_i - \frac{1}{2}\sum i^2\Delta^2\}$$

This belongs to one-parameter exponential family with sufficient statistic $T(\mathbf{x}) = \sum_i ix_i$ and $Q(\Delta) = \Delta$. This family has monotone likelihood ratio in $T(\mathbf{x})$. Using KR theorem UMP size-$\alpha$ test for testing $H_0 : \Delta \leq 0$ against $H_1 : \Delta > 0$ is given by

$$\phi(T(\mathbf{x})) = \begin{cases} 1 & \text{if } T > t_0 \\ 0 & \text{otherwise} \end{cases}$$

where, $t_0$ is obtained by size condition $E_{\Delta=0}[\phi(T)] = \alpha$

We have, $T = \sum iX_i$. Let $Y_i = i\ X_i$. The distribution of $Y_i$ is $N(i^2\Delta, i^2)$ since $X_i$ is $N(i\Delta, 1)$. This gives $T = \sum iX_i = \sum Y_i \sim N(\sum i^2\Delta, i^2)$ and $T|H_0 \sim N(0, \sum i^2)$.

Therefore, $t_0$ is determined by

$$P_{\Delta=0}\{T > t_0\} = \alpha$$

$$P_0\Big\{\frac{T}{\sqrt{\sum i^2}} > \frac{t_0}{\sqrt{\sum i^2}}\Big\} = \alpha$$

where $T/\sqrt{\sum i^2} \sim N(0,1)$. We get $t_0/\sqrt{\sum i^2} = z_\alpha$ or $t_0 = z_\alpha\sqrt{\sum i^2} = z_\alpha\sqrt{\frac{n(n+1)(2n+1)}{6}}$.

**Example 3.3.14.** *Consider a sample $X_1, X_2, \dots X_n$ from $G(\alpha,\ \beta)$. Show that $G(\alpha,\ \beta)$ family has monotone likelihood ratio when $\alpha$ is fixed.*

***Solution:*** Let $\alpha = \alpha_0$ (fixed) and $\beta_1 < \beta_2$. Consider

$$\frac{f(\mathbf{x}|\,\beta_2)}{f(\mathbf{x}|\,\beta_1)} = \frac{\left(\frac{1}{\Gamma(\alpha_0)\beta_2^{\alpha_0}}\right)^n \exp\{-(\sum x_i/\beta_2)\}(\prod x_i)^{\alpha_0-1}}{\left(\frac{1}{\Gamma(\alpha_0)\beta_1^{\alpha_0}}\right)^n \exp\{-(\sum x_i/\beta_1)\}(\prod x_i)^{\alpha_0-1}}$$

$$= \left(\frac{\beta_1}{\beta_2}\right)^{\alpha_0} \exp\left\{\left(\frac{1}{\beta_1} - \frac{1}{\beta_2}\right)\sum x_i\right\} \text{ where } \alpha_0 > 0 \text{ and } \beta > 0$$

note that $(\frac{1}{\beta_1} - \frac{1}{\beta_2}) > 0$, therefore, $f(\cdot|\beta_2)/f(\cdot|\beta_1)$ is non-decreasing in $T(\mathbf{x}) = \sum x_i$. Also $G(\alpha_0, \beta)$ belong to one-parameter exponential family.

Next if we fix $\beta = \beta_0$ and consider $\alpha_1 < \alpha_2$ then

$$\frac{f(\cdot|\alpha_2)}{f(\cdot|\alpha_1)} = \frac{(\Gamma(\alpha_1))^n\ \beta_0^{n\alpha_1}}{(\Gamma(\alpha_2))^n\ \beta_0^{n\alpha_2}} (\prod x_i)^{\alpha_2-\alpha_1} = c(\alpha_1,\ \alpha_2,\ \beta_0)(\prod x_i)^{\alpha_2-1}$$

We note $f(\cdot|\alpha_2)/f(\cdot|\alpha_1)$ for $\alpha_1 < \alpha_2$ is an increasing function in $\prod x_i$. We therefore, see that gamma family, with one parameter fixed, has monotone likelihood ratio in $\sum x_i$ and in $\prod x_i$ when $\alpha$ fixed and $\beta$ fixed respectively.

**Example 3.3.15.** *Let $X_1, \dots, X_n$ be a sample from $G(\alpha,\ \beta)$ with density*

$$f(x|\alpha, \beta) = \frac{1}{\Gamma(\alpha)\beta^\alpha} x^{\alpha-1}\ e^{-x/\beta};\quad x > 0;\quad \alpha,\ \beta > 0$$

*Show that there exists a UMP test for testing*

(a) $H_0 : \beta \le \beta_0$ *against* $H_1 : \beta > \beta_0$ *when $\alpha$ is given.*

(b) $H_0 : \alpha \le \alpha_0$ *against* $H_1 : \alpha > \alpha_0$ *when $\beta$ is given.*

***Solution:*** (a) We have seen in either case that the above family has monotone likelihood ratio. In the first case $Q(\beta) = -1/\beta$ and $T(\mathbf{x}) = \sum x_i$. The UMP test for testing $H_0 : \beta \le \beta_0$ against $H_1 : \beta > \beta_0$ would be given by

$$\phi(T) = \begin{cases} 1 & \text{if } T > t_0 \\ 0 & \text{otherwise} \end{cases}$$

where, $t_0$ is obtained s.t.

$$E_{\beta_0}[\phi(T)] = \alpha$$

where, $T = \sum X_i$. Each $X_i \sim G(\alpha_0,\ \beta)$ for fixed $\alpha$ and $X_i|H_0 \sim G(\alpha_0, \beta_0)$. Therefore,

$$T|H_0 = \sum X_i|H_0 \sim G(n\alpha_0, \beta_0).$$

This gives

$$\int_{t_0}^{\infty} G(n\alpha_0,\ \beta_0)\, dy = 1 - \alpha$$

One could obtain $t_0$ from incomplete gamma distribution table.

(b) In this case $T(\mathbf{x}) = \sum \log x_i$ and $Q(\alpha) = (\alpha - 1)$. The UMP test for testing $H_0 : \alpha \leq \alpha_0$ would be given by

$$\phi(T) = \begin{cases} 1 & \text{if } T > t_0 \\ 0 & \text{otherwise} \end{cases}$$

where, $t_0$ is obtained such that

$$E_{\alpha_0}[\phi(T)] = \alpha$$

$t_0$ could be obtained by calculating the distribution of $T = \sum \log X_i | H_0$.

**Example 3.3.16.** *Let $X_1, X_2, \ldots, X_n$ be a random sample been drawn from*

$$f(x|\theta) = \frac{1}{\theta}\, e^{-x/\theta} \qquad x \geq 0, \quad \theta > 0$$

*Find a UMP size-$\alpha$ test of $H_0 : \theta \leq 1$ against $H_1 : \theta > 1$.*

***Solution:*** The joint density of $X_1, X_2, \ldots, X_n$ is given by

$$\frac{1}{\theta^n}\, e^{-1/\theta \sum x_i}$$

This family belongs to the exponential family with $Q(\theta) = -1/\theta$ and $T(\mathbf{x}) = \sum x_i$. Therefore, this family has MLR in $T(\mathbf{x})$. Here, $\sum_1^n X_i \sim G(n, \theta)$. The UMP test for testing $H_0 : \theta \leq 1$ against $H_1 : \theta > 1$ is given by

$$\phi(T) = \begin{cases} 1 & \text{if } T > t_0 \\ 0 & \text{otherwise} \end{cases}$$

where, $t_0$ is obtained by

$$E_{\theta_0=1}[\phi(T)] = \alpha \quad \text{or} \quad \int_{t_0}^{\infty} G(n, 1)\, dy = \alpha$$

where, $t_0$ would be obtained from tables of incomplete gamma distribution.

**Example 3.3.17.** *Let $X_1, X_2, \ldots, X_n$ be a random sample from beta distribution $Be(\alpha, \beta)$. Show that this family has monotone likelihood ratio for $\alpha$ fixed.*

***Solution:*** The density is given by

$$f(x|\alpha, \beta) = \frac{\Gamma(\alpha + \beta)}{\Gamma(\alpha)\Gamma(\beta)} x^{\alpha-1}\, (1 - x)^{\beta-1}\, I_{[0,1]}(x).$$

Given $\alpha = \alpha_0$ , for $\beta_1 < \beta_2$

$$A(\mathbf{x}) = \frac{f(\mathbf{x}|\beta_2)}{f(\mathbf{x}|\beta_1)} = \Big(\frac{\Gamma(\beta_1)\,\Gamma(\alpha_0+\beta_2)}{\Gamma(\beta_2)\,\Gamma(\alpha_0+\beta_1)}\Big)\cdot\Big\{\prod(1-x_i)\Big\}^{\beta_2-1}$$

Note $A(\mathbf{x})$ is an increasing function in the statistic $T(\mathbf{x}) = \prod(1-x_i)$, therefore, Beta family with $\alpha$ fixed has monotone likelihood ratio. Note for $\beta$ fixed Beta family has monotone likelihood ratio in $T(\mathbf{x}) = \prod x_i$.

**Example 3.3.18.** *Let $X \sim \mathcal{H}(n, m, M)$. Show that this family has monotone likelihood ratio by assuming $m$ is the only unknown parameter.*

***Solution:*** The density is given by

$$f(x|m) = \frac{\binom{n}{x}\binom{M-n}{m-x}}{\binom{M}{m}}, \qquad x = max(0,\ m+n-M), \ldots min(m,\ n).$$

Considering $m_1 < m_2$ or $m < m+1$ we have

$$k(x) = \frac{p(x|m+1)}{p(x|m)} = \frac{\binom{n}{x}\binom{M-n}{m+1-x}}{\binom{M}{m+1}} \cdot \frac{\binom{M}{m}}{\binom{n}{x}\binom{M-n}{m-x}}$$

$$= \frac{\frac{1}{(m+1-x)}\cdot\frac{1}{(M-m)}}{\frac{1}{(M-n)-(m-x)}\cdot\frac{1}{m+1}} = \Big(\frac{m+1}{M-m}\Big)\cdot\Big(\frac{M-n-m+x}{m+1-x}\Big) = c\cdot\frac{(a+x)}{(b-x)}$$

where, $c = \dfrac{(m+1)}{(M-n)}$, $a = M-n-m$, $b = m+1$ and $a,\ b,\ c > 0$. It implies that as $x$ increases, $k(x)$ also increase. This can also be shown by differentiating $k(x)$ w.r.t. $x$, we get

$$k' = c\Big[\frac{(a+x)}{(b\quad x)^2} + \frac{1}{(b\quad x)}\Big]$$

Here $b - x = m+1-x > 0$, since $x = 0, 1, \ldots min(m, n)$ implies $k' > 0$. This shows that $k(x)$ is an increasing function in $x$.

Further that if $m_2 = m_1 + l$, then

$$k(x) = \frac{f(x|m_2)}{f(x|m_1)} = \frac{f(x|m_1+1)}{f(x|m_1)}\cdot\frac{f(x|m_1+2)}{f(x|m_1+1)}\cdots\frac{f(x|m_1+l)}{f(x|m_1+l-1)}$$

which is a product of the functions of the type considered as just before. Since each of these functions are increasing in $x$, hence product is also increasing in $x$.

Hence, hypergeometric distribution has MLR in $x$.

**Example 3.3.19.** *Consider a sample $X_1, X_2, \ldots, X_n$ from the family of distribution $\mathcal{P}$, with density*

$$f(x|\theta) = c(\theta)\ h(x)\ I_{(-\infty,\ \theta)}(x)$$

*Show that $\mathcal{P}$ has monotone likelihood ratio.*

***Solution:*** For $\theta_1 < \theta_2$

$$A(\mathbf{x}) = \frac{f(\mathbf{x}|\theta_2)}{f(\mathbf{x}|\theta_1)} = \Big(\frac{c(\theta_2)}{c(\theta_1)}\Big)^n \frac{I_{(-\infty,\,\theta_2)}(\max x_i)}{I_{(-\infty,\,\theta_1)}(\max x_i)}$$

$$= \begin{cases} \Big(\frac{c(\theta_2)}{c(\theta_1)}\Big)^n & -\infty < \max x_i < \theta_1 \\ \infty & \theta_1 < \max x_i < \theta_2 \end{cases}$$

which shows $A(\mathbf{x})$ is increasing in $T(\mathbf{x}) = \max x_i$, therefore, the family $\mathcal{P}$ has monotone likelihood ratio.

**Example 3.3.20.** *Show that double exponential family of distribution*

$$f(x|\alpha,\ \beta) = \frac{1}{2\beta}\exp\Big\{\frac{-|x-\alpha|}{\beta}\Big\}$$

*has monotone likelihood ratio, when $\alpha$ is unknown and $\beta$ is known.*

***Solution:*** Let $\beta = \beta_0$ and $\alpha_1 < \alpha_2$, we have

$$k(x) = \frac{f(x|\alpha_2)}{f(x|\alpha_1)} = \frac{\exp\{-\frac{|x-\alpha_2|}{\beta_0}\}}{\exp\{-\frac{|x-\alpha_1|}{\beta_0}\}} = \exp\{\frac{1}{\beta_0}[|x-\alpha_1| - |x-\alpha_2|]\}$$

Consider cases

(a) If $(x-\alpha_i) \le 0$ for $i = 1, 2$

$$k(x) = \exp\Big\{\frac{-(x-\alpha_1)+(x-\alpha_2)}{\beta_0}\Big\} = \exp\{(\alpha_1-\alpha_2)/\beta_0\} = \text{constant}$$

(b) If $(x-\alpha_1) \ge 0$ and $(x-\alpha_2) < 0$

$$k(x) = \exp\Big\{\frac{1}{\beta_0}((x-\alpha_1)+(x-\alpha_2))\Big\} = \exp\Big\{\frac{2x-\alpha_1-\alpha_2}{\beta_0}\Big\}$$

which is non-decreasing in $x$ and $k(x) \to \exp\{(\alpha_2-\alpha_1)/\beta_0\}$ as $x \uparrow \alpha_2$.

(c) If $(x-\alpha_i) \ge 0$ for $i = 1, 2.$

$$k(x) = e^{(\alpha_2-\alpha_1)/\beta_0} = \text{constant}.$$

From (a), (b) and (c) it is clear that as $x \uparrow \alpha_1$ in $(-\infty, \alpha_1)$, $x \uparrow \alpha_2$ in $(\alpha_1, \alpha_2)$ and $x \uparrow +\infty$ in $(\alpha_2, \infty)$, $k(x)$ rests at $e^{(\alpha_1-\alpha_2)/\beta_0}$ and increases to $e^{(\alpha_2-\alpha_1)/\beta_0}$, and becomes constant $e^{(\alpha_2-\alpha_1)/\beta_0}$ lastly. In other words, $k(x)$ is non-decreasing in $x$ and therefore, the double exponential family $\mathcal{P}$ has monotone likelihood ratio in $x$.

**Example 3.3.21.** *Consider a sample $X_1, \ldots, X_n$ drawn from the negative exponential family with density*

$$f(x|\,\theta) = e^{-(x-\theta)}\ \mathrm{I}_{(\theta,\infty)}(x)$$

*Show this family has monotone likelihood ratio.*

***Solution:*** Let $\theta_1 < \theta_2$, and denote $X_{(1)} = \min X_i$

$$k(\mathbf{x}) = \frac{f(\mathbf{x}|\theta_2)}{f(\mathbf{x}|\theta_1)} = \frac{\exp\{-\sum(x_i - \theta_2)\}\,\mathrm{I}_{(\theta_2,\,\infty)}(x_{(1)})}{\exp\{-\sum(x_i - \theta_1)\}\,\mathrm{I}_{(\theta_1,\,\infty)}(x_{(1)})}$$

$$k(\mathbf{x}) = \begin{cases} 0 & \text{if } \theta_1 < x_{(1)} < \theta_2 \\ \exp\{n(\theta_2 - \theta_1)\} & \text{if } \theta_2 < x_{(1)} < \infty \end{cases}$$

$k(\mathbf{x})$ is non-decreasing in $x_{(1)}$. Therefore, negative exponential family has monotone likelihood ratio in $x_{(1)}$.

**Example 3.3.22.** *Show that the Cauchy $\mathcal{C}(\theta, 1)$ distribution is without monotone likelihood ratio.*

***Solution:*** Let $\theta_1 < \theta_2$

$$k(x) = \frac{f(x|\,\theta_2)}{f(x|\,\theta_1)} = \frac{\frac{1}{\pi}\frac{1}{1+(x-\theta_2)^2}}{\frac{1}{\pi}\frac{1}{1+(x-\theta_1)^2}}; \quad x \in \mathbb{R}^1$$

$$= \frac{1+(x-\theta_1)^2}{1+(x-\theta_2)^2} = \frac{1/x^2 + (1-\theta_1/x)^2}{1/x^2 + (1-\theta_2/x)^2}$$

Note that $k(x) \to 1$ as $x \to \pm\infty$ and $k(x) = \dfrac{1+\theta_1^2}{1+\theta_2^2} \neq 1$ when $x = 0$ shows that $k(x)$ is *not monotone*. Hence, Cauchy family does not have monotone likelihood ratio

**Example 3.3.23.** *Show that Cauchy $\mathcal{C}(0, \theta)$ has no monotone likelihood ratio.*

***Solution:*** The density of $\mathcal{C}(\alpha,\ \beta)$ is given by

$$\frac{\beta}{\pi} \cdot \frac{1}{\beta^2 + (x-\alpha)^2}, \quad \beta > 0.$$

Let $\theta_1 < \theta_2$, we have

$$k(x) = \frac{f(x|\,\theta_2)}{f(x|\,\theta_1)} = \frac{\frac{\theta_2}{\pi} \cdot \frac{1}{\theta_2^2 + x^2}}{\frac{\theta_1}{\pi} \cdot \frac{1}{\theta_1^2 + x^2}}$$

$$= \frac{\theta_2}{\theta_1} \cdot \frac{\theta_1^2 + x^2}{\theta_2^2 + x^2} = \left(\frac{\theta_2}{\theta_1}\right) \cdot \frac{1 + \theta_1^2/x^2}{1 + \theta_2^2/x^2}$$

Note that, $k(x) \to \left(\frac{\theta_2}{\theta_1}\right) > 1$ as $x \to \pm\infty$ and at $x = 0$, $k(x) = \frac{\theta_1}{\theta_2} < 1$. Therefore, $k(x)$ is not monotone in $x$, and hence $\mathcal{C}(0, \theta)$ has no monotone likelihood ratio.

The density of $|X|$ shall be given by

$$\begin{aligned} f_{|X|}(x) &= f_X(-x) + f_X(x) \\ &= \frac{\theta}{\pi} \cdot \frac{1}{\theta^2 + x^2} + \frac{\theta}{\pi} \cdot \frac{1}{\theta^2 + x^2} = 2 \cdot \frac{\theta}{\pi} \cdot \frac{1}{\theta^2 + x^2}. \\ \text{Let} \quad \theta_1 < \theta_2 \quad \lambda(x) &= \frac{f_{|X|}(x|\,\theta_2)}{f_{|X|}(x|\,\theta_1)} = \frac{\theta_2}{\theta_1} \cdot \frac{\theta_1^2 + x^2}{\theta_2^2 + x^2} \end{aligned}$$

$\lambda(x)$ at $|X| = 0$ is $\frac{\theta_1}{\theta_2} < 1 \cdot \lambda(x) \to \frac{\theta_2}{\theta_1} > 1$ as $|x| \to \infty$. This shows that the distribution of the sufficient statistic $|X|$ has monotone likelihood ratio.

**Example 3.3.24.** *Show that the logistic family has monotone likelihood ratio with location parameter $\theta$.*

***Solution:*** The density is given by

$$f(x|\theta) = \frac{e^{-x-\theta}}{(1 + e^{-x-\theta})^2} = \frac{1}{2(1 + \cosh(x - \theta))}$$

Let $\theta_1 < \theta_2$,

$$\begin{aligned} k(x) &= \frac{f(x|\theta_2)}{f(x|\theta_1)} = \frac{1 + \cosh(x - \theta_1)}{1 + \cosh(x - \theta_2)} \\ &= \frac{2\cosh^2(x - \theta_1)/2}{2\cosh^2(x - \theta_2)/2}. \end{aligned}$$

On differentiating $k(x)$ with respect to $x$, we get

$$\begin{aligned} k'(x) = \frac{\partial}{\partial x} \frac{f(x|\theta_2)}{f(x|\theta_1)} = \Big[\Big(&\cosh^2(x - \theta_2)/2 \cdot 2\cosh(x - \theta_1)/2 \cdot \\ &\sinh(x - \theta_1)/2 \cdot \frac{1}{2} - \cosh^2(x - \theta_1)/2 \cdot 2\cosh(x - \theta_2)/2 \cdot \\ &\sinh(x - \theta_2)/2 \cdot 1/2\Big)\Big] \Big/ \cosh^4 \frac{(x - \theta_2)}{2} \end{aligned}$$

$$= \cosh\frac{(x-\theta_1)}{2}\cosh\frac{(x-\theta_2)}{2}\Big[\cosh\frac{(x-\theta_2)}{2}\sinh\frac{(x-\theta_1)}{2}$$

$$-\cosh\frac{(x-\theta_1)}{2}\sinh\frac{(x-\theta_2)}{2}\Big]$$

$$= \frac{\cosh\frac{(x-\theta_1)}{2}\cosh\frac{(x-\theta_2)}{2}\cdot[\sinh(\frac{x-\theta_1}{2}-\frac{x-\theta_2}{2})]}{\cosh^4\frac{(x-\theta_2)}{2}}$$

$$= \frac{\cosh\frac{(x-\theta_1)}{2}\cosh(\frac{x-\theta_2}{2})\cdot\sinh(\frac{\theta_2-\theta_1}{2})}{\cosh^4\frac{(x-\theta_2)}{2}}$$

Since $\theta_2 > \theta_1$, $\sinh\frac{(\theta_2-\theta_1)}{2} > 0$, $\cosh^4(\frac{x-\theta_2}{2}) > 0, \cosh\frac{(x-\theta_1)}{2}$ and $\cosh\frac{x-\theta_2}{2}$ is always positive since $\cosh(-x) = \cosh(x)$, giving $k'(x)$ as positive. Therefore, $k(x)$ is non-decreasing in $x$ and $\mathcal{P}$ has monotone likelihood ratio.

*An alternative method:* Let $\theta_1 < \theta_2$, we have

$$k(x) = \frac{f(x|\,\theta_2)}{f(x|\,\theta_1)} = \frac{e^{-x-\theta_2}}{(1+e^{-x-\theta_2})^2}\cdot\frac{(1+e^{-x-\theta_1})^2}{e^{-x-\theta_1}}$$

$$= e^{\theta_1-\theta_2}\left(\frac{1+e^{-x-\theta_1}}{1+e^{-x-\theta_2}}\right)^2$$

Now, $k(x) < k(x')$ iff

$$e^{\theta_1-\theta_2}\left(\frac{1+e^{-x-\theta_1}}{1+e^{-x-\theta_2}}\right)^2 < e^{\theta_1-\theta_2}\left(\frac{1+e^{-x'-\theta_1}}{1+e^{-x'-\theta_2}}\right)^2$$

or

$$\frac{1+e^{-x-\theta_1}}{1+e^{-x-\theta_2}} < \frac{1+e^{-x'-\theta_1}}{1+e^{-x'-\theta_2}}$$

or

$$(1+e^{-x-\theta_1})(1+e^{-x'-\theta_2}) < (1+e^{-x'-\theta_1})(1+e^{-x-\theta_2})$$

or

$$e^{-x}(e^{-\theta_1}-e^{-\theta_2}) < e^{-x'}(e^{-\theta_1}-e^{-\theta_2})$$

or

$$e^{-x} < e^{-x'}(\text{since } \theta_1 < \theta_2 \text{ implies } e^{-\theta_1}-e^{-\theta_2} > 0)$$

or

$$-x < -x' \quad \text{or} \quad x > x'$$

which shows that $k(x)$ is monotonically decreasing in $x$.

**Example 3.3.25.** *For the logistic distribution with location parameter $\theta$, with density*

$$f(x|\theta) = \frac{e^{-x-\theta}}{(1+e^{-x-\theta})^2}, \quad -\infty < x < \infty, \; -\infty < \theta < \infty$$

*Find a UMP test of size-$\alpha$ for testing $H_0 : \theta \le \theta_0$ against $H_1 : \theta > \theta_0$.*

***Solution:*** We have already shown in Example 3.2.24 that this family has MLR in $T(x) = -x$. Thus, the UMP test for testing

$$H_0 : \theta \leq \theta_0 \text{ against } H_1 : \theta > \theta_0$$

would be given by

$$\phi(x) = \begin{cases} 1 & \text{if } x < x_0 \\ 0 & \text{if } x \geq x_0 \end{cases}$$

where, $x_0$ would be determined by the size condition, i.e.

$$E_{\theta_0}[\phi(X)] = \alpha$$

or

$$P_{\theta_0}\{X < x_0\} = \alpha$$

$$\int_{x_0}^{\infty} \frac{e^{-x-\theta_0}}{(1+e^{-x-\theta_0})^2} dx = 1 - \alpha$$

By putting, $1 + e^{-x-\theta_0} = t$, we get $-e^{-x-\theta_0} dx = dt$,

$$\int_{1+e^{-x_0-\theta_0}}^{1} -\frac{1}{t^2}\, dt = 1 - \alpha$$

or

$$1 - \frac{1}{1+e^{-x_0-\theta_0}} = 1 - \alpha$$

$e^{-x_0-\theta_0} = 1/\alpha - 1$ or $-x_0 - \theta_0 = \log(1/\alpha - 1)$ or $x_0 = -\log(1/\alpha - 1) - \theta_0$
Therefore, UMP test for testing $H_0 : \theta \leq \theta_0$ against $H_1 : \theta > \theta_0$ would be given by

$$\phi(x) = \begin{cases} 1 & \text{if } x < -\log(1/\alpha - 1) - \theta_0 \\ 0 & \text{if } x \geq -\log(1/\alpha - 1) - \theta_0 \end{cases}$$

**Example 3.3.26.** *Show that the family of distributions given by*

$$f(x|\theta) = c(\theta)h(x) \cdot I_{(\pi_1(\theta),\, \pi_2(\theta))}(x)$$

*has monotone likelihood ratio provided $\pi_1(\theta)$ and $\pi_2(\theta)$ are non-decreasing function of $\theta$.*

***Solution:*** Let $\theta_1 < \theta_2$, we have

$$k(x) = \frac{f(x|\,\theta_2)}{f(x|\,\theta_1)} = \frac{c(\theta_2)\, I_{(\pi_1(\theta_2),\, \pi_2(\theta_2))}(x)}{c(\theta_1) I_{(\pi_1(\theta_1),\, \pi_2(\theta_1))}(x)}$$

*Case I:* If $\pi_1(\theta_2) < \pi_2(\theta_1)$

$$k(x) = \begin{cases} 0 & \text{if } \; x \in (\pi_1(\theta_1),\, \pi_1(\theta_2)) \\ \frac{c(\theta_2)}{c(\theta_1)} & \text{if } \; x \in (\pi_1(\theta_2),\, \pi_2(\theta_1)) \\ \infty & \text{if } \; x \in (\pi_2(\theta_1),\, \pi_2(\theta_2)) \end{cases}$$

*Case II:* If $\pi_2(\theta_1) < \pi_1(\theta_2)$

$$k(x) = \begin{cases} 0 & \text{if } \; x \in (\pi_1(\theta_1), \pi_2(\theta_1)) \\ \text{not defined} & \text{if } \; x \in (\pi_2(\theta_1), \pi_1(\theta_2)) \\ \infty & \text{if } \; x \in (\pi_1(\theta_2), \pi_2(\theta_2)) \end{cases}$$

In both these cases, $k(x)$ is increasing in $x$, therefore, the above family $\mathcal{P}$ has monotone likelihood ratio.

**Example 3.3.27.** *Let $X \sim U(\theta,\ \theta + 1)$. Show that the uniform distribution has monotone likelihood ratio.*

***Solution:*** Let $\theta_1 < \theta_2$, consider

$$k(x) = \frac{f(x|\ \theta_2)}{f(x|\ \theta_1)} = \frac{I_{(\theta_2,\ \theta_2+1)}(x)}{I_{(\theta_1,\ \theta_1+1)}(x)}$$

Now, there arise two cases,

*Case I:* When $\theta_1 < \theta_2 < \theta_1 + 1 < \theta_2 + 1$ (Figure 3.2), consider

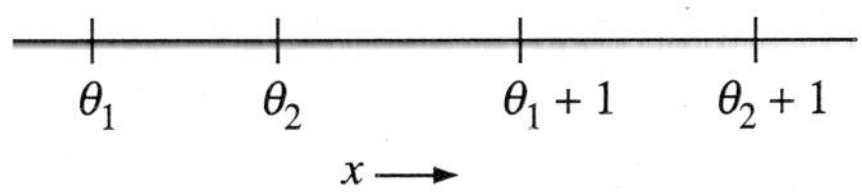


**Figure 3.2:** Support of the distributions $U(\theta_1, \theta_1 + 1)$ and $U(\theta_2, \theta_2 + 1)$ for the case $\theta_2 < \theta_1 + 1$.

$$k(x) = \frac{f(x|\theta_2)}{f(x|\theta_1)} = \begin{cases} 0/0(\text{undefined}) & \text{if } x < \theta_1 \\ 0/1 = 0 & \text{if } \theta_1 < x < \theta_2 \\ 1/1 = 1 & \text{if } \theta_2 < x < \theta_1 + 1 \\ 1/0 = \infty & \text{if } \theta_1 + 1 < x < \theta_2 + 1 \\ 0/0 = (\text{undefined}) & \text{if } \theta_2 + 1 < x \end{cases}$$

Clearly, $k(x)$ is non-decreasing function in $x$ for which the ratio of the densities is defined, i.e. $(\theta_1,\ \theta_2 + 1)$.

*Case II:* When $\theta_1 < \theta_1 + 1 < \theta_2 < \theta_2 + 1$ (Figure 3.3.)

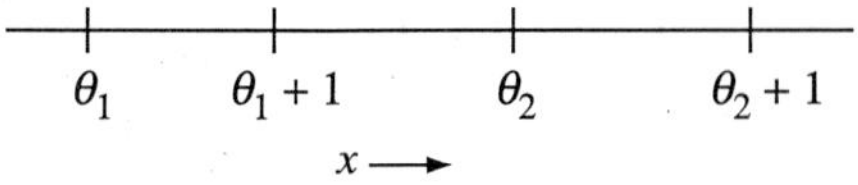


**Figure 3.3:** Support of the distributions $U(\theta_1, \theta_1+1)$ and $U(\theta_2, \theta_2+1)$ for the case $\theta_1 + 1 < \theta_2$.

$$k(x) = \frac{f(x|\theta_2)}{f(x|\theta_1)} = \begin{cases} 0/0(\text{undefined}) & \text{if } x < \theta_1 \\ 0/1 = 0 & \text{if } \theta_1 < x < \theta_1 + 1 \\ 0/0(\text{undefined}) & \text{if } \theta_1 + 1 < x < \theta_2 \\ 1/0 = \infty & \text{if } \theta_2 < x < \theta_2 + 1 \\ 0/0(\text{undefined}) & \text{if } \theta_2 + 1 < x \end{cases}$$

$k(x)$ is non-decreasing in $x$ in the set of existence $(\theta_1, \theta_2 + 1)$. On combining Cases (I) and (II), shown by Figs. 3.2 and 3.3, respectively, we conclude that $k(x)$ is non-decreasing in $(\theta_1, \theta_2 + 1)$, therefore, $U(\theta, \theta + 1)$ has monotone likelihood ratio in $T(\mathbf{x}) = x$.

**Example 3.3.28.** ([Ferguson, 1967] [54]) *The second part of Karlin and Rubin theorem gives that for $\alpha > 0$ the test of the form as given in the theorem is UMP for testing $H_0 : \theta \leq \theta_0$ against $H_1 : \theta > \theta_0$. Construct a counter example (for $\alpha = 0$) to this statement.*

***Solution:*** Here we need to show that the test of the form as given in the theroem at $\alpha = 0$ is not UMP for testing the above hypothesis. For this consider $X \sim U(\theta, \theta+1)$ such that $\theta_1 < \theta_1 + 1 < \theta_2 < \theta_2 + 1$ for testing $\theta = \theta_1$ against $\theta = \theta_2$, $\theta_1 < \theta_2$, UMP size 0 test in KR theorem is given by

$$\phi(x) = \begin{cases} 1 & \text{if } x \geq \theta_2 + 1 \\ 0 & \text{if } x < \theta_2 + 1 \end{cases}$$

so that its size is $\alpha = \int_{x \geq \theta_2 + 1} I_{(\theta_1,\ \theta_1+1)}(x)\, dx = 0$ and the power is

$$\int_{x \geq \theta_2 + 1} I_{(\theta_2,\ \theta_2+1)}(x)\, dx = 0$$

Next, consider another test

$$\phi'(x) = \begin{cases} 1 & \text{if } x > \theta_2 \\ 0 & \text{otherwise} \end{cases}$$

of size $\alpha = \int_{x > \theta_2} I_{(\theta_1,\ \theta_1+1)}(x)\, dx = 0$ and power $\int_{x > \theta_2} I_{(\theta_2,\ \theta_2+1)}(x)\, dx = 1$, which shows that $\phi(x)$ is not UMP. This sets an counter example to the second part of Karlin and Rubin theorem.

**Example 3.3.29.** *Find a UMP test for testing $H_0 : \theta \leq \theta_0$ against $H_1 : \theta > \theta_0$ for $U(\theta,\ \theta+1)$ in no data problem.*

***Solution:*** Let us recall that single observation on $X$ is called no data problem. The UMP test is given by

$$\phi(x) = \begin{cases} 1 & \text{if } x > x_0 \\ 0 & \text{if } x \leq x_0 \end{cases}$$

where, $x_0$ is obtained so that

$$E_{\theta_0}\phi(X) = \alpha$$

$$\int_{x>x_0} I_{(\theta_0,\ \theta_0+1)}(x)\, dx = \alpha \quad \text{or} \quad \int_{x_0}^{\theta_0+1} dx = \alpha$$

or, $x_0 = \theta_0 + 1 - \alpha$, therefore, the UMP test is given by

$$\phi(x) = \begin{cases} 1 & \text{if } x > \theta_0 + 1 - \alpha \\ 0 & \text{if } x \leq \theta_0 + 1 - \alpha \end{cases}$$

Additionally, if we shall consider the dual testing problem $H_0 : \theta \geq \theta_0$ against $H_1 : \theta < \theta_0$. UMP size-$\alpha$ test for this dual problem is given by

$$\phi(x) = \begin{cases} 1 & \text{if } x < x_0 \\ 0 & \text{if } x \geq x_0 \end{cases}$$

s.t.

$$E_{\theta_0}\phi(x) = \alpha$$

or

$$\int_{x<x_0} I_{(\theta_0,\theta_0+1)}(x)dx = \alpha$$

$$\int_{\theta_0}^{x_0} dx = x_0 - \theta_0 = \alpha; x_0 = \theta_0 + \alpha$$

Therefore, the test shall be given by

$$\phi(x) = \begin{cases} 1 & \text{if } x < \theta_0 + \alpha \\ 0 & \text{if } x \geq \theta_0 + \alpha \end{cases}$$

**Example 3.3.30.** *Consider a testing problem $H_0 : \theta \leq \theta_0$ against $H_1 : \theta > \theta_0$ on the basis of a sample $X_1, \ldots, X_n$ from $U(\theta,\ \theta+1)$. Find out a UMP size-$\alpha$ test for the data problem $U(\theta, \theta+1)$.*

***Solution:*** Let the order statistic corresponding to the sample $X_1, X_2, \ldots, X_n$ be given by $Y_1 < Y_2 < \cdots < Y_n$ and the joint distribution of $Y_i$ and $Y_j$ order statistic is given by

$$g(Y_i, Y_j) = \frac{n!}{(i-1)!(j-i-1)!(n-j)!}[F(y_i)]^{i-1}[F(y_j) - F(y_i)]^{j-i-1}$$
$$[1 - F(y_j)]^{n-j} f(y_i) \cdot f(y_j) \qquad \text{for } i < j, \;\; Y_i < Y_j.$$

Let $T_1 = Y_1 = \min X_i$; $T_2 = Y_n = \max X_i$. The joint density of $(T_1, T_2)$ be given by

$$g(t_1,\, t_2) = \frac{n!}{(1-1)!(n-1-1)!(n-n)!}[F(t_1)]^{1-1}$$
$$[F(t_2) - F(t_1)]^{n-1-1}[1 - F(t_2)]^{n-n} f(t_1) f(t_2).$$

We get

$$g(t_1, t_2) = n(n-1)[F(t_2) - F(t_1)]^{n-2} f(t_1) \cdot f(t_2)$$

where

$$F(t) = t - \theta \;\text{ if }\; \theta < t < \theta + 1$$

gives

$$g(t_1, t_2) = n(n-1)[t_2 - t_1]^{n-2} \text{ for } \theta < t_1 < t_2 < \theta + 1$$

Let us consider the likelihood ratio for $\theta_1 < \theta_2$

*Case I:* If $\theta_1 + 1 < \theta_2$ (Figure 3.4) then

$$\frac{g(t_1, t_2|H_1)}{g(t_1, t_2|H_0)} = \begin{cases} 0 & \text{if } \theta_1 < t_1 < t_2 < \theta_1 + 1 \\ \infty & \text{if } \theta_2 < t_1 < t_2 < \theta_2 + 1 \end{cases}$$

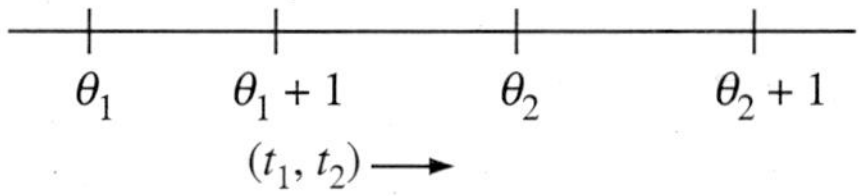


**Figure 3.4:** Support of the distributions $U(\theta_1, \theta_1 + 1)$ and $U(\theta_2, \theta_2 + 1)$ for the case $\theta_1 + 1 < \theta_2$.

*Case II:* If $\theta_2 < \theta_1 + 1$ (Figure 3.5) then

$$\frac{g(t_1, t_2|H_1)}{g(t_1, t_2|H_0)} = \begin{cases} 0 & \text{if } \theta_1 < t_1 < t_2 < \theta_2 \\ 1 & \text{if } \theta_2 < t_1 < t_2 < \theta_1 + 1 \\ \infty & \text{if } \theta_1 + 1 < t_1 < t_2 < \theta_2 + 1 \end{cases}$$

We see that in both the cases the distribution of $(T_1,\, T_2)$ has monotone likelihood ratio in $(t_1,\, t_2)$. Karlin and Rubin theorem gives UMP test for testing $H_0 : \theta \le 0$ against $H_1 : \theta > 0$

$$\phi(t_1,\, t_2) = \begin{cases} 1 & \text{if } k < t_1 < t_2 \;\text{ and }\; t_2 < 1 \\ 0 & \text{if } \;t_1 < k \text{ and } t_2 < 1 \end{cases}$$

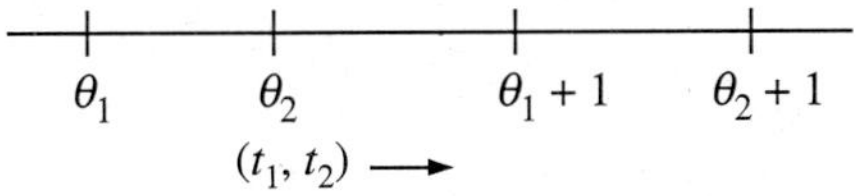


**Figure 3.5:** Support of the distributions $U(\theta_1, \theta_1 + 1)$ and $U(\theta_2, \theta_2 + 1)$ for the case $\theta_2 < \theta_1 + 1$.

where, $k$ is determined by

$$E_{\theta=0}^{T_1,T_2}[\phi(T_1, T_2)] = \alpha$$

$$\int_{t_2}\int_{t_1} \phi(t_1, t_2) g(t_1, t_2) dt_1 dt_2 = \alpha$$

$$\int_k^1 \int_k^{t_2} n(n-1)(t_2 - t_1)^{n-2}\, dt_1\, dt_2 = \alpha$$

Let, $t_2 - t_1 = y$ or $dt_1 = -dy$

$$-n(n-1)\int_k^1 \int_{t_2-k}^0 y^{n-2}\, dy\, dt_2 = \alpha$$

$$-n(n-1)\int_k^1 \left[\frac{y^{n-1}}{n-1}\right]_{t_2-k}^0 dt_2 = \alpha$$

$$n\int_k^1 (t_2 - k)^{n-1} dt_2 = \alpha$$

or

$$n \cdot \left.\frac{(t_2 - k)^n}{n}\right|_k^1 = \alpha$$

or

$$(1-k)^n = \alpha; \quad k = 1 - \alpha^{1/n}$$

Therefore, UMP size-$\alpha$ test is given by

$$\phi_0(t_1, t_2) = \begin{cases} 1 & \text{if } 1 - \alpha^{1/n} < t_1 < t_2 < 1 \\ 0 & \text{otherwise} \end{cases}$$

**Example 3.3.31.** *Let $X_1, \ldots, X_n$ be a random sample drawn from uniform distribution $U(0,\ \theta)$. Find out a UMP size-$\alpha$ test for testing* (a) $H_0 : \theta \le \theta_0$ *against* $H_1 : \theta > \theta_0$, (b) $H_0 : \theta = \theta_0$ *against* $H_1 : \theta \ne \theta_0$.

***Solution:*** Let us consider $\theta_0 < \theta_1$ and the likelihood ratio

$$k(\mathbf{x}) = \frac{f(\mathbf{x}|\theta_1)}{f(\mathbf{x}|\theta_0)} = \frac{(1/\theta_1)^n I_{(T \le \theta_1)}}{(1/\theta_0)^n I_{(T \le \theta_0)}}$$

where $T = \max x_i$.

$$k(\mathbf{x}) = \begin{cases} \left(\dfrac{\theta_0}{\theta_1}\right)^n & \text{if } T \in (0, \theta_0) \\ \infty & \text{if } T \in (\theta_0, \theta_1) \end{cases}$$

which shows that $k(\mathbf{x})$ is non-decreasing in $T$, therefore, $U(0,\ \theta)$ has monotone ratio in $T$. By Karlin and Rubin theorem the UMP size-$\alpha$ test for testing $H_0 : \theta \leq \theta_0$ against $H_1 : \theta > \theta_0$ is given by

$$\phi(t) = \begin{cases} 1 & \text{if } t > t_0 \\ 0 & \text{otherwise} \end{cases}$$

where $t_0$ is determined by

$$E_{\theta_0}\phi(T) = \alpha$$

The density of $T$ is given by

$$g(t) = n[F(t)]^{n-1}f(t)$$

where $F$ is the distribution function of $X$. We have

$$F(t) = \int_0^t \frac{1}{\theta}dy = \frac{t}{\theta}$$

which gives

$$g(t) = n \cdot \left(\frac{t}{\theta}\right)^{n-1} \cdot \frac{1}{\theta} = \frac{nt^{n-1}}{\theta^n}$$

$t_0$ is obtained by size condition

$$E_{\theta_0}\phi(T) = \alpha \quad \text{or} \quad \int_{t_0}^{\theta_0} \frac{nt^{n-1}}{\theta_0^n}\, dt = \alpha$$

$$\frac{n}{\theta_0^n} \cdot \frac{t^n}{n}\bigg|_{t_0}^{\theta_0} = \alpha \quad \text{or} \quad \left(\frac{\theta_0}{\theta_0}\right)^n - \left(\frac{t_0}{\theta_0}\right)^n = \alpha; \quad t_0 = \theta_0(1-\alpha)^{1/n}$$

Therefore, the UMP size-$\alpha$ test is given by

$$\phi(t) = \begin{cases} 1 & \text{if } t > \theta_0(1-\alpha)^{1/n} \\ 0 & \text{otherwise} \end{cases}$$

The power of this test is given by

$$\beta_\phi(\theta) = \int_{\theta_0(1-\alpha)^{1/n}}^{\theta_1} g(t|\theta_1)\, dt = \frac{n}{\theta_1^n}\int_{\theta_0(1-\alpha)^{(1/n)}}^{\theta_1} t^{n-1}dt$$

$$= \frac{n}{\theta_1^n} \cdot \frac{t^n}{n}\bigg|_{\theta_0(1-\alpha)^{1/n}}^{\theta_1} = 1 - \left(\frac{\theta_0}{\theta_1}\right)^n(1-\alpha).$$

**Example 3.3.32.** *Whether there are more than one UMP tests for testing $H_0 : \theta = \theta_0$ against $H_1 : \theta = \theta_1 (\theta_1 > \theta_0)$ for $U(0, \theta)$? Discuss.*

***Solution:*** By Remark 2.2.7, the best test will be the function of the sufficient statistic, $T = \max X_i$ for $U(0, \theta)$; in addition to it is also minimal sufficient. Therefore, we consider

$$k(t) = \frac{g(t,\ \theta_1)}{g(t,\ \theta_0)} = \frac{\frac{nt^{n-1}}{\theta_1^n} I_{(0,\ \theta_1)}(t)}{\frac{nt^{n-1}}{\theta_0^n} I_{(0,\ \theta_0)}(t)} = \left(\frac{\theta_0}{\theta_1}\right)^n \frac{I_{(0,\ \theta_1)}(t)}{I_{(0,\ \theta_0)}(t)}$$

$$= \begin{cases} \left(\frac{\theta_0}{\theta_1}\right)^n & \text{if } 0 < t < \theta_0 \\ \infty & \text{if } t > \theta_0 \end{cases}$$

We see that $k(t)$ is an increasing function in $t$; and further the distribution of $k(T)|H_0$ is given by

$$P_{H_0}(k(T) \leq y) = G_{H_0}(y) = \begin{cases} 0 & \text{if } y < \left(\frac{\theta_0}{\theta_1}\right)^n \\ 1 & \text{if } y \geq \left(\frac{\theta_0}{\theta_1}\right)^n \end{cases}$$

Therefore, the NP lemma best test of size-$\alpha$ is given by

$$\phi(t) = \begin{cases} 1 & \text{if } k(t) > k \\ \gamma(t) & \text{if } k(t) = k \\ 0 & \text{if } k(t) < k \end{cases}$$

where $(k, \ \gamma(t))$ are calculated by the condition

$$E_{\theta_0}\phi(T) = \alpha$$

or

$$P_{H_0}[k(T) \leq k_\alpha] - \gamma_\alpha P_{\theta_0}[k(T) = k_\alpha] = 1 - \alpha$$

If one chooses $k_\alpha = \left(\frac{\theta_0}{\theta_1}\right)^n$, then we get $\gamma_\alpha = \alpha$ and MP test of size-$\alpha$ is given by

$$\phi(t) = \begin{cases} 1 & \text{if } k(t) > \left(\frac{\theta_0}{\theta_1}\right)^n \Rightarrow t > \theta_0 \\ \alpha & \text{if } k(t) > \left(\frac{\theta_0}{\theta_1}\right)^n \Rightarrow 0 < t < \theta_0 \end{cases}$$

or

$$\phi(t) = \begin{cases} 1 & \text{if } t > \theta_0 \\ \alpha & \text{if } 0 < t < \theta_0 \end{cases}$$

The size of this test is $\alpha$ and power at $\theta_1$

$$\beta_\psi(\theta_1) = E_{\theta_1}\phi(T) = \int_{\theta_0}^{\theta_1} g(t|\theta_1)dt + \alpha \int_0^{\theta_0} g(t|\theta_1)dt$$

$$= \frac{t^n}{\theta_1^n}\bigg|_{\theta_0}^{\theta_1} + \alpha \frac{t^n}{\theta_1^n}\bigg|_0^{\theta_0} = 1 - \left(\frac{\theta_0}{\theta_1}\right)^n + \alpha\left(\frac{\theta_0}{\theta_1}\right)^n$$

$$= 1 - \left(\frac{\theta_0}{\theta_1}\right)^n (1 - \alpha)$$

The test $\phi$ is, therefore, UMP of size-$\alpha$ for testing $H_0 : \theta \leq \theta_0$ against $H_1 : \theta > \theta_0$. Note the test $\phi$ attains the same power as by the KR test in Example 3.3.31.

Next, consider a test $\phi_1$ defined by

$$\phi_1(t) = \begin{cases} 1 & \text{if } t > \theta_0 \\ \gamma(t) & \text{if } 0 < t < \theta_0 \end{cases}$$

where, $0 \leq \gamma(t) < 1$ so that $\int_0^{\theta_0} \gamma(t) \frac{nt^{n-1}}{\theta_0^n} \, dt = \alpha$.
The power of the test $\phi_1(t)$ at $\theta_1$ is given by

$$\begin{aligned}\beta_{\phi_1}(\theta_1) &= \int_{\theta_0}^{\theta_1} \frac{nt^{n-1}}{\theta_1^n} \, dt + \int_0^{\theta_0} \gamma(t) \, \frac{nt^{n-1}}{\theta_1^n} \, dt \\ &= 1 - \left(\frac{\theta_0}{\theta_1}\right)^n + \left(\frac{\theta_0}{\theta_1}\right)^n \int_0^{\theta_0} \gamma(t) \frac{nt^{n-1}}{\theta_0^n} \, dt \\ &= 1 - \left(\frac{\theta_0}{\theta_1}\right)^n + \left(\frac{\theta_0}{\theta_1}\right)^n \alpha \\ &\qquad \text{(by the size condition)} \\ &= 1 - \left(\frac{\theta_0}{\theta_1}\right)^n (1 - \alpha)\end{aligned}$$

This shows that there are several size-$\alpha$ tests given by $\int_0^{\theta_0} \gamma(t) \cdot \frac{nt^{n-1}}{\theta_0^n} \, dt = \alpha$ which attain the same power as attained by KR UMP test of size-$\alpha$; and we obtain another test $\phi_1$ which is UMP size-$\alpha$ test for the same testing problem. Further, let $\gamma(t)$ be given by

$$\gamma(t) = \begin{cases} 0 & \text{if } 0 < t < a \\ 1 & \text{if } a \leq t < \theta_0 \end{cases}$$

where $\alpha$ is obtained by

$$E_{\theta_0}[\phi_1(T)] = \alpha$$

$$\int_a^{\theta_0} \frac{nt^{n-1}}{\theta_0^n} \, dt = \alpha$$

or

$$\left.\frac{t^n}{\theta_0^n}\right|_a^{\theta_0} = \alpha$$

or

$$1 - \left(\frac{a}{\theta_0}\right)^n = \alpha$$

or

$$(1 - \alpha)^{1/n} \cdot \theta_0 = a$$

and the test $\phi_1$ in this case is given by

$$\phi_1(t) = \begin{cases} 1 & \text{if } t > \theta_0(1-\alpha)^{1/n} \\ 0 & \text{otherwise} \end{cases}$$

Note $\phi_1$ has the same power as of KR UMP size-$\alpha$ test. Similarly, if we take

$$\gamma(t) = \begin{cases} 1 & \text{if } 0 < t < b \\ 0 & \text{if } b \le t < \theta_0 \end{cases}$$

leads to a test

$$\phi(t) = \begin{cases} 1 & \text{if } 0 < t < \theta_0 \alpha^{1/n} \\ 0 & \text{otherwise} \end{cases}$$

which is further a UMP test of size-$\alpha$ for testing $H_0 : \theta \le \theta_0$ against $H_1 : \theta > \theta_0$. This shows that the UMP size-$\alpha$ test is not unique. Therefore, one could state that the UMP test

$$\phi(t) = \begin{cases} 1 & \text{if } t > \theta_0 \\ \alpha & \text{if } t \le \theta_0 \end{cases}$$

is not admissible.

**Example 3.3.33.** *For the family of distribution*

$$f(x|\,\theta) = \theta\,(\theta + x)^{-2}, \qquad x \ge 0;\;\; \theta > 0$$

*obtain the UMP test for testing* (a) $H_0 : \theta = 2$ *against* $H_1 : \theta > 2$ *and* (b) $H_0 : \theta \le 2$ *against* $H_1 : \theta > 2$

***Solution:*** (a) Consider

$$\begin{aligned} A(x) &= \frac{f(x|\theta_1)}{f(x|2)} \quad \text{so that } \theta_1 > 2 \\ &= \frac{\theta_1}{2}\frac{(2+x)^2}{(\theta_1+x)^2} \\ A'(x) &= \frac{\theta}{2}\cdot\frac{2(2+x)(\theta_1+x)(\theta_1-2)}{(\theta_1+x)^4} > 0 \quad \text{since } \theta_1 > 2 \end{aligned}$$

This shows that $f(x|\theta_1)/f(x|\theta_2)$ is an increasing function of $x$. Therefore, best test for testing $\theta = 2$ against $\theta = \theta_1$ is given by

$$\phi(x) = \begin{cases} 1 & \text{if } x > k \\ 0 & \text{otherwise} \end{cases}$$

where $k$ is obtained by

$$E_2\phi(X) = \alpha \;\text{ or }\; P_2[X > k] = \alpha \;\text{ this gives }\; k = 2(1/\alpha - 1)$$

Note the test $\phi$ is independent of the choice of alternative $\theta_1$, therefore, the same test is UMP of size-$\alpha$ for testing $H_0 : \theta = 2$ against $H_1 : \theta > 2$.
(b) Let $\theta_1 < \theta_2$, consider

$$\frac{f_{\theta_2}(x)}{f_{\theta_1}(x)} = \frac{\theta_2 \left(\theta_2 + x\right)^{-2}}{\theta_1 \left(\theta_1 + x\right)^{-2}} = \lambda(x) \quad \text{(say)}$$

Consider two points $x$ and $x'$ for which

$$h(x) < h(x')$$

$$\frac{\theta_2 \left(\theta_2 + x\right)^{-2}}{\theta_1 \left(\theta_1 + x\right)^{-2}} < \frac{\theta_2 \left(\theta_2 + x'\right)^{-2}}{\theta_1 \left(\theta_1 + x'\right)^{-2}}$$

$$\left(\frac{\theta_1 + x}{\theta_2 + x}\right)^2 < \left(\frac{\theta_1 + x'}{\theta_2 + x^1}\right)^2$$

$$\theta_1\theta_2 + \theta_1 x' + x\theta_2 + xx' < \theta_1\theta_2 + \theta_1 x + \theta_2 x' + xx'$$

$$x(\theta_2 - \theta_1) < x'(\theta_2 - \theta_1)$$

$$x < x' \text{ since } \theta_2 - \theta_1 > 0$$

This shows $f_{\theta_2}/f_{\theta_1}$ is increasing in $x$ and the UMP test for testing $H_0 : \theta \leq 2$ against $H_1 : \theta > 2$ is given by

$$\phi(x) = \begin{cases} 1 & \text{if } x > x_0 \\ 0 & \text{otherwise} \end{cases}$$

where, $x_0$ is obtained by

$$E_{\theta_0}[\phi(X)] = \alpha$$

or

$$2\int_{x_0}^{\infty} (2 + x)^{-2}\, dx = \alpha$$

or

$$2 \cdot \left.\frac{(2 + x)^{-1}}{-1}\right|_{x_0}^{\infty} = \alpha$$

gives

$$x_0 = 2/\alpha - 2 = 2(1/\alpha - 1)$$

So the UMP test for testing $H_0 : \theta \leq 2$ against $H_1 : \theta > 2$ is given by

$$\phi(x) = \begin{cases} 1 & \text{if } x > 2(1/\alpha - 1) \\ 0 & \text{if } x \leq 2(1/\alpha - 1) \end{cases}$$

**Example 3.3.34.** *Consider a random sample of size n from $U(0, \theta)$. Suggest a UMP size-$\alpha$ test for testing $H_0 : \theta = \theta_0$ against $H_1 : \theta \neq \theta_0$.*

***Solution:*** The testing problem $H_0 : \theta = \theta_0$ against $H_1 : \theta \neq \theta_0$ is called two-sided testing problem which we would discuss in detail in chapter 4. In the present example a simple attempt is made by utilizing the techniques developed in this chapter to identify a UMP size-$\alpha$ test for this two-sided testing problem. For this we put up the two-sided testing problem $\theta = \theta_0$ against $\theta \neq \theta_0$ as the union of two one-sided testing problems namely, $\theta = \theta_0$ against $\theta > \theta_0$ and $\theta = \theta_0$ against $\theta < \theta_0$. We have already given a UMP size-$\alpha$ test for testing $\theta = \theta_0$ against $\theta > \theta_0$ in Example 3.3.32, namely:

$$\phi_1(t) = \begin{cases} 1 & \text{if } \ t > \theta_0 \\ \gamma(t) & \text{if } \ 0 < t < \theta_0 \end{cases} \tag{3.21}$$

where $\gamma(t)$ is chosen so that, $\int_0^{\theta_0} \gamma(t) \frac{nt^{n-1}}{\theta_0^n}\, dt = \alpha$.

Next, consider the testing problem $H_0 : \theta = \theta_0$ against $H_1 : \theta < \theta_0$ and for some $\theta_1$ in $H_1$ take

$$k(t) = \begin{cases} \left(\frac{\theta_0}{\theta_1}\right)^n & \text{if } \ 0 < t < \theta_1 \\ 0 & \text{if } \ \theta_1 < t < \theta_0 \end{cases}$$

which means the monotone likelihood ratio $k(t)$ is decreasing in $t$; the UMP test of size-$\alpha$, therefore, is given by

$$\phi_2(t) = \begin{cases} \gamma(t) & \text{if } \ 0 < t < \theta_1 \\ 0 & \text{if } \ \theta_1 \leq t < \theta_0 \end{cases}$$

where, $\gamma(t)$ is obtained such that $\int_0^{\theta_1} \gamma(t) \frac{nt^{n-1}}{\theta_0^n}\, dt = \alpha$ , where $\theta_1$ in $H_1$. The power of the test $\phi_2$ is given by, $\beta_{\phi_2}(\theta_1) = \int_0^{\theta_1} \gamma(t) \cdot \frac{nt^{n-1}}{\theta_1^n}\, dt = \left(\frac{\theta_0}{\theta_1}\right)^n \int_0^{\theta_1} \gamma(t) \cdot \frac{nt^{n-1}}{\theta_0}\, dt = \left(\frac{\theta_0}{\theta_1}\right)^n \cdot \alpha < 1$(since $\theta_1 < \theta_0 < 1$). Note that the test $\phi_2$ depends on particular $\theta_1$ chosen from $H_1$ and we get different tests $\phi_2$ for different choices of $\theta_1$ in $H_1$. To come out of this problem we take $\gamma(t) = 1$ for $0 < t < a < \theta_1$ and modify the test $\phi_2$ as

$$\phi_2(t) = \begin{cases} 1 & \text{if } \ 0 < t < a < \theta_1 \\ 0 & \text{if } \ a \leq t \leq \theta_0 \end{cases}$$

where, $a$ is obtained by $\int_0^a \frac{nt^{n-1}}{\theta_0^n}\, dt = \alpha$, $\left(\frac{a}{\theta_0}\right)^n = \alpha$ or $a = \theta_0 \cdot \alpha^{1/n}$. Further, the power of the test $\phi_2$ is obtained as

$$\begin{aligned} \beta_{\phi_2}(\theta_1) &= \int_0^a \frac{nt^{n-1}}{\theta_1^n}\, dt \\ &= \left(\frac{a}{\theta_1}\right)^n = \left(\frac{\theta_0}{\theta_1}\right)^n \alpha \quad \text{if } \ a = \theta_0\, \alpha^{1/n} < \theta_1 \\ &= 1 \qquad\qquad\qquad\quad\ \text{if } \ a = \theta_0\, \alpha^{1/n} > \theta_1 \end{aligned}$$

Therefore, the UMP size-$\alpha$ test for testing $H_0 : \theta = \theta_0$ against $H_1 : \theta < \theta_0$ is given by

$$\phi_2(t) = \begin{cases} 1 & \text{if } \; 0 < t < \theta_0 \cdot \alpha^{1/n} \\ 0 & \text{if } \; \theta_0 \cdot \alpha^{1/n} \leq t < \theta_0 \end{cases} \tag{3.22}$$

which is seen to be independent of a particular alternative $\theta_1$ chosen.

We can now combine the test $\phi_1$ in Eq. (3.21) and $\phi_2$ in Eq. (3.22) as a proposed test for testing $\theta = \theta_0$ against $\theta \neq \theta_0$

$$\phi(t) = \begin{cases} 1 & \text{if } \; 0 < t < \theta_0\, \alpha^{1/n} \text{ and } t > \theta_0 \\ 0 & \text{if } \; \theta_0\, \alpha^{1/n} < t \leq \theta_0 \end{cases}$$

then $\phi(t)$ is of size-$\alpha$ and has the power $\beta_\phi(\theta) = \int_0^\theta \frac{nt^{n-1}}{\theta^n} dt = 1$ if $\theta < \theta_0 \alpha^{1/n}$ and $\int_0^{\theta_0 \alpha^{1/n}} \frac{nt^{n-1}}{\theta^n}\, dt = \left(\frac{\theta_0}{\theta}\right)^n \cdot \alpha$ if $\theta_0 \alpha^{1/n} < \theta \leq \theta_0$ and $\int_0^{\theta_0 \alpha^{1/n}} \frac{nt^{n-1}}{\theta^n}\, dt + \int_{\theta_0}^{\theta} \frac{nt^{n-1}}{\theta}\, dt = \alpha \cdot \left(\frac{\theta_0}{\theta}\right)^n + 1 - \left(\frac{\theta_0}{\theta}\right)^n = 1 - \left(\frac{\theta_0}{\theta}\right)^n (1-\alpha)$ if $\theta > \theta_0$. Therefore, this test $\phi$ is UMP size-$\alpha$ test for testing $H_0 : \theta = \theta_0$ against $H_1 : \theta \neq \theta_0$.

## *Review Questions*

**3.1** (a) For a one-sided testing problem define (i) size of a test (ii) power function of a test (iii) UMP test (iv) UMPU tests.

(b) State and prove Karlin Rubin theorem.

**3.2** What do you mean by the family of distribution having a monotone likelihood ratio(MLR)? Explain its relevance in constructing a UMP test with an example.

**3.3** (a) Define a family of distributions having monotone likelihood ratio. Show that the family of Cauchy distributions $\{\mathcal{C}(\theta, 1),\ \theta \in \mathbb{R}^1\}$, does not have the monotone likelihood ratio.

(b) Show that one-parameter exponential family

$$f(\mathbf{x}|\theta) = \exp\{Q(\theta)T(\mathbf{x}) \; + \; S(\mathbf{x}) + D(\theta)\}$$

has MLR in $T(\mathbf{x})$, where, $Q(\theta)$ is non-decreasing.

**3.4** Let $p(x|\theta)$ be a pdf with monotone likelihood ratio in $T(x)$ where $\theta$ is a real parameter. Show that for testing $H_0 : \theta \leq \theta_0$ against $H_1 : \theta > \theta_0$, there exists a UMP test given by

$$\phi(x) = \begin{cases} 1 & \text{if } \; T(x) > c \\ \gamma & \text{if } \; T(x) = c \\ 0 & \text{if } \; T(x) < c \end{cases}$$

where $c$ and $\gamma$ are determined by $E_{\theta_0}\{\phi(X)\} = \alpha$.

Furthermore, if $\beta(\theta) = E_\theta\{\phi(X)\}$ is the power function of the above test, show that:

(a) $\beta(\theta)$ is strictly increasing for all $\theta$ for which $\beta(\theta) < 1$.

(b) For all $\theta'$, the test determined above is UMP for testing $H_0 : \theta \leq \theta'$ against $H_1 : \theta > \theta'$ at level $\alpha' = \beta(\theta')$

(c) Give an application of the result (a) in deriving the UMP test.

**3.5** Given a random sample of size $n$ from Bernoulli $(1, \theta)$ distribution, find the UMP size-$\alpha$ test of $H_0 : \theta = \theta_0$ against $H_1 : \theta > \theta_0$. Derive the power function $\beta(\theta)$ of the test.

**3.6** (a) When is a family of pdf's said to have MLR in some statistic $T(\mathbf{x})$? If $X_1, X_2, \ldots, X_n$ is a random sample from exponential distribution with mean $\theta$, verify whether the family of exponential distribution has MLR in some statistic $T(\mathbf{x})$. Obtain UMP test of size-$\alpha$ for testing $H_0 : \theta \leq \theta_0$ against $H_1 : \theta > \theta_0$.

(b) Let $X_1, X_2, \ldots, X_n$ be a random sample from a pdf

$$f(x \mid \theta) = \begin{cases} \theta\, x^{\theta-1} & \text{if } 0 \leq x \leq 1,\ \theta > 0 \\ 0 & \text{otherwise} \end{cases}$$

Obtain a level-$\alpha$ UMP test for testing $H_0 : \theta = 2$ against $H_1 : \theta > 2$. Determine also its power function and sketch its graph.

**3.7** Given the two possible distribution for $X$ (labelled $\theta_1$ and $\theta_2$) in the following probability table, determine a statistic $T$ such that the likelihood ratio is monotone in $T$.

| | $x_1$ | $x_2$ | $x_3$ | $x_4$ | $x_5$ |
|---|---|---|---|---|---|
| $\theta_1$ | 0.2 | 0.3 | 0.1 | 0.3 | 0.1 |
| $\theta_2$ | 0.3 | 0.1 | 0.3 | 0.2 | 0.1 |

Determine the most powerful test (a) in terms of $T$ (b) in terms of $x'$. Determine the most powerful test of size 0.3 and compare its power with that of critical region $\{x_4\}$.

**3.8** Prove the following:

(a) A family of distributions $\{f_\theta,\ \theta \in \Theta\}$ has monotone likelihood ratio in $x$ if and only if

$$\frac{\partial^2 \log f_\theta(x)}{\partial\theta\, \partial x} \geq 0 \qquad \forall\ \theta \text{ and } \forall\ x$$

if this mixed derivative exists.

(b) The equivalent form of this necessary and sufficient condition is that

$$f_\theta(x)\, \frac{\partial^2 f_\theta(x)}{\partial\theta\, \partial x} \geq \frac{\partial f_\theta(x)}{\partial\theta} \cdot \frac{\partial f_\theta(x)}{\partial x} \qquad \forall\ \theta \text{ and } x$$

**3.9** Let $X_1, X_2, \ldots, X_n$ be a random sample from a Poisson distribution with parameter $\theta$. Obtain UMP test of $H_0 : \theta = \theta_0$ against $H_1 : \theta > \theta_0$ at a level $\alpha$. Show that the power function of the test is monotonic increasing in $\theta$. Is this test unbiased for the alternative $\theta_1 (< \theta_0)$? Explain your answer.

**3.10** A laboratory is testing $n$ components of a computer simultaneously. The failure times (or length of life) of these components are independently and identically distributed with the density

$$f(x;\ \theta) = \frac{1}{2\theta}\ \exp\{-x/2\theta\}, \quad x \geq 0,\ \ \theta > 0$$

Each component is immediately replaced by a new one. Let $Y_i,\ i = 1, 2, \ldots$ denote the waiting time (measured from some fixed time) for the $i^{th}$ replacement to take place. Observation is continued until $r (< n)$ replacements are made. On the basis of observations $Y_1, Y_2, \ldots, Y_r$, determine a uniformly most powerful size-$\alpha$ test for testing $H_0 : \theta \geq \theta_0$ against $H_1 : \theta < \theta_0$ where, $\theta_0$ is some given number.

Also, derive the distribution of the test statistic you use.

**3.11** State the role of sufficient statistic in constructing tests for composite hypothesis. Let $X_1, X_2, \ldots, X_n$ be a random sample from a normal population $N(\mu,\ \sigma^2)$, $\mu$ being known. Find UMP of for $H_0 : \sigma \leq \sigma_0$ against $H_1 : \sigma > \sigma_0$.

**3.12** (a) When is a real parameter family of probability densities said to have monotone likelihood ratio? Verify whether the following families of densities have this property or not

$$\text{(i) } f(x,\ \theta) = \frac{1}{\theta},\quad \theta > 0 \qquad \text{(ii) } f(x,\ \theta) = \frac{1}{\pi\ [1 + (x - \theta)^2]}$$

(b) Let $X_1, \ldots, X_n$ be a random sample from $N(\mu,\ \sigma^2)$ where $\sigma^2$ is known. Obtain the UMP test for

$$H_0 : \mu \leq \mu_0 \text{ against } H_1 : \mu > \mu_0$$

at a level $\alpha$. Show that the power function of the test is monotonically increasing in $n$.

**3.13** Let $X_1, X_2, \ldots, X_n$ be independent random variables with density of an exponential distribution with mean $\theta$, i.e.

$$f(x;\theta) = \begin{cases} 1/\theta e^{-x/\theta} & \text{if } x \geq 0 \\ 0 & \text{if } x < 0 \end{cases}$$

where, $\theta$ is unknown.

Based on a random sample of size 31, find a UMP test for $\alpha = 0.05$ to test $H_0 : \theta = 10$ against $H_1 : \theta > 10$.

**3.14** (a) When is a family of densities said to have monotone likelihood ratio? Show that the one-parameter exponential family of densities belong to this class of MLR densities.

(b) On the basis of a random sample of size $n$ from distribution with pdf

$$f_\theta(x) = \begin{cases} \theta e^{-\theta x} & \text{if } x > 0, \;\; \theta > 0 \\ 0 & \text{otherwise} \end{cases}$$

Derive the MP critical region for testing $H_0 : \theta = \theta_0$ against $H_1 : \theta = \theta_1 (> \theta_0)$. Will this region be UMP against $H_1 : \theta > \theta_0$? Will this region be also MP against $H_1 : \theta = \theta_2 (< \theta_0)$?

(c) Let $X_1, X_2, \ldots, X_n$ be a random sample from a distribution with pmf $p_\theta(x) = \theta^x (1-\theta)^{1-x}$, if $x = 0, 1$ $(0 < \theta < 1)$. Find the UMP critical region of size-$\alpha$, for testing $H_0 : \theta = \theta_0$ against $H_1 : \theta > \theta_0$.

**3.15** Let $X$ have a probability mass function

$$P_M = P(X = x) = \frac{\binom{M}{x}\binom{N-M}{n-x}}{\binom{N}{n}}; \quad x \geq \max(0, M + n - N)$$
$$\text{and} \;\; x \leq \min(M, n)$$

Show that the family $\{P_M\}$ has a monotone likelihood ratio in $x$. Hence, obtain a uniformly most powerful test (UMPT) of size-$\alpha$ for $H_0 : M \leq M_0$ against $H_1 : M > M_0$.

**3.16** If $X$ has the pareto distribution $P(c, \tau)$ with density,

$$f(x|c, \tau) = \frac{c\tau^c}{x^{c+1}}, \quad 0 < \tau < x, \; c = 0$$

(a) If $X$ has distribution $P(c, \tau)$, then show that $Y = \log X$ has exponential distribution $E(\xi, b)$ with $\xi = \log \tau, \; b = 1/c$.

(b) If $X_1, \ldots, X_n$ is a sample from $P(c, \tau)$. Use $(a)$ to obtain UMP test of (i) $H_0 : \tau = \tau_0$ against $H_1 : \tau \neq \tau_0$ when $b$ is known ; (ii) $H_0 : c = c_0, \; \tau = \tau_0$ against $c > c_0, \; \tau > \tau_0$.

**3.17** A random variable $X$ has Weibull distribution $W(b, \; c)$ with density

$$\frac{c}{b}\left(\frac{x}{b}\right)^{c-1} e^{-(x/b)^c}, \quad x > 0, \;\; b, \; c > 0$$

If $X_1, \ldots, X_n$ is a sample from $W(b, \; c)$, with the shape parameter $c$ known, show that there exist a UMP test of $H_0 : b \leq b_0$ against $H_1 : b > b_0$ and give its form.

**3.18** Consider a single observation $X$ from $W(1, \; c)$, i.e.

$$c\, x^{c-1} e^{-x^c} \qquad x > 0, \; c > 0$$

(a) Show the MP test for testing $H_0 : c = 1$ against $H_1 : c = 2$ is given by

$$\phi(x) = \begin{cases} 1 & \text{if } x < k_1, \text{ and } x > k_2 \\ 0 & \text{otherwise} \end{cases}$$

Show how to determine $k_1$ and $k_2$.
[***Hint:*** Consider

$$A(x) = \frac{f(x|c_1)}{f(x|c_0)} = \frac{c_1}{c_0} x^{c_1 - c_0} \exp\{-(x^{c_1} - x^{c_0})\}$$
$$= 2x \exp\{-(x^2 - 1)\}$$

A(x) is increasing if $x < 1$ and decreasing if $x > 1$]

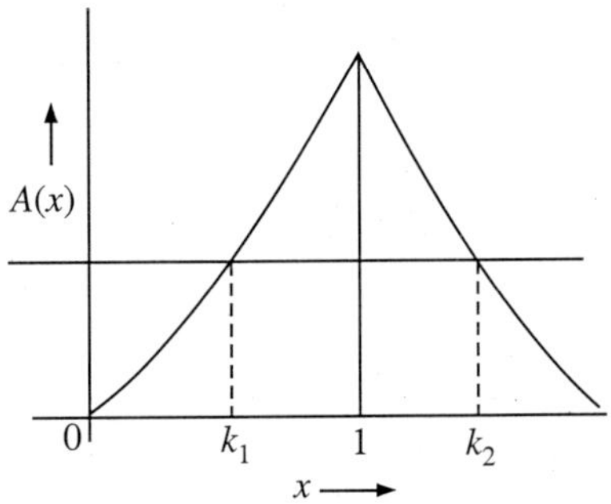


**Figure 3.6:**

(b) Generalize (a) to arbitrary alternative $c > 1$, and show that a UMP test of $H_0 : c = 1$ against $H_1 : c > 1$ does not exist.

(c) Show for any $c_1 > 1$, the power function of the MP test of $H_0 : c = 1$ against $c = c_1$ is an increasing function of $c$.

**3.19** Let $X_1, \ldots, X_n$ be a sample from inverse gaussian distribution $I(\mu, \tau)$ with density

$$\sqrt{\frac{\tau}{2\pi x^3}} \exp\{-\frac{\tau}{2x\mu^2}(x - \mu)^2\}, \quad x > 0; \quad \tau, \ \mu > 0$$

Show that there exists a UMP test for testing

(a) $H_0 : \mu \leq \mu_0$ against $H_1 : \mu > \mu_0$ when $\tau$ is known.

(b) $H_0 : \tau \leq \tau_0$ against $H_1 : \tau > \tau_0$ when $\mu$ is known.
In each case give the form of the rejection region.

**3.20** Consider the uniform $U(\theta, \ \theta + 1)$.

(a) Show that the family has monotone likelihood ratio, hence write down the form of a UMP test of its size for testing $H_0 : \theta \leq 0$ against $H_1 : \theta > 0$.

(b) Let $X_1, X_2, \ldots, X_n$ be a sample of size $n$ from the above population. Show that a UMP size-$\alpha$ test for the above hypothesis against the above alternative exists in the form

$$\phi(x_1, \ldots, x_n) = \begin{cases} 0 & \text{if } \min X_i < k \text{ and } \max X_i < 1 \\ 1 & \text{otherwise} \end{cases}$$

Find the value of $k$ that makes this a size-$\alpha$ test.

**3.21** (a) If the loss function satisfies certain regularity conditions and the distribution of random variable $X$ has monotone likelihood ratio, then show that the class of one-sided test given by Karlin-Rubin theorem is essentially complete.

(b) Let $X_1, X_2, \ldots, X_n$ be a random sample from the rectangular distribution:

$$f(x|\theta) = \frac{1}{\theta}, \qquad 0 \le x \le \theta$$

Obtain a UMP test for testing $H_0 : \theta = 1$ against $H_1 : \theta \neq 1$.

**3.22** (a) Let $\theta$ be a real parameter and the random variable $x$ have probability density with MLR in $T(x)$. Determine a size-$\alpha$ UMP test of $H_0 : \theta \le \theta_0$ against $H_1 : \theta > \theta_0$.

(b) Let $X_1, X_2, \ldots, X_n$ be a random sample from a rectangular distribution $r(0, \theta)$. Show that for testing $H_0 : \theta = \theta_0$ against $H_1 : \theta > \theta_0$, any critical region $W$ for which $P_{\theta_0}(W) = \alpha$ and which necessarily includes the sample point if $\max(x_1, \ldots, x_n) > \theta_0$ is UMP at level $\alpha$.

**3.23** Given a random sample $X_1, X_2, \ldots, X_n$ from a uniform distribution $U(\theta, \theta')$, find the form of a best test of size-$\alpha$ for $H_0 : \theta = \theta_0$ against $H_1 : \theta = \theta_1$, when $\theta_1 > \theta_0$ ($\theta_0$ and $\theta_1$ are pre-assigned values). Show that there exist a uniformly most powerful test if the alternative hypothesis is $H_1 : \theta > \theta_0$.

# Chapter 4

# Two-sided Uniformly Most Powerful Tests and UMP Unbiased Tests

## 4.1 INTRODUCTION

In Chapter 3, we learnt that UMP test of a one-sided hypothesis testing problem exists in the class of all size-$\alpha$ tests when the family of distributions have monotone likelihood ratio. In this chapter, we consider the problem of finding a UMP test of size-$\alpha$ of two-sided testing problems

(i) $H_0 : \theta \leq \theta_1$ or $\theta \geq \theta_2 (\theta_1 < \theta_2)$
against $H_1 : \theta_1 < \theta < \theta_2$

(ii) $H_0 : \theta_1 \leq \theta \leq \theta_2$
against $H_1 : \theta < \theta_1$ or $\theta > \theta_2$

(iii) $H_0 : \theta = \theta_0$
against $H_1 : \theta \neq \theta_0$

For the problem of type (i) when a class of size-$\alpha$ tests is considered, and the family is one-parameter exponential distributions, a UMP test has been shown to exist in Section 4.2. But, unfortunately, under these conditions, a UMP test does not exist for problems (ii) and (iii). Whereas, if the class of size-$\alpha$ tests is reduced to a class by taking only the unbiased tests and the family of distributions is Polya type-3, we will learn in Section 4.3 and 4.4, that a UMP test exists for testing problems of the type (ii) and (iii).

**Definition 4.1.1.** A family of distributions $\mathcal{P} = \{P_\theta, \theta \in \Theta\}$ is known as one-parameter exponential family if its density is given by (with respect to some common measure $\mu$)

$$f_\theta(x \mid \theta) = c(\theta) \cdot \exp\{Q(\theta)T(x)\} \cdot h(x) \tag{4.1}$$

where $Q$ is strictly monotone.

A real life application of the testing problem of type $H_0 : \theta \leq \theta_1$ or $\theta \geq \theta_2$ against $H_1 : \theta_1 < \theta < \theta_2$ could be, when one wishes to test whether a given measuring instrument is properly balanced. In this case the null hypothesis $\theta \leq \theta_1$ or $\theta \geq \theta_2$ states that the instrument is out-of-balance. The probability of type I error becomes the probability to declare whether the instrument is within the prescribed limits of errors, whereas the fact is, it is not. This is a fatal error since incorrect weighing may results into heavy economic losses and bad reputation to company, so it must be timely controlled. On the other hand, on account of probability of type II error, i.e. we accept $H_0$ when it is false or we declare that the instrument is out-of-balance (whereas we know that it is not) it is only an opportunity loss. Therefore, we see that the probability of type I error is more serious as compared to type II error.

For the above two-sided testing problem we would, therefore, search for a test whose power $E_\theta \phi(X)$ is smallest in $\theta < \theta_1$ or $\theta > \theta_2$, and largest in $\theta_1 \leq \theta \leq \theta_2$ when compared to any other test $\phi$ in the class of level $\alpha$ tests. A test $\phi$ for this testing problem is known as a two-sided test if it is of the form

$$\phi(x) = \begin{cases} 1 & \text{if } x_1 < x < x_2 \\ \gamma_i & \text{if } x = x_i\,; \quad i = 1, 2. \\ 0 & \text{if } x < x_1 \quad \text{or} \quad x > x_2 \end{cases} \tag{4.2}$$

for some suitable values of $x_1,\ x_2$ s.t., $x_1 \leq x_2$ and $0 \leq \gamma_i \leq 1,\ i = 1, 2$. Note that $x_1$ may be equal to $x_2$ and there would be just a randomization factor $\gamma$ on the boundary point $x_1 = x_2 = x_0$. In such a case there would be no critical region. Further, if $x_1 = -\infty$, the corresponding critical region is given by $(-\infty,\ x_2)$ and if $x_2 = +\infty$ the corresponding critical region is given by $(x_1,\ \infty)$ and the two-sided tests with such critical regions become one-sided tests. Therefore, we see that the class of two-sided tests contains the class of one-sided tests as its subclass.

## 4.2 TWO-SIDED UMP TESTS FOR TESTING $H_0 : \theta \leq \theta_1$ OR $\theta \geq \theta_2$ VERSUS $H_1 : \theta_1 < \theta < \theta_2$

Theorem 4.2.1 states the existence of a UMP test for testing two-sided hypothesis $H_0 : \theta \leq \theta_1$ or $\theta \geq \theta_2$ against $H_1 : \theta_1 < \theta < \theta_2$ when the distribution of $X$ belongs to one-parameter exponential family. The proof of the theorem has been given following the lines of Lehmann, 1986 [130].

**Theorem 4.2.1.** (a) *Let the distribution of $X$ belongs to $\mathcal{P} = \{P_\theta,\ \theta \in \Theta\}$ is one-parameter exponential family of distributions, the density corresponding to $P_\theta$ is given by (4.1). Let the family $\mathcal{P}$ admits a sufficient statistic $T = T(X)$ whose distribution again belongs to one parameter exponential family and is* *given by*

$$dP_\theta(t) = C(\theta)\exp\{Q(\theta)t\}d\nu(t) \tag{4.3}$$

*with* $Q(\theta)$ *strictly increasing. Consider the testing problem* $H_0 : \theta \leq \theta_1$ *or* $\theta \geq \theta_2 (\theta_1 < \theta_2)$ *against* $H_1 : \theta_1 < \theta < \theta_2$*, the test*

$$\phi_0[T(x)] = \begin{cases} 1 & \text{if } c_1 < T(x) < c_2 \quad (c_1 < c_2) \\ \gamma_i & \text{if } T(x) = c_i; \quad i = 1, 2. \\ 0 & \text{if } T(x) < c_1 \text{ or } T(x) > c_2 \end{cases} \tag{4.4}$$

*where,* $\gamma_1,\ \gamma_2,\ c_1,\ c_2$ *are determined by*

$$E_{\theta_1}\phi_0[T(X)] = E_{\theta_2}\phi_0[T(X)] = \alpha \tag{4.5}$$

*is UMP test of size-*$\alpha$ *in* $C_\alpha$*, where* $C_\alpha$ *is defined as*

$$C_\alpha = \{\phi \in \mathcal{D} \,|\, E_{\theta_1}\phi[T(X)] = \alpha = E_{\theta_2}\phi[T(X)]\}$$

(b) *The test in* (a) *minimizes* $E_\theta\phi(X)$ *for all* $\theta < \theta_1$ *and* $\theta > \theta_2$ *among all the tests in* $\mathcal{C}_\alpha$.
(c) *For* $0 < \alpha < 1$*, the power function of this test has a maximum at a point* $\theta_0$ *between* $\theta_1$ *and* $\theta_2$ *and decreases strictly as* $\theta$ *tends away from* $\theta_0$ *in either direction, unless there exist two values* $t_1,\ t_2$ *such that*

$$P_\theta\{T(X) = t_1\} + P_\theta\{T(X) = t_2\} = 1 \quad \forall\, \theta \tag{4.6}$$

*Proof.* (a) The attention is restricted to the tests which are the function of the sufficient statistic $T(X)$ for the given two-sided testing problem, since such a statistic would contain as much information on $\theta$ as the observation $X$ originally contained. Consider the class of tests

$$C_\alpha = \{\phi \in \mathcal{D} : E_{\theta_1}\phi(T) = \alpha;\ E_{\theta_2}\phi(T) = \alpha\}$$

and the set $S$ of points

$$S = \{(E_{\theta_1}\phi(T),\ E_{\theta_2}\phi(T)) \text{ for variations over all critical functions } \phi\}$$

corresponding to the trivial test $\phi(t) \equiv \alpha$, rejecting $H_0$ irrespective of the value of $T(X) = t$, the diagonal line $\{(\alpha, \alpha) : E_{\theta_1}\phi(T) = \alpha, E_{\theta_2}\phi(T) = \alpha\}$ is contained in $S$. Further, there exists a most powerful test of size-$\alpha$ for testing $\theta_1$ against $\theta_2$ by part (a) of Theorem 2.2.1, with its power $E_{\theta_2}\phi(T) = u_2 > E_{\theta_1}\phi(T) = \alpha$ by Remark 2.2.8. This shows that if $(\alpha, \alpha)$ for $\alpha$, $0 < \alpha < 1$, is the point of $S$, there exists a point $(\alpha, u_2)$, $u_2 > \alpha$ in $S$. The point $(1-\alpha, 1-u_2)$ belongs to the set $S$ since if $\phi$ is a test, $(1-\phi)$ is also a test. Therefore, there exists a point $(\alpha, u_1)$, $u_1 < \alpha$, in $S$ for $\alpha$, $0 < \alpha < 1$. Since $S$ is convex, and it contain points $(\alpha, u_1), (\alpha, u_2)$, it also contain points on the line joining these two points. This shows that each point

$(\alpha, \alpha)$, $0 < \alpha < 1$, is an interior point of $S$ and thus generalized Neyman-Pearson lemma (Theorem 2.3.1 of Section 2.3) applies. According to the part (d) of the Theorem 2.3.1, p. 44, $(\alpha, \alpha)$ is an interior point of $S$, then there exist constants $k_1$ and $k_2$ and a test $\phi_0$ in $C_\alpha$ satisfying

$$\phi_0(T) = \begin{cases} 1 & \text{if } f_\theta(x) > \sum_{i=1}^{2} k_i f_{\theta_i}(x) \\ 0 & \text{if } f_\theta(x) < \sum_{i=1}^{2} k_i f_{\theta_i}(x) \end{cases} \tag{4.7}$$

The condition given in Eq. (4.7) holds a.e. $\mu$ and it is a necessary condition for a test in $C_\alpha$ to maximizes $E_\theta \phi(T)$ at each $\theta$, $\theta_1 < \theta < \theta_2$. The critical region in Eq. (4.7) may be written as

$$c(\theta)\exp\{Q(\theta)t\} > k_1 c(\theta_1)\exp\{Q(\theta_1)t\} + k_2 c(\theta_2)\exp\{Q(\theta_2)t\}$$

or

$$k_1 \frac{c(\theta_1)}{c(\theta)} \exp\{(Q(\theta_1) - Q(\theta))t\} + k_2 \frac{c(\theta_2)}{c(\theta)} \exp\{(Q(\theta_2) - Q(\theta))t\} < 1$$

Let

$$a_1 = k_1 \cdot \frac{c(\theta_1)}{c(\theta)}; \quad b_1 = Q(\theta_1) - Q(\theta) < 0$$

and

$$a_2 = k_2 \cdot \frac{c(\theta_2)}{c(\theta)}; \quad b_2 = Q(\theta_2) - Q(\theta) > 0$$

since $Q$ is monotonically increasing)

i.e., $b_1 < 0 < b_2$, therefore, the condition or the critical region reduces to

$$a_1 \exp\{b_1 t\} + a_2 \exp\{b_2 t\} < 1$$

If both $a$'s are negative then this test always rejects $H_0$ and if either of the $a$ is non-positive and the other is positive then the left hand side is strictly monotone in $t$. The test, therefore, becomes

$$\phi_0(T(x)) = \begin{cases} 1 & \text{if } T(x) > t_0 \\ 0 & \text{if } T(x) < t_0 \end{cases} \tag{4.8}$$

when $a_1 \leq 0$, or

$$\phi_0(T(x)) = \begin{cases} 1 & \text{if } T(x) < t_0 \\ 0 & \text{if } T(x) > t_0 \end{cases} \tag{4.9}$$

when $a_1 > 0$

Further, the distribution of $T$, $P^T$, has monotone likelihood ratio Karlin and Rubin theorem holds and we state that the power function $E_\theta \phi(T)$ of the test in Eq. 4.8 or Eq. 4.9 is strictly monotone. Therefore, the condition

$E_{\theta_1}\phi_0(T) = E_{\theta_2}\phi_0(T) = \alpha$ cannot be satisfied, and we conclude that both $a$'s must be positive, which gives the rejection region

$$a_1 \exp\{b_1 t\} + a_2 \exp\{b_2 t\} < 1 \Rightarrow c_1 < T(x) < c_2$$

for some $c_1$ and $c_2$, since the function $a_1 \exp\{b_1 t\} + a_2 \exp\{b_2 t\}$ is convex (check its second derivative) and it tends to $\infty$ as $|t| \to \infty$. Hence, the test $\phi_0$ is of the form of Eq. (4.4). The constants $c_i$'s and $\gamma_i$'s in $\phi_0$ are uniquely obtained by Eq. (4.5), as asserted in Theorem 4.2.2. This test $\phi_0$ in Eqs. (4.4) and (4.5) with $k_1,\ k_2 \geq 0$ maximizes $E_\theta\phi(T)$ at each $\theta,\ \theta_1 < \theta < \theta_2$, among all the tests satisfying $E_\theta\phi(T) \leq \alpha,\ i = 1, 2$, by the application of generalized Neyman-Pearson (Theorem 2.3.1, part (b)). Since this result is independent of the choice of $\theta$ such that $\theta_1 < \theta < \theta_2$, the test $\phi_0$ in Eqs. (4.4) and (4.5) is UMP level $\alpha$ test for testing $H_0 : \theta \leq \theta_1$ or $\theta \geq \theta_2$ against $H_1 : \theta_1 < \theta < \theta_2$ if we show

$$E_\theta\phi_0(T) \leq \alpha \text{ for all } \theta,\ \theta < \theta_1 \text{ and } \theta \geq \theta_2$$

This clearly holds from (b) of this Theorem 4.2.1, by comparing $\phi_0$ with $\phi(T) \equiv \alpha$.
(b) Consider the problem of minimizing $E_\theta\phi(T)$ for $\theta < \theta_1$; and applying generalized Neyman-Pearson lemma part (Theorem 2.3.1, part (d)), there exists constants $k_1$ and $k_2$ and a test $\phi_0$ in $C_\alpha$ so that

$$\phi_0(t) = \begin{cases} 1 & \text{if } f_\theta(t) < k_1 f_{\theta_1}(t) + k_2 f_{\theta_2}(t) \\ 0 & \text{if } f_\theta(t) > k_1 f_{\theta_1}(t) + k_2 f_{\theta_2}(t) \end{cases}$$

The critical region of the test $\phi_0$ may be written as

$$c(\theta)\exp\{Q(\theta)t\} < k_1 c(\theta_1)\exp\{Q(\theta_1)t\} + k_2 c(\theta_2)\exp\{Q(\theta_2)t\}$$

On dividing throughout by $k_1 c(\theta_1)\exp\{Q(\theta_1)t\}$, we get

$$\frac{c(\theta)}{k_1 c(\theta_1)} \exp\{(Q(\theta) - Q(\theta_1))t\} - \frac{k_2\, c(\theta_2)}{k_1 c(\theta_1)} \cdot \exp\{(Q(\theta_2) - Q(\theta_1))t\} < 1$$

or

$$a_1 \exp\{b_1 t\} + a_2 \exp\{b_2 t\} < 1; \qquad (b_1 < 0 < b_2)$$

where

$$a_1 = \frac{c(\theta)}{k_1 c(\theta_1)}; \qquad b_1 = Q(\theta) - Q(\theta_1) < 0$$

and

$$a_2 = -\frac{k_2 c(\theta_2)}{k_1 c(\theta_1)}; \qquad b_2 = Q(\theta_2) - Q(\theta_1) > 0$$

This gives rise to the test $\phi_0$ in Eq. (4.4), which has been shown as a UMP test in $C_\alpha$ for testing $H_0$ against $H_1$. Further, the test $\phi_0$ in Eq. (4.4) is unique provided $P\{T = c_1\} = P\{T = c_2\} = 0$, since the first and second

conditions in $\phi_0$ are also necessary by generalized Neyman-Pearson lemma (Theorem 2.3.1, part (d)).
(c) Since $Q(\theta)$ in Eq. (4.3) is strictly increasing, therefore, we can reparametrize the density Eq. (4.3) by putting $\eta = Q(\theta)$

$$dP_\eta(t) = c(Q^{-1}(\eta)) \exp\{\eta t(x)\} \cdot d\gamma(t)$$

It is for this reason, here we assume $Q(\theta) = \theta$ without loss of generality. Since the above family is one parameter exponential family, the power function, $E_\theta \phi(T)$, of every critical function is continuous in $\theta$. The continuity of the power function of the test $\phi_0$ in Eq. (4.4) and that $\phi_0$ is UMP in $\mathcal{C}_\alpha$ as shown in (a) of this theorem either implies a point $\theta_0$ between $\theta_1$ and $\theta_2$ so that $\beta_{\phi_0}(\theta)$ attains maximum at $\theta_0$ and strictly decreases as $\theta$ moves away from $\theta_0$ in either direction and that (c) of this theorem holds, or there exist three points $\theta_3,\ \theta_4,\ \theta_5,\ \theta_3 < \theta_4 < \theta_5$ in the region $(\theta_1, \theta_2)$ such that

$$\beta_{\phi_0}(\theta_3) = \beta_{\phi_0}(\theta_5) = k \text{ (say) } \text{ and } \beta_{\phi_0}(\theta_4) \le k$$

$k$ can not take value 0 or 1 since if $k = 0$, we get

$$\beta_{\phi_0}(\theta_3) = \int \phi_0(t) c(\theta) \exp\{\theta\, t\} d\gamma(t) = 0$$

showing $\phi_0(t) = 0$ a.e. $\mu$. This implies

$$E_{\theta_1}[\phi_0(T)] = 0$$

that contradicts $E_{\theta_1}[\phi_0(T)] = \alpha \in (0,1)$; and if $k = 1$, we get $\phi_0(t) = 1$ a.e. $\mu$, $E_{\theta_1}[\phi_0(T)] = 1$ contradicts $E_{\theta_1}[\phi_0(T)] = \alpha \in (0,1)$. Therefore, we exclude the values $k = 0$ and 1 and consider $0 < k < 1$. Corollary (2.3.1) gives

$$\beta_{\phi_0}(\theta_4) > k$$

unless (4.6) holds, $P_{\theta_3}$, $P_{\theta_4}$ and $P_{\theta_5}$ are linearly independent, which is a contradiction to the assumption $\beta_{\phi_0}(\theta_4) \le k$. Therefore, (c) holds. □

**Theorem 4.2.2.** (Lehmann (1986) [130]) *Let $\mathcal{P}$ be the family of densities $P_\theta(x)$ on the real line with monotone likelihood ratio in $t$. Let $\phi(t)$ be a function with single change in sign. In other words, there exists a value $t = t_0$ such that*

$$\phi(t) \le 0 \quad \textit{for} \quad t < t_0$$

*and*

$$\phi(t) \ge 0 \quad \textit{for} \quad t \ge t_0$$

*so that $P_\theta\{\phi(t) \ne 0\} > 0$. Let $P_\theta(x) > 0$ for all $\theta$ and for all $x$ and $\dfrac{P_{\theta'}(x)}{P_\theta(x)}$ is strictly increasing in $t$ for $\theta < \theta'$. Under these assumptions*

(a) *If the tests $\phi$ and $\phi'$ satisfy (4.4) with $c_i$, $\gamma_i$ and $c_i'$, $\gamma_i'$ $i = 1, 2$ respectively, where $\beta_\phi(\theta_1) = \beta_{\phi'}(\theta_1)$ and either $c_1' > c_1$ or $c_1' = c_1$ and $\gamma_1' < \gamma_1$ ($\phi'$ lies to the right of $\phi$),*

$$\beta_\phi(\theta) < \beta_{\phi'}(\theta) \quad \text{for} \quad \theta > \theta_1$$

*or*

$$\beta_\phi(\theta) > \beta_{\phi'}(\theta) \quad \text{for} \quad \theta < \theta_1$$

(b) *If the tests $\phi$ and $\phi'$ satisfy (4.4) and (4.5), then $\phi = \phi'$ a.e. $\mu$.*

### 4.2.1 Determination of the Two-sided UMP Test in Theorem 4.2.1

We will discuss now as to how the UMP size-$\alpha$ test $\phi_0$ in Theorem 4.2.1 is computed by utilizing the results of Theorem 4.2.2. The constants $c_1$, $c_2$, $\gamma_1$ and $\gamma_2$ in $\phi_0$ are obtained subject to the conditions given in Eq. (4.5), namely,

$$\beta_{\phi_0}(\theta_1) = \beta_{\phi_0}(\theta_2) = \alpha$$

We shall start with some guess values $c_1'$, $\gamma_1'$ and find $c_2'$, $\gamma_2'$ such that $\beta_{\phi'}(\theta_1) = \alpha$. Then calculate $\beta_{\phi'}(\theta_2)$ which is usually either too low or too high. If $\beta_{\phi'}(\theta_2) < \alpha$ then correct acceptance region would be to the right of the trial region considered, that is, choose now $c_1 > c_1'$ or $c_1 = c_1'$ and $\gamma_1 < \gamma_1'$ and conversely if $\beta_{\phi'}(\theta_2) > \alpha$. Repeat the process by replacing trial values $c_1'$, $\gamma_1'$ by $c_1$, $\gamma_1$ so obtained. We would continue this process till we get $\beta_\phi(\theta_2) = \alpha$ and this way we get unique values of $c_1$, $\gamma_1$, $c_2$, $\gamma_2$ (see Lehmann 1986 [130]).

**Example 4.2.1.** *Consider a random sample $X_1, X_2, \ldots, X_n$ drawn from $N(\theta, \sigma^2)$ $\sigma^2$, known. Find out a UMP size-$\alpha$ test for testing $H_0 : \theta \le \theta_1$ or $\theta \ge \theta_2$ against $H_1 : \theta_1 < \theta < \theta_2$. Also, find a UMP test on the basis of a sample of size 16 for testing $H_0 : \theta \le 1$ or $\theta \ge 2$ against $H_1 : 1 < \theta < 2$ at 5% levwl of significance.*

***Solution:*** The UMP size-$\alpha$ test for testing $H_0 : \theta \le \theta_1$ or $\theta \ge \theta_2$ against $H_1 : \theta_1 < \theta < \theta_2$ will be a function of the sufficient statistic $\bar{X}$ for $\theta$ and is given by

$$\phi_0(\bar{x}) = \begin{cases} 1 & \text{if } x_1 < \bar{x} < x_2 \\ 0 & \text{otherwise} \end{cases}$$

where $x_1$ and $x_2$ are obtained by

$$E_{\theta_1}[\phi_0(\bar{X})] = \alpha = E_{\theta_2}[\phi_0(\bar{X})] \;\text{ or }\; \beta_{\phi_0}(\theta_1) = \alpha = \beta_{\phi_0}(\theta_2) \tag{4.10}$$

Note $\phi_0$ is non-randomized since the distribution of $\bar{X}$ is continuous. Consider the power function of the test $\phi_0$ at some point $\theta$

$$\begin{aligned} \beta_{\phi_0}(\theta) &= P_\theta[x_1 < \bar{X} < x_2] \\ &= \Phi\Big(\frac{\sqrt{n}}{\sigma}(x_2 - \theta)\Big) - \Phi\Big(\frac{\sqrt{n}}{\sigma}(x_1 - \theta)\Big) \end{aligned}$$

where $\bar{X} \sim N(\theta, \sigma^2/n)$ and $\Phi$ is cumulative distribution function of normal distribution. We show here that the power function $\beta_{\phi_0}(\theta)$ is symmetric about $\frac{x_1 + x_2}{2}$. For this we show

$$\beta_{\phi_0}\left(\frac{x_1 + x_2}{2} - \alpha\right) = \beta_{\phi_0}\left(\frac{x_1 + x_2}{2} + \alpha\right) \text{ for every } \alpha > 0$$

Consider

$$\begin{aligned}
\beta_{\phi_0}\left(\frac{x_1 + x_2}{2} - \alpha\right) &= \Phi\left(\frac{\sqrt{n}}{\sigma}\left(x_2 - \overline{\frac{x_1 + x_2}{2} - \alpha}\right)\right) \\
&\quad - \Phi\left(\frac{\sqrt{n}}{\sigma}\left(x_1 - \overline{\frac{x_1 + x_2}{2} - \alpha}\right)\right) \\
&= \Phi\left(\frac{\sqrt{n}}{\sigma}\left(\frac{x_2 - x_1}{2} + \alpha\right)\right) - \Phi\left(\frac{\sqrt{n}}{\sigma}\left(\frac{x_1 - x_2}{2} + \alpha\right)\right) \\
&= \Phi\left(\frac{\sqrt{n}}{\sigma}\left(\frac{x_2 - x_1}{2} - \alpha\right)\right) - \Phi\left(\frac{\sqrt{n}}{\sigma}\left(\frac{x_1 - x_2}{2} - \alpha\right)\right) \\
&\qquad \text{(by the symmetry of normal distribution)} \\
&= \Phi\left(\frac{\sqrt{n}}{\sigma}\left(x_2 - \overline{\frac{x_1 + x_2}{2} + \alpha}\right)\right) - \Phi\left(\frac{\sqrt{n}}{\sigma}\left(x_1 - \overline{\frac{x_1 + x_2}{2} + \alpha}\right)\right) \\
&= \beta_{\phi_0}\left(\frac{x_1 + x_2}{2} + \alpha\right)
\end{aligned}$$

Further, the condition Eq. 4.10 shows that the power function of the test $\phi_0$, $\beta_{\phi_0}(\theta)$ at $\theta_1$ and $\theta_2$ attains the same value $\alpha$. This along with the symmetry of $\beta_{\phi_0}(\theta)$ about $\frac{x_1 + x_2}{2}$ gives that $\theta_1$ and $\theta_2$ must be situated at equal distances on either sides, i.e.

$$\frac{x_1 + x_2}{2} = \frac{\theta_1 + \theta_2}{2} \quad \text{or} \quad x_1 = \frac{\theta_1 + \theta_2}{2} - d, \; x_2 = \frac{\theta_1 + \theta_2}{2} + d$$

The constant $d$ is obtained by the condition Eq. 4.10. $E_{\theta_1}\phi_0(\bar{X}) = \alpha$ gives

$$\Phi\left(\frac{\sqrt{n}}{\sigma}(x_2 - \theta_1)\right) - \Phi\left(\frac{\sqrt{n}}{\sigma}(x_1 - \theta_1)\right) = \alpha$$

$$\Phi\left[\frac{\sqrt{n}}{\sigma}\left(\frac{\theta_2 - \theta_1}{2} + d\right)\right] - \Phi\left[\frac{\sqrt{n}}{\sigma}\left(\frac{\theta_2 - \theta_1}{2} - d\right)\right] = \alpha$$

On setting $n = 16, \; \sigma = 1, \; \theta_1 = 1, \; \theta_2 = 2$ and $\alpha = 0.05$, we get

$$\Phi[4(0.5 + d)] - \Phi[4(0.5 - d)] = 0.05$$

$$\Phi[2 + 4d] - \Phi[2 - 4d] = 0.05$$

gives $d = 0.1$. We then have

$$x_1 = 1.5 - 0.1 = 1.4, \quad \text{and} \quad x_2 = 1.5 + 0.1 = 1.6$$

Finally, the UMP test for testing $H_0$ against $H_1$ at 5% level is given by

$$\phi_0(\bar{x}) = \begin{cases} 1 & \text{if } 1.4 < \bar{x} < 1.6 \\ 0 & \text{otherwise} \end{cases}$$

**Example 4.2.2.** *Consider a random sample $X_1, X_2, \ldots, X_n$ from $N(\theta, \sigma^2)$, $\theta$ known. Find out a UMP size-$\alpha$ test for testing $H_0 : \sigma \leq \sigma_1$ or $\sigma \geq \sigma_2$ against $H_1 : \sigma_1 < \sigma < \sigma_2$.*

***Solution:*** The UMP test for testing $H_0 : \sigma \leq \sigma_1$ or $\sigma \geq \sigma_2$ against $H_1 : \sigma_1 < \sigma < \sigma_2$ is based on the sufficient statistic $T = \sum(x_i - \theta)^2$ for $\sigma^2$. It is given by

$$\phi_0(T) = \begin{cases} 1 & \text{if } x_1 < T < x_2 \\ 0 & \text{otherwise} \end{cases}$$

so that $E_{\sigma_1}\phi_0(T) = \alpha = E_{\sigma_2}\phi_0(T)$

$$P_{\sigma_1}[x_1 < T < x_2] = P_{\sigma_2}[x_1 < T < x_2] = \alpha$$

$$P\left[\frac{x_1}{\sigma_1^2} < \chi_n^2 < \frac{x_2}{\sigma_1^2}\right] = P[\frac{x_1}{\sigma_2^2} < \chi_n^2 < \frac{x_2}{\sigma_2^2}] = \alpha$$

since $\frac{T}{\sigma_2} \sim \chi_n^2$. On setting $\frac{x_1}{\sigma_1^2} = a_1$, $\frac{x_2}{\sigma_1^2} = a_2$, $\frac{x_1}{\sigma_2^2} = b_1$, $\frac{x_2}{\sigma_2^2} = b_2$ we get

$$x_1 = a_1\sigma_1^2 = b_1\sigma_2^2, \quad \text{and} \quad x_2 = a_2\sigma_1^2 = b_2\sigma_2^2$$

which implies $\frac{a_1}{a_2} = \frac{b_1}{b_2} = \frac{x_1}{x_2}$. Therefore, $a_1$, $a_2$ and $b_1$, $b_2$ are so chosen that

$$P[a_1 < \chi_n^2 < a_2] = P[b_1 < \chi_n^2 < b_2] = \alpha$$

and $\frac{a_1}{a_2} = \frac{b_1}{b_2} = \frac{x_1}{x_2}$

## 4.3 TWO-SIDED TESTS FOR TESTING $H_0 : \theta_1 \leq \theta \leq \theta_2$ and $H_0 : \theta = \theta_0$

In previous section we have seen that there exists a UMP test in the class of size-$\alpha$ tests, $C_\alpha$, for testing $H_0 : \theta \leq \theta_1$ or $\theta \geq \theta_2$ against $H_1 : \theta_1 < \theta < \theta_2$ when the distribution of $X$ belongs to the exponential family. But unfortunately an UMP test in the class of size-$\alpha$ tests does not exist for testing $H_0 : \theta_1 \leq \theta \leq \theta_2$ $(\theta_1 \leq \theta_2)$ against $H_1 : \theta < \theta_1$ or $\theta > \theta_2$, or $H_0 : \theta = \theta_0$ against the alternatives $H_1 : \theta \neq \theta_0$ in an exponential family We consider an example that illustrates this situation.

**Example 4.3.1.** *Let $X_1, \ldots, X_n$ be iid $N(\theta, \sigma^2)$ where $\sigma^2$ is known. Consider the testing problem $H_0 : \theta = \theta_0$ against $H_1 : \theta \neq \theta_0$. Show that a UMP size-$\alpha$ test for testing this problem does not exists.*

***Solution :*** Since the family of joint pdfs of $X_1, \ldots, X_n$ has an monotone likelihood ratio in $T(\mathbf{X}) = \sum_1^n X_i$, the UMP size-$\alpha$ test, by Karlin-Rubin theorem, for testing $H_0 : \theta = \theta_0$ against $H_1 : \theta < \theta_0$ is given by

$$\phi_1(\mathbf{x}) = \begin{cases} 1 & \text{if } \bar{x} < \theta_0 - \frac{\sigma}{\sqrt{n}} z_\alpha \\ 0 & \text{otherwise} \end{cases}$$

The power function of the test $\phi_1$ is given by

$$\beta_{\phi_1}(\theta) = P_\theta\Big(\bar{X} < \theta_0 - \frac{\sigma}{\sqrt{n}} z_\alpha\Big)$$

which is a decreasing function of $\theta$. Note that $\beta_\phi(\theta_0) = \alpha$. Similarly the UMP size-$\alpha$ test for testing $H_0 : \theta = \theta_0$ against $H_1 : \theta > \theta_0$ is given by

$$\phi_2(\mathbf{x}) = \begin{cases} 1 & \text{if } \bar{x} > \theta_0 + \frac{\sigma}{\sqrt{n}} z_\alpha \\ 0 & \text{otherwise} \end{cases}$$

$\beta_{\phi_2}(\theta_0) = \alpha$. Consider any $\theta_2 > \theta_0$

$$\begin{aligned} \beta_{\phi_2}(\theta_2) &= P_{\theta_2}(\bar{X} > \theta_0 + \frac{\sigma}{\sqrt{n}} z_\alpha) \\ &= P_{\theta_2}\Big(\frac{\bar{X} - \theta_2}{\sigma/\sqrt{n}} > \frac{\theta_0 - \theta_2}{\sigma/\sqrt{n}} + z_\alpha\Big) \\ &> P_{\theta_2}(Z > z_\alpha) \qquad (Z \sim N(0,1), \;\; \theta_0 - \theta_2 < 0) \\ &= P_{\theta_2}(Z < -z_\alpha) \\ &> P_{\theta_2}\Big(\frac{\bar{X} - \theta_2}{\sigma/\sqrt{n}} < -z_\alpha + \frac{\theta_0 - \theta_2}{\sigma/\sqrt{n}}\Big) \\ &= P_{\theta_2}\Big(\bar{X} < \theta_0 - \frac{\sigma}{\sqrt{n}} z_\alpha\Big) = \beta_{\phi_1}(\theta_2) \end{aligned}$$

Similarly for any $\theta_2 < \theta_0$

$$\beta_{\phi_2}(\theta_2) < \beta_{\phi_1}(\theta_2)$$

Thus $\phi_1$ is not UMP size-$\alpha$ test for testing $H_0 : \theta = \theta_0$ against $H_1 : \theta > \theta_0$ since $\phi_2$ has higher power than of $\phi_1$ at each $\theta > \theta_0$ and $\phi_2$ is not UMP size-$\alpha$ test for testing $H_0 : \theta = \theta_0$ against $H_1 : \theta < \theta_0$ since $\phi_1$ has higher power than of $\phi_2$ at each $\theta < \theta_0$. Therefore, UMP size$\alpha$ test does not exist in this problem.

The above example illustrates the non-existence of a UMP size-$\alpha$ test in $\mathcal{C}_\alpha$ for testing $H_0 : \theta_1 \le \theta \le \theta_2$ against $H_1 : \theta \le \theta_1$ or $\theta > \theta_2$ or $H_0 : \theta = \theta_0$ against $H_0 : \theta \neq \theta_0$. In this case, on imposing a desirable property of a test called unbiasedness, the class $\mathcal{C}_\alpha$ reduces to $\mathcal{U}_\alpha$ as a class of all size-$\alpha$ unbiased tests. We discuss the existence of a UMP test in $\mathcal{U}_\alpha$ for these testing problems in Section 4.4 in the background of the results obtained in the present section for one parameter exponential family with density given in Eq. (4.1) (with respect to a common measure $\mu$).

Here-in-after, we would restrict our attention to a sufficient statistic $T$ in the density Eq. (4.1) whose distribution is given by

$$f_T(t \mid \theta) = c(\theta) \exp\{\theta t\}$$

with respect to a measure $\nu(t)$, which also belongs to the family of one parameter exponential family. We say a test is of a two-sided form if it is given by

$$\phi(T(x)) = \begin{cases} 1 & \text{if } T(x) < c_1 \text{ or } T(x) > c_2 \\ \gamma_i & \text{if } T(x) = c_i; \quad i = 1, 2. \\ 0 & \text{if } c_1 < T(x) < c_2 \end{cases} \tag{4.11}$$

for some $c_1 \leq c_2$ and $0 \leq \gamma_i \leq 1$, $i = 1, 2$. We see in the following theorem that a two-sided test of the form Eq. (4.11) is better as compared to any other test when they have the same power on the boundaries of $H_0 : \theta_1 \leq \theta \leq \theta_2$ and $H_1 : \theta < \theta_1$ or $\theta > \theta_2$, namely at $\theta_1$ and $\theta_2$.

**Theorem 4.3.1.** (Ferguson (1967)[54]) *Suppose that $X$ follows one parameter exponential family. Then given any test $\phi$ and $\theta_1$, $\theta_2 \in \Theta$, with $\theta_1 < \theta_2$, there exists a two-sided test $\phi'$ of the form Eq. (4.11) for which*

$$E_{\theta_1}\phi'(T) = E_{\theta_1}\phi(T) \textit{ and } E_{\theta_2}\phi'(T) = E_{\theta_2}\phi(T)$$

*Moreover,*

$$E_\theta\phi'(T) - E_\theta\phi(T) = \begin{cases} \leq 0 & \textit{for } \theta_1 < \theta < \theta_2 \\ \geq 0 & \textit{for } \theta < \theta_1 \textit{ and } \theta > \theta_2 \end{cases}$$

Consider next, the two-sided testing problem $H_0 : \theta = \theta_0$ against $H_1 : \theta \neq \theta_0$. It is a known result that the power function of any test $\phi$, $E_\theta\phi(T)$, is an analytic function of $\theta$ when the distribution of $T$ belongs to one-parameter exponential family (subsection 1.6.1 with $k = 1$, Chapter 1). Therefore, $E_\theta\phi(T)$ is differentiable with respect to $\theta$ a.e. $\nu$. Furthermore, if the derivative has been assumed to be allowed to pass beneath the integral sign, we then have

$$\frac{d}{d\theta} E_\theta\phi(T) = \frac{d}{d\theta} \int \phi(t) c(\theta) e^{\theta t} dt = \int \phi(t)[c'(\theta) + tc(\theta)] e^{\theta t} dt$$

We shall now find out $c'(\theta)$. Note that

$$\int c(\theta) e^{\theta t}\, dt = 1$$

On differentiating this with respect to $\theta$, we get

$$\int [c'(\theta) + tc(\theta)] e^{\theta t}\, dt = 0$$

or

$$\frac{c'(\theta)}{c(\theta)} + E_\theta T = 0$$

which gives

$$c'(\theta) = -c(\theta) E_\theta T$$

On putting the value of $c'(\theta)$ in $\frac{d}{d\theta} E_\theta \phi(T)$, we get

$$\begin{aligned}\frac{d}{d\theta} E_\theta \phi(T) &= -E_\theta T \cdot \int \phi(t) c(\theta) e^{\theta t}\, dt + \int t \cdot \phi(t) \cdot c(\theta) e^{\theta t} dt \\ &= E_\theta T \phi(T) - E_\theta \phi(T) \cdot E_\theta T\end{aligned}$$

The expression for $\frac{d}{d\theta} E_\theta \phi(X)$ gives slope to the power function at some points $\theta$. For a two-sided test $\phi'$ to be better than any other test $\phi$, they must have the same power at $\theta = \theta_0$ and $\phi'$ have no smaller power, $E_\theta \phi'(T) \geq E_\theta \phi(T),\ \forall\ \theta \neq \theta_0$. Theorem 4.3.2, states the necessary condition for the two sided test $\phi'$ to be as good as $\phi$ by having same slopes to their power functions at $\theta = \theta_0$.

**Theorem 4.3.2.** (Ferguson (1967)[54]) *Let $X$ belong to the one parameter exponential family. Then, given any test $\phi$ and $\theta_0 \in \Theta$, there exists a two-sided test $\phi'$ of the form given in Eq. (4.11) for which*

$$E_{\theta_0} \phi'(T) = E_{\theta_0} \phi(T)$$

*and*

$$\frac{d}{d\theta} E_\theta \phi'(T) \Big|_{\theta=\theta_0} = \frac{d}{d\theta} E_\theta \phi(T) \Big|_{\theta=\theta_0}$$

*Moreover,*

$$E_\theta \phi'(T) \geq E_\theta \phi(T) \forall \theta \in \Theta.$$

In order to understand the shape-relationship of power functions of the tests $\phi$ and $\phi'$ (of Theorem 4.3.2), three possible patterns have been plotted in Figure 4.1. One of these patterns (shown in Figure 4.1) would be followed by the power functions of the tests $\phi$ and $\phi'$.

### 4.3.1 Loss Function in Two-sided Testing Problem

We shall assume that the loss functions for the two-sided testing problems $H_0 : \theta_1 \leq \theta \leq \theta_2$ against $H_1 : \theta < \theta_1$ or $\theta > \theta_2$ must satisfy

$$L(\theta, a_1) - L(\theta, a_0) \geq 0 \text{ if } \theta_1 < \theta < \theta_2$$

and

$$L(\theta, a_1) - L(\theta, a_0) \leq 0 \text{ if } \theta < \theta_1 \text{ or } \theta > \theta_2 \tag{4.12}$$

where, $\theta_1 < \theta_2;\ \theta_1, \theta_2 \in \Theta \subseteq \mathbb{R}^1$.

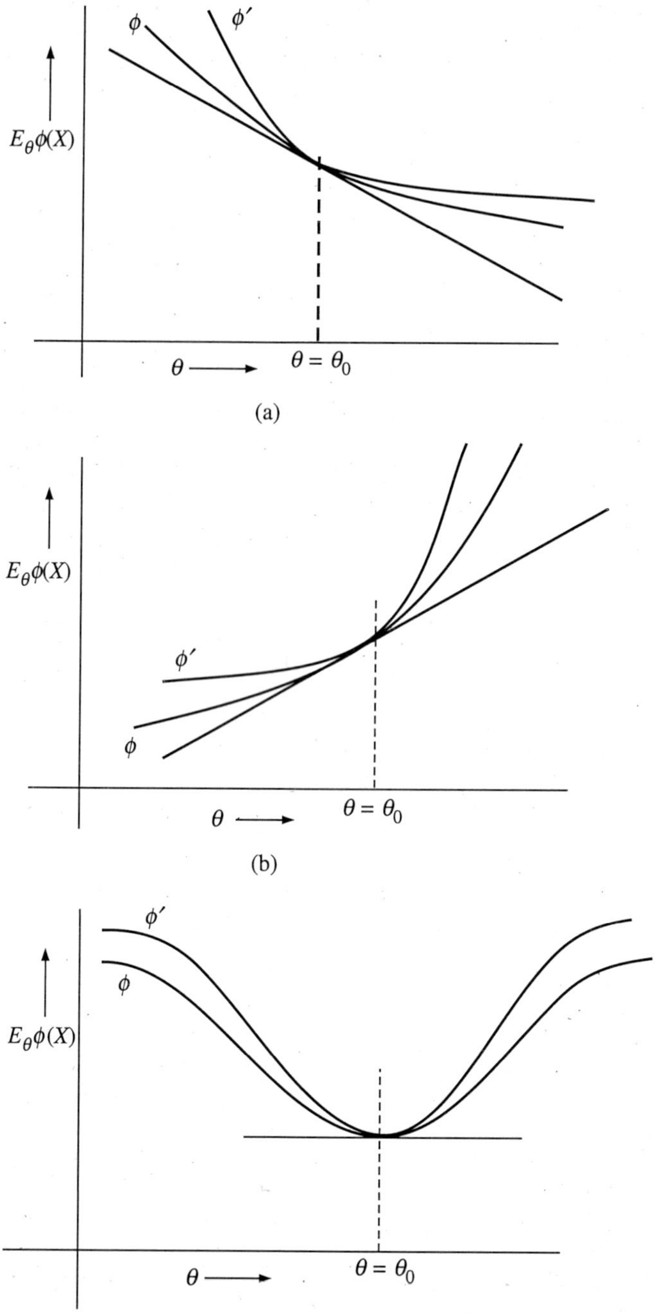


**Figure 4.1:** Comparative plot of power functions of the tests $\phi$ and $\phi'$.

The loss function for the testing problem $H_0 : \theta = \theta_0$ against $H_1 : \theta \neq \theta_0$ ($\theta_1 = \theta_2 = \theta_0$) must satisfy

$$L(\theta_0, a_1) - L(\theta_0, a_0) > 0$$

and

$$L(\theta, a_1) - L(\theta, a_0) \ < 0 \ \text{ for } \ \theta \neq \theta_0 (= \theta_1 = \theta_2) \tag{4.13}$$

The loss function in Eq. (4.12) tells us that if $\theta_1 < \theta < \theta_2$ we prefer to take action $a_0$ and, if $\theta < \theta_1$ or $\theta > \theta_2$ we prefer to take action $a_1$; and the loss function in Eq. (4.13) tells that if $\theta_1 = \theta_2 = \theta_0$ we prefer to take action $a_0$, and if $\theta \neq \theta_0$, we prefer $a_1$.

### 4.3.2 Risk Function in Two-sided Testing Problem

Given any two tests $\phi$ and $\phi'$, the difference in their risk functions is given by

$$R(\theta, \phi') - R(\theta, \phi) = [L(\theta, a_1) - L(\theta, a_0)][E_\theta \phi'(T) - E_\theta \phi(T)]$$

The class of two-sided tests forms an essentially complete class when loss function satisfies the inequalities Eqs. (4.12) or (4.13). The result is formally given in Theorem 4.3.3.

**Theorem 4.3.3.** (Ferguson, 1967[54]) *Let the distribution of $X$ belongs to one parameter exponential family and let the loss function follows the inequalities given in Eqs. (4.12) and (4.13) for some $\theta_1 \leq \theta_2$. Then the class of two-sided tests is essentially complete.*

*Proof.* The difference in the risk functions of the tests $\phi$ and $\phi'$ is given by

$$R(\theta, \phi') - R(\theta, \phi) = [L(\theta, a_1) - L(\theta, a_0)][E_\theta \phi'(T) - E_\theta \phi(T)]$$

Consider any test $\phi$. We know from Theorem 4.3.1 when $\theta_1 < \theta_2$ that $\phi'$ has no larger power than of $\phi$ in $\theta_1 < \theta < \theta_2$ and no smaller power in $\theta < \theta_1$ and $\theta > \theta_2$. This, along with the given loss inequalities, gives the risk differences to be non-positive. Similarly, when we consider $\theta_1 = \theta_2$, Theorem 4.3.2 gives $\phi'$ has same power as of $\phi$ at $\theta = \theta_0$ and has no smaller power at $\theta \neq \theta_0$. This, along with the given loss inequalities, gives the risk differences again to be non-positive. In both the cases $\phi'$ proves to be as good as $\phi$. This proves the class of two-sided tests forms an essentially complete class. □

## 4.4 UNIFORMLY MOST POWERFUL UNBIASED TESTS FOR TWO-SIDED TESTING PROBLEMS

It has been seen that a UMP size-$\alpha$ test does not exist for either of the two-sided hypothesis testing problems $H_0 : \theta_1 \leq \theta \leq \theta_2$ against $H_1 : \theta < \theta_1$ or

$\theta > \theta_2$ and $H_0 : \theta = \theta_0$ against $H_1 : \theta \neq \theta_0$ . In other words, class of level $\alpha$ tests $\mathcal{C}_\alpha$ did not contain a UMP member in it. It is in this reference a desirable restriction on $\mathcal{C}_\alpha$ need to be imposed in order to get a smaller class of tests, where the possibility of existence of a UMP test could be explored. This restriction is known as unbiasedness of a test and has been defined as follows:

**Definition 4.4.1. (Unbiased Tests)** A size-$\alpha$ test $\phi$ for testing $H_0 : \theta \in \Theta_0$ against $H_1 : \theta \in \Theta_1$ is said to be unbiased if

$$E_\theta \phi(X) \geq \alpha \qquad \forall \quad \theta \in \Theta_1.$$

This requirement on a test tells us that the probability of rejecting a false hypothesis is never smaller than the probability of rejecting a true hypothesis. Therefore, the condition is treated as a desirable requirement on a test.

Class of all size-$\alpha$ unbiased tests is denoted by $\mathcal{U}_\alpha$. Clearly, the class of level $\alpha$ tests $\mathcal{C}_\alpha$ contains the class of size-$\alpha$ unbiased tests, $\mathcal{U}_\alpha$, i.e. $\mathcal{C}_\alpha \supset \mathcal{U}_\alpha$. We would now search for a UMP test in such a reduced class $\mathcal{U}_\alpha$.

**Definition 4.4.2. (UMP size-$\alpha$ Unbiased Test)** A test $\phi_0$ having maximum power at each $\theta \in \Theta_1$ from and among the tests in $\mathcal{U}_\alpha$, is said to be UMP size-$\alpha$ unbiased test.

## 4.4.1 UMP Unbiased Size-$\alpha$ Test for $H_0 : \theta_1 \leq \theta \leq \theta_2$ against $H_1 : \theta < \theta_1$ or $\theta > \theta_2$

The results discussed here are due to Lehmann and Scheffe, 1950, 1955 [32] where the distribution of $X$ has been assumed to follow one parameter exponential family. Let $T$ be a sufficient statistic for $\theta$ in this distribution. We have seen that the distribution of $T$ is again a one parameter exponential family, therefore, attention has been restricted to the class of tests which are functions of the sufficient statistic $T$. As we know from Chapter 1 that for this family of distributions, the power function of any test $\phi$, $E_\theta \phi(T)$, is an analytic function of $\theta$ and therefore continuous in $\theta$. Using this, the class of size-$\alpha$ unbiased tests has been defined as

$$\mathcal{U}_\alpha = \big\{\phi \in \mathcal{D} | \sup_{\theta_1 \leq \theta \leq \theta_2} E_\theta \phi(T) = \alpha \text{ and } E_\theta \phi(T) \geq \alpha \; \forall \; \theta < \theta_1 \text{ or } \theta > \theta_2\big\}$$

$$= \big\{\phi \in \mathcal{D} | E_{\theta_1} \phi(T) = \alpha = E_{\theta_2} \phi(T), \; E_\theta \phi(T) \leq \alpha \;\; \forall \; \theta_1 < \theta < \theta_2$$

and

$$E_\theta \phi(T) \geq \alpha \; \forall \; \theta < \theta_1 \text{ or } \theta > \theta_2\big\}.$$

Given a test $\phi(t) \equiv \alpha$ in $\mathcal{U}_\alpha$, we get a two-sided test $\phi'$ from Theorem 4.3.1, such that

$$E_{\theta_1} \phi'(T) = \alpha = E_{\theta_2} \phi'(T)$$

Moreover,

$$E_\theta \phi'(T) - \alpha = \begin{cases} \leq 0 & \text{for } \theta_1 < \theta < \theta_2 \\ \geq 0 & \text{for } \theta < \theta_1 \text{ or } \theta > \theta_2 \end{cases}$$

or

$$E_{\theta_1} \phi'(T) = \alpha = E_{\theta_2} \phi'(T)$$
(from the continuity of power function)

and

$$E_\theta \phi'(T) \geq \alpha \quad \text{for } \theta < \theta_1 \text{ or } \theta > \theta_2$$

The above conditions clearly show the existence of a two-sided test $\phi'$ in $\mathcal{U}_\alpha$. Note that the two sided test $\phi'$ is obtained by the first condition of power functions at $\theta_1$ and $\theta_2$ being equal to $\alpha$.

Similarly, if we consider some other test $\phi$ from $\mathcal{U}_\alpha$, Theorem 4.3.1 gives a two-sided test $\phi''$ in $\mathcal{U}_\alpha$ such that

$$E_{\theta_1} \phi''(X) = E_{\theta_1} \phi(X) = \alpha = E_{\theta_2} \phi''(X) = E_{\theta_2} \phi(X),$$
$$E_\theta \phi(X) \leq \alpha \text{ and } E_\theta \phi''(X) \leq \alpha \ \forall\ \theta_1 < \theta < \theta_2;$$
$$E_\theta \phi(X) \geq \alpha, \ E_\theta \phi''(X) \geq \alpha \ \forall\ \theta < \theta_1 \ \textit{or} \ \theta > \theta_2$$

and

$$\begin{aligned} E_\theta \phi''(T) &\leq E_\theta \phi(T) \quad \text{for } \theta_1 < \theta < \theta_2 \\ &\geq E_\theta \phi(T) \quad \text{for } \theta < \theta_1 \text{ or } \theta > \theta_2 \end{aligned}$$

and $\phi''$ is obtained by

$$E_{\theta_1} \phi''(T) = E_{\theta_2} \phi''(T) = \alpha$$

The obtained two-sided test $\phi''$ is no different from the previously obtained two-sided test $\phi'$, since both are of the same form and their defining conditions are also same. Therefore, we get same sets of values of $c_1$, $c_2$, $\gamma_1$ and $\gamma_2$ for both the tests $\phi'$ and $\phi''$. In other words, on application of Theorem 4.3.1 over and again, it gives the same two-sided test as good as the test $\phi$. Therefore, UMP size-$\alpha$ unbiased test $\phi'$ in $\mathcal{U}_\alpha$ for testing $H_0 : \theta_1 \leq \theta \leq \theta_2$ against $H_1 : \theta < \theta_1$ or $\theta > \theta_2$ is given by

$$\phi'(T) = \begin{cases} 1 & \text{if } T < c_1, \text{ or } T > c_2 \\ \gamma_i & \text{if } T = c_i;\ i = 1, 2 \\ 0 & \text{if } c_1 < T < c_2 \end{cases}$$

where, $c_1, c_2, \gamma_1$ and $\gamma_2$ are obtained by

$$E_{\theta_1} \phi'(T) = \alpha = E_{\theta_2} \phi'(T)$$

### 4.4.2 UMP Unbiased size-$\alpha$ Test for $H_0 : \theta = \theta_0$ against $H_1 : \theta \neq \theta_0$

The results discussed here are due to (Lehmann and Scheffe, 1950, 1955 [132]). Let the distributional assumptions be same as in the subsection 4.4.1. Where the power function of any test $\phi$, $E_\theta\phi(T)$, is continuous in $\theta$. Let us consider a class of size-$\alpha$ unbiased tests for testing $H_0 : \theta = \theta_0$ against $H_1 : \theta \neq \theta_0$ denoted by $\mathcal{U}_\alpha$. The conditions of unbiasedness

$$E_\theta\phi(T) \geq \alpha \qquad \text{for all} \quad \theta \neq \theta_0$$

and the differentiability of $E_\theta\phi(T)$ (since $E_\theta\phi(T)$ is an analytic function of $\theta$) give together the condition

$$\frac{d}{d\theta}E_\theta\phi(T)\Big|_{\theta=\theta_0} = 0$$

Therefore, class of size-$\alpha$ unbiased tests, $\mathcal{U}_\alpha$, would be given by

$$\mathcal{U}_\alpha = \{\phi \in \mathcal{D} | E_{\theta_0}\phi(X) = \alpha \;\text{ and }\; \frac{d}{d\theta}E_\theta\phi(X)\Big|_{\theta=\theta_0} = 0\}$$

Note that the tests in $\mathcal{U}_\alpha$ will have their power functions of the type as shown in Figure 4.2.

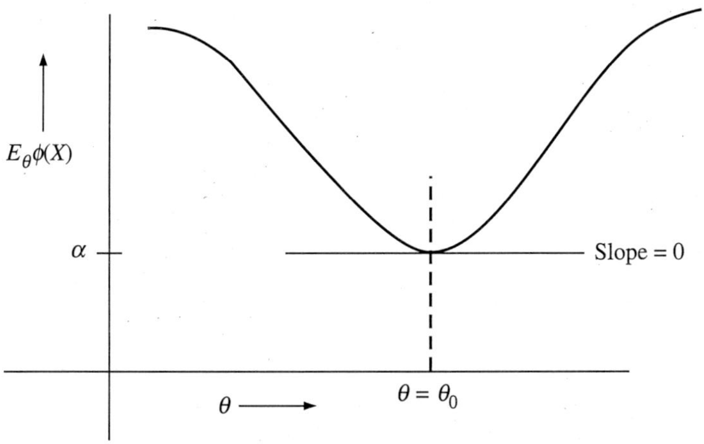


**Figure 4.2:** Plot of the power function of some test $\phi$ in $\mathcal{U}_\alpha$.

However, these shapes cannot be of the types as shown in Figures 4.3 and 4.4 since the condition of unbiasedness is violated, note $E_\theta\phi(T) < \alpha$ for $\theta > \theta_0$ in Figure 4.3, and $E_\theta\phi(T) < \alpha$ for $\theta < \theta_0$ in Figure 4.4.

We shall now show that the two-sided test in Eq. (4.11) is UMP for testing $H_0 : \theta = \theta_0$ against $H_1 : \theta \neq \theta_0$. Given a test $\phi(t) \equiv \alpha$ in $\mathcal{U}_\alpha$, Theorem 4.3.2 gives a two-sided test $\phi'$ for which

$$E_{\theta_0}\phi'(T) = E_{\theta_0}\phi(T) = \alpha$$

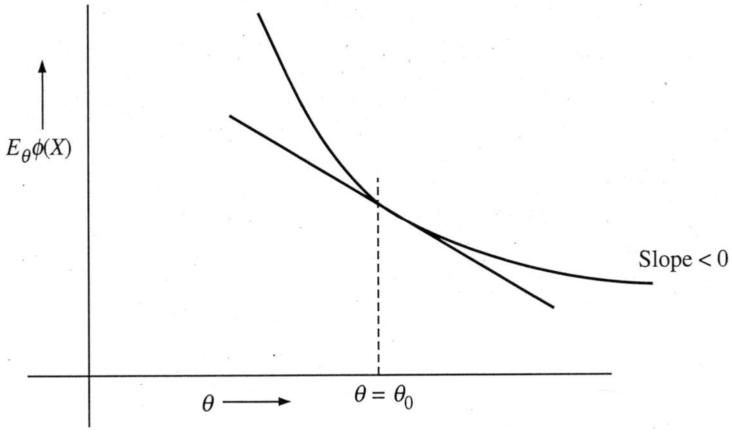


**Figure 4.3:** Plot of the power function of some test $\phi$ not in $\mathcal{U}_\alpha$.

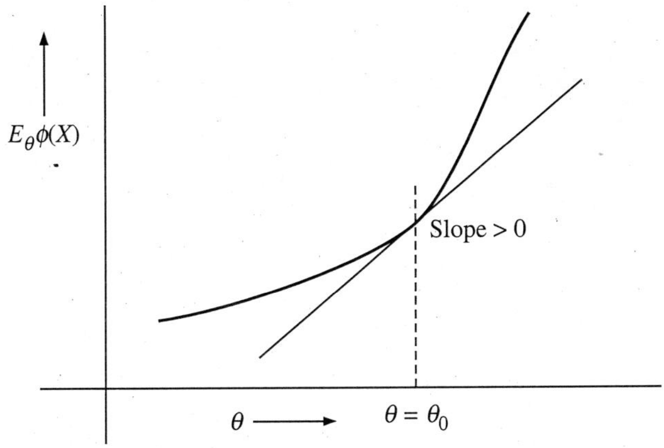


**Figure 4.4:** Plot of the power function of some test $\phi$ not in $\mathcal{U}_\alpha$.

and

$$\frac{d}{d\theta}E_\theta\phi'(x)\bigg|_{\theta=\theta_0} = \frac{d}{d\theta}E_\theta\phi(X)\bigg|_{\theta=\theta_0} = 0;$$

Moreover,

$$E_\theta\phi'(T) \geq E_\theta\phi(T) = \alpha \qquad \forall\ \theta$$

For any other test $\phi$ in $\mathcal{U}_\alpha$, Theorem 4.3.2 gives the same two-sided test $\phi'$ as good as $\phi$ since the defining conditions are same. Therefore, the two-sided test $\phi'$ so obtained is given by

$$\phi'(T) = \begin{cases} 1 & \text{if } T < c_1, \text{ or } T > c_2 \\ \gamma_i & \text{if } T = c_i; \ i = 1, 2. \\ 0 & \text{if } c_1 < T < c_2 \end{cases}$$

where, $c_1, c_2, \gamma_1, \gamma_2$ are obtained by $E_{\theta_0}\phi'(T) = \alpha$ and $E_{\theta_0}T\phi'(T) = \alpha\ E_{\theta_0}T$.

Such a test $\phi'$ is, therefore, UMP size-$\alpha$ unbiased test in $\mathcal{U}_\alpha$ for testing $H_0 : \theta = \theta_0$ against $H_1 : \theta \neq \theta_0$.

We shall now discuss few examples on finding UMP unbiased size-$\alpha$ tests for two-sided testing problems.

## 4.5 Solved Examples

**Example 4.5.1.** (Ferguson (1967)[54] *Let $X \sim \beta(\theta, 1)$ and suppose that the loss function is in the form of Eq. (4.12) for testing the hypothesis*

$$H_0 : 1 \leq \theta \leq 2 \text{ against } H_1 : \theta < 1 \text{ or } \theta > 2$$

*A test $\phi$ is given for which $E_{\theta_1}\phi(X) = 0.5$ and $E_{\theta_2}\phi(X) = 0.3$. Find a two-sided test $\phi'$ which is as good as the given test $\phi$.*

***Solution:*** Given any test $\phi$, we have two-sided test $\phi'$ for which

$$R(\theta, \phi') - R(\theta, \phi) = [L(\theta, a_1) - L(\theta, a_0)] \cdot [E_\theta \phi'(X) - E_\theta \phi(X)]$$

Using the loss inequality given in Eq. (4.12) and from Theorem 4.3.1 we get

$$R(\theta, \phi') - R(\theta, \phi) = \begin{cases} \geq 0 \cdot \leq 0 & \text{for } \theta_1 < \theta < \theta_2 \\ \leq 0 \cdot \geq 0 & \text{for } \theta < \theta_1 \text{ or } \theta > \theta_2 \end{cases}$$

Which gives

$$R(\theta, \phi') \leq R(\theta, \phi) \quad \forall \quad \theta \in \Theta$$

Showing that $\phi'$ is as good as $\phi$ where $\phi'$ is a two sided test obtained in Theorem 4.3.1 by knowing constants $x_1, x_2, \gamma_1$ and $\gamma_2$ by the conditions

$$E_{\theta_1}\phi'(X) = 0.5; \text{ at } \theta_1 = 1$$

$$E_{\theta_2}\phi'(X) = 0.3; \text{ at } \theta_2 = 2$$

Here $\gamma_1$ and $\gamma_2$ are zero since $X$ follows a continuous distribution. Since $X \sim \beta(\theta, 1)$

$$f(x|\,\theta) = \frac{\Gamma(\theta+1)}{\Gamma(\theta)\Gamma(1)}\, x^{\theta-1}\,(1-x)^{1-1}; \quad 0 < x < 1$$

$$= \theta x^{\theta-1}; \quad 0 < x < 1$$

$$E_{\theta_1=1}\phi'(X) = 0.5 \qquad \text{gives } \int_0^{x_1} dx + \int_{x_2}^1 dx = 0.5;$$

$$1 - \int_{x_1}^{x_2} dx = 0.5 \quad \int_{x_1}^{x_2} dx = 0.5; \quad x_2 - x_1 = 0.5 \tag{4.14}$$

The second condition gives

$$
\begin{aligned}
E_{\theta_2=2}\phi'(X) &= 0.3 \\
\int_0^{x_1} 2x\,dx + \int_{x_2}^1 2x\,dx &= 0.3 \\
\int_0^1 2x\,dx - \int_{x_1}^{x_2} 2x\,dx &= 0.3 \\
2\frac{x^2}{2}\Big|_0^1 - 2\cdot\frac{x^2}{2}\Big|_{x_1}^{x_2} &= 0.3 \\
x_2^2 - x_1^2 &= 0.7
\end{aligned}
$$

or

$$
\begin{aligned}
(x_2 - x_1)(x_2 + x_1) = (x_2 + x_1) \times 0.5 &= 0.7 \\
x_1 + x_2 &= 1.4 \qquad (4.15)
\end{aligned}
$$

From Eqs. (4.14) and (4.15), $x_1 = 0.45$, $x_2 = 0.95$. Therefore, the two-sided test $\phi'$, which is as good as $\phi$ is given by

$$
\phi'(x) = \begin{cases} 1 & \text{if} \quad x < 0.45 \quad \text{or} \quad x > 0.95 \\ 0 & \text{if} \quad 0.45 < x < 0.95 \end{cases}
$$

**Example 4.5.2.** (Ferguson (1967)[54]) *Let $X \sim \beta(\theta, 1)$ and let $\theta_1 = 1$. Consider the two-sided hypothesis testing problem $H_0 : \theta(= \theta_0) = \theta_1 = 1$ against $H_1 : \theta \neq 1$.*
*Given any test $\phi$ with $E_{\theta_1}\phi(X) = 0.10$*

*and*
$$
\frac{d}{d\theta} E_\theta\phi(X)\Big|_{\theta=\theta_1} = 0
$$

*Find a two-sided test $\phi'$ which is as good as $\phi$.*

***Solution:*** From loss inequalities given in Eq. (4.13) and Theorem 4.3.2, we get a two-sided test $\phi'$ which is as good as $\phi$. The test $\phi'$ is obtained by the conditions

$$
E_{\theta_1}\phi'(X) = E_{\theta_1}\phi(X) = 0.10; \quad \text{at} \quad \theta_1 = 1
$$

and

$$
\frac{d}{d\theta} E_\theta\phi'(X)\Big|_{\theta=\theta_1} - \frac{d}{d\theta} E_\theta\phi(X)\Big|_{\theta=\theta_1} - 0
$$

or

$$
\int_0^{x_1} dx + \int_{x_2}^1 dx = 0.10
$$

or

$$
1 - \int_{x_1}^{x_2} dx = 0.10; \qquad \int_{x_1}^{x_2} dx = 0.9
$$

or

$$x_2 - x_1 = 0.90.$$

The second condition gives

$$E_{\theta_1} X\phi(X) = E_{\theta_1}\phi(X) E_{\theta_1} X$$

$$\int_0^{x_1} x\,dx + \int_{x_2}^1 x\,dx = 0.1\int_0^1 x\,dx = 0.1\frac{x^2}{2}\Big|_0^1 = 0.05$$

or

$$\frac{1}{2} - \int_{x_1}^{x_2} x\,dx = 0.05$$

$$\frac{x^2}{2}\Big|_{x_1}^{x_2} = 0.45;\ (x_2 - x_1)(x_2 + x_1) = 0.9$$

$x_1 + x_2 = 1$ gives along with $x_2 - x_1 = 0.90,\ x_1 = 0.05;\ x_2 = 0.95$. We get a two-sided test $\phi'$ which is as good as $\phi$

$$\phi'(x) = \begin{cases} 1 & \text{if } x < 0.05 \text{ or } x > 0.95 \\ 0 & \text{if } 0.05 < x < 0.95 \end{cases}$$

**Example 4.5.3.** *Let $X_1, X_2, \ldots, X_n$ be a random sample drawn from $N(\theta, 1)$. Find out a UMP size-$\alpha$ unbiased test for testing*

(a) *$H_0 : \theta_1 \le \theta \le \theta_2$ against $H_1 : \theta < \theta_1$ or $\theta > \theta_2$.*

(b) *$H_0 : 1 \le \theta \le 2$ against $H_1 : \theta < 1$ or $\theta > 2$, at 5% level of significance when $n = 16,\ \sigma^2 = 1$.*

(c) *$H_0 : \theta = \theta_0$ against $H_1 : \theta \ne \theta_0$.*

***Solution:*** (a) The non-randomized UMP size-$\alpha$ unbiased test for testing $H_0 : \theta_1 \le \theta \le \theta_2$ against $H_1 : \theta < \theta_1$ or $\theta > \theta_2$ will be a function of the sufficient statistic $\bar{X}$ for $\theta$

$$\phi_0(\bar{x}) = \begin{cases} 1 & \text{if } \bar{x} < x_1 \text{ or } \bar{x} > x_2 \\ 0 & \text{if } x_1 \le \bar{x} \le x_2 \end{cases} \tag{4.16}$$

where $x_1, x_2$ are obtained by

$$E_{\theta_1}\phi_0(\bar{X}) = \alpha = E_{\theta_2}\phi_0(\bar{X}) \tag{4.17}$$

The power function of the test $\phi_0$ is given by

$$\beta_{\phi_0}(\theta) = E_\theta\phi_0(\bar{X}) = P_\theta[N(\theta, \sigma^2/n) < x_1] + P_\theta[N(\theta, \sigma^2/n) > x_2]$$

or

$$\beta_{\phi_0}(\theta) = 1 - \Phi\Big(\frac{\sqrt{n}}{\sigma}(x_2 - \theta)\Big) + \Phi\Big(\frac{\sqrt{n}}{\sigma}(x_1 - \theta)\Big) \tag{4.18}$$

Following the lines of Example 4.5.1, we easily show that $\beta_{\phi_0}(\theta)$ is symmetric about $\frac{x_1+x_2}{2}$. Further, by the condition given in Eq. (4.17), the power function of the test $\phi_0$, $\beta_{\phi_0}(\theta)$, attains equal value $\alpha$ at $\theta_1$ and $\theta_2$. This, along with the symmetry of the power function about $\frac{x_1+x_2}{2}$, implies that the points $\theta_1$ and $\theta_2$ are situated at equal distances from $\frac{x_1+x_2}{2}$ on either sides, i.e.

$$\frac{x_1+x_2}{2} = \frac{\theta_1+\theta_2}{2} = \bar{\theta} \text{ or } x_1 = \bar{\theta} - c \text{ and } x_2 = \bar{\theta} + c$$

Here, the constant $c$ is obtained by the condition given in Eq. (4.17) where

$$E_{\theta_1}\phi_0(\bar{X}) = \alpha \text{ gives}$$

$$P[N(\theta_1, \sigma^2/n) < \bar{\theta} - c] + P[N(\theta_1, \sigma^2/n) > \bar{\theta} + c] = \alpha$$

$$\text{or} \qquad \int_{\bar{\theta}-c}^{\bar{\theta}+c} N(\theta_1, \sigma^2/n)\, d\bar{x} = 1 - \alpha;$$

or

$$\int_{\frac{\sqrt{n}}{\sigma}\left(\frac{\theta_2-\theta_1}{2}-c\right)}^{\frac{\sqrt{n}}{\sigma}\left(\frac{\theta_2-\theta_1}{2}+c\right)} N(0,1)\, dy = 1 - \alpha$$

Let

$$\frac{\theta_2-\theta_1}{2} = l_0, \quad \text{we have} \int_{\frac{\sqrt{n}}{\sigma}(l_0-c)}^{\frac{\sqrt{n}}{\sigma}(l_0+c)} N(0,1)\, dy = 1 - \alpha$$

and

$$E_{\theta_2}\phi_0(\bar{X}) = \alpha \text{ gives} \int_{\frac{\sqrt{n}}{\sigma}(-l_0-c)}^{\frac{\sqrt{n}}{\sigma}(-l_0+c)} N(0,1)\, dy = 1 - \alpha$$

Both of these conditions give the same $c$ since $N(0, 1)$ is symmetric about 0. Given $\theta_1$, $\theta_2$, $n$ and $\sigma^2$ the constant $c$ is found so that the area under normal (0, 1) probability curve around $\frac{\sqrt{n}}{\sigma}c$-neighbourhood of the point $\frac{\sqrt{n}}{\sigma}l_0$ is $1-\alpha$ (refer Figure 4.5).
(b) For this case condition given in Eq. (4.17) gives

$$\Phi\left(\frac{\sqrt{n}}{\sigma}(x_2-\theta_1)\right) - \Phi\left(\frac{\sqrt{n}}{\sigma}(x_1-\theta_1)\right) = 1-\alpha$$
$$= \Phi\left(\frac{\sqrt{n}}{\sigma}(x_2-\theta_2)\right) - \Phi\left(\frac{\sqrt{n}}{\sigma}(x_1-\theta_2)\right)$$

As explained in (a)

$$x_1 = \frac{\theta_1+\theta_2}{2} - d, \quad x_2 = \frac{\theta_1+\theta_2}{2} + d$$

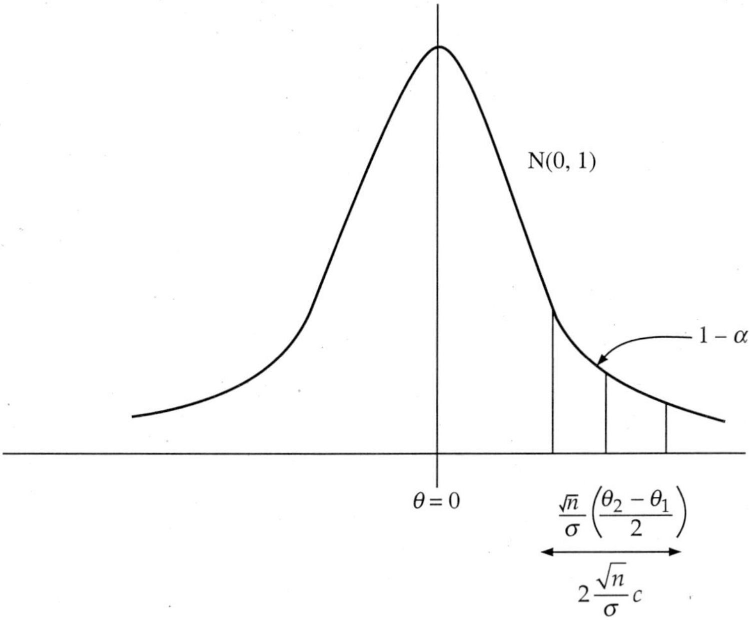


**Figure 4.5:** Critical region.

We get

$$\Phi\left(\frac{\sqrt{n}}{\sigma}\left(\frac{\theta_2-\theta_1}{2}+d\right)\right)-\Phi\left(\frac{\sqrt{n}}{\sigma}\left(\frac{\theta_2-\theta_1}{2}-d\right)\right)$$

$$=1-\alpha=\Phi\left(\frac{\sqrt{n}}{\sigma}\left(\frac{\theta_1-\theta_2}{2}+d\right)\right)-\Phi\left(\frac{\sqrt{n}}{\sigma}\left(\frac{\theta_1-\theta_2}{2}-d\right)\right)$$

For $n = 16$, $\sigma = 1$, $\alpha = 0.05$, we get

$$\Phi\left(4\left(\frac{1}{2}+d\right)\right)-\Phi\left(4\left(\frac{1}{2}-d\right)\right)=0.95$$

or

$$\Phi[2+4d]-\Phi[2-4d]=0.95$$

This gives $d = 0.911$; and UMP unbiased test for testing $H_0$ against $H_1$ at 5% level of significance is given by

$$\phi_0(\bar{x})=\begin{cases}1 & \text{if } \bar{x}<0.589 \text{ or } \bar{x}>2.411\\ 0 & \text{otherwise}\end{cases} \tag{4.19}$$

(c) Consider, now the testing problem $H_0 : \theta = \theta_0$ against $H_1 : \theta \neq \theta_0$, the UMP unbiased size-$\alpha$ test in this case is given by

$$\phi_0(\bar{x})=\begin{cases}1 & \text{if } \bar{x}<x_1 \text{ or } \bar{x}>x_2\\ 0 & \text{if } x_1<\bar{x}<x_2\end{cases}$$

$x_1, x_2$ are obtained by

$$E_{\theta_0}\phi_0(\bar{X}) = \alpha \quad \text{and} \quad E_{\theta_0}\left[\bar{X}\phi_0(\bar{X})\right] = \alpha\, E_{\theta_0}[\bar{X}]$$

The second condition gives

$$\frac{d}{d\theta}E_\theta\phi_0(\bar{X})\Big|_{\theta=\theta_0} = \frac{d}{d\theta}\int_{-\infty}^{x_1} N(\theta, \sigma^2/n)\, d\bar{x}\Big|_{\theta=\theta_0} + \frac{d}{d\theta}\int_{x_2}^{\infty} N(0, \sigma^2/n)\, d\bar{x}\Big|_{\theta=\theta_0} = 0$$

or

$$\int_{-\infty}^{\bar{x}_1}(\bar{x}-\theta)N(\theta, \sigma^2/n)\, d\bar{x}\Big|_{\theta=\theta_0} + \int_{x_2}^{\infty}(\bar{x}-\theta)N(\theta, \sigma^2/n)\big|_{\theta=\theta_0}\, d\bar{x} = 0$$

$$\int_{-\infty}^{\infty}(\bar{x}-\theta_0)N(\theta_0, \sigma^2/n)\, d\bar{x} - \int_{x_1}^{x_2}(\bar{x}-\theta_0)N(\theta_0, \sigma^2/n)\, d\bar{x} = 0$$

or

$$\int_{x_1}^{x_2}(\bar{x}-\theta_0)N(\theta_0, \sigma^2/n)\, d\bar{x} = 0$$

Since the normal distribution $N(\theta_0, \sigma^2/n)$ is symmetric about the location parameter $\theta_0$, the above integral will be zero if and only if $x_1$ and $x_2$ are equidistant from $\theta_0$ on either sides, i.e.

$$x_1 = \theta_0 - c$$

and

$$x_2 = \theta_0 + c$$

$c$ may be obtained by the size condition

$$E_{\theta_0}\phi_0(\bar{X}) = \alpha$$

or

$$\int_{\theta_0-c}^{\theta_0+c} N(\theta_0, \sigma^2/n)\, d\bar{x} = 1-\alpha$$

or

$$\int_{-\frac{\sqrt{n}}{\sigma}c}^{\frac{\sqrt{n}}{\sigma}c} N(0,1)\, dy = 2\int_0^{\frac{\sqrt{n}}{\sigma}c} N(0,1)\, dy = 1-\alpha$$

or

$$\int_0^{\frac{\sqrt{n}}{\sigma}c} N(0,1)\, dy = \frac{1-\alpha}{2}$$

or

$$P\left(N(0,1) > \frac{\sqrt{n}}{\sigma}c\right) = \frac{1}{2} - \frac{1-\alpha}{2} = \alpha/2$$

We get $c$ as $z_{\alpha/2}\cdot\frac{\sigma}{\sqrt{n}}$ from normal distribution table where $z_{\alpha/2}$ is the upper $\alpha/2$th quantile of $N(0,1)$. Finally, UMP unbiased test of size-$\alpha$ for testing $H_0 : \theta = \theta_0$ against $H_1 : \theta \neq \theta_0$ is given by

$$\phi_0(\bar{x}) = \begin{cases} 1 & \text{if } \bar{x} < \theta_0 - z_{\alpha/2}\cdot\frac{\sigma}{\sqrt{n}} \text{ or } \bar{x} > \theta_0 + z_{\alpha/2}\cdot\frac{\sigma}{\sqrt{n}} \\ 0 & \text{if } \theta_0 - z_{\alpha/2}\cdot\frac{\sigma}{\sqrt{n}} < \bar{x} < \theta + z_{\alpha/2}\cdot\frac{\sigma}{\sqrt{n}} \end{cases}$$

**Example 4.5.4.** *Let $X_1, \ldots, X_n$ be a random sample drawm from $N(\theta, \sigma^2)$, $\theta$ known. Find out a UMP unbiased size-$\alpha$ test for testing*

(a) $H_0 : \sigma_1 \leq \sigma \leq \sigma_2$ *against* $H_1 : \sigma < \sigma_1$ *or* $\sigma > \sigma_2$.

(b) $H_0 : \sigma = \sigma_0$ *against* $H_1 : \sigma \neq \sigma_0$.

***Solution:*** (a) UMP unbiased test will be a function of the sufficient statistic $T = \sum(x_i - \theta)^2$ for $\sigma^2$. It is given by

$$\phi_0(T) = \begin{cases} 1 & \text{if } T < x_1 \text{ or } T > x_2 \\ 0 & \text{otherwise} \end{cases}$$

so that

$$P\left[\frac{x_1}{\sigma_1^2} < \chi_n^2 < \frac{x_2}{\sigma_1^2}\right] = P\left[\frac{x_1}{\sigma_2^2} < \chi_n^2 < \frac{x_2}{\sigma_2^2}\right] = 1 - \alpha$$

$a_1$, $a_2$ and $b_1$, $b_2$ are so chosen that

$$P[a_1 < \chi_n^2 < a_2] = P[b_1 < \chi_n^2 < b_2] = 1 - \alpha$$

and $\frac{a_1}{a_2} = \frac{b_1}{b_2} = \frac{x_1}{x_2}$
(b) UMP unbiased test in this case is given by

$$\phi_0(T) = \begin{cases} 1 & \text{if } T < x_1 \text{ or } T > x_2 \\ 0 & \text{otherwise} \end{cases}$$

so that

$$E_{\sigma_0}\phi_0(T) = \alpha$$

and

$$E_{\sigma_0}[T\, \phi_0(T)] = \alpha \cdot E_{\sigma_0}[T]$$

On simplification of the second condition, we get

$$\int_{-\infty}^{x_1} tf(t|\sigma_0)dt + \int_{x_2}^{\infty} tf(t|\sigma_0)dt = \alpha E_{\sigma_0}[T]$$

$$E_{\sigma_0}[T] - \int_{x_1}^{x_2} tf(t|\sigma_0)dt = \alpha E_{\sigma_0}[T]$$

$$\int_{x_1}^{x_2} tf(t|\sigma_0)dt = (1 - \alpha) E_{\sigma_0}[T]$$

On setting $U = \frac{T}{\sigma_0^2}$, $\frac{x_1}{\sigma_0^2} = a_1$, $\frac{x_2}{\sigma_0^2} = a_2$, we get

$$\int_{a_1}^{a_2} uf_n(u)du = n(1 - \alpha)$$

or

$$\int_{a_1}^{a_2} u^{n/2} \exp\{-u/2\} du = n(1-\alpha)$$

Integration by parts gives

$$\frac{1}{\Gamma(\frac{n}{2})2^{n/2}}\left[-2u^{n/2}\exp\{-u/2\}\Big|_{a_1}^{a_2} + \frac{n}{2}\cdot 2.\int_{a_1}^{a_2} u^{n/2-1}\exp\{-u/2\}du\right] = n(1-\alpha)$$

On using the first condition $E_{\sigma_0}\phi_0(T) = \alpha$, we get

$$\frac{1}{\Gamma(\frac{n}{2})2^{n/2}}\left[-2u^{n/2}\exp\{-u/2\}\right]_{a_1}^{a_2} + n(1-\alpha) = n(1-\alpha)$$

or

$$a_1^{n/2}\exp\left\{-\frac{a_1}{2}\right\} = a_2^{n/2}\exp\left\{-\frac{a_2}{2}\right\}$$

Therefore, we choose $a_1,\ a_2$ s.t.

$$a_1^{n/2}\exp\left\{-a_1/2\right\} = a_2^{n/2}\exp\{-a_2/2\}$$

and

$$\int_{a_1}^{a_2} f_n(u)du = 1-\alpha$$

where $f_n(u)$ is the density of $\chi_n^2$ distribution. The UMP unbiased size-$\alpha$ test is, therefore, given by

$$\phi_0(T) = \begin{cases} 1 & \text{if } T < a_1 \text{ or } T > a_2 \\ 0 & \text{otherwise} \end{cases}$$

## *Review Questions*

**4.1** Explain most powerful, uniformly most powerful and uniformly most powerful unbiased tests with examples. Prove that most powerful tests are unbiased.

**4.2** Explain the concept of an unbiased test. Examine that whether a MP test is necessarily unbiased.

**4.3** Define MP and UMP region. Compare them and show that MP test is necessarily unbiased.

**4.4** Explain the concepts of uniformly most powerful test and unbiased test. Show that the UMP tests are unbiased. Show that the usual t-test for testing the hypothesis $\mu = \mu_0$ against $\mu \neq \mu_0$ of a normal population, $\sigma^2$ unknown, is UMP unbiased.

**4.5** Examine the existence of UMP test for testing $H_0 : \mu \leq \mu_0$ or $\mu > \mu_1 (\mu_1 > \mu_0)$ against $H_1 : \mu_0 < \mu < \mu_1$ based on a random sample of size $n$ from $N(\mu,\ 1)$.

**4.6** (a) Let $X$ follows one parameter exponential distribution, $f_\theta(x), \theta \in \Theta$. Consider a random sample $X_1, X_2 \ldots, X_n$ from this family to test the hypothesis $H_0 : \theta_1 \leq \theta \leq \theta_2$ against $H_1 : \theta < \theta_1$ or $\theta > \theta_2$. State the UMP unbiased size-$\alpha$ test and prove that it is UMP in the class of level $\alpha$ unbiased tests.

(b) Further, let $X \sim N(\theta, 1)$. Suggest the UMP unbiased size-$\alpha$ test for the testing problem in (a).

**4.7** Consider the problem of testing $H_0 : \theta = \theta_0$ against $H_1 : \theta \neq \theta_0$ for the family of distributions of the form $f(x|\theta) = c(\theta)h(x)\exp\{\theta x\}$. Prove that a two-sided test of the form:

$$\phi(x) = \begin{cases} 1 & \text{if } x < x_1 \text{ or } x > x_2 \\ \gamma_i & \text{if } x = x_i,\ i = 1, 2. \\ 0 & \text{if } x_1 < x < x_2 \end{cases}$$

where $x_1, x_2, \gamma_1$ and $\gamma_2$ are so chosen that $E_{\theta_0}\phi(X) = \alpha$ and $E_{\theta_0}X\phi(X)$ $= \alpha E_{\theta_0}\phi(X)$ is UMP unbiased.

**4.8** Let $X \sim N(\theta, 1)$. Prove that for testing $H_0 : \theta = 5$ against $H_1 : \theta \neq 5$, the two-sided test, with $x_1$ and $x_2$ equidistant from $\theta_0$, would be UMP unbiased of its size.

**4.9** (a) Explain the concepts of UMPU tests and show that the MP and UMP tests of size-$\alpha$ are unbiased.

(b) Use NP lemma to construct the best test for testing $\sigma^2 = 1$ against $\sigma^2 > 1$, when the sample is from $N(0, \sigma^2)$. Is this test UMP? Is it unbiased ? Give reasons?

**4.10** Let $X_1, X_2, \ldots, X_n$ be a sample from $N(0, \sigma^2)$. Consider the testing problem $H_0 : \sigma = \sigma_0$ against $H_1 : \sigma \neq \sigma_0$. Show that the test

$$\phi(\mathbf{x}) = \begin{cases} 1 & \text{if } \dfrac{\sum x_i^2}{\sigma_0^2} < c_1 \text{ or } \dfrac{\sum x_i^2}{\sigma_0^2} > c_2 \\ 0 & \text{otherwise} \end{cases}$$

is UMP unbiased of size-$\alpha$, where, $c_i$'s are determined by

$$\int_{c_1}^{c_2} \chi^2_{(n)}(y)\, dy = 1 - \alpha \text{ and } \int_{c_1}^{c_2} y\,\chi^2_{(n)}(y)\, dy = n(1 - \alpha)$$

Show unless $n$ is very small or $\sigma_0$ close to 0 or $\infty$, the latter condition reduces to

$$\int_0^{c_1} \chi^2_{(n)}(y) dy = \int_{c_2}^{\infty} \chi^2_{(n)}(y) dy = \alpha/2$$

and gives equal tail test.

**4.11** (a) Define the following terms in connection with testing of hypothesis: Critical region, statistical test, two types of errors and unbiasedness. Explain why unbiasedness is considered a desirable property for a test. Show that MP test and UMP test (if one exists) are necessarily unbiased.

(b) Let $X_1, X_2, \ldots, X_n$ be a random sample from a Poisson distribution with parameter $\theta$. Obtain UMP test of $H_0 : \theta = \theta_0$ against $H_1 : \theta > \theta_0$ at a level $\alpha$. Show that the power function of the test is monotonic increasing in $\theta$. Is this test unbiased for the alternative $\theta_1 (< \theta_0)$? Explain your answer.

**4.12** (a) Suppose that $W_0$ is defined by:

$$W_0 \ : \ \{x : f_\theta(x) > k_1 f_{\theta_0}(x) + k_2 f'_\theta(x)\}$$

Where, $k_1$ and $k_2$ are constants such that:

$$\int_{W_0} f_{\theta_0}(x)\, dx = \alpha \quad \text{and} \quad \int_{W_0} f'_{\theta_0}(x)\, dx = 0$$

Then prove that $W_0$ is a UMPU C.R. of size-$\alpha$ for testing $H_0 : \theta = \theta_0$ against $H_1 : \theta \neq \theta_0$.

(b) Obtain UMPU critical region for testing $H_0 : \mu = \mu_0$ against $H_1 : \mu \neq \mu_0$, if $(x_1, \ldots, x_n)$ is a random sample of size $n$ from $N(\mu,\ \sigma^2)$, when variance $\sigma^2$ is assumed to be known.

# Chapter 5

# UMP Tests for Multiparameter Case

## 5.1 INTRODUCTION

In the present chapter we will discuss the testing problem that involves a parameter vector $\boldsymbol{\theta}$ in $k$-parameter exponential family, where $X \sim f_{\boldsymbol{\theta}}$, $\boldsymbol{\theta} \in \Theta \subseteq \mathbb{R}^k$. Let the testing problem be stated as $H_0 : \boldsymbol{\theta} \in \Theta_0$ against $H_1 : \boldsymbol{\theta} \in \Theta_1$, where only one component in the parameter vector is involved in testing, while the rest $(k-1)$ are unknown. These unknown parameters are known as *nuisance parameters*. The density of $k$-parameter exponential family is given by

$$f(x|\,\boldsymbol{\theta}) = c(\boldsymbol{\theta})h(x)\exp\Big\{\sum_{i=1}^{k}\theta_i t_i(x)\Big\} \tag{5.1}$$

In this case the power function of any test $\phi$, $\beta_\phi(\boldsymbol{\theta}) = E_{\boldsymbol{\theta}}\phi(X)$ is continuous in $\boldsymbol{\theta}$ (as derived vide the results of Chapter 1). Let the sets $\Theta_0$ and $\Theta_1$ be disjoint such that $\Theta_0 \cup \Theta_1 = \Theta$ and the boundary region be defined as $\Theta_\beta = \overline{\Theta}_0 \cap \overline{\Theta}_1$, where $\overline{\Theta}_0$ and $\overline{\Theta}_1$ are the closure sets (the sets having points of the set and their limit points). Therefore, the power of a size-$\alpha$ unbiased test equals $\alpha$ at every $\boldsymbol{\theta} \in \Theta_\beta$. Such tests are called $\alpha$-similar tests on the boundary $\Theta_\beta$.

**Definition 5.1.1. ($\alpha$-similar Test)** A test $\phi$ is said to be $\alpha$-similar on a set $\Theta_\beta$ if $E_{\boldsymbol{\theta}}\phi(X) = \alpha \;\; \forall \;\; \boldsymbol{\theta} \in \Theta_\beta$. The class of $\alpha$-similar tests is denoted by $S_\alpha$, $S_\alpha = \{\phi \in \mathcal{D} : E_{\boldsymbol{\theta}}\phi(X) = \alpha \;\; \forall \;\; \boldsymbol{\theta} \in \Theta_\beta\}$.

For example, let $X \sim N(\theta, \sigma^2)$, $\sigma^2$ unknown $H_0 : \theta_1 \leq \theta \leq \theta_2$ against $H_1 : \theta < \theta_1$ or $\theta > \theta_2$, then the boundary set is given by

$$\Theta_\beta = \{(\theta, \sigma^2) \, : \, \theta = \theta_1 \text{ and } \theta = \theta_2, \; \sigma^2 > 0\}$$

A set is said to be similar on a set $\Theta_\beta \subseteq \Theta$, if it is $\alpha$-similar on $\Theta_\beta$ for some $\alpha$, $0 \leq \alpha \leq 1$.

It is clear that there exists atleast one similar test on every $\Theta_\beta$, namely $\phi(x) = \alpha,\ 0 \le \alpha \le 1$.

**Definition 5.1.2. (UMP $\alpha$-similar Test)** A test $\phi_0$ is said to be UMP $\alpha$-similar test of $H_0 : \boldsymbol{\theta} \in \Theta_0$ against $H_1 : \boldsymbol{\theta} \in \Theta_1$ in the class $\mathcal{S}_\alpha = \{\phi \in \mathcal{D} : E_{\boldsymbol{\theta}}\phi(X) = \alpha\ \ \forall\ \boldsymbol{\theta} \in \Theta_\beta\}$ if it has maximum power at each point $\boldsymbol{\theta} \in \Theta_1$ when compared to all other tests in $\mathcal{S}_\alpha$.

The objective of this chapter, is to find out a UMP unbiased size-$\alpha$ test $\phi_0$ from

$$\mathcal{U}_\alpha = \{\phi \in \mathcal{D} : \sup_{\boldsymbol{\theta}\in\Theta_0} E_{\boldsymbol{\theta}}\phi(X) = \alpha \text{ and } E_{\boldsymbol{\theta}}\phi(X) \ge \alpha\ \forall\ \boldsymbol{\theta} \in \Theta_1\}$$

for testing $H_0 : \boldsymbol{\theta} \in \Theta_0$ against $H_1 : \boldsymbol{\theta} \in \Theta_1$, when some nuisance parameters are involved in the testing.

## 5.2 UMP UNBIASED TEST FROM $\alpha$-SIMILAR TESTS AND $\alpha$-SIMILAR TESTS WITH NEYMAN STRUCTURE

We may easily note that $\mathcal{S}_\alpha$ is usually a bigger class as compared to $\mathcal{U}_\alpha$ since if the power function of every test $\phi$ is continuous, then a test $\phi$ in $\mathcal{U}_\alpha$ is also in $\mathcal{S}_\alpha$, i.e. $\mathcal{U}_\alpha \subset \mathcal{S}_\alpha$. It has been observed that finding a UMP test in $\mathcal{S}_\alpha$ is easier as compared to obtain it from $\mathcal{U}_\alpha$. We then search for a UMP test in $\mathcal{S}_\alpha$, a bigger class, provided it becomes UMP test in $\mathcal{U}_\alpha$(a smaller class). Theorem 5.2.1 provides an answer.

**Theorem 5.2.1.** *If for every test $\phi$ of $H_0 : \boldsymbol{\theta} \in \Theta_0$ against $H_1 : \boldsymbol{\theta} \in \Theta_1$, the power function $E_{\boldsymbol{\theta}}\phi(X)$ is continuous in $\boldsymbol{\theta}$, if $\phi_0$ is UMP in $\mathcal{S}_\alpha$ and is of size-$\alpha$ for testing $H_0$ against $H_1$, then $\phi_0$ is UMP in $\mathcal{U}_\alpha$, i.e. $\phi_0$ is UMP unbiased size-$\alpha$ test.*

*Proof.* Size of the test $\phi_0$ gives $E_{\boldsymbol{\theta}}\phi_0(X) \le \alpha\ \forall\ \boldsymbol{\theta} \in \Theta_0$. Note the test $\phi(x) \equiv \alpha$ is a member in $\mathcal{S}_\alpha$; $\phi_0$ is UMP in $\mathcal{S}_\alpha$ gives $E_{\boldsymbol{\theta}}\phi_0(X) \ge \alpha\quad \forall\ \boldsymbol{\theta} \in \Theta_1$. This shows that $\phi_0$ is unbiased and therefore $\phi_0 \in \mathcal{U}_\alpha$. The continuity of power function of every test $\phi$ gives that if $\phi$ is unbiased of size $\alpha$, it is $\alpha$-similar, i.e. $\mathcal{U}_\alpha \subset \mathcal{S}_\alpha$. The test $\phi_0$ is UMP in $\mathcal{U}_\alpha$, since UMP property remains preserved from bigger to smaller class, provided that the test $\phi$ belongs to the smaller class. Hence proved. □

In the light of Theorem 5.2.1 for a given testing problem, let us search for a UMP test in $\mathcal{S}_\alpha$, a bigger class and check whether the power function of every test is continuous in $\theta$. If the result is positive, we then check whether the UMP test is of size-$\alpha$. If the result is yes, such a test would be performed to check UMP in $\mathcal{U}_\alpha$. Therefore, in the subsequent sections we will start with finding a UMP test in $\mathcal{S}_\alpha$ for a given testing problem that involves nuisance parameters, and finally end up with a UMP test in $\mathcal{U}_\alpha$.

We assume that the family of distributions, $f_{\boldsymbol{\theta}}, \boldsymbol{\theta} \in \Theta$, admits a sufficient statistic $T$ for $\boldsymbol{\theta} \in \Theta_\beta$.

**Definition 5.2.1. (Neyman Structure)** Let T be a sufficient statistic for $\boldsymbol{\theta} \in \Theta_\beta$. A $\alpha$-similar test $\phi$ is said to have *Neyman structure* if

$$E(\phi(X)|\,T = t) = \alpha \;\; a.e.\; t \text{ on } P_{\boldsymbol{\theta}},\; \boldsymbol{\theta} \in \Theta_\beta$$

We shall note that a test $\phi$ having Neyman structure is also $\alpha$-similar since, $E_{\boldsymbol{\theta}}\phi(X) = E_{\boldsymbol{\theta}}^T E^{X|T}(\phi(X)|T) = \alpha;\ \forall\ \boldsymbol{\theta} \in \Theta_\beta$, but an $\alpha$-similar test would not necessarily have Neyman structure. Thus, the class of $\alpha$-similar tests having Neyman structure denoted by $\mathcal{N}_\alpha$ is contained in $\mathcal{S}_\alpha$, i.e $\mathcal{N}_\alpha \subseteq \mathcal{S}_\alpha$.

### 5.2.1 Construction of Similar Test with Neyman Structure

We search for a UMP test in $\mathcal{N}_\alpha$ instead of in $\mathcal{S}_\alpha$, since it is analytically easy to find a UMP test in $\mathcal{N}_\alpha$. Therefore, it becomes necessary to construct a similar test having Neyman structure. For this, we fix $T = t$ and get a partition on the sample space $\mathfrak{X}$ on which $\{x \in \mathfrak{X}\,|\,T = t\}$. Define a test $\phi$ on this partition so that $E(\phi(X)\,|\,T = t) = \alpha$. Then it is checked whether this holds for all values of $t$. If the condition is true then we have to obtain a test $\phi$ with a Neyman structure, and if the condition is not true, try for other test and see whether the given condition is satisfied. We continue the process till we get a test having Neyman structure. Many such tests could be constructed to constitute the class $\mathcal{N}_\alpha$.

Sometimes it is easier to find out a UMP test in $\mathcal{N}_\alpha$ (a smaller class) as compared to $\mathcal{S}_\alpha$ (a bigger one). One is then interested in knowing as to when would such a UMP test in $\mathcal{N}_\alpha$ be also UMP in $\mathcal{S}_\alpha$. The following Corollary 5.2.1 provides an answer:

**Corollary 5.2.1.** *If $T$ is a boundedly complete sufficient statistic for $\boldsymbol{\theta} \in \Theta_\beta$, then every similar test would have Neyman structure.*

*Proof.* Let us consider a $\alpha$-similar test $\phi$, i.e.

$$E_{\boldsymbol{\theta}}\phi(X) = \alpha\ \forall\ \boldsymbol{\theta} \in \Theta_\beta.$$

If the same is written as

$$E_{\boldsymbol{\theta}}^T(E^{X\,|\,T}\phi(X)|\,T) = \alpha\ \forall\ \boldsymbol{\theta} \in \Theta_\beta$$

or

$$E_{\boldsymbol{\theta}}^T(E^{X\,|\,T}\phi(X)|\,T - \alpha) = 0\ \forall\ \boldsymbol{\theta} \in \Theta_\beta.$$

Note $E^{X|T}$ does not index $\boldsymbol{\theta}$ since $T$ is a sufficient statistic. Boundedly completeness of $T$ gives

$$E^{X|T}(\phi(X)|T) = \alpha\ \forall\ \boldsymbol{\theta} \in \Theta_\beta$$

which shows that the $\alpha$-similar test $\phi$ has Neyman structure. □

The importance of Neyman structure is that it permits us to reduce the problem of finding a UMP $\alpha$-similar test for a composite hypothesis involving nuisance parameters to a familiar problem of finding a UMP test amongst the types of testing problems discussed in the previous chapters for a single parameter.

## 5.3 UMP UNBIASED TEST FOR ONE-SIDED TESTING PROBLEM

The results obtained in this section are the result Lehmann and Seheffe (1950, 1955) [132]) where the original testing problem is addressed on the basis of a sample $X_1, \ldots, X_n$ from $f(x|\boldsymbol{\theta})$ in Eq. (5.1) with $n \geq k$. The joint sufficiency of the statistics $T_1, T_2, \ldots, T_k$ for the parameter $\boldsymbol{\theta}$ results into the consideration of the joint density of $\mathbf{T} = (T_1, T_2, \ldots, T_k)$ given by

$$f_T(t|\,\boldsymbol{\theta}) = c(\boldsymbol{\theta})h(\mathbf{t})\exp\{\sum_{i=1}^{k}\theta_i t_i\} \tag{5.2}$$

Let us now consider the testing problem $H_0 : \boldsymbol{\theta} \in \Theta_0$ against $H_1 : \boldsymbol{\theta} \in \Theta_1$ where

$$\Theta_0 = \{\boldsymbol{\theta} \in \Theta : \theta_1 \leq \theta_1^0;\ \theta_2,\ \cdots,\ \theta_k \text{ are } (k-1) \text{ free parameters}\}$$

$$\Theta_1 = \{\boldsymbol{\theta} \in \Theta : \theta_1 > \theta_1^0;\ \theta_2,\ \cdots,\ \theta_k \text{ are } (k-1) \text{ free parameters}\}$$

This testing problem is known as unconditional testing problem. Further, consider the testing problem $H_0 : \theta_1 \leq \theta_1^0$ against $H_1 : \theta_1 > \theta_1^0$, that involves only one parameter $\theta_1$; this problem is called a conditional testing problem. The terms used here as unconditional and conditional derive their reference from the consideration of joint distribution of sufficient statistics $T_1,\ \ldots,\ T_k$ and conditional distribution of $T_1$ given $T_2, \ldots, T_k$, used in the development of this section. The conditional testing problem requires elimination of nuisance parameters $\theta_2, \ldots, \theta_k$, from the joint density $f_T(t|\boldsymbol{\theta})$ in Eq. (5.2). For each fixed $\theta_1$, $(T_2, \ldots, T_k)$ is a sufficient statistic for $(\theta_2, \ldots, \theta_k)$ whose joint density is given by

$$f_{T_2,\ldots,T_k}(t_2, \ldots, t_k|\,\boldsymbol{\theta}) = c(\boldsymbol{\theta})\Big[\int h(\mathbf{t})\exp\{\theta_1 t_1\}\,dt_1\Big]\exp\{\sum_{i=2}^{k}\theta_i t_i\}$$

This gives the conditional density of $T_1|\ T_2, \ldots, T_k$

$$f_{T_1|\,T_2,\ldots,T_k}(t_1|\theta_1) = \Big[\int h(\mathbf{t})\ \exp\{\theta_1 t_1\}dt_1\Big]^{-1} h(\mathbf{t})\exp\{\theta_1 t_1\}$$

We see that the conditional density of $T_1|\ T_2, \ldots, T_k$ is one-parameter exponential family and is independent of $\theta_2, \ldots, \theta_k$. Therefore, Karlin and

Rubin theorem could be applied in the conditional testing problem of testing $H_0 : \theta_1 \leq \theta_1^0$ against $H_1 : \theta_1 > \theta_1^0$ to get a UMP unbiased size-$\alpha$ test

$$\phi_0(t_1, \ldots, t_k) = \begin{cases} 1 & \text{if } t_1 > z(t_2, \ldots, t_k) \\ \gamma(t_2, \ldots, t_k) & \text{if } t_1 = z(t_2, \ldots, t_k) \\ 0 & \text{if } t_1 < z(t_2, \ldots, t_k) \end{cases}$$

where, $\gamma$ and $z$ are the functions of $t_2, \ldots, t_k$ such that

$$E_{\theta_1^0}(\phi_0(\mathbf{T})|\, T_2, \ldots, T_k) = \alpha$$

Clearly, the test $\phi_0$ has maximum conditional power for $\theta_1 > \theta_1^0$ and minimum conditional power for $\theta_1 \leq \theta_1^0$ in the class of tests $\mathcal{C} = \{\phi \in \mathcal{D} : \sup_{\theta_1 \leq \theta_1^0} E_{\theta_1}(\phi(T)\,|\,T_2, \ \ldots, \ T_k) = \alpha\}$. Let us define a class of $\alpha$-similar tests on the boundary $\Theta_\beta$ by $\mathcal{S}_\alpha = \{\phi \in \mathcal{D} : E_{\boldsymbol{\theta}}\phi(\mathbf{T}) = \alpha \forall \ \boldsymbol{\theta} \in \Theta_\beta\}$ for the original (unconditional) testing problem. The boundary set has been defined as $\Theta_\beta = \{\boldsymbol{\theta} : \theta_1 = \theta_1^0\}$. If we define a class of $\alpha$-similar tests having Neyman structure, $\mathcal{N}_\alpha$, by $\mathcal{N}_\alpha = \{\phi \in \mathcal{D} : E_{\theta_1^0}(\phi(\mathbf{T})|\, T_2, \ldots, T_k) = \alpha \ a.e. \ t_1, \ldots, t_k$ under $f(\mathbf{t}\,|\,\boldsymbol{\theta}), \boldsymbol{\theta} \in \Theta_\beta\}$. We then get $\mathcal{S}_\alpha \subset \mathcal{N}_\alpha$ and finally $\mathcal{S}_\alpha = \mathcal{N}_\alpha$ since by definition of Neyman structure and similar tests we have already noted $\mathcal{N}_\alpha \subset \mathcal{S}_\alpha$. The maximum conditional power attained by the test $\phi_0$ in $\mathcal{S}_\alpha = \mathcal{N}_\alpha$ at each $\theta_1 > \theta_1^0$ gives

$$\begin{aligned} E_{\boldsymbol{\theta}}\phi_0(\mathbf{T}) &= E_{\boldsymbol{\theta}}^{T_2,\ldots,T_k}(E_{\theta_1}^{T_1|T_2,\ldots,T_k}\phi_0(\mathbf{T})) \\ &\geq E_{\boldsymbol{\theta}}^{T_2,\ldots,T_k}(E_{\theta_1}^{T_1|T_2,\ldots,T_k}\phi(\mathbf{T})) \\ &= E_{\boldsymbol{\theta}}\phi(\mathbf{T}) \ \ \forall \ \ \boldsymbol{\theta} \in \Theta_1, \ \ (\theta_1 > \theta_1^0) \end{aligned}$$

which shows that $\phi_0$ has attained the maximum unconditional power over $\Theta_1$, i.e. $\phi_0$ is UMP $\alpha$-similar. Further, for $\boldsymbol{\theta} \in \Theta_0, \ \theta_1 < \theta_1^0$

$$E_{\boldsymbol{\theta}}\phi_0(\mathbf{T}) = E_{\boldsymbol{\theta}}^{T_2,\ldots,T_k}(E_{\theta_1}^{T_1|T_2,\ldots,T_k}\phi_0(\mathbf{T})) \leq \alpha$$

shows that $\phi_0$ is of size-$\alpha$ in the unconditional testing problem. Since $\phi_0$ is UMP $\alpha$-similar in $S_\alpha$ and of size-$\alpha$ it is UMP unbiased size-$\alpha$ test in $\mathcal{U}_\alpha$ for the original unconditional testing problem by Theorem 5.2.1. Every $\alpha$-similar test in $\mathcal{S}_\alpha$ would have Neyman structure by Corollary 5.2.1 since $(T_2, \ldots, T_k)$ is complete, hence boundedly complete sufficient statistics for $\boldsymbol{\theta} \in \Theta_\beta$.

## 5.4 UMP UNBIASED TESTS FOR TWO-SIDED TESTING PROBLEMS

### 5.4.1 UMP Unbiased Test for $H_0 : \theta_1^{(1)} \leq \theta_1 \leq \theta^{(2)}$ against $H_1 : \theta_1 < \theta_1^{(1)}$ or $\theta_1 > \theta_1^{(2)}$

Let $X \sim f(x\,|\,\boldsymbol{\theta}), \ \theta \in \Theta \subseteq E^k$ be $k$-parameter exponential family of distributions as given in Eq. (5.1). Consider a testing problem $H_0 : \theta \in \Theta_0$

against $H_1 : \theta \in \Theta_1$, where, $\Theta_0 = \{\boldsymbol{\theta} \in \Theta : \theta_1^{(1)} \leq \theta_1 \leq \theta_1^{(2)}\}$ and $\Theta_1 = \{\boldsymbol{\theta} \in \Theta : \theta_1 < \theta_1^{(1)}$ or $\theta_1 > \theta_1^{(2)}\}$ referred to as unconditional testing problem (Ferguson (1967)[54]). For this testing problem we would search for a UMP unbiased size-$\alpha$ test from the class of all size-$\alpha$ unbiased tests defined by $\{\phi \in \mathcal{D} : \sup_{\boldsymbol{\theta}\in\Theta_0} E_{\boldsymbol{\theta}}\phi(T) = \alpha$ and $E_{\boldsymbol{\theta}}\,\phi(T) > \alpha,\ \boldsymbol{\theta} \in \Theta_1\}$. If we assume that $T_2, \ldots, T_k$ are given, we may treat the conditional problem of testing $H_0 : \theta_1^{(1)} \leq \theta_1 \leq \theta_1^{(2)}$ against $H_1 : \theta_1 < \theta_1^{(1)}$ or $\theta_1 > \theta_1^{(2)}$ based on the conditional distribution of $T_1$ given $T_2, \ldots, T_k$. This conditional distribution is one-parameter exponential family of distributions, therefore, by Karlin and Rubin theorem a UMP unbiased size-$\alpha$ test for the conditional testing problem $H_0$ against $H_1$ is given by

$$\phi_0(t_1, \ldots, t_k) = \begin{cases} 1 & \text{if } t_1 < z_1(t_2, \ldots, t_k) \text{ or } t_1 > z_2(t_2, \ldots, t_k) \\ \gamma_i(t_2, \ldots, t_k) & \text{if } t_1 = z_i(t_2, \ldots, t_k);\ i = 1, 2 \\ 0 & \text{if } z_1(t_2, \ldots, t_k) < t_1 < z_2(t_2 \ldots, t_k) \end{cases} \tag{5.3}$$

where $z_1$, $z_2$, $\gamma_1$ and $\gamma_2$ are chosen such that

$$E_{\theta_1^{(1)}}(\phi(\mathbf{T})|\,T_2, \ldots, T_k) = \alpha = E_{\theta_1^{(2)}}(\phi(\mathbf{T})|\,T_2, \ldots, T_k)$$

From the results on two-sided testing problems for one parameter exponential family discussed in Chapter 4, the test $\phi_0$ has maximum conditional power at every $\theta_1 < \theta_1^{(1)}$ or $\theta_1 > \theta_1^{(2)}$ and smallest conditional power at every $\theta_1^{(1)} \leq \theta_1 \leq \theta_2^{(2)}$ in the class of size-$\alpha$ unbiased tests $\mathcal{U}_\alpha = \{\phi \in \mathcal{D} : \sup_{\theta_1^{(1)}<\theta_1<\theta_1^{(2)}} E_{\theta_1}(\phi(\mathbf{T})|\,T_2, \ldots, T_k) = \alpha,\ E_{\theta_1}(\phi(\mathbf{T})|\,T_2, \ldots, T_k) > \alpha$ for all $\theta_1 < \theta_1^{(1)}$ or $\theta_1 > \theta_1^{(2)}$ and $E_{\theta_1^{(1)}}(\phi(\mathbf{T})|\,T_2, \ldots, T_k) = \alpha = E_{\theta_1^{(2)}}(\phi(\mathbf{T})|T_2, \ldots, T_k)\}$. $\mathcal{U}_\alpha$ for conditional testing problem is identical to the class of size-$\alpha$ unbiased tests for unconditional testing problem since the statistic $(T_2, \ldots, T_k)$ is boundedly complete and sufficient for $\boldsymbol{\theta} \in \Theta_\beta$. Further, any test in $\mathcal{U}_\alpha$ for testing $H_0$ against $H_1$ would be $\alpha$-similar on the boundary $\Theta_\beta = \{\boldsymbol{\theta} : \theta_1 = \theta_1^{(1)}$ or $\theta_1 = \theta_1^{(2)}\}$, i.e. such a test would belong to the class of $\alpha$-similar tests, $\mathcal{S}_\alpha = \{\phi \in \mathcal{D} : E_{\boldsymbol{\theta}}\phi(\mathbf{T}) = \alpha$ for all $\boldsymbol{\theta} \in \Theta_\beta\}$. This gives $\mathcal{U}_\alpha \subset \mathcal{S}_\alpha$. Any test in $\mathcal{S}_\alpha$ must have Neyman structure by Corollary 5.2.1 since $(T_2, \ldots, T_k)$ is boundedly complete sufficient statistic for $(\theta_2, \ldots, \theta_k)$ for each fixed $\theta_1 = \theta_1^{(1)}$ or $\theta_1 = \theta_1^{(2)}$, i.e. such a test would belong to $\mathcal{N}_\alpha = \{\phi \in \mathcal{D} : E_{\theta_1^{(1)}}(\phi(\mathbf{T})|\,T_2, \ldots, T_k) = \alpha = E_{\theta_1^{(2)}}(\phi(\mathbf{T})|\,T_2, \ldots, T_k)$ a.e. $(t_2, \ldots, t_k)$ under all distributions $f(t_2, \ldots, t_k|\boldsymbol{\theta})$, $\boldsymbol{\theta} \in \Theta_\beta\}$. This shows $\mathcal{S}_\alpha = \mathcal{N}_\alpha$. In $\mathcal{N}_\alpha = \mathcal{S}_\alpha$ the test $\phi_0$ has maximum conditional power at each $\theta_1 < \theta_1^{(1)}$ or $\theta_1 > \theta_1^{(2)}$ which gives

$$\begin{aligned} E_{\boldsymbol{\theta}}\phi_0(T) &= E_{\boldsymbol{\theta}}(E_{\theta_1}(\phi_0(\mathbf{T})|\,T_2, \ldots, T_k)) \\ &\geq E_{\boldsymbol{\theta}}(E_{\theta_1}(\phi(\mathbf{T})|\,T_2, \ldots, T_k)) = E_{\boldsymbol{\theta}}\phi(T) \end{aligned}$$

showing that $\phi_0$ has attained maximum unconditional power at each $\boldsymbol{\theta} \in \Theta_1$, therefore, $\phi_0$ is UMP in $\mathcal{S}_\alpha$. The test $\phi_0$ in $\mathcal{N}_\alpha = \mathcal{S}_\alpha$ has minimum conditional power at each $\theta_1^{(1)} \leq \theta_1 \leq \theta_1^{(2)}$

$$E_{\boldsymbol{\theta}}\phi_0(T) = E_{\boldsymbol{\theta}}(E_{\theta_1}(\phi_0(\mathbf{T})|\, T_2, \ldots, T_k)) \leq \alpha$$

showing that $\phi_0$ is a test of size-$\alpha$. Therefore, by Theorem 5.2.1, the test $\phi_0$ is UMP in $\mathcal{U}_\alpha$ for unconditional testing problem. We finally conclude that $\phi_0$ is UMP unbiased size-$\alpha$ test.

### 5.4.2 UMP Unbiased Test for $H_0 : \theta_1 = \theta_1^{(0)}$ against $H_1 : \theta_1 \neq \theta_1^{(0)}$

Let us consider the unconditional testing problem $H_0 : \boldsymbol{\theta} \in \Theta_0$ against $H_1 : \boldsymbol{\theta} \in \Theta_1$ where $\Theta_0 = \{\boldsymbol{\theta} : \theta_1 = \theta_1^{(0)}\}$ and $\Theta_1 = \{\boldsymbol{\theta} : \theta_1 \neq \theta_1^{(0)}\}$ (Ferguson, 1967[54]). The corresponding conditional testing problem will be given by $H_0 : \theta_1 = \theta_1^{(0)}$ against $H_1 : \theta_1 \neq \theta_1^{(0)}$. The class of size-$\alpha$ unbiased tests for testing unconditional problem is given by

$$\mathcal{U}_\alpha = \{\phi \in \mathcal{D} : \sup_{\boldsymbol{\theta}\in\Theta_0} E_{\boldsymbol{\theta}}\phi(\mathbf{T}) = \alpha \text{ and } E_{\boldsymbol{\theta}}\phi(\mathbf{T}) \geq \alpha \ \ \forall\, \boldsymbol{\theta} \in \Theta_1\}$$

$$= \left\{\phi \in \mathcal{D} : E_{\boldsymbol{\theta}}\phi(\mathbf{T}) = \alpha \ \forall\, \boldsymbol{\theta} \in \Theta_\beta \text{ and } \frac{\partial}{\partial\theta_1} E_{\boldsymbol{\theta}}\phi(\mathbf{T})\Big|_{\theta_1=\theta_1^{(0)}} = 0\right\}$$

We see that a test in $\mathcal{U}_\alpha$ must not only be $\alpha$-similar but further slope to its power function at $\theta_1 = \theta_1^{(0)}$ must also be zero. The zero slope condition, the second condition in $\mathcal{U}_\alpha$, may also be written as

$$E_{\boldsymbol{\theta}}((\phi(\mathbf{T}) - \alpha)T_1)\Big|_{\theta_1=\theta_1^{(0)}} = 0 \tag{5.4}$$

Further, any $\alpha$-similar test in $\mathcal{U}_\alpha$ must have Neyman structure since $T_2, \ldots, T_k$ is complete sufficient statistic for $\boldsymbol{\theta} \in \Theta_\beta$ given by Corollary 5.2.1. Therefore, the first condition in $\mathcal{U}_\alpha$, namely

$$E_{\boldsymbol{\theta}}\phi(\mathbf{T}) = \alpha \text{ for all } \boldsymbol{\theta} \in \Theta_\beta$$

reduces to

$$E_{\theta_1^{(0)}}(\phi(\mathbf{T})|T_2, \ldots, T_k) = \alpha \tag{5.5}$$

using Eq. (5.5), Eq. (5.4) reduces to

$$E_{\theta_1^{(0)}}((\phi(\mathbf{T}) - \alpha)T_1|T_2, \ldots, T_k)\Big|_{\theta_1=\theta_1^{(0)}} = 0 \tag{5.6}$$

except perhaps for a set of probability zero. Using Eqs. (5.5) and (5.6) the class of tests $\mathcal{U}_\alpha$ is equivalently written as

$$\mathcal{U}_\alpha = \{\phi \in \mathcal{D} : E_{\theta_1^{(0)}}(\phi(\mathbf{T})|T_2, \ldots, T_k) = \alpha$$

and

$$E_{\theta_1^{(0)}}((\phi(\mathbf{T})-\alpha)T_1|T_2,\ldots,T_k)=0\}$$

By the result of Chapter 4, the two-sided test in $\phi_0$ in Eq. (5.3) that satisfies Eq. (5.5) and Eq. (5.6) (where $\phi_0 \in \mathcal{U}_\alpha$) has maximum conditions power for all $\theta_1 \neq \theta_1^{(0)}$. Then at $\boldsymbol{\theta} \in \Theta_1$, the unconditional power

$$\begin{aligned}E_{\boldsymbol{\theta}}\phi_0(\mathbf{T}) &= E_{\boldsymbol{\theta}}(E_{\theta_1}(\phi_0(\mathbf{T})|T_2,\ldots,T_k))\\ &\geq E_{\boldsymbol{\theta}}(E_{\theta_1}(\phi(\mathbf{T})|T_2,\ldots,T_k)) = E_{\boldsymbol{\theta}}\phi(\mathbf{T})\end{aligned}$$

This shows that $\phi_0$ is UMP, i.e. $\phi_0$ has greatest the unconditional power. Further, for $\boldsymbol{\theta} \in \Theta_0$

$$E_{\boldsymbol{\theta}}\phi_0(\mathbf{T}) = E_{\boldsymbol{\theta}}(E_{\theta_1^{(0)}}(\phi_0(\mathbf{T})|T_2,\ldots,T_k)) = \alpha$$

This shows that $\phi_0$ is of size-$\alpha$ in the unconditional problem. Therefore, $\phi_0$ is UMP unbiased size-$\alpha$ test for the unconditional testing problem.

## 5.5 UMP UNBIASED TESTS FOR A LINEAR COMBINATION OF $k$-PARAMETERS

We shall consider a testing problem when it concerns testing for a parameter which is a linear combination of $k$-parameters of an exponential family. Define

$$\theta^* = \sum_{i=1}^{k} c_i\theta_i, \quad c_1 \neq 0$$

A $k$-parameter exponential family may be written as

$$\begin{aligned}f_T(\mathbf{t}|\boldsymbol{\theta}) &= c(\boldsymbol{\theta})h(\mathbf{t})\exp\{\sum_{i=1}^{k}\theta_i t_i\}\\ &= c(\boldsymbol{\theta})h(\mathbf{t})\exp\{\theta^*\frac{t_1}{c_1}+\sum_{j=2}^{k}\theta_j(t_j-\frac{c_j}{c_1}t_1)\}\\ &= f_{(\frac{T_1}{c_1},\, T_2-(\frac{c_2}{c_1})T_1,\ldots,T_k-(\frac{c_k}{c_1})T_1)}\left(\frac{t_1}{c_1},\, t_2-\frac{c_2}{c_1}t_1,\ldots,t_k-\frac{c_k}{c_1}t_1\middle|\theta^*,\theta_2,\ldots,\theta_k\right)\end{aligned}$$

This is a $k$-parameter exponential family with parameters $(\theta^*,\ \theta_2,\ldots,\theta_k)$ and the corresponding complete sufficient statistic has been given by $(\frac{T_1}{c_1}, T_2 - \frac{c_2}{c_1}T_1,\ldots,T_k-\frac{c_k}{c_1}T_1)$. Now if the hypothesis involves $\theta^*$, we proceed similarly as we did for $\theta_1$ in the previous subsections, and finally get a UMP unbiased size-$\alpha$ test for unconditional testing problem.

## 5.6 ON FINDING UMP UNBIASED TESTS

If has been seen in the previous sections that finding a UMP unbiased size-$\alpha$ test for $k$-parameter exponential family, one requires to calculate the conditional distribution of $T_1$ given $T_2, \ldots, T_k$ which is often not easy. A much simpler approach is based on a statistic $V(\mathbf{T})$ so that it is independent of $(T_2, \ldots, T_k)$, increasing in $T_1$ for every fixed value of $(T_2, \ldots, T_k)$ and linear in $T_1$ where $(T_2, \ldots, T_k)$ is jointly complete sufficient statistic for $(\theta_2, \ldots, \theta_k)$. The characterization of such a statistic is achieved through an ancillary statistic $V$ determined by a well known Basu's theorem.

**Theorem 5.6.1.** (Basu (1955)) *Let $X_1, X_2, \ldots, X_n$ be a random sample from a family of distributions $\mathcal{P} = \{f(x,\theta),\ \theta \in \Theta\}$ and let $T$ be a boundedly complete sufficient statistic for $\theta$. If $Z$ is any statistic then $T$ and $Z$ are independent if and only if the distribution of $Z$ is independent of $\theta$, i.e. $Z$ is ancillary.*

Under this approach the test obtained as a function of a single statistic $V$ is equivalent to the conditional test in terms of $T_1$ given $t_2, \ldots, t_k$. The advantage of using such a test is its unconditional nature in terms of a single statistic $V$, making it more convenient to construct. Lehmann(1986, Chapter 5, Section 1) has discussed this approach in much detail. We shall outline the main results and defer their proofs for the purpose of their quick applications. Readers who are interested in further details may refer to Lehmann Chapter 5.

(a) Let us consider the testing problem:

$$H_0 : \boldsymbol{\theta} \in \Theta_0; \quad \Theta_0 = \{(\theta_1, \ldots, \theta_k) : \theta_1 \leq \theta_1^0\}$$

$$\text{against} \quad H_1 : \boldsymbol{\theta} \in \Theta_1; \quad \Theta_1 = \{(\theta_1, \ldots, \theta_k) : \theta_1 > \theta_1^0\}$$

The procedure suggests to find out such a $V = V(\mathbf{T})$ which is independent of $(T_2, \ldots, T_k)$ when $\theta_1 = \theta_1^0$ and which is monotone in $T_1$ for each fixed value of $(T_2 = t_2, \ldots, T_k = t_k)$. We have already seen that $(T_2, \ldots, T_k)$ is boundedly complete for $\boldsymbol{\theta} \in \Theta_\beta$. Lehmann had shown that if the distribution of such a $V$ does not depend on $(\theta_2, \ldots, \theta_k)$ then $V$ is independent of $(T_2, \ldots, T_k)$. Therefore, one is required to suggest, such a $V$ whose distribution does not depend on $(\theta_2, \ldots, \theta_k)$ and that it is monotone in $T_1$ for each fixed $(t_2, \ldots, t_k)$. The UMP unbiased size-$\alpha$ test for testing $H_0 : \boldsymbol{\theta} \in \Theta_0$ against $H_1 : \boldsymbol{\theta} \in \Theta_1$ is given by

$$\phi_0(v) = \begin{cases} 1 & \text{if } v > v_0 \\ \gamma_0 & \text{if } v = v_0 \\ 0 & \text{if } v < v_0 \end{cases}$$

where $v_0$, $\gamma_0$ does not depend on $(t_2, \ldots, t_k)$ and are obtained by

$$E_{\theta_0}^V[\phi_0(V)] = \alpha$$

(b) Let us now consider the testing problem

$$\begin{aligned} & H_0 : \boldsymbol{\theta} \in \Theta_0; \quad \Theta_0 = \{(\theta_1, \ldots, \theta_k) : \theta_1^{(1)} \leq \theta_1 \leq \theta_1^{(2)}\} \\ \text{against} \quad & H_1 : \boldsymbol{\theta} \in \Theta_1; \quad \Theta_1 = \{(\theta_1, \ldots, \theta_k) | \theta_1 < \theta_1^{(1)} \text{ or } \theta_1 > \theta_1^{(2)}\} \end{aligned}$$

Lehmann suggests to find out a $V$ which is independent of $(T_2, \ldots, T_k)$ when $\theta_1 = \theta_1^{(1)}$ and $\theta_1 = \theta_1^{(2)}$ or alternatively such a $V$ whose distribution does not depend on $(\theta_2, \ldots, \theta_k)$, and $V$ must be monotone in $T_1$ for each fixed $t_2, \ldots, t_k$. Then UMP unbiased size-$\alpha$ test for the two-sided testing problem is given by

$$\phi_0(v) = \begin{cases} 1 & \text{if } v < v_1 \text{ or } v > v_2 \\ \gamma_i & \text{if } v = v_i, i = 1, 2 \\ 0 & \text{if } v_1 < v < v_2 \end{cases}$$

where, $v_1$, $v_2$, $\gamma_1$, $\gamma_2$ are obtained by

$$E_{\theta_1^{(1)}}[\phi_0(V)] = \alpha = E_{\theta_1^{(2)}}[\phi_0(V)]$$

(c) Let us now consider the two-sided testing problem

$$\begin{aligned} & H_0 : \boldsymbol{\theta} \in \Theta_0; \quad \Theta_0 = \{(\theta_1, \ldots, \theta_k) : \theta_1 = \theta_1^{(0)}\} \\ \text{against} \quad & H_1 : \boldsymbol{\theta} \in \Theta_1; \quad \Theta_1 = \{(\theta_1, \ldots, \theta_k) : \theta_1 \neq \theta_1^{(0)}\} \end{aligned}$$

Lehmann suggests to find out a $V(\mathbf{T})$ which is independent of $(T_2, \ldots, T_k)$ when $\theta_1 = \theta_1^{(0)}$ or in other words a $V$ whose distribution does not depend on $(\theta_2, \ldots, \theta_k)$ and that $V$ is linear in $T_1$ for each fixed $t_2, \ldots, t_k$, i.e.

$$v(\mathbf{t}) = a(t_2, \ldots, t_k)t_1 + b(t_2, \ldots, t_k) \text{ with } a(t_2, \ldots, t_k) > 0$$

Then the UMP unbiased size-$\alpha$ test would be given by

$$\phi_0(v) = \begin{cases} 1 & \text{if } v < v_1 \text{ or } v > v_2 \\ \gamma_i & \text{if } v = v_i; \quad i = 1, 2. \\ 0 & \text{if } v_1 < v < v_2 \end{cases}$$

where, $v_1$, $v_2$, $\gamma_1$ and $\gamma_2$ are obtained by

$$E_{\theta_1^{(0)}}[\phi_0(V)] = \alpha$$

and

$$E_{\theta_1^{(0)}}[V\phi_0(V)] = \alpha E_{\theta_1^{(0)}}(V)$$

We now consider few classical examples that would explain conditional approach using Neyman structure and the unconditional approach based on an ancillary statistic used by Lehmann.

## 5.7 Solved Examples

**Example 5.7.1.** (Ferguson (1967)[54]) *Consider a random sample* $X_1, X_2, \ldots,$ $X_n$ *from* $N(\mu, \sigma^2)$, *when both* $\mu$ *and* $\sigma^2$ *are unknown. Find the UMP unbiased size-*$\alpha$ *test for testing* $H_0 : \mu \leq 0$ *against* $H_1 : \mu > 0$.

***Solution:*** **Conditional approach:** The joint distribution of $X_1, \ldots, X_n$ is given by

$$f_{\mathbf{X}}(\mathbf{x}|\,\mu, \sigma^2) = \Big(\frac{1}{2\pi\sigma^2}\Big)^{n/2} \exp\Big\{-\frac{n\mu^2}{2\sigma^2}\Big\} \exp\Big\{\frac{\mu}{\sigma^2}\sum x_i - \frac{1}{2\sigma^2}\sum x_i^2\Big\}$$

which gives

$$f_{\mathbf{T}}(\mathbf{t}|\boldsymbol{\theta}) = c(\mu, \sigma) \cdot (h(\mathbf{x}) \equiv 1) \cdot \exp\{\theta_1 t_1 + \theta_2 t_2\}$$

where

$$\begin{aligned} k &= 2 \\ \theta_1 &= \frac{\mu}{\sigma^2} \quad ; \quad t_1 = \sum x_i \\ \theta_2 &= -\frac{1}{2\sigma^2}; \quad t_2 = \sum x_i^2 \end{aligned}$$

The hypothesis $H_0 : \mu \leq \mu_0,\ \sigma^2 > 0$ against $H_1 : \mu > \mu_0,\ \sigma^2 > 0$ could be rewritten as $H_0 : \theta_1 \leq 0,\ \theta_2 < 0$ against $H_1 : \theta_1 > 0,\ \theta_2 < 0$. This testing problem is known as unconditional testing problem. By using the results of section 5.3, an UMP unbiased size-$\alpha$ test for this testing problem would be given by

$$\phi_0(t_1, t_2) = \begin{cases} 1 & \text{if } t_1 > z(t_2) \\ 0 & \text{if } t_1 \leq z(t_2) \end{cases}$$

This test is non-randomized since the distribution of $T_1$ given $T_2$ is continuous where $z(t_2)$ is obtained by

$$P_{\theta_1=0}\{T_1 > z(t_2)|T_2 = t_2\} = \alpha$$

The distribution of $(\frac{T_2}{\sigma^2})|_{\theta_1=0}$ is $\chi_n^2 = G(\frac{n}{2}, 2)$ or $T_2|_{\theta_1=0}$ is distributed as $\frac{1}{\sigma^2} f_{\frac{T_2}{\sigma^2}}(\frac{t_2}{\sigma^2})$, where $f$ is the density of gamma distribution $G(\frac{n}{2}, 2)$. Therefore, the conditional distribution of $X_1, \ldots, X_n$ given $T_2 = t_2$ becomes

$$
\begin{aligned}
f_{\mathbf{X}|\,T_2=t_2}(\mathbf{x}|\,t_2) &= \frac{f_{\mathbf{X}}(\mathbf{x}|(\mu, \sigma^2))}{\frac{1}{\sigma^2} f_{\frac{T_2}{\sigma^2}}(t_2|\sigma^2)} \\
&= \frac{\left(\frac{1}{2\pi\sigma^2}\right)^{n/2} e^{-\frac{1}{2\sigma^2} t_2}}{\frac{1}{\sigma^2} \frac{1}{\Gamma(\frac{n}{2})\, 2^{n/2} e^{-\frac{t_2}{2\sigma^2}} (t_2)^{n/2-1}}} \\
&= c(\sigma) \cdot \left(\frac{1}{\sqrt{t_2}}\right)^{n-2} \\
&= f_{T_1|\,t_2}(t_1|\,t_2)
\end{aligned}
$$

and we get the distribution of $T_1$ given $T_2 = t_2$ when $\theta_1 = 0$, which is uniform on the sphere $T_2 = \sum X_i^2 = t_2$. Thus $\sqrt{t_2}$ is a scale parameter for the conditional distribution of $T_1|\,t_2$. It follows that $z(t_2)/\sqrt{t_2}$ in

$$P_{\theta_1=0}\left\{\frac{T_1}{\sqrt{t_2}} > \frac{z(t_2)}{\sqrt{t_2}}\middle| T_2 = t_2\right\} = \alpha$$

must be a constant; and the resulting UMP unbiased test will be of the type $\frac{t_1}{\sqrt{t_2}} > c$. Let us denote $\bar{x} = t_1/n$ and $s^2 = \sum(x_i - \bar{x})^2/n = \sum x_i^2/n - \bar{x}^2 = t_2/n - (t_1/n)^2$. On writing $\frac{t_1}{\sqrt{t_2}} = \frac{t_1/\sqrt{n}}{\sqrt{t_2/n}} = \frac{\sqrt{n}\bar{x}}{\sqrt{s^2+\bar{x}^2}} = \frac{\sqrt{n}}{\sqrt{1+(\frac{s}{\bar{x}})^2}}$, we note that it is increasing function in $\frac{\bar{x}}{s}$. The equivalent critical region becomes of the form $\frac{\bar{x}}{s} > c$. Under the null hypothesis $\theta_1 = 0$ ($\mu = 0$), $\sqrt{n}\cdot\bar{x}/\sigma \sim N(0,1)$ and $\sum(x_i - \bar{x})^2/\sigma^2 = \frac{ns^2}{\sigma^2} \sim \chi^2_{n-1}$ independently. This gives

$$\frac{N(0,1)}{\sqrt{\chi^2/df}} \sim t_{df}, \quad \text{i.e} \quad \frac{\sqrt{n}\bar{x}/\sigma}{\sqrt{\frac{ns^2/\sigma^2}{n-1}}} = \sqrt{n-1}\,\frac{\bar{x}}{s} \sim t_{n-1}.$$

Therefore, the UMP unbiased size-$\alpha$ test would finally be given by

$$\phi_0(\mathbf{x}) = \begin{cases} 1 & \text{if } \sqrt{n-1}\,\frac{\bar{x}}{s} > c \\[2ex] 0 & \text{if } \sqrt{n-1}\,\frac{\bar{x}}{s} < c \end{cases}$$

where, the constant $c$ is obtained by

$$E_{\theta_0}[\phi_0(\mathbf{X})] = \alpha$$

$$\int_c^\infty f(t_{n-1})\,dt = \alpha$$

where $f(t_{n-1})$ is the pdf of $t$-distribution with $(n-1)$ degrees of freedom and $c$ is the upper $\alpha^{\text{th}}$ quantile of $t_{n-1}$ distribution.

**Lehmann's procedure** (Lehmann (1986)[130]) Let us solve the problem by Lehmann procedure. Here we find out a statistic $V$ such that

(a) $V = h(T_1, T_2)$ whose distribution does not depend on $\sigma^2$ for fixed $\theta_1 = \theta_1^{(0)}$ or in other words $V$ is independent of $T_2$, and

(b) $V$ is monotone in $T_1$ for each given $t_2$.

Let us define

$$V = f(X_1 - \theta_1^{(0)}, \ldots, X_n - \theta_1^{(0)}),\ \theta_1^{(0)} \text{ is 0 here.}$$

where, $f$ is scale invariant, i.e. it satisfies

$$f(cx_1, \ldots, cx_n) = f(x_1, \ldots, x_n)\ \forall\ c > 0$$

Therefore, $V$ remains unchanged if each $X_i - \theta_1^{(0)}$ is replaced by $\dfrac{X_i - \theta_1^{(0)}}{\theta_2} = \dfrac{X_i - \mu_0}{\sigma}$. Since $V$ is a function of $\dfrac{X_i - \mu_0}{\sigma}$, the distribution of $V$ would then depend on the distribution of $\dfrac{X_i - \mu_0}{\sigma}$. But for fixed $\theta_1 = \theta_1^{(0)}$ $(\mu = \mu_0)$, the distribution of $\dfrac{X_i - \mu_0}{\sigma}$ is $N(0, 1)$, which is independent of $\theta_2$, (i.e. $\sigma^2$). Therefore, for fixed $\theta_1 = \theta_1^{(0)}$, the distribution of $V$ is independent of $\theta_2$. We have

$$\begin{aligned}
V &= f\Big(\frac{X_1 - \theta_1^{(0)}}{\theta_2}, \ldots, \frac{X_n - \theta_1^{(0)}}{\theta_2}\Big) \\
&= \frac{\overline{X} - \theta_1^{(0)}}{\sqrt{\sum(X_i - \overline{X})^2}} = \frac{\overline{X}}{\sqrt{\sum(X_i - \overline{X})^2}} \quad (\text{since } \theta_1^{(0)} = 0) \\
&= \frac{T_1/n}{\sqrt{T_2^2 - nT_1^2}} = c \cdot \frac{\sqrt{n}\bar{x}/\sigma^2}{\sqrt{\frac{ns^2/\sigma^2}{(n-1)}}} = c\sqrt{(n-1)}\,\frac{\bar{x}}{s} \\
&= c \cdot \frac{N(0,1)}{\sqrt{\chi_{n-1}^2/(n-1)}}\bigg|_{\theta_1 = 0} \sim t_{(n-1)}
\end{aligned}$$

$V$ is, therefore, independent of $T_2$ when $\theta_1 = \theta_1^{(0)} = 0$ and monotonically increasing in $T_1$ for each fixed $T_2 = t_2$. The UMP unbiased size-$\alpha$ test would now be given by

$$\phi_0(v) = \begin{cases} 1 & \text{if } v > v_0 \text{ or } \sqrt{n-1}\,\frac{\bar{x}}{s} > c \\ 0 & \text{if } v < v_0 \text{ or } \sqrt{n-1}\,\frac{\bar{x}}{s} \le c \end{cases}$$

where, $c$ is obtained by

$$\int_c^\infty t_{n-1}(t)\, dt = \alpha$$

Finally, we see that the UMP unbiased size-$\alpha$ test obtained by conditional approach and Lehmann's approach leads to the same test. This has also been realized that the $V$- statistic approach due to Lehmann, resulted into a considerable reduction of problem, since the distribution of $V$ did not depend on $\theta_2 = -\frac{1}{2\sigma^2}$ (a nuisance parameter) and have an unconditional distribution instead a conditional distribution.

**Example 5.7.2.** *Let $X \sim N(\mu, \sigma^2)$ where both $\mu$ and $\sigma^2$ are unknown. A random sample $(X_1, \ldots, X_n)$ has been drawn from this population to test the hypothesis*

$$H_0 : \mu = 0 \quad \textit{against} \quad H_1 : \mu \neq 0$$

*Find out a UMP unbiased size-$\alpha$ test for the above unconditional testing problem.*

***Solution:*** **Conditional approach:** The UMP unbiased size-$\alpha$ test is given by

$$\phi_0(t_1, t_2) = \begin{cases} 1 & \text{if } \; t_1 < z_1(t_2) \;\; \text{or} \;\; t_1 > z_2(t_2) \\ 0 & \text{if } \; z_1(t_2) < t_1 < z_2(t_2) \end{cases}$$

where $z_1(t_2)$ and $z_2(t_2)$ are obtained by

$$E_{\theta_1^{(0)}}[\phi_0(T_1, T_2)|T_2] = \alpha$$

and

$$E_{\theta_1^{(0)}}[(\alpha - \phi_0(T_1, T_2))T_1|T_2] = 0$$

The zero slope condition gives

$$\begin{aligned} \alpha E_{\mu=0}(T_1|\,T_2) &= E_{\mu=0}(\,T_1\,\phi_0(T_1,\,T_2)|\,T_2) \\ &= E_{\mu=0}(T_1|\,T_2) - \int_{z_1(t_2)}^{z_2(t_2)} t_1 f(t_1|\,t_2)\,dt_1\Big|_{\mu-0} \end{aligned}$$

We have already derived the distribution of $T_1|\,t_2$ under $H_0 : \mu = 0$

$$f_{T_1|\,T_2=t_2}(t_1|\,t_2) = \frac{\Gamma(n/2)}{\pi^{n/2}}\left(\frac{1}{t_2}\right)^{n/2-1}$$

which gives $E_{\mu=0}(T_1|\,T_2) = 0$. We now have

$$\int_{z_1(t_2)}^{z_2(t_2)} t_1\,f(t_1|\,t_2)\,dt_1 = 0$$

or

$$z_2^2(t_2) - z_1^2(t_2) = 0$$

$$(z_2(t_2) + z_1(t_2))(z_2(t_2) - z_1(t_2)) = 0$$

which gives either $z_1(t_2) = z_2(t_2)$ or, $z_1(t_2) = -z_2(t_2)$

The first condition is ruled out since the entire range of $t_1$ becomes a critical region. The second, therefore, is acceptable. Using the result of the previous example that $\sqrt{t_2}$ is the scale parameter in the distribution of $T_1|t_2$ under $H_0 : \mu = 0$ and that $z_1(t_2) = -z_2(t_2)$, the UMP unbiased test $\phi_0(T_1, T_2)$ is given by

$$\phi_0(t_1, t_2) = \begin{cases} 1 & \text{if } \left|\frac{t_1}{\sqrt{t_2}}\right| > c \\ 0 & \text{otherwise} \end{cases}$$

we have also seen that $\frac{t_1}{\sqrt{t_2}}$ is increasing in $\sqrt{n-1}\,\frac{\bar{x}}{s}$, therefore, the critical region may now be written as $\left|\sqrt{n-1}\,\frac{\bar{x}}{s}\right| > c$

The UMP unbiased size-$\alpha$ test for two-sided unconditional problem would be given by

$$\phi_0(\mathbf{x}) = \begin{cases} 1 & \text{if } |\sqrt{n-1}\,\frac{\bar{x}}{s}| > c \\ 0 & \text{if } |\sqrt{n-1}\,\frac{\bar{x}}{s}| \le c \end{cases}$$

where $c$ is obtained by

$$E_{\mu=0}\phi_0(\mathbf{X}) = \alpha$$

The null distribution of $\sqrt{n-1}\,\frac{\bar{x}}{s}$ is $t_{n-1}$, which is symmetric about 0, and $c$ is obtained by

$$\int_c^\infty t_{n-1}(y)\,dy = \frac{\alpha}{2}$$

where $c$ could easily be read from $t_{n-1}$ ($t$-distribution) table.

**Lehmann's approach:** Consider, $V$ as

$$\begin{aligned} V &= f(X_1 - \theta_1^{(0)}, \ldots, X_n - \theta_1^{(0)}) \\ &= f(X_1 - \mu_0, \ldots, X_n - \mu_0) \end{aligned}$$

where

$$f(c\mathbf{x}) = f(\mathbf{x}) \;\; \forall\; c > 0$$

and

$$V = \frac{\overline{X} - \mu_0}{\sqrt{\sum(X_i - \mu_0)^2}} = \frac{\overline{X}}{\sqrt{\sum X_i^2}}$$

(since $\mu_0 = 0$)

$$= \frac{nT_1}{\sqrt{T_2}} = c \cdot \sqrt{n-1}\frac{\overline{X}}{S} \sim t_{n-1}$$

The distribution of $V$ is independent of $\sigma^2$, therefore, $V$ is independent of $T_2$. $V$ is linear in $T_1$ for each fixed $t_2$. Hence, Lehmann's conditions are satisfied and UMP unbiased size-$\alpha$ test, based on $V$, is given by

$$\phi_0(v) = \begin{cases} 1 & \text{if } v < v_1 \text{ or } v > v_2 \\ 0 & \text{if } v_1 < v < v_2 \end{cases} \quad \text{or} \quad \phi_0(\mathbf{x}) = \begin{cases} 1 & \text{if } |\sqrt{n-1}\frac{\bar{x}}{s}| > c \\ 0 & \text{if } |\sqrt{n-1}\frac{\bar{x}}{s}| < c \end{cases}$$

Since the distribution of $V|\,H_0$ is $t_{n-1}$ which is symmetric about 0, $c$ would be obtained from

$$\int_c^{\infty} t_{n-1}(y)\,dy = \frac{\alpha}{2}$$

**Example 5.7.3.** *Consider the previous example and the testing problem*

$$H_0 : \sigma \leq \sigma_0 \textit{ against } H_1 : \sigma > \sigma_0$$

*Find out a UMP unbiased size-$\alpha$ test for the above testing problem.*

***Solution:*** Here, $k = 2$ $\quad \theta_1 = -1/2\sigma^2; \qquad \theta_2 = n\mu/\sigma^2$

$$T_1 = \sum X_i^2; \qquad T_2 = \sum X_i$$

Define

$$V = f(X_1, \ldots, X_n)$$

such that

$$f(\mathbf{x} + c) = f(\mathbf{x}) \quad \forall \text{ real } c$$

We get one such $V$ as

$$V = f(X_1 - \mu, \ldots, X_n - \mu)$$

where $E(X_i) = \mu$. For fixed $\sigma = \sigma_0$, the distribution of $X_i - \mu \sim N(0, \sigma_0^2)$ is independent of $\mu$ that implies that the distribution of $V$ is independent of $\mu$. It, therefore, follows that any such statistic $V = \sum(X_i - \bar{X})^2$ is independent of $T_2 = \sum X_i$. This is true for all $\sigma$. Further

$$V = \sum(X_i - \overline{X})^2 = \sum X_i^2 - n\overline{X}^2$$

$$= T_1 - \frac{T_2^2}{n} = c \cdot \frac{\sum(X_i - \bar{X})^2}{\sigma_0^2} \sim \chi^2_{n-1}$$

It could be seen, in the above expression that $V$ is monotonically increasing in $T_1$ for each $T_2 = t_2$. Therefore, the UMP unbiased test would be given by

$$\phi_0(v) = \begin{cases} 1 & \text{if } v > c \\ 0 & \text{if } v \leq c \end{cases} \quad \text{or} \quad \phi_0(\mathbf{x}) = \begin{cases} 1 & \text{if } \dfrac{\sum(x_i - \bar{x})^2}{\sigma_0^2} > c \\ 0 & \text{if } \dfrac{\sum(x_i - \bar{x})^2}{\sigma_0^2} \leq c \end{cases}$$

where $c$ is obtained by

$$\int_c^{\infty} \chi^2_{n-1}(y)\,dy = \alpha$$

**Example 5.7.4.** *Consider the previous example and the testing problem*

$$H_0 : \sigma = \sigma_0 \textit{ against } H_1 : \sigma \neq \sigma_0$$

*Find out a UMP unbiased test of size-$\alpha$ for testing $H_0$ against $H_1$.*

***Solution:*** We had seen that $V = \sum(X_i - \overline{X})^2 = T_1 - T_2^2/n$ is linear in $T_1$ for each fixed $T_2 = t_2$. Therefore, a UMP unbiased size-$\alpha$ test is given by

$$\phi_0(v) = \begin{cases} 1 & \text{if } v < v_1 \text{ or } v > v_2 \\ 0 & \text{if } v_1 < v < v_2 \end{cases}$$

$$\text{or} \quad \phi_0(\mathbf{x}) = \begin{cases} 1 & \text{if } \frac{\sum(x_i - \bar{x})^2}{\sigma_0^2} < v_1 \text{ or } \frac{\sum(x_i - \bar{x})^2}{\sigma_0^2} > v_2 \\ 0 & \text{otherwise} \end{cases}$$

where $v_1$ and $v_2$ are obtained by the first condition $E_{\sigma_0}\phi_0(V) = \alpha$, i.e.

$$\int_{v_1}^{v_2} \chi^2_{n-1}(y)\, dy = 1 - \alpha \tag{5.7}$$

while the second condition gives

$$E_{\sigma_0}[V\phi_0(V, t_2)|\, t_2] = \alpha\, E_{\sigma_0}[V|\, t_2]$$

or

$$E_{\sigma_0}[V\phi_0(V)] = \alpha E_{\sigma_0}[V] \tag{5.8}$$

since $V$ is independent of $t_2$ and that $V \sim \chi^2_{n-1} = G(\frac{n-1}{2}, 2)$ that gives $E(V) = (n-1)$. The above expression may be rewritten as

$$(n-1) - E_{\sigma_0}[V\phi_0(V)] = (n-1) - \alpha(n-1)$$

or

$$E_{\sigma_0}[V] - E_{\sigma_0}[V\phi_0(V)] = E_{\sigma_0}[V(1 - \phi_0(V))] = (n-1)(1-\alpha)$$

or

$$\frac{1}{n-1}\int_{v_1}^{v_2} y\,\chi^2_{n-1}(y)\, dy = (1-\alpha) \tag{5.9}$$

$v_1$ and $v_2$ may be chosen so that the conditions given in Eqs. (5.7) and (5.9) are satisfied.

**Example 5.7.5.** *Let $X_1, \ldots, X_m$ and $Y_1, \ldots, Y_n$ be independent samples from $N(\mu, \sigma^2)$ and $N(\eta, \tau^2)$, respectively. Find a UMP unbiased test of size-$\alpha$ for testing*

$$H_0 : \frac{\tau^2}{\sigma^2} \le \Delta_0 \ \textit{against}\ H_1 : \frac{\tau^2}{\sigma^2} > \Delta_0$$

***Solution:*** The joint density of sample observations is given by

$$f_{\mathbf{x},\mathbf{y}}(\mathbf{x},\, \mathbf{y}|\, \mu,\, \eta,\, \sigma^2,\, \tau^2) = c(\mu,\, \eta,\, \sigma^2,\, \tau^2)$$
$$\exp\{-\frac{1}{2\tau^2}\sum y_i^2 - \frac{1}{2\sigma^2}\sum x_i^2 + \frac{n\eta}{\tau^2}\bar{y} + \frac{m\mu}{\sigma^2}\bar{x}\}$$

$$\text{where} \quad k = 4,\ \theta_1 = -1/2\tau^2,\ \theta_2 = -1/2\sigma^2,\ \theta_3 = \frac{n\eta}{\tau^2},\ \theta_4 = \frac{m\mu}{\sigma^2};$$
$$T_1 = \sum Y_i^2,\ \ T_2 = \sum X_i^2\ \ T_3 = \overline{Y},\ \ T_4 = \overline{X}.$$

Let us now consider $\theta^* = \sum_{i=1}^{4} a_i\theta_i$ for comparing the variances of two normal populations with

$$a_1 = 1,\ a_2 = -\frac{1}{\Delta_0},\ a_3 = a_4 = 0$$

we get

$$\theta^* = \theta_1 - \frac{\theta_2}{\Delta_0} = -\frac{1}{2\tau^2} + \frac{1}{2\sigma^2\Delta_0}$$

so that $\theta^* \le 0$ gives $H_0 : \tau^2/\sigma^2 \le \Delta_0$. Therefore, the hypothesis in the transformed problem becomes $H_0 : \theta^* \le 0$, where the transformed parameter vector is $(\theta^*, \theta_2, \ldots, \theta_k)$ and the corresponding variables are

$$\begin{aligned}[T_1/a_1,\, T_2 - (a_2/a_1)T_1,\, T_3 - (a_3/a_1)T_1,\, T_4 - (a_4/a_1)T_1] \\ &= [T_1,\, T_2 + T_1/\Delta_0,\, T_3,\, T_4] = [T_1^*,\, T_2^*,\, T_3^*,\, T_4^*] \\ &= \left[\sum Y_i^2, \sum X_i^2 + (1/\Delta_0)\sum Y_i^2, \overline{Y}, \overline{X}\right]\end{aligned}$$

Let us define, under $H_0 : \tau^2/\sigma^2 = \Delta_0$

$$V = \frac{\sum(Y_i - \overline{Y})^2/\Delta_0}{\sum(X_i - \overline{X})^2} = \frac{\sum(Y_i - \overline{Y})^2/\tau^2}{\sum(X_i - \overline{X})^2/\sigma^2}$$

The numerator and denominator, in the above expression are distributed as $\chi^2_{n-1}$ and $\chi^2_{m-1}$ respectively. This shows that the distribution of $V|H_0$ is independent of $\theta_2, \theta_3, \theta_4$ or $\sigma, \xi$ or $\eta$ and, therefore, $V$ is independent of $(T_2 + T_1/\Delta_0, T_3, T_4)$. We shall now check whether, for each fixed $(t_2 + t_1/\Delta_0, t_3, t_4)$, $V$ is monotone in $T_1$. Consider

$$V = \frac{(T_1^* - n\,T_3^{*2})/\Delta_0}{T_2^* - (1/\Delta_0)T_1^* - m\,T_4^*}$$

on differentiating $V$ with respect to $T_1^*$ we get

$$\begin{aligned}\frac{\partial V}{\partial T_1^*} &= \frac{1/\Delta_0}{(\cdot)} + \frac{(T_1^* - nT_3^{*2})/\Delta_0 \cdot (-1)(-1/\Delta_0)}{(\cdot)^2} \\ &= \frac{1}{\Delta_0(\cdot)}\left[1 + \frac{(T_1^* - nT_3^{*2})}{\Delta_0(\cdot)}\right] = \frac{1}{\Delta_0^2(\cdot)^2}[\Delta_0(T_2^* - mT_4^*) - nT_3^{*2}] \\ &= \frac{1}{\Delta_0^2(\cdot)^2}\left[\sum(X_i - \overline{X})^2 + \sum(Y_i - \overline{Y})^2\right] > 0\end{aligned}$$

which shows that $V$ is an increasing function in $T_1^*$ for each fixed $(t_2^*,\, t_3^*,\, t_4^*)$. Therefore, UMP unbiased test is given by

$$\phi_0(v) = \begin{cases} 1 & \text{if } v > v_0 \\ 0 & \text{if } v \le v_0 \end{cases}$$

where

$$V = \frac{\sum(Y_i - \overline{Y})^2/\Delta_0(n-1)}{\sum(X_i - \overline{X})^2/(m-1)} = \frac{\chi^2_{(n-1)}/(n-1)}{\chi^2_{(m-1)}/(m-1)} \sim F_{n-1,\,m-1}$$

and $v_0$ is determined by $\int_{v_0}^{\infty} F_{n-1,\,m-1}(y)\,dy = \alpha$.

**Example 5.7.6.** *Let $X_1, \ldots, X_m$ and $Y_1, \ldots, Y_n$ be independent sample from $N(\mu, \sigma^2)$ and $N(\eta, \tau^2)$ respectively. Find out a UMP unbiased test of size-$\alpha$ for testing*

$$H_0 : \tau^2/\sigma^2 = \Delta_0 \quad \textit{against} \quad H_1 : \tau^2/\sigma^2 \neq \Delta_0$$

***Solution:*** The two-sided testing problem

$$H_0 : \tau^2/\sigma^2 = \Delta_0 \quad \text{against} \quad H_1 : \tau^2/\sigma^2 \neq \Delta_0$$

may be restated as

$$H_0 : \theta^* = 0 \ \text{ against } \ H_1 : \theta^* \neq 0.$$

We shall now consider $V$ under $\tau^2/\sigma^2 = \Delta_0$ as

$$V = \frac{\sum(Y_i - \overline{Y})^2/\Delta_0}{\sum(X_i - \overline{X})^2 + (1/\Delta_0)\sum(Y_i - \overline{Y})^2}$$

On dividing numerator and denominator by $\sigma^2$, we get

$$V = \frac{\sum(Y_i - \overline{Y})^2/\tau^2}{\sum(X_i - \overline{X})^2/\sigma^2 + \sum(Y_i - \overline{Y})^2/\tau^2}$$

Let

$$W_1 = \sum(Y_i - \overline{Y})^2/\tau^2 \sim \chi^2_{n-1}$$

and

$$W_2 = \sum(X_i - \overline{X})^2/\sigma^2 \sim \chi^2_{m-1}$$

we get

$$V = \frac{W_1}{W_1 + W_2} = \frac{W_1/W_2}{1 + W_1/W_2}$$

Let

$$Y = \frac{W_1}{W_2}$$

and

$$\frac{(m-1)}{(n-1)}Y = \frac{W_1/(n-1)}{W_2/(m-1)} \sim F_{n-1,m-1}$$

we get

$$V = \frac{Y}{1+Y} = \frac{1}{1+\frac{1}{Y}} = \frac{1}{1 + \frac{1}{[\frac{(m-1)}{n-1}Y]\,\frac{(n-1)}{(m-1)}}}$$

$$= \frac{1}{1 + \frac{(m-1)}{(n-1)}F_{m-1,\,n-1}} \sim B\left(\frac{n-1}{2}, \frac{m-1}{2}\right)$$

We see that the distribution of $V$ under $\tau^2/\sigma^2 = \Delta_0$ is independent of $\sigma^2$, $\eta$ and $\mu$. Therefore, $V$ is independent of $T_2^*$, $T_3^*$, $T_4^*$ under $H_0 : \tau^2/\sigma^2 = \Delta_0$. Further, writing $V$ as

$$\begin{aligned} V &= \frac{\sum Y_i^2 - n\overline{Y}^2}{\Delta_0 \sum X_i^2 - n\Delta_0 \overline{X}^2 + \sum Y_i^2 - n\overline{Y}^2} \\ &= \frac{T_1^* - nT_3^{*2}}{\Delta_0 T_2^* - T_1^* - n\Delta_0 T_4^{*2} + T_1^* - nT_3^{*2}} \\ &= a(T_2^*, T_3^*, T_4^*)\, T_1^* \,+\, b(T_2^*, T_3^*, T_4^*) \end{aligned}$$

and we see that $V$ is linear in $T_1^*$. Following Lehmann's approach UMP unbiased test is given by

$$\phi_0(v) = \begin{cases} 1 & \text{if } \; v < v_1 \text{ or } v > v_2 \\ 0 & \text{if } \; v_1 < v < v_2 \end{cases}$$

where, $v_1, v_2$ are obtained by

$$E_{\theta^*=0}[\phi_0(V)] = \alpha$$

and

$$E_{\theta^*=0}[V\phi_0(V)] = \alpha E_{\theta^*=0}[V]$$

Here

$$E_0[V] = \frac{n-1}{m+n-2}$$

The lower condition can be written as

$$E_0[V] - E_0[V\phi_0(V)] = (1-\alpha)\, E_0[V]$$

$$E_0[V(1-\phi_0(V))] = (1-\alpha)\,\frac{(n-1)}{(m+n-2)}$$

or

$$\int_{v_1}^{v_2} v\, B_{(\frac{1}{2}(n-1),\frac{1}{2}(m-1))}(v)\, dv = (1-\alpha)\,\frac{(n-1)}{(m+n-2)}$$

Let us consider

$$\begin{aligned} vB_{\frac{1}{2}(n-1),\frac{1}{2}(m-1)}(v) &= \\ &\frac{\frac{(\frac{m+n}{2}-1)(\frac{m+n}{2}-2)!}{(\frac{m+n}{2}-1)}}{\Gamma(\frac{1}{2}(m-1))(\frac{n-1}{2}-1)!\frac{(\frac{n}{2}-\frac{1}{2})}{(\frac{n}{2}-\frac{1}{2})}} v^{\frac{1}{2}(n-3)+1=\frac{n+1}{2}-1}(1-v)^{\frac{1}{2}(m-3)} \\ &= \frac{\Gamma(\frac{m+n}{2})}{\Gamma(\frac{1}{2}(m-1))(\frac{n+1}{2})!}\,\frac{(\frac{n-1}{2})}{(\frac{m+n}{2}-1)}\, v^{\frac{n+1}{2}-1}\,(1-v)^{\frac{1}{2}(m-3)} \\ &= \frac{n-1}{m+n-2}\, B_{\frac{n+1}{2},\,\frac{m-1}{2}}(v) \end{aligned}$$

Now, using the above identity

$$\int_{v_1}^{v_2} \frac{n-1}{m+n-2} B_{\frac{n+1}{2},\,\frac{m-1}{2}}(v)\,dv = (1-\alpha)\frac{(n-1)}{(m+n-2)}$$

or

$$\int_{v_1}^{v_2} B_{\frac{n+1}{2},\,\frac{m-1}{2}}(v)\,dv = 1-\alpha$$

Size condition gives

$$\int_{v_1}^{v_2} B_{\frac{1}{2}(n-1),\,\frac{1}{2}(m-1)}(v)\,dv = 1-\alpha$$

Finally, $v_1$ and $v_2$ are obtained satisfying the above two conditions.

**Example 5.7.7.** (Lehmann (1986)[130]) *Let $X_1, \ldots, X_m$ and $Y_1, \ldots, Y_n$ be independent samples from $N(\mu, \sigma^2)$ and $N(\eta, \tau^2)$ respectively. Find out a UMP unbiased test of size-$\alpha$ for testing*

(a) $H_0 : \eta - \mu \leq 0$ *against* $H_1 : \eta - \mu > 0$
(b) $H_0 : \eta - \mu = 0$ *against* $H_1 : \eta - \mu \neq 0$

*assuming equality of population variances,* $\sigma^2 = \tau^2$.

***Solution:*** The hypothesis testing problem of equality of means $\mu$ and $\eta$ of two normal populations, when the variances $\sigma^2$ and $\tau^2$ are both unknown, is known as **Behrens-Fisher problem**. This cannot be solved by the method discussed in the previous section. The principle of likelihood ratio tests or the principle of invariance could be used as an alternative approach to solve this problem. We consider here a simple case where population variances $\sigma^2$ and $\tau^2$ are assumed to be equal, i.e. $\sigma^2 = \tau^2$. The joint density of the $x$'s and $y$'s in this case would be given by

$$c(\mu,\,\eta,\,\sigma)\exp\{\frac{\eta}{\sigma^2}\sum y_i + \frac{\mu}{\sigma^2}\sum x_i - \frac{1}{2\sigma^2}(\sum x_i^2 + \sum y_i^2)\}$$

Here

$$\theta_1 = \eta/\sigma^2, \qquad \theta_2 = \mu/\sigma^2, \qquad \theta_3 = -1/2\sigma^2$$

and the sufficient statistics are given by

$$T_1 = \sum Y_i, \quad T_2 = \sum X_i, \quad T_3 = \sum X_i^2 + \sum Y_i^2$$

The hypothesis $H_0 : \eta = \mu$ does not directly involve $\theta_1,\ \theta_2,\ \theta_3$. Some rearrangement of terms in the joint density of $x's$ and $y's$ gives

$$c(\mu, \eta, \sigma)\ \exp\Big\{\frac{m\mu\overline{x} + n\eta\overline{y}}{\sigma^2} - \frac{1}{2\sigma^2}(\sum x_i^2 + \sum y_i^2)\Big\}$$

But the identity $m\mu\overline{x} + n\eta\overline{y}$ may be written as

$$m\mu\bar{x} + n\eta\bar{y} = \frac{(\bar{y}-\bar{x})(\eta-\mu)}{\frac{1}{m}+\frac{1}{n}} + \frac{(m\bar{x}+n\bar{y})(m\mu+n\eta)}{m+n}$$

Therefore,

$$c(\mu,\eta,\sigma)\ \exp\Big\{\frac{(\eta-\mu)}{(\frac{1}{m}+\frac{1}{n})\sigma^2}(\bar{y}-\bar{x})+\frac{m\mu+n\eta}{(m+n)\sigma^2}\cdot(m\bar{x}+n\bar{y}) \\ -\frac{1}{2\sigma^2}(\sum x_i^2+\sum y_i^2)\Big\}$$

After re-parameterization, we get

$$\theta_1^*=\frac{(\eta-\mu)}{(\frac{1}{m}+\frac{1}{n})\sigma^2},\quad \theta_2^*=\frac{m\mu+n\eta}{(m+n)\sigma^2},\quad \theta_3^*=-\frac{1}{2\sigma^2}$$

and the sufficient statistics

$$T_1^*=\overline{Y}-\overline{X},\quad T_2^*=m\overline{X}+n\overline{Y},\quad T_3^*=\sum X_i^2+\sum Y_i^2$$

(a) The hypothesis may be restated as

$$H_0:\theta_1^*\le 0 \ \text{ against } \ H_1:\theta_1^*>0$$

We define

$$V=\frac{\overline{Y}-\overline{X}}{\sqrt{\sum(X_i-\overline{X})^2+\sum(Y_i-\overline{Y})^2}}=\frac{\overline{Y}-\overline{X}}{\sqrt{\sum X_i^2+\sum Y_i^2-m\overline{X}^2-n\overline{Y}^2}}$$

$$=\frac{T_1^*}{\sqrt{T_3^*-\frac{1}{m+1}T_2^{*2}-\frac{mn}{m+n}T_1^{*2}}}$$

which shows that $V$ is monotonically increasing function in $T_1^*$. Further

$$V=C\cdot\frac{\overline{Y}-\overline{X}/\sqrt{(\frac{1}{m}+\frac{1}{n})\sigma^2}}{\sqrt{\frac{\sum(X_i-\overline{X})^2+(Y_i-\overline{Y})^2}{(m+n-2)\sigma^2}}}=C\cdot\frac{N\left(\frac{n-\mu}{\sqrt{(\frac{1}{m}+\frac{1}{n})\sigma^2}},1\right)}{\sqrt{\frac{\chi^2_{(m+n-2)}}{(m+n-2)}}}$$

$$V=C\cdot t_{(m+n-2);\,\delta},\quad \text{where } \ \delta=\frac{\eta-\mu}{\sqrt{(\frac{1}{m}+\frac{1}{n})}\ \sigma}$$

: non-central-t distribution with noncentrality parameter $\delta$.
Under $\eta=\mu$, we have $V\sim t_{(m+n-2)}$.

This shows that $V$ is independent of $\mu$ or $\sigma$, therefore, $V$ is independent of $(T_2^*,T_3^*)$.

Now, following Lehmann, UMP unbiased test for the above testing problem will be given by

$$\phi(v)=\begin{cases}1 & \text{if } \ v>v_0\\ 0 & \text{if } \ v\le v_0\end{cases}$$

Here

$$V = \frac{(\overline{Y} - \overline{X})/\sqrt{\frac{1}{m} + \frac{1}{n}}}{\sqrt{[\sum(X_i - \overline{X})^2 + \sum(Y_i - \overline{Y})^2]/(m+n-2)}} \sim t_{(m+n-2)}$$

under $\eta = \mu$ and the constant $v_0$ is obtained by $\int_{v_0}^{\infty} t_{m+n-2}(v)\, dv = \alpha$.

(b) We shall now consider the testing problem $H_0 : \theta_1^* = 0$ against $H_1 : \theta_1^* \neq 0$. The statistic $V$ defined as above would not work in this case, since it is not linear in $T_1^*$. We shall, therefore, define a new statistic $V'$ as

$$V' = \frac{\overline{Y} - \overline{X}}{\sqrt{\sum X_i^2 + \sum Y_i^2 - \dfrac{(\sum X_i + \sum Y_i)^2}{m+n}}}$$

which is related to $V$ through

$$V = \frac{V'}{\sqrt{1 - \dfrac{mn}{m+n} V'^2}}$$

We have shown $V$ to be independent of $(T_2^*, T_3^*)$ when $\eta = \mu$ and $V'$ is a function of $V$, therefore, $V'$ becomes independent of $(T_2^*, T_3^*)$. Further

$$V' = \frac{T_1^*}{\sqrt{T_3^* - \dfrac{T_2^{*2}}{m+n}}}$$

We have that $V'$ is linear in $T_1^*$, and therefore, the conditions for the use of Lehmann's approach are satisfied. The UMP unbiased test for the above two-sided testing problem shall now be given by

$$\phi_0(v') = \begin{cases} 1 & \text{if } v' < v_1' \text{ or } v' > v_2' \\ 0 & \text{if } v_1' < v' < v_2' \end{cases}$$

where $v_1', v_2'$ are obtained by $E_{\eta=\mu}[\phi_0(V')] = \alpha$.
But the distribution of $V'$ when $\eta = \mu$ is symmetric about 0, the slope zero condition gives, $v_1' = -v_2'$. The test $\phi_0$ can now be written as

$$\phi_0(v') = \begin{cases} 1 & \text{if } |v'| > v_0' \\ 0 & \text{if } |v'| < v_0' \end{cases}$$

Since

$$V = \frac{V'}{\sqrt{1 - \dfrac{mn}{m+n} V'^2}}$$

the absolute value of $V$ is an increasing function of $|V'|$, the above test $\phi_0$ can now equivalently be written as

$$\phi_0(v) = \begin{cases} 1 & \text{if } |v| > v_0 \\ 0 & \text{if } |v| < v_0 \end{cases}$$

where
$$v|_{\eta=\mu} \sim t_{(m+n-2)}$$

the constant $v_0$ can be obtained by the size condition. The symmetry of the null distribution of $v|H_0$, i.e. $t_{(m+n-2)}$ about 0 help us in determining $v_0$ by

$$\int_{v_0}^{\infty} t_{m+n-2}(y)\, dy = \alpha/2$$

**Example 5.7.8.** (Hoel, [1945]) *Comparing two Poisson populations: Let $X$ and $Y$ be random variables with $X$ and $Y$ independent and $X \sim P(\lambda), Y \sim P(\mu)$. Find out a UMP unbiased test of size-$\alpha$ for testing:*

| | | | |
|---|---|---|---|
| (a) | $H_0 : \lambda \le \mu$ | against | $H_1 : \lambda > \mu$ |
| (b) | $H_0 : \lambda = \mu$ | against | $H_1 : \lambda \ne \mu$ |
| (c) | $H_0 : \lambda = 2\mu$ | against | $H_1 : \lambda \ne 2\mu$ |
| (d) | $H_0 : \lambda \le \mu^2$ | against | $H_1 : \lambda > \mu^2$ |
| (e) | $H_0 : \lambda \le k\mu$ | against | $H_1 : \lambda > k\mu$ |
| (f) | $H_0 : \mu \le \lambda + 1$ | against | $H_1 : \mu > \lambda + 1$ |

***Solution:*** The joint density function of random variables $X$ and $Y$ is given by

$$f_{X,Y}(x, y|\, \lambda, \mu) = \frac{e^{-\lambda}\lambda^x}{x!} \cdot \frac{e^{-\mu}\mu^y}{y!} = \frac{e^{-(\lambda+\mu)}}{x!y!} \exp\{x \log \lambda + y \log \mu\}$$
$$\text{for } x = 0, 1, \ldots \text{ and } y = 0, 1, \ldots$$

Here
$$\theta_1 = \log \lambda, \quad \theta_2 = \log \mu$$

and
$$T_1 = X, \quad T_2 = Y$$

We can find a UMP unbiased test for the testing problem of the type $\theta^* = a_1 \log \lambda + a_2 \log \mu$ , a linear combination of the parameters $\theta_1$ and $\theta_2$. Different hypotheses may be written in terms of $\theta^*$ as shown further:

| | Hypothesis | Hypothesis involving $\theta^*$ |
|---|---|---|
| (a) | $\lambda \le \mu$ | $\theta^* = \log \lambda - \log \mu \le 0$ |
| (b) | $\lambda = \mu$ | $\theta^* = 0$ |
| (c) | $\lambda = 2\mu$ | $\theta^* = \log 2$ (since, $\log \lambda - \log \mu = \log 2$ gives, $\lambda/\mu = 2$) |
| (d) | $\lambda \le \mu^2$ | $\theta^* = \log \lambda - 2 \log \mu$, i.e. $\theta^* \le 0$ |
| (e) | $\lambda = k\mu$ | $\theta^* = \log k$ |
| (f) | $\mu \le \lambda + 1$ | it cannot be represented in terms of $\theta^*$ since the hypotheses cannot be expressed aslinear combination of $\log \lambda$ and $\log \mu$ |

It is now clear that $(\theta_1, \theta_2)$ are now changed to $(\theta^*, \theta_2)$ and $T_1, T_2 = (X, Y)$ transformed to $[T_1^*, T_2^*] = [T_1/a_1,\ T_2 - (a_2/a_1)T_1] = [X,\ X+Y]$. We get a UMP unbiased test for any of the hypotheses [From (a) to (f)] that would be conditional on $X + Y = T$. The conditional distribution of $X|X + Y = t$

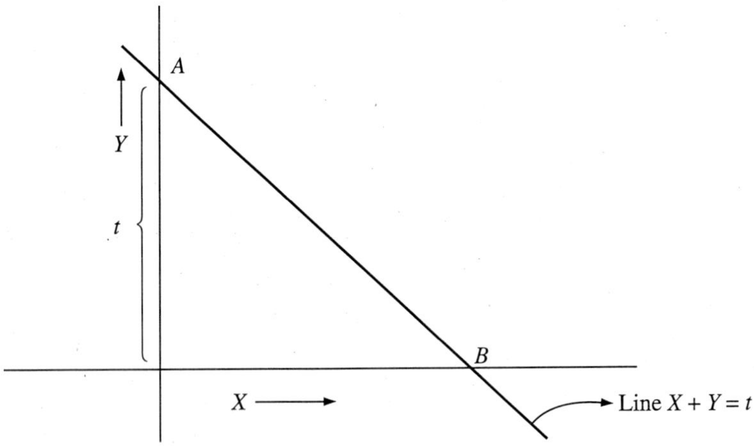


**Figure 5.1:** Plot of the line $X + Y = t$.

would now be calculated. Given $X + Y = t$, $X$ would take values from the line segment $AB$ in the positive quadrant (Figure 5.1). The marginal distribution of $X + Y$ will be given by $P(\lambda + \mu)$. The conditional distribution of $X|X + Y = t$ is given by

$$P\{X = x|X + Y = t\} = \frac{P\{X = x,\ Y = y\}}{P\{X + Y = t\}}$$

$$= \frac{\dfrac{e^{-(\lambda+\mu)}}{x!y!}\exp\{x\log(\lambda/\mu) + (x+y)\log\mu\}}{\dfrac{e^{-(\lambda+\mu)}}{t!}(\lambda+\mu)^t}$$

$$= \frac{t!}{x!(t-x)!}\exp\left\{x\log\frac{\lambda}{\mu} + (x+y)\log\mu - t\log(\lambda+\mu)\right\}$$

$$P\{X = x|X+Y = t\} = \binom{t}{x}\exp\left\{x\log\frac{\lambda}{\mu} + (x+y)\log\frac{\mu}{\lambda+\mu}\right\}$$

$$= \binom{t}{x}\exp\left\{x\log\frac{\lambda}{\lambda+\mu} + y\log\frac{\mu}{\lambda+\mu}\right\}$$

$$= \binom{t}{x}\left(\frac{\lambda}{\lambda+\mu}\right)^x\left(\frac{\mu}{\lambda+\mu}\right)^{t-x} \sim B\left(t, \frac{\lambda}{\lambda+\mu}\right) = B(t,\ p)$$

where

$$p = \frac{\lambda}{\lambda+\mu}$$

If we consider the hypothesis testing problem given in Example 5.7.8 part (e)

$$H_0 : \lambda \leq k\mu \;\text{ against }\; H_1 : \lambda > k\mu$$

we write

$$H_0 : \theta^* \leq \log k \quad \text{against } H_1 : \theta^* > \log k$$

But if we write the above hypothesis that involves $p$, we get

$$H_0 : \frac{\mu}{\lambda} \geq \frac{1}{k} \;\text{ or} H_0 : \frac{\mu}{\lambda} + 1 \geq \frac{1}{k} + 1$$

$$H_0 : \frac{1}{\frac{\mu}{\lambda} + 1} \leq \frac{1}{\frac{1}{k} + 1} \;\text{ or }\; H_0 : p \leq \frac{k}{1+k} \;\text{ against }\; H_1 : p > \frac{k}{1+k}$$

UMP unbiased test for this testing problem would now be given by

$$\phi_0(x,t) = \begin{cases} 1 & \text{if } x \geq x_0(t) \\ 0 & \text{if } x < x_0(t) \end{cases}$$

where, $x_0(t)$ is obtained by $E_{p=\frac{k}{k+1}}[\phi_0(X,T)|T = t] = \alpha$.
or

$$P_{\frac{k}{k+1}}[X \geq x_0(t)|\, X + Y = t] = \alpha$$

where

$$X|\,t\Big|_{p=\frac{k}{k+1}} \sim B\Big(t,\; \frac{k}{1+k}\Big)$$

Similarly, we can find out UMP unbiased test for the two-sided hypothesis of the type

$$H_0 : p = \frac{k}{k+1} \;\text{ against }\; H_1 : p \neq \frac{k}{k+1}$$

(*Note:* Solve the other parts of the question as an exercise.)

**Example 5.7.9.** *Let $X$ and $Y$ be random variables with joint density*

$$f_{X,Y}(x,y|\,\lambda,\mu) = \lambda\mu\, e^{-\lambda x - \mu y} I_{(0,\,\infty)}(x) I_{(0,\,\infty)}(y)$$

*Find out a UMP unbiased test of size-$\alpha = 0.20$ for testing*

$$H_0 : \lambda \leq \mu + 1 \;\text{ against }\; H_1 : \lambda > \mu + 1$$

***Solution:*** The null hypothesis is

$$H_0 : \lambda - \mu \leq 1.$$

In the joint density

$$\theta_1 = -\lambda,\;\; \theta_2 = -\mu, \qquad T_1 = X,\;\; T_2 = Y.$$

Here

$$\theta^* = a_1\,\theta_1 + a_2\theta_2 = -a_1\,\lambda - a_2\,\mu$$

with

$$a_1 = -1 \text{ and } a_2 = 1$$

so that $\theta^* = \lambda - \mu$. The null hypothesis in terms of $\theta^*$ can now be written as

$$H_0 : \theta^* \leq 1 \text{ against } H_1 : \theta^* > 1$$

The joint density, after the necessary re-parametrization, be given by

$$\begin{aligned}
&\lambda\mu \exp\{\theta^* T_1^* + \theta_2 T_2^*\} \\
&= \lambda\mu \exp\{(\lambda - \mu)T_1 / -1 + (-\mu)(T_2 - \frac{1}{-1}T_1)\} \\
&= \lambda\mu \exp\{-(\lambda - \mu)\, x - \mu\,(x + y)\}
\end{aligned}$$

Let $T = X + Y$, the joint density of $(X, T)$ be given by

$$f_{(X,\,T)}(x\,, t|\, \lambda,\, \mu) = \lambda\mu \exp\{-\lambda x - \mu(t - x)\}$$

The marginal density of $T$ becomes

$$\begin{aligned}
f_T(t) &= \int_0^\infty \lambda\mu \exp\{-\lambda x - \mu(t - x)\} dx \\
&= \lambda\mu\, e^{-\mu t} \int_0^\infty \exp\{-(\lambda - \mu)x\} dx
\end{aligned}$$

or

$$\begin{aligned}
f_T(t) &= \lambda\mu e^{-\mu t} \Big[ -\frac{e^{-(\lambda-\mu)x}}{\lambda - \mu} \Big]_0^\infty \\
&= \frac{\lambda\mu}{\lambda - \mu} e^{-\mu t}\; I_{(0,\,\infty)}(t)
\end{aligned}$$

Now, the conditional density of $x|\,t$ is given by

$$\begin{aligned}
f_{X|\,t}(x|\,t) &= \frac{f_{X,\,T}(x, t)}{f_T(t)} \\
&= \frac{\lambda\mu\, e^{-\lambda x - \mu(t-x)}}{\frac{\lambda\mu}{\lambda-\mu}\, e^{-\mu t}} \\
&= (\lambda - \mu)\, e^{-(\lambda-\mu)x}
\end{aligned}$$

Therefore, the UMP unbiased test becomes

$$\phi_0(x, t) = \begin{cases} 1 & \text{if } x > x_0(t) \\ 0 & \text{if } x \leq x_0(t) \end{cases}$$

where, $x_0(t)$ is obtained by

$$E_{\theta^*=1}[\phi_0(X,T)|T=t] = 0.20$$

$$\int_{x_0(t)}^{\infty} e^{-x}dx = -e^{-x}\Big|_{x_0(t)}^{\infty}$$

$$= e^{-x_0} = 0.20$$

or

$$-x_0 = \log(0.20)$$

or

$$x_0 = \log 1/0.2 = \log 5$$

And the test we get

$$\phi_0(x) = \begin{cases} 1 & \text{if } x > \log 5 \\ 0 & \text{if } x \le \log 5 \end{cases}$$

is UMP unbiased of size 0.20 for the given testing problem.

**Example 5.7.10.** *Let $X$ and $Y$ be independent random variables with geometric distribution*

$$f_{X,Y}(x,y|\theta_1,\theta_2) = (1-\theta_1)(1-\theta_2)\theta_1^x\theta_2^y;\ x = 0,1,\ldots\quad y = 0,1,\ldots$$

*where $0 < \theta_1 < 1$ and $0 < \theta_2 < 1$. Find out a UMP unbiased test of size-$\alpha = 0.20$ for testing $H_0 : \theta_1 = \theta_2$ against $H_1 : \theta_1 \neq \theta_2$.*

***Solution:*** The joint density of the random variables $X$ and $Y$ is given by

$$f_{X,Y}(x,y|\theta_1,\theta_2) = (1-\theta_1)(1-\theta_2)\exp\{x\log\theta_1 + y\log\theta_2\}$$

Here

$$\begin{aligned} \theta_1 &= \log\theta_1, & \theta_2 &= \log\theta_2 \\ T_1 &= X, & T_2 &= Y \end{aligned}$$

Let us define

$$\theta^* = a_1\theta_1 + a_2\theta_2 = a_1\log\theta_1 + a_2\log\theta_2$$

We take

$$a_1 = 1, \qquad a_2 = -1$$

$$\theta^* = \log\theta_1 - \log\theta_2$$

$$H_0 : \theta_1 = \theta_2 \text{ can be written as } \ H_0 : \theta^* = 0$$

The statistic $(T_1, T_2) = (X, Y)$ transforms into

$$(T_1/a_1,\, T_2 - (a_2/a_1)T_1) = (T_1,\, T_1 + T_2) = (X,\, X+Y)$$

Let $T = X + Y$, the joint density of $X$ and $T$ be given by

$$f_{X,T}(x,\, t|\theta_1,\, \theta_2) = (1-\theta_1)(1-\theta_2)\exp\{x\log\theta_1 + (t-x)\log\theta_2\}$$

The marginal density of $T$ is calculated as

$$f_T(t|\,\theta_1,\,\theta_2) = \sum_{x=0}^{t}(1-\theta_1)\,(1-\theta_2)\,\theta_1^x\,\theta_2^{(t-x)}$$

$$= (1-\theta_1)(1-\theta_2)\,\theta_2^t\,\textstyle\sum_{x=0}^{t}\left(\frac{\theta_1}{\theta_2}\right)^x$$

$$= (1-\theta_1)(1-\theta_2)\,\theta_2^t\,\frac{(\frac{\theta_1}{\theta_2})^t - 1}{(\frac{\theta_1}{\theta_2}) - 1}$$

Under the null hypothesis $\theta_1 = \theta_2 = \theta$, we have

$$f_{X,T}(x, t|\,\theta) = (1-\theta)^2\,\theta^t$$

and

$$f_T(t|\,\theta) = (1-\theta)^2\theta^t\,t$$

Therefore, the conditional distribution of $X|\,t$ under $H_0 : \theta_1 = \theta_2 = \theta$ is given by

$$f_{(X|\,t)}(x|\,t;\theta) = \frac{1}{t}, \quad x = 0, 1, \ldots, t$$

Therefore, UMP unbiased test shall be given by

$$\phi_0(x,t) = \begin{cases} 1 & \text{if } x > x_0(t) \\ \gamma & \text{if } x = x_0(t) \\ 0 & \text{if } x < x_0(t) \end{cases} \tag{5.10}$$

where $\gamma$ and $x_0(t)$ is obtained by

$$E_{\theta_1=\theta_2=\theta}[\phi_0(X,\, T)|\,T = t] = \alpha$$

$$P_\theta[X > x_0(t)|t] + \gamma\,P_\theta[X = x_0(t)|t] = \alpha$$

$$\gamma\cdot\frac{1}{t} + \sum_{x_0(t)+1}^{t}\frac{1}{t} = \alpha$$

$$\frac{\gamma}{t} + \frac{1}{t}(t - x_0(t)) = \alpha$$

$$\frac{x_0(t)}{t} - \frac{\gamma}{t} = 1-\alpha$$

If one gets $x_0(t)$ such that

$$\frac{x_0(t)}{t} = 1-\alpha \quad \text{or} \quad x_0(t) = t(1-\alpha)$$

one chooses $\gamma = 0$; and if

$$\frac{x_0(t)}{t} - \frac{1}{t} \leq 1 - \alpha < \frac{x_0(t)}{t}$$

then we choose, $x_0(t)$ and $\gamma = x_0 - t(1-\alpha)$.

From the above constants in Eq. (5.10) we get the UMP unbiased test. If we consider

$$\varphi(\theta_1, \theta_2) = a_1 \log \theta_1 + a_2 \log \theta_2 = 0$$
$$\theta_1^{a_1} \cdot \theta_2^{a_2} = 1$$

The calculations in this example could be applied to the functions of the type $\theta_1^{a_1} \cdot \theta_2^{a_2} = 1$ to get a UMP unbiased test. If we set $a_1 = 1,\ a_2 = -1$, we have $\dfrac{\theta_1}{\theta_2} = 1$ which gives $\log \theta_1 - \log \theta_2 = \phi_1(\theta_1,\ \theta_2) = 0$. Therefore, the hypotheses $H_0 : \theta_1 = \theta_2$ and $H_0 : \phi_1(\theta_1, \theta_2) = 0$ are equivalent.

## *Review Questions*

**5.1** (a) Define uniformly most powerful unbiased tests.
(b) Describe how you would obtain a uniformly most powerful unbiased test by considering tests having Neyman Structure. State and prove any results needed in the discussion. Give an example in which the above ideas can be applied to get uniformly most powerful unbiased test.

**5.2** Let the power function of every test $\phi$ of $H_0 : \theta \in \Theta_0$ against $H_1 : \theta \in \Theta_1$ be continuous in $\theta$. Then show that a UMP $\alpha$-similar test is UMP unbiased provided that its size is $\alpha$ for testing $H_0$ against $H_1$.

**5.3** (a) In the context of composite parametric null hypothesis $H_0$, explain the term *similar test* and test having Neyman structure. Bring out the relationship between the two concepts.

(b) Give an application of the concept of similar tests in $k$-parameter exponential family in deriving UMPU test. Give an example.

(c) A populations is dichotomized according to the presence or absence of each of two attributes $A$ and $B$. Indicate the assumptions and derive a small sample test of independence of the two attributes.

**5.4** State and prove the necessary and sufficient conditions for all similar tests of the above problem to have Neyman structure.

**5.5** Let $X_1, \ldots, X_n$ be $n$ independent observations from a normal distribution $N(\mu, \sigma^2)$ when $\mu$ and $\sigma^2$ are both unknown. Obtain a UMP unbiased test for: $H_0 : \mu \leq 0$ against $H_1 : \mu > 0$

**5.6** (a) Discuss the relevance of similar tests in finding the best unbiased test for testing these composite hypothesis.
(b) Obtain a UMP unbiased test for testing the composite hypothesis $H_0 : \sigma \leq 1$ against the alternative hypothesis $H_1 : \sigma > 1$ on the basis of a random sample of size $n$ from the normal distribution $N(\mu,\ \sigma^2)$.

**5.7** Obtain a UMP unbiased test for testing the composite hypothesis: $H_0 : \sigma \geq 1$ against the alternative $H_1 : \sigma < 1$ on the basis of a random sample of size $n$ from the normal distribution $N(\mu, \sigma^2)$.

**5.8** Let $X$ be distributed as

$$f_{\theta,\gamma}(x) = c(\theta, \gamma) \exp\{\theta\mu(x) + \sum_{i=1}^{k} \gamma_j T_j(x)\} \cdot d\mu(x); \quad (\theta, \gamma) \in \mathbb{R}^{k+1}$$

a $(k+1)$ parameter exponential family, here, $\boldsymbol{\gamma} = (\gamma_1, \gamma_2, \ldots, \gamma_k)$ and $\mathbf{T} = (T_1, \ldots, T_k)$. Consider the testing problem (unconditional), $H_0 : \theta_1 \leq \theta \leq \theta_2,\ \boldsymbol{\gamma}$ against $H_1 : \theta < \theta_1$ or $\theta > \theta_2, \boldsymbol{\gamma}$. Show that the conditional test

$$\phi(u, t) = \begin{cases} 1 & \text{when } u < c_1(t) \text{ or } u > c_2(t) \\ \gamma_i(t) & \text{when } u = c_i(t), i = 1, 2. \\ 0 & \text{when } c_1(t) < u < c_2(t) \end{cases}$$

where, $c_i'$s and $\gamma_i'$s are determined by

$$E_{\theta_1}[\phi(U, T)|\, t] = E_{\theta_2}[\phi(U, T)|\, t] = \alpha$$

is UMP unbiased for unconditional testing problem. Note here, $(U, T)$ are jointly sufficient for $(\theta, \boldsymbol{\gamma})$.

**5.9** Let $X \sim F_{\boldsymbol{\theta}}(x)$ be a $k$-parameter exponential family. Let a sample $X_1, X_2, \ldots, X_n$ be drawn from $F$, $n \geq k$. Find out UMP unbiased test for testing the following hypothesis

$$H_0 : \boldsymbol{\theta} \in \Theta_0 = \{\boldsymbol{\theta}|\, \theta_1 \leq \theta_1^0\} \text{ against } H_1 : \boldsymbol{\theta} \in \Theta_1 = \{\boldsymbol{\theta}|\, \theta_1 > \theta_1^0\}$$

**5.10** Discuss the role of tests having Neyman structure in testing when $\Theta \subset \mathbb{E}^k$ and $\boldsymbol{\theta}$ is unknown. How does this help in getting a size-$\alpha$ UMP unbiased tests for testing $H_0 : \theta_1 \leq \theta_1^{(0)}$ against $H_1 : \theta_1 > \theta_1^{(0)}$.

**5.11** Suppose $X_1$ and $X_2$ are independent poisson random variables with parameter $\lambda_1$, $\lambda_2$ respectively, and $\theta = \lambda_1/\lambda_2$. Consider testing $H_0 : \theta = \theta_0$ against $H_1 : \theta > \theta_0$, where $\theta_0$ is a preassigned value. Find

(a) A locally most powerful test of $H_0$ against $H_1$ when $\lambda_2$ is known.

(b) A uniformly most powerful similar test of $H_0$ against $H_1$ when $\lambda_1$ and $\lambda_2$ are unknown.

**5.12** (a) Let $X$ and $Y$ be independently distributed with poisson distributions $P(\lambda)$ and $P(\mu)$. Work out for the UMP unbiased test of $H_0 : \mu \leq \lambda$ against $H_1 : \lambda = 0.1$, $\mu = 0.2$. Also, find the power of UMP unbiased test at level of significance $\alpha = 0.1$.

(b) Write a brief note on testing for the hypothesis of independence in $2 \times 2$ contingency table against any alternative of your choice.

**5.13** Let $X$ and $Y$ be random variable with joint density

$$f_{X,Y}(x, y\, \lambda,\, \mu) = \lambda\mu\, e^{-\lambda x - \mu y}\, \mathrm{I}_{(0,\infty)}\,(x) \cdot \mathrm{I}_{(0,\infty)}\,(y)$$

Find a UMP unbiased test of size-$\alpha = 0.20$ for testing :
(a) $H_0 : \lambda \leq \mu + 1$ against $H_1 : \lambda > \mu + 1$ (b) $H_0 : \lambda \geq 2\mu$ against $H_1 : \lambda < 2\mu$.

**5.14** (a) Let $X_1, \ldots, X_m$ be independent poisson variables with parameters $\lambda_1, \ldots, \lambda_m$. Show that the test which rejects the null hypothesis $\sum_{j=1}^{m} \lambda_j \leq a$ when $\sum_{j=1}^{m} X_j > c$, in favour of the alternative hypothesis $\sum_{j=1}^{m} \lambda_j > a$, is a uniformly most powerful test of its size.

(b) Let $X_1, \ldots, X_m$ and $Y_1, \ldots, Y_n$ be independent random samples and let $\mu$ and $\nu$ denote the location parameters of the distributions of $X_1$ and $Y_1$ respectively. Discuss the problem of testing the null hypothesis $H_0 : \mu = \nu$ against the alternative $H_1 : \mu \neq \nu$ when (i) the random variables (r.v.s) $X$ and $Y$ are normally distributed and (ii) the r.v.s. $X$ and $Y$ have continuous distributions.

# Chapter 6

# Principle of Invariance in Testing of Hypothesis

## 6.1 INTRODUCTION

Principle of invariance like the principle of sufficiency is another way of data summarization where the problem of testing of hypothesis reduces into much simpler problem. Roughly, under this principle we define a group of transformations $\mathcal{G}$, from sample space onto itself, so that under the group $\mathcal{G}$, the family of distributions $\{P_\theta,\ \theta \in \Theta\}$ and the testing problem $H_0 : \theta \in \Theta_0$ against $H_1 : \theta \in \Theta_1$ remain invariant. Further, we define a class of tests where these remain in the same class under the transformations. Such a class of tests is referred to as class of invariant tests. A UMP test in this class, if it exists, is called an UMP invariant test for a given testing problem. A great reduction of the problem towards finding an UMP invariant test is obtained in this chapter, where it is shown that instead of considering a class of invariant tests one could restrict attention to a class of tests which are function of a special statistic known as maximal invariant statistic.

In Chapter 5, we discussed about the testing problem that involves nuisance parameters. In this, UMP unbiased tests were obtained by using conditional distributions, since these tests were having a Neyman structure. Handling of these conditional distributions were often not easy. Here we introduce the principle of invariance that simplifies such problems and provides relatively simple alternative approach towards finding a UMP test.

We shall now discuss the invariance principle in detail. Let $\mathfrak{X}$ be the sample space, $\mathfrak{X} \subseteq \mathbb{R}^n$, $\Theta$ and $\mathcal{A}$ be parameter and action spaces respectively; the family of distributions corresponding to the random variable $\mathbf{X}$, taking its values in $\mathfrak{X}$, be given by $\{P_\theta,\ \theta \in \Theta\}$. Let $\mathcal{G}$ be a group of measurable transformations from $\mathfrak{X}$ into itself. The assumption of measurability of $g \in \mathcal{G}$ has been made to ensure that $g(\mathbf{X})$ becomes a random variable, whenever $\mathbf{X}$ is a random variable. Some definitions related to the principle of invariance which are essential for studying its applications in testing of hypothesis are as follows:

**Definition 6.1.1. (Invariant Family of Distributions)** The family of distributions $\{P_\theta,\, \theta \in \Theta\}$ is said to be invariant under a group of transformations $\mathcal{G}$ if for every $g \in \mathcal{G}$ and $\theta \in \Theta$, there exists some $\theta' \in \Theta$ such that the distribution of $g(\mathbf{X})$ is given by $P_{\theta'}$ whenever the distribution of $\mathbf{X}$ is given by $P_\theta$. We see that the invariance of a family of distributions $\{P_\theta,\, \theta \in \Theta\}$ under $\mathcal{G}$ means the transformed random variable $g(\mathbf{X})$ finds its distribution in the same family, but with a changed parameter $\theta'$. The two conditions by which a family is said to be invariant are as follows:

(a) For every measurable set $A \in \mathfrak{X}$

$$P_\theta^{\mathbf{X}}\{g(\mathbf{X}) \in A\} = P_{\theta'}^{g(\mathbf{X})}\{\mathbf{X} \in A\} \tag{6.1}$$

(b) For every (integrable) real-valued $\phi$

$$E_\theta^{\mathbf{X}}\phi(g(\mathbf{X})) = E_{\theta'}^{g(\mathbf{X})}\phi(\mathbf{X}) \tag{6.2}$$

We note that the induced transformations $\bar{g}$ on $\Theta$ onto itself also form a group $\overline{\mathcal{G}} = \{\bar{g} : g \in \mathcal{G}\}$.

**Definition 6.1.2. (Invariant Decision Problem)** A decision problem $(\Theta, A, L)$ is said to be invariant under a group of transformations $\mathcal{G}$ if

(a) the family $\{P_\theta,\, \theta \in \Theta\}$ is invariant, and
(b) loss function is invariant under $\mathcal{G}$, i.e. for every $g \in \mathcal{G}$ and $a \in \mathcal{A}$ there exists $a' \in \mathcal{A}$ such that

$$L(\theta, a) = L(\bar{g}(\theta),\, a') \;\forall\; \theta \in \Theta$$

Subsequently, the induced transformation $\widetilde{g}$ on $\mathcal{A}$ into itself becomes a group denoted by $\widetilde{G} = \{\widetilde{g} : g \in \mathcal{G}\}$.

## 6.2 INVARIANT DECISION RULES

Let us consider a decision problem that is invariant under a group of transformations $\mathcal{G}$ on the sample space $\mathfrak{X}$. Let $X$ follow some distribution $P_\theta, \theta \in \Theta$. Let us consider two problems, the first, where $X \sim P_\theta,\; \theta \in \Theta$, random observable $X$ takes on a value $x_0$ and an statistician decides to choose an action $a_0 = \hat{\theta}(x_0) = d(x_0) \in \mathcal{A}$ with a loss $L(\theta, a_0)$, (call this problem as original problem), and the second where he defines another random variable $Y = g(X) \sim P_\phi, \phi \in \Theta$ with $\phi = \bar{g}(\theta)$ and chooses $b = \hat{\theta}(g(x_0)) = d(g(x_0)) \in \mathcal{A}$ with loss $L(\bar{g}(\theta), b)$ when $Y = g(x_0)$, call this problem as *transformed problem.* By utilizing the fact that the loss function is invariant, the statistician can choose $b = \widetilde{g}(a_0) = \widetilde{g}(d(x_0))$ such that $L(\phi,\, b) = L(\bar{g}(\theta),\, \widetilde{g}(a_0)) = L(\theta,\, a_0)$

and claim that both the problems are identical. In other words, he could even equivalently choose action $\widetilde{g}(a_0)$ whenever he observes $X = g(x_0)$ in the original problem. Therefore, the decision rule must satisfy

$$d(g(x_0)) = \widetilde{g}(d(x_0)) \qquad \forall \ g \in \mathcal{G}, \ \forall \ x_0 \in \mathfrak{X} \tag{6.3}$$

such rules are called *invariant decision rules.* The definition of invariant decision rule indicates that if $d(x_0)$ is a decision rule for making an inference on $\theta$, $d(g(x_0))$ shall be the appropriate decision rule for related inference on $\bar{g}_\theta$.

**Example 6.2.1.** *Let $X \sim P_\theta$, where $\theta$ is a location parameter or in other words, $P_\theta$ is a location family. By definition, $P_\theta$ must be some function of $(x - \theta)$. Let the random observable takes some value $x$ and the statistician decides to choose $a_0 = \hat{\theta}(x_0) = d(x_0)$ with loss function $L(\theta, a) = c(\theta - a)^2$. Now consider $Y = g(X) = X + c$ for some $g \in \mathcal{G}$ with distribution function $P_{\theta'}$, $\theta' \in \Theta$, with $\theta' = \bar{g}(\theta) = \theta + c$ since $P_Y(y|\,\theta') = P(y - \theta') = P(y - c - \theta) = P(y - (c + \theta)) \Rightarrow \theta' = \theta + c$ (since the family $P_\theta$ is invariant). If $Y = g(x_0) = x_0 + c$ has been observed, statistician decides to choose a action $b = d(g(x_0)) = d(x_0 + c)$ for which $L(\theta', b) = L(\bar{g}(\theta), b) = L(\theta, a) \ \forall \ \theta$. Invariance of loss function suggests a choice $b = \widetilde{g}(a_0) = a_0 + c$ in $\mathcal{A}$ would be such that $L(\theta', b) = c(\theta' - b)^2 = c(\theta + c - b)^2 = c(\theta + c - a_0 - c)^2 = c(\theta - a_0)^2 = L(\theta, a_0)$. Therefore, if the statistician observes $X = g(x_0) = x + c$ in the original problem the statistician would choose $\widetilde{g}(a_0) = a_0 + c$, therefore, invariant decision rule must satisfy*

$$d(g(x_0)) = \widetilde{g}(d(x_0)) \quad \textit{or} \qquad d(x_0 + c) = d(x_0) + c$$

### 6.2.1 Invariant Behavioural Decision Rule

A behavioural decision rule $\delta \in \mathcal{D}$ is said to be invariant if for all $x \in \mathfrak{X}$ and all $g \in \mathcal{G}$, $\delta(g(x)) = \widetilde{g}\ \delta(x)$, where by $\widetilde{g}\ \delta$ we meant that $\widetilde{g}Z$ has the distribution $\widetilde{g}\ \delta$ when $Z$ has distribution $\delta$.

#### Risk function of an invariant decision rule

Let us assume that that the parameter space $\Theta$ breaks up into equivalence classes by the relation $\bar{g}$ in $\bar{\mathcal{G}}$. Such classes are known as *orbits.* The important property of an invariant decision rule is that its risk function is constant on these orbits or

$$R(\theta, \delta) = R(\bar{g}(\theta), \delta) \quad \forall \ \theta \in \Theta \ \text{ and } \forall \ \bar{g} \in \bar{\mathcal{G}}$$

In case $\bar{\mathcal{G}}$ is transitive over $\Theta$, then for every $\theta_1$ and $\theta_2$ from $\Theta$ there exists some $\bar{g}$ in $\bar{\mathcal{G}}$ so that $\bar{g}\theta_1 = \theta_2$. In this case, the risk of invariant decision rule at $\theta_2$ is given by

$$R(\theta_2, \delta) = R(\bar{g}\theta_1, \delta) = R(\theta_1, \delta) \tag{6.4}$$

which is same as risk of invariant decision rule $\delta$ at $\theta_1$. This shows the risk of an invariant decision rule is independent of $\theta$ when $\bar{\mathcal{G}}$ over $\Theta$ is transitive. Clearly, whenever the risk of every invariant decision rule is constant, one should choose a rule as an optimal invariant decision rule for which this constant is minimum. Such a rule is referred to as *minimum risk invariant decision rule.*

Whenever $\bar{\mathcal{G}}$ is not transitive, even though the problem of minimization of risk $R(\theta, \delta)$ over the space $\Theta$ reduces into its minimization only over the orbits of $\Theta$.

## 6.3 INVARIANCE IN TESTING OF HYPOTHESIS PROBLEMS

Let us consider $\Theta$ as a parameter space a general hypothesis testing problem $H_0 : \theta \in \Theta_0$ against $H_1 : \theta \in \Theta$ with $\Theta_0 \cap \Theta_1 = \{\phi\}$, $\Theta_0 \cup \Theta_1 = \Theta$, $A$ as action space having two points $\{a_0, a_1\}$ and a loss function used in testing of hypothesis

$$L(\theta, a_0) = \begin{cases} c_{00}(0) & \text{if } \theta \in \Theta_0 \\ c_{01}(1) & \text{if } \theta \in \Theta_1 \end{cases}$$

and
$$L(\theta, a_1) = \begin{cases} c_{10}(1) & \text{if } \theta \in \Theta_0 \\ c_{11}(0) & \text{if } \theta \in \Theta_1 \end{cases} \tag{6.5}$$

where, $c_{00} < c_{01}$ and $c_{11} < c_{10}$. With the loss function as in Eq. (6.5), let the decision problem $(\Theta, A, L)$ be given as invariant under a group of transformations $\mathcal{G}$ on $\mathfrak{X}$ into itself and the corresponding induced group of transformations be denoted by $\overline{\mathcal{G}}$ and $\widetilde{\mathcal{G}}$ on $\Theta$ and $\mathcal{A}$ respectively. In this case, the loss function is invariant if and only if $\widetilde{g}$ is an identity transformation, i.e. $\widetilde{g}(a) = a \;\forall\; \widetilde{g} \in \widetilde{\mathcal{G}}$ and $\bar{g}(\Theta_0) = \Theta_0$ and $\bar{g}(\Theta_1) = \Theta_1$; and further the family of distributions is invariant if both the families $\{P_\theta, \theta \in \Theta_0\}$ and $\{P_\theta, \theta \in \Theta_1\}$ are invariant. Note that the testing problem and the decision rule does not change under the transformations $\mathcal{G}$ whenever the loss function and family of distributions are invariant.

Therefore, under the testing setup of the present section, a behavioural decision rule (a test $\phi$) is said to be invariant if for all $x \in \mathfrak{X}$ and $g \in \mathcal{G}$

$$\phi(g(x)) = \widetilde{g}(\phi(x)) = \phi(x)$$

We shall now define a special statistics that helps in reducing the problem of hypothesis testing to a great extent.

**Maximal invariant statistics**

Let $\mathfrak{X}$ be a sample space and $\mathcal{G}$ be a group of transformations on $\mathfrak{X}$. A function $T(x)$ on $\mathfrak{X}$ is said to be maximal invariant with respect to $\mathcal{G}$ if

$$\text{(Invariance)}T(g(x)) = T(x) \quad \forall\ x \in\ X \text{ and } g \in \mathcal{G} \tag{6.6}$$

$$\text{(Maximality)}T(x_1) = T(x_2) \text{ implies } x_1 = g(x_2) \text{ for some } g \in \mathcal{G} \tag{6.7}$$

Equation (6.6) says that $T$ is constant on orbits, Eq. (6.7) says that each orbit gets a different value under $T$, i.e. $T$ distinguishes orbits.

## 6.4 UMP INVARIANT TESTS

We shall now discuss how a UMP invariant test is obtained, but before this we shall discuss some results needed.

**Theorem 6.4.1.** *Let $\mathfrak{X}$ be the sample space and let $\mathcal{G}$ be a group of transformations on $\mathfrak{X}$ and let $T(x)$ be maximal invariant with respect to $\mathcal{G}$. A test function $\phi(x)$ is invariant with respect to $\mathcal{G}$ if and only if $\phi$ is a function of $T(x)$.*

*Proof.* (a)*If part:* Given that $\phi$ is function of $T(x)$, i.e.

$$\phi(x) = h(T(x))$$

Now consider

$$\begin{aligned}\phi(g(x)) &= h(\,T(g(x))\,)\\ &= h(T(x)) \qquad \text{since } T \text{ is invariant}\\ &= \phi(x)\end{aligned}$$

so that $\phi$ is invariant.
(b) *Only if part:* Suppose $\phi$ is invariant, i.e. if we have $x_1, x_2 \in \mathfrak{X}$ so that $x_1 = g(x_2)$ for some $g \in \mathcal{G}$

$$\phi(x_1) = \phi(x_2)$$

also

$$T(x_1) = T(x_2) \qquad \text{since } T \text{ is invariant on orbits}$$

which shows that $\phi$ is a function of $T$. □

*Remark* 6.4.1. The result obtained from Theorem 6.4.1 part (b) reduces the testing problem to a great extent as now the class of invariant tests has reduced to the class of all such tests which are function of maximal invariant statistic $T(x)$.

**Theorem 6.4.2.** *Suppose a statistical decision problem is invariant under a group $\mathcal{G}$ and let $v(\theta)$ be a maximal invariant under $\overline{\mathcal{G}}$. Then if $T(x)$ is invariant under $\mathcal{G}$, the distribution of $T(X)$ depends only on $v(\theta)$*

*Proof.* Consider two parameters $\theta, \theta'$ from the same orbit, i.e. $\theta' = \bar{g}(\theta)$ for some $\bar{g} \in \overline{\mathcal{G}}$. Consider the probability

$$P_{\theta'}^{g(X)}\{T(X) \in A\} = P_{\theta}^{X}\{T(g(X)) \in A\}$$
(since the decision problem is invariant)
$$= P_{\theta}^{X}\{T(X) \in A\}$$
(since $T(x)$ is invariant)

so that $P_\theta\{T(X) \in A\}$ is constant on the orbits of $\overline{\mathcal{G}}$, i.e. it is invariant. On using Theorem 6.4.1, the distribution of $T(X)$, i.e. $P_\theta\{T(A) \in A\}$, as a function of $\theta$, will be the function of the maximal invariant statistic $v(\theta)$. Therefore, the distribution of $T(X)$ depends only on $v(\theta)$. □

The direct application of Theorem 6.4.1 is that the risk of an invariant decision rule is constant on the orbits of $\Theta$. Therefore, minimization problem of risk, with respect to $\theta$ over the space of $\Theta$, for an optimal choice of invariant decision rule, converts into relatively a simple problem of minimization of risk over the orbits (since $P_\theta\{T(X) \in A\}$ is constant on orbits).

**Theorem 6.4.3. (Leading to UMP Invariant Tests)** *Let $X_1, X_2, \ldots, X_n$ be a random sample drawn from $F_X(x|\,\theta)$ for testing the hypothesis*

$$H_0 : F_{\mathbf{X}}(\mathbf{x}|\,\theta) = G_0(\mathbf{x} - \theta) \quad \textit{against} \quad H_1 : F_{\mathbf{X}}(\mathbf{x}|\,\theta) = G_1(\mathbf{x} - \theta)$$

*where $G_0$ and $G_1$ are some known distribution functions. The UMP invariant test for testing $H_0$ against $H_1$ is given by*

$$\phi(\mathbf{y}) = \begin{cases} 1 & \textit{if } \dfrac{\int_{-\infty}^{\infty} dG_1(y_1 + z, \ldots, y_{n-1} + z, z)}{\int_{-\infty}^{\infty} dG_0(y_1 + z, \ldots, y_{n-1} + z, z)} > k \\ 0 & \textit{otherwise} \end{cases}$$

*Proof.* The family $F_X(\mathbf{x}|\theta)$ is a location family which is invariant under a group of transformations $\mathcal{G}$

$$\mathcal{G} = \{g \,:\, g_c(\mathbf{x}) = \mathbf{x} + c, \quad c \in \mathbb{R}^1\}$$

In this problem, the statistic

$$\mathbf{Y} = (Y_1, \ldots, Y_{n-1}) = (X_1 - X_n, \ldots, X_i - X_n, \ldots, X_{n-1} - X_n)$$

is maximal invariant. Using the Remark 6.4.1, the class of invariant tests is given by

$$I_\alpha = \{\phi(\mathbf{y}) : E\phi(\mathbf{Y}) = \alpha\}$$

We may easily note that the distribution of $\mathbf{Y}$, $\int_{-\infty}^{\infty} dG_i(y_1+z, \ldots, y_{n-1}+z, z)$ under the hypothesis $H_i$, $i = 0, 1$, is independent of $\theta$. The original testing problem has now reduced to a simple versus simple hypothesis problem.

Therefore, the NP lemma gives the best test

$$\phi(\mathbf{y}) = \begin{cases} 1 & \text{if } \dfrac{\int_{-\infty}^{\infty} dG_1(y_1+z,\ldots,y_{n-1}+z,z)}{\int_{-\infty}^{\infty} dG_0(y_1+z,\ldots,y_{n-1}+z,z)} > k \\ 0 & \text{otherwise} \end{cases}$$

and, since it belongs to $\mathcal{I}_\alpha$, it is UMP invariant test. The constant $k$ is obtained by size condition. □

The examples in Section 6.5 would further explain the application of the results discussed in this section.

## 6.5 SOLVED EXAMPLES

**Example 6.5.1.** *Obtain maximal invariant statistics when $\mathfrak{X} = E_n$ and the group of transformations $\mathcal{G}$ is*

(a) *Location or translations group*

$$\mathcal{G} = \{g : g_c(x_1, x_2, \ldots, x_n) = (x_1 + c, \ldots, x_n + c)\}$$

(b) *Scale group*

$$\mathcal{G} = \{g : g_c(\mathbf{x}) = c\mathbf{x};\ \textit{where } c > 0\}$$

(c) *Location and scale translations group*

$$\mathcal{G} = \{g : g_{a,b}(\mathbf{x}) = a\mathbf{x} + b; a > 0\}$$

(d) *Linear orthogonal transformations group*

$$\mathcal{G} = \{g : g(\mathbf{x}) = A\mathbf{x} \textit{ such that } A'A = 0\}$$

(e) *Permutation group*

$$\mathcal{G} = \{g : g(\mathbf{x}) = (x_{i1}, \ldots, x_{in}), \text{is some permutation of} (1, 2, \ldots, n)\}$$

***Solution:*** (a) The statistic

$$T(\mathbf{x}) = (x_1 - x_n, \ldots, x_{n-1} - x_n)$$

satisfies the conditions of invariance and maximality, namely Eqs. (6.6) and (6.7) of Section 6.3, therefore, $T(\mathbf{x})$ is maximal invariant.

(b) Proceeding similarly as in (a), the statistic

$$T(\mathbf{x}) = \begin{cases} \mathbf{x}/z & \text{if } z \neq 0 \\ 0 & \text{if } z = 0 \end{cases}$$

where, $z^2 = \mathbf{x}'\mathbf{x}$ may easily be seen to satisfy the conditions (6.6) and (6.7) of section 6.3, therefore is a maximal invariant statistic.

(c) The statistic

$$T(\mathbf{x}) = \begin{cases} \dfrac{\mathbf{x} - \bar{x}}{s} & \text{if } s \neq 0 \\ 0 & \text{if } s = 0 \end{cases}$$

where,

$$\bar{x} = \frac{1}{n}\sum x_i; s^2 = \frac{1}{n}\sum (x_i - \bar{x})^2$$

is maximal invariant when $\mathcal{G}$ is a group of location and scale transformations.

(d) Similarly, the statistic

$$T(\mathbf{x}) = \mathbf{x}'\mathbf{x}$$

is maximal invariant under the group $\mathcal{G}$ of linear orthogonal transformations.

(e) The statistic

$$T(\mathbf{x}) = (x_{(1)}, x_{(2)}, \ldots, x_{(n)})$$

is maximal invariant under the group $\mathcal{G}$ as permutation group.

**Example 6.5.2.** *Let $X_1$ and $X_2$ be two iid random variables drawn to test the hypothesis $H_0 : F_X(x|\,\theta) : N(\theta, 1)$ against $H_1 : F_X(x|\,\theta) : \mathcal{C}(\theta, 1)$ (with semi-interquartile range 1)*

*Show that*
$$\phi(x_1, x_2) = \begin{cases} 1 & \text{if } |x_1 - x_2| > k \\ 0 & \text{if } |x_1 - x_2| < k \end{cases}$$

*is UMP invariant test of $H_0$ against $H_1$.*

***Solution:*** We may note that $\theta$ is a location parameter of the distributions under the null and the alternative hypotheses, therefore, the conditions of Theorem 6.4.3 hold. Further under a group of transformations

$$\mathcal{G} = \{g_c : g_c(\mathbf{x}) = \mathbf{x} + c, \quad c \in \mathbb{R}^1\}$$

$g_c(\mathbf{x})\big|_{H_0} \sim N(\theta + c, 1)$ and $g_c(\mathbf{x})|_{H_1} \sim \mathcal{C}(\theta + c, 1)$, $\theta + c \in \Theta$. This implies that the distributions $\{N(\theta, 1),\ \theta \in \Theta = \mathbb{R}^1\}$ and $\{\mathcal{C}(\theta, 1),\ \theta \in \Theta = \mathbb{R}^1\}$ are invariant under the null and the alternative hypotheses respectively. Therefore, under $\mathcal{G}$ the testing of hypothesis problem is invariant.

Let us now define a statistic

$$\mathbf{Y} = (Y_{n-1}) = Y_1 = X_1 - X_2$$

Consider

$$\mathbf{Y}(g(\mathbf{X})) = \mathbf{Y}(\mathbf{X} + c) = (X_1 + c) - (X_2 + c) = X_1 - X_2 = \mathbf{Y}(\mathbf{X})$$

showing that $\mathbf{Y}$ is invariant. Next, consider

$$\mathbf{Y}(\mathbf{X}) = \mathbf{Y}(\mathbf{X}')$$

or

$$X_1 - X_2 = X_1' - X_2' \text{ or } X_1 = X_1' + (X_2 - X_2') = X_1' + c$$

where

$$c = (X_2 - X_2')$$

which implies, $g_c(\mathbf{x}') = \mathbf{x}$ for c $= (x_2 - x_2')$ showing that $\mathbf{Y}$ is maximal. Let us consider the class of invariant tests of size-$\alpha$

$$I_\alpha = \{\phi \in \mathcal{D} : \phi(g_c(\mathbf{x})) = \phi(\mathbf{x}), \ \forall \ c \in \mathbb{R}^1 \text{ and } \sup_{\theta \in \Theta_0} E_\theta \phi(\mathbf{X}) = \alpha\}$$

$$= \{\phi \in \mathcal{D} : \phi \text{ as functions of } \mathbf{Y} \text{ and } \sup_{\theta \in \Theta_0} E_\theta \phi(\mathbf{Y}) = \alpha\}$$

Here, $I_\alpha$ is the class of all size-$\alpha$ tests which are functions of maximal invariant statistic $\mathbf{Y}$.

Consider the joint distribution of $(X_1, X_2)|\, H_0$

$$f_{X_1,X_2}(x_1, x_2|\,\theta) = \frac{1}{2\pi} \exp\{-\frac{1}{2}\sum_{i=1}^{2}(x_i - \theta)^2\}$$

Let

$$y_1 = x_1 - x_2 \text{ and } z = x_2$$

which gives

$$x_1 = y_1 + z, \ x_2 = z$$

$$f_{Y_1,\,Z}(y_1 + z,\, z) = \frac{1}{2\pi} \exp\Big\{-\frac{1}{2}(y_1 + z - \theta)^2 - \frac{1}{2}(z - \theta)^2\Big\}$$

$$f_{Y_1}(y_1) = \int_{\mathbb{R}^1} \frac{1}{2\pi} \exp\Big\{-\frac{1}{2}[(y_1 + z - \theta)^2 + (z - \theta)^2]\} \, dz$$

Let

$$w = z - \theta \text{ gives, } dw = dz$$

$$f_{Y_1}(y_1) = \frac{1}{2\pi} \int_{\mathbb{R}^1} \exp\Big\{-\frac{1}{2}[(y_1 + w)^2 + w^2]\Big\} \, dw$$

$$= \frac{1}{2\pi} \exp\Big\{-\frac{1}{2}y_1^2\Big\} \int \exp\Big\{-[y_1 w + w^2]\Big\} \, dw$$

$$= \frac{1}{2\pi} \exp\{-\frac{1}{2}y_1^2\} \int \exp\Big\{-\Big[\Big(\frac{y_1}{2}\Big)^2 + y_1 w + w^2 - \Big(\frac{y_1}{2}\Big)^2\Big]\Big\} \, dw$$

$$= \frac{1}{2\pi} \exp\{(\frac{y_1}{2})^2\} \int \exp\{-(w + y_1/2)^2\} \, dw$$

On putting

$$w = z - \theta$$

$$\begin{aligned} f_{Y_1}(y_1) &= \frac{1}{2\pi} \exp\{-(\tfrac{y_1}{2})^2\} \int \exp\Big\{-\frac{(\sqrt{2})^2}{2}(z - (\theta - y_1/2))^2\Big\}\, dz \\ &= \frac{1}{\sqrt{2\pi}\sqrt{2}} \exp\Big\{-\Big(\frac{y_1}{2}\Big)^2\Big\} \int_{\mathbb{R}^1} \exp\Big\{-\Big(\frac{1}{2(\frac{1}{\sqrt{2}})^2}\Big)\Big(z - \Big(\theta - \frac{y_1}{2}\Big)\Big)^2\Big\}\, dz \\ &= \frac{1}{\sqrt{2\pi}\sqrt{2}} \exp\Big\{-(\frac{1}{2.2})y_1^2\Big\} \sim N(0, 2), \quad y_1 \in \mathbb{R}^1 \end{aligned}$$

Therefore, we see that the distribution of $\mathbf{Y} = Y_1|_{H_0} \sim N(0,2)$ which is independent of $\theta$.

Next, the joint distribution of $X_1$, $X_2$ under $H_1 : X \sim \mathcal{C}(\theta, 1)$ is given by

$$f_{X_1, X_2}(x_1, x_2 | \theta) = \frac{1}{\pi} \cdot \frac{1}{1 + (x_1 - \theta)^2} \cdot \frac{1}{\pi} \cdot \frac{1}{1 + (x_2 - \theta)^2}$$

Let

$$Y_1 = X_1 - X_2 \text{ and } Z = X_2$$

We have

$$X_1 = Y_1 + Z, \qquad X_2 = Z$$

We get

$$f_{Y_1, Z}(y_1 + z, z) = \frac{1}{\pi^2} \cdot \frac{1}{1 + (y_1 + z - \theta)^2} \cdot \frac{1}{1 + (z - \theta)^2}$$

and

$$\begin{aligned} f_{Y_1}(y_1) &= \frac{1}{\pi^2} \int_{-\infty}^{\infty} \frac{1}{1 + (y_1 + z - \theta)^2} \cdot \frac{1}{1 + (z - \theta)^2}\, dz \\ &= \frac{1}{\pi^2} \cdot \frac{2}{y_1^2 + 2^2} \end{aligned}$$

which is again independent of $\theta$ and we see that the distribution of $\mathbf{Y}$ under either hypotheses does not depend on parameter $\theta$ and have different distributions say $G_0$ and $G_1$ respectively. Therefore, we see that the invariance principle reduces the original testing problem to a simple versus simple hypothesis for testing $H_0 : F_{\mathbf{Y}}(\mathbf{y}) \sim N(0, 2)$ against $H_1 : F_{\mathbf{Y}}(\mathbf{y}) \sim \frac{1}{\pi^2} \cdot \frac{2}{y_1^2 + 2^2}$. For this problem, the NP lemma gives the MP size-$\alpha$ test by

$$\phi_0(\mathbf{y}) = \begin{cases} 1 & \text{if } \dfrac{f_{Y_1}(y_1 | H_1)}{f_{Y_1}(y_1 | H_0)} > k \\ 0 & \text{otherwise} \end{cases}$$

where, $k$ is obtained by the size condition

$$E_{H_0}\phi_0(\mathbf{Y}) = \alpha$$

On writing

$$\lambda(\mathbf{y}) = \frac{f_{Y_1}(y_1|\, H_1)}{f_{Y_1}(y_1|\, H_0)} = \frac{\frac{1}{\pi^2}\cdot\frac{2}{y_1^2+2^2}}{\frac{1}{\sqrt{2\pi}\sqrt{2}}\sqrt{e^{-\frac{1}{2}\frac{y_1^2}{2}}}} = c\cdot\frac{e^{\frac{|y_1|^2}{4}}}{|y_1|^2+4}$$

Now, differentiating $\lambda(\mathbf{y})$ with respect to $|y_1|$ we get

$$\begin{aligned}\frac{\partial\lambda(\mathbf{y})}{\partial|y_1|} &= c\cdot\frac{(|y_1|^2+4)\cdot 2|y_1|/4\cdot e^{|y_1|^2/4} - e^{\frac{|y_1|^2}{4}}\cdot 2|y_1|}{(|y_1|^2+4)^2}\\ &= c\cdot\frac{2|y_1|e^{|y_1|^2/4}(|y_1|^2/4+1-1)}{(|y_1|^2+4)^2}\\ &= c\cdot\frac{|y_1|^3 e^{|y_1|^2/4}}{(|y_1|^2+4)^2} > 0\end{aligned}$$

which shows that $\lambda(\mathbf{y})$ is an increasing function in $|y_1|$, therefore, $\lambda(\mathbf{y}) > k$ implies $|y_1| > k'$ for some $k'$. The UMP invariant test is now given by

$$\phi_0(\mathbf{y}) = \begin{cases} 1 & \text{if } |y_1| > k' \\ 0 & \text{otherwise} \end{cases}$$

where, $k'$ is determined by

$$E_{H_0}\phi_0(\mathbf{Y}) = \alpha$$

$$\int_{|y_1|>k} N(0,1)\, dy_1 = \alpha$$

Symmetry of the normal distribution about zero gives

$$\int_k^\infty N(0,2)\, dy_1 = \alpha/2$$

Let

$$w = y_1/\sqrt{2} \;\text{ then }\; \int_{k/\sqrt{2}}^\infty N(0,1)\, dw = \alpha/2$$

and we get

$$k/\sqrt{2} = z_{\alpha/2}; \qquad \text{or } \; k = \sqrt{2}\cdot z_{\alpha/2}$$

**Example 6.5.3.** *Let $X_1, \ldots, X_n$ be iid from $F_X(x|\,\theta)$ to test the hypothesis*

$$H_0 : F_X(x|\,\theta) : N(\theta, 1) \;\; \textit{against} \;\; H_1 : F_X(x|\,\theta) : e^{-e^{(x-\theta)}} + (x-\theta)$$

*Find out the form of the UMP invariant test of $H_0$ against $H_1$.*

***Solution:*** It can easily be seen that $\theta$ is the location parameter in the densities under both the hypotheses. Therefore, this problem is similar to the one we have discussed in Example 6.5.2. Let $\mathcal{G}$ be a group under location transformations. The distributions under the null and the alternative hypotheses could easily be shown to be invariant, leaving the testing of hypothesis problem invariant. Let the statistic

$$\mathbf{Y} = (Y_1, Y_2, \ldots, Y_{n-1}) = (X_1 - X_n, \ldots, X_{n-1} - X_n)$$

be maximal invariant. (The remaining solution has been left as an exercise).

**Example 6.5.4.** *Let $X_1, \ldots, X_n$ be iid sample drawn from $N(\mu, \sigma^2)$ to test the hypothesis*

$$H_0 : \sigma^2 \geq \sigma_0^2, \quad \mu \in \mathbb{R}^1 \quad \text{against} \quad H_1 : \sigma^2 < \sigma_0^2, \quad \mu \in \mathbb{R}^1.$$

*Show that*

$$\phi(\mathbf{x}) = \begin{cases} 1 & \text{if } \sum(x_i - \bar{x})^2 < k \\ 0 & \text{if } \sum(x_i - \bar{x})^2 > k \end{cases}$$

*is a UMP invariant test of $H_0$ against $H_1$.*

***Solution:*** Consider the group of translations

$$\mathcal{G} = \{g_c |\, g_c(\mathbf{x}) = \mathbf{x} + c, \ c \neq 0\}$$

The family $\{N(\mu, \sigma^2)\}$ remains invariant under $\mathcal{G}$. The families of distributions $\{N(\mu, \sigma^2) : (\mu, \sigma^2) \in \Theta_0\}$ and $\{N(\mu, \sigma^2) : \theta \in \Theta_1\}$ remain invariant since $V(g_c(X)) = V(X)$, i.e. $V(X + C) = V(X)$. This makes the testing of hypothesis problem invariant. $(\bar{X}, \sum(X_i - \bar{X})^2)$ is jointly sufficient for $(\mu, \sigma^2)$ and that under $g_c(\mathbf{x}) = \mathbf{x} + c$ this changes to $(\bar{X} + c, \sum(X_i - \bar{X})^2)$. This suggests that $\sum(X_i - \bar{X})^2$ is maximal invariant. The class of invariant tests $I_\alpha$ will be the class of tests which are function of maximal invariant statistic $\sum(X_i - \bar{X})^2$. We shall now consider the distribution of $T = \sum(X_i - \bar{X})^2$. We know that $\sum(X_i - \bar{X})/\sigma^2 \sim \chi^2_{n-1}$, therefore,

$$f_T(t|\, \sigma^2) = \frac{1}{\Gamma((n-1)/2)\, 2^{(n-1)/2}} e^{-t/2\sigma^2} \left(\frac{t}{\sigma^2}\right)^{\frac{(n-1)}{2} - 1} \cdot |J|$$

where

$$|J| = |1/\sigma^2| = \frac{1}{\sigma^2}$$

We get

$$f_T(t|\, \sigma^2) = \frac{\sigma^{-(n-1)}}{\Gamma((n-1)/2)\, 2^{(n-1)/2}} e^{-t/2\sigma^2} t^{(n-3)/2}$$

We know that this family has monotone likelihood ratio in $T$. Therefore, Karlin and Rubin theorem gives UMP test for testing $H_0 : \sigma^2 \geq \sigma_0^2$ against $H_1 : \sigma^2 < \sigma_0^2$ as

$$\phi_0(t) = \begin{cases} 1 & \text{if } t \leq k \\ 0 & \text{if } t > k \end{cases}$$

where $t = \sum_{i=1}^{n}(x_i - \bar{x})^2$ and the constant $k$ is determined by

$$P_{\sigma_0^2}\{T \leq k\} = P_{\sigma_0^2}\left\{\frac{T}{\sigma_0^2} \leq \frac{k}{\sigma_0^2}\right\} = \alpha$$

or

$$P_{\sigma_0^2}\left\{\chi_{n-1}^2 > \frac{k}{\sigma_0^2}\right\} = 1 - \alpha$$

which gives

$$\frac{k}{\sigma_0^2} = \chi^2_{n-1,\,1-\alpha}, \quad \text{i.e. } k = \sigma_0^2\,\chi^2_{n-1,\,1-\alpha}$$

The test $\phi_0$ is UMP invariant of size-$\alpha$. The same test has already been shown as UMP unbiased while discussing similar tests with Neyman structure.

**Example 6.5.5.** *Consider $T \sim f_T(t|\,\delta)$, non-central t-distribution with n degrees of freedom and $\delta$ as non-centrality parameter. Show that the ratio*

$$\frac{f_T(t|\,\delta)}{f_T(t|\,0)}$$

*is a non-decreasing function of t when $\delta > 0$.*

***Solution:*** If $X \sim N(\mu, \sigma^2)$ and $\frac{Y}{\sigma^2} \sim \chi^2_{(n)}$, $X$, and $Y$ are independent, we define

$$T = \frac{X}{\sqrt{Y/n}} = \frac{X/\sigma}{\sqrt{Y/\sigma^2 n}} \sim t_{n,\delta};\ \delta = \mu/\sigma$$

where, $\delta$ is non-centrality parameter and the corresponding density is given by

$$f_T(t, n, \delta) = \frac{n^{n/2} e^{-\delta^2/2}}{\sqrt{\pi}\,\Gamma(\frac{n}{2})(n + t^2)^{\frac{(n+1)}{2}}} \sum_{s=0}^{\infty} \Gamma\left(\frac{n+s+1}{2}\right) \cdot \frac{\delta^s}{s!} \cdot \left(\frac{2t^2}{n+t^2}\right)^{s/2}$$

and when $\delta = 0$ we have

$$f_T(t, n, 0) = \frac{n^{n/2}\,\Gamma(\frac{(n+1)}{2})}{\sqrt{\pi}\,\Gamma(n/2)(n+t^2)^{(n+1)/2}}$$

If we consider the ratio

$$\begin{aligned} L &= \frac{f_T(t, n, \delta)}{f_T(t, n, 0)} \\ &= \frac{e^{-\delta^2/2}}{\Gamma(n+1)/2} \sum_{s=0}^{\infty} \Gamma\left(\frac{n+s+1}{2}\right) \frac{\delta^s}{s!} \left(\frac{2t^2}{n+t^2}\right)^{s/2} \end{aligned}$$

On differentiating $L$ with respect to $t$ we get

$$\frac{\partial L}{\partial t} = \frac{e^{-\delta^2/2}}{\Gamma(n+1)/2}\sum_{s=0}^{\infty}\Gamma\Big(\frac{n+s+1}{2}\Big)\frac{\delta^s}{s!}\cdot\frac{s}{2}\cdot\Big(\frac{2t^2}{n+t^2}\Big)^{s/2-1}$$
$$\cdot\Big\{\frac{(n+t^2)4t-2t^2\cdot 2t}{(n+t^2)^2}\Big\}$$
$$= \frac{e^{-\delta^2/2}}{\Gamma(n+1)/2}\sum_{s=0}^{\infty}\Gamma\Big(\frac{n+s+1}{2}\Big)\frac{\delta^s}{s(s-1)!}\cdot\frac{s}{2}\cdot\frac{(n+t^2)}{2t^2}$$
$$\cdot\Big(\frac{2t^2}{n+t^2}\Big)^{s/2}\cdot\frac{4nt}{(n+t^2)^2}$$
$$\frac{\partial L}{\partial t} = \frac{e^{-\delta^2/2}}{\Gamma\frac{(n+1)}{2}}\sum_{s=0}^{\infty}\Gamma\Big(\frac{n+s+1}{2}\Big)\frac{\delta^s}{(s-1)!}\Big(\frac{2t^2}{n+t^2}\Big)^{s/2}\frac{n}{t(n+t^2)}$$
$$= \frac{e^{-\delta^2/2}}{\Gamma\frac{(n+1)}{2}}\sum_{s=1}^{\infty}\Gamma\Big(\frac{n+s+1}{2}\Big)\frac{\delta^s}{(s-1)!}2^{s/2}\cdot n\frac{t^{s-1}}{(n+t^2)^{s/2+1}}$$
$$> 0 \text{ when } \delta > 0 \text{ and } t > 0$$

which shows that the ratio $f_T(t,n,\delta)/f_T(t,n,0)$ is non-decreasing function of $t$ when $\delta > 0$ and $t > 0$.

**Example 6.5.6.** *Let $T \sim f_T(t,n,\delta)$ be a non-central t-distribution with n degrees of freedom and δ non-centrality parameter. Show that*

$$\frac{f_{|T|}(t,n,\delta)}{f_{|T|}(t,n,0)}$$

*is an increasing function of t for $t > 0$.*

***Solution:*** Consider the ratio

$$L = \frac{f_{|T|}(t,n,\delta)}{f_{|T|}(t,n,0)} = \frac{f_T(t,n,\delta)+f_T(-t,n,\delta)}{f_T(t,n,0)+f_T(-t,n,0)}$$
$$= \frac{2n^{n/2}e^{-\delta^2/2}\sum_{s=0}^{\infty}\Gamma(\frac{n+s+1}{2})\frac{\delta^s}{s!}(\frac{2t^2}{n+t^2})^{s/2}/\sqrt{\pi}\,\Gamma(n/2)(n+t^2)^{\frac{n+1}{2}}}{2n^{n/2}\Gamma(\frac{n+1}{2})/\sqrt{\pi}\,\Gamma(n/2)(n+t^2)^{(n+1)/2}}$$
$$L = \frac{e^{-\delta^2/2}}{\Gamma\frac{(n+1)}{2}}\sum_{s=0}^{\infty}\Gamma\frac{(n+s+1)}{2}\frac{\delta^s}{s!}\Big(\frac{2t^2}{n+t^2}\Big)^{s/2}$$

On differentiating $L$ with respect to $t$ we get

$$\begin{aligned}\frac{\partial L}{\partial t} &= \frac{e^{-\delta^2/2}}{\Gamma\frac{(n+1)}{2}} \sum_{s=0}^{\infty} \Gamma\frac{(n+s+1)}{2} \cdot \frac{\delta^s}{s!}\frac{s}{2}\left(\frac{2t^2}{(n+t^2)}\right)^{s/2-1} \left\{\frac{4nt}{(n+t^2)^2}\right\} \\ &= \frac{e^{-\delta^2/2}}{\Gamma\frac{(n+1)}{2}} \sum_{s=1}^{\infty} \Gamma\frac{(n+s+1)}{2} \frac{\delta^s}{(s-1)!} 2^{s/2} \cdot \frac{t^{s-1}}{(n+t^2)^{s/2+1}} \\ &> 0 \text{ when } \delta > 0 \text{ and } t > 0\end{aligned}$$

This shows that the ratio $f_{|T|}(t,n,\delta)/f_{|T|}(t,n,0)$ is an increasing function of $t$ when $\delta > 0$ and $t > 0$.

**Example 6.5.7.** *Consider $X \sim N(\mu, \sigma^2)$, both $\mu$, $\sigma^2$ are unknown. Find out a UMP invariant test for the testing problem*

$$H_0 : \mu \leq 0 \text{ against } H_1 : \mu > 0$$

*on the basis of a random sample $X_1, \ldots, X_n$ from $N(\mu, \sigma^2)$.*

***Solution:*** Consider the group of scale transformations

$$\mathcal{G} = \{g|\, g_c(\mathbf{x}) = c\mathbf{x},\ c > 0\}$$

giving

$$E[g_c(X)] = E(cX) = c\mu$$

and

$$V[g_c(X)] = c^2\sigma^2.$$

The families $\{N(\mu,\sigma^2)|\,(\mu,\sigma^2) \in \Theta_0\}$ and $\{N(\mu,\sigma^2)|\,(\mu,\sigma^2) \in \Theta_1\}$ are invariant under the transformations $g_c(\mathbf{x})$, leading to invariance of the testing problem under these scale transformations $g_c(\mathbf{x})$.

Let $U = \sqrt{n}\bar{X}$ and $V = \sum(X_i - \bar{X})^2$. We know that $(U, V)$ is jointly sufficient for $(\mu, \sigma^2)$. We have seen the testing problem is invariant under the changes of scale, hence under the group of transformations

$$g_c(U, V) = (cU, c^2V), \quad \text{where} \quad c > 0$$

We shall define a maximal invariant statistic

$$\begin{aligned}T &= \frac{U}{\sqrt{V/(n-1)}} \\ &= \frac{U/\sigma}{\sqrt{V/\sigma^2(n-1)}} \sim \frac{N(\frac{n\mu}{\sigma}, 1)}{\sqrt{\chi^2_{n-1}/(n-1)}} \sim t_{n-1,\,\delta}\end{aligned}$$

where $\delta = \frac{n\mu}{\sigma}$ is the non-centrality parameter.

Note that

$$T(g_c(U, V)) = \frac{cU}{\sqrt{c^2V/(n-1)}} = \frac{U}{\sqrt{V/(n-1)}} = T(U, V)$$

shows that $T$ is invariant. Let us take any two points $(U_1, V_1)$ and $(U_2, V_2)$ then $T(U_1, V_1) = T(U_2, V_2)$

$$\frac{U_1}{\sqrt{V_1/(n-1)}} = \frac{U_2}{\sqrt{V_2/(n-1)}}$$

or

$$U_1 = \sqrt{\frac{V_1}{V_2}} \cdot U_2$$

Let

$$c = \sqrt{\frac{V_1}{V_2}}$$

We get

$$\sqrt{n}\frac{\sum X_{1i}}{n} = \frac{c\sqrt{n}\sum X_{2i}}{n}$$

or

$$X_{1i} = cX_{2i} \quad \text{for} \quad i = 1, \ldots, n$$

which gives for a given $c$

$$x_1 = g_c(x_2)$$

showing that $T$ is maximal. Therefore, $T$ is a maximal invariant statistic.

The problem of finding UMP invariant test for $H_0 : \mu \leq 0$ against $H_1 : \mu > 0$ becomes the problem of testing $H_0 : \delta \leq 0$ against $H_1 : \delta > 0$, where $\delta$ is non-centrality parameter of non-central t-distribution with $n-1$ degrees of freedom which is the distribution of maximal invariant statistic $T$. We have seen distribution of $T$ has monotone likelihood ratio. Therefore, Karlin and Rubin theorem gives

$$\phi_0(t) = \begin{cases} 1 & \text{if } \ t > t_0 \\ 0 & \text{otherwise} \end{cases}$$

a UMP invariant test of size-$\alpha$, where $t_0$ is obtained by

$$E_{\delta=0}[\phi_0(T)] = \alpha$$

$$\int_{t_0}^{\infty} t_{n-1}(y)\, dy = \alpha$$

An alternative way of showing the above test is UMP invariant. Consider the testing problem, $H_0 : \delta = 0$ against $H_1 : \delta = \delta_1,\ \delta_1 > 0$. NP lemma gives the MP test by

$$L = \frac{f_T(t, n-1, \delta_1)}{f_T(t, n-1, 0)} > K$$

But we have already shown $L$ as an increasing function of $t$ when $\delta > 0$. Therefore, best test is given by

$$t > K$$

The same test is UMP for $H_0 : \delta = 0$ against $H_1 : \delta > 0$ since it is independent of the alternative $\delta$. The family of $t_{n-1,\,\delta}$ has MLR in $T$, by Karlin and Rubin theorem, the above test $\phi_0(t)$ has non-decreasing power function in $\delta$. This gives $\phi_0(t)$ is UMP for $H_0 : \delta \leq 0$ against $H_1 : \delta > 0$. Therefore, $\phi_0(t)$ is UMP invariant for this testing problem.

**Example 6.5.8.** *Let $X \sim N(\mu, \sigma^2)$ where, both $\mu$ and $\sigma^2$ are unknown. Let $X_1, \ldots, X_n$ be a random sample from $N(\mu, \sigma^2)$ to test the hypothesis*

$$H_0 : \mu = 0 \quad \textit{against} \quad H_1 : \mu \neq 0$$

*Find out a UMP invariant test.*

***Solution:*** Consider the group of transformations

$$\mathcal{G} = \{g_c |\, g_c(\mathbf{x}) = c\mathbf{x}, \quad c \neq 0\}$$

$\mathcal{G}$ for the sufficient statistics $(U, V)$ be given by

$$\mathcal{G} = \{g_c(U, V) |\, g_c(U, V) = (cU, c^2V); \quad c \neq 0\}$$

Consider the statistic

$$|T| = \frac{|U|}{\sqrt{V/(n-1)}}$$

Take $g_c(U, V) = (cU, c^2V)$ for some $c \neq 0$ and consider

$$|T(g_c(U, V))| = \frac{|cU|}{\sqrt{c^2V/(n-1)}} = \frac{|U|}{\sqrt{V/(n-1)}} = |T(U, V)|$$

which shows $|T|$ is invariant under $\mathcal{G}$. Now, consider

$$|T(U_1, V_1)| = |T(U_2, V_2)|$$

$$\frac{|U_1|}{\sqrt{V_1/(n-1)}} = \frac{|U_2|}{\sqrt{V_2/(n-1)}}$$

$$|U_1| = \sqrt{\frac{V_1}{V_2}}\,|U_2| \quad \text{where} \quad c = \sqrt{\frac{V_1}{V_2}}$$

$$\left|\sqrt{n}\frac{\sum_1^n X_{1i}}{n}\right| = c\left|\sqrt{n}\frac{\sum_1^n X_{2i}}{n}\right|$$

which gives

$$X_{1i} = c\,X_{2i} \qquad \forall\ i = 1, \ldots, n \ \text{ or } \ \mathbf{X}_1 = g_c(\mathbf{X}_2)$$

This shows that $|T|$ is maximal. Therefore, the considered statistic $|T|$ is maximal invariant. We shall now consider a class of tests which are the function of maximal invariant statistic $|T|$, defined by

$$I_\alpha = \{\phi |\, E_{\delta=0}\phi(T) = \alpha\}$$

The testing problem now becomes

$$H_0 : \delta = 0 \;\text{ against }\; H_1 : \delta \neq 0$$

or

$$H_0 : \delta = 0 \;\text{ against }\; H_1 : |\delta| > 0$$

NP lemma gives the best test for the above testing problem as

$$\phi_0(t) = \begin{cases} 1 & \text{if } \dfrac{f_{|T|}(t, n-1, |\delta|)}{f_{|T|}(t, n-1, 0)} > k \\ 0 & \text{otherwise} \end{cases}$$

We have already noted that $L = \dfrac{f_{|T|}(t,\, n-1,\, |\delta|)}{f_{|T|}(t,\, n-1,\, 0)}$ is increasing in $|t|$ for $|\delta| > 0$. The UMP invariant test would now be given by

$$\phi_0(t) = \begin{cases} 1 & \text{if } |T| > t_0 \\ 0 & \text{otherwise} \end{cases}$$

where, $t_0$ is determined by

$$E_{\delta=0}[\phi_0(T)] = \alpha$$

$$\int_{t_0}^{\infty} t_{n-1}(w)\, dw = \alpha/2$$

**Example 0.5.9.** *Let $X_1, \ldots, X_m$ and $Y_1, \ldots, Y_n$ be independent samples from populations with distributions $N(\mu, \sigma^2)$ and $N(\eta, \sigma^2)$ respectively. Find out UMP invariant tests for the following hypotheses.*

(a) $H_0 : \mu \leq \eta$ *or* $\eta - \mu \geq 0$ *against* $H_1 : \mu > \eta$ *or* $\eta - \mu < 0$

(b) $H_0 : \mu = \eta$ *or* $\eta - \mu = 0$ *against* $H_1 : \mu \neq \eta$ *or* $\eta - \mu \neq 0$.

***Solution:*** The joint distribution of $X_1, \ldots, X_m$ and $Y_1, \ldots, Y_n$ is given by

$$f_{\mathbf{X},\mathbf{Y}}(\mathbf{x}, \mathbf{y} |\, \mu, \eta, \sigma^2) = \left(\frac{1}{2\pi\sigma^2}\right)^{(m+n)/2} \cdot \exp\{-\tfrac{m\mu^2 + n\eta^2}{\sigma^2}\}$$

$$\cdot \exp\{+\frac{\mu}{\sigma^2} m\overline{x} + \frac{\eta}{\sigma^2} n\overline{y} - \frac{1}{2\sigma^2}\sum x_i^2 - \frac{1}{2\sigma^2}\sum y_i^2\}$$

$\left(\overline{X}, \overline{Y}, S = \sqrt{\sum(X_i - \overline{X})^2 + \sum(Y_i - \overline{Y})^2}\right)$ are jointly sufficient for $(\mu,\, \eta,\, \sigma)$. If we consider

$$g_c(\mathbf{X},\, \mathbf{Y}) = (\mathbf{x} + c,\, \mathbf{y} + c)$$

we have

$$g_c(\bar{X}, \bar{Y}, S) = (\bar{X} + c, \bar{Y} + c, S)$$

Under this transformation, the joint distribution of $\mathbf{X}, \mathbf{Y}$ under $H_0$ and $H_1$ remains invariant, therefore, the testing problem is invariant. The data could be summarized by using maximal invariant statistics $\overline{Y} - \overline{X}$ and $S$. Further, if we consider the scale transformation

$$g_c(\mathbf{X}, \mathbf{Y}) = (c\mathbf{X}, c\mathbf{Y}),\ c \neq 0$$

we have

$$g_c(\overline{X}, \overline{Y}, S) = (c\bar{X}, c\bar{Y}, cS)$$

The joint distributions of $(\mathbf{X}, \mathbf{Y})$ under $H_0$ and $H_1$ are still invariant leaving the testing problem as invariant. This transformation reduces the data to maximal invariant statistic

$$T = \frac{\overline{Y} - \overline{X}}{S}$$

We shall now restrict ourselves to the invariant tests which are the functions of the maximal invariant statistic $T$, i.e.

$$I_\alpha = \{\phi \in \mathcal{D} : E_{H_0}\phi(T) = \alpha\}$$

Consider

$$T = \frac{\overline{Y} - \overline{X}}{S} = \frac{(\overline{Y} - \overline{X})/\sigma\sqrt{\frac{1}{m} + \frac{1}{n}}}{S/\sigma\sqrt{m + n - 2}} = \frac{N\left(\frac{\eta - \mu}{\sigma\sqrt{\frac{1}{m} + \frac{1}{n}}}, 1\right)}{\sqrt{\frac{\chi^2_{m+n-2}}{(m+n-2)}}} \sim t_{m+n-2,\, 1,\, \delta} \quad (6.8)$$

where

$$\delta = \frac{\eta - \mu}{\sigma\sqrt{1/m + 1/n}}$$

is the non-centrality parameter. In terms $\delta$, the hypotheses in (a) and (b) may be restated as

(a) $H_0 : \delta < 0$

against $\quad H_1 : \delta > 0$

(b) $H_0 : \delta = 0$

against $\quad H_1 : \delta \neq 0$

Consider (a) and note that the distribution of $T$ in Eq. (6.8) has monotone likelihood ratio. Therefore, by Kertin-Rubin theorem, a UMP invariant test for testing problem in (a) is given by

$$\phi_0(t) = \begin{cases} 1 & \text{if } t < c \\ 0 & \text{otherwise} \end{cases}$$

where $c$ is obtained by

$$\int_{-\infty}^{c} t_{n-1,\delta=0}(w)\,dw = \alpha \quad \text{or} \quad \int_{c}^{\infty} t_{n-1,0}(w)\,dw = 1-\alpha$$

Analogously, the UMP invariant test for testing two-sided problem in (b) is given by

$$\phi_0(t) = \begin{cases} 1 & \text{if } |t| \geq c \\ 0 & \text{otherwise} \end{cases}$$

so that $c$ is obtained by $\int_c^\infty t_{n-1,\,0}(w)\,dw = \alpha/2$, since $t_{n-1,\,0}$ is symmetric about zero.

## *Review Questions*

**6.1** Show that hypothesis testing problem is invariant if it leaves the families of distributions $\{P_\theta,\,\theta \in \Theta_0\}$ and $\{P_\theta,\,\theta \in \Theta_1\}$ both invariant and $\tilde{g}(a) = a$.

**6.2** Define an invariant testing problem and a maximal invariant statistic. An invariant test has constant risk function on those subsets in the parameter space for which the maximal invariant parameter under the group of transformation $\overline{\mathcal{G}}$ is constant. Hence, prove that the sign test is UMP invariant for the bivariate single sample problem of location against the two-sided alternatives.

**6.3** Define the concept of invariance in hypothesis testing. Prove that a test $\phi(x)$ is invariant with respect to a group of transformations on the sample space if the same were a function of maximal invariant.

**6.4** (a) Define a maximal invariant function under a group of transformations.

(b) A statistical decision problem is invariant under a group $\mathcal{G}$. $\nu(\theta)$ is a maximal invariant on $\Theta$ with respect to $\overline{\mathcal{G}}$. Prove that if $h(x)$ is invariant under $\mathcal{G}$, the distribution of $h(X)$ depends only on $\nu(\theta)$.

(c) $X = (X_1, X_2, \ldots, X_n)$ has density of the form $f(x_1-\theta, x_2-\theta, \ldots, x_n-\theta)$ where $\theta \in \mathbb{R}^1$ is unknown. It is desired to test $H_0 : f = f_0$ versus $f = f_1$ where $f_0$ and $f_1$ are known. The loss is $0-1$. Show that this problem is invariant under

$$\mathcal{G} = \{g_c : g_c(x_1, x_2, \ldots, x_n) = (x_1+c, \ldots, x_n+c)\};$$

(d) Show how the use of maximal invariant function reduces it to a problem of testing a simple hypothesis against a simple alternative.

**6.5** (a) Define an invariant decision problem and an invariant decision function. Give an example in which sufficiency and invariance lead to the same reduction of data.

(b) Consider testing $H_0 : (X_1, \ldots, X_n)$ has a distribution function $G_0(x_1 - \theta, \ldots, x_n - \theta)$ against $H_1 : (X_1, \ldots, X_n)$ has a distribution function $G_1(x_1 - \theta, \ldots, x_n - \theta)$ where $\theta$ is unknown but $G_0$ and $G_1$ are known.

Show that the problem is invariant under change of location. Find a maximal invariant and the uniformly most powerful invariant test.

**6.6** Let $X_1, \ldots, X_n$ be random variables whose distribution depends on a parameter $\theta$. Consider the problem of testing the hypothesis that the distribution of $X_1, X_2, \ldots, X_n$ is $G_0(x_1 - \theta, x_2 - \theta, \ldots, x_n - \theta)$ against the alternative $G_1(x_1 - \theta, x_2 - \theta, \ldots, x_n - \theta)$, where $G_0$ and $G_1$ are known distribution functions and $-\infty < \theta < \infty$. Can you find a best test of size-$\alpha$ for the above problem? Determine an invariant test for the problem and state whether you could find a best test of size-$\alpha$ in this class; state reason.

**6.7** Let $X_1, X_2$ be independent identically distributed random variables, let $H_0$ be the hypothesis that the underlying distribution is $N(\theta, 1)$, a normal distribution with variance unity, and let $H_1$ be the hypothesis that the underlying distribution is $\mathcal{C}(\theta, 1)$, a Cauchy distribution with semi-interquartile range unity. Show that

$$\phi(x_1, x_2) = \begin{cases} 1 & \text{if } |x_1 - x_2| > k \\ 0 & \text{if } |x_1 - x_2| < k \end{cases}$$

is a UMP invariant test of $H_0$ against $H_1$.

**6.8** Assume that $\mathbf{x} = (x_1, \ldots, x_n)$ is a random sample from $N(\theta, \sigma^2)$ distribution both $\theta$ and $\sigma^2$ unknown. It is desired to test $H_0 : \sigma^2 \geq 1$ against $H_1 : \sigma^2 < 1$ under $0 - 1$ loss function.

(a) After reducing to the sufficient statistic $(\overline{X}, S^2)$, the sample mean and the sample variance, show that the problem is invariant under the location group of transformations

$$\mathcal{G} = \{g_c : c \in \mathbb{E}^1,\ g_c(\overline{x}, S^2) = (\overline{x} + c, S^2)\}$$

(b) Show that $T(\overline{X}, S^2) = S^2$ is a maximal invariant.

(c) Show that the UMP invariant test is to reject $H_0$ if $S^2 < K$ and accept $H_0$ otherwise, where $k$ is a constant which depends on the desired error probabilities.

**6.9** What do you mean by invariance and maximality of invariance in testing of hypothesis? Let $X_1, \ldots, X_n$ be iid $N(\theta, \sigma^2)$ and consider testing $H_0 : \sigma^2 \geq 1$ against $H_1 : \sigma^2 < 1$. Show that:

$$\phi(\mathbf{x}) = \begin{cases} 1 & \text{if } \sum(x_i - \overline{x})^2 < k \\ 0 & \text{if } \sum(x_i - \overline{x})^2 > k \end{cases}$$

is UMP invariant test of $H_0$ against $H_1$.

# Chapter 7

# Likelihood Ratio Tests

## 7.1 INTRODUCTION

In previous chapters we have seen that UMP or UMP-unbiased tests existed only for some special families of distributions, while they do not exist for other families. Further, computations of UMP unbiased tests in $k$-parameter exponential family discussed in Chapter 5, are usually complex. Since these are $\alpha$-similar tests having Neyman structure, therefore, involves conditional distributions. Neyman and Pearson(1928) suggested a simple method for testing a general testing problem. Consider

$$\mathbf{X} \sim f_{\mathbf{X}}(\mathbf{x}|\,\boldsymbol{\theta}), \quad \boldsymbol{\theta} \in \Theta \subseteq \mathbb{R}^k \tag{7.1}$$

and a general testing problem

$$H_0 : \boldsymbol{\theta} \in \Theta_0 \text{ against } H_1 : \boldsymbol{\theta} \in \Theta_1 \tag{7.2}$$

then the likelihood ratio test for testing the problem in Eq. (7.2) is defined as

$$\lambda(\mathbf{x}) = \frac{\sup_{\boldsymbol{\theta}\in\Theta_0} L(\boldsymbol{\theta}, \mathbf{x})}{\sup_{\boldsymbol{\theta}\in\Theta} L(\boldsymbol{\theta}, \mathbf{x})}$$

Here, $L(\boldsymbol{\theta}, \mathbf{x})$ is the likelihood function of $\mathbf{x}$. The numerator measures the best possibility that the observation $\mathbf{X}$ comes from some population under the null hypothesis, and the denominator measures the best possibility of $\mathbf{X}$ to come from some population covered under the entire parameter space $\Theta$.

Higher values of the numerator correspond to the better explanation of $\mathbf{X}$ given by $H_0$ as compared to overall best possible explanation of $\mathbf{X}$, that results into larger values in $\lambda$ leading to acceptance of $H_0$. Indeed, smaller values of $\lambda$ leads to the rejection of $H_0$. Therefore, the critical region would be of the type $\lambda(\mathbf{x}) < c$. The constant $c$ is determined by

$$\sup_{\boldsymbol{\theta}\in\Theta_0} P_{\boldsymbol{\theta}}\{\mathbf{X} : \lambda(\mathbf{X}) < c\} = \alpha$$

If the distribution of $\lambda$ is continuous then the size $\alpha$ is exactly attained and no randomization on the boundary is needed, whereas if the distribution is discrete, the size may not attain $\alpha$ and one may require randomization.

It is easy to verify the following results:

Result 1: For simple versus simple hypothesis, NP tests and Likelihood ratio tests are equivalent.

Result 2: The likelihood ratio test is a function of every sufficient statistic for $\boldsymbol{\theta}$ if it exists.

Likelihood ratio test is a classical test criterion for a general hypothesis testing problem and has intuitively appealing definition. Moreover, this criterion proves to be a powerful alternative for testing vector valued parameters that involve nuisance parameters. Generally, the likelihood ratio tests result into optimal tests, whenever they exist, but theoretically they do not have statistical nice properties. It is the simplicity of this procedure that has earned its wide applicability and popularity. Yet a difficulty arises, while computing the exact null distribution of the test statistic $\lambda$, since it is quite complex to arrive at and the computation of cut-off point $c$ becomes difficult except for cases in normal population where things are much simple. Therefore, a study of large sample properties of $\lambda$ becomes necessary where maximum likelihood estimators follow normal distribution under certain regularity conditions. These large sample properties of $\lambda$ has been discussed in the following section.

## 7.2 ASYMPTOTIC PROPERTIES OF LIKELIHOOD RATIO TESTS

We consider here a general hypothesis testing problem that concerns a vector of parameters, $H_0 : \boldsymbol{\theta} \in \Theta_0$ against $H_1 : \boldsymbol{\theta} \in \Theta_1$, where $\Theta \subseteq \mathbb{E}^k$ and $m$ parameters out of $k$ are specified in the null hypothesis, $\Theta_0$ and $\Theta_1 \subseteq \mathbb{E}^{k-m}$. We draw a random sample $X_1, \ldots, X_n$ from $F_{\boldsymbol{\theta}}$ to test this hypothesis under the regularity conditions of Cramer-Rao lower bound. Large sample properties of likelihood ratio test are discussed in the following theorems.

**Theorem 7.2.1. (Asymptotic Distribution of Likelihood Ratio Test)** *Under $H_0$ the asymptotic distribution of $-2\log_e \lambda$ is $\chi^2_f$, where $f$ is the difference between the number of free parameters in $\Theta$ and the number of free parameters in $\Theta_0$* (Gupta et al. (1985)[78] and Cramer (1946)[36]).

*Proof.* Consider $\theta$ as a single parameter. Let $\hat{\theta}$ be a maximum likelihood estimator of $\theta$. We know from the large sample properties of maximum likelihood estimators that its asymptotic variance under the regularity conditions is equal to the Cramer-Rao lower bound. In this case

$$\frac{\partial \log L}{\partial \theta} = c(\theta)[\hat{\theta} - \theta]$$

which gives

$$c(\theta) = 1/V_\theta(\hat{\theta}) = -E_\theta[\partial^2 \log L/\partial\theta^2]$$

On putting the value of $c(\theta)$ in the above expression, we get

$$\frac{\partial \log L}{\partial \theta} = -(\hat{\theta} - \theta)E_\theta\left[\frac{\partial^2 \log L}{\partial \theta^2}\right] \tag{7.3}$$

On integrating Eq. (7.1) w.r.t. $\theta$, we get

$$L(\theta) = k(\theta)\exp\left\{\frac{1}{2}(\hat{\theta} - \theta)^2 E_\theta\left[\frac{\partial^2 \log L}{\partial \theta^2}\right]\right\} \tag{7.4}$$

Now, extending this result to the case when $\boldsymbol{\theta}$ is a vector, $\boldsymbol{\theta} \in \Theta \subseteq \mathbb{E}^k$, the condition in Eq. (7.4) changes to

$$\frac{\partial \log L}{\partial \boldsymbol{\theta}} = (\hat{\boldsymbol{\theta}} - \boldsymbol{\theta})'\mathbf{V}^{-1} \tag{7.5}$$

where

$$\mathbf{V}^{-1} = ||V^{ij}|| \quad \text{where elements are shown by}$$

$$V^{ii} = -E_{\boldsymbol{\theta}}\left[\frac{\partial^2 \log L}{\partial \theta_i^2}\right], \quad V^{ij} = -E_\theta\left[\frac{\partial^2 \log L}{\partial \theta_i \partial \theta_j}\right]$$

On integrating the Eq. (7.5) throughout with respect to $\boldsymbol{\theta}$, we get

$$L(\boldsymbol{\theta}) = k(\boldsymbol{\theta})\ \exp\{-\frac{1}{2}(\hat{\boldsymbol{\theta}} - \boldsymbol{\theta})'\mathbf{V}^{-1}(\hat{\boldsymbol{\theta}} - \boldsymbol{\theta})\} \tag{7.6}$$

We see in Eqs. (7.4) and (7.6), under the regularity conditions, that the likelihood function takes the form of density of maximum likelihood estimator, in Eqs. (7.6), it is multivariate normal distribution with dispersion matrix $\mathbf{V}$ for large $n$. The likelihood ratio test, for large $n$ it takes the value

$$\lambda = \frac{\sup_{\boldsymbol{\theta}\in\Theta_0} L(\boldsymbol{\theta})}{\sup_{\boldsymbol{\theta}\in\Theta} L(\boldsymbol{\theta})}$$

When $L(\boldsymbol{\theta})$ is as in Eq. (7.6). Here there are $m$ parameters which are specified under $H_0$ and $(k - m)$ are unspecified parameters known as nuisance parameters. We may write $\boldsymbol{\theta}' = (\boldsymbol{\theta}'_m, \boldsymbol{\theta}'_{k-m})$ in $L(\boldsymbol{\theta})$. Where $\hat{\boldsymbol{\theta}}$ is a maximum likelihood estimator of $\boldsymbol{\theta}$ we have, $\sup_{\boldsymbol{\theta}\in\Theta} L(\boldsymbol{\theta}) = L(\hat{\boldsymbol{\theta}}) = L(\hat{\boldsymbol{\theta}}_m, \hat{\boldsymbol{\theta}}_{k-m}) \propto 1$ on taking $L(\boldsymbol{\theta})$ as in Eq. (7.6). Further, the maximum of $L(\boldsymbol{\theta})$ over $\Theta_0$ or under $H_0 : \boldsymbol{\theta}_m = \boldsymbol{\theta}_{m_0}$(say) is attained at maximum likelihood estimator $\hat{\boldsymbol{\theta}}_{k-m}$ of $\boldsymbol{\theta}_{k-m}$ which by Eq. (7.6)

$$\sup_{\boldsymbol{\theta}\in\Theta_0} L(\boldsymbol{\theta}) = L(\boldsymbol{\theta}_{m_0}, \hat{\boldsymbol{\theta}}_{k-m|m_0}) \propto \exp\{-\frac{1}{2}(\hat{\boldsymbol{\theta}}_m - \boldsymbol{\theta}_{m_0})'\mathbf{V}_m^{-1}(\hat{\boldsymbol{\theta}}_m - \boldsymbol{\theta}_{m_0})\}$$

where $\hat{\boldsymbol{\theta}}_{k-m|m_0}$ is the maximum likelihood estimator of $\boldsymbol{\theta}$ when $\boldsymbol{\theta}_m$ and is fixed at $\boldsymbol{\theta}_{m_0}$ under $H_0$. The index $m$ in the right hand side expression indicates the dimension of the multivariate normal distribution. Hence, likelihood ratio test is defined as

$$\lambda = \frac{L(\boldsymbol{\theta}_{m_0}, \hat{\boldsymbol{\theta}}_{k-m})}{L(\hat{\boldsymbol{\theta}}_m, \hat{\boldsymbol{\theta}}_{k-m|m_0})} \tag{7.7}$$

$$= \exp\{-\frac{1}{2}(\hat{\boldsymbol{\theta}}_m - \boldsymbol{\theta}_{m_0})'\mathbf{V}_m^{-1}(\hat{\boldsymbol{\theta}}_m - \boldsymbol{\theta}_{m_0})\}$$

Thus, we have

$$-2\log\lambda = (\hat{\boldsymbol{\theta}}_m - \boldsymbol{\theta}_{m_0})'\mathbf{V}_m^{-1}(\hat{\boldsymbol{\theta}}_m - \boldsymbol{\theta}_{m_0})$$

We know that

$$\hat{\boldsymbol{\theta}}_m \sim N_m(\boldsymbol{\theta}_m, \mathbf{V}_m)$$

$$\hat{\boldsymbol{\theta}}_m - \boldsymbol{\theta}_{m_0} \sim N_m(\boldsymbol{\theta}_m - \boldsymbol{\theta}_{m_0}, \mathbf{V}_m)$$

$$\mathbf{V}_m^{-1}(\hat{\boldsymbol{\theta}}_m - \boldsymbol{\theta}_{m_0}) \sim N_m(\mathbf{V}_m^{-1}(\boldsymbol{\theta}_m - \boldsymbol{\theta}_{m_0}), \mathbf{I}) \tag{7.8}$$

Therefore,

$$(\hat{\boldsymbol{\theta}}_m - \boldsymbol{\theta}_{m_0})'\mathbf{V}_m^{-1}(\hat{\boldsymbol{\theta}}_m - \boldsymbol{\theta}_{m_0}) \sim \chi^2_{m,\delta} \tag{7.9}$$

where, the $-2\log\lambda = \delta$ is the non-centrality parameter

$$\delta = (\boldsymbol{\theta}_m - \boldsymbol{\theta}_{m_0})'\mathbf{V}_m^{-1}(\boldsymbol{\theta}_m - \boldsymbol{\theta}_{m_0})$$

Therefore, $-2\log_e\lambda \sim \chi^2_{m,\delta}$, a non-central $\chi^2$ with $m$ degrees of freedom (as many as the number of parameters being specified in the null hypothesis) with non-centrality parameter being equal to $\delta$. Under $H_0$, $\delta = 0$ and $-2\log_e\lambda \sim \chi^2_m$, a central $\chi^2$ distribution with $m$ degrees of freedom. □

We shall now discuss the second asymptotic property of likelihood ratio tests, namely, consistency, when a very general condition is satisfied. However, the formal definition of consistency of a test has been given in Section 9.3.

**Theorem 7.2.2.** *Likelihood ratio test is consistent under a very general condition.*

*Proof.* From Eq. (7.7) asymptotic value of $\lambda$ is

$$\lambda = \frac{\sup_{\boldsymbol{\theta}\in\Theta_0} L(\boldsymbol{\theta})}{\sup_{\boldsymbol{\theta}\in\Theta} L(\boldsymbol{\theta})} = \frac{L(\boldsymbol{\theta}_{m_0}, \hat{\boldsymbol{\theta}}_{(k-m)|m_0})}{L(\hat{\boldsymbol{\theta}}_m, \hat{\boldsymbol{\theta}}_{k-m})}$$

where, $\hat{\boldsymbol{\theta}}_m$ and $\hat{\boldsymbol{\theta}}_{k-m|m_0}$ are maximum likelihood estimators. We assume that a general condition holds under which a maximum likelihood estimator is consistent. This gives

$$\lambda = \frac{L(\boldsymbol{\theta}_{m_0}, \hat{\boldsymbol{\theta}}_{(k-m)|m_0})}{L(\hat{\boldsymbol{\theta}}_m, \hat{\boldsymbol{\theta}}_{k-m})} \xrightarrow{p} \frac{L(\boldsymbol{\theta}_{m_0}, \boldsymbol{\theta}_{k-m})}{L(\boldsymbol{\theta}_m, \boldsymbol{\theta}_{k-m})} \tag{7.10}$$

where, $\boldsymbol{\theta}_m$ is the true value of the parameters being specified as $\boldsymbol{\theta}_{m_0}$ under the null hypothesis and $\boldsymbol{\theta}_{(k-m)|m_0}$ is the true value of the nuisance parameters. Further, critical region corresponding to the likelihood ratio test is given by $\lambda < c$. We see from Eq. (7.10) $\lambda \xrightarrow{p} 1$ under $H_0 : \boldsymbol{\theta}_m = \boldsymbol{\theta}_{m_0}$. This gives the cut-off point $c \to 1$. By noting $\lambda \xrightarrow{p} 1$ for some $0 \leq< 1$ under the alternative hypothesis, we have

$$P_{\boldsymbol{\theta}}(\lambda \leq c) \to 1 \quad \text{for each } \boldsymbol{\theta} \in \Theta_1$$

and

$$P_{\boldsymbol{\theta}}(\lambda \leq k) \to 1 \quad \text{for each } \boldsymbol{\theta} \in \Theta_0$$

This show that likelihood ratio test is consistent under the above assumption.

□

## 7.3 SOLVED EXAMPLES

The likelihood ratio tests are useful, especially when $\boldsymbol{\theta}$ is a vector of parameters and the testing involves only some of them. The remaining parameters behave as nuisance parameters. Treatment to such situations has already been discussed at length, while discussing similar tests and similar tests with Neyman structure (Chapter 5). Use of such tests is not convenient, since they involve conditional distribution which is often not easy to compute. Whereas, one advantage of using these tests has been that they are UMP or UMP unbiased of size-$\alpha$. On the other hand, likelihood ratio test criterion, though not having small sample properties, is very popular because of its computational simplicity. We would illustrate this by some examples.

**Example 7.3.1.** *Let $X$ be a Binomial $b(n,p)$ random variable. Find the size-$\alpha$ likelihood ratio test for testing $H_0 : p \leq p_0$ against $H_1 : p > p_0$.*

***Solution:*** The likelihood ratio test statistic is given by

$$\lambda(x) = \frac{\sup_{p \leq p_0} L(p,x)}{\sup_{0 \leq p \leq 1} L(p,x)} = \frac{\sup_{p \leq p_0} \binom{n}{x} p^x (1-p)^{n-x}}{\sup_{0 \leq p \leq 1} \binom{n}{x} p^x (1-p)^{n-x}}$$

The function $p^x(1-p)^{n-x}$ increases in $p$, achieves maximum at $p = x/n$, and then starts decreasing. Therefore,

$$\lambda(x) = \begin{cases} \dfrac{p_0^x (1-p_0)^{n-x}}{(x/n)^x [1-(x/n)]^{n-x}} & \text{if } p_0 < x/n \\ 1 & \text{if } p_0 > x/n \end{cases}$$

We shall note that $\lambda(x) \leq 1$ when $x > np_0$ and $\lambda(x) = 1$ when $x < np_0$. This shows that $\lambda(x)$ is a decreasing function of $x$. Therefore, the LR critical region is given by $x > k$ corresponding to $\lambda(x) < c$. This gives

$$\phi(x) = \begin{cases} 1 & \text{if } x > k \\ 0 & \text{otherwise} \end{cases}$$

where, $k$ is obtained by

$$\sup_{p \le p_0} E_p \phi(X) = \alpha \quad \text{or} \quad P_{p_0}\{X > k\} = \alpha$$

Since $X$ is discrete random variable, $k$ is obtained such that

$$P_{p_0}\{X > k\} \le \alpha < P_{p_0}\{X > k - 1\}$$

*Remark* 7.3.1. If the distribution of $X$ belongs to the one-parameter exponential family, then the LR test for one-sided testing problem becomes identical to the UMP test, obtained by applying Karlin-Rubin theorem discussed in Chapter 3. Note that the test in Example 7.3.1 is UMP since a Binomial distribution belongs to one parameter exponential family.

**Example 7.3.2.** *Let $X_1, \ldots, X_n$ be a random sample of size n from a normal population with mean $\mu$ and variance $\sigma^2$.*

(a) $H_0 : \mu = \mu_0$ *against* $H_1 : \mu \ne \mu_0$ *when $\sigma^2$ is known.*

(b) $H_0 : \mu = \mu_0$ *against* $H_1 : \mu \ne \mu_0$ *when $\sigma^2$ is unknown.*

***Solution:*** (a) The testing problem is $H_0 : \mu = \mu_0$ against $H_1 : \mu \ne \mu_0$ and when $\sigma^2$ is known.

$$\begin{aligned}\sup_{\theta \in \Theta_0} L(\theta, \mathbf{x}) &= L(\mu_0, \mathbf{x}) \quad (\text{since } \Theta_0 = \{\mu_0\}) \\ &= \left(\frac{1}{2\pi\sigma^2}\right)^{n/2} \exp\{-\sum_1^n (x_i - \mu_0)^2/2\sigma^2\}\end{aligned}$$

and

$$\sup_{\theta \in \Theta} L(\theta, \mathbf{x}) = \sup_{\mu \in \mathbb{R}^1} L(\mu, \mathbf{x}) \quad (\text{since } \Theta = \{\mu | \mu \in \mathbb{R}^1\})$$

we know that $\bar{x}$ is MLE of $\mu$, therefore,

$$\sup_{\theta \in \Theta} L(\theta, \mathbf{x}) = \left(\frac{1}{2\pi\sigma^2}\right)^{n/2} \exp\{-\sum_1^n (x_i - \bar{x})^2/2\sigma^2\}$$

This gives

$$\lambda(\mathbf{x}) = \frac{\exp\{-\sum_1^n (x_i - \mu_0)^2/2\sigma^2\}}{\exp\{-\sum_1^n (x_i - \bar{x})^2/2\sigma^2\}} = \exp\{-\frac{n}{2\sigma^2}(\bar{x} - \mu_0)^2\}$$

The rejection region $\lambda(\mathbf{x}) < c$ gives

$$-\frac{n}{2\sigma^2}(\bar{x} - \mu_0)^2 < c' \quad \text{or} \quad \left|\frac{\sqrt{n}(\bar{x} - \mu_0)}{\sigma}\right| > k$$

Thus, likelihood ratio test is given by

$$\phi(\bar{x}) = \begin{cases} 1 & \text{if } |\frac{\sqrt{n}(\bar{x}-\mu_0)}{\sigma}| > k \\ 0 & \text{otherwise} \end{cases}$$

where, the constant $k$ is obtained by the size condition

$$E_{\mu_0}[\phi(\bar{X})] = \alpha$$

or

$$P_{\mu_0}\Big[\Big|\frac{\sqrt{n}(\bar{X}-\mu_0)}{\sigma}\Big| > k\Big] = \alpha$$

Under $H_0 : \mu = \mu_0$, the statistic $\frac{\bar{X}-\mu_0}{\sigma/\sqrt{n}}$ follows $N(0,1)$ distribution, which is symmetric about 0, therefore, $k$ is obtained by

$$P_{\mu_0}\Big[\frac{(\bar{X}-\mu_0)}{\sigma/\sqrt{n}} > k\Big] = \alpha/2$$

This gives $k$ as the upper $\alpha/2^{\text{th}}$ quantile of $N(0,1)$ distribution denoted by $z_{\alpha/2}$. Finally, the test is given by

$$\phi(\bar{x}) = \begin{cases} 1 & \text{if } \Big|\frac{\sqrt{n}(\bar{x}-\mu_0)}{\sigma}\Big| > z_{\alpha/2} \\ 0 & \text{otherwise} \end{cases}$$

(b) The testing problem is $H_0 : \mu = \mu_0$ against $H_1 : \mu \neq \mu_0$ and $\sigma^2$ is not known. Here,

$$\Theta_0 = \{(\mu,\sigma^2)|\mu = \mu_0,\ \sigma^2 > 0\} \text{ and } \Theta = \{(\mu,\sigma^2)|\mu \in \mathbb{R}^1, \sigma^2 > 0\}$$

In this case,

$$\sup_{\boldsymbol{\theta}\in\Theta_0} L(\boldsymbol{\theta},\mathbf{x}) = \sup_{\sigma^2>0} L(\sigma^2,\mathbf{x}) = \sup_{\sigma^2>0}\Big(\frac{1}{2\pi\sigma^2}\Big)^{n/2}\exp\{-\frac{1}{2\sigma^2}\textstyle\sum_1^n (x_i-\mu_0)^2\}$$

MLE of $\sigma^2$ given $\mu = \mu_0$ is given by

$$s_0^2 = \frac{1}{n}\sum_1^n (x_i-\mu_0)^2$$

This gives

$$\sup_{\sigma^2>0} L(\sigma^2,\mathbf{x}) = \Big(\frac{1}{2\pi s_0^2}\Big)^{n/2}\exp\{-n/2\}$$

Further

$$\sup_{\boldsymbol{\theta}\in\Theta} L(\boldsymbol{\theta},\mathbf{x}) = \sup_{\mu,\sigma^2} L((\mu,\sigma^2),\mathbf{x})$$

$$= \sup_{\mu,\sigma^2}\Big(\frac{1}{2\pi\sigma^2}\Big)^{n/2}\exp\{-\frac{1}{2\sigma^2}\sum_1^n (x_i-\mu)^2\}$$

The MLE of $\mu$ and $\sigma^2$ are given by $\bar{x}$ and $1/n\sum_1^n(x_i - \bar{x})^2 = (n-1)s^2/n$, where, $\bar{x} = 1/n\sum_1^n x_i$ and $s^2 = \frac{1}{n-1}\sum_1^n(x_i - \bar{x})^2$. This gives,

$$\sup_{\mu,\sigma^2} L((\mu,\sigma^2),\mathbf{x}) = \left(\frac{1}{2\pi\frac{n-1}{n}s^2}\right)^{n/2} \exp\{-n/2\}$$

Hence, the likelihood ratio test statistic is given by

$$\lambda(\mathbf{x}) = \frac{\sup_{\sigma^2>0} L(\sigma^2,\mathbf{x})}{\sup_{\mu,\sigma^2} L((\mu,\sigma^2),\mathbf{x})} = \frac{\left(\frac{1}{2\pi s_0^2}\right)^{n/2}\exp\{-n/2\}}{\left(\frac{1}{2\pi\frac{(n-1)}{n}s^2}\right)^{n/2}\exp\{-n/2\}}$$

$$= \left(\frac{(n-1)s^2}{ns_0^2}\right)^{n/2}$$

If we consider

$$ns_0^2 = \textstyle\sum_1^n(x_i - \mu_0)^2 = \sum_1^n(x_i - \bar{x} + \bar{x} - \mu_0)^2$$
$$= n(\bar{x} - \mu_0)^2 + \textstyle\sum(x_i - \bar{x})^2$$

or

$$ns_0^2 = n(\bar{x} - \mu_0)^2 + (n-1)s^2$$

The LR critical region is given by

$$\lambda(\mathbf{x}) < c$$

$$\left(\frac{(n-1)s^2}{ns_0^2}\right)^{n/2} < c \quad \text{or} \quad \frac{ns_0^2}{s^2} > c'$$

On using the relation $ns_0^2 = n(\bar{x} - \mu_0)^2 + (n-1)s^2$ and the critical region $\frac{ns_0^2}{s^2} > c'$, we have

$$\frac{n(\bar{x} - \mu_0)^2}{s^2} + (n-1) > c'$$

or

$$\frac{n(\bar{x} - \mu_0)^2}{s^2} > c''$$

or

$$\left|\frac{\sqrt{n}(\bar{x} - \mu_0)}{s}\right| > k \qquad \text{for some } k$$

The likelihood ratio test is given by

$$\phi(\bar{x}, s) = \begin{cases} 1 & \text{if } \left|\frac{\sqrt{n}(\bar{x} - \mu_0)}{s}\right| > k \\ 0 & \text{otherwise} \end{cases}$$

where, $k$ would be obtained by

$$E_{\mu_0}[\phi(\bar{X}, S)] = \alpha$$

or

$$P_{\mu_0}\left\{\left|\frac{\sqrt{n}(\bar{X} - \mu_0)}{S}\right| > k\right\} = \alpha$$

But

$$\left.\frac{\dfrac{\bar{X} - \mu_0}{\sigma/\sqrt{n}}}{\sqrt{\dfrac{(n-1)S^2}{\sigma^2}\Big/(n-1)}}\right|_{H_0} = \left.\frac{N(0,1)}{\sqrt{\dfrac{\chi^2_{(n-1)}}{(n-1)}}}\right|_{H_0} \sim t_{n-1}$$

which gives

$$\left.\frac{\sqrt{n}(\bar{X} - \mu_0)}{S}\right|_{H_0} \sim t_{n-1}$$

We know that the distribution $t_{n-1}$ is symmetric about 0, therefore,

$$P_{\mu_0}\left\{\frac{\sqrt{n}(\bar{X} - \mu_0)}{S} > k\right\} = \alpha/2$$

this gives $k$ as upper $\alpha/2^{\text{th}}$ quantile of $t$-distribution at $(n-1)$ degrees of freedom denoted by $k = t_{\alpha/2,\, n-1}$. The LR test of size-$\alpha$ is, therefore, given by

$$\phi(\bar{x}, s) = \begin{cases} 1 & \text{if } \left|\dfrac{\sqrt{n}(\bar{x} - \mu_0)}{s}\right| > t_{\alpha/2, n-1} \\ 0 & \text{otherwise} \end{cases}$$

**Example 7.3.3.** *Let $X_1, \ldots, X_n$ be a random sample of size n from a normal population with mean $\mu$ and variance $\sigma^2$. Find out the likelihood ratio test of*

(a) $H_0 : \mu \le \mu_0$ *against* $H_1 : \mu > \mu_0$ *when* $\sigma^2$ *is known.*

(b) $H_0 : \mu \le \mu_0$ *against* $H_1 : \mu > \mu_0$ *when* $\sigma^2$ *is unknown.*

***Solution:*** (a) The testing problem is $H_0 : \mu \le \mu_0$ against $H_1 : \mu > \mu_0$, when $\sigma^2$ is known. Here

$$\Theta_0 = \{\mu | -\infty < \mu \le \mu_0\} \text{ and } \Theta = \{\mu | \, \mu \in \mathbb{R}^1\}$$

Now, consider

$$\sup_{\boldsymbol{\theta} \in \Theta_0} L(\theta, \mathbf{x}) = \sup_{\mu \le \mu_0} L(\mu, \mathbf{x})$$

The MLE of $\mu$ for $\mu \in \Theta_0$ is

$$\mu_{ML} = \begin{cases} \mu_0 & \text{if } \bar{x} \ge \mu_0 \\ \bar{x} & \text{if } \bar{x} < \mu_0 \end{cases}$$

This gives

$$\sup_{\mu \le \mu_0} L(\mu, \mathbf{x}) = \begin{cases} (\frac{1}{2\pi\sigma^2})^{n/2} \exp\{-1/2\sigma^2 \sum (x_i - \mu_0)^2\} & \text{if } \bar{x} \ge \mu_0 \\ (\frac{1}{2\pi\sigma^2})^{n/2} \exp\{-1/2\sigma^2 \sum (x_i - \bar{x})^2\} & \text{if } \bar{x} < \mu_0 \end{cases}$$

Next, consider

$$\sup_{\boldsymbol{\theta} \in \Theta} L(\theta, \mathbf{x}) = \sup_{\mu} L(\mu, \mathbf{x})$$

The MLE of $\mu$ is given by $\bar{x}$, which gives

$$\sup_{\mu} L(\mu, \mathbf{x}) = \left(\frac{1}{2\pi\sigma^2}\right)^{n/2} \exp\{-1/2\sigma^2 \sum (x_i - \tilde{x})^2\}$$

The likelihood ratio test would now be given by

$$\lambda(\mathbf{x}) = \begin{cases} \exp\{-1/2\sigma^2 \sum (x_i - \mu_0)^2 + 1/2\sigma^2 \sum (x_i - \bar{x})^2\} & \text{if } \bar{x} \ge \mu_0 \\ 1 & \text{if } \bar{x} < \mu_0 \end{cases}$$

$$= \begin{cases} \exp\{-\frac{n}{2\sigma^2}(\bar{x} - \mu_0)^2\} & \text{if } \bar{x} \ge \mu_0 \\ 1 & \text{if } \bar{x} < \mu_0 \end{cases}$$

We know that the critical region is $\lambda(\mathbf{x}) \le c$. If $c = 1$, then $P_{\mu_0}(\lambda(\mathbf{X}) \le 1) = 1$, which is a contradiction to size $\alpha$, $0 < \alpha < 1$. This implies that $c < 1$ and $\bar{x} < \mu_0$ would be the part of the acceptance region while $\bar{x} \ge \mu_0$ will be the part of the rejection region. The condition that

$$\lambda(\mathbf{x}) < c$$

would imply

$$-\frac{1}{2\sigma^2}(\bar{x} - \mu_0)^2 < c' \quad \text{or} \quad \frac{n(\bar{x} - \mu_0)^2}{\sigma^2} > c''$$

or

$$\left|\frac{\sqrt{n}(\bar{x} - \mu_0)}{\sigma}\right| > k$$

The LR test is, therefore, given by

$$\phi(\bar{x}) = \begin{cases} 1 & \text{if } \dfrac{\sqrt{n}(\bar{x} - \mu_0)}{\sigma} > k \\ 0 & \text{otherwise} \end{cases}$$

where, $k$ is obtained by

$$E_{\mu_0}[\phi(\bar{X})] = \alpha$$

or

$$P_{\mu_0}\left\{\frac{\sqrt{n}(\bar{X} - \mu_0)}{\sigma} > k\right\} = \alpha$$

we know that

$$\left.\frac{\sqrt{n}(\bar{X} - \mu_0)}{\sigma}\right|_{H_0: \mu = \mu_0} \sim N(0, 1)$$

Therefore, $k$ is upper $\alpha^{\text{th}}$ quantile of $N(0,1)$ distribution denoted by $z_\alpha$. Finally, the LR test is given by

$$\phi(\bar{x}) = \begin{cases} 1 & \text{if } \dfrac{\sqrt{n}(\bar{x}-\mu_0)}{\sigma} > z_\alpha \\ 0 & \text{otherwise} \end{cases}$$

(b) Consider the testing problem

$$H_0 : \mu \leq \mu_0 \text{ against } H_1 : \mu > \mu_0$$

when $\sigma^2$ is unknown. In this case

$$\Theta_0 = \{(\mu, \sigma^2) | -\infty < \mu \leq \mu_0, \sigma^2 > 0\}$$

and

$$\Theta = \{(\mu, \sigma^2) | \mu \in \mathbb{R}^1 \text{ and } \sigma^2 > 0\}$$

For $(\mu, \sigma^2) \in \Theta_0$, the maximum likelihood estimator of $\mu$ and $\sigma^2$ is given by

$$\mu_{ML} = \begin{cases} \mu_0 & \text{if } \bar{x} \geq \mu_0 \\ \bar{x} & \text{if } \bar{x} < \mu_0 \end{cases}$$

$$\sigma^2_{ML} = \begin{cases} s_0^2 & \text{if } \bar{x} \geq \mu_0 \\ \dfrac{(n-1)s^2}{n} & \text{if } \bar{x} < \mu_0 \end{cases}$$

This gives $\sup_{(\mu,\sigma^2)\in\Theta_0} L((\mu, \sigma^2), \mathbf{x})$

$$= \begin{cases} (\frac{1}{2\pi s_0^2})^{n/2} \exp\{-\frac{1}{2s_0^2}\sum_1^n (x_i - \mu_0)^2\} & \text{if } \bar{x} \geq \mu_0 \\ \left(\frac{1}{2\pi \frac{(n-1)s^2}{n}}\right)^{n/2} \exp\left\{-\frac{1}{2\frac{(n-1)s^2}{n}}\sum_1^n (x_i - x)^2\right\} & \text{if } x < \mu_0 \end{cases}$$

$$= \begin{cases} (\frac{1}{2\pi s_0^2})^{n/2} \exp\{-n/2\} & \text{if } \bar{x} \geq \mu_0 \\ \left(\frac{1}{2\pi \frac{(n-1)s^2}{n}}\right)^{n/2} \exp\{-n/2\} & \text{if } \bar{x} < \mu_0 \end{cases}$$

For $(\mu, \sigma^2) \in \Theta$, the maximum likelihood estimators would be $\mu_{ML} = \bar{x}$ and $\sigma^2_{ML} = \dfrac{(n-1)s^2}{n}$. This gives

$$\sup_{(\mu,\sigma^2)\in\Theta} L((\mu, \sigma^2), \mathbf{x}) = \left(\frac{1}{2\pi \frac{(n-1)s^2}{n}}\right)^{n/2} \exp\{-n/2\}$$

Therefore, the likelihood ratio test would now be given by

$$\lambda(\mathbf{x}) = \frac{\sup_{(\mu,\sigma^2)\in\Theta_0} L((\mu, \sigma^2), \mathbf{x})}{\sup_{(\mu,\sigma^2)\in\Theta} L((\mu, \sigma^2), \mathbf{x})}$$

$$= \begin{cases} \left(\dfrac{(n-1)s^2}{ns_0^2}\right)^{n/2} & \text{if } \bar{x} \geq \mu_0 \\ 1 & \text{if } \bar{x} < \mu_0 \end{cases}$$

Since, $0 < \alpha < 1$, the observations $\mathbf{x}$ for which $\bar{x} < \mu_0$ must lie in the acceptance region while $\bar{x} \geq \mu_0$ would be the part of the rejection region. The rejection region corresponding to the likelihood ratio test is given by

$$\lambda(\mathbf{x}) < c$$

$$\left[\frac{(n-1)s^2}{ns_0^2}\right]^{n/2} < c$$

or

$$\frac{ns_0^2}{s^2} > c'$$

But we have seen

$$ns_0^2 = n(\bar{x} - \mu_0)^2 + (n-1)s^2$$

or

$$\frac{ns_0^2}{s^2} = \frac{n(\bar{x} - \mu_0)^2}{s^2} + (n-1)$$

The critical region could be equivalently written as

$$\frac{n(\bar{x} - \mu_0)^2}{s^2} > c''$$

or

$$\frac{\sqrt{n}(\bar{x} - \mu_0)}{s} > k$$

since $\bar{x} \geq \mu_0$ is the part of the critical region)

Therefore, likelihood ratio test is given by

$$\phi(\bar{x}, s) = \begin{cases} 1 & \text{if } \dfrac{\sqrt{n}(\bar{x} - \mu_0)}{s} > k \\ 0 & \text{otherwise} \end{cases}$$

where, $k$ is obtained by

$$E_{\mu_0}[\phi(\bar{X}, S)] = \alpha$$

or

$$P_{\mu_0}\left\{\frac{\sqrt{n}(\bar{X} - \mu_0)}{S} > k\right\} = \alpha$$

We know that $\dfrac{\sqrt{n}(\bar{X} - \mu_0)}{S} \sim t_{n-1}$. Hence, $k$ is the upper $\alpha$ quantile of the $t_{n-1}$ distribution, i.e. $k = t_{\alpha,n-1}$. Finally, likelihood ratio test is given by

$$\phi(\bar{x}, s) = \begin{cases} 1 & \text{if } \dfrac{\sqrt{n}(\bar{x} - \mu_0)}{s} > t_{\alpha,n-1} \\ 0 & \text{otherwise} \end{cases}$$

**Example 7.3.4.** *Let $X_1, \ldots, X_n$ be a random sample of size n from a normal population with mean $\mu$ and variance $\sigma^2$. Find out the likelihood ratio test of*

(a) $H_0 : \mu \geq \mu_0$ *against* $H_1 : \mu < \mu_0$ *when* $\sigma^2$ *is known*
(b) $H_0 : \mu \geq \mu_0$ *against* $H_1 : \mu < \mu_0$ *when* $\sigma^2$ *is unknown*

***Solution:*** (a) $H_0 : \mu \geq \mu_0$ against $H_1 : \mu < \mu_0$ when $\sigma^2$ is known. Here

$$\Theta_0 = \{\mu | \, \mu_0 \leq \mu < +\infty\} \text{ and } \Theta = \{\mu | \, \mu \in \mathbb{R}^1\}$$

The MLE of $\mu$, when $\mu \in \Theta_0$ is given by

$$\mu_{ML} = \begin{cases} \mu_0 & \text{if } \bar{x} \leq \mu_0 \\ \bar{x} & \text{if } \bar{x} > \mu_0 \end{cases}$$

and MLE of $\mu$, when $\mu \in \Theta$ is given by $\mu_{ML} = \bar{x}$ . This gives the LR test

$$\lambda(\mathbf{x}) = \begin{cases} \exp\{-\frac{n}{2\sigma^2}(\bar{x} - \mu_0)^2\} & \text{if } \bar{x} \leq \mu_0 \\ 1 & \text{if } \bar{x} > \mu_0 \end{cases}$$

By the arguments given in (b) we have $\bar{x} > \mu_0$ in the acceptance region while $\bar{x} \leq \mu_0$ in the rejection region. The likelihood ratio test would be given by

$$\lambda(\mathbf{x}) < c$$

or

$$\frac{-n(\bar{x} - \mu_0)^2}{2\sigma^2} < c \text{ or } \frac{n(\bar{x} - \mu_0)^2}{\sigma^2} > c'$$

$$\frac{\sqrt{n}(\bar{x} - \mu_0)}{\sigma} < -c'' \quad (\text{since } \bar{x} \leq \mu_0)$$

where, $c''$ would be obtained by

$$P_{\mu_0}\Big\{\frac{\sqrt{n}(\bar{X} - \mu_0)}{\sigma} < -c''\Big\} = \alpha \text{ or } P_{\mu_0}\Big\{\frac{\sqrt{n}(\bar{X} - \mu_0)}{\sigma} \geq -c''\Big\} = 1 - \alpha$$

where $-c'' = z_{1-\alpha}$. Hence, likelihood ratio test is given by

$$\phi(\bar{x}) = \begin{cases} 1 & \text{if } \frac{\sqrt{n}(\bar{x} - \mu_0)}{\sigma} < z_{1-\alpha} \\ 0 & \text{otherwise} \end{cases}$$

(b) $H_0 : \mu \geq \mu_0$ against $H_1 : \mu < \mu_0$ when $\sigma^2$ is unknown. Here

$$\Theta_0 = \{(\mu, \sigma^2) | \, \mu_0 \leq \mu < \infty, \ \sigma^2 > 0\}$$

$$\Theta = \{(\mu, \sigma^2) | \, \mu \in \mathbb{R}^1, \ \sigma^2 > 0\}$$

The MLE of $(\mu, \sigma^2) \in \Theta_0$ would be given by

$$\mu_{ML} = \begin{cases} \mu_0 & \text{if } \bar{x} \leq \mu_0 \\ \bar{x} & \text{if } \bar{x} > \mu_0 \end{cases} \quad \text{and} \quad \sigma^2_{ML} = \begin{cases} s_0^2 & \text{if } \bar{x} \leq \mu_0 \\ \frac{(n-1)s^2}{n} & \text{if } \bar{x} > \mu_0 \end{cases}$$

Further, for $(\mu, \sigma^2) \in \Theta$, the MLE of $\mu$ and $\sigma^2$ are given by $\mu_{ML} = \bar{x}$ and $\sigma^2_{ML} = \dfrac{(n-1)s^2}{n}$. Therefore, the likelihood ratio test becomes

$$\lambda(\mathbf{x}) = \begin{cases} \left(\dfrac{(n-1)s^2}{ns_0^2}\right)^{n/2} & \text{if } \bar{x} \leq \mu_0 \\ 1 & \text{if } \bar{x} > \mu_0 \end{cases}$$

The critical region corresponding to likelihood ratio test would be given by

$$\frac{\sqrt{n}(\bar{x} - \mu_0)}{s} < -k \quad (\text{since } \bar{x} \leq \mu_0 \text{ to the part of the critical region})$$

where, $k$ is obtained by

$$P_{\mu_0}\left\{\frac{\sqrt{n}(\bar{X} - \mu_0)}{S} < -k\right\} = \alpha$$

or

$$P_{\mu_0}\left\{\frac{\sqrt{n}\,(\bar{X} - \mu_0)}{S} \geq -k\right\} = 1 - \alpha$$

This gives $-k = t_{1-\alpha,n-1}$. Finally, likelihood ratio test takes the form

$$\phi(\bar{x}, s) = \begin{cases} 1 & \text{if } \dfrac{\sqrt{n}(\bar{x} - \mu_0)}{s} < t_{1-\alpha,n-1} \\ 0 & \text{otherwise} \end{cases}$$

The results of the Examples 7.3.2, 7.3.3, 7.3.4 have summarized in Table 7.1:

**Table 7.1:** Likelihood ratio tests concerning mean of a normal population (t-test).

| $H_0$ | $H_1$ | *Likelihood ratio test at $\alpha$ level* ($\sigma^2$ *known*) | ($\sigma^2$ *unknown*) |
|---|---|---|---|
| $\mu = \mu_0$ | $\mu \neq \mu_0$ | $\left\lvert\frac{\sqrt{n}(\bar{x}-\mu_0)}{\sigma}\right\rvert > z_{\alpha/2}$ | $\left\lvert\frac{\sqrt{n}(\bar{x}-\mu_0)}{s}\right\rvert > t_{\alpha/2,n-1}$ |
| $\mu \leq \mu_0$ | $\mu > \mu_0$ | $\frac{\sqrt{n}(\bar{x}-\mu_0)}{\sigma} > z_\alpha$ | $\frac{\sqrt{n}(\bar{x}-\mu_0)}{s} > t_{\alpha,n-1}$ |
| $\mu \geq \mu_0$ | $\mu < \mu_0$ | $\frac{\sqrt{n}(\bar{x}-\mu_0)}{\sigma} < z_{1-\alpha}$ | $\frac{\sqrt{n}(\bar{x}-\mu_0)}{s} < t_{1-\alpha,n-1}$ |

**Example 7.3.5.** *Let $X_1, X_2, \ldots, X_m$ and $Y_1, Y_2, \ldots, Y_n$ be independent random samples drawn from $N(\mu_1, \sigma_1^2)$ and $N(\mu_2, \sigma_2^2)$ respectively. Obtain the likelihood ratio test of*

$$H_0 : \mu_1 = \mu_2, \;\; \sigma_1^2 > 0, \; \sigma_2^2 > 0 \;\; \textit{against} \;\; H_1 : \mu_1 \neq \mu_2, \;\; \sigma_1^2 > 0, \; \sigma_2^2 > 0.$$

*When $\sigma_1^2$ and $\sigma_2^2$ are known.*

***Solution:*** when $\sigma_1^2$ and $\sigma_2^2$ are known. In this case

$$\Theta_0 = \{\mu_1 = \mu_2 = \mu \; : \; \mu \in \mathbb{R}^1\}$$

$$\Theta = \{(\mu_1, \mu_2) \qquad : \mu_1, \; \mu_2 \in \mathbb{R}^1\}$$

The likelihood function for $(\mu_1, \mu_2) \in \Theta$ is given by

$$L((\mu_1, \mu_2), \mathbf{x}, \mathbf{y}) = \Big(\frac{1}{2\pi\sigma_1^2}\Big)^{m/2} \exp\{-\frac{1}{2\sigma_1^2}\sum_1^m (x_i - \mu_1)^2\}\Big(\frac{1}{2\pi\sigma_2^2}\Big)^{n/2}$$

$$\cdot \exp\{-\frac{1}{2\sigma_2^2}\sum_1^n (y_i - \mu_2)^2\}$$

On taking log, we get

$$\log L((\mu_1, \mu_2), \mathbf{x}, \, \mathbf{y}) = -\frac{m}{2}\log(2\pi\sigma_1^2) - \frac{1}{2\sigma_1^2}\textstyle\sum_1^m (x_i - \mu_1)^2$$

$$-\frac{n}{2}\log(2\pi\sigma_2^2) - \frac{1}{2\sigma_2^2}\textstyle\sum_1^n (y_i - \mu_2)^2$$

ML estimators of $\mu_1, \mu_2$ are given by the following equations:

$$\frac{\partial}{\partial\mu_1}\log L = 0 \;\; \text{gives} \;\; \mu_{1ML} = \frac{1}{m}\textstyle\sum_1^m X_i = \bar{X}$$

and

$$\frac{\partial}{\partial\mu_2}\log L = 0 \;\; \text{gives} \;\; \mu_{2ML} = \frac{1}{n}\textstyle\sum_1^n Y_i = \bar{Y}$$

This gives

$$\sup_{(\mu_1,\mu_2)\in\Theta} L((\mu_1, \mu_2), \mathbf{x}, \mathbf{y}) = \Big(\frac{1}{2\pi\sigma_1^2}\Big)^{m/2} \exp\{-\frac{1}{2\sigma_1^2}\sum_1^m (x_i - \bar{x})^2\}$$

$$\times \Big(\frac{1}{2\pi\sigma_2^2}\Big)^{n/2} \exp\{-\frac{1}{2\sigma_2^2}\sum_1^n (y_i - \bar{y})^2\}$$

Further, the likelihood function for $\mu \in \Theta_0$ is given by

$$L(\mu, \mathbf{x}, \mathbf{y}) = \Big(\frac{1}{2\pi\sigma_1^2}\Big)^{m/2}\Big(\frac{1}{2\pi\sigma_2^2}\Big)^{n/2} e^{-\frac{1}{2\sigma_1^2}\sum_1^m (x_i-\mu)^2 - \frac{1}{2\sigma_2^2}\sum_1^n (y_i-\mu)^2}$$

On taking log, we get

$$\log L(\mu, \mathbf{x}, \mathbf{y}) = -\frac{m}{2}\log(2\pi\sigma_1^2) - \frac{n}{2}\log(2\pi\sigma_2^2)$$
$$\cdot -\frac{1}{2\sigma_1^2}\sum_1^m (x_i-\mu)^2 - \frac{1}{2\sigma_2^2}\sum_1^n (y_i-\mu)^2$$

The ML estimator for $\mu$ is obtained by

$$\frac{\partial}{\partial\mu}\log L = 0 \quad \text{or} \quad \frac{1}{\sigma_1^2}\left(\sum_1^m x_i - m\mu\right) + \frac{1}{\sigma_2^2}\left(\sum_1^n y_i - n\mu\right) = 0$$

or

$$\frac{1}{\sigma_1^2}\sum_1^m x_i + \frac{1}{\sigma_2^2}\sum_1^n y_i = \left(\frac{m}{\sigma_1^2} + \frac{n}{\sigma_2^2}\right)\mu$$

or

$$\mu_{ML} = \frac{m\bar{X}/\sigma_1^2 + n\bar{Y}/\sigma_2^2}{(m/\sigma_1^2 + n/\sigma_2^2)} = \frac{\sigma_1^2/m\bar{Y} + \sigma_2^2/n\bar{X}}{(\sigma_1^2/m + \sigma_2^2/n)}$$

This gives

$$\sup_{\mu\in\Theta_0} L(\mu, \mathbf{x}, \mathbf{y}) = \left(\frac{1}{2\pi\sigma_1^2}\right)^{m/2}\left(\frac{1}{2\pi\sigma_2^2}\right)^{n/2}$$
$$\exp\{-\frac{1}{2\sigma_1^2}\sum_1^m (x_i - \mu_{ML})^2 - \frac{1}{2\sigma_2^2}\sum_1^n (y_i - \mu_{ML})^2\}$$

ML test $\lambda(\mathbf{x})$ is given by

$$\lambda(\mathbf{x}, \mathbf{y}) = \Big\{\exp\{-\frac{1}{2\sigma_1^2}\{\sum_1^m (x_i-\bar{x})^2 + m(\bar{x}-\mu_{ML})^2\} - \frac{1}{2\sigma_2^2}\{\sum_1^n (y_i-\bar{y})^2$$
$$+ n(\bar{y}-\mu_{ML})^2\}\}\Big\} \Big/ \Big\{\exp\{-\frac{1}{2\sigma_1^2}\sum_1^m (x_i-\bar{x})^2 - \frac{1}{2\sigma_2^2}\sum_1^n (y_i-\bar{y})^2\}\Big\}$$
$$= \exp\{-\frac{1}{2\sigma_1^2}m(\bar{x}-\mu_{ML})^2 - \frac{1}{2\sigma_2^2}n(\bar{y}-\mu_{ML})^2\}$$
$$= \exp\Big\{-\frac{1}{2\sigma_1^2}m\cdot\left(\frac{\sigma_1^2/m(\bar{x}-\bar{y})}{\sigma_1^2/m+\sigma_2^2/n}\right)^2 - \frac{1}{2\sigma_2^2}n\cdot\left(\frac{\sigma_2^2/n(\bar{y}-\bar{x})}{\sigma_1^2/m+\sigma_2^2/n}\right)^2\Big\}$$
$$= \exp\Big\{-\frac{1}{2}\left(\frac{\sigma_1^2}{m}+\frac{\sigma_2^2}{n}\right)\left(\frac{\bar{y}-\bar{x}}{\sigma_1^2/m+\sigma_2^2/n}\right)^2\Big\}$$

LR test is given by

$$\lambda(\mathbf{x}, \mathbf{y}) < c$$

or

$$\left(\frac{\bar{Y}-\bar{X}}{\sigma_1^2/m+\sigma_2^2/n}\right)^2 > c$$

or

$$\left|\frac{\bar{Y}-\bar{X}}{\sqrt{\sigma_1^2/m+\sigma_2^2/n}}\right| > k$$

We know that, $\bar{X} \sim N(\mu_1, \sigma_1^2/m)$ and $\bar{Y} \sim N(\mu_2, \sigma_2^2/n)$; $\bar{X}$ and $\bar{Y}$ are independent. Therefore, $\bar{Y} - \bar{X} \sim N(\mu_2 - \mu_1, \sigma_1^2/m + \sigma_2^2/n)$. This gives

$$\frac{(\bar{Y}-\bar{X})-(\mu_2-\mu_1)}{\sqrt{\sigma_1^2/m+\sigma_2^2/n}} \sim N(0,1)$$

or under $H_0 : \mu_1 = \mu_2$

$$(\bar{Y}-\bar{X})/\sqrt{\sigma_1^2/m+\sigma_2^2/n} \sim N(0,1)$$

Using the distribution of LR test statistic under $H_0$ and its size-$\alpha$ condition gives $k$ as $\alpha/2^{\text{th}}$ quantile of $N(0,1)$ distribution denoted by $z_{\alpha/2}$. Finally, the likelihood ratio test test takes the form

$$\phi(\bar{x},\bar{y}) = \begin{cases} 1 & \text{if } \dfrac{|\bar{x}-\bar{y}|}{\sqrt{\sigma_1^2/m+\sigma_2^2/n}} > z_{\alpha/2} \\ 0 & \text{otherwise} \end{cases}$$

Similarly, LR test for testing

$$H_0 : \mu_1 \le \mu_2 \text{ against } H_1 : \mu_1 > \mu_2$$

is given by

$$\phi(\bar{x},\bar{y}) = \begin{cases} 1 & \text{if } \dfrac{\bar{x}-\bar{y}}{\sqrt{\sigma_1^2/m+\sigma_2^2/n}} > -z_{\alpha} \\ 0 & \text{otherwise} \end{cases}$$

and LR test for testing

$$H_0 : \mu_1 > \mu_2 \text{ against } H_1 : \mu < \mu_2$$

would be given by

$$\phi(\bar{x},\bar{y}) = \begin{cases} 1 & \text{if } \dfrac{\bar{x}-\bar{y}}{\sqrt{\sigma_1^2/m+\sigma_2^2/n}} < -z_{\alpha} \\ 0 & \text{otherwise} \end{cases}$$

Note if $\sigma_1^2$, $\sigma_2^2$ are unknown and $\sigma_1^2 \neq \sigma_2^2$, one can easily see that the maximization of the likelihood function $L(\mu, \sigma_1^2, \sigma_2^2)$ for variations in $\mu, \sigma_1^2$ and $\sigma_2^2$ results into finding the roots of a cubic equation when it is solved for ML estimate of $\mu$, which becomes a complicated function of sample observations. This makes $\lambda(\mathbf{x}, \mathbf{y})$ and its distribution under $H_0$ complex. As a result the problem becomes unsolvable and popularly known as *Behrens Fisher problem.* This problem becomes solvable when we assume $\sigma_1^2 = \sigma_2^2 = \sigma^2$ and has been discussed in Example 7.3.6:

**Example 7.3.6.** *Let $X_1, X_2, \ldots, X_m$ and $Y_1, Y_2, \ldots, Y_n$ be independent random samples drawn from $N(\mu_1, \sigma_1^2)$ and $N(\mu_2, \sigma_2^2)$ respectively. Obtain the likelihood ratio test of*

(a) $H_0 : \mu_1 = \mu_2$ *against* $H_1 : \mu_1 \neq \mu_2$
(b) $H_0 : \mu_1 \leq \mu_2$ *against* $H_1 : \mu_1 > \mu_2$

*when population variances are equal i.e.* $\sigma_1^2 = \sigma_2^2 = \sigma^2$ *but unknown.*

***Solution:*** (a) In this case

$$\Theta_0 = \{(\mu, \sigma^2) \, : \, \mu \in \mathbb{R}^1, \; \sigma^2 > 0\}$$

and

$$\Theta = \{(\mu_1, \mu_2, \sigma^2) \, : \, \mu_1, \mu_2 \in \mathbb{R}^1 \text{and} \;\; \sigma^2 > 0\}$$

The likelihood function for $(\mu_1,\, \mu_2,\, \sigma^2) \in \Theta$ is given by

$$L((\mu_1, \mu_2, \sigma^2), \mathbf{x}, \, \mathbf{y}) = \left(\frac{1}{2\pi\sigma^2}\right)^{(m+n)/2}$$
$$\exp\{-\frac{1}{2\sigma^2}\{\textstyle\sum_1^m (x_i - \mu_1)^2 + \sum_1^n (y_i - \mu_2)^2\}\}$$

On taking the log, we get

$$\log L = -\frac{(m+n)}{2}\log(2\pi\sigma^2) - \frac{1}{2\sigma^2}\{\textstyle\sum_1^m (x_i - \mu_1)^2 + \sum_1^n (y_i - \mu_2)^2\}$$

The ML estimators for $(\mu_1, \mu_2, \sigma^2) \in \Theta$ are given by

$$\frac{\partial}{\partial \mu_1}\log L = 0 \;\; \text{gives} \;\; \mu_{1ML} = \bar{X}$$

$$\frac{\partial}{\partial \mu_2}\log L = 0 \;\; \text{gives} \;\; \mu_{2ML} = \bar{Y}$$

and

$$\frac{\partial}{\partial \sigma^2}\log L = 0 \;\; \text{gives} \;\; -\frac{(m+n)}{2} \cdot \frac{1}{2\pi\sigma^2} \cdot 2\pi$$
$$+ \frac{1}{2(\sigma^2)^2}\{\textstyle\sum_1^m (X_i - \mu_1)^2 + \sum_1^n (Y_i - \mu_2)^2\} = 0$$

$$\sigma^2_{ML} = \frac{1}{m+n}[\textstyle\sum_1^m (X_i - \mu_{1ML})^2 + \sum_1^n (Y_i - \mu_{2ML})^2]$$

or

$$\sigma^2_{ML} = \frac{1}{m+n}[\textstyle\sum_1^m (X_i - \bar{X})^2 + \sum_1^n (Y_i - \bar{Y})^2]$$
$$= \frac{1}{m+n}[ms_1^2 + ns_2^2]$$

On substituting these ML estimators in the likelihood equation, we get

$$L((\mu_1, \mu_2, \sigma^2), \mathbf{x}, \mathbf{y}) = \Big(\frac{m+n}{2\pi(ms_1^2 + ns_2^2)}\Big)^{(m+n)/2} \cdot \exp\{-\frac{1}{2}(m+n)\}$$

Consider the likelihood function for $(\mu, \sigma^2) \in \Theta_0$

$$L((\mu, \sigma^2), \mathbf{x}, \mathbf{y}) = \Big(\frac{1}{2\pi\sigma^2}\Big)^{\frac{(m+n)}{2}} \exp\{-\frac{1}{2\sigma^2}\{\sum_1^m (x_i - \mu)^2 + \sum_1^n (y_i - \mu)^2\}\}$$

or

$$\log L = -\frac{(m+n)}{2}\log(2\pi\sigma^2) - \frac{1}{2\sigma^2}\{\textstyle\sum_1^m (x_i - \mu)^2 + \sum_1^n (y_i - \mu)^2\}$$

ML estimator for $\mu$ is given by

$$\frac{\partial}{\partial\mu}\log L = 0 \ \text{ gives } \ \frac{1}{\sigma^2}\Big\{\sum_1^m (x_i - \mu) + \sum_1^n (y_i - \mu)\Big\} = 0$$

$$(m\bar{X} + n\bar{Y}) - (m+n)\mu = 0$$

or

$$\mu_{ML} = \frac{m\bar{X} + n\bar{Y}}{m+n}$$

and ML estimator for $\sigma^2 (\frac{\partial}{\partial\sigma^2}\log L = 0)$ is given by

$$-\frac{(m+n)}{2} \cdot \frac{1}{2\pi\sigma^2} \cdot 2\pi + \frac{1}{2(\sigma^2)^2}\{\sum_1^m (x_i - \mu)^2 + \sum_1^n (y_i - \mu)^2\} = 0$$

or $\sigma^2_{ML} - \dfrac{1}{(m+n)}[\sum_1^m (x_i - \mu_{ML})^2 + \sum_1^n (y_i - \mu_{ML})^2]$

$$= \frac{1}{(m+n)}[\textstyle\sum_1^m (x_i - \bar{x})^2 + m(\bar{x} - \mu_{ML})^2 + \sum_1^n (y_i - \bar{y})^2 + n(\bar{y} - \mu_{ML})^2]$$

Here,

$$(\bar{x} - \mu_{ML})^2 = \Big(\bar{x} - \frac{m\bar{x} + n\bar{y}}{m+n}\Big)^2 = \Big(\frac{n(\bar{x} - \bar{y})}{m+n}\Big)^2$$

and

$$\Big(\bar{y} - \mu_{ML}\Big)^2 = \Big(\bar{y} - \frac{m\bar{x} + n\bar{y}}{m+n}\Big)^2 = \Big(\frac{m(\bar{y} - \bar{x})}{m+n}\Big)^2$$

This gives

$$\sigma^2_{ML} = \frac{1}{(m+n)}\Big[ms_1^2 + m \cdot \Big(\frac{n(\bar{x} - \bar{y})}{m+n}\Big)^2 + ns_2^2 + n\Big(\frac{m(\bar{y} - \bar{x})}{m+n}\Big)^2\Big]$$

$$= \frac{1}{m+n}[ms_1^2 + ns_2^2 + \frac{mn}{m+n}(\bar{y} - \bar{x})^2]$$

Therefore,

$$\sup_{(\mu,\sigma^2)\in\Theta_0} L((\mu,\sigma^2),\mathbf{x},\mathbf{y}) = \Big(\frac{m+n}{2\pi[ms_1^2+ns_2^2+\frac{mn}{m+n}(\bar{y}-\bar{x})^2]}\Big)^{(m+n)/2} \cdot e^{-\frac{(m+n)}{2}}$$

The likelihood ratio test is now given by

$$\begin{aligned}\lambda(\mathbf{x},\mathbf{y}) &= \frac{\sup_{(\mu,\sigma^2)\in\Theta_0} L((\mu,\sigma^2),\mathbf{x})}{\sup_{(\mu_1,\mu_2,\sigma^2)\in\Theta} L((\mu_1,\mu_2,\sigma^2),\mathbf{x})} \\ &= \Big(\frac{ms_1^2+ns_2^2}{ms_1^2+ns_2^2+\frac{mn}{m+n}(\bar{y}-\bar{x})}\Big)^{(m+n)/2} \\ &= \Big\{\frac{1}{\big(1+\frac{mn(\bar{y}-\bar{x})^2}{(m+n)(ms_1^2+ns_2^2)}\big)}\Big\}^{(m+n)/2}\end{aligned}$$

We know, $\bar{X} \sim N(\mu_1, \sigma^2/m)$ and $\bar{Y} \sim N(\mu_2, \sigma^2/n)$. We have now, $\bar{Y}-\bar{X} \sim N(\mu_2-\mu_1, \sigma^2(\frac{1}{m}+\frac{1}{n}))$ or

$$\frac{(\bar{Y}-\bar{X})-(\mu_2-\mu_1)}{\sigma\sqrt{1/m+1/n}} \sim N(0,1)$$

$$\frac{1}{\sigma^2}\sum_1^m (X_i-\bar{X})^2 \sim \chi^2_{m-1}$$

and

$$\frac{1}{\sigma^2}\sum_1^n (Y_i-\bar{Y})^2 \sim \chi^2_{n-1}$$

or

$$\frac{1}{\sigma^2}\{\sum_1^m (X_i-\bar{X})^2 + \sum_1^n (Y_i-\bar{Y})^2\} \sim \chi^2_{m+n-2}$$

or

$$\frac{1}{\sigma^2}\{ms_1^2+ns_2^2\} \sim \chi^2_{m+n-2}$$

Therefore, under $H_0 : \mu_1 = \mu_2$

$$t = \frac{(\bar{Y}-\bar{X})/\sigma\sqrt{1/m+1/n}}{\sqrt{\frac{1}{\sigma^2}\{ms_1^2+ns_2^2\}\frac{1}{m+n-2}}} \sim t_{m+n-2}$$

or

$$t = \frac{\sqrt{\frac{mn}{m+n}}(\bar{Y}-\bar{X})}{\sqrt{\frac{(ms_1^2+ns_2^2)}{m+n-2}}} \sim t_{m+n-2}$$

The statistic $\lambda(\mathbf{x},\mathbf{y})$ is now written as

$$(\lambda(\mathbf{x},\mathbf{y}))^{2/(m+n)} = \frac{1}{1+\frac{t^2}{m+n-2}} \quad \text{or} \quad \lambda^{2/(m+n)} = \frac{m+n-2}{(m+n-2)+t^2}$$

Therefore, the likelihood ratio test is given by

$$\lambda \leq c \quad \text{or} \quad t^2 > c' \quad \text{or} \quad |t| \geq k$$

where, $k$ is obtained by

$$P_\mu\{|T| \geq k\} = \alpha$$

where, $k$ is an upper $\alpha/2^{\text{th}}$ quantile of $t_{m+n-2}$ distribution which is denoted by $t_{\alpha/2,\, m+n-2}$. Finally, LR test is given by

$$\phi(\mathbf{x}, \mathbf{y}) = \begin{cases} 1 & \text{if } \dfrac{|\bar{y} - \bar{x}|}{s\sqrt{\frac{1}{m} + \frac{1}{n}}} > t_{\alpha/2, m+n-2} \\ 0 & \text{otherwise} \end{cases}$$

where, $s = \frac{1}{m+n-2}(ms_1^2 + ns_2^2)$
(b) Proceeding similarly as in (a) one gets the LR test of

$$H_0 : \mu_1 \leq \mu_2 \quad \text{against} \quad H_1 : \mu > \mu_2$$

The LR test, in this case, is given by

$$\phi(\mathbf{x}, \mathbf{y}) = \begin{cases} 1 & \text{if } \dfrac{|\bar{x} - \bar{y}|}{s\sqrt{\frac{1}{m} + \frac{1}{n}}} > t_{\alpha, m+n-2} \\ 0 & \text{otherwise} \end{cases}$$

Analogously, for testing $H_0 : \mu_1 \geq \mu_2$ against $H_1 : \mu < \mu_2$ the LR test is given by

$$\phi(\mathbf{x}, \mathbf{y}) = \begin{cases} 1 & \text{if } \dfrac{|\bar{x} - \bar{y}|}{s\sqrt{\frac{1}{m} + \frac{1}{n}}} < -t_{\alpha, m+n-2} \\ 0 & \text{otherwise} \end{cases}$$

The results of Examples 7.3.5 and 7.3.6 have been summarized in Table 7.2:

**Table 7.2:** Likelihood ratio tests for comparing means of two normal populations ($t$-test)

| | | | *Rejection region of LR test* | |
|---|---|---|---|---|
| | $H_0$ | $H_1$ | $\sigma_1^2, \sigma_2^2$ *are known* | $\sigma_1^2, \sigma_2^2$ *are unknown but* $\sigma_1^2 = \sigma_2^2$ |
| 1. | $\mu_1 = \mu_2$ | $\mu_1 \neq \mu_2$ | $\frac{\lvert\bar{x}-\bar{y}\rvert}{\sqrt{\frac{\sigma_1^2}{m}+\frac{\sigma_2^2}{n}}} > z_{\alpha/2}$ | $\frac{\lvert\bar{x}-\bar{y}\rvert}{s\sqrt{\frac{1}{m}+\frac{1}{n}}} > t_{\alpha/2,m+n-2}$ |
| 2. | $\mu_1 \leq \mu_2$ | $\mu_1 > \mu_2$ | $\frac{\bar{x}-\bar{y}}{\sqrt{\frac{\sigma_1^2}{m}+\frac{\sigma_2^2}{n}}} > z_\alpha$ | $\frac{\bar{x}-\bar{y}}{s\sqrt{\frac{1}{m}+\frac{1}{n}}} > t_{\alpha,m+n-2}$ |
| 3. | $\mu_1 \geq \mu_2$ | $\mu_1 < \mu_2$ | $\frac{\bar{x}-\bar{y}}{\sqrt{\frac{\sigma_1^2}{m}+\frac{\sigma_2^2}{n}}} < -z_\alpha$ | $\frac{\bar{x}-\bar{y}}{s\sqrt{\frac{1}{m}+\frac{1}{n}}} < -t_{\alpha,m+n-2}$ |

**Example 7.3.7.** *Let $X_{11}, \ldots, X_{1n_1}$ be a random sample from $N(\mu_1, \sigma^2)$, and$X_{21}$, $\ldots, X_{2n_2}$ be from $N(\mu_2, \sigma^2), \ldots, X_{k1}, \ldots, X_{kn_k}$ be from $N(\mu_k, \sigma^2)$. Further, let these samples be independent from each other, drawn from homoscedastic populations ($\sigma_1^2 = \cdots = \sigma_k^2 = \sigma^2$ (say)). Find out the likelihood ratio test of*

$$H_0: \ \mu_1 = \mu_2 = \cdots = \mu_k = \mu (say)$$

$$H_1: \ \text{not all } \mu_i's \text{ are equal}$$

***Solution:*** Here

$$\Theta = \{(\mu_1, \ldots, \mu_k, \sigma^2) \ : \ \mu_i \in \mathbb{R}^1, i = 1, \ldots, k, \sigma^2 > 0\}$$

and

$$\Theta_0 = \{(\mu_1, \ldots, \mu_k, \sigma^2) \ : \ \mu \in \mathbb{R}^1 \ \text{ and } \ \sigma^2 > 0\}$$

The likelihood equation for $(\mu_1, \ldots, \mu_k, \sigma^2) \in \Theta$ would be given by

$$L((\mu_1, \ldots, \mu_k, \sigma^2), \mathbf{x}) = \left(\frac{1}{2\pi\sigma^2}\right)^{n/2} \exp\{-\frac{1}{2\sigma^2} \sum_1^k \sum_1^{n_i} (x_{ij} - \mu_i)^2\}$$

where, $n = \sum_1^k n_i$. The ML estimators for $(\mu_1, \ldots, \mu_k, \sigma^2)$ in $\Theta$ has been given by

$$\frac{\partial}{\partial \mu_i} \log L = 0 \ \text{ implies } \ \sum_{j=1}^{n_i} (x_{ij} - \mu_i) = 0$$

or

$$\mu_{i_{ML}} = \bar{x}_i \quad (i = 1, 2, \ldots, k) \ \text{ and } \ \frac{\partial}{\partial \sigma^2} \log L = 0$$

This implies

$$-\frac{n}{2} \frac{1}{2\pi\sigma^2} \cdot 2\pi + \frac{1}{2} \frac{1}{(\sigma^2)^2} \sum_1^k \sum_1^{n_i} (x_{ij} - \mu_i)^2 = 0$$

$$\sigma^2_{ML} = \frac{1}{n} \sum_1^k \sum_1^{n_i} (x_{ij} - \mu_{i_{ML}})^2 = \frac{1}{n} \sum_1^k \sum_1^{n_i} (x_{ij} - \bar{x}_i)^2 = S_W/n$$

where, $S_W$ is called *within sample sum of squares*. Now, consider the likelihood function for $(\mu, \sigma^2) \in \Theta_0$

$$L((\mu, \sigma^2), \mathbf{x}) = \left(\frac{1}{2\pi\sigma^2}\right)^{n/2} \exp\{-\sum_i^k \sum_{j=1}^{n_i} (x_{ij} - \mu)^2 / 2\sigma^2\}$$

On taking log of $L$, we get

$$\log L = -\frac{n}{2} \log(2\pi\sigma^2) - \frac{1}{2\sigma^2} \sum_1^k \sum_1^{n_i} (x_{ij} - \mu)^2$$

ML estimator of $\mu$ would be the solution of

$$\frac{\partial}{\partial\mu}\log L = 0 \text{ implies } -\frac{1}{2\sigma^2}\cdot 2\sum_1^k\sum_1^{n_i}(x_{ij}-\mu) = 0$$

or

$$\mu_{ML} = \sum_1^k\sum_1^{n_i} x_{ij}/n = \sum_1^k n_i\bar{x}_i/n = \bar{x}$$

ML estimator of $\sigma^2$ is given by

$$\frac{\partial}{\partial\sigma^2}\log L = 0 \text{ implies } -\frac{n}{2}\cdot\frac{1}{2\pi\sigma^2}\cdot 2\pi + \frac{1}{2(\sigma^2)^2}\sum\sum(x_{ij}-\mu)^2 = 0$$

$$\sigma^2_{ML} = \sum_1^k\sum_1^{n_i}(x_{ij}-\bar{x})^2/n = S_T/n$$

where, $S_T$ is called total sum of squares. We must note that

$$\sup_{(\mu_1,\ldots,\mu_k,\sigma^2)\in\Theta} L((\mu_1,\ldots,\mu_k,\sigma^2),\mathbf{x}) = \left(\frac{n}{2\pi S_W}\right)^{n/2}\exp\{-n/2\}$$

and

$$\sup_{(\mu,\sigma^2)\in\Theta_0} L((\mu,\sigma^2),\mathbf{x}) = \left(\frac{n}{2\pi S_T}\right)^{n/2}\exp\{-n/2\}$$

Therefore, the likelihood ratio test is given by

$$\lambda(\mathbf{x}) = \frac{\sup_{(\mu,\sigma^2)\in\Theta_0} L((\mu,\sigma^2),\mathbf{x})}{\sup_{(\mu_1,\ldots,\mu_k,\sigma^2)\in\Theta} L((\mu_1,\ldots,\mu_k,\sigma^2),\mathbf{x})} = \left(\frac{S_W}{S_T}\right)^{n/2}$$

Here

$$S_T = \sum_1^k\sum_1^{n_i}(x_{ij}-\bar{x})^2 = \sum_i\sum_j(x_{ij}-\bar{x}_i+\bar{x}_i-\bar{x})^2$$

$$= \sum\sum(x_{ij}-\bar{x}_i)^2 + \sum_1^k n_i(\bar{x}_i-\bar{x})^2 = S_W + S_B$$

where, $S_B = \sum_1^k n_i(\bar{x}_i-\bar{x})^2$ is called *between samples sum of squares.* Therefore, the likelihood ratio test is given by

$$\lambda(\mathbf{x}) = \left(\frac{S_W}{S_T}\right)^{n/2} = \left(\frac{S_W}{S_W+S_B}\right)^{n/2} = \frac{1}{(1+S_B/S_W)^{n/2}}$$

The critical region of LR test $\lambda\,(\mathbf{x}) \; < \; c$ would imply $S_B/S_W > c'$.

$$\text{or} \quad \frac{S_B/(k-1)}{S_W/(n-k)} > k \quad \text{or} \quad \frac{\text{MSB}}{\text{MSW}} > k$$

where, MSB is called mean square between samples and MSW is called mean square within sample. Under $H_0$, the distribution of $S_B$ and $S_W$ is given by,

$$S_B \sim \chi^2_{(k-1)} \text{ and } S_W \sim \chi^2_{(n-k)}$$

Therefore,

$$F = \frac{\text{MSB}}{\text{MSW}}$$

is distributed as $F$ with $(k-1, n-k)$ degree of freedom. Using this distribution the constant $k$ in the LR test would be upper $\alpha$ quantile of $F$-distribution with $(k-1, n-k)$ degrees of freedom and would be indicated by $F_{\alpha\,;\,k-1,n-k}$. Therefore, LR test takes the form

$$\phi(\mathbf{x}) = \begin{cases} 1 & \text{if } \dfrac{MSB}{MSW} > F_{\alpha,k-1,n-k} \\ 0 & \text{otherwise} \end{cases}$$

**Example 7.3.8.** *Let a random sample $X_1, \ldots, X_n$ has been drawn from a normal population $N(\mu, \sigma^2)$. Obtain a likelihood ratio test of*

$$H_0 : \sigma^2 = \sigma_0^2 \text{ against } H_1 : \sigma \neq \sigma_0^2.$$

*when population mean $\mu$ is known.*

***Solution:*** In this case

$$\Theta_0 = \{\sigma^2 |\ \sigma^2 = \sigma_0^2\} \quad \text{and} \quad \Theta = \{\sigma^2 |\ \sigma^2 > 0\}$$

Here

$$\sup_{\sigma^2 \in \Theta_0} L(\sigma^2, \mathbf{x}) = \left(\frac{1}{2\pi\sigma_0^2}\right)^{n/2} \exp\{-\frac{1}{2\sigma_0^2}\sum_1^n (x_i - \mu)^2\}$$

Likelihood function for $\sigma^2 \in \Theta$ is given by

$$L(\sigma^2, \mathbf{x}) = \left(\frac{1}{2\pi\sigma^2}\right)^{n/2} \exp\{-\frac{1}{2\sigma^2}\sum_1^n (x_i - \mu)^2\}$$

or

$$\log L = -\frac{n}{2}\log(2\pi\sigma^2) - \frac{1}{2\sigma^2}\sum_1^n (x_i - \mu)^2$$

$$\frac{\partial \log L}{\partial \sigma^2} = 0 \text{ gives } -\frac{n}{2} \cdot \frac{1}{2\pi\sigma^2} \cdot 2\pi + \frac{1}{2(\sigma^2)^2}\sum_1^n (x_i - \mu)^2 = 0$$

$$\sigma^2_{ML} = \frac{1}{n}\sum_1^n (x_i - \mu)^2$$

Therefore,

$$\sup_{\sigma^2 \in \Theta} L(\sigma^2, \mathbf{x}) = \left(\frac{n}{2\pi \sum_1^n (x_i - \mu)^2}\right)^{n/2} \exp\{-n/2\}$$

The likelihood ratio statistic is given by

$$\begin{aligned}\lambda(\mathbf{x}) &= \frac{\sup_{\sigma^2 \in \Theta_0} L(\sigma^2, \mathbf{x})}{\sup_{\sigma^2 \in \Theta} L(\sigma^2, \mathbf{x})} \\ &= \left(\frac{\sum_1^n (x_i - \mu)^2}{n\sigma_0^2}\right)^{n/2} \exp\{-\frac{1}{2\sigma_0^2}\sum_1^n (x_i - \mu)^2 - n/2\}\end{aligned}$$

The critical region $\lambda(\mathbf{x}) < c$ implies

$$\left(\frac{\sum (x_i - \mu)^2/\sigma_0^2}{n}\right)^{n/2} \exp\{-\frac{1}{2}(\sum (x_i - \mu)^2/\sigma_0^2 - n)\} < c$$

Let $\sum (x_i - \mu)^2/\sigma_0^2 = \chi^2$ then we have $(\chi^2)^{n/2} e^{-\frac{1}{2}\chi^2} < c(ne^{-1})^{n/2} = \lambda_0$. If we plot $(\chi^2)^{n/2} \exp\{-\frac{1}{2}\mathfrak{X}^2\}$ against $\chi^2$ and find out $\chi^2$ for which $(\chi^2)^{n/2} \exp\{-\frac{1}{2}\mathfrak{X}^2\} < \lambda_0$ as shown in Figure 7.1.

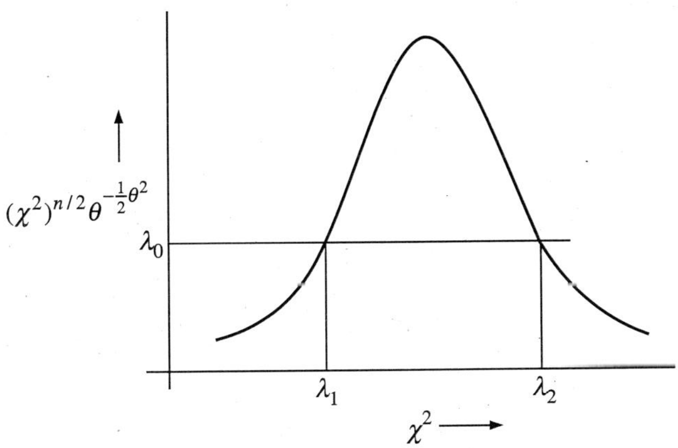


**Figure 7.1:** Plot for determination of $\lambda_1$ and $\lambda_2$.

Figure 7.1 shows the critical regions $0 < \chi^2 < \lambda_1$ or $\lambda_2 < \chi^2 < \infty$ corresponding to the critical region $\lambda((x)) < c$.

We know that under $H_0$, the statistic $\chi^2 = \sum (x_i - \mu)^2/\sigma_0^2$ follows $\chi^2$-distribution with $n$ degrees of freedom. Therefore, $\lambda_1$ and $\lambda_2$ are obtained from the size condition

$$P_{\sigma_0^2}(\chi^2 < \lambda_1) + P_{\sigma_0^2}(\chi^2 > \lambda_2) = \alpha$$

Although $\chi^2$ is not a symmetric distribution, but for the matter of simplicity, equal error probabilities $\alpha/2$ are attached to both left and right sided critical regions. The size condition gives $\lambda_1 = \chi^2_{n,1-\alpha/2}$ and $\lambda_2 = \chi^2_{n,\,\alpha/2}$. Therefore, the LR test is given by

$$\phi(\mathbf{x}) = \begin{cases} 1 & \text{if } \sum_1^n (x_i - \mu)^2/\sigma_0^2 \le \chi^2_{n,1-\alpha/2} \\ & \text{or } \sum_1^n (x_i - \mu)^2/\sigma_0^2 \ge \chi^2_{n,\alpha/2}. \\ 0 & \text{otherwise} \end{cases}$$

Similarly, LR test for testing $H_0 : \sigma^2 \le \sigma_0^2$ against $H_1 : \sigma^2 > \sigma_0^2$, has been given by

$$\phi(\mathbf{x}) = \begin{cases} 1 & \text{if } \sum_1^n (x_i - \mu)^2/\sigma_0^2 \ge \chi^2_{n,\alpha} \\ 0 & \text{otherwise} \end{cases}$$

and for, $H_0 : \sigma^2 \ge \sigma_0^2$ against $H_1 : \sigma^2 < \sigma_0^2$ the LR test is given by

$$\phi(\mathbf{x}) = \begin{cases} 1 & \text{if } \sum_1^n (x_i - \mu)^2/\sigma_0^2 \le \chi^2_{n,1-\alpha} \\ 0 & \text{otherwise} \end{cases}$$

**Example 7.3.9.** *Let us consider a random sample $X_1, \ldots, X_n$ from a Normal population $N(\mu, \sigma^2)$. Obtain a likelihood ratio test of*

$$H_0 : \sigma^2 = \sigma_0^2 \quad \textit{against} \quad H_1 : \sigma \ne \sigma_0^2$$

*when population mean $\mu$ is unknown.*

***Solution:*** In this case

$$\Theta_0 = \{(\mu, \sigma^2) \mid \mu \in \mathbb{R}^1 \ \text{ or } \ \sigma^2 = \sigma_0^2\}$$

$$\Theta = \{(\mu, \sigma^2) \mid \mu \in \mathbb{R}^1 \ \text{ or } \ \sigma^2 > 0\}$$

The likelihood function for $(\mu, \sigma^2) \in \Theta_0$ has been given by

$$L((\mu, \sigma_0^2), \mathbf{x}) = \Big(\frac{1}{2\pi\sigma_0^2}\Big)^{n/2} \exp\{-\frac{1}{2\sigma_0^2} \sum_1^n (x_i - \mu)^2\}$$

$$\log L = -\frac{n}{2} \log(2\pi\sigma_0^2) - \frac{1}{2\sigma_0^2} \sum_1^n (x_i - \mu)^2$$

The MLE for $\mu$ is obtained by

$$\frac{\partial}{\partial \mu} \log L = 0 \ \text{ implies } \ \mu_{ML} = \bar{x}$$

which gives

$$\sup_{(\mu, \sigma_0^2) \in \Theta_0} L((\mu, \sigma_0^2), \mathbf{x}) = \Big(\frac{1}{2\pi\sigma_0^2}\Big)^{n/2} \exp\{-\frac{(n-1)s^2}{2\sigma_0^2}\}$$

Further, the likelihood function for $(\mu, \sigma^2) \in \Theta$ is

$$L((\mu,\sigma^2),\mathbf{x}) = \Big(\frac{1}{2\pi\sigma^2}\Big)^{n/2} \exp\{-\frac{1}{2\sigma^2}\sum_1^n (x_i-\mu)^2\}$$

or

$$\log L = -\frac{n}{2}\log(2\pi\sigma^2) - \frac{1}{2\sigma^2}\textstyle\sum_1^n (x_i-\mu)^2$$

ML estimates for $\mu$ and $\sigma^2$ are

$$\frac{\partial}{\partial\mu}\log L = 0 \;\text{ gives }\; \mu_{ML} = \bar{x} \;\text{ and }\; \frac{\partial}{\partial\sigma}\log L = 0 \;\text{ gives }\; \sigma^2_{ML} = \frac{(n-1)s^2}{n}$$

which gives

$$\sup_{(\mu,\sigma^2)\in\Theta} L((\mu,\sigma^2),\mathbf{x}) = \Big(\frac{n}{2\pi(n-1)s^2}\Big)^{n/2}\exp\{-n/2\}$$

Therefore, likelihood ratio is

$$\lambda(\mathbf{x}) = \Big(\frac{(n-1)s^2}{n\sigma_0^2}\Big)^{n/2}\exp\{-\tfrac{1}{2}\big[\tfrac{(n-1)s^2}{\sigma^2} - n\big]\}$$

We know that under $H_0$ , the statistic

$$\chi^2 = \frac{(n-1)s^2}{\sigma_0^2} \sim \chi^2_{(n-1)}$$

The LR test in terms of $\chi^2$ would be given by

$$\lambda(\mathbf{x}) = \Big(\frac{\chi^2}{n}\Big)^{n/2} e^{-\frac{1}{2}(\chi^2-n)} < c$$

or

$$(\chi^2)^{n/2}e^{-\frac{1}{2}\chi^2} < c\cdot(n-e^{-1})^{n/2} = c'$$

Equivalent to this, we get the two critical regions $0 < \chi^2 < \lambda_1$, or $\lambda_2 < \chi^2 < \infty$, where $\lambda_1$ and $\lambda_2$ are obtained by

$$P_{\sigma_0^2}(\chi^2 < \lambda_1) + P_{\sigma_0^2}(\chi^2 > \lambda_2) = \alpha$$

Distributing the error probability equally in tails, we get

$$\lambda_1 = \chi^2_{n-1,1-\alpha/2} \;\text{ and }\; \lambda_2 = \chi^2_{n-1,\alpha/2}$$

The LR test would finally be given by

$$\phi(\mathbf{x}) = \begin{cases} 1 & \text{if } \dfrac{(n-1)s^2}{\sigma_0^2} \le \chi^2_{n-1,1-\alpha/2} \\ & \text{or } \dfrac{(n-1)s^2}{\sigma_0^2} \ge \chi^2_{n-1,\,\alpha/2} \\ 0 & \text{otherwise} \end{cases}$$

Similarly, LR test for $H_0 : \sigma^2 \leq \sigma_0^2$ against $H_1 : \sigma^2 > \sigma_0^2$ is given by

$$\phi(\mathbf{x}) = \begin{cases} 1 & \text{if } \dfrac{(n-1)s^2}{\sigma_0^2} \geq \chi^2_{n-1,\alpha} \\ 0 & \text{otherwise} \end{cases}$$

and for $H_0 : \sigma^2 \geq \sigma_0^2$ against $H_1 : \sigma^2 < \sigma_0^2$ is given by

$$\phi(\mathbf{x}) = \begin{cases} 1 & \text{if } \dfrac{(n-1)s^2}{\sigma_0^2} \leq \chi^2_{n-1,1-\alpha} \\ 0 & \text{otherwise} \end{cases}$$

Table 7.3 summarizes the results.

**Table 7.3:** Likelihood ratio tests for variance of a normal population ($\chi^2$-tests)

| $H_0$ | $H_1$ | *Rejection region of LR test at level* $\alpha$ | |
|---|---|---|---|
| | | $\mu$ *is known* | $\mu$ *is unknown* |
| $\sigma^2 = \sigma_0^2$ | $\sigma^2 \neq \sigma_0^2$ | $\frac{\sum_1^n (x_i-\mu)^2}{\sigma_0^2} \leq \chi^2_{n,1-\alpha/2}$ or $\frac{\sum_1^n (x_i-\mu)^2}{\sigma_0^2} \geq \chi^2_{n,\alpha/2}$ | $\frac{(n-1)s^2}{\sigma_0^2} \leq \chi^2_{n-1,1-\alpha/2}$ or $\frac{(n-1)s^2}{\sigma_0^2} \geq \chi^2_{n-1,\alpha/2}$ |
| $\sigma^2 \leq \sigma_0^2$ | $\sigma^2 > \sigma_0^2$ | $\frac{\sum_1^n (x_i-\mu)^2}{\sigma_0^2} \geq \chi^2_{n,\alpha}$ | $\frac{(n-1)s^2}{\sigma_0^2} \geq \chi^2_{n-1,\alpha}$ |
| $\sigma^2 \geq \sigma_0^2$ | $\sigma^2 < \sigma_0^2$ | $\frac{\sum_1^n (x_i-\mu)^2}{\sigma_0^2} \leq \chi^2_{n,1-\alpha}$ | $\frac{(n-1)s^2}{\sigma_0^2} \leq \chi^2_{n-1,1-\alpha}$ |

Let us consider two normal populations $N(\mu_1, \sigma_1^2)$ and $N(\mu_2, \sigma_2^2)$ for testing the equality of their variances.

**Example 7.3.10.** *Let* $X_1, \ldots, X_m$ *and* $Y_1, \ldots, Y_n$ *be two independent samples drawn from* $N(\mu_1, \sigma_1^2)$ *and* $N(\mu_2, \sigma_2^2)$ *respectively. Find out the likelihood ratio test of*

(a) $H_0 : \sigma_1^2 = \sigma_2^2$ against $H_1 : \sigma_1^2 \neq \sigma_2^2$

(b) $H_0 : \sigma_1^2 \leq \sigma_2^2$ against $H_1 : \sigma_1^2 > \sigma_2^2$ when $\mu_1$ and $\mu_2$ are unknown.

***Solution:*** (a) Here

$$\Theta_0 = \{(\mu_1, \mu_2, \sigma^2) : \mu_i \in \mathbb{R}^1, i = 1, 2;\ \sigma^2 > 0$$

and

$$\Theta = \{(\mu_1, \mu_2, \sigma_1^2, \sigma_2^2) : \mu_i \in \mathbb{R}^1, i = 1, 2;\ \sigma_1^2 > 0, \sigma_2^2 > 0\}$$

The likelihood equation for $(\mu_1, \mu_2, \sigma_1^2, \sigma_2^2)$ is given by

$$L((\mu_1, \mu_2, \sigma_1^2, \sigma_2^2), \mathbf{x}, \mathbf{y}) = \left(\frac{1}{2\pi\sigma_1^2}\right)^{m/2} \exp\{-\frac{1}{2\sigma_1^2}\sum_1^m (x_i - \mu_1)^2\}$$

$$\cdot \left(\frac{1}{2\pi\sigma_2^2}\right)^{n/2} \exp\{-\frac{1}{2\sigma_2^2}\sum_1^n (y_i - \mu_2)^2\}$$

$$\log L = -\frac{m}{2}\log(2\pi\sigma_1^2) - \left\{\frac{1}{2\sigma_1^2}\textstyle\sum_1^m (x_i - \mu_1)^2\right\}$$

$$-\frac{n}{2}\log(2\pi\sigma_2^2) - \left\{\frac{1}{2\sigma_2^2}\textstyle\sum_1^n (y_i - \mu_2)^2\right\}$$

The ML estimators of $\mu_1, \mu_2, \sigma_1^2, \sigma_2^2$ are obtained from

$$\frac{\partial}{\partial\mu_1}\log L = 0 \;\text{ gives }\; \mu_{1ML} = \bar{x}; \quad \frac{\partial}{\partial\mu_2}\log L = 0 \;\text{ gives }\; \mu_{2ML} = \bar{y}$$

$$\frac{\partial}{\partial\sigma_1^2}\log L = 0 \;\text{ gives }\; \sigma_{1ML}^2 = \frac{1}{m}\textstyle\sum_1^m (x_i - \mu_{1ML})^2 = \dfrac{(m-1)s_1^2}{m}$$

and

$$\frac{\partial}{\partial\sigma_2^2}\log L = 0 \;\text{ gives }\; \sigma_{2ML}^2 = \frac{(n-1)s_2^2}{n}$$

Therefore,

$$\sup_{(\mu_1,\mu_2,\sigma_1^2,\sigma_2^2)\in\Theta} L((\mu_1, \mu_2, \sigma_1^2, \sigma_2^2), \mathbf{x}, \mathbf{y}) = \left(\frac{m}{2\pi(m-1)s_1^2}\right)^{m/2}$$

$$\cdot \left(\frac{n}{2\pi(n-1)s_2^2}\right)^{n/2} \exp\{-\frac{1}{2}(m+n)\}$$

The likelihood equation for $(\mu_1, \mu_2, \sigma^2) \in \Theta_0$ is given by

$$L((\mu_1, \mu_2, \sigma^2), \mathbf{x}, \mathbf{y}) = \left(\frac{1}{2\pi\sigma^2}\right)^{(m+n)/2} \exp\Big\{-\frac{1}{2\sigma^2}\{\textstyle\sum_1^m (x_i - \mu_1)^2 + \sum_1^n (y_i - \mu_2)^2\}\Big\}$$

$$\log L = -\frac{(m+n)}{2}\log(2\pi\sigma^2) - \frac{1}{2\sigma^2}\{\textstyle\sum_1^m (x_i - \mu_1)^2 + \sum_1^n (y_i - \mu_1)^2\}$$

$$\frac{\partial \log L}{\partial\mu_1} = 0 \;\text{ gives }\; \mu_{1ML} = \bar{x}; \quad \frac{\partial \log L}{\partial\mu_2} = 0 \;\text{ gives }\; \mu_{2ML} = \bar{y}$$

and

$$\frac{\partial}{\partial\sigma^2}\log L = 0$$

gives

$$-\frac{(m+n)}{2\sigma^2}+\frac{1}{2(\sigma^2)^2}\{\textstyle\sum_1^m(x_i-\mu_1)^2+\sum_1^n(y_i-\mu_2)^2\}$$

or

$$\sigma^2_{ML}=\frac{1}{m+n}\Big\{\frac{(m-1)s_1^2}{m}+\frac{(n-1)s_2^2}{n}\Big\}$$

This gives

$$\sup_{(\mu_1,\mu_2,\sigma^2)\in\Theta_0}=\Bigg(\frac{(m+n)}{2\pi\{\frac{(m-1)s_1^2}{m}+\frac{(n-1)s_2^2}{n}\}}\Bigg)^{(m+n)/2}\exp\{-\frac{1}{2}(m+n)\}$$

and the LR test becomes

$$\lambda(\mathbf{x},\mathbf{y})=\frac{\sup_{(\mu_1,\mu_2,\sigma^2)\in\Theta_0}L((\mu_1,\mu_2,\sigma^2),\mathbf{x},\mathbf{y})}{\sup_{(\mu_1,\mu_2,\sigma_1^2,\sigma_2^2)\in\Theta}L((\mu_1,\mu_2,\sigma_1^2,\sigma_2^2),\mathbf{x},\mathbf{y})}$$

$$=(m+n)^{(m+n)/2}\frac{\left(\frac{(m-1)s_1^2}{m}\right)^{m/2}\left(\frac{(n-1)s_2^2}{n}\right)^{n/2}}{\left\{\frac{(m-1)s_1^2}{m}+\frac{(n-1)s_2^2}{n}\right\}^{(m+n)/2}}$$

Now, under the null hypothesis $H_0:\sigma_1^2=\sigma_2^2=\sigma^2$, consider the statistic

$$F=\frac{(m-1)s_1^2/(m-1)}{(n-1)s_2^2/(n-1)}=\frac{s_1^2}{s_2^2}\sim F_{(m-1),(n-1)}$$

On writing $\lambda$ in terms of $F$, we have

$$\lambda(\mathbf{x},\mathbf{y})=(m+n)^{(m+n)/2}\frac{\left(\frac{(m-1)ns_1^2}{(n-1)ms_2^2}\right)^{m/2}}{\left(1+\frac{(m-1)ns_1^2}{(n-1)ms_2^2}\right)^{(m+n)/2}}$$

$$=(m+n)^{(m+n)/2}\frac{\left(\frac{(m-1)n}{(n-1)m}F\right)^{m/2}}{\left(1+\frac{(m-1)n}{(n-1)m}F\right)^{(m+n)/2}}$$

Therefore, $\lambda(\mathbf{x},\mathbf{y})<c$ could be seen to be equivalent to $F<c_1$ or $F>c_2$. These constants $c_1$ and $c_2$ are obtained by the size condition

$$P_{\sigma_1^2=\sigma_2^2}\{F\le c_1\}=P_{\sigma_1^2=\sigma_2^2}\{F\ge c_2\}=\alpha/2$$

This gives, $c_1=F_{m-1,\,n-1;1-\alpha/2}$ and $c_2=F_{m-1,\,n-1;\,\alpha/2}$. The likelihood ratio test is, therefore, given by

$$\phi(\mathbf{x},\mathbf{y})=\begin{cases}1 & \text{if } s_1^2/s_2^2\le F_{m-1,n-1;\,1-\alpha/2}\\ & \text{or } s_1^2/s_2^2\ge F_{m-1,n-1;\,\alpha/2}\\ 0 & \text{otherwise}\end{cases}$$

(b) Similarly, one could obtain LR test for testing $H_0 : \sigma_1^2 \leq \sigma_2^2$ against $H_1 : \sigma_1^2 > \sigma_2^2$ as

$$\phi(\mathbf{x}, \mathbf{y}) = \begin{cases} 1 & \text{if } s_1^2/s_2^2 \geq F_{m-1,n-1;\alpha} \\ 0 & \text{otherwise} \end{cases}$$

and for $H_0 : \sigma_1^2 \geq \sigma_2^2$ against $H_1 : \sigma_1^2 < \sigma_2^2$ as

$$\phi(\mathbf{x}, \mathbf{y}) = \begin{cases} 1 & \text{if } s_1^2/s_2^2 \leq F_{m-1,n-1;1-\alpha} \\ & \text{or } s_2^2/s_1^2 \geq F_{n-1,m-1;\alpha} \\ 0 & \text{otherwise} \end{cases}$$

Table 7.4 summarizes the results of $F$-tests:

**Table 7.4:** Results of $F$-tests

| $H_0$ | $H_1$ | *Likelihood ratio test at level* $\alpha$ | |
|---|---|---|---|
| | | $\mu_1, \mu_2$ *are known* | $\mu_1, \mu_2$ *are unknown* |
| $\sigma_1^2 = \sigma_2^2$ | $\sigma_1^2 \neq \sigma_2^2$ | $\frac{\sum_1^m (x_i - \mu_1)^2/m}{\sum_1^n (y_j - \mu_2)^2/n} \geq F_{m,n;\alpha/2}$ or $\leq F_{m,n;1-\alpha/2}$ | $\frac{s_1^2}{s_2^2} \geq F_{m-1,n-1;\alpha/2}$ or $\frac{s_1^2}{s_2^2} \leq F_{m-1,n-1,;1-\alpha/2}$ |
| $\sigma_1^2 \leq \sigma_2^2$ | $\sigma_1^2 > \sigma_2^2$ | $\frac{\sum_1^m (x_i - \mu_1)^2/m}{\sum_1^n (y_j - \mu_2)^2/n} \geq F_{m,n;\alpha}$ | $\frac{s_1^2}{s_2^2} \geq F_{m-1,n-1;\alpha}$ |
| $\sigma_1^2 \geq \sigma_2^2$ | $\sigma_1^2 < \sigma_2^2$ | $\frac{\sum_1^n (y_j - \mu_2)^2/n}{\sum_1^m (x_i - \mu_1)^2/m} \geq F_{n,m;\alpha}$ | $\frac{s_2^2}{s_1^2} \geq F_{n-1,m-1;\alpha}$ |

**Example 7.3.11.** *Let there be $k$ normal populations with different unspecified means and variances. Let $X_{11}, \ldots, X_{1n_1}, \ldots, X_{k1}, \ldots, X_{kn_k}$ be random samples drawn from each of these populations respectively and let these samples be mutually independent. Find out the likelihood ratio test of*

$$H_0 : \sigma_1^2 = \sigma_2^2 = \ldots, = \sigma_k^2 = \sigma^2$$
$$H_1 : \textit{not all } \sigma_i^2 \textit{ s are equal}$$

***Solution:*** Here

$$\Theta = \{(\mu_1, \ldots, \mu_k; \sigma_1^2, \ldots, \sigma_k^2) \mid \mu_i \in \mathbb{R}^1 \text{ and } \sigma_i^2 > 0,\ i = 1, \ldots, k\}$$

and

$$\Theta_0 = \{(\mu_1, \ldots, \mu_k; \sigma^2) \mid \mu_i \in \mathbb{R}^1 \text{ for } i = 1, \ldots, k \text{ and } \sigma^2 > 0\}$$

Likelihood equation for $(\mu_1, \ldots, \mu_k; \sigma_1^2, \ldots, \sigma_k^2) \in \Theta$ is given by

$$L(\boldsymbol{\mu}, \boldsymbol{\sigma}^2, \mathbf{x}) = \prod_{i=1}^{k} \{(1/2\pi\sigma_i^2)^{n_i/2} \exp\{-\frac{1}{2\sigma_i^2} \sum_{j=1}^{n_i} (x_{ij} - \mu_i)^2\}\}$$

ML estimators of $\mu_i$'s and $\sigma_i^2$'s are then given by

$$\mu_{iML} = \bar{x}_i \quad \text{and} \quad \sigma_{iML}^2 = \frac{1}{n_i}\sum_{j=1}^{n_i}(x_{ij} - \bar{x}_i)^2 = \frac{(n_i - 1)s_i^2}{n_i}$$

This gives

$$\sup_{(\boldsymbol{\mu},\boldsymbol{\sigma}^2)\in\Theta} L(\boldsymbol{\mu}, \boldsymbol{\sigma}^2; \mathbf{x}) = \prod_{i=1}^{k}\Big(\frac{n_i}{2\pi(n_i - 1)s_i^2}\Big)^{n_i/2} e^{-n_i/2}$$

$$= e^{-n/2}\prod_{i=1}^{k}\Big(\frac{n_i}{2\pi(n_i - 1)s_i^2}\Big)^{n_i/2} \text{where } n = \sum_{1}^{k} n_i$$

The likelihood equation for $(\boldsymbol{\mu}, \boldsymbol{\sigma}^2) \in \Theta_0$ is given by

$$L(\boldsymbol{\mu}, \boldsymbol{\sigma}^2; \mathbf{x}) = \Big(\frac{1}{2\pi\sigma^2}\Big)^{n/2} \exp\{-\frac{1}{2\sigma^2}\sum_{i}\sum_{j}(x_{ij} - \mu_i)^2\}$$

The MLE for $\mu_i$'s and $\sigma^2$'s are then given by

$$\mu_{iML} = \bar{x}_i; \quad \sigma_{ML}^2 = \frac{1}{n}\sum_i\sum_j(x_{ij} - \bar{x}_i)^2 = \frac{1}{n}\sum_i(n_i - 1)s_i^2$$

This gives

$$\sup_{(\boldsymbol{\mu},\sigma^2)\in\Theta_0} L(\boldsymbol{\mu}, \sigma^2; \mathbf{x}) = \Big(\frac{n}{2\pi\sum_i(n_i - 1)s_i^2}\Big)^{n/2} e^{-n/2}$$

Therefore, the likelihood ratio test statistic is given by

$$\lambda(\mathbf{x}) = \frac{\sup_{(\boldsymbol{\mu},\sigma^2)\in\Theta_0} L(\boldsymbol{\mu}, \sigma^2; \mathbf{x})}{\sup_{(\boldsymbol{\mu},\boldsymbol{\sigma}^2)\in\Theta} L(\boldsymbol{\mu}, \sigma^2; \mathbf{x})}$$

$$= \frac{\prod_{i=1}^{k}((n_i - 1)s_i^2/n_i)^{n_i/2}}{(\frac{1}{n}\sum_{i=1}^{k}(n_i - 1)s_i^2)^{n/2}}$$

Let

$$\frac{1}{n}\sum_{i=1}^{k}(n_i - 1)s_i^2 = \frac{1}{n}\sum_i\sum_j(x_{ij} - \bar{x}_i)^2 = s^2$$

This gives

$$\lambda(\mathbf{x}) = \frac{\prod_{i=1}^{k}((n_i - 1)s_i^2/n_i)^{n_i/2}}{(s^2)^{\sum n_i/2}} = \prod_{i=1}^{k}\Big(\frac{(n_i - 1)}{n_i}\frac{s_i^2}{s^2}\Big)^{n_i/2}$$

The distribution of the statistic obtained in $\lambda(\mathbf{x})$ is difficult to calculate. Therefore, we could only say about its asymptotic distribution i.e. $-2\log_e\lambda \sim$

$\mathfrak{X}^2_{2k-(k+1)=(k-1)}$ for large $n_i$'s. It has also been seen that this approximate result holds good even for small $n_i'$s. However, Bartlett [11] suggested the following approximation

$$\chi^2 = \frac{-2\log\lambda(\mathbf{x})}{1+\frac{1}{3(k-1)}[\sum_i(1/n_i)-\frac{1}{\sum n_i}]}$$

Here $\lambda(\mathbf{x})$ has been considered as

$$\prod_{i=1}^{k}\Big(\frac{(n_i-1)}{n_i}\frac{s_i^2}{s^2}\Big)^{(n_i-1)/2}$$

This gives

$$\chi^2 = \frac{\sum_{i=1}^{k}(n_i-1)\log_e(\frac{n_i s^2}{(n_i-1)s_i^2})}{1+\frac{1}{3(k-1)}[\sum_i(1/n_i)-\frac{1}{\sum n_i}]} \sim \chi^2_{(k-1)}$$

The critical region corresponding to this test is given by

$$\chi^2 \geq c \quad \text{where} \quad c = \chi^2_{(k-1),\,\alpha}$$

## *Review Questions*

**7.1** Describe the rationale of likelihood ratio test and mention some of its important properties. Show that the two sample t-test is a likelihood ratio test.

**7.2** Show that likelihood ratio tests are consistent under regularity conditions. State these conditions clearly.

**7.3** Derive the asymptotic distribution of the likelihood ratio statistic under the null hypothesis for testing a composite hypothesis with $r$ degrees of freedom against a composite alternative with $n(> r)$ d.f.

**7.4** Give an example of likelihood ratio test which is uniformly most powerful unbiased.

**7.5** Derive the asymptotic distribution of likelihood ratio test criterion for testing a simple null hypothesis in the one-parameter family of densities.

(a) Describe the regularity conditions under which asymptotic properties of likelihood ratio test are discussed.

(b) If $\hat{\theta} \sim N\Big(\theta_0, \frac{1}{n\beta^2(\theta_0,\theta_0)}\Big)$ for large $n$. Under the above regularity conditions then show

$$\lim_{n\to\infty} P(-2\log\lambda_H < \chi^2|\, H_0) = \frac{1}{\sqrt{2\pi}}\int_0^{\chi^2} u^{-1/2}e^{-1/2u}\, du$$

**7.6** Let $X_1, X_2, \ldots, X_n$ be a random sample from normal density with variance one and unknown mean $\mu$. Find out the likelihood ratio test of the hypothesis $H_0 : \mu = 3$ against the alternative $\mu \neq 3$.

**7.7** Obtain the likelihood ratio test for testing the equality of means of $k(> 2)$ normal populations having the same variance.

**7.8** A sample of size $n$ is drawn from each of the three normal populations whose variances are known, show how you will test the hypothesis that their means are in arithmetic progression, (i.e $\mu_1 + \mu_3 = 2\mu_2$).

(a) Show that likelihood ratio test is function of sufficient statistic for $\theta$.

(b) Let $X_1, X_2, \ldots, X_n$ be a random sample from normal distribution $N(\theta, \sigma^2)$, where both $\theta$ and $\sigma$ are unknown. Find the likelihood ratio test of

$$H_0 : \sigma = \sigma_0 \quad \text{against} \quad H_1 : \sigma \neq \sigma_0$$

Examine whether the test is unbiased.

**7.9** Let $X_1, X_2, \ldots, X_m$ and $Y_1, Y_2, \ldots, Y_n$ be independent samples from $N(\mu_1, \sigma_1^2)$ and $N(\mu_2, \sigma_2^2)$ respectively. Consider the testing problem

$$H_0 : \sigma_1^2 = \sigma_2^2 \quad \text{vs.} \quad H_1 : \sigma_1^2 \neq \sigma_2^2$$

and $\mu_1$ and $\mu_2$ are unknown. Show that the likelihood ratio test shall be given by

$$\frac{s_1^2}{s_2^2} \geq F_{m-1,n-1,\alpha/2} \ \text{ if } \ s_1^2 \geq s_2^2$$

**7.10** Let $X_1, X_2, \ldots, X_n$ be drawn from $N(\mu, \sigma^2)$ both $\mu, \sigma^2$ are unknown. Employing the likelihood ratio test criterion obtain the two-tailed $t$-test of

$$H_0 : \mu = \mu_0 \qquad H_1 : \mu \neq \mu_0$$

also determine the power function of the test.

**7.11** Pumpkins were grown under two experimental conditions. Two random samples of 11 and 9 pumpkins show the sample standard deviations of their weights as 0.8 and 0.5 respectively. Assuming that the weight distributions are normal, test the hypothesis that the true variances are equal, against the alternative that they are not, at the 90% level. [Assume that $P(F_{10,8} \geq 3.35) = 0.05$ and $P(F_{8,10} \geq 3.07) = 0.05$]

**7.12** Let $X_1, X_2, \ldots, X_n$ be iid $b(1, \theta)$ random variables. Obtain a level $\alpha$ likelihood ratio test of $H_0 : \theta \leq \theta_0$ against $H_1 : \theta > \theta_0$.

**7.13** Let $X$ be a binomial $b(n, p)$ random variable. Develop the level $\alpha$ likelihood ratio test of $H_0 : p \leq p_0$ against $H_1 : p > p_0$.

**7.14** Obtain the likelihood ratio test procedure for testing the null hypothesis that $x$ and $y$ are independent against the alternative that they are not, when $x$ and $y$ are jointly distributed as bivariate normal and a set of observations $(x_i, y_i), i = 1, \ldots, n$ are given. Modify the test procedure when $x$ and $y$ are positively correlated.

**7.15** Let $X_1$ and $X_2$ follow binomial distributions with parameters $(n_1, p_1)$ and $(n_2, p_2)$ respectively independent of each other. Describe large sample test procedure for testing the hypothesis $H_0 : p_1 = p_2$ against $H_1 : p_1 \neq p_2$. Hence, find $100(1 - \alpha)\%$ confidence interval of $p_1 - p_2$ in large sample.

# Chapter 8

# Confidence Estimation and Testing of Hypothesis

## 8.1 INTRODUCTION

In the present chapter the connection between tests and confidence intervals of the parameter $\theta$ has been discussed. Here, we consider a random vector $\mathbf{X}$ whose probability distribution is given by $P_\theta$ which is a distribution in the family $\mathcal{P} = \{P_{\boldsymbol{\theta}} \, : \, \boldsymbol{\theta} \in \Theta \subseteq \mathbb{R}^k\}$. We, next, consider a family of subsets $S(\mathbf{x})$ of $\Theta$, which depends on $\mathbf{x}$ and independent of $\boldsymbol{\theta}$, called a family of random sets.

**Definition 8.1.1. ($(1-\alpha)$-Level Confidence Sets)** Let $\boldsymbol{\theta} \in \Theta \subseteq \mathbb{R}^k$ and $0 < \alpha < 1$. A family of random subsets $S(\mathbf{x})$ of $\Theta$ is called a *family of confidence sets at confidence level* $(1-\alpha)$ *if*

$$P_{\boldsymbol{\theta}}\{S(\mathbf{X}) \ni \boldsymbol{\theta}\} \geq 1 - \alpha \qquad \forall\, \boldsymbol{\theta} \in \Theta \tag{8.1}$$

The quantity

$$\inf_{\boldsymbol{\theta} \in \Theta} P_{\boldsymbol{\theta}}\{S(\mathbf{X}) \ni \boldsymbol{\theta}\}$$

is called *confidence coefficient* associated with random set $S(\mathbf{X})$.

**Definition 8.1.2. (Uniformly Most Accurate Family of Confidence Sets)** A family of confidence sets $\{S(\mathbf{x})\}$ is said to be a UMA family of confidence sets if

$$P_{\boldsymbol{\theta}}\{S(\mathbf{X}) \ni \boldsymbol{\theta}\} \geq 1 - \alpha \qquad \forall \;\; \boldsymbol{\theta} \in \Theta$$

and
$$P_{\boldsymbol{\theta}'}\{S(\mathbf{X}) \ni \boldsymbol{\theta}\} \leq P_{\boldsymbol{\theta}'}\{S'(\mathbf{X}) \ni \boldsymbol{\theta}\} \qquad \forall\, \boldsymbol{\theta}, \boldsymbol{\theta}' \in \Theta \tag{8.2}$$

for all $S'(\mathbf{X})$ satisfying the Eq. (8.1) i.e. $S'(\mathbf{X})$ is any other family of $(1-\alpha)$ level confidence sets.

We shall see that the acceptance region, $AR(\boldsymbol{\theta})$, of size-$\alpha$ test and a family of $(1-\alpha)$ level confidence sets $S(\mathbf{X})$ imply each other. Here, we shall restrict our discussion only to non-randomized size-$\alpha$ tests.

Let us consider a testing problem $H_0 : \theta \in \Theta_0$ versus $H_1 : \theta \in \Theta_1$ denoted by $H_0(\Theta_0)$ and $H_1(\Theta_1)$ respectively. Let the class of level-$\alpha$ tests be denoted by

$$\begin{aligned}\mathcal{C}_\alpha &= \{\phi \in \mathcal{D} : \sup_{\theta\in\Theta_0} E_\theta\phi(X) \le \alpha\} \\ &= \{A \in \mathbb{R}^n : \inf_{\theta\in\Theta_0} P_\theta(A) \ge 1-\alpha\} \\ &= \{S(\mathbf{x}) : \min_{\theta\in\Theta_0} P_\theta(S(\mathbf{X}) \ni \theta) \ge 1-\alpha\}\end{aligned}$$

This shows that a class of $\alpha$-level tests for testing $(\alpha, H_0(\Theta_0), H_1(\Theta_1))$ and of confidence sets $S(\mathbf{x}) \subset \Theta_0$ at level $(1-\alpha)$ imply each other. The UMP size-$\alpha$ test with its acceptance region $A(\theta_0)$ gives

$$P_\theta(\mathbf{X} \in A(\theta_0)) \le P_\theta(\mathbf{X} \in A^*(\theta_0)) \;\; \forall\, \theta \in \Theta_1(\theta \in H_1(\Theta_1))$$

or

$$P_\theta(S(\mathbf{X}) \ni \theta_0) \le P_\theta(S^*(\mathbf{X}) \ni \theta_0) \;\; \forall\, \theta \in \Theta_1$$

Therefore, acceptance region corresponding to a UMP size-$\alpha$ test, $A(\Theta_0)$ minimizes

$$P_\theta(S(\mathbf{X}) \ni \theta') \;\; \forall\, \theta \in H_1(\Theta_1) \;\text{ and for every } \theta' \text{ in } \Theta_0.$$

*Therefore, the family of confidence sets corresponding to a UMP acceptance region is UMA family at $(1-\alpha)$ level.*

## 8.2 UMP SIZE-$\alpha$ ACCEPTANCE REGION AND UMA $(1-\alpha)$ LEVEL CONFIDENCE SETS

We shall now give an important result that establishes a correspondence between UMP size- $\alpha$ acceptance region and UMA $(1-\alpha)$ level family of confidence sets. Let us consider the null hypothesis $H_0 : \theta = \theta_0$. Denote it by $H_0(\theta_0)$ against any one or two-sided alternative denote it by $H_1(\theta_0)$.

**Theorem 8.2.1.** *Let $A(\theta_0)$, $\theta_0 \in \Theta$ denotes the acceptance region of a size-$\alpha$ test of $H_0(\Theta_0)$. For each observation $\mathbf{x} = (x_1, \ldots, x_n)$, let $S(\mathbf{x})$ denotes the set*

$$S(\mathbf{x}) = \{\theta : \mathbf{x} \in A(\theta),\; \theta \in \Theta\}$$

*Then $S(\mathbf{x})$ is a $(1-\alpha)$ level family of confidence sets for $\theta$. Further, if $A(\theta_0)$ is UMP for the above problem, $(\alpha, H_0(\theta_0), H_1(\theta_0))$, then $S(\mathbf{X})$ is UMA $(1-\alpha)$ level family of confidence sets, i.e $S(\mathbf{X})$ minimizes*

$$P_\theta\{S(\mathbf{X}) \ni \theta'\} \qquad \forall\, \theta \in H_1(\theta')$$

*among all $(1-\alpha)$ level families of confidence sets.*

*Proof.* Let us consider size-$\alpha$ acceptance region $A(\theta)$ such that

$$P_\theta\{\mathbf{X} \in A(\theta)\} \geq 1 - \alpha \qquad \forall \quad \theta \in H_0(\theta_0)$$

This may be equivalently written as

$$P_\theta\{S(\mathbf{X}) \ni \theta\} \geq 1 - \alpha$$

This $S(\mathbf{X})$, by Definition 8.1.1, is a family of $(1 - \alpha)$ level confidence sets. This establishes the correspondence between a size-$\alpha$ acceptance region and family of confidence sets for $\theta$ at level $(1 - \alpha)$.

Let us consider $A^*(\theta)$ as any other size-$\alpha$ acceptance region or

$$P_\theta\{\mathbf{X} \in A^*(\theta)\} \geq 1 - \alpha$$

The corresponding $(1 - \alpha)$ level family of confidence sets is given by $S^*(\mathbf{x})$ so that

$$P_\theta\{S^*(\mathbf{X}) \ni \theta\} \geq 1 - \alpha$$

It is given that $A(\theta_0)$ is a UMP size-$\alpha$ acceptance region, or

$$P_\theta\{\mathbf{X} \in A(\theta_0)\} \leq P_\theta\{\mathbf{X} \in A(\theta_0^*)\} \qquad \forall\, \theta \in H_1(\theta_0)$$

further, $S(\mathbf{X})$ has been given as the family of confidence sets corresponding to $A(\theta_0)$, we then have

$$P_\theta\{S(\mathbf{X}) \ni \theta_0\} \leq P_\theta\{S^*(\mathbf{X}) \ni \theta_0\} \quad \forall\, \theta \in H_1(\theta_0)$$

Since $A^*(\theta)$ was taken as an arbitrary size-$\alpha$ acceptance region, therefore, the $(1 - \alpha)$ level family of confidence sets $S(\mathbf{X})$ corresponding to UMP size-$\alpha$ acceptance region $A(\theta_0)$ is the one that minimizes $P_\theta\{S(\mathbf{X}) \ni \theta_0\}$ (the probability that $S(\mathbf{X})$ captures the false value of the parameter while true value being $\theta$) over $\theta \in H_1(\theta_0)$. This completes the proof. □

## 8.3 UNBIASED CONFIDENCE SETS

A family $\{S(\mathbf{x})\}$ of confidence sets for a parameter $\theta$ is said to be unbiased at level $(1 - \alpha)$ if

$$P_\theta\{S(\mathbf{X}) \ni \theta\} \geq 1 - \alpha \quad \forall\, \theta \in \Theta$$

: ($S(\mathbf{x})$ traps the true parameter value with probability at least $(1 - \alpha)$)

and $$P_{\theta'}\{S(\mathbf{X}) \ni \theta\} \leq 1 - \alpha \quad \forall\, \theta,\ \theta' \in \Theta.$$

: ($S(\mathbf{x})$ traps a false parameter value with probability at most $(1 - \alpha)$)

If $S^*(\mathbf{X})$ is a family of $(1 - \alpha)$ level unbiased confidence sets that minimizes

$$P_\theta\{S(\mathbf{X}) \ni \theta'\} \qquad \forall\, \theta,\ \theta' \in \Theta$$

then $S^*(\mathbf{X})$ is called uniformly most accurate unbiased (UMAU) family of confidence sets at level $(1-\alpha)$

Now, Theorem 8.3.1 states the relations between UMP unbiased size-$\alpha$ acceptance region and UMAU family of confidence sets at level $1-\alpha$.

**Theorem 8.3.1.** *Consider the testing problem $H_0 : \theta = \theta_0$ (denoted by $H_0(\theta_0)$) against $H_1 : \theta \neq \theta_0$ (denoted by $H_1(\theta_0)$) for each $\theta_0 \in \Theta$. Let $A(\theta_0)$ be the UMP unbiased size-$\alpha$ acceptance region for this problem. Then $S(\mathbf{x}) = \{\theta | \mathbf{x} \in A(\theta)\}$ is a UMA unbiased family of confidence sets at level $1-\alpha$.*

*Proof.* Let the UMP unbiased size-$\alpha$ test be given by $\phi_0(\mathbf{x})$. Unbiasedness gives

$$E_{\theta'}\phi_0(X) \geq \alpha \qquad \forall\ \theta' \in H_1(\theta_0)$$

or

$$E_{\theta'}(1-\phi_0(X)) \leq 1-\alpha \qquad \forall\ \theta' \in H_1(\theta_0)$$

or

$$P_{\theta'}(\mathbf{X} \in A(\theta)) \leq 1-\alpha$$

or

$$P_{\theta'}(S(\mathbf{X}) \ni \theta) \leq 1-\alpha$$

shows that $S(\mathbf{X})$ *is unbiased.*

Next, consider any other unbiased size-$\alpha$ test $\phi^*(\mathbf{x})$, with acceptance region $A^*(\theta)$; we get a corresponding $(1-\alpha)$ level family of unbiased confidence sets $S^*(\mathbf{X})$, i.e.

$$P_{0'}(S^*(\mathbf{X}) \ni \theta) \leq 1-\alpha \qquad \forall\ \theta' \in H_1(\theta_0)$$

The test $\phi_0(\mathbf{x})$ has been given to be UMP, therefore,

$$E_{\theta'}[\phi_0(\mathbf{X})] \geq E_{\theta'}[\phi^*(\mathbf{X})] \qquad \forall\ \theta' \in H_1(\theta_0)$$

or

$$E_{\theta'}[1-\phi_0(\mathbf{X})] \leq E_{\theta'}[1-\phi^*(\mathbf{X})]$$

or

$$P_{\theta'}[\mathbf{X} \in A(\theta)] \leq P_{\theta'}[\mathbf{X} \in A^*(\theta)]$$

or

$$P_{\theta'}\{S(\mathbf{X}) \ni \theta\} \leq P_{\theta'}\{S^*(\mathbf{X}) \ni \theta\} \qquad \forall\ \theta' \in H_1(\theta_0)$$

This follows $S(\mathbf{X})$ is UMA unbiased family of confidence sets at level $(1-\alpha)$. □

## 8.4 MINIMUM EXPECTED LENGTH AND UNBIASED CONFIDENCE SETS

Uniformly shortest length confidence intervals usually do not exist among all $(1-\alpha)$ level confidence intervals even for most commonly used distributions. Therefore, this cannot be taken as a measure of precision of a confidence interval. In this light Pratt, 1961 [163] had suggested to take expected length of a confidence interval as a measure of its precision. He had then shown that the minimum expected length of a confidence interval is attained when one restricts only to unbiased confidence intervals. This is met when one restricts to a class of unbiased tests in case of two-sided testing problems or in case of testing problems that involve nuisance parameters, where for certain families UMP unbiased tests exist. The result of Theorem 8.4.1 result has been derived from Pratt (1961)[163]: that is being presented in a form of a theorem:

**Theorem 8.4.1.** *Let* $X \sim f_\theta$, $\theta \in \Theta \subseteq \mathbb{R}^1$*; let* $S(\mathbf{X})$ *be* $(1-\alpha)$ *level confidence intervals of finite length, that is, let* $S(\mathbf{X}) = (\underline{\theta}(\mathbf{X}), \bar{\theta}(\mathbf{X}))$ *and that* $(\bar{\theta}(\mathbf{X}) - \underline{\theta}(\mathbf{X})$ *is a random variable which is finite. Then*

$$E_\theta[\bar{\theta}(\mathbf{X}) - \underline{\theta}(\mathbf{X})] = \int_{\theta' \neq \theta} P_\theta\{S(\mathbf{X}) \ni \theta'\} d\theta' \quad \forall\ \theta \in \Theta$$

*or, in simple words, the expected length of the confidence interval is* $P_\theta(S(\mathbf{X}) \ni \theta')$ *averaged over all false values of* $\theta' \neq \theta$.

*Proof.* Consider the interval

$$\bar{\theta} - \underline{\theta} = \int_{\underline{\theta}}^{\bar{\theta}} d\theta'$$

Taking expectation on both the sides

$$E_\theta\{\bar{\theta}(\mathbf{X}) - \underline{\theta}(\mathbf{X})\} = E_\theta\Big\{\int_{\underline{\theta}}^{\bar{\theta}} d\theta'\Big\} = \int_{\mathcal{X}}\Big\{\int_{\underline{\theta}}^{\bar{\theta}} d\theta'\Big\} f_\theta(\mathbf{x})\, d\mathbf{x}$$

$$= \int\Big\{\int_{\underline{\theta}(\mathbf{x})}^{\bar{\theta}(\mathbf{x})} f_\theta(\mathbf{x}) d\mathbf{x}\Big\} d\theta' = \int_{\theta' \neq \theta} P_\theta\{S(\mathbf{x}) \ni \theta'\}\, d\theta' \quad \forall\ \theta \in \Theta.$$

Hence proved. □

If a test $\phi_0$ is UMP unbiased of size-$\alpha$ in the class of all size-$\alpha$ unbiased tests, then correspondingly we have a UMAU confidence interval of $\theta$ at level $(1-\alpha)$, $S(\mathbf{X})$, that minimizes $P_\theta\{S(\mathbf{X}) \ni \theta'\}$ for all false parameter values $\theta' \neq \theta$ that it captures. Subsequently, Pratt [163] had shown that such a UMAU $(1-\alpha)$ level family of confidence sets, $S(\mathbf{X})$, in the class of all families of $(1-\alpha)$ level unbiased confidence sets minimizes the expected length of the confidence intervals, $E_\theta^{\mathbf{X}} S(\mathbf{X})$, which is taken as a reasonable measure of precision of confidence intervals.

# 8.5 GUENTHER PROCEDURE FOR FINDING A $(1-\alpha)$ LEVEL UNBIASED CONFIDENCE INTERVAL

Guenther, 1971[77] has suggested a procedure of finding a $(1-\alpha)$ level family of unbiased confidence intervals. Let $X_1, \ldots, X_n$ be a sample drawn from a continuous pdf $f(x|\theta)$. Let $T(\mathbf{x}, \theta)$ be a pivot and suppose

$$P_\theta\{\lambda_1(\alpha) < T(\mathbf{X}, \theta) < \lambda_2(\alpha)\} = 1-\alpha$$

which can be written in the form of a confidence interval

$$P_\theta\{\underline{\theta}(\mathbf{X}) < \theta < \bar{\theta}(\mathbf{X})\} = 1-\alpha$$

Further, unbiasedness of $(1-\alpha)$ level confidence interval implies

$$P_\theta\{\underline{\theta}(\mathbf{X}) < \theta' < \bar{\theta}(\mathbf{X})\} < 1-\alpha \quad \forall\, \theta' \neq \theta$$

Let us define

$$\begin{aligned} P(\theta, \theta') &= P_\theta\{\underline{\theta}(\mathbf{X}) < \theta' < \bar{\theta}(\mathbf{X})\} \\ &= P\{\gamma(\theta, \theta')\} \end{aligned}$$

Assuming this probability depends on some function $\gamma$ of $\theta$ and $\theta'$. The above conditions may be restated in terms of $\gamma$ by

$$P(\gamma) = \begin{cases} = 1-\alpha & \text{if } \theta' = \theta \\ < 1-\alpha & \text{if } \theta' \neq \theta \end{cases}$$

i.e. $P(\gamma)$ attains maximum at $\theta' = \theta$. $\lambda_1$ and $\lambda_2$ may finally be obtained by solving

$$P_{\theta'=\theta}(\gamma) = 1-\alpha \quad \text{and} \quad \frac{\partial}{\partial \theta'} P_{\theta'}(\gamma)\Big|_{\theta'=\theta} = 0$$

# 8.6 SOLVED EXAMPLES

**Example 8.6.1.** *Let $X$ follows one parameter exponential family. Consider the testing problem $(\alpha, H_0(\Theta_0), H_1(\Theta_1))$ defined as*

$$H_0 : \theta = \theta_0 \quad \textit{against} \quad H_1 : \theta < \theta_0$$

*Find out a UMP size-$\alpha$ acceptance region and the corresponding UMA confidence sets at level $1-\alpha$.*

***Solution:*** The density function of the one parameter exponential family is given by

$$f_X(x|\,\theta) = c(\theta) \cdot h(x)\, e^{Q(\theta)T(x)}$$

where, $Q(\theta)$ is a non-decreasing function of $\theta$. On applying Karlin and Rubin theorem the UMP size-$\alpha$ test for testing $H_0 : \theta = \theta_0$ against $H_1 : \theta < \theta_0$ has been given by

$$\phi_0(T(x)) = \begin{cases} 1 & \text{if } T \leq t \\ 0 & \text{if } T > t \end{cases}$$

where, $t$ is obtained from

$$E_{\theta_0}\phi_0(T) = \alpha \quad \text{or} \quad P_{\theta_0}[T \leq t] = \alpha$$

which shows that $t$ is a function of $\theta_0$. The corresponding UMP size-$\alpha$ acceptance region will be given by

$$A(\theta_0) = \{x : T > t(\theta_0)\}$$

Since $A(\theta_0)$ is UMP size-$\alpha$ acceptance region

$$P_{\theta'}\{T(X) \leq t(\theta_0)\} \geq P_{\theta_0}\{T(X) \leq t(\theta_0)\} = \alpha \;\forall\; \theta' < \theta_0$$
$$\text{i.e. } \theta' \in H_1(\Theta_1)$$

But

$$P_{\theta'}\{T(X) \leq t(\theta')\} = \alpha$$

This gives

$$P_{\theta'}\{T(X) \leq t(\theta_0)\} \geq P_{\theta'}\{T(X) \leq t(\theta')\} \text{ for } \theta' < \theta_0$$

which implies $t(\theta_0) \geq t(\theta')$. This shows that, $t(\theta)$ is a non-decreasing function of $\theta$. We have now

$$\begin{aligned} S(x) &= \{\theta : x \in A(\theta)\} = \{\theta | T(x) > t(\theta)\} \\ &= \{\theta : \theta < t^{-1}(T(x))\} \quad \text{(since t is non-decreasing)} \\ &= (-\infty,\; t^{-1}(T(x))) \end{aligned}$$

where, $t^{-1}$ is defined as

$$t^{-1}(T(x)) = \sup_{\theta}\{\theta | \, t(\theta) \leq T(x)\}$$

**Example 8.6.2.** *Let $X$ be a random variable with the density*

$$f_X(x|\,\theta) = \begin{cases} \dfrac{1}{\theta} \cdot e^{-x/\theta} & \textit{if } x > 0 \\ 0 & \textit{otherwise} \end{cases}$$

*where $\theta > 0$. Consider the testing problem $H_0 : \theta = \theta_0$ against $H_1 : \theta < \theta_0$. Find out a UMA $(1-\alpha)$ level family of confidence sets corresponding to size-$\alpha$ UMP test.*

***Solution:*** The given family belongs to the one parameter exponential family. The UMP size-$\alpha$ acceptance region is given by

$$\begin{aligned} A(\theta) &= \{x : T(x) \geq c(\theta)\} \\ &= \{x : x \geq c(\theta)\} \end{aligned}$$

where, we choose $c(\theta)$ by

$$P_{\theta_0}(A(\theta_0)) = 1 - \alpha$$

or

$$\int_0^{c(\theta_0)} \frac{1}{\theta_0} e^{-x/\theta_0} dx = \alpha$$

$$\frac{1}{\theta_0}\left[-\theta_0 e^{-x/\theta_0}\right]_0^{c(\theta_0)} = \alpha$$

or

$$-e^{-c(\theta_0)/\theta_0} + 1 = \alpha$$

or

$$c(\theta_0) = \theta_0 \cdot \log \frac{1}{1-\alpha}, \qquad 0 < \alpha < 1$$

Therefore, the corresponding UMA family of $1 - \alpha$ level of confidence sets is given by

$$\begin{aligned} S(x) = \{\theta : x \in A(\theta)\} &= \left\{\theta : x \geq \theta \log \frac{1}{1-\alpha}\right\} \\ &= \left\{\theta : \theta \leq \frac{x}{\log \frac{1}{1-\alpha}}\right\} = \left(0, \frac{x}{\log(\frac{1}{1-\alpha})}\right] \qquad (\text{since}\, \theta > 0) \end{aligned}$$

**Example 8.6.3.** *Let $X_1, \ldots, X_n$ be a sample from $N(\mu, \sigma^2)$ where both $\mu$ and $\sigma^2$ are unknown. For testing $H_0 : \mu = \mu_0$ against $H_1 : \mu \neq \mu_0$. Find the UMA unbiased family of confidence sets for $\mu$ at level $(1 - \alpha)$.*

*Solution:* We have seen that the UMP unbiased size-$\alpha$ test for the testing problem is given by

$$\phi(\mathbf{x}) = \begin{cases} 1 & \text{if } \dfrac{|\sqrt{n-1}(\bar{x} - \mu_0)|}{s} > c \\ 0 & \text{otherwise} \end{cases}$$

where, $\bar{x} = \frac{1}{n}\sum x_i$, $s^2 = \frac{1}{n}\sum(x_i - \bar{x})^2$.
The constant c is obtained by the size condition

$$E_{\mu_0}[\phi(\mathbf{X})] = \alpha$$

or

$$E_{\mu_0}[1 - \phi(\mathbf{X})] = 1 - \alpha$$

or

$$P_{\mu_0}\left\{\left|\frac{\sqrt{n-1}(\bar{x}-\mu_0)}{s}\right|\leq c\right\}=1-\alpha$$

We get $c = t_{n-1,\,\alpha/2}$. Thus, the acceptance region corresponding to UMP unbiased size-$\alpha$ test for testing $H_0 : \mu = \mu_0$ against $H_1 : \mu \neq \mu_0$ is given by

$$A(\mu_0) = \left\{\mathbf{x} \,:\, \left|\frac{\sqrt{n-1}(\bar{x}-\mu_0)}{s}\right|\leq t_{n-1,\,\alpha/2}\right\}$$

On using Theorem 8.3.1, the corresponding UMAU family of confidence sets at level $1-\alpha$, is

$$\begin{aligned}
S(\mathbf{x}) &= \{\mu \,:\, \mathbf{x} \in A(\mu)\} \\
&= \left\{\mu \,:\, \left|\frac{\sqrt{n-1}(\bar{x}-\mu)}{s}\right|\leq t_{n-1,\,\alpha/2}\right\} \\
&= \left(-t_{n-1,\,\alpha/2} \leq \frac{\sqrt{n-1}(\bar{x}-\mu)}{s} \leq +t_{n-1,\,\alpha/2}\right) \\
&= \left(\bar{x} - \frac{s}{\sqrt{n-1}}\,t_{n-1,\,\alpha/2} \leq \mu \leq \bar{x} + \frac{s}{\sqrt{n-1}}\,t_{n-1,\,\alpha/2}\right)
\end{aligned}$$

**Example 8.6.4.** *Let $X_1, \ldots, X_n$ be a sample from $N(\mu, \sigma^2)$, where $\sigma^2$ is known for testing $H_0 : \mu = \mu_0$ against $H_1 : \mu \neq \mu_0$. Find a UMA $(1-\alpha)$ level confidence sets for $\mu$.*

***Solution:*** For testing the hypothesis

$$H_0 : \mu = \mu_0 \quad \text{against} \quad H_1 : \mu \neq \mu_0$$

the UMP unbiased size-$\alpha$ test is given by

$$\phi(\mathbf{x}) = \begin{cases} 1 & \text{if } \dfrac{\sqrt{n}|(\bar{x}-\mu_0)|}{\sigma} > c \\ 0 & \text{otherwise} \end{cases}$$

This test is known as $z$-test. The constant c is determined by the size condition

$$E_{\mu_0}[\phi(\mathbf{X})] = \alpha$$

or

$$P_{\mu_0}\left\{\frac{\sqrt{n}|\bar{X}-\mu_0|}{\sigma} > c\right\}= \alpha/2$$

which gives

$$c = z_{\alpha/2}$$

Thus, the acceptance region corresponding to this UMP unbiased size-$\alpha$ test is given by

$$A(\mu_0) = \left\{\mathbf{x} : \frac{\sqrt{n}\,|(\bar{x}-\mu_0)|}{\sigma} \leq z_{\alpha/2}\right\}$$

By utilizing Theorem 8.3.1, the UMA unbiased family of confidence sets $S(\mathbf{X})$ at level $(1-\alpha)$ is finally given by

$$\begin{aligned} S(\mathbf{x}) &= \{\mu : \mathbf{x} \in A(\mu)\} \\ &= \left(-z_{\alpha/2} \leq \frac{\sqrt{n}(\bar{x}-\mu)}{\sigma} \leq z_{\alpha/2}\right) \\ &= \left(-\frac{\sigma}{\sqrt{n}}\, z_{\alpha/2} \leq (\mu - \bar{x}) \leq \frac{\sigma}{\sqrt{n}}\, z_{\alpha}\right) \\ &= \left(\bar{x} - \frac{\sigma}{\sqrt{n}}\, z_{\alpha/2} \leq \mu \leq \bar{x} + \frac{\sigma}{\sqrt{n}}\, z_{\alpha/2}\right) \end{aligned}$$

**Example 8.6.5.** *Let $X_1, \ldots, X_n$ be a sample from $U(0, \theta)$. Consider the testing problem*

$$H_0 : \theta = \theta_0 \quad \textit{against} \quad H_1 : \theta \neq \theta_0$$

*Find out a UMA family of confidence intervals for $\theta$ at level $(1-\alpha)$.*

***Solution:*** The UMP unbiased size-$\alpha$ test for the above testing problem is given by

$$\phi(\mathbf{x}) = \begin{cases} 1 & \text{if } \max(x_1, \ldots, x_n) < c_1 \\ & \text{or } \max(x_1, \ldots, x_n) > c_2 \\ 0 & \text{otherwise} \end{cases}$$

Let us denote $M_n = \max(X_1, \ldots, X_n)$ and let $c_1$ and $c_2$ be obtained by the size condition

$$E_{\theta_0}[\phi(M_n)] = \alpha \quad \text{or} \quad \int_{c_1}^{c_2} g_{M_n}(y)|_{\theta=\theta_0}\, dy = 1-\alpha$$

where, the density of $M_n$ is given by $g_{M_n}(y)|_{\theta=\theta_0} = ny^{n-1}\theta^{-n}$. Let $\alpha$ be divided equally in tails, we get $c_1$ and $c_2$ such that

$$\int_0^{c_1} ny^{n-1}\theta_0^{-n} dy = \alpha/2 = \int_{c_2}^{\theta_0} ny^{n-1}\theta_0^{-n} dy$$

We have

$$n\theta_0^{-n} \frac{y^n}{n}\bigg|_0^{c_1} = \alpha/2$$

$$c_1^n = \theta_0^n.\alpha/2 \quad \text{or} \quad c_1 = \theta_0(\alpha/2)^{1/n}$$

and

$$n\theta_0^{-n} \frac{y^n}{n}\bigg|_{c_2}^{\theta_0} = \alpha/2$$

$$\theta_0^n - c_2^n = \theta_0^n \cdot \alpha/2$$

$$c_2^n = (1-\alpha/2)\theta_0^n \quad \text{or} \quad c_2 = \theta_0(1-\alpha/2)^{1/n}$$

The corresponding acceptance region is given by

$$A(\theta_0) = \{\mathbf{x} \,:\, \theta_0(\alpha/2)^{1/n} \le M_n \le \theta_0(1-\alpha/2)^{1/n}\}$$

Utilizing the result of the theorem 8.3.1, the UMA unbiased family of $(1-\alpha)$ level confidence sets is given by

$$\begin{aligned} S(\mathbf{x}) &= \{\theta \,:\, \mathbf{x} \in A(\theta)\} \\ &= \{\mathbf{x} \,:\, \theta_0(\alpha/2)^{1/n} \le M_n \le \theta_0(1-\alpha/2)^{1/n}\} \\ &= \Big((\alpha/2)^{1/n} \le \frac{M_n}{\theta} \le (1-\alpha/2)^{1/n}\Big) \\ &= \Big(\frac{1}{(1-\alpha/2)^{1/n}} \le \frac{\theta}{M_n} \le \frac{1}{(\alpha/2)^{1/n}}\Big) \\ &= \Big(\frac{M_n}{(1-\alpha/2)^{1/n}} \le \theta \le \frac{M_n}{(\alpha/2)^{1/n}}\Big) \end{aligned}$$

**Example 8.6.6.** *Let $X_1, \ldots, X_n$ be a sample drawn from $N(\mu_0, \sigma^2)$, where, $\sigma^2$ is unknown and $\mu = \mu_0$ is known. Test the hypothesis*

$$H_0 : \sigma = \sigma_0 \quad \textit{against} \quad H_1 : \sigma \neq \sigma_0$$

*and find out a UMA unbiased family of confidence intervals for $\sigma^2$ at level $(1-\alpha)$.*

***Solution:*** The UMP unbiased test for the testing problem $H_0 : \sigma = \sigma_0$ against $H_1 : \sigma \neq \sigma_0$ is given by

$$\phi(\mathbf{x}) = \begin{cases} 1 & \text{if } \dfrac{\sum(x_i-\mu_0)^2}{\sigma^2} < c_1 \\ & \text{or } \dfrac{\sum(x_i-\mu_0)^2}{\sigma^2} > c_2 \\ 0 & \text{otherwise} \end{cases}$$

where, constants $c_1$ and $c_2$ are determined by the size condition

$$E_{\sigma_0}[\phi(\mathbf{X})] = \alpha$$

or

$$P_{\sigma_0}\Big\{c_1 \le \frac{\sum(X_i-\mu_0)^2}{\sigma_0^2} \le c_2\Big\} = 1-\alpha$$

$c_1$ and $c_2$ and chosen as

$$\int_0^{c_1} \chi_n^2(y)\,dy = \alpha/2 = \int_{c_2}^{\infty} \chi_n^2(y)\,dy$$

which gives

$$c_1 = \chi^2_{n,\,(1-\alpha/2)};\ c_2 = \chi^2_{n,\,\alpha/2}$$

Thus, the acceptance region corresponding to UMP unbiased size-$\alpha$ test $\phi(\mathbf{x})$ for testing $H_0 : \sigma = \sigma_0$ against $H_1 : \sigma \neq \sigma_0$ is given by

$$A(\sigma_0) = \{\mathbf{x} : \chi^2_{n,(1-\alpha/2)} \leq \frac{\sum(x_i - \mu_0)^2}{\sigma^2} \leq \chi^2_{n,\alpha/2}\}$$

Further, by utilizing the result of Theorem 8.3.1, UMAU $(1 - \alpha)$ level family of confidence sets $S(\mathbf{x})$ is given by

$$\begin{aligned} S(\mathbf{x}) &= \{\sigma : \mathbf{x} \in A(\sigma)\} \\ &= \left(\chi^2_{n,(1-\alpha/2)} \leq \frac{\sum(x_i - \mu_0)^2}{\sigma^2} \leq \chi^2_{n,\alpha/2}\right) \\ &= \left(\frac{\sum(x_i - \mu_0)^2}{\chi^2_{n,\alpha/2}} \leq \sigma^2 \leq \frac{\sum(x_i - \mu_0)^2}{\chi^2_{n,(1-\alpha/2)}}\right) \end{aligned}$$

**Example 8.6.7.** *Let $X_1, \ldots, X_m$ and $Y_1, \ldots, Y_n$ be independent samples from $N(\mu, \sigma^2)$ and $N(\theta, \sigma^2)$ respectively. Consider the testing problem*

$$H_0 : \mu - \theta = \delta \quad \text{against} \quad H_1 : \mu - \theta \neq \delta$$

*Find out a UMA family of unbiased confidence intervals for $(\mu - \theta)$ at level $(1 - \alpha)$.*

***Solution:*** Here, $\mu, \theta$ and $\sigma^2$ are unknown. We have already shown the following test as UMP unbiased of size-$\alpha$

$$\phi(\mathbf{x}, \mathbf{y}) = \begin{cases} 1 & \text{if} \quad \dfrac{|\bar{x} - \bar{y} - \delta|/\sqrt{(\frac{1}{m} + \frac{1}{n})}}{\sqrt{\{\sum(x_i - \bar{x})^2 + \sum(y_i + \bar{y})^2\}/m + n - 2}} > c \\ 0 & \text{otherwise} \end{cases} \tag{8.3}$$

The constant $c$ is determined by the size condition

$$E_{\mu-\theta=\delta}[\phi(\mathbf{X}, \mathbf{Y})] = \alpha$$

$$P_{\mu-\theta=\delta}\left[\frac{|\overline{X} - \overline{Y} - \delta|/\sqrt{(\frac{1}{m} + \frac{1}{n})}}{s_p} > c\right] = \alpha$$

where

$$s_p^2 = \frac{1}{m + n - 2}\{\sum(x_i - \bar{x})^2 + \sum(y_i - \bar{y})^2\}$$

and

$$c = t_{m+n-2,\alpha/2}$$

Therefore, the acceptance region, corresponding to the UMP unbiased test in Eq. (8.3) is given by

$$A(\delta) = \left\{(\mathbf{x}, \mathbf{y}) : \frac{|\bar{x} - \bar{y} - \delta|/\sqrt{(\frac{1}{m} + \frac{1}{n})}}{s_p} \leq t_{m+n-2,\alpha/2}\right\}$$

By utilizing the result of Theorem 8.3.1, the UMAU $(1-\alpha)$ level family of confidence sets $S(\mathbf{X})$ is given by

$$S(\mathbf{x}) = \{\delta : (\mathbf{x}, \mathbf{y}) \in A(\delta)\}$$

$$S(\mathbf{x}) = \left\{-t_{m+n-2,\,\alpha/2} \leq \frac{(\bar{x}-\bar{y})-\delta}{s_p\sqrt{\frac{1}{m}+\frac{1}{n}}} \leq t_{m+n-2,\,\alpha/2}\right\}$$

$$= \left\{(\bar{x}-\bar{y}) - s_p\sqrt{\frac{1}{m}+\frac{1}{n}}\,t_{m+n-2,\alpha/2} \leq \delta(=\mu-\theta)\right.$$

$$\left.\leq (\bar{x}-\bar{y}) + s_p\sqrt{\frac{1}{m}+\frac{1}{n}}\,t_{m+n-2,\,\alpha/2}\right\}$$

**Example 8.6.8.** *Let $X_1, \ldots, X_n$ be a sample from $N(\mu, \sigma^2)$ where, $\mu$ and $\sigma^2$ are both unknown. Show that*

$$S(\mathbf{X}) = \left(\overline{X} - t_{n-1,\,\alpha/2}\frac{S}{\sqrt{n-1}}, \overline{X} + t_{n-1,\,\alpha/2}\frac{S}{\sqrt{n-1}}\right)$$

*is minimum expected length confidence interval.*

***Solution:*** Let us consider the pivot

$$T(\mathbf{X}, \mu) = \frac{\overline{X}-\mu}{S/\sqrt{n-1}} \sim t_{(n-1)}$$

where

$$S^2 = \frac{1}{n}\sum_{i=1}^{n}(X_i - \overline{X})^2$$

We know from the theory of confidence interval estimation that the given confidence interval $S(\mathbf{X})$ is of shortest length and that this is UMAU confidence interval that corresponds to UMP unbiased test of size-$\alpha$. Therefore, by utilizing the results of Theorem 8.4.1, $S(\mathbf{X})$ is confidence interval with minimum expected length, i.e. $E_\theta^{\mathbf{X}} S(\mathbf{X})$.

**Example 8.6.9.** *Let $X_1, \ldots, X_n$ be a random sample drawn from $N(\mu, \sigma^2)$. Find out $(1-\alpha)$ level family of unbiased confidence intervals for $\sigma^2$ by using Guenther procedure.*

***Solution:*** Consider the pivot

$$T(\mathbf{X}, \sigma^2) = \frac{nS^2}{\sigma^2} \sim \chi^2_{n-1} \text{ where } S^2 = \frac{1}{n}\sum_{1}^{n}(X_i - \bar{X})^2$$

We have

$$P_{\sigma^2}\left\{\lambda_1 < \frac{nS^2}{\sigma^2} < \lambda_2\right\} = 1-\alpha$$

or

$$P_{\sigma^2}\Big\{n\cdot\frac{S^2}{\lambda_2}<\sigma^2<n\cdot\frac{S^2}{\lambda_1}\Big\}=1-\alpha$$

Consider

$$P(\theta,\theta')=P(\sigma^2,\sigma'^2)=P_{\sigma^2}\Big\{n\cdot\frac{S^2}{\lambda_2}<\sigma'^2<n\cdot\frac{S^2}{\lambda_1}\Big\}$$

Let

$$\gamma=\frac{\sigma'^2}{\sigma^2};\quad P(\sigma^2,\sigma'^2)=P_{\sigma^2}\Big\{\frac{1}{\lambda_2}\frac{nS^2}{\sigma^2}<\frac{\sigma'^2}{\sigma^2}<\frac{1}{\lambda_1}\frac{nS^2}{\sigma^2}\Big\}$$

$$P(\sigma^2,\sigma'^2)=P_{\sigma^2}\Big\{\frac{T(\mathbf{X},\sigma^2)}{\lambda_2}<\gamma<\frac{T(\mathbf{X},\sigma^2)}{\lambda_1}\Big\}$$

or

$$P(\gamma)=P\Big\{\lambda_1\gamma<T(\mathbf{X},\sigma^2)<\lambda_2\gamma\Big\}$$

We have

$$P(1)=1-\alpha\qquad \text{if }\ \sigma'^2=\sigma^2$$

$$\frac{\partial}{\partial\gamma}P(\gamma)\Big|_{\gamma=1}=\lambda_2 f_{n-1}(\lambda_2)-\lambda_1 f_{n-1}(\lambda_1)=0 \tag{8.4}$$

where, $f_{n-1}$ is the pdf of $T_\sigma$ which is $\chi^2_{n-1}$. Tate and Klett (1959)[200] have solved Eq. (8.4) for $\lambda_1$ and $\lambda_2$ numerically.

Therefore, $(1-\alpha)$ level unbiased confidence interval shall be given by

$$\left(n\frac{S^2}{\lambda_2},\ n\frac{S^2}{\lambda_1}\right)$$

**Example 8.6.10.** *Discuss whether the unbiased confidence interval for $\sigma^2$, obtained in Example 8.6.9, minimizes the expected length, i.e. $E[S(\mathbf{X})]$.*

*Solution:* We consider here the testing problem

$$H_0:\sigma=\sigma_0,\quad \mu\in\mathbb{R}^1\quad\text{against}\quad H_1:\sigma\neq\sigma_0,\quad \mu\in\mathbb{R}^1$$

We know that a UMP unbiased size-$\alpha$ test for the above testing problem is given by

$$\phi_0(\mathbf{x})=\begin{cases}1 & \text{if }\ \dfrac{\sum(x_i-\bar{x})^2}{\sigma_0^2}<c_1\ \text{ or }\ >c_2\\[2ex] 0 & \text{otherwise}\end{cases}$$

where, the constants $c_1, c_2$ are obtained by the following two conditions

$$E_{\sigma_0}[\phi_0(\mathbf{X})]=\alpha \tag{8.5}$$

and

$$E_{\sigma_0}[\mathbf{X}\phi_0(\mathbf{X})] = \alpha E_{\sigma_0}[\mathbf{X}] \tag{8.6}$$

We know that

$$\left.\frac{nS^2}{\sigma}\right|_{H_0:\sigma^2=\sigma_0^2} \sim \chi^2_{n-1}$$

Therefore, the Eqs. (8.5) and (8.6) reduce to

$$\text{(a)} \qquad \int_{c_1}^{c_2} \chi^2_{n-1}(y)\, dy = 1 - \alpha \tag{8.7}$$

$$\text{and (b)} \qquad (n-1) - \int_{c_1}^{c_2} y\, \chi^2_{n-1}(y)\, dy = (n-1)\alpha \tag{8.8}$$

or

$$\frac{1}{(n-1)} \int_{c_1}^{c_2} y\, \chi^2_{n-1}(y)\, dy = (1-\alpha)$$

Now consider the identity

$$y\, \chi^2_{n-1}(y) = (n-1)\, \chi^2_{n+1}(y)$$

From condition (b) we get

$$\int_{c_1}^{c_2} \chi^2_{n+1}(y)\, dy = 1 - \alpha$$

$$= \int_{c_1}^{c_2} \chi^2_{n-1}(y)\, dy \quad \text{(by condition (a) on size)}$$

Usually in practice the type I error $\alpha$ is divided equally in tails of $\chi^2_{n-1}$ distribution, we get $c_1$ and $c_2$ as:

$$\int_0^{c_1} \chi^2_{n-1}(y)\, dy = \int_{c_2}^{\infty} \chi^2_{n-1}(y)\, dy = \alpha/2$$

so that

$$c_1 = \chi^2_{n-1,\, 1-\alpha/2}; \quad c_2 = \chi^2_{n-1,\, \alpha/2}$$

Subsequently, UMPU size-$\alpha$ acceptance region is given by

$$A(\sigma_0) = \left\{\mathbf{x} : c_1 < \frac{nS^2}{\sigma_0^2} < c_2\right\}$$

Therefore, the corresponding UMAU $(1-\alpha)$ level confidence interval is given by

$$S(\mathbf{x}) = \left(n\,\frac{S^2}{c_2},\, n\,\frac{S^2}{c_1}\right)$$

Note that $c_1$ and $c_2$ are obtained by the conditions

$$\int_{c_1}^{c_2} \chi^2_{n-1}(y)\, dy = 1 - \alpha$$

or

$$P_{\sigma_0^2}\left(c_1 < n \cdot \frac{S^2}{\sigma_0^2} < c_2\right) = 1 - \alpha$$

which is equivalent to $P(1) = 1 - \alpha$. Further, consider

$$\frac{1}{(n-1)} \int_{c_1}^{c_2} y\, \chi^2_{n-1}(y)\, dy = 1 - \alpha$$

On differentiating it with respect to $y$, we get

$$c_2 f_{n-1}(c_2) - c_1 f_{n-1}(c_1) = 0$$

Therefore, we see that the family of $(1-\alpha)$ level unbiased confidence intervals following Guenther's procedure and UMAU $(1-\alpha)$ level confidence intervals are identical. It is, therefore, the obtained interval minimizes the expected length, i.e. $ES(\mathbf{X})$. Further, $(1-\alpha)$ level shortest length confidence intervals is obtained by getting $c_1, c_2$ (or $\lambda_1, \lambda_2$) so that

$$P(c_1 < f_{n-1} < c_2) = 1 - \alpha \quad \text{and} \quad c_1^2 f_{n-1}(c_1) = c_2^2 f_{n-1}(c_2)$$

If we compare the conditions for obtaining UMAU $(1-\alpha)$ level minimum expected length confidence intervals with that of shortest length confidence intervals, the length of the farmer is considerably large as compared to the latter. It has been investigated that for large $n$ both the lengths of confidence intervals are approximately same.

## *Review Questions*

**8.1** Explain how the method of confidence intervals is connected with the theory of testing of hypotheses. Illustrate your answer with an example.

**8.2** Obtain the shortest length confidence interval for the mean of a normal population with unknown variance.

**8.3** What are uniformly most accurate confidence sets? Bring out the relationship between uniformly most accurate (UMA) confidence sets of confidence coefficient $(1-\alpha)$ and uniformly most powerful non-randomized tests of level $\alpha$.

**8.4** Let $A(\theta_0)$ be acceptance region of a UMP test of size-$\alpha$ of the hypothesis $H_0 : \theta = \theta_0$ against $H_1 : \theta \in \overline{H}(\theta_0)$. Find out the uniformly most accurate family of confidence sets at level $(1-\alpha)$.

**8.5** Let $X_1, \ldots, X_n$ be a sample from $N(\mu, \sigma^2)$, where both $\mu$ and $\sigma^2$ are unknown. For testing

$$H_0 : \mu = \mu_0 \quad \text{against} \quad H_1 : \mu \neq \mu_0$$

the UMP unbiased size-$\alpha$ test is given by

$$\phi(\mathbf{x}) = \begin{cases} 1 & \text{if } \dfrac{\sqrt{n}|\bar{x} - \mu_0|}{s} > c \\ 0 & \text{otherwise} \end{cases}$$

where $$\bar{x} = \frac{1}{n}\sum_{1}^{n} x_i, \; s^2 = \frac{1}{n-1}\sum_{1}^{n}(x_i - \bar{x})^2$$

Find out UMA unbiased family of confidence sets at level $1 - \alpha$.

**8.6** (a) Let $x_1, x_2, \ldots, x_n$ be a sample from $N(\mu, \sigma^2)$ where, both $\mu$ and $\sigma^2$ are unknown. Consider the testing problem $H_0 : \mu = \mu_0$ versus $H_1 : \mu \neq \mu_0$. Show by using Basu's theorem, the test

$$\phi(\mathbf{x}) = \begin{cases} 1 & \text{if } \dfrac{\sqrt{n}|\bar{x} - \mu_0|}{s} \\ 0 & \text{otherwise} \end{cases}$$

is UMP unbiased size-$\alpha$ test.

(b) Find out uniformly most accurate unbiased family of confidence sets at level $1 - \alpha$. Also, state the theorems, results, etc. used.

(c) Find out $S(\mathbf{X})$, a family of $1 - \alpha$ level confidence intervals, which minimizes the expected length $E[S(\mathbf{X})]$. State the theorems, results used.

**8.7** Let the parameter space $\Theta$ be the real line, and let the random variable $X$ be $N(\theta - 1, 1)$ if $\theta < 0$, $N(0, 1)$ if $\theta = 0$ and $N(\theta + 1, 1)$ if $\theta > 0$. Find a uniformly most accurate family of confidence sets for $\theta$ at confidence level $1 - \alpha$.

**8.8** Find the uniformly most accurate unbiased (UMAU) confidence interval for $\sigma^2$ at level $1 - \alpha$ from testing of $H_0 : \sigma = \sigma_0$ against $H_1 : \sigma \neq \sigma_0$ on the basis of likelihood ratio test when a sample $x_1, x_2, \ldots, x_n$ has been drawn from $N(\mu, \sigma^2)$, where both $\mu$ and $\sigma^2$ are unknown.

**8.9** (a) Investigate the relationship between interval estimation and hypothesis testing.

(b) Let $X_1, X_2, \ldots, X_n$ be a random sample from:

$$f(x, \theta) = e^{-(x-\theta)} \quad ; \quad \text{x} > \theta$$

Find the shortest length confidence interval for $\theta$ at level $(1 - \alpha)$.

# Chapter 9

# Non-parametric Tests

## 9.1 INTRODUCTION

The subject matter of statistics is usually divided into two categories, namely—*descriptive statistics* and *inductive statistics*. Descriptive statistics relates to the data summarizing statistics, e.g., mean, median, and variance. On the other hand, when a sample is drawn from the population to infer some of its characteristics, the subject matter is called the inductive statistics or statistical inference.

The entire body of classical inference is based on the assumptions imposed on the underlying population. In other words, the tests developed in classical inference are valid so long as these assumptions are satisfied, keeping apart the robustness issues. This domain of study is termed as *parametric testing procedures*. Sometimes, in real life situations, these assumptions are not met and causes break down of parametric procedures. Under these circumstances the alternatively developed procedures are known as *distribution-free or non-parametric procedures*. In the distribution free inference (both for testing and estimation) the procedures involve a function of sample observations so that its distribution does not depend on the underlying population distribution. It is in this sense that such procedures are known as distribution free, since the distribution of the test statistic is free from the population distribution. In addition to it, the non-parametric tests are developed for such hypothesis testing problems which are not the statements of the population parameter. The hypothesis concerning the median cannot be considered as a non-parametric testing problem in the strict sense, since median is itself a parameter; but it is taken as a valid non-parametric testing problem since the distribution of the test statistics does not involve the parent population distribution. Despite these inconsistencies, we would make no distinction between these non-parametric procedures while developing the theory on non-parametric testing, in the present and the following chapters.

## 9.2 EMERGING DEFINITION OF NON-PARAMETRICS

The non-parametrics is the study of the inference problems where the specific assumptions on the underlying populations are replaced by some very general assumptions, and further that the study is based on some function of sample observations, i.e., statistics whose distribution could be obtained without the knowledge of the underlying population distribution. The assumptions that are required on the underlying population are very general in nature, e.g., population be continuous or its distribution be symmetric. In non-parametric inference we consider some function of the actual magnitude of the observations and ignore the actual magnitudes in developing these procedures, e.g., the sample observations here may be replaced by their relative ranks in the sample. Some function of these ranks may be taken as a test statistic whose distribution can be determined by assuming only very general assumptions on the underlying population. These tests may relate to whatever parameters are relevant and adaptable such as median for a location parameter. These procedures are basically distribution-free and are broadly known as non-parametric tests. It can be noted that the parametric and non-parametric procedures are analogous both relating to location, and identical in case of a continuous and symmetric populations.

### 9.2.1 Merits of Non-parametric Testing Procedures

(a) NP procedures involve simple calculations, therefore, these are quick and easy to apply;

(b) NP involves much simpler and less sophisticated mathematics to derive the distribution of the test statistics as one requires these in parametric testing. In most cases NP tests are the discrete random variables with non-zero probabilities, assigned only to a finite number of values and its exact sampling distribution could easily be calculated by simple combinatorial mathematics;

(c) The asymptotic distribution of the NP test statistic under $H_0$ is usually known, e.g., normal and chi-square;

(d) The assumptions on underlying population are so general that these absorb the inappropriate and indiscriminate uses of NP tests by untrained users;

(e) NP procedures are based on sample ranks and not on the actual magnitude of the sample observations, therefore, the inferences are unaffected in case of dirty data. It is for this reason that these procedures may be less-expensive and time saving;

(f) Some new types of problems relating to sample-distribution characteristics are solvable with NP tests.

In non-parametrics, the actual observations on the sample are ignored and apparently it seems that we have deliberately ignored the available information. As a result, we expect to pay its price by loosing on efficiency. However, the related literatures suggest that we do not loose any thing, since the information embodied in the actual magnitude of the observations that have been ignored is actually irrelevant to the distribution of the underlying population and which is not relevant to the distribution-free tests. It is for this reason that the NP tests are almost as efficient as their counterpart parametric tests where the actual magnitude of observations are fully utilized.

## 9.3 PERFORMANCE OF NP TESTS

The performance of any NP test depends on many factors, e.g., sample size and significance level. Box and Anderson have given the criterion of the performance of a test that it should be sensitive to change in the specific factors being tested, referred to as *power* and it should be insensitive to changes in extraneous factors which are most likely expected in practice referred to as *robustness.* Generally, robustness is taken as a performance criterion of parametric tests and power for non-parametric tests. But the power calculations are usually complex since it requires the distribution of the test statistic under the alternative hypothesis which are very general. Therefore, we shall discuss only those which are universally accepted as a performance criterion. These are defined as follows:

**Definition 9.3.1. (Consistency)** A test is said to be consistent for a specified alternative, if the power of the test, when the alternative is true, approaches one (1) as the sample size approaches infinity.

**Definition 9.3.2. (Pitman Efficiency)** Pitman efficiency is an objective criterion of judging the performance of two or more tests. Box and Anderson have stated that the power is the measure of accuracy of tests.

The Pitman efficiency of a test A relative to a test B, where both tests have same simple null hypothesis, the same type of critical region, and the same significance level, i.e., $\alpha$, is the ratio of $n_b$, the number of observations employed by test B, to $n_a$, the number of observations required by test A to equal its power to that of B.

$$\text{PE of A relative to B} = \frac{n_b}{n_a}$$

Pitman efficiency generally depends on the selected significance level, hypothesis, and $n_b$, it is difficult to calculate and interpret. This difficulty could be dealt with in many cases by defining a type of limiting power efficiency, that we shall discuss in Section 9.4.

## 9.4 ASYMPTOTIC RELATIVE EFFICIENCY

Let $T$ and $T^*$ be two consistent tests of $H_0$ against $H_1$ at significance level $\alpha$. The asymptotic relative efficiency (ARE) of $T$ relative to $T^*$ is the limiting value of the ratio $n^*/n$, where $n$ is the number of observations required by test $T$ to equal its power $\gamma$ to that of test $T^*$ based on $n^*$ observations, simultaneously $n^* \to \infty$ and $H_1 \to H_0$. This limiting number is usually independent of the choices of $\alpha$ and $\gamma$ or even the values of the parameters in the neighbourhood of the hypothesized value. Since this is single number well-defined and its interpretation is possible, it is for this reason that it is a well accepted comparison criterion, even though it is a large sample property.

### 9.4.1 Formal Definition of ARE

Let $T_n$ and $T_n^*$ be two statistics based on $n$ observations to test the hypothesis

$$H_0 : \theta \in \Theta_0 \quad \text{against} \quad H_1 : \theta \in \Theta_1$$

where

$$\Theta = \{\theta_0, \theta_1, \ldots, \theta_n, \ldots, \}; \theta_0 \in \Theta_0, \theta_1, \ldots, \theta_n, \cdots \in \Theta_1$$

so that the points $\theta_0, \theta_1, \ldots, \theta_n, \ldots$ form a sequence $\{\theta_n\}$ such that

$$\lim_{n \to \infty} \theta_n = \theta_0$$

Let the sequences of test statistics $\{T_n\}$ and $\{T_n^*\}$ be on the same significance level $\alpha$ and $\{n_i\}$ and $\{n_i^*\}$ be two monotonically increasing sequences of positive integers such that

$$\lim_{i \to \infty} \beta_{T_{n_i}}(\theta_i) = \lim \beta_{T_{n_i}}(\theta_i) = \gamma$$

where $0 < \gamma < 1$ and $\beta_{T_{n_i}}(\cdot)$ is the power of the test $T_{n_i}$ at the point $\theta_i$.

Then the asymptotic relative efficiency of the test $T$ relative to $T^*$ is defined as

$$ARE(T, T^*) = \lim_{i \to \infty} \frac{n_i^*}{n_i}$$

if this limit exists and is constant for all sequences $\{n_i\}$ and $\{n_i^*\}$ [we refer Fraser, 1957, p 270][66].

### 9.4.2 Constructive Definition of ARE and Some Results on its Calculations

Let us consider two sequences of consistent tests $\{T_n\}$ and $\{T_n^*\}$ both of size-$\alpha$ for testing the hypothesis

$$H_0 : \theta = \theta_0 \quad \text{against} \quad H_1 : \theta > \theta_0$$

From $\Theta_1 = \{\theta \mid \theta > \theta_0\}$ we take a monotonic decreasing sequence of numbers $\theta_1, \theta_2, \ldots$ which converges to $\theta_0$ from above, so that $\lim_{n \to \infty} \theta_n = \theta_0$. Let the tests $T_n$ and $T_n^*$ be of the form $t_n \geq t_{n,\alpha}$ and $t_n^* \geq t_{n,\alpha}^*$ where, $t_{n,\alpha}$ and $t_{n,\alpha}^*$ are chosen such that

$$P_{\theta_0}(T_n \geq t_{n,\alpha}) = \alpha \quad \text{and} \quad P_{\theta_0}(T_n \geq t_{n,\alpha}^*) = \alpha$$

we shall give some regularity conditions for $T_n$, which would analogously hold for $T_n^*$.

(a) $\frac{d}{d\theta}E(T_n)$ exists and is non-zero for $\theta = \theta_0$ and is continuous at $\theta_0$.

(b) There exists a positive constant $c$ such that

$$\lim_{n\to\infty} \frac{\frac{d}{d\theta}E(T_n)|_{\theta=\theta_0}}{\sqrt{n}\,\sigma(T_n)|_{\theta=\theta_0}} = c$$

(c) There exists a sequence of alternatives $\{\theta_n\}$ such that for some constant $d > 0$, we have

(i) $\theta_n = \theta_0 + \frac{d}{\sqrt{n}}$

(ii) $\lim_{n\to\infty} \frac{\frac{d}{d\theta}E(T_n)|_{\theta=\theta_n}}{\frac{d}{d\theta}E(T_n)|_{\theta=\theta_0}} = 1$

(iii) $\lim_{n\to\infty} \frac{\sigma(T_n)|_{\theta=\theta_n}}{\sigma(T_n)|_{\theta=\theta_0}} = 1$

(d) $\lim_{n\to\infty} P_{\theta_n}\left\{\frac{T_n - E(T_n)|_{\theta=\theta_n}}{\sigma(T_n)|_{\theta=\theta_n}} \le z\right\} = \phi(z)$

**Theorem 9.4.1.** (Gibbons, 1971, p 270, [71]) *Under the above four regularity conditions, the limiting power of the test $T_n$ is*

$$\lim_{n\to\infty} \beta_{T_n}(\theta_n) = 1 - \phi(z_\alpha - dc)$$

*where, $z_\alpha$ is the number obtained so that $1 - \phi(z_\alpha) = \alpha$*

*Proof.* The limiting power would be given by

$$\lim_{n\to\infty} P_{\theta_n}(T_n \ge t_{n,\alpha}) = \lim_{n\to\infty} P_{\theta_n}\left\{\frac{T_n - E(T_n)|_{\theta=\theta_n}}{\upsilon(T_n)|_{\theta=\theta_n}} \ge \frac{t_{n,\alpha} - E(T_n)|_{\theta=\theta_n}}{\sigma(T_n)|_{\theta=\theta_n}}\right\} = 1 - \phi(z)$$

where

$$z = \lim_{n\to\infty} \frac{t_{n,\alpha} - E(T_n)|_{\theta=\theta_n}}{\sigma(T_n)|_{\theta=\theta_n}}$$

$$z = \lim_{n\to\infty}\left\{\frac{t_{n,\alpha} - E(T_n)|_{\theta=\theta_n}}{\sigma(T_n)|_{\theta=\theta_0}} \cdot \frac{\sigma(T_n)|_{\theta=\theta_0}}{\sigma(T_n)|_{\theta=\theta_n}}\right\}$$

$$= \lim_{n\to\infty}\left\{\frac{t_{n,\alpha} - E(T_n)|_{\theta=\theta_n}}{\sigma(T_n)|_{\theta=\theta_0}}\right\}$$

(from the regularity condition (c) (iii) of subsection 9.4.2)

Expanding $E(T_n)|_{\theta=\theta_n}$ in a Taylor's series about $\theta_0$, we get

$$E(T_n)|_{\theta=\theta_n} = E(T_n)|_{\theta=\theta_0} + (\theta_n - \theta_0) \cdot \frac{d}{d\theta} E(T_n)\Big|_{\theta=\theta_0} + \epsilon$$

where

$$\begin{aligned}
\epsilon &= \frac{(\theta_n - \theta_0)^k}{k!} \frac{d^k}{d\theta^k} E(T_n)\big|_{\theta=\theta_0}; k = 2, 3, \ldots \\
&= \frac{d^k}{k!} \cdot \frac{1}{n^{k/2}} \cdot \frac{d^k}{d\theta^k} E(T_n)|_{\theta=\theta_0};\ k = 2, 3, \ldots \\
&\to 0 \text{ as } n \to \infty
\end{aligned}$$

On putting the value of $E(T_n)|_{\theta=\theta_n}$ in the expression of $z$, we get

$$\begin{aligned}
z &= \lim_{n\to\infty} \left\{ \frac{t_{n,\,\alpha} - E(T_n)|_{\theta=\theta_0}}{\sigma(T_n)|_{\theta=\theta_0}} - \frac{(\theta_n - \theta_0)\frac{d}{d\theta} E(T_n)|_{\theta=\theta_0} + \epsilon}{\sigma(T_n)|_{\theta=\theta_0}} \right\} \\
&= \lim_{n\to\infty} \left\{ \frac{t_{n,\,\alpha} - E(T_n)|_{\theta=\theta_0}}{\sigma(T_n)|_{\theta=\theta_0}} - \lim_{n\to\infty} d \cdot \frac{\frac{d}{d\theta} E(T_n)|_{\theta=\theta_0}}{\sqrt{n}\sigma(T_n)|_{\theta=\theta_0}} - \lim_{n\to\infty} \frac{\epsilon}{\sigma(T_n)|_{\theta=\theta_0}} \right\} \\
&\qquad \text{(from the regularity condition (c)(i)))} \\
&= \lim_{n\to\infty} \left\{ \frac{t_{n,\alpha} - E(T_n)|_{\theta=\theta_0}}{\sigma(T_n)|_{\theta=\theta_0}} \right\} - dc \quad \text{(from condition (b))}
\end{aligned}$$

The test $T_n$ is given to be of size-$\alpha$

$$\begin{aligned}
\alpha = \lim_{n\to\infty} P_{\theta_0}(T_n \geq t_{n,\,\alpha}) &= \lim_{n\to\infty} P_{\theta_0} \left\{ \frac{T_n - E(T_n)|_{\theta=\theta_0}}{\sigma(T_n)|_{\theta=\theta_0}} \right. \\
&\qquad \left. \geq \frac{t_{n,\,\alpha} - E(T_n)|_{\theta=\theta_0}}{\sigma(T_n)|_{\theta=\theta_0}} \right\} \\
&= 1 - \phi\left\{ \lim_{n\to\infty} \left\{ \frac{t_{n,\,\alpha} - E(T_n)|_{\theta=\theta_0}}{\sigma(T_n)|_{\theta=\theta_0}} \right\} \right\} \text{ [from condition (d)]}
\end{aligned}$$

This gives

$$\lim_{n\to\infty} \frac{t_{n,\,\alpha} - E(T_n)|_{\theta=\theta_0}}{\sigma(T_n)|_{\theta=\theta_0}} = z_\alpha$$

We get

$$z = z_\alpha - dc$$

And finally, we get the limiting power

$$\lim_{n\to\infty} \beta_{T_n}(\theta_n) = 1 - \phi(z_\alpha - dc)$$

□

**Theorem 9.4.2.** *Let $T_n$ and $T_n^*$ be two tests satisfying the four regularity conditions (a)–(d), subsection 9.4.2, the ARE of $T_n$ relative to $T_n^*$ is*

$$ARE(T, T^*) = \lim_{n\to\infty} \frac{e(T_n)}{e(T_n^*)}$$

*where*

$$e(T_n) = \frac{[\frac{d}{d\theta}E(T_n)]^2}{\sigma^2(T_n)|_{\theta=\theta_0}}$$

*$e(T_n)$ is called the efficacy of the test statistic $T_n$ when the test $T_n$ is used to test the hypothesis $H_0 : \theta = \theta_0$.*

*Proof.* The limiting powers of the tests $T_n$ and $T_n^*$ are

$$1 - \phi(z_\alpha - dc) \quad \text{and} \quad 1 - \phi(z_\alpha - d^*c^*)$$

The limiting powers be equal if

$$z_\alpha - dc = z_\alpha - d^*c^* \quad \text{or} \quad \frac{d^*}{d} = \frac{c}{c^*}$$

Let the sequence of alternatives for the tests $T_n$ and $T_n^*$ be given by $\{\theta_n\}$ and $\{\theta_n^*\}$ as mentioned in 9.4.2(c). These sequences would be same if

$$\theta_n = \theta_n^* \quad \text{or} \quad \theta_0 + \frac{d}{\sqrt{n}} = \theta_0 + \frac{d^*}{\sqrt{n^*}} \quad \text{or} \quad \frac{d^*}{d} = \left(\frac{n^*}{n}\right)^{1/2}$$

ARE is defined as the limit of the ratio of the sample sizes when the limiting power and sequence of alternatives are the same for both tests

$$\begin{aligned}
ARE(T; T^*) &= \frac{n^*}{n} = \left(\frac{d^*}{d}\right)^2 = \left(\frac{c}{c^*}\right)^2 \\
&= \lim_{n\to\infty} \left[\frac{\frac{d}{d\theta}E(T_n)|_{\theta=\theta_0}}{\sqrt{n}\,\sigma(T_n)|_{\theta=\theta_0}} \cdot \frac{\sqrt{n}\,\sigma(T_n^*)|_{\theta=\theta_0}}{\frac{d}{d\theta}E(T_n^*)|_{\theta=\theta_0}}\right]^2 \\
&= \lim_{n\to\infty} \frac{[\frac{d}{d\theta}E(T_n)|_{\theta=\theta_0}]^2}{\sigma^2(T_n)|_{\theta=\theta_0}} \Bigg/ \frac{[\frac{d}{d\theta}E(T_n^*)|_{\theta=\theta_0}]^2}{\sigma^2(T_n^*)|_{\theta=\theta_0}} \\
&= \lim_{n\to\infty} \frac{e(T_n)}{e(T_n^*)}
\end{aligned}$$

□

We note that ARE is independent of the quantities $\alpha$ and $\gamma$. Therefore, ARE does not suffer the disadvantage the power efficiency suffers from.

## 9.5 SOLVED EXAMPLES

**Example 9.5.1.** *Calculate the efficacy of sign test and student's t-test for testing one sample problem of location*

$$H_0 : F_X(x) = F_{X-\theta}(x - \theta)$$

*against one or two-sided alternatives, where $F_{X-\theta}$ is some continuous distribution with median 0. Also, calculate the AREs for sign test against student's t-test for the following populations:*

(a) $F_X$ *as* $N(\theta, \sigma^2)$

(b) $F_X$ *as* $u(\theta - 1/2, \theta + 1/2)$

(c) $F_X$ *as double exponential distribution,* $DE(\lambda, \theta)$ *with density* $f_X(x) = \frac{1}{2}\lambda e^{-\lambda|x-\theta|}$

*and interpret the results.*

***Solution:*** The model stated in the null hypothesis is called a single sample location model. For $F_{X-\theta}$ as continuous with median 0, the model in the hypothesis tells that $F_X$ has median $\theta = 0$. Therefore, the null hypothesis may be restated as

$$H_0 : \theta = 0$$

against an appropriate alternative.

To test this hypothesis, a single sample of size $n$, $X_1, \ldots, X_n$ is drawn from the population $F_X$ and a suitable non-parametric test is then applied. We will learn these non-parametric tests in more detail in Chapters 10 to 12. In the present example, the non-parametric test named sign test has been considered for testing $H_0 : \theta = 0$. Sign test is defined as $S$, the number of positive observations in the sample $X_1, X_2, \ldots, X_n$. The statistics $S$ is distributed as

$$S \sim b(n, p), \quad \text{where } p = P(X > 0) = 1 - F_X(0)$$

We have

$$E(S) = np \quad \text{and} \quad V(S) = np(1 - p)$$

Let us now find

$$\left.\frac{dp}{d\mu}\right|_{\mu=0} = \left.\frac{d}{d\mu}[1 - F_X(0)]\right|_{\mu=0}$$

Now under the model $F_X(x) = F(x - \theta)$ we have, $F_X(0) = F(-\theta)$, and

$$\left.\frac{dp}{d\mu}\right|_{\mu=0} = \left.\frac{d}{d\mu}[1 - F(-\mu)]\right|_{\mu=0} = \left.f(\mu)\right|_{\mu=0} = f(0) = f_X(\mu)$$

$$\text{(since } f_X(x) = f(x - \mu))$$

Further, under $H_0 : \mu = 0, \quad p = 1/2$, so that

$$V(S)|_{\mu=0} = n/4$$

Therefore, the efficacy of sign test is calculated as

$$e(S) = \frac{\left[\frac{d}{d\mu}E(S)\right]^2}{\sigma^2(S)|_{\mu=0}} = \frac{[nf_X(\mu)]^2}{n/4}$$

$$= 4nf_X^2(\mu) = 4nf^2(0)$$

The parametric test for this testing problem is the single sample student's $t$ test if $F_{X-\theta}$ is continuous and symmetric about 0; in this case mean and median of the distribution $F_X$ becomes $\mu = \theta = 0$, where, $\mu$ and $\sigma^2$ are the mean and the variance of $F_X$. The hypothesis may be stated as

$$H_0 : \mu = 0 \text{ (mean} = 0)$$

The test will be given by

$$T_n^* = \frac{\sqrt{n}\,\bar{x}}{s_n} \quad \text{where,} \quad s_n^2 = \frac{1}{n-1}\sum_{i=1}^{n}(x_i - \bar{x})^2$$

For large $n$, note that

$$\lim_{n\to\infty}\left(\frac{s_n}{\sigma}\right) = 1, \quad \text{and rewriting } T_n^* \text{ by}$$

$$T_n^* = \frac{\sqrt{n}\bar{x}}{\sigma}\,\frac{\sigma}{s_n} = \left[\frac{\sqrt{n}(\bar{x} - \mu)}{\sigma} + \frac{\sqrt{n}\mu}{\sigma}\right]\frac{\sigma}{s_n}$$

gives

$$T_n^* = \frac{\sqrt{n}\bar{x}}{\sigma}, \text{ a } z\text{-test for } \sigma \text{ known.}$$

The asymptotic moments of $T_n^*$ are

$$E(T_n^*) = \frac{\sqrt{n}\mu}{\sigma} \quad \text{and} \quad V(T_n^*) = \frac{N\text{Var}(\bar{X})}{\sigma^2} = 1$$

and

$$\frac{d}{d\mu}E(T_n^*)\bigg|_{\mu=0} = \frac{\sqrt{n}}{\sigma}$$

Therefore, the efficacy of student's t-test is given by

$$e(T_n^*) = \frac{[\frac{d}{d\mu}E(T_n^*)]^2}{\sigma^2(T_n^*)|_{\mu=0}} = \frac{n}{\sigma^2}$$

and

$$\text{ARE }(S, T_n^*) = \lim_{n\to\infty} \frac{e(S)}{e(T_n^*)}$$

$$= \lim_{n\to\infty} \frac{4nf^2(0)}{n/\sigma^2} = 4\sigma^2 f^2(0)$$

$$= [2\sigma f(0)]^2$$

(a) $F_X$ is $N(\theta, \sigma^2)$

$$F_X(x) = \phi\Big(\frac{x-\theta}{\sigma}\Big) \quad \text{or} \quad F(x) = \phi\Big(\frac{x}{\sigma}\Big)$$

$$f(0) = \frac{1}{\sqrt{2\pi}\sigma}, \; e(S) = 4n \cdot \frac{1}{2\pi\sigma^2} = \frac{2n}{\pi\sigma^2}$$

$$e(T_n^*) = n/\sigma^2$$

$$\text{ARE }\; (S, T_n^*) = \lim_{n\to\infty} \frac{e(S)}{e(T_n^*)} = \lim_{n\to\infty} \frac{2n/\pi\sigma^2}{n/\sigma^2}$$

$$= \frac{2}{\pi} = \frac{200}{314}$$

The interpretation of ARE calculated as above is that if, while using normal-theory $z$-test, one requires a sample of size 200 to attain a fixed power $\gamma$ at a fixed level of significance $\alpha$, then he must raise the sample size to 314 on using the sign test to attain the same power $\gamma$ and size-$\alpha$.

(b) $F_X(x)$ is uniform, $U(\theta - 1/2, \theta + 1/2)$. This gives

$$f_X(x) = 1 \text{if } \; \theta - 1/2 < x < \theta + 1/2$$

For $\theta = 0$, we have

$$f(x) = 1 \quad \text{if } \; -1/2 < x < 1/2$$

or

$$f(0) = 1 \quad \text{if } \; -1/2 < x < 1/2$$

We shall now calculate $\sigma^2$ for $f_X(x)$

$$\sigma^2 = EX^2 - \{E(X)\}^2$$

$$E[X] = \int_{\theta-1/2}^{\theta+1/2} x\,dx = \frac{x^2}{2}\Big|_{\theta-1/2}^{\theta+1/2} = \frac{1}{2}\Big[(\theta+1/2)^2 - (\theta-1/2)^2\Big]$$

$$= \frac{1}{2}\Big[\theta^2 + \theta + \frac{1}{4} - \theta^2 + \theta - \frac{1}{4}\Big] = \theta$$

and

$$E[X^2] = \int_{\theta-1/2}^{\theta+1/2} x^2 dx = \frac{1}{3}\Big[x^3\Big]_{\theta-1/2}^{\theta+1/2} = \frac{1}{3}[(\theta+1/2)^3 - (\theta-1/2)^3]$$

$$= \frac{1}{3}\Big[\Big(\theta^3 + \frac{3}{2}\theta^2 + \frac{3}{4}\theta + \frac{1}{8}\Big) - \Big(\theta^3 - \frac{3}{2}\theta^2 + \frac{3}{4}\theta - \frac{1}{8}\Big)\Big]$$

$$= \frac{1}{3}\Big[3\theta^2 + \frac{1}{4}\Big] = \Big[\theta^2 + \frac{1}{12}\Big]$$

Therefore,

$$\sigma^2 = EX^2 - \{E(X)\}^2 = \theta^2 + \frac{1}{12} - \theta^2 = 1/12$$

The efficacy of normal-theory test is given by

$$e(T_n^*) = n/\sigma^2 = 12n$$

Next, the efficacy of sign test is given by

$$e(S) = 4nf^2(0) = 4n \qquad (\text{since } f(0) = 1)$$

The ARE of sign test relative to normal theory test would be given by

$$\text{ARE } (S, T_n^*) = \lim_{n\to\infty} \frac{e(S)}{e(T_n^*)} = \lim_{n\to\infty} \frac{4n}{12n}$$
$$= 1/3 = 100/300$$

with the same interpretation as in (a).

(c) $F_X(x)$ follows double exponential distribution $DE(\lambda, \theta)$. Therefore, the density is given by

$$f_X(x) - \frac{1}{2}\lambda e^{-\lambda|x-\theta|}$$

and corresponding to $\theta = 0$, we have

$$f(x) = \frac{1}{2}\lambda e^{-\lambda|x|} \text{ and } f(0) = \frac{1}{2}\lambda$$

We shall now find $\sigma^2$ corresponding to $f_X(x)$

$$\sigma^2 = E\{X^2\} - \{E\{X\}\}^2$$

$$E\{X\} = \int x \cdot \frac{1}{2}\lambda e^{-\lambda|x-\theta|} dx$$

Readers are advise to calculate the ARE of sign test as compared to its counterpart normal theory test and interpret.

**Example 9.5.2.** *Consider two random samples $X_{11}, \ldots, X_{1n_1}$ of size $n_1$ from the population $G_1$ and $X_{21}, \ldots, X_{2n_2}$ of size $n_2$ from the population $G_2$ respectively. Assume that the sample sizes $n_1$ and $n_2$ from the respective populations $G_1$ and $G_2$ bear a definite ratio to the total sample size, i.e.*

$$\lim_{k\to\infty} n_{(k)} = \infty, \quad \lim_{k\to\infty} \frac{n_{1(k)}}{n_{(k)}} = f_1, \ \textit{and} \ \lim_{k\to\infty} \frac{n_{2(k)}}{n_{(k)}} = f_2$$

*where $f_1$ and $f_2$ are such that $0 < f_1 < 1$, $0 < f_2 < 1$ and $f_1 + f_2 = 1$. Calculate the efficacies of non-parametric Wilcoxon-Mann-Whitney test $T_W$ (or U statistic) and the classical two-sample student's t test for testing the identical distributions*

$$H_0 : G_1(x) = G_2(x) \ \ \forall x$$

*under the location problem with the distribution model*

$$G_2(x) = G_1(x - \theta)$$

*Also, calculate ARE of Wilcoxon-Mann-Whitney Test relative to student's t test.*

***Solution:*** We assume that the populations $G_1$ and $G_2$ are absolutely continuous distributions. Under the above distribution model, the null hypothesis may be stated as

$$H_0 : \theta = 0$$

against the alternative $\theta > 0$. Here, the alternative we mean $X_2$ is stochastically larger than $X_1$ or $G_2$ is located to the right of $G_1$

$$P[X_1 < X_2] > P[X_1 > X_2]$$

or
$$\int_{-\infty}^{\infty} G_1(x)\, dG_2(x) > 1/2$$

or
$$\int_{-\infty}^{\infty} [2G_1(x) - 1]\, dG_2(x) > 0$$

Denoting $\int_{-\infty}^{\infty} [2G_1(x) - 1]\, dG_2(x) = \Delta_W(G_1, G_2)$, the alternative hypothesis may be stated as

$$H_1 : \Delta_W(G_1, G_2) > 0$$

Under $H_0 : G_2(x) = G_1(x) \ \forall x$, we have $\Delta_W(G_1, G_2) = 0$. This gives $H_0 : \Delta_W(G_1, G_2) = 0$ (Refer sense-III of Section 11.2).
Under the assumptions, $\frac{n_1}{n} \to f_1$ and $\frac{n_2}{n} \to f_2$, such that, $0 < f_1 < 1$, $0 < f_2 < 1$, $f_1 + f_2 = 1$, the theory developed in the present chapter for calculating efficacy and ARE remains applicable to the two sample case (Refer Section 11.1).

The Wilcoxon-Mann-Whitney test for testing $\Delta_W = 0$ against $\Delta_W > 0$ has been defined by

$$T_W = \sum_{i=1}^{n_2} S_i = \sum_{i=1}^{n_2} R_{2i} \tag{9.1}$$

where $R_{21}, R_{22}, \ldots, R_{2n_2}$ are the ranks of the second sample observations and $S_1, S_2, \ldots, S_{n_2}$ are the corresponding ordered values. An alternative description of this test is more convenient for many purposes. For this define

$$u(x_1, x_2) = \begin{cases} 1 & \text{if } x_1 < x_2 \\ 0 & \text{otherwise} \end{cases} \tag{9.2}$$

And consider the sum

$$U = \sum_{i=1}^{n_1} \sum_{j=1}^{n_2} u(x_{1i}, x_{2j}) \tag{9.3}$$

$U$ is called $U$-statistic and its relation with $T_W$ is given by

$$U = T_W - \frac{n_2(n+1)}{2} \tag{9.4}$$

This shows $T_W$ and $U$ are related and that $T_W$ and $U$ could be used interchangeably for testing $H_0$ against $H_1$ (for more details, refer to Section 11.4).

The class of distributions $(G_1(x), G_2(x))$ under the location model $G_2(x) = G_1(x-\theta)$ may be represented by $(G_0(x)G_0(x-\theta))$, $\theta > 0$. In these notations, the mean of $U$-statistic

$$E(U|\theta) = n_1 n_2 P(X_1 < X_2) = n_1 n_2 \int_{-\infty}^{\infty} G_1(x)\, dG_2(x)$$

$$= n_1 n_2 \int_{-\infty}^{\infty} G_0(x+\theta)\, dG_0(x)$$

so that

$$\frac{d}{d\theta} E(U|\theta)|_{\theta=0} - n_1 n_2 \int_{-\infty}^{\infty} g_0^2(x)\, d(x) \tag{9.5}$$

where $g_0(x)$ is the density corresponding to $G_0(x)$, since $G_0$ is absolutely continuous, and

$$V(U|\theta)|_{\theta=o} = \frac{n_1 n_2 (n+1)}{12} \tag{9.6}$$

(See Section 11.4.1)

The efficacy of $U$-statistic is then given by

$$\text{Efficacy of } U = \frac{[\frac{d}{d0} E(U)|H_0]^2}{V(U|H_0)}$$

$$= \frac{(n_1 n_2 \int_{-\infty}^{\infty} [g_0(x)]^2\, dx)^2}{n_1 n_2 (n+1)/12}$$

$$= \frac{12\, n_1 n_2 (\int_{-\infty}^{\infty} [g_0(x)]^2\, d(x))^2}{n+1}$$

The classical student's $t$- test for testing $\theta = \mu_2 - \mu_1 = 0$($\mu_1$ and $\mu_2$ are the population means of $G_1$ and $G_2$ respectively) for large sample $n = n_1 + n_2$ and based on two sample mean $\bar{X}_1$ and $\bar{X}_2$ is given by

$$Z = \frac{\bar{X}_2 - \bar{X}_1}{\sqrt{\frac{s_1^2}{n_1} + \frac{s_2^2}{n_2}}}\Bigg|_{H_0} \xrightarrow{\mathcal{L}} N(0,1) \tag{9.7}$$

For the location model with elements $(G_1, G_2) = (G_0(x), G_0(x - \theta))$, the asymptotic moments of $Z$ are

$$E(Z|\theta) = \frac{\sqrt{n_1 n_2}\theta}{\sqrt{n}\sigma(G_0)}; \; V(Z|\theta) = 1 \tag{9.8}$$

where $\sigma(G_0)$ is the standard deviation of $G_0(x)$ for which we assume that the second moment exists. Therefore,

$$\frac{d}{d\theta}E(Z|\theta)|_{\theta=0} = \frac{\sqrt{n_1 n_2/n}}{\sigma(G_0)}$$

$$V(Z|\theta)|_{H_0} = 1$$

This gives

$$\text{Efficacy of } Z = \frac{[\frac{d}{d\theta}E(Z|\theta)|_{\theta=0}]^2}{V(Z|H_0)} = \frac{n_1 n_2}{n\sigma^2(G_0)}$$

The ARE of Mann-Whitney test (or $U$-test) relative to student's $t$ test for any population $G_1 = G_0$ with variance $\sigma^2(G_0)$ satisfying the location model is given by

$$\lim_{n\to\infty}\frac{e(U)}{e(Z)} = \frac{\frac{12n_1 n_2}{n+1}\left(\int_{-\infty}^{\infty}[g_0(x)]^2\, d(x)\right)^2}{\frac{n_1 n_2}{n\sigma^2(G_0)}}$$

$$= 12\sigma^2(G_0)\left[\int_{-\infty}^{\infty}[g_0(x)]^2\, d(x)\right]^2$$

## Review Questions

**9.1** Consider the one-sample location problem with

$$H_o : F_X(x) = F(x - \theta)$$

where $F$ is some continuous distribution with median 0. Note $\theta$ is the median of $F_X$ and $H_0 : \theta = 0$

(a) $F_X$ is $N(\theta, \sigma^2)$

(b) $F_X(x)$ is uniform $U(\theta - 1/2, \theta + 1/2)$
(c) $F_X(x)$ is double exponential distribution $DE(\lambda, \theta)$ with density

$$f_X(x) = \frac{1}{2}\lambda e^{-\lambda|x-\theta|}$$

calculate the efficacy of the Wilcoxon Signed-rank test $T^+$ statistic (Refer Section 10.8.1) for the distributions in (a), (b) and (c). Also, calculate ARE for populations in (a), (b) and (c) of $T^+$ with respect to the Sign-test (Refer Section 10.6) statistic $S$ and $T^+$ with respect to student's $t$ test statistic $T_n^*$.

**9.2** Consider the two sample problem of location for testing

$$H_0 : G_1(x) = G_2(x) \;\; \forall x$$

under the location model $G_2(x) = G_1(x-\theta)$, $\theta \geq 0$ where $G_1$ is given by the distributions given in Questions 9.1(a), 9.1(b) and 9.1(c). Calculate the efficacies of two sample Wilcoxon-Mann-Whitney test and student's $t$ test and show that the ARE of Wilcoxon-Mann-Whitney test with respect to Student's $t$-test is given by $3/\pi$, 1 and $3/2$ for the populations in 9.1(a), 9.1(b) and 9.1(c), respectively.

# Chapter 10

# Univariate Single-sample Problem of Location

## 10.1 INTRODUCTION

It is assumed in parametric inference that the form of the parent population distribution is known and the null hypothesis concerns some hypothesized value of the parameter. For example, the classical t-test assumes the underlying parent population distribution is normal. But there are some real situations where justification for such an assumption is weak and, therefore, one needs to check whether the distribution is of the given form. The tests for such type of problems are known as goodness-of-fit tests. For testing

$$H_0: \; F_X(x) = F_0(x) \quad \forall \; x \quad \text{against} \quad H_1: \; F_X(x) \neq F_0(x) \quad \text{at least for one } x$$

there could be two situations; one in which $F_0$ is completely specified and the second, where $F_0$ is not completely specified, i.e. some parameters are unknown. In the first case the null hypothesis is known as simple and in the second case it is composite, where unknown parameters need to be estimated by some suitable method of estimation. In every case the alternative hypothesis is composite. Therefore, rejection of $H_0$ does help us to understand what distribution the underlying population follows. Practically, goodness-of-fit is performed with the hope that the null hypothesis would be accepted.

We shall discuss two goodness-of-fit tests here namely the classical Karl Pearson $\chi^2$- test of fit, the oldest non-parametric test given by Karl Pearson in 1900 [165] in Section 10.2 and Kolmogorov-Smirnov test; Smirnov (1948)[197], Goodman (1954)[74] in Section 10.4 as an early development.

In some cases one is interested in testing for a location parameter $\theta$, say the median of some population $G_X$ continuous in the vicinity of the median $Md$, $H_0 : Md = \mu_0$, against an appropriate alternative. If the sample information is available on the nominal scale, Sign test is used for testing $H_0 : Md = \mu_0$. This has been discussed in Sections 10.6 and 10.7. Further, if $G_X$ is symmetric and continuous, and sample data is available on the interval scale or at least on ordinal scale, Wilcoxon Signed-Rank test is used for testing $Md = \mu_0$. This has been discussed in Section 10.8. Intuitively, Wilcoxon Signed-Rank test is superior to the Sign test since it utilizes relative position of sample observations whereas Sign test ignores the actual magnitudes.

## 10.2 CHI-SQUARE GOODNESS-OF-FIT TEST

Let the random variable $X$ follow some unknown distribution $F_X$. We shall be interested in testing the hypothesis that $F_X$ has a given form $F_0$, say,

i.e. $H_0 : F_X(x) = F_0(x) \; \forall \, x$ against $H_1 : F_X(x) \neq F_0(x)$ for at least one $x$

where, $F_0$ is completely specified.

To test the above hypothesis, let a random sample of size $n$ be drawn from $F_X$. Let the range of $X$ be divided into $k$ disjoint Borel measurable sets $C_1, C_2, \ldots, C_k$ so that $\cup_{i=1}^{k} C_i \subset \mathbb{R}^1$. Most often, data collected may be classified into some natural categories more particularly when the distribution is discrete and when continuous, the experimenter chooses his own classification, and obviously some information is lost. Lesser the number of classes more is the information loss. Under $H_0$, let $P(X \in C_i) = p_i, \; i = 1, \ldots, k$ where, $p_i$ be the probability that a random observation $X$ will be classified into the $i$th category. Let $O_j$ = number of $X_i$'s classified in $C_j$, $j = 1, \ldots, k$, $i = 1, 2, \ldots, n$. The joint distribution of $(O_1, O_2, \ldots, O_{k-1})$ follows multinomial distribution with parameters $(n, p_1, p_2, \ldots, p_{k-1})$. Here, $O_k = n - O_1 - O_2 \cdots - O_{k-1}$ and $p_k = 1 - p_1 \cdots - p_{k-1}$. The expected frequency in the $i$th class shall be given by $E_i = np_i$. This is a frequency in the $i$th category under the null hypothesis. When we assume null hypothesis to be true, there shall be close agreement between observed and expected frequencies, except for sampling variations. Considering the deviations $(O_i - E_i)$ as a measure of disagreement between observed and expected frequencies or in other words, as a criterion for rejecting $H_0$, Karl Pearson (1900) suggested the given as:

$$\chi^2 = \sum_{i=1}^{k} \frac{(O_i - E_i)^2}{E_i} \tag{10.1}$$

This is known as chi-square goodness-of-fit test. Indeed, large value of $\chi^2$ would indicate the lack of agreement is too high to have occurred by chance.

### 10.2.1 The Null Distribution of $\chi^2$

We have seen that the observed frequencies $O_1, O_2, \ldots, O_k$ follow multinomial distribution with parameters $n, \; p_1, p_2, \ldots, p_k$. The likelihood function of the parameters has been given by

$$L(p_1, p_2, \ldots, p_k; O_1, O_2, \ldots, O_k) = \prod_{i=1}^{k} p_i^{O_i}$$

where

$$O_i = 0, 1, \ldots, n, \quad \sum_{i=1}^{k} O_i = n, \quad \sum_{i=1}^{k} p_i = 1$$

When $F_0$ is completely specified, the class probabilities $p_i$ could be calculated utilizing $F_0$. In this case, the null hypothesis can be written as

$$H_0 : p_i = p_i^0 = E_i/n, \quad i = 1, 2, \ldots, k$$

The likelihood ratio test for testing this $H_0$, would be given by

$$\lambda(\mathbf{O}) = \frac{\sup_{\mathbf{p}\in\Theta_0} L(\mathbf{p}; \mathbf{O})}{\sup_{\mathbf{p}\in\Theta} L(\mathbf{p}; \mathbf{O})}$$

Let $\hat{p}_i$ be the maximum-likelihood estimate of $p_i$, given by $\hat{p}_i = O_i/n$. This gives

$$\lambda(\mathbf{O}) = \frac{\prod_{i=1}^{k}(p_i^0)^{O_i}}{\prod_{i=1}^{k}(\hat{p}_i)^{O_i}} = \prod_{i=1}^{k}\left(\frac{p_i^0}{\hat{p}_i}\right)^{O_i}$$

From the asymptotic theory for LR test, (refer to Chapter 7) we have seen that the asymptotic distribution of $-2\log\lambda(\mathbf{O})$ follows $\chi^2$ with $(k-1)$ degrees of freedom; note that $\sum_{i=1}^{k} p_i = 1$ leaves $(k-1)$ parameters in $\Theta$ to be estimated independently. We shall now show that, for large $n$, $-2\log\lambda$ and $\chi^2$, as given by Pearson, are equivalent. Let us now consider

$$-2\log\lambda(\mathbf{O}) = -2\sum O_i\,(\log p_i^0 - \log\widehat{p}_i)$$

Expanding $\log p_i$ about $\widehat{p}_i = O_i/n$ by Taylor's expansion, we get

$$\log p_i = \log p_i\big|_{p_i=\widehat{p}_i} + (p_i - \widehat{p}_i)\cdot\frac{\partial}{\partial p_i}\log p_i\big|_{p_i=\widehat{p}_i}$$
$$+\frac{(p_i-\widehat{p}_i)^2}{2!}\,\frac{\partial^2}{\partial p_i^2}\log p_i\big|_{p_i=\widehat{p}_i} + R_n$$

or

$$\log p_i - \log O_i/n = (p_i - O_i/n)\frac{n}{O_i} - (p_i - O_i/n)^2\cdot\frac{n^2}{2\,O_i^2} + R_n$$

where

$$R_n = \sum_{j=3}^{\infty}(-1)^{j+1}(p_i - O_i/n)^j\cdot\frac{n^j}{j!\,O_i^j}$$

or

$$-2\sum_{i=1}^{k} O_i(\log p_i - \log O_i/n) = -2\sum_{i=1}^{k} O_i(p_i - O_i/n)\frac{n}{O_i}$$

$$+2\sum_{i=1}^{k} O_i(p_i - O_i/n)^2\frac{n^2}{2O_i^2} - 2\sum_{i=1}^{k}\sum_{j=3}^{\infty}(-1)^{j+1}O_i(p_i - O_i/n)^j\frac{n^j}{j!\,O_i^j}$$

$$-2\log\lambda(\mathbf{O}) = 0 + \sum_{i=1}^{k}\frac{(np_i - O_i)^2}{O_i} + R_n' \text{ where } R_n' \to 0\ n \to \infty.$$

Thus, we see that$-2\log\lambda(\mathbf{O})$ and $\chi^2$ are asymptotically equivalent. Therefore, we conclude that the likelihood ratio test statistic $\chi^2$ given in Eq. (10.1) for testing $H_0 : p_i = p_i^0$ follows $\chi^2$ chi-square distribution with $(k-1)$ degrees of freedom.

If the calculated value of $\chi^2$ is greater than upper $\alpha^{th}$ quantile of $\chi^2$- distribution, then null hypothesis $H_0$ is rejected at $\alpha$-level of significance.

The asymptotic null distribution of the test statistic $\chi^2$ holds good only when at least 80% cells have their expected frequency of at least 5. If this requirement is not met for any category, the adjacent classes are merged together so that their expected frequencies raises to at least 5. As a result of this, the degrees of freedom is then reduced by as many as classes merged.

### 10.2.2 The Null Distribution of $\chi^2$ when $H_0$ is Composite

This situation arises when $F_0$ is not completely specified, the parameters specifying $F_0$ are unknown and, therefore, the null hypothesis becomes composite. For example, when one is interested in testing whether a sample has come from normal population with mean $\mu$ and variance $\sigma^2$ when $\mu$ and $\sigma^2$ are unknown. Let us call this distribution as $F_{\boldsymbol{\theta}}$, $\boldsymbol{\theta} \in \mathbb{R}^s$. The probabilities $p_i = P_{\boldsymbol{\theta}}\{X \in C_i\}$ for some category $C_i$ cannot be calculated and so are the expected frequencies, unless the parameters $\boldsymbol{\theta} = (\theta_1, \ldots, \theta_s)$ are estimated from sample observations. Let $\widehat{\theta}_1, \ldots, \widehat{\theta}_s$ be MLE's of $\theta_1, \theta_2, \ldots, \theta_s$. The expected frequencies for a set of $k$ disjoint categories, $C_1, C_2, \ldots, C_k$ would be estimated from the data by $\widehat{e}_i = n_i\widehat{p}_i^{\,0}$ , where $\widehat{p}_i^{\,0}$ are MLE's of the $p_i^0$ under $H_0$. Proceeding the same way as in the previous subsection, the corresponding likelihood ratio test is given by

$$\lambda(\mathbf{O}) = \frac{\sup_{\mathbf{p}\in\Theta_0} L(\mathbf{p};\mathbf{O})}{\sup_{\mathbf{p}\in\Theta} L(\mathbf{p};\mathbf{O})} = \frac{L(\widehat{p_1}^0, \widehat{p_2}^0, \ldots \widehat{p_k}^0)}{L(\widehat{p}_1, \widehat{p}_2, \ldots \widehat{p}_k)}$$

Further, asymptotically equivalent statistic could be obtained as

$$\chi^2 = \sum_{i=1}^{k}\frac{(O_i - n_i\widehat{p}_i^0)^2}{n_i\widehat{p}_i^0}$$

This is popularly known as goodness-of-fit statistic; which follows chi-square distribution with $(k-1-s)$ degrees of freedom, where $s$ is the number of independent parameters in $F_0$, estimated from the grouped data for estimating $p_i^0$s. We shall discuss some examples to elaborate this testing procedure.

**Example 10.2.1.** *A computer program is written to generate random numbers, X, uniformly in the interval* $0 \le X \le 10$. *From 250 consecutive values, the following data are obtained:*

| $X$ value : | 0 – 1.99 | 2 – 3.99 | 4 – 5.99 | 6 – 7.99 | 8 – 9.99 |
|---|---|---|---|---|---|
| Frequency : | 38 | 55 | 54 | 41 | 62 |

*Do these data offer any evidence that the program is not properly written?*

***Solution:*** The null hypothesis here is

$$H_0 : X \sim U(0,10) \quad \text{against} \quad H_1 : X \nsim U(0,10)$$

In words, the hypothesis may be stated as

$H_0$: The program has been properly written and it generates proper random variables from the given interval $0 \le X \le 10$.
against $H_1$: The program has not been properly written. Here,

$$p_1^0 = P\{X \in (0,1.99)|H_0\} = \int_0^{1.99} \frac{1}{10}\,dx = \frac{1.99}{10} = 0.199$$

$$p_2^0 = \frac{3.99-2}{10} = \frac{1.99}{10} = 0.199; \quad p_3^0 = 0.199 = p_4^0 = p_5^0$$

The observed and expected frequencies are given as:

| $X$ value | 0 – 1.99 | 2 – 3.99 | 4 – 5.99 | 6 – 7.99 | 8 – 9.99 |
|---|---|---|---|---|---|
| *Observed frequency* | 38 | 55 | 54 | 41 | 62 |
| *Expected frequency* ($E_i = Np_i$) | 49.75 | 49.75 | 49.75 | 49.75 | 49.75 |

and the calculated value of $\chi^2$-statistic is

$$\chi^2 = \sum_{i=1}^{5} \frac{(O_i - E_i)^2}{E_i} = 7.2475$$

The tabulated value of $\chi^2$ with $5-1=4$ degrees of freedom at 5% level of significance is given by 9.488. Since calculated value of $\chi^2$ is less than the tabulated value, therefore, we accept the null hypothesis at 5% level and conclude that the data has not enough evidence to reject $H_0$ and infer that the program is properly written.

**Example 10.2.2.** *An experiment consists of tossing a coin until the first head shows up. One hundred repetitions of this experiment are performed. The frequency distribution of the number of trials required for the first head is as follows:*

| Number of trials | 1 | 2 | 3 | 4 | 5 or more |
|---|---|---|---|---|---|
| Frequency | 40 | 32 | 15 | 7 | 6 |

*Can we conclude that the coin is fair?*

***Solution:*** Let $X$ be the number of failures preceding the first success. Total number of trials to get the first success would be $X+1$. To test the hypothesis

$$H_0 : X \sim NB(1, 1/2)$$

$$p_0^0 = P_{1/2}\{X = 0\} = pq^x = p(1-p)^0 = p = \frac{1}{2} = 0.5$$

$$p_1^0 = P_{1/2}\{X = 1\} = pq^1 = p(1-p) = \frac{1}{4} = 0.25$$

$$p_2^0 = P_{1/2}\{X = 2\} = pq^2 = p(1-p)^2 = \frac{1}{2} \cdot \frac{1}{4} = \frac{1}{8} = 0.125$$

$$p_3^0 = P_{1/2}\{X = 3\} = \frac{1}{2} \cdot \frac{1}{2^3} = \frac{1}{16} = 0.0625$$

$$p_4^0 = P_{1/2}\{X = 4\} = 1 - \frac{1}{2} - \frac{1}{4} - \frac{1}{8} - \frac{1}{16} = \frac{1}{16} = 0.0625$$

The observed and expected frequencies are given by

| $X$ : Number of failures preceded the 1st success | 0 | 1 | 2 | 3 | 4 |
|---|---|---|---|---|---|
| Observed frequency | 40 | 32 | 15 | 7 | 6 |
| Expected frequency | 50 | 25 | 12.5 | 6.25 | 6.25 |

This gives

$$\chi^2 = \sum_{i=0}^{4} \frac{(O_i - E_i)^2}{E_i} = 2.88$$

The tabulated value of $\chi^2_{4,\,0.05} = 9.488$.

Since calculated value of $\chi^2 < \chi^2$-tabulated, therefore, the null hypothesis that the underlying distribution is $NB(1, 1/2)$ has been accepted at 5% level of significance. We conclude, therefore, the coin is fair.

**Example 10.2.3.** *Fit a binomial distribution to the following data:*

| $x$ | 0 | 1 | 2 | 3 | 4 |
|---|---|---|---|---|---|
| Frequency | 8 | 46 | 55 | 40 | 11 |

***Solution:*** Here, we are to test the composite hypothesis

$$H_0 : X \sim b(4, p),\ 0 < p < 1$$

The parameter $p$ is unknown, therefore, $F_0$ is unspecified. We shall estimate $p$ by ML estimation procedure. This gives

$$\hat{p} = \frac{0 \times 8 + 1 \times 46 + 2 \times 55 + 3 \times 40 + 4 \times 11}{160 \times 4} = \frac{320}{640} = 0.5$$

Let us now estimate

$$\hat{p}_0^0 = P_{\hat{p}}\{X = 0\} = \binom{4}{0}\hat{p}^0(1-\hat{p})^{4-0} = (1-0.5)^4 = 0.0625$$

We may note that

$$\frac{P_{\hat{p}}\{X = x+1\}}{P_{\hat{p}}\{X = x\}} = \frac{n-x}{x+1}\frac{\hat{p}}{(1-\hat{p})}$$

Hence, we get

$$P_{\hat{p}}\{X = 1\} = \hat{p}_1^0 = \frac{4-0}{0+1}\cdot\frac{0.5}{1-0.5}\cdot\hat{p}_0^0 = 0.25$$

$$\hat{p}_2^0 = \frac{n-1}{1+1}\cdot\hat{p}_1^0 = \frac{4-1}{1+1}\cdot 0.25 = \frac{3}{2}\times 0.25 = \frac{0.75}{2} = 0.375$$

$$\hat{p}_3^0 = \frac{n-2}{2+1}\cdot\hat{p}_2^0 = \frac{4-2}{2+1}\times 0.375 = \frac{2}{3}\cdot 0.375 = 0.25$$

$$\hat{p}_4^0 = 1 - \hat{p}_0^0 - \hat{p}_1^0 - \hat{p}_2^0 - \hat{p}_3^0 = 1 - 0.0625 - 0.25 - 0.375 - 0.25 = 0.0625$$

The observed and expected frequencies are shown in the following table:

| $x$ | 0 | 1 | 2 | 3 | 4 |
|---|---|---|---|---|---|
| Observed frequency | 8 | 46 | 55 | 40 | 11 |
| Expected frequency $\hat{E}_i = 160 \cdot \hat{p}_i^0$ | 10 | 40 | 60 | 40 | 10 |

The calculated value of $\chi^2$ is, therefore,

$$\chi^2 = \sum_{i=0}^{4}\frac{(O_i - E_i)^2}{E_i} = 1.8167$$

Further, the tabulated value of $\chi^2_{4,\,0.05} = 9.488$. Since chi-square calculated is less than the tabulated value, we accept the hypothesis. We, therefore, conclude that the binomial distribution fits well in the given data.

# 10.3 EMPIRICAL DISTRIBUTION FUNCTION

Let $X_1, X_2, \ldots, X_n$ be a random sample from some unknown population distribution $F$. We arrange the sample observations into order statistics $X_{(1)}, X_{(2)}, \ldots, X_{(n)}$. Consider each of these order statistics as jump point with jump amount of $1/n$ at each point. Consider, then a step function $S_n(x)$ which is increased by the amount $1/n$ at each of its jump points. More formally, it is defined as

$$S_n(x) = \begin{cases} 1 & \text{if } x < X_{(1)} \\ k/n & \text{if } X_{(k)} \leq x < X_{(k+1)} \\ & \quad \text{for } k = 1, 2, \ldots, n-1 \\ 0 & \text{if } x \geq X_{(n)} \end{cases} \tag{10.2}$$

The function $S_n$ is known as empirical (sample) distribution function of the given sample.

Since $S_n$ is a function of sample observations $X_1, \ldots, X_n$, therefore, $S_n$ is also a random variable. We shall now discuss its distribution and moments.

## 10.3.1 Probability Distribution of $S_n$

Let us define a random indicator function,

$$\delta_{X_i}(t) = \begin{cases} 1 & \text{if } X_i \leq t \\ 0 & \text{otherwise} \end{cases} \tag{10.3}$$

$\delta_{X_i}$ are $n$ Bernoulli random variables with $\theta$ as probability of success, $P\{\delta_{X_i}(t) = 1\} = P\{X_i \leq t\} = F_X(t)$. The empirical distribution $S_n$ as a function of $\delta_{X_i}$, can now be written as

$$S_n(x) = \sum_{i=1}^{n} \frac{\delta_{X_i}(x)}{n}$$

Now, $nS_n(x) = \sum_{i=1}^{n} \delta_{X_i}(x)$, the sum of the $n$ independently distributed Bernoulli random variables, would follow Binomial distribution with probability of success $\theta = F_X(x)$. In other words, the distribution of $S_n$ would be given by

$$P[nS_n(x) = j] = P[S_n(x) = j/n] = \binom{n}{j} \theta^j (1-\theta)^{(n-j)},$$
$$j = 0, 1, \ldots, n, \quad \theta = F_X(x)$$

## 10.3.2 Moments of $S_n$

We have seen that $nS_n(x) \sim b(n, \theta)$, therefore,

$$E[nS_n(X)] = n\theta \quad \text{or} \quad E[S_n(X)] = \theta$$

and

$$V[n\,S_n(X)] = n\theta(1-\theta) \quad \text{or} \quad V[S_n(X)] = \frac{F_X(x)[1-F_X(x)]}{n}$$

### 10.3.3 Some Asymptotic Results of $S_n$

Since, $\delta_{X_i}(x)$ are iid with $E[\delta_{X_i}(x)] = \theta < \infty$, by strong law of large numbers, sample mean, $\frac{1}{n}\sum_{i=1}^{n}\delta_{X_i}(x)$ would converge to $E[\delta_{X_i}(x)] = \theta$ in probability. In other words,

$$S_n(x) = \frac{1}{n}\sum_{i=1}^{n}\delta_{X_i}(x) \xrightarrow{p} F_X(x)$$

This shows that the sequence of estimators $\{S_n\}$ is consistent for $\theta = F_X(x)$. The property of convergence of this type is for each individual value of $x$. Glivenko-Cantelli had considered the convergence, that was discussed for all values of $x$ together, instead for each individual $x$.

Glivenko-Cantelli had shown $S_n$ converges to $F_X$ uniformly, i.e. for every $\varepsilon > 0$

$$\lim_{n\to\infty} P[\sup_{-\infty<x<\infty} |S_n(x) - F_X(x)| > \varepsilon] = 0$$

The proof of asymptotical result is beyond the scope of this book, therefore, deferred. For proof and other details, readers may refer to Fisz (1963)[62].

Now, consider the random variable $nS_n$, with its finite mean and variance, the standard central limit theorem gives

$$\frac{nS_n(x) - E[nS_n(x)]}{\sqrt{V[nS_n(x)]}} \to N(0,1) \qquad \text{for large } n$$

or

$$\frac{nS_n(x) - nF_n(x)}{\sqrt{nF_n(x)[1-F_X(x)]}} = \frac{\sqrt{n}[S_n(x) - F_X(x)]}{\sqrt{F_X(x)[1-F_X(x)]}} \to N(0,1) \text{ for large } n$$

In other words

$$\lim_{n\to\infty} P\Big\{\frac{\sqrt{n}[S_n(x) - F_X(x)]}{\sqrt{F_X(x)[1-F_X(x)]}} \le t\Big\} = P\{N(0,1) \le t\} = \phi(t)$$

## 10.4 KOLMOGOROV-SMIRNOV ONE-SAMPLE TEST

We have seen, while discussing chi-square goodness-of-fit test, that $n$ observations were categorized into $k$ groups. The observed and expected frequencies were compared in order to test the goodness-of-fit hypothesis. There was certainly a loss of information while grouping. Alternatively, the difference between the empirical and expected distribution functions on every $n$ observations may be used as a criterion for testing goodness-of-fit. By utilizing these deviations, Kolmogorov-Smirnov suggested the single-sample test for testing $H_0 : F_X(x) = F_0(x)\ \forall x$ against $H_1 : F_X(x) \neq F_0(x)$ for at least one $x$

$$D_n = \sup_x |S_n(x) - F_0(x)|$$

here, $D_n$ is a two-sided test. Kolmogorov-Smirnov one-sided test statistics are defined as $D_n^+ = \sup_x [S_n(x) - F_0(x)]$ for testing the alternative $H_1 : F_X(x) \geq F_0(x)\ \ \forall\ x$, with strict inequality for at least one $x$; and

$$D_n^- = \sup_x [F_0(x) - S_n(x)]$$

for testing the alternative $H_1 : F_X(x) \leq F_0(x)\ \ \forall\ x$, with strict inequality for at least one $x$.

The main non-parametric feature of these statistics is that its probability distribution does not depend on the parent population distribution $F_X$, as long as $F_X$ is continuous. This has been proved in Theorem 10.4.1:

**Theorem 10.4.1.** *The statistics, $D_n$, $D_n^+$ and $D_n^-$ are distribution free whenever population cdf $F_0$ is continuous.*

*Proof.* $D_n$ is defind as

$$D_n = \sup_x [S_n(x) - F_0(x)] = \max_x (D_n^+, D_n^-)$$

The empirical distribution has been defined as

$$S_n(x) = \frac{i}{n} \ \text{ if } \ X_{(i)} \leq x < X_{(i+1)} \ \text{ for } i = 0, 1, \ldots, n$$

where, two extreme order statistics are $X_{(0)} = -\infty$ and $X_{(n+1)} = +\infty$. We now have

$$\begin{aligned} D_n^+ &= \sup_x [S_n(x) - F_0(x)] = \max_{0 \leq i \leq n} \sup_{X_{(i)} \leq x < X_{(i+1)}} [S_n(x) - F_0(x)] \\ &= \max_{0 \leq i \leq n} \sup_{X_{(i)} \leq x < X_{(i+1)}} \left[\frac{i}{n} - F_0(x)\right] = \max_{0 \leq i \leq n} \left[\frac{i}{n} - \inf_{X_{(i)} \leq x < X_{(i+1)}} F_0(x)\right] \\ &= \max_{0 \leq i \leq n} \left[\frac{i}{n} - F_0(X_{(i)})\right] = \max\left\{\max_{1 \leq i \leq n} \left[\frac{i}{n} - F_0(X_{(i)})\right], 0\right\} \end{aligned}$$

Similarly,

$$D_n^- = \sup_x [F_0(x) - S_n(x)] = \max\left\{\max_{1 \leq i \leq n} \left[F_0(X_{(i)}) - \frac{i-1}{n}\right], 0\right\}$$

and, now we can write

$$D_n = \max\left\{0,\ \max_{1 \leq i \leq n} \left[\frac{i}{n} - F_0(X_{(i)})\right],\ \max_{1 \leq i \leq n} \left[F_0(X_{(i)}) - \frac{i-1}{n}\right]\right\}$$

Clearly, Kolmogorov statistics $D_n^+, D_n^-$ and $D_n$ depend on the random variable $F_0(X_{(i)}), i = 1, 2, \ldots, n$, which, by probability-integral transformation, are order statistics from uniform distribution on (0, 1) independent of $F_0$ as long as $F_0$ is continuous. Therefore, Kolmogorov statistics are independent of $F_0$. □

For the purpose of testing we require the sampling distribution of $D_n$. This is stated in Theorem, 10.4.2, the proof of which is omitted in view of the level at which the book addresses the subject matter. The interested readers may refer Gibbons (1971)[71] and Wilks, 1962[215] for the proof of Theorem 10.4.2:

**Theorem 10.4.2.** *For $D_n = \sup_x[S_n(x) - F_0(x)]$ where, $F_0$ is any continuous cdf, we have*

$$P\Big(D_n < \frac{1}{2n} + v\Big) = \begin{cases} 0 & \text{for } v \leq 0 \\ \int_{1/2n-v}^{1/2n+v} \int_{3/2n-v}^{3/2n+v} \cdots & \text{for } 0 < v < \frac{2n-1}{2n} \\ \int_{2n-1/2n-v}^{2n-1/2n+v} f(u_1, u_2, \ldots u_n) du_n, \ldots, du_1 & \\ 1 & \text{for } v \geq \frac{2n-1}{2n} \end{cases}$$

*where*

$$f(u_1, u_2, \ldots, u_n) = \begin{cases} n! & \text{for } 0 < u_1 < u_2 < \ldots u_n < 1 \\ 0 & \text{otherwise} \end{cases}$$

The values of $D_{n,\,\alpha}$ so that $P[D_n > D_{n,\alpha}] = \alpha$ for $\alpha = 0.01$ and $\alpha = 0.05$ have been tabulated by Birnbaum (1952)[19] for some selected values of $n$.

Kolmogorov (1933)[105] derived the asymptotic distribution of $D_n$, the proof of which is complicated. Although, Smirnov(1939)[195] had given a simple proof, we discuss the Theorem 10.4.3 without proof:

**Theorem 10.4.3.** *If $F_X$ is any continuous distribution function, then for every $l \geq 0$*

$$\lim_{n\to\infty} P(D_n \leq \frac{l}{\sqrt{n}}) = L(l)$$

*where*

$$L(l) = 1 - 2\sum_{i=1}^{\infty}(-1)^{i-1}e^{-2i^2l^2}$$

Smirnov (1948)[197] has tabulated the function $L(l)$. Birnbaum (1952)[19], Gibbons (1971)[71], had shown that the exact and approximate values of $D_{n,\,\alpha}$ such that $P(D_n > D_{n,\,\alpha}) = \alpha$ for $\alpha = 0.01,\ 0.05$ are very close for sample sizes exceeding 35.

Since the one-sided Kolmogorov-Smirnov statistics do not depend on $F_X$, their use in non-parametric testing is very useful. Testing based on them requires their sampling distributions. The sampling distributions of $D_n^+$ and $D_n^-$ are easy to obtain as compared to that of $D_n$, therefore, the sampling distribution of $D_n^+$ has been stated in Theorem 10.4.4 without proof. The sampling distribution of $D_n^-$ is easily obtained by symmetry.

**Theorem 10.4.4.** *If $F_X$ is any continuous cdf, then*

$$P(D_n^+ < c) = \begin{cases} 0 & \text{for } \; c \leq 0 \\ \int_{1-c}^{1} \int_{(n-1)/n-c}^{u_n} \cdots & \text{for } \; 0 < c < 1 \\ \int_{2/n-c}^{u_3} \int_{1/n-c}^{u_2} f(u_1, u_2, \ldots u_n)\; du_1, \ldots du_n & \\ 1 & \text{for } \; c \geq 1 \end{cases}$$

*where*

$$f(u_1, u_2, \ldots, u_n) = \begin{cases} n! & \text{for } \; 0 < u_1 < u_2 < \ldots u_n < 1 \\ 0 & \text{otherwise} \end{cases}$$

Birnbaum and Tingey, 1952[20] have tabulated the values of $D_{n,\alpha}^+$ for some selected values of $n$ and $\alpha$ so that $P[D_n^+ > D_{n,\alpha}^+] \leq \alpha$. Smirnov have discussed the asymptotic distribution of $D_n^+$, which is given in Theorem 10.4.5 without proof:

**Theorem 10.4.5.** *If $F_X$ is any continuous distribution, then for every $l \geq 0$*

$$\lim_{n \to \infty} P\left(D_n^+ \leq \frac{l}{\sqrt{n}}\right) = 1 - e^{-2l^2}$$

Consider, $P(D_n^+ \leq l/\sqrt{n})$, which can equivalently be written as $P(4nD_n^{+2} \leq 4l^2)$, $l \geq 0$ or $\lim_{n\to\infty} P(4nD_n^{+2} \leq 4l^2) = 1 - e^{-2l^2}$, $l \geq 0$ This gives

$$\lim_{n \to \infty} P(4nD_n^{+2} \leq z) = 1 - e^{-z/2}, \quad z \geq 0$$

which is the distribution function of $\chi^2$ distribution with 2 degrees of freedom. This shows $4nD_n^{+2} \sim \chi^2(2)$ and one could conveniently use $4nD_n^{+2}$ statistic for large $n$.

**An illustration of the result of Theorem 10.4.5:** We shall use Theorem 10.4.5 to approximate $D_{n,\alpha}^+$ for large $n$. Considering $\alpha = 0.05$, $4nD_n^{+2} \sim \chi^2_{2,.05}$, this gives,

$$4nD_n^{+2} = 5.99 \quad \text{or} \quad D_{n,.05}^+ = \sqrt{\frac{5.99}{4n}} = \frac{2.4474}{2\sqrt{n}} = \frac{1.22}{\sqrt{n}}$$

$$\text{for } \; n = 35, \quad \text{we get} \quad D_{n,0.05}^+ = \frac{1.22}{\sqrt{35}} = 0.2062$$

For convenience, the results of the Section 10.4 have been summarized in Table 10.1.

**Table 10.1:** Kolmogorov-Smirnov one-sided critical regions for different alternatives

| $H_0$ | $H_1$ | *Kolmogorov-Smirnov goodness-of-fit test size-α critical region* |
|---|---|---|
| $F_X(x) = F_0(x)$ | $F_X(x) \neq F_0(X)$ for some $x$ | $D_n > D_{n,\alpha}$ |
| $F_X(x) = F_0(x)$ | $F_X(x) \geq F_0(X)$ at least for one $x$ | $D_n^+ > D_{n,\alpha}^+$ |
| $F_X(x) = F_0(x)$ | $F_X(x) \leq F_0(X)$ at least for one $x$ | $D_n^- > D_{n,\alpha}^-$ |

On testing the large sample theory and Glivenko-Cantelli lemma, the tests in Table 10.1 could be shown as consistent against their respective alternatives. This large sample property of Kolmogorov-Smirnov statistics is being reported here without proof.

**Example 10.4.1.** *A machine working correctly cuts pieces of wire to a mean length of 10.5 cm with a standard deviation of 0.15 cm. Sixteen samples of wire were drawn at random from a production batch and measured with the following results(centimeters):*

| 10.4 | 10.6 | 10.1 | 10.3 | 10.2 | 10.9 | 10.5 | 10.8 |
|---|---|---|---|---|---|---|---|
| 10.6 | 10.5 | 10.7 | 10.2 | 10.7 | 10.3 | 10.4 | 10.5 |

*Test the hypothesis that the machine is working correctly, i.e. the data fits $N(10.5,\ 0.15)$ at $\alpha = 0.05$ by using Kolmogorov-Smirnov goodness-of-fit test.*

***Solution:*** The null hypothesis to be tested is given by

$$H_0 : F_X(x) = F_0(x) \text{ where } F_0(x) \text{ is cdf of } N(10.5, 0.15)$$

$$\text{against } H_1 : F_X(x) \neq F_0(x) \text{ for some } x$$

The result is tabulated in Table 10.2:

**Table 10.2:** Computation of Kolmogrov-Smirnov statistic

| $x$ | $\frac{x-10.5}{\sqrt{0.15}}$ | $F_0(x) =$ $P\ N(0,1) \leq \frac{x-10.5}{\sqrt{0.15}}$ | $S_n(x)$ | $\lvert S_n(x) - F_0(x)\rvert$ |
|---|---|---|---|---|
| 10.1 | −1.03 | 0.1515 | $1/16 = 0.0625$ | 0.089 |
| 10.2 | −0.77 | 0.2206 | $3/16 = 0.1875$ | 0.0331 |
| 10.3 | −0.52 | 0.3015 | $5/16 = 0.3125$ | 0.011 |
| 10.4 | −0.26 | 0.3974 | $7/16 = 0.4375$ | 0.0401 |
| 10.5 | 0.00 | 0.5 | $10/16 = 0.625$ | 0.125 |
| 10.6 | +0.26 | 0.6026 | $12/16 = 0.75$ | 0.1474 |
| 10.7 | +0.52 | 0.6985 | $14/16 = 0.875$ | 0.1765 |
| 10.8 | + 0.77 | 0.7794 | $15/16 = 0.9375$ | 0.1581 |
| 10.9 | +1.03 | 0.8486 | $16/16 = 1$ | 0.1514 |

$$D_{16} = \sup_x |S_n(x) - F_0(x)| = 0.1765$$

At $\alpha = 0.05$ the tabulated value of $D_{16,0.05}$ is 0.327. Since $0.1765 < 0.325$, we accept the null hypothesis that the machine is working correctly, at 5% level of significance.

### 10.4.1 Comparison of Chi-square and Kolmogorov-Smirnov Tests

We compare the two tests of goodness-of-fit in Table 10.3:

**Table 10.3:** Comparison table of Chi-square and Kolmorgorov-Smirnov test

| *Chi-square test* | *Kolmogorov-Smirnov test* |
|---|---|
| This groups the data and often loses information through grouping. | This treats individual sample observations directly. |
| This test is designed mainly for large samples. | Applicable even in the case of small samples. |
| It allows the estimation of unknown parameters in $F_0$. Then suggests a test with modified degrees of freedom. | This test has no such provision. |
| This can be used in both the cases—when data are in the form of natural categories or continuous. | This test essentially assumes the continuity of the parent cdf Therefore, it provides more refined analysis of data. It is conservative in the sense that it is more prone towards accepting $H_0$ when applied in case $F_X$ is not continuous. |

## 10.5 SIGN TEST

In some problems we are interested in testing for location parameter of some population $G_X$. Such problems are known as single-sample problems of location and concern the testing for population median

$$H_0 : Md = \mu_0 \tag{10.4}$$

against a corresponding one or two-sided alternative on the value of $Md$.

Let the underlying population be denoted by $G_X(x)$. Also, $\Omega$ be class of all conceivable possibilities $G$. We shall discuss a test for testing $H_0 : Md = \mu_0$ against an appropriate alternative which is popularly known as sign test. The assumptions under which the sign test has been developed are stated as follows:

(a) The underlying population $G_X(x)$, with unknown median ($Md$), is univariate and continuous at least in the vicinity of median ($Md$). In other words, $P(X = Md) = 0$;

(b) The sample observations $X_1, \ldots, X_n$ are independently drawn from $G_X(x)$, i.e.

$$F_{(X_1,\ldots,X_n)}(x_1, \ldots, x_n) = \prod_{i=1}^{n} G(x_i)$$

Let $\Gamma$ be the class of all univariate continuous distributions. Suppose a sample $X_1, \ldots, X_n$ of size $n$ has been drawn from $G_X(x)$ so that $G_X \in \Gamma$. The hypotheses mentioned in Eq. (10.4) could now be written in terms of $G$

$$\gamma = \{G : G(\mu_0) = 1/2\}$$

$$\Gamma_1 = \{G : G(\mu_0) < 1/2\} \quad (Md > \mu_0)$$

such that $\gamma$ and $\Gamma_1$ are the subsets of $\Gamma$. Our problem is to test the hypothesis

$$H_0 : G \in \gamma \qquad \text{against} \quad H_1 : G \in \Gamma_1$$

We shall discuss the one-sided test for the alternative $G(\mu_0) < 1/2$ (or, $Md > \mu_0$), and treatments to other alternatives would derive accordingly.

Since each $G \in \Gamma$ is continuous, there would be at least one point $x$ at which $G(x) = 1/2$. In fact this would hold for all points $x$ belonging to interval $I$. Any such point then represents a median of the distribution $G$. We can define $\gamma$ as a subset of $G's$ for which at least one of the median is $\mu_0$; and $\Gamma_1$ contains those $G's$ for which all the medians exceed $\mu_0$. In the loose terms, we can say that the problem is of testing that the distribution is located at $\mu_0$ against the alternative that it is located to the right of $\mu_0$.

We shall take $\mu_0 = 0$. This, however, does not entail any loss in generality since for $\mu_0 \neq 0$ we can replace $X_1, \ldots, X_n$ by $X_1 - \mu_0, \ldots, X_n - \mu_0$ and $\mu_0$ by 0.

Finally, we note that the hypothesis can generally be concerned with the p-quantile of the distribution $G_X$ instead of median. The treatment then would call for obvious modifications. We shall confine ourselves exclusively to the use of median.

Under the hypothesis $G(\mu_0 = 0) = 1/2$, i.e. $Md = \mu_0 = 0$, we have

$$P\{X_1 \leq 0\} = P\{X_1 > 0\} = 1/2$$

and under the alternatives of interest

$$P\{X_1 > 0\} = 1 - G(0) > 1/2$$

Let $S$ denote a random variable that represents number of positive values among $X_1, \ldots, X_n$. Under $H_0$, $S$ will be binomially distributed with parameters $(n, 1/2)$ and under an admissible alternative $G, S$ will be distributed as binomial with parameters $(n, 1 - G(0) > 1/2)$. The large values of $S$ would indicate that the median is located to right of 0, i.e. $Md > 0$, thus rejecting $H_0$. The small values of $S$ would favour the null hypothesis. Therefore, $S$ could distinguish between null and the alternative hypotheses and its distribution under $H_0$ is $b(n, 1/2)$, completely known, thus satisfying the requirement of a statistic to *be test statistic.*

Let $\beta(s) = P\{S \leq s \,|\, H_0\}$ represent the cdf of the binomial distribution with parameters $(n, 1/2)$. Let $s_\alpha$ be the number such that

$$1 - \beta(s_\alpha) < \alpha, \quad \text{i.e.} \quad P\{S > s_\alpha |\, H_0\} < \alpha$$

and

$$1 - \beta(s_\alpha - 1) \geq \alpha, \quad \text{i.e.} \quad P(S > s_\alpha - 1) = P(S \geq s_\alpha \,|\, H_0) \geq \alpha$$

Then we define the test $\phi$ as

$$\phi(S) = \begin{cases} 1 & \text{if } \; S > s_\alpha \\ a & \text{if } \; S = s_\alpha \\ 0 & \text{if } \; S < s_\alpha \end{cases} \tag{10.5}$$

where, $a$ is a number, $0 < a \leq 1$, so that $E\{\phi(S)|\, H_0\} = \alpha$, the specified significance level.
Clearly,

$$E\{\phi(S)|H_0\} = P\{S > s_\alpha|H_0\} + aP\{S = s_\alpha|H_0\} = \alpha$$

$$\begin{aligned} a &= \frac{\alpha - P\{S > s_\alpha|H_0\}}{P\{S = s_\alpha|H_0\}} = \frac{\alpha - P\{S > s_\alpha|H_0\}}{P(S \geq s_\alpha|H_0) - P(S > s_\alpha|H_0)} \\ &= \frac{\alpha - (1 - \beta(s_\alpha))}{(1 - \beta(s_\alpha - 1) - (1 - \beta(s_\alpha)))} = \frac{\alpha + \beta(s_\alpha) - 1}{\beta(s_\alpha) - \beta(s_\alpha - 1)} \end{aligned}$$

The sign test defined in Eq. (10.5) is known as randomized sign test at exact level $\alpha$. Otherwise, when one can afford to use a non-randomized sign test, defined as

$$\phi(S) = \begin{cases} 1 & \text{if } \; S > s_\alpha \\ 0 & \text{if } \; S \leq s_\alpha \end{cases}$$

In this case the probability of the first kind of error may be slightly less than $\alpha$.

### 10.5.1 Optimality of Sign Test

We shall now show that one-sided sign test is UMP among all level $\alpha$ distribution free tests of the hypothesis $H_0 : G \in \gamma$ against $G \in \Gamma_1$. We shall describe a general technique which is often useful in spotting the most powerful level $\alpha$ test for $H_0 : G \in \gamma$ against a simple alternative $G_1$. From the set $\gamma$ we try to find a cdf which resembles $G_1$ most closely. (often this would be a weighted average of the cdfs of $\gamma$ rather than a member of $\gamma$. For the application we have in mind, however, we would not consider this possibility). Let this cdf be $G_0$. We then find the most powerful test for the simple hypothesis $G = G_0$ against the simple alternative $G = G_1$ by an application of Neyman-Pearson lemma. If $G_0$ and $G_1$ possess the densities $g_0$ and $g_1$, respectively with respect to some common measure $\mu$, then by the application of this lemma for a sample of size $n$ the most powerful test for $G = G_0$ against $G = G_1$ is given by

$$\phi(x_1, \ldots, x_n) = \begin{cases} 1 & \text{if } \prod g_1(x_i) > k \prod g_0(x_i) \\ a & \text{if } \prod g_1(x_i) = k \prod g_0(x_i) \\ 0 & \text{if } \prod g_1(x_i) < k \prod g_0(x_i) \end{cases}$$

where the numbers $k > 0$ and $0 \leq a \leq 1$ are to be so chosen that the test has exact level $\alpha$ for $G = G_0$. We then check if this test has level $\alpha$ for all $G \in \gamma$. In many situations, from intuitive consideration, we can find a $G_0$ for which this is realized. As the class of tests $\phi$ which are of level $\alpha$ for testing $G = G_0$ includes the class of tests which are of level $\alpha$ for testing $H_0 : G \in \gamma$ as subclass, if the test, most powerful against $G_1$ in the larger class, also belongs to the smaller class, it is necessarily most powerful against $G_1$ in the smaller class. Thus, if the test $\phi$ is of level $\alpha$ for all $G \in \gamma$ it is the most powerful level $\alpha$ test for $H_0 : G \in \gamma$ against $G_1$. If further this test is independent of $G_1 \in \Gamma_1$, the test is UMP test against $G \in \Gamma_1$. The solution of the problem lies in the correct choice of $G_0$.

Now coming back to the main problem, let us write any $G \in \Gamma$ as

$$G(x) = G(0)\, G^-(x) + \{1 - G(0)\}\, G^+(x) \quad \text{where } \; 0 < G(0) < 1$$

$$G^-(x) = \begin{cases} \dfrac{1}{G(0)}\, G(x) & \text{for } \; x \leq 0 \\ 1 & \text{for } \; x > 0 \end{cases}$$

The shape of $G^-$ is shown in Figure 10.1.

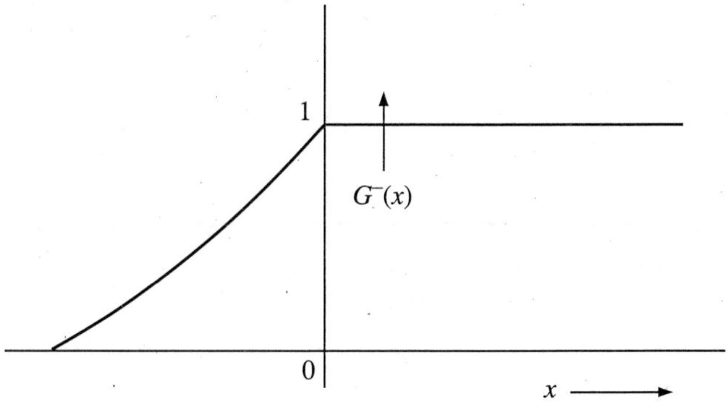


**Figure 10.1:** Distribution $G^-$.

and

$$G^+(x) = \begin{cases} 0 & \text{for } x \le 0 \\ \dfrac{G(x) - G(0)}{1 - G(0)} & \text{for } x > 0 \end{cases}$$

The shape of $G^+$ is shown in Figure 10.2.

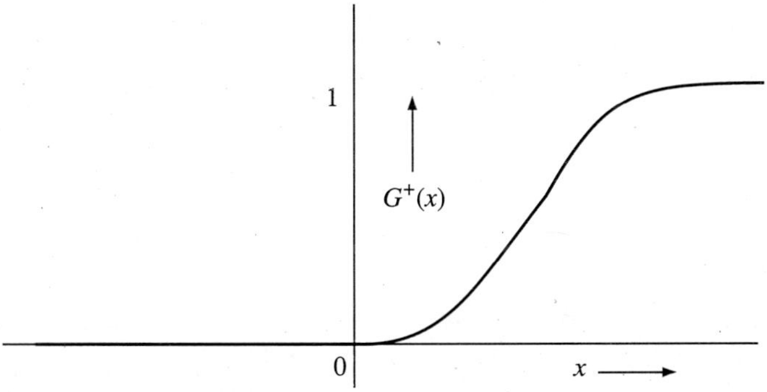


**Figure 10.2:** Distribution $G^+$.

Clearly, among the cdf's $G^-(x)$ and $G^+(x)$, the distribution $G^-(x)$ has its total probability confined to the negative half, and the distribution $G^+(x)$ has its total probability confined to the positive half of the real axis. In fact, if $X$ denotes the random variable having cdf $G(x)$, $G^-(x)$ and $G^+(x)$ represent the conditional distribution of $X$ given that $X \le 0$ and $X > 0$ respectively. For $G(0) = 0$, we take $G(x) = G^+(x)$ and choose any arbitrary cdf with total probability confined to $(-\infty, 0)$ for $G^-(x)$. For $G(0) = 1$, we take $G(x) = G^-(x)$ and choose any arbitrary cdf with total probability confined to $(0, \infty)$ for $G^+(x)$.

Now, we choose an arbitrary $G_1(x) \in \Gamma_1$. As has been defined $G(x)$, we can write

$$P(X \le x) = P(X \le x | X \le 0) \cdot P(X \le 0) + P(X \le x | X > 0) \cdot P(X > 0)$$

$$G_1(x) = G_1(0)\, G_1^-(x) + [1 - G_1(0)]\, G_1^+(x)$$

From $\gamma$ we are to choose a cdf which resembles $G_1(x)$ most closely. It seems that

$$G_0(x) = \frac{1}{2}\{G_1^-(x) + G_1^+(x)\}$$

would be the best choice

$$G_0(0) = \frac{1}{2}[G_1^-(0) + G_1^+(0)] = \frac{1}{2}[1 + 0] = 1/2$$

so that $G_0(x) \in \gamma$ and clearly

$$G_0(x) = G_0^-(x) \cdot G_0(0) + G_0^+(x) \cdot [1 - G_0(x)]$$
$$= \frac{1}{2}[G_0^-(x) + G_0^+(x)] \tag{10.6}$$

But

$$G_0(x) = \frac{1}{2}[G_1^-(x) + G_1^+(x)] \tag{10.7}$$

Therefore, on comparing Eqs. (10.6) and (10.7), we get

$$G_1^-(x) = G_0^-(x)$$

and

$$G_1^+(x) = G_0^+(x)$$

i.e. conditional distribution of $G_1$ and $G_0$ are same, but distribution functions are different.

We shall next find out the most powerful level $\alpha$ test for the simple null hypothesis $G_0(x)$ against the simple alternative $G_1(x)$.

Let the densities of $G_1^-(x)$ and $G_1^+(x)$ with respect to some common measure $\mu$ be $g_1^-(x)$ and $g_1^+(x)$. (For instance, by Radon-Nikodym theorem, $1/2\,\{G_1^-(x) + G_1^+(x)\}$ corresponds to such a measure). Then clearly

$$g_1^-(x) = 0 \quad \text{for} \quad x > 0; \quad g_1^+(x) = 0 \quad \text{for} \quad x \le 0$$

Also, the densities of $G_1(x)$ and $G_0(x)$ w.r.t. the same measure will be given by

$$g_1(x) = G_1(0)\, g_1^-(x) + \{1 - G_1(0)\} g_1^+(x)$$
$$g_0(x) = \frac{1}{2}\{g_1^-(x) + g_1^+(x)\}$$

Now by the way $\phi(\mathbf{x})$ has been defined earlier for a sample of size $n$ the MP test of $G_0(x)$ against $G_1(x)$ would be given by the critical function $\phi(\mathbf{x})$, where

$$\phi(\mathbf{x}) = \begin{cases} 1 & \text{if } \dfrac{\prod_{i=1}^n g_1(x_i)}{\prod_{i=1}^n g_0(x_i)} > k \\ a & \text{if } (\cdot) = k \\ 0 & \text{if } (\cdot) < k \end{cases}$$

Now, consider

$$\frac{\prod_{i=1}^n g_1(x_i)}{\prod_{i=1}^n g_0(x_i)} > k \quad \text{or} \quad \prod_{i=1}^n g_1(x_i) > k \prod_{i=1}^n g_0(x_i)$$

$$\prod_{i=1}^n [G_1(0)\, g_1^-(x_i) + \{1 - G_1(0)\}\, g_1^+(x_i)] > k \prod_{i=1}^n \frac{1}{2}[g_1^-(x_i) + g_1^+(x_i)] \tag{10.8}$$

Suppose the number of positive values among $x_1, x_2, \ldots, x_n$ is $s$, and let $x_i > 0$ for $i = i_1, \ldots, i_s$ and $x_i \leq 0$ for $i \neq i_1, i_2, \ldots, i_s$. Then, because $g_1^-(x) = 0$ for $x > 0$ and $g_1^+(x) = 0$ for $x \leq 0$, we can write the inequality in Eq. (10.8) as

$$\prod_{i=i_1,\ldots,i_s} [G_1(0)\, g_1^-(x_i) + \{1 - G_1(0)\} g_1^+(x_i)] \times$$

$$\prod_{i\neq i_1,\ldots,i_s} [G_1(0) g_1^-(x_i) + \{1 - G_1(0)\} g_1^+(x_i)]$$

$$> k \prod_{i=i_1,\ldots,i_s} \frac{1}{2} [g_1^-(x_i) + g_1^+(x_i)] \cdot \prod_{i\neq i_1,\ldots,i_s} \frac{1}{2} [g_1^-(x_i) + g_1^+(x_i)]$$

or

$$\{1 - G_1(0)\}^s \prod_{i=i_1,\ldots,i_s} g_1^+(x_i) \{G_1(0)\}^{n-s} \prod_{i\neq i_1,\ldots,i_s} g_1^-(x_i)$$

$$> k/2^n \prod_{i=i_1,\ldots,i_s} g_1^+(x_i) \prod_{i\neq i_1,\ldots,i_s} g_1^-(x_i)$$

We shall note that either $X_i s$ would be positive or negative, but not zero, i.e. ties do not occur since the cdf's $G$ are all continuous.

Now for any sample points $\mathbf{X} = \mathbf{x}$ at which

$$\textstyle\prod_{i=i_1,\ldots,i_s} g_1^+(x_i) \prod_{i\neq i_1,\ldots,i_s} g_1^-(x_i) = 0$$

both $\prod g_1^+(x_i)$ and $\prod g_1^-(x_i)$ are zero. Therefore, for the set of points for which $\prod g_1^+(x_i) = 0$ and $\prod g_1^-(x_i) = 0$ hold, have probability measure zero under both $G_0$ and $G_1$. So it does not matter what value $\phi$ attains at these points. Thus, we may ignore the possibility $(\cdot) \times (\cdot) = 0$ all together. Then

$$\phi(\mathbf{x}) = \begin{cases} 1 & \text{for } [1 - G_1(0)]^s [G_1(0)]^{n-s} > \frac{k}{2^n} \\ a & \text{for } [1 - G_1(0)]^s [G_1(0)]^{n-s} = \frac{k}{2^n} \\ 0 & \text{for } [1 - G_1(0)]^s [G_1(0)]^{n-s} < \frac{k}{2^n} \end{cases}$$

Now, consider

$$\left[\frac{1 - G_1(0)}{G_1(0)}\right]^s [G_1(0)]^n \quad \text{and } G_1 \in \Gamma_1$$

since, $\dfrac{1 - G_1(0)}{G_1(0)} > 1$, shows that $\left[\dfrac{1 - G_1(0)}{G_1(0)}\right]^s$ is an increasing function in $s$ and so $[1 - G_1(0)]^s [G_1(0)]^{n-s}$ is an increasing function in $s$. Therefore,

$$\phi(x_1, \ldots, x_n) = \begin{cases} 1 & \text{for } S > k \\ a & \text{for } S = k \\ 0 & \text{for } S < k \end{cases} \tag{10.9}$$

where $a$ and $k$ are constants and are to be so chosen that $\phi(x_1, \ldots, x_n) = \phi(S)$ is of size-$\alpha$. Hence, the test $\phi(\mathbf{x})$ in Eq. (10.9) can be written as a function of $S$, i.e $\phi(S)$. Thus, the test in Eq. (10.9) is most powerful for testing $G_0$ against $G_1$. Now for all $G \in \gamma$, the distribution of $S$ has the same distribution as it had for $G_0$. Therefore, this test $\phi$ in Eq. (10.9) has size-$\alpha$ for all $G \in \gamma$ and thus strictly distribution free. Hence, it is a level $\alpha$ most powerful test for the composite hypothesis $H_0 : G \in \gamma$ against $G_1$. But the test does not depend in any way on $G_1$. So, the one-sided sign test, given as above, is UMP against $\Gamma_1$ among all level $\alpha$ (distribution-free) tests of $H_0 : G \in \gamma$. It follows that the test is also unbiased against alternatives $\Gamma_1$.

When the set of alternatives is $\Gamma_1 = \{G : G_1(\mu_0) > \frac{1}{2}\}$ the inequality in $\phi(S)$ gets changed and the left hand tail sign test becomes UMP.

### 10.5.2 Case of Discontinuous Parent cdf

We shall now discuss the case when $G \in \Gamma$ is discontinuous at 0, i.e. $P(X = 0) = +\text{ve}$ whenever $X \sim G_X(x)$. Therefore, more realistic is to test now

$$H_0 : P\{X < 0\} = P\{X > 0\} \quad \text{or} \quad G(0-0) = 1 - G(0) \quad \text{or} \quad p_G^- = p_G^+$$

Consider, one-sided alternative

$$H_1 : G(0-0) < 1 - G(0) \quad (\text{median } > 0) \quad \text{or} \quad p_G^- < p_G^+$$

Let, $S$ be the total number of positive observations and $T$ be the total number of zero observations. Let

$$p_G^- = G(0-0); \; p_G^0 = \{G(0) - G(0-0)\}$$

$$p_G^+ = 1 - G(0) = 1 - p_G^- - p_G^0$$

Now, the joint distribution of $S$ and $T$ would be given by

$$P\{S = s,\ T = t|G\} = \frac{n!}{s!\ t!\ (n-s-t)!}\ \{p_G^-\}^{n-s-t}\ \{p_G^0\}^t\ \{p_G^+\}^s$$

$$\begin{aligned} P\{S = s|T = t\} &= \frac{P\{S = s,\ T = t\}}{P\{T = t\}} \\ &= \frac{\frac{n!}{s!\ t!\ (n-s-t)!}\{p_G^-\}^{n-s-t}\{p_G^0\}^t\ \{p_G^+\}^s}{\binom{n}{t}\{p_G^0\}^t\{p_G^+ + p_G^-\}^{n-t}} \\ &= \frac{(n-t)!}{s!(n-t-s)!}\left(\frac{p_G^+}{p_G^+ + p_G^-}\right)^s\left(\frac{p_G^-}{p_G^+ + p_G^-}\right)^{n-s-t} \\ &\sim b\left(n-t,\ \frac{p_G^+}{p_G^+ + p_G^-} = P_G^+\right) \end{aligned}$$

We can now write $H_0$ and $H_1$ as

$$H_0 : P_G^+ = 1/2 \text{ versus } H_1 : P_G^+ > 1/2$$

Consider the test

$$\phi(S|T=t) = \begin{cases} 1 & \text{if } S > s_\alpha(t) \\ a(t) & \text{if } S = s_\alpha(t) \\ 0 & \text{if } S < s_\alpha(t) \end{cases}$$

$s_\alpha$ and $a(t)$ are determined by the size condition, i.e.

$$E\{\phi(S|T=t)|H_0\} = \alpha \qquad \text{for every } t$$

or

$$E\{\phi(S|T=t)|G\} = \alpha \quad \forall\, G \in \gamma$$

It can be shown that $\phi(S|t)$ is UMP unbiased among all level $\alpha$ test of $H_0$ against $H_1$

Any $G \in \Gamma$ can be expressed as

$$G(x) = p_G^- \, G^-(x) + p_G^0 \, G^0(x) + p_G^+ \, G^+(x)$$

Consider any $G_1 \in \Gamma - \gamma$ and consider the class

$$\Gamma^* = \{G \,|\, p^- \, G_1^-(x) + p^0 \, G_1^0(x) + p^+ \, G_1^+(x)\}$$

where,

$$0 < p^-,\ p^0,\ p^+ < 1 \text{ and } p^- + p^0 + p^+ = 1$$

For a sample $x_1, \ldots, x_n$ of size $n$

$$\begin{aligned}\prod_{i=1}^{n} G(x_i) &= (p_G^-)^{n-s-t} \prod_{\substack{i \neq i_1,\ldots,i_s \\ \text{and } i \neq i_1',\ldots,i_t'}} G_1^-(x_i) \cdot (p_G^0)^t \\ &\quad \cdot \prod_{i - i_1',\ldots,i_t'} G_1^0(x_i) \cdot (p_G^+)^s \prod_{i = i_1,\ldots,i_s} G_1^+(x_i) \\ &= \Bigg\{ \prod_{\substack{i \neq i_1,\ldots,i_s \text{ and} \\ i \neq i_1',\ldots,i_t'}} G_1^-(x_i) \prod_{i = i_1',\ldots,i_t'} G_1^0(x_i) \\ &\quad \cdot \prod_{i = i_1,\ldots,i_s} G_1^+(x_i) \Bigg\} \cdot (p_G^-)^{n-s-t} \cdot (p_G^0)^t \cdot (p_G^+)^s\end{aligned}$$

The expressions in $\{\cdot\}$ are like $h(\mathbf{x})$ and $(p_G^-)^{n-s-t} \cdot (p_G^0)^t \cdot (p_G^+)^s$ as $g_\theta(T(\mathbf{x}))$ in the factorization theorem, therefore, $(S, T)$ are jointly sufficient for the class $\Gamma^*$ and we will be confining our attention to tests $\phi$ that depend on $(S, T)$. By the method of similar tests discussed in Chapter 5, the test $\phi(S|T=t)$ is UMP unbiased for $H_0 : p_G^- = p_G^+$ against $p_G^- < p_G^+$ within $\Gamma^*$. This test is of level $\alpha$ for testing $H_0$ under the original set up and does not depend on $G$. Therefore, the test $\phi(S|T=t)$ is UMP unbiased for the original problem.

## 10.6 THE TWO-SIDED SIGN TEST

In this we consider the testing problem

$$H_0 : G \in \gamma = \{G|G(0) = 1/2\} \ (M_d = 0)$$
$$\text{against} \quad H_1 : G \in \Gamma_1 = \{G|G(0) \neq 1/2\} \ (i.e.\ M_d \neq 0)$$

For this problem it shall be reasonable to reject $H_0$ when $S$ is too small or too large, i.e.

$$\phi(S) = \begin{cases} 1 & \text{for } S < s_1 \text{ or } S > s_2 \\ a_i & \text{for } S = s_i,\ i = 1, 2 \\ 0 & \text{for } s_1 < S < s_2 \end{cases} \tag{10.10}$$

where, $s_1$ and $s_2$ are numbers such that

$$P\{S < s_1|H_0\} < \alpha/2 \leq P\{S \leq s_1|H_0\}$$

From the symmetry of the distribution $S|H_0$, (i.e. binomial $(n, 1/2)$ about $E(S|H_0) = n/2$), we expect $s_1$ and $s_2$ to be equidistant from $n/2$ and that $P\{S = s_1|H_0\} = P\{S = s_2|H_0\}$. In other words

$$n/2 - s_1 = s_2 - n/2 \qquad \text{or} \qquad n = s_1 + s_2$$

or

$$n/2 = \frac{s_1 + s_2}{2}$$

The constants $a_1, a_2$ s.t. $0 < a_1, a_2 < 1$ and $s_1$ and $s_2$ are chosen so that the test $\phi(S)$ has level $\alpha$

$$P(S < s_1|H_0) + a_1\, P(S = s_1|H_0) + P(S > s_2|H_0) + a_2\, P(S = s_2|H_0) = \alpha$$

Hence, because of symmetry

$$a_1 = \frac{\alpha/2 - P\{S < s_1|H_0\}}{P\{S = s_1|H_0\}} \quad \text{and} \quad a_2 = \frac{\alpha/2 - P\{S > s_2|H_0\}}{P\{S = s_2|H_0\}}$$

which makes $a_1$ and $a_2$ equal.

For the given testing problem of two-sided hypothesis testing there does not exist any uniformly most powerful test. However, the test given is UMP within the class of all unbiased tests of level $\alpha$, i.e. among the class of tests $\phi'$ for which

$$E\{\phi'|G\} \leq \alpha \ \ \forall\, G \in \gamma \ \text{ and } \ E\{\phi'|G\} \geq \alpha \quad \forall\, G \in \Gamma - \gamma$$

We can write any $G \in \Gamma$ in terms of $G(0)$, $G^-(x)$ and $G^+(x)$. Let us take a particular alternative $G_1(x) \in \Gamma - \gamma$ and consider the cdfs $G_1^-(x)$ and $G_1^+(x)$ obtained from it. Consider

$$\Gamma^* = \{G : p\, G_1^-(x) + (1-p)\, G_1^+(x),\ 0 < p < 1,\ p \neq 1/2\}$$

$\Gamma^* \subset \Gamma$, $\Gamma^*$ has only cdf common with $\gamma$ namely, that for $p = 1/2$. So if we restrict ourself to $\Gamma^*$, the above problem of testing reduces to

$$H_0 : p = 1/2 \ \text{ against } \ H_1 : p \neq 1/2$$

Now, supposing we are able to show the existence of UMP unbiased test $\phi_0(x_1, \ldots, x_n)$ for the reduced problem and suppose this test is found to be:

(a) Of level $\alpha$ for testing $H_0 : G \in \gamma$
(b) Independent of particular $G_1$ considered

By (a) test $\phi_0$ would be a level $\alpha$ unbiased test for $H_0 : G \in \gamma$ against $G_1$ (i.e. $p\,G_1^-(x) + (1-p)\,G_1^+(x)$ with $p = G_1(0)$) and by (b) $\phi_0$ is level $\alpha$ unbiased test of $H_0$ against $\Gamma - \gamma$. Now any level $\alpha$ unbiased test for $H_0 : G \in \gamma$ against $\Gamma - \gamma$ is of level $\alpha$ unbiased for the hypothesis $G = \frac{1}{2}\{G_1^-(x) + G_1^+(x)\}$ against the alternative $p\,G_1^-(x) + (1-p)\,G_1^+(x)$, $0 < p < 1$, $p \neq 1/2$. Therefore, as $\phi_0$ has maximum power against $G_1$ within the class of all level $\alpha$ unbiased tests of $G = \frac{1}{2}\{G_1^-(x) + G_1^+(x)\}$ against the alternatives $p\,G_1^-(x) + (1-p)\,G_1^+(x)$, it must have maximum power against $G_1$ among all level $\alpha$ unbiased tests of $H_0 : G \in \gamma$ against $G_1 \in \Gamma - \gamma$. But by (b) this is true whatever $G_1$. Hence, $\phi_0$ would be UMP among all tests of $H_0 : G \in \gamma$ against $\Gamma - \alpha$.

Now for the problem of testing $p = 1/2$ against $p \neq 1/2$ a UMP test actually exists. This may be seen by first noting that the number $S$ of positive observations represents a sufficient statistic for the class of distributions $\{p\,G_1^-(x) + (1-p)\,G_1^+(x),\ 0 < p < 1\}$. This may be seen by noting that

$$\begin{aligned}
&\prod_{i=1}^{n} [p\,G_1^-(x_i) + (1-p)\,G_1^+(x_i)] \\
&\qquad = (1-p)^s \prod_{i=i_1,\ldots,i_s} G_1^+(x_i) \cdot p^{n-s} \prod_{i \neq i_1,\ldots,i_s} G_1^-(x_i) \\
&\qquad = \Big\{ \prod_{i=i_1,\ldots,i_s} G_1^+(x_i) \cdot \prod_{i \neq i_1,\ldots,i_s} G_1^-(x_i) \Big\} (1-p)^s p^{n-s}
\end{aligned}$$

by factorization theorem $S$ is a sufficient statistic. This suggests that we may consider only such tests that are the function of $S$. Now, $S \sim b(n, 1-p)$. Under this set up for testing $p = 1/2$ against $p \neq 1/2$ there exists a UMP unbiased test, which is precisely the test given in Eq. (10.10). This follows by an application of the general theory UMP unbiased test for one parameter exponential families. The test ofcourse satisfies conditions (a) and (b).

## 10.7 THE USE OF RANKS

We have seen that the use of sign test required the data to be available on the nominal scale. Even if the data were on the interval scale, we could have reduced it to the nominal scale for the analysis, to increase the speed and ease of calculations. Intuitively, such a loss of information usually results into loss in power.

Let us now add another assumption of symmetry to the parent population, apart from its continuity. This assumption is not as strong as the assumption that the parent population follows normal distribution, because every normal distribution is symmetric, but not every symmetric distribution is normal. If a distribution is symmetric, then the mean (if its exists) coincides with the median, because both are located exactly in the middle of the distribution at the line of symmetry. One consequence of adding this assumption to the model is that any inference concerning the median would also hold good for mean.

A second consequence of adding the assumption of symmetry to the model is that the required scale of measurement has changed from ordinal to interval. With an ordinal scale of measurement, two observations of the random variable need only to be distinguished on the basis of their measurements as to which is larger and which is smaller. It is not necessary to know that which one is farthest from the median, such as when the two observations are on the opposite sides of the median. If the assumption of symmetry is meaningful one, the distance from the median is a meaningful measurement. As a result, the scale of measurement is more than just ordinal, it is interval.

One other assumption is included in the model that the random variable is continuous. The continuity assumption is made so that we may consider the distribution of the test statistic, if no ties occur. In practice, ties do occur, so we shall include a modification for ties along with each test whenever possible.

### 10.7.1 The Wilcoxon Signed-Rank Test (WSRT)

We have seen that the sign test only uses the signs of the difference between each observation and hypothesized value of median $\mu_0$, the magnitude of these observations were ignored. If such informations are available, a test statistic which takes into account these individual relative magnitudes might be expected to give better performance. Wilcoxon Signed-Rank Test is the test which takes into account both *signs* and *magnitudes* of these differences.

Let us consider the assumptions in more detail:

(a) The parent population from which the sample has been drawn is symmetric about the location parameter.

Now, a random sample of size $n$ has been drawn from a population. Let the median of the population be $\mu_0$. Then by the symmetry of the population, we mean

$$P(X \leq \mu_0 - c) = P(X \geq \mu_0 + c) \qquad \forall\, c > 0$$

or, if we put

$$D_i = X_i - M_d = X_i - \mu_0$$

The differences are symmetrically distributed about zero so that the positive and negative differences of equal absolute magnitude have the same probability of occurrence, i.e.

$$P(D_i \leq -c) = P(D_i \geq +c) = 1 - P(D_i < c)$$

This assumption has changed the scale of measurement from ordinal to interval.

(b) The population is assumed to be continuous so that we may discard zero or tie values from the analysis as

$$P(D_i = 0) = 0 \quad \text{or} \quad P(X_i - \mu_0 = 0) = 0 \quad \text{or} \quad P(X_i = \mu_0) = 0$$

(c) Due to the symmetry of the parent population the measurement scale is interval. Therefore, we can put the data in the increasing order.

**Test statistic**

Let $x_1, \ldots, x_n$ be a sample of size $n$ drawn from a univariate, continuous and symmetric population, which is symmetric about its location parameter.

Then we shall be interested in one of the following testing problems:

$$H_0 : M_d = 0 \text{ against } H_1^{(1)} : M_d > 0 \text{ one-sided testing problem.}$$

or against

$$H_1^{(2)} : M_d < 0 \text{ one-sided testing problem.}$$

or against

$$H_1^{(3)} : M_d \neq 0 \text{ two-sided testing problem.}$$

Now, define

$$D_i = X_i - \mu_0$$

then $D_i$ is a random variable and $H_0$ can now be stated as

$$H_0 : Md_{(D_i)} = 0 \quad \text{against} \quad H_1 : Md_{(D_i)} > 0$$

Now, $D_1, D_2, \ldots, D_n$ is a new set of random variables and its distribution is continuous and symmetric about zero. We have

(a) $P(D_i = 0) = 0$
(b) $P(D_i \leq -c) = P(D_i \geq c)$

Find $|D_i|$ $\forall\ i = 1, 2, \ldots, n$; $|D_i|$ are the order statistics. Let the increasing order of $|D_i|$ be

$$|D'_1|, |D'_2|, \ldots, |D'_n|$$

and their ranks will be $1, 2, \ldots, n$, respectively.
Define

$$Z_{(i)} = \begin{cases} 1 & \text{if } D'_i > 0 \\ 0 & \text{if } D'_i < 0 \end{cases}$$

Now, we define

$$T^+ : \text{sum of ranks of} |D_i'| \text{ for which } D_i' > 0$$

$$T^+ = \sum_{i=1}^{n} iZ_{(i)}$$

$T^+$ will be a test-statistic if we know its distribution under $H_0 : Md_{(D_i)} = 0$ and it can distinguish between $H_0$ and $H_1$ since larger values of $T^+$ will lead to the rejection of $H_0$. We shall discuss the distribution of $T^+|H_0$ along with certain other properties. Define

$$T^- : \text{sum of ranks over } |D_i'| \text{ for which } D_i' < 0$$

and since

$$T^+ + T^- = \sum_{i=1}^{n} i = \frac{n(n+1)}{2}$$

is constant, a test statistic could either be based on $T^+$ or $T^-$ or even any linear combination of each of these. All of these would be equivalent criterion.

Hence, $T^+$ could be used as a test statistic for testing $H_0$ against $H_1$

$$\phi(T^+) = \begin{cases} 1 & \text{if } T^+ > t_\alpha^+ \\ a & \text{if } T^+ = t_\alpha^+ \\ 0 & \text{if } T^+ < t_\alpha^+ \end{cases}$$

**First two moments of WSRT**

In the expression of $T^+$, $Z_i$s are involved. Since $Z_i$s are associated with $D_i$s and $D_i$s are associated with $X_i$s and $X_i$s are independent, so $Z_i$s are also independent. We know that $Z_{(i)}$ is a Bernoulli random variable, but they are not identically distributed as $P(D_1' > 0), P(D_2' > 0), \ldots, P(D_n' > 0)$ are all different, or, $P(Z_{(1)} > 0), P(Z_{(2)} > 0), \ldots, P(Z_{(n)} > 0)$ are all different. Then

$$E(Z_{(i)}) = 1.\, P(D_i' > 0) = \theta_i$$

$$V(Z_{(i)}) = E\{Z_{(i)}^2\} - [E\{Z_{(i)}\}]^2 = \theta_i - \theta_i^2 = \theta_i(1 - \theta_i)$$

Let

$$\begin{aligned}\theta_i &= P(D_i' > 0)\\ &= P(i^{th} \text{ order statistic amongst} |D_1'|, \ldots, |D_n'| \\ &\qquad\qquad \text{corresponds to positive values})\\ &= \int_0^\infty \frac{n!}{(i-1)!\,(n-i)!}[F_{|D|}(u)]^{i-1}[1-F_{|D|}(u)]^{n-i} f_D(u)\,du\\ &= n\binom{n-1}{i-1}\int_0^\infty [F_D(u)-F_D(-u)]^{i-1}\\ &\qquad\qquad [1-F_D(u)+F_D(-u)]^{n-i} f_D(u)\,du\end{aligned}$$

Under $H_0$, the distribution of $D_i'$s are symmetric about 0, gives

$$F_D(-u) = 1 - F_D(u).$$

And now

$$\theta_i|H_0 = n\binom{n-1}{i-1}\int_0^\infty (2F_D(u)-1)^{i-1}(2(1-F_D(u)))^{n-i} f_D(u)\,du$$

Let

$$2F_D(u) - 1 = y$$

On differentiating both the sides, we get

$$2f_D(u)\,du = dy$$

and

$$2(1-F_D(u)) = 1 + (1-2F_D(u)) = 1-(2F_D(u)-1) = 1-y$$

On putting these values in $\theta_i|H_0$, we get

$$\begin{aligned}\theta_i|H_0 &= \frac{n}{2}\binom{n-1}{i-1}\int_0^\infty y^{i-1}(1-y)^{n-i}\,dy\\ &= \frac{n}{2}\binom{n-1}{i-1} Be(i,\, n-i+1)\\ &= \frac{n}{2}\binom{n-1}{i-1}\frac{\Gamma(i)\Gamma(n-i+1)}{\Gamma(n+1)}\\ &= \frac{n}{2}\;\frac{(n-1)!}{(i-1)!\,(n-i)!}\cdot\frac{(i-1)!\,(n-i)!}{n!} = \frac{1}{2}\\ &\qquad\qquad (\text{since } \Gamma(n) = (n-1)!)\end{aligned}$$

We shall now write

$$E(T^+|H_0) = E(\sum_{i=1}^{n} i\, Z_{(i)}|H_0) = \sum_{i=1}^{n} i\, E(Z_{(i)})|H_0 = \sum_{i=1}^{n} i\, \theta_i|H_0$$

$$= \frac{1}{2}\,\frac{n(n+1)}{2} = \frac{n(n+1)}{4}$$

and

$$V(T^+|H_0) = \sum_{i=1}^{n} i^2\, V(Z_i|H_0) = \sum_{i=1}^{n} i^2.\,[\theta_i\,(1-\theta_i)]$$

$$= \frac{1}{4}\,\frac{n(n+1)(2n+1)}{6} = \frac{n(n+1)(2n+1)}{24}$$

The same may be written as

$$E\Big(\frac{2T^+}{n(n+1)}\Big|H_0\Big) = \frac{1}{2} \quad \text{and} \quad V\Big(\frac{2T^+}{n(n+1)}\Big|H_0\Big) = \frac{(2n+1)}{6\,n\,(n+1)}$$

### Consistency of one-sided WSRT

We shall now show that WSRT is consistent against the specified alternative $H_1 : Md_{(D)} > 0$. The form of one-sided WSRT is

$$\phi(T^+) = \begin{cases} 1 & \text{if } T^+ > t_\alpha^+ \\ a & \text{if } T^+ = t_\alpha^+ \\ 0 & \text{if } T^+ < t_\alpha^+ \end{cases}$$

Then the power function under $H_1$ can be defined as

$$\beta[\phi(T_n^+)|H_1] = P[T^+ > t_\alpha^+|H_1] + a\, P[T^+ = t_\alpha^+|H_1]$$

$$\geq P[T^+ > t_\alpha^+|H_1]$$

$$= P\Big[\frac{2T^+}{n(n+1)} - \frac{1}{2} > \frac{2t_\alpha^+}{n(n+1)} - \frac{1}{2}\Big|H_1\Big]$$

Now

$$\lim_{n\to\infty} V\Big(\frac{2T^+}{n(n+1)}\Big|H_0\Big) = \lim_{n\to\infty} \frac{(2n+1)}{6n(n+1)} = \lim_{n\to\infty} \frac{(2+1/n)}{6(1+n)} = 0$$

here

$$\frac{2T^+}{n(n+1)} = \frac{T^+}{\frac{n(n+1)}{2}} = \frac{\text{sum of ranks of } |D_i'| \text{ for which } D_i' > 0 \text{ in the sample}}{\text{total sum of ranks}}$$

$$= \text{sample average of ranks of } |D_i'| \text{ corresponding to } D_i' > 0$$

and the fact $V\left(\frac{2T^+}{n(n+1)}\Big|H_0\right) \to 0$ as $n \uparrow \infty$, by the central limit theorem, sample average of ranks approaches to population average of ranks of $|D_i'|$s for which $D_i' > 0$. So

$$\lim_{n\to\infty} \beta[\phi(T_n^+)|H_1] \geq P\Big[\lim_{n\to\infty}\left(\frac{2T^+}{n(n+1)}\right)-\frac{1}{2} > \lim_{n\to\infty}\frac{2t_\alpha^+}{n(n+1)} - \frac{1}{2}\Big|H_1\Big]$$

$$= \Big[\{\text{population average of ranks of}|D_i'| \text{ for } D_i' > 0\} - \frac{1}{2} > 0\Big| H_1\Big]$$

Note that

$$\frac{\frac{2T^+}{n(n+1)} - E\left(\frac{2T^+}{n(n+1)}\right)}{\sqrt{V\left(\frac{2T^+}{n(n+1)}\right)}} \sim N(0,1)$$

i.e.,

$$\frac{\frac{2T^+}{n(n+1)} - \frac{1}{2}}{\sqrt{\frac{(2n+1)}{6n(n+1)}}} \sim N(0,1) \text{ and } \frac{\frac{2t_\alpha^+}{n(n+1)} - \frac{1}{2}}{\sqrt{\frac{2n+1}{6n(n+1)}}} = Z_\alpha$$

Therefore,

$$\lim_{n\to\infty}\left(\frac{2t_\alpha^+}{n(n+1)} - \frac{1}{2}\right) = z_\alpha \cdot \lim_{n\to\infty}\sqrt{\frac{2+1/n}{6(n+1)}} = 0$$

Therefore, the power, $\lim_{n\to\infty}\beta[\phi(T^+)|H_1] \geq P[\text{Population}Md_{(D_i)} > 0|H_1 : Md_{(D_i)} > 0] = 1$. Hence, one-sided WSRT is consistent under some specified alternative $H_1$.

**Consistency of two-sided WSRT**

We shall now show that the two-sided WSRT is consistent against the alternatives $H_1 : Md_{(D_i)} \neq 0$. Let us consider the two-sided testing problem

$$H_0 : Md_{(D_i)} = 0 \text{ against } H_1 : Md_{(D_i)} \neq 0$$

The two-sided WSRT would be given by

$$\phi(T_n^+) = \begin{cases} 1 & \text{if } T_{n,\alpha}^+ < t_{1,n,\alpha}^+ \text{ or } T_{n,\alpha}^+ > t_{2,n,\alpha}^+ \\ a & \text{if } T_{n,\alpha}^+ = t_{i,n,\alpha}^+ i = 1,2 \\ 0 & \text{if } t_{1,n,\alpha}^+ < T_{n,\alpha}^+ < t_{2,n,\alpha}^+ \end{cases}$$

Now, considering the limiting power under the specified $H_1$, we have

$$\lim_{n\to\infty}\beta(\phi(T_n^+)|H_1) \geq P\Big[\lim_{n\to\infty}\frac{2T_n^+}{n(n+1)} - \frac{1}{2} < \lim_{n\to\infty}\frac{2t_1^+}{n(n+1)} - \frac{1}{2}\Big|H_1\Big] + P\Big[\lim_{n\to\infty}\frac{2T_n^+}{n(n+1)} - \frac{1}{2} > \lim_{n\to\infty}\frac{2t_2^+}{n(n+1)} - \frac{1}{2}\Big|H_1\Big]$$

$$= P[\{\text{Popln. av. of rank of } |D'_i| \text{ assctd. with } D'_i > 0\} < 1/2|H_1]$$
$$+ P[\{\text{Popln. av. of ranks of } |D'_i| \text{ assctd. with } D'_i > 0\} > 1/2|H_1]$$
$$= 1$$

Hence, two-sided WSRT is consistent for given alternatives $H_1$.

### Comparison of WSRT and Sign test

A brief account of comparison between WSRT and Sign test has been given in Table 10.4. These comparisons have been made on the types of populations assumed, the scale of measurements, signs and magnitudes required for applications of these test statistics.

**Table 10.4:** Comparison of WSRT and Sign Test

| *WSRT* | *Sign test* |
|---|---|
| (1) WSRT may only be used when sample is drawn from the parent population which is continuous and symmetric about its location parameter. | While Sign test may be used even when parent population is not symmetric. |
| (2) The data must be on the interval scale. | While it may be used even when the data is on the nominal scale with categories of positive and negative signs. |
| (3) It utilizes *sign* and *relative position* (rank) of the observation. | While it utilizes signs of the observations and ignores the magnitude. |
| (4) It is sum of ranks of $\|D'_i\|$ for which $D'_i > 0$. | While this is sum of positive signs for which $D'_i > 0$. |

### The null distribution of $T^+$ (i.e. $P[T^+ = t|H_0]$)

We have

$$T^+ = \sum_{i=1}^{n} iZ_{(i)} = \mathbf{I}'\mathbf{Z}$$

$$\mathbf{I}' = (1, 2, \ldots, n) \quad \mathbf{Z}' = (Z_{(1)}, Z_{(2)}, \ldots, Z_{(n)})$$

It is clear that $T^+$ may take values $0, 1, \ldots, \frac{n(n+1)}{2}$. $T^+$ is regulated by the values of $\mathbf{Z}$, so it is sufficient to consider the space of $\mathbf{Z}$ instead of taking the space of $T^+$. Total number of points in the space of $\mathbf{Z}$ is equal to $2^n$ since $Z_{(i)}$ can take values 0 and 1. And since

$$P[Z_{(i)} = 1|H_0] = P[D'_i > 0|H_0] = \theta_i|H_0 = 1/2$$

and

$$P[Z_{(i)} = 0|H_0] = P[D_i' < 0|H_0] = 1 - \theta_i|H_0 = 1 - 1/2 = 1/2$$

Therefore, each of these distinguishable arrangements are equally likely under $H_0$. Thus, the null probability distribution of $T^+$ shall be given by

$$P(T^+ = t|H_0) = \frac{u(t)}{2^n}$$

where, $u(t)$: number of ways to assign 1 and 0 signs to the first $n$ integers such that the sum of positive integers equals $t$.

We must note that the unique value of $T^+$ can be obtained by different values of **Z**, but unique value of **Z** gives unique value of $T^+$.

**Symmetry of the distribution of $T^+$ under $H_0$**

The null distribution of $T^+$ has been given by

$$P(T^+ = t) = \frac{u(t)}{2^n}$$

where, $u(t)$ is the number of ways to assign 1 and 0 digits to the first $n$ integers such that the sum of the positive integers equals $t$. Every assignment occurs with equal probability and every assignment has a conjugate assignment with 1 replaced by 0 and 0 by 1, we have

$$P(T^+ = t) = P(T^+ = \sum_{i-1}^{n} i(1 - Z_{(i)}))= P\Big(T^+ = 2 \cdot \frac{n(n+1)}{4} - t\Big)$$

This shows that the null distribution of $T^+$ is symmetric about $\frac{n(n+1)}{4}$.

**Formulation of table to calculate $P[T^+ = t|H_0]$**

Let us consider a sample of size $n = 3$. We shall see how the null distribution of $T^+$ is calculated. Different combinations of 1's and 0's in **Z** would determine the value of $T^+$ ranging from $(0, \frac{n(n+1)}{2})$ or $(0, 6)$. Table 10.5 explains the calculations of the null distribution of $T^+$.

$$P[T^+ = t|H_0] = P\Big[T^+ = \frac{n(n+1)}{2} - t\Big|H_0\Big] = \frac{u(t)}{2^n}$$

Since the null distribution of $T^+$ is symmetric about $\theta = \frac{n(n+1)}{4}$, therefore, it would be sufficient to determine the half null distribution of $T^+$.

**Table 10.5:** Null distribution of $T^+$

| $T^+ = t$ | *Number of possible values of* $\mathbf{Z}'s$ *which give* $T^+ = t$ | $u(t)$ | $P[T^+ = t \mid H_0]$ |
|---|---|---|---|
| 0 | (0,0,0) | 1 | $1/2^3$ |
| 1 | (1,0,0) | 1 | $1/2^3$ |
| 2 | (0,1,0) | 1 | $1/2^3$ |
| 3 | (1,1,0);(0,0,1) | 2 | $2/2^3$ |
| 4 | (1,0,1) | 1 | $1/2^3$ |
| 5 | (0,1,1) | 1 | $1/2^3$ |
| 6 | (1,1,1) | 1 | $1/2^3$ |

**On use of the same distribution of $T^+$ and $T^-$**

For hypothesis testing by WSRT, the entire distribution of $T^+|H_0$ is not necessary. Because of the fact $T^+ + T^- = \dfrac{n(n+1)}{2}$, the large values of $T^+$ corresponds to the smaller values of $T^-$. Moreover, the distribution of $T^+$ and $T^-$ are the same as

$$P(T^+ \geq c) = P\Big(T^+ - \frac{n(n+1)}{4} \geq c - \frac{n(n+1)}{4}\Big)$$

$$= P\Big(T^+ - \frac{n(n+1)}{4} \leq \frac{n(n+1)}{4} - c\Big)$$

$$\text{(by the symmetry of } T^+|H_0 \text{ about } \frac{n(n+1)}{4})$$

$$= P(T^+ - \frac{n(n+1)}{2} \leq -c)$$

$$= P(-T^- \leq -c) = P(T^- \geq c)$$

It is a matter of choice and convenience as to which statistics among $T^+$ and $T^-$ could be used since their null distributions are the same. Apart from this, it is more convenient to work with smaller sums. It is with this reason that right sided critical regions are suggested to be converted into left sided critical regions. Let

$$H_0 : Md = \mu_0$$

$t_\alpha$ is obtained by

$$P(T^+ \leq t_\alpha) = \alpha$$

The appropriate critical region would be

$$T^- \leq t_\alpha \quad \text{for } H_1 : Md > \mu_0 \text{ and } T^+ \leq t_\alpha \quad \text{for } H_1 : Md < \mu_0$$

$$T^+ \leq t_{\alpha/2} \quad \text{or } T^- \leq t_{\alpha/2} \qquad \text{for } H_1 : Md \neq \mu_0$$

This is because if $H_0 : Md = \mu_0$ against $H_1 : Md > \mu_0$, the critical region will be $T^+ \geq t_\alpha$

$$P[T^+ \geq t_\alpha | H_0] = P[-T^+ \leq -t_\alpha | H_0]$$

$$= P\Big[\frac{n(n+1)}{2} - T^+ \leq \frac{n(n+1)}{2} - t_\alpha | H_0\Big]$$

$$= P[T^- \leq t_\alpha^- | H_0]$$

**Calculation of critical value ($t_{\alpha,n}$)**

Consider the testing problem

$$H_0 : Md = \mu_0 \quad \text{against} \quad H_1 : Md < \mu_0$$

The WSRT is given by

$$\phi(T^+) = \begin{cases} 1 & \text{if } T^+ < t_{n,\alpha} \\ a & \text{if } T^+ = t_{\alpha,n} \\ 0 & \text{if } T^+ > t_{\alpha,n} \end{cases}$$

where, $t_{\alpha,n}$ is determined by

$$E[\phi(T_n^+) | H_0] = \alpha$$

or

$$\frac{1}{2^n} [u(0) + u(1) + \ldots, +u(t_{\alpha,n})] = \alpha$$

$$u(0, 1, \ldots, t_{\alpha,n}) = \alpha \cdot 2^n$$

where, $u(0, 1, \ldots, t_\alpha)$ : total number of points $\mathbf{Z}$ in the space of $\mathbf{Z}$ which gives $T^+ = 0$ or $1$ or $2, \ldots, t_{\alpha,n}$.

## 10.8 Solved Examples

**Example 10.8.1.** *Let* $n = 3$, $\alpha = 0.25$; $2^n\alpha = 2^3 \times 0.25 = 8 \times 0.25 = 2$, *Find out* $t_{\alpha,n}$, *so that* $u(0, 1, \ldots, t_{\alpha,n}) = 2$.

***Solution:*** Null distribution of $T^+$ has been calculated in Table 10.6, from which we get $t_{\alpha,n} = 1$ so that $u(0, 1) = 2$.

**Table 10.6:** Null distribution of $T^+$ and critical value $t_{\alpha,n}$

| $T^+ = t$ | $\mathbf{Z}'s$ s.t.$\mathbf{I}'\mathbf{Z} = t$ | $u(t)$ | $u(0,1,\ldots,t_\alpha)$ |
|---|---|---|---|
| 0 | (0,0,0) | 1 | 1 |
| 1 | (1,0,0) | 1 | $2 = u(0,1)$ |
| 2 | (0,1,0) | 1 | 3 |
| 3 | (1,1,0); (0,0,1) | 2 | 5 |
| 4 | $(\cdots)$ | 1 | 7 |
| 5 | $(\cdots)$ | 1 | 8 |
| 6 | $(\cdots)$ | 1 | 9 |

We shall now consider another example with larger value of $n$.

**Example 10.8.2.** *Suppose $n = 8$ and let the testing problem be*

$$H_0 : Md = \mu_0 \quad \textit{against} \quad H_1 : Md < \mu_0$$

*Find out $t_\alpha$ at level $\alpha$=0.05.*

***Solution:*** We have $\alpha = 0.05$, which gives

$$u(0,1,\ldots,t_\alpha) = 2^8 \times 0.05 = 256 \times 0.05 = 12.8$$

**Table 10.7:** Null distribution of $T^+$ and critical value $t_{\alpha,n}$

| $T^+ = t$ | No. of $\mathbf{Z}'s$ which gives $T^+ = t$ | $u(t)$ | $u(0,1,\ldots,t_\alpha)$ |
|---|---|---|---|
| 0 | (0,0,0,0,0,0,0,0) | 1 | 1 |
| 1 | (1,0,0,0,0,0,0,0) | 1 | 2 |
| 2 | (0,1,0,0,0,0,0,0) | 1 | 3 |
| 3 | (1,1,0,0,0,0,0,0); (0,0,1,0,0,0,0,0) | 2 | 5 |
| 4 | (1,0,1,0,0,0,0,0); (0,0,0,1,0,0,0,0) | 2 | 7 |
| 5 | 5; 2,3; 1,4 | 3 | 10 |
| 6 | 6; 2,4;1,5;1,2,3 | 4 | 14 |
| . | . | . | . |
| . | . | . | . |
| . | . | . | . |

From Table 10.7, we get $t_\alpha$ s.t. $u(0,1,\ldots,t_{\alpha,n}) \leq 2^n \cdot \alpha = 12.8$, $t_\alpha = 5$, the size at $t_{\alpha,n}$

$$P(T^+ \leq 5|H_0) = \frac{10}{256} = 0.039 < 0.05$$

and if we take $t_\alpha = 6$, we get

$$P(T^+ \leq 6|H_0) = 12/256 > 0.05$$

Therefore, the exact level of significance at which WSRT is carried out is 0.039, slightly below 0.05.

The formula $P[T_n^+ = t|H_0]$ with $0 < k \leq \dfrac{n(n+1)}{2}$ is needed when the null distribution of $T^+$ is required for several samples of different sizes. Let WSRT, $T_n^+$, be based on $n$ observations. And let the distribution of $T_{n-1}^+$, be known. Let $X_n$ is observed at the $n^{th}$ draw, and $|D_n| = |X_n - \mu_0|$, we can assume without loss of generality that $|D_n| > |D_i| \;\; \forall i = 1, \ldots, n-1$. In this case, $r(|D_n|) = n$.

The event $[T_n^+ = t]$ occurs if $D_n < 0$ and $T_{n-1}^+ = t$ or $D_n > 0$ and $T_{n-1}^+ = t - n$.
Therefore,

$$\begin{aligned} P[T_n^+ = t|H_0] &= P[T_{n-1}^+ = t - n|D_n > 0] \cdot P(D_n > 0) \\ &\quad + P[T_{n-1}^+ = t|D_n < 0] \cdot P(D_n < 0) \\ &= \frac{u_{n-1}(t-n)}{2^{n-1}} \cdot \frac{1}{2} + \frac{u_{n-1}(t)}{2^{n-1}} \cdot \frac{1}{2} \\ &= \frac{1}{2^n}[u_{n-1}(t-n) + u_{n-1}(t)] \end{aligned}$$

Here, we assume

$$u_n(t) = 0 \quad \text{if} \;\; t < 0 \quad \text{or} \;\; t > \frac{n(n+1)}{2}$$

**Example 10.8.3.** Gibbons (1971)[71] *Prove that the Wilcoxon-Signed-Rank statistic $T^+ - T^-$ based on a set of non-zero observations $X_1, X_2, \ldots, X_n$ can be written symbolically in the form*

$$\sum_{1 \leq i} \sum_{\leq j \leq n} sgn(X_i + X_j)$$

*where*

$$sgn(x) = \begin{cases} 1 & \text{if } x > 0 \\ -1 & \text{if } x < 0 \end{cases}$$

***Solution:*** Let us define

$$S^*(X_j, X_i) = \begin{cases} -1 & \text{if } X_i < 0 \text{ and } |X_j| > |X_i| \\ 0 & \text{if } X_i > 0 \end{cases}$$

for $i = 1, 2, \ldots, n, \;\; j \neq i = 1, \ldots, n$.

$$\begin{aligned} \sum_{\substack{j=1 \\ j \neq i}} S^*(X_j, X_i) &= \begin{cases} -(\text{number of observations } X_j, j \neq i = 1, 2, \ldots, n \\ \text{for which } |X_j| > |X_i| \text{ and } X_i < 0) \\ 0 \qquad \text{if } X_i > 0, \; i = 1, 2, \ldots, n \end{cases} \\ &= \begin{cases} -(R_i - 1) & \text{if } X_i < 0 \\ 0 & \text{if } X_i > 0 \end{cases} \end{aligned}$$

or

$$R_i = 1 - \sum_{j \neq i=1}^{n} S^*(X_j, X_i) \text{ (where, } R_i \text{ is the rank of } |X_i|s,$$

$$i = 1, \ldots, n \text{ for which } X_i < 0)$$

By the definition of $T^-$

$$T^- = \sum_{\substack{i=1 \\ x_i<0}}^{n} R_i = \sum_{\substack{i=1 \\ x_i<0}}^{n} \left[- \sum_{j \neq i=1}^{n} S^*(X_j, X_i) + 1\right]$$

or

$$T^- = -\sum_{i=1}^{n} \sum_{\substack{j \neq i=1 \\ x_i<0}}^{n} S^*(X_j, X_i) + (n - s)$$

where, $s$ is the number of positive observations.

or

$$T^- = -\sum_{i=1}^{n}\Big[\sum_{j<i} S^*(X_j, X_i) + \sum_{j>i} S^*(X_j, X_i)\Big] + (n - s)$$

$$= -\sum_{i=1}^{n}\Big[\sum_{j>i} S^*(X_j, X_i) + \sum_{j>i} S^*(X_i, X_j)\Big] + (n - s)$$

$$= -\sum_{i=1}^{n}\sum_{j>i}\{S^*(X_j, X_i) + S^*(X_i, X_j)\} + (n - s)$$

Let us define

$$S'(X_i, X_j) = S^*(X_j, X_i) + S^*(X_i, X_j)$$

Therefore,

$$S'(X_i, X_j) = \begin{cases} -1 & \text{if } \begin{cases} \text{if } X_i < 0 \text{ and } |X_j| > |X_i| \\ \text{or} \\ \text{if } X_j < 0 \text{ and } |X_i| > |X_j| \end{cases} \\ 0 & \text{otherwise} \end{cases}$$

Let us now define

$$S(X_i, X_j) = \begin{cases} 1 & \text{if} \begin{cases} X_i > 0 \text{ and } |X_j| < |X_i| \\ \text{or} \\ X_j > 0 \text{ and } |X_i| < |X_j| \end{cases} \\ 0 & \text{otherwise} \end{cases}$$

Using this, we can express WSRT as

$$T^+ = \sum_{i=1}^{n}\sum_{j>i} S(X_i, X_j) + s$$

where, $s$ is the number of positive observations. Let us now calculate

$$T^+ - T^- = +\sum_{i=1}^{n}\sum_{j>i} S'(X_i, X_j) + s + \sum_{i=1}^{n}\sum_{j>i} S(X_i, X_j) - (n-s)$$

$$= \sum_{i=1}^{n}\sum_{j>1}\{S'(X_i, X_j) + S(X_i, X_j)\} + s - (n-s)$$

But

$$S(X_i, X_j) + S'(X_i, X_j) = sgn(X_i + X_j)$$

$$= \begin{cases} 1 & \text{if } X_i + X_j > 0 \\ -1 & \text{if } X_i + X_j < 0 \end{cases}$$

Therefore,

$$T^+ - T^- = \sum_{i=1}^{n}\sum_{j>i} sgn(X_i + X_j) + s - (n-s)$$

For $i = j$, we have

$$sgn(X_i + X_j) = \begin{cases} 1 & \text{if } 2X_i > 0 \\ -1 & \text{if } 2X_i < 0 \end{cases}$$

$$= \begin{cases} 1 & \text{if } X_i > 0 \\ -1 & \text{if } X_i < 0 \end{cases}$$

$$\sum_{i=1}^{n}\sum_{j=i} sgn(X_i + X_j) = \text{ no. of +ve signs - no. of -ve signs} = s - (n-s)$$

Hence,

$$T^+ - T^- = \sum_{i=1}^{n}\sum_{j>i} sgn(X_i + X_j) + \sum_{i=1}^{n}\sum_{j=i} sgn(X_i + X_j)$$

$$= \sum_{1 \le i \le j \le n}{}' sgn(X_i + X_j)$$

## Review Questions

**10.1** It is desired to test, whether the number of gamma rays emitted per second by a certain radio active substance, is a random variable having the poisson distribution with $\lambda = 2.4$. Use the following data obtained for 300 one seconds intervals to test this null hypothesis at the 0.05 level of significance.

(Given $\chi^2_{0.05,7} = 14.067$, $\chi^2_{0.05,6} = 12.592$, $\chi^2_{0.05,5} = 11.070$)

| No. of gamma rays | 0 | 1 | 2 | 3 | 4 | 5 | 6 | 7 or more |
|---|---|---|---|---|---|---|---|---|
| Frequency | 19 | 48 | 66 | 74 | 44 | 35 | 10 | 4 |

**10.2** Justify the use of chi-square as test of goodness-of-fit. A set of 6 similar coins was tossed together 640 times and the frequency $f(x)$ of the tosses giving $x$ heads was found to be as follows: Fitting a suitable distribution

| $x$ | 0 | 1 | 2 | 3 | 4 | 5 | 6 |
|---|---|---|---|---|---|---|---|
| $f(x)$ | 13 | 62 | 145 | 194 | 153 | 64 | 9 |

to the data, carry out the test of goodness-of-fit as far as you can without the use of any statistical table and state how you would proceed further.

**10.3** Describe chi-square and Kolmogorov test for goodness-of-fit, stating necessary assumption for both one and two-sided alternatives and compare. Indicate how the Kolmogorov statistic may be used to set a confidence band for the distribution function.

**10.4** Describe the premises in which non-parametric tests are appropriate. Discuss the common non-parametric test of location.

**10.5** Describe clearly (a) one-sample sign test and (b) paired-sample Sign test. State the assumptions and nature of hypothesis being tested in each case.

**10.6** (a) Define sign test giving details on testing problem, the model, the hypothesis and the decision rule. What is its parametric counterpart?

(b) Prove that the one-sided sign test is UMP among all level $\alpha$ distribution free tests of the hypothesis

$$H_0 : G \in \gamma \text{ against } H_1 : G \in \Gamma$$
$$\text{where } \gamma = \{G|G(\mu_0) = 1/2\} \text{ and } \Gamma = \{G|G(\mu_0) < 1/2\};$$

$\mu_0$ being the median of the distribution $G$.

**10.7** Obtain $100(1-\alpha)\%$ confidence interval for the population median based on the sign test.

**10.8** Discuss Wilcoxon Signed-Rank test, and examine its consistency.

**10.9** Describe (a) the sign test (b) Wilcoxon Signed-Rank test for the median of a population. Show how these can be adapted to the case of paired samples. Which of the two tests for paired samples would you use in different practical situations and why?

**10.10** Ten students were given a test in mathematics. They were given a month's further tuition and a second test of equal difficulty was held at the end of it. If $\theta$ is the median of population of differences, make a

| Roll number | 1 | 2 | 3 | 4 | 5 | 6 | 7 | 8 | 9 | 10 |
|---|---|---|---|---|---|---|---|---|---|---|
| Marks of test I | 9 | 12 | 8 | 14 | 2 | 7 | 8 | 11 | 9 | 11 |
| Marks of test II | 15 | 20 | 9 | 17 | 5 | 8 | 11 | 9 | 13 | 9 |

sign test for testing the null hypothesis $H_0 : \theta = 0$ against alternative $H_1 : \theta > 0$ (you are given : probability of 2 or fewer minus signs in 10 independent trials with $p = 0.5$ is 0.055).

**10.11** (a) What is meant by a consistent test? Prove that one-sided Wilcoxon's Signed-Rank test is consistent.

(b) Explain conversion of right-sided critical region to left-sided critical region. What is its importance?

(c) Derive the recursion formula for finding $P[T_n^+ = k|H_0]$.

**10.12** Two experimental drugs developed for the treatment of hypertension were administered to seven pairs of patients. The drop in diastolic pressure for each patient (in millimeters of mercury) is recorded below:

| Drug 1 | 10 | 16 | 10 | 4 | 2 | 14 | 4 |
|---|---|---|---|---|---|---|---|
| Drug 2 | 6 | 20 | 8 | 12 | 8 | 4 | 15 |

Apply Wilcoxon Signed-Rank test to see if there was any difference in the effectiveness of the drugs. (For $n = 7$ and $\alpha = 0.10$, the critical value c for two sided test is 4).

# Chapter 11

# Univariate Two-Sample Problem of Location and Scale

## 11.1 INTRODUCTION

In this chapter we shall consider two univariate continuous populations $G_1$ and $G_2$ and shall be concerned with the data which consist of two independent samples drawn from each of them. Not only the observations within each sample are independent but also between samples. Let us consider the random samples $X_{11}, \ldots, X_{1n_1}$ of size $n_1$ from $G_1$ and $X_{21}, \ldots, X_{2n_2}$ of size $n_2$ from $G_2$, respectively.

In a two-sample problem one is usually interested in the hypothesis that these two populations are identical, i.e.

$$H_0 : G_1(x) = G_2(x) \quad \forall\ x \tag{11.1}$$

against some specified alternative. We shall discuss all working types of alternatives in the Section 11.2.

Let us introduce some notations required for the development of theory for this testing problem:

**Definition 11.1.1. (Distribution Function)** The distribution function shall be given by

$$G = \{G_1(x),\, G_2(x)\} \tag{11.2}$$

**Definition 11.1.2. (Sample Size)** We shall draw a sample of size $n_1$ from the first population $G_1$ and $n_2$ from the second population $G_2$ and

$$n_1 + n_2 = n : \text{ is the total sample size}$$

**Definition 11.1.3. (Test Function)** The test function for the testing problem in Eq. (11.2) shall depend on the two samples of size $n_1$ and $n_2$.

A sequence of total sample sizes shall be represented by $\{n_{(k)}\}$ and corresponding to any such sequence let there exist subsequences $\{n_{1(k)}\}$ and $\{n_{2(k)}\}$ of individual sample sizes $n_1$ and $n_2$.

We shall throughout assume that the sample sizes from the respective populations bear a definite ratio to the total sample size. Hence,

$$\lim_{k\to\infty} n_{(k)} = \infty$$

$$\lim_{k\to\infty} \frac{n_{1(k)}}{n_{(k)}} = f_1 \text{ and } \lim_{k\to\infty} \frac{n_{2(k)}}{n_{(k)}} = f_2$$

where, $f_1$ and $f_2$ are the numbers such that

$$0 < f_1 < 1, \quad 0 < f_2 < 1 \quad \text{and } f_1 + f_2 = 1$$

We shall also denote the sequence of test functions by

$$\phi = \{\phi_{n(k)}\}$$

corresponding to the sequence of total sample size $\{n_{(k)}\}$.

**Definition 11.1.4. (Consistency)** A sequence of test functions $\{\phi_{n(k)}\}$ is said to be consistent against the alternative $G$ if $\lim_{k\to\infty} \beta_{\phi_{n(k)}}(G) = 1$ where $n_{(k)} = n_{1(k)} + n_{2(k)}$.

**Definition 11.1.5. (Asymptotic Power)** The asymptotic power of a sequence of tests $\phi = \{\phi_{n(k)}\}$ for a sequence of alternatives $\{G_{(k)}\}$ is defined as $\lim_{k\to\infty} \beta_{\phi_{n(k)}}(G_{(k)})$.

**Definition 11.1.6. (Asymptotic Relative Efficiency)** Suppose for the same testing problem there are two test functions $\phi$ and $\phi^*$. Let $\{G_{(k)}\}$ be the sequence of alternatives and $\{n_{(k)}\}, \{n^*_{(k)}\}$ be the sequence of sample sizes on which the tests $\phi$ and $\phi^*$ are respectively based. Suppose further that the following conditions are satisfied:

(a) $\lim_{k\to\infty} \beta_{\phi_{\{n(k)\}}}(G) = \lim_{k\to\infty} \beta_{\phi_{\{n^*(k)\}}}(G) = \alpha;\ \forall\ G \in \gamma$

(b) $\lim_{k\to\infty} \beta_{\phi_{\{n(k)\}}}(G_{(k)}) = \lim_{k\to\infty} \beta_{\phi_{\{n^*(k)\}}}(G_{(k)}) = \beta,$

where $G_{(k)} \in \{G_{(k)}\}$ and $G_{(k)} \in \Gamma_1 = \Gamma - \gamma$

(c) $\lim_{k\to\infty} \frac{n_{1(k)}}{n_{(k)}} = f_1;\ \lim_{k\to\infty} \frac{n_{2(k)}}{n_{(k)}} = f_2$

$0 < f_1, f_2 < 1;\ f_1 + f_2 = 1$

Under the conditions given in (a), (b) and (c), Asymptotic Relative Efficiency (ARE) of the test $\phi$ relative to $\phi^*$ for the common sequence of alternatives $\{G_{(k)}\}$ has been defined as

$$ARE(\phi,\, \phi^*) = \lim_{k\to\infty} \frac{n^*_{(k)}}{n_{(k)}}$$

provided the limit exists and is independent of $\alpha$, $\beta$, $f_1$, $f_2$ and the particular sequence $\{n_{(k)}\}$ and $\{n^*_{(k)}\}$ chosen.

## 11.2 FIVE STANDARD SENSES OF ALTERNATIVES

We shall discuss the five standard senses of alternative hypothesis in which one population is said to be located to the right of the other.

In the univariate two sample problem we draw one sample $X_{11}, \ldots, X_{1n_1}$ of size $n_1$ from a continuous population $G_1$ and second sample $X_{21}, X_{22}, \ldots,$ $X_{2n_2}$ of size $n_2$ from the second continuous population $G_2$. We wish to test the hypothesis

$$H_0 : G_1(x) = G_2(x) \qquad \forall\ x$$

Let us define a class $\gamma = \{(G_1,\, G_2)|G_1(x) = G_2(x)\ \ \forall\ x\}$. The null hypothesis may now be written as

$$H_0 : (G_1, G_2) \in \gamma$$

The alternative may be written as

$$H_1 : G_2(x) \text{ is located to right of } G_1(x)$$

Now, define $\quad \Gamma_1 = \{(G_1, G_2)|G_2(x) \text{ is located to the right of } G_1\}$

The alternative may be rewritten as

$$H_1 : (G_1, G_2) \in \Gamma_1$$

We shall now discuss different senses of the above alternatives $\Gamma_1$.

**Sense-I:** In this case $G_2$ can be obtained by shifting $G_1(x)$ by a positive quantity $\theta > 0$ towards right, i.e.

$$G_2(x) = G_1(x - \theta) \text{ for } \theta > 0, \ \ \forall\ x$$

This situation is explained in Figure 11.1.

In this case, the set of alternatives has been denoted by $\Gamma_1^{(1)}$ and defined as:

$$\Gamma_1^{(1)} = \{(G_1, G_2) : G_2(x) = G_1(x - \theta)\ \forall\, x \in \mathbb{R}^1 \text{ and } \theta > 0\}$$

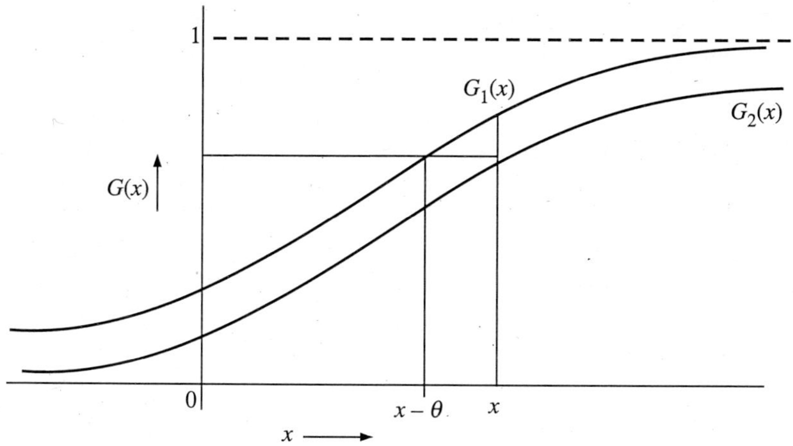


**Figure 11.1:** Sense-I.

**Sense-II:** This is a situation when we say $G_2(x)$ is stochastically larger than $G_1$ or $G_2$ dominates $G_1$ when $G_2$ differs $G_1$ not only in terms of location, but in the functional form as well. The set of alternatives is denoted by $\Gamma_1^{(2)}$. This situation is shown in Figure 11.1.

$$\begin{aligned}\Gamma_1^{(2)} = \{(G_1, G_2)\ :\ & G_2(x) = G_1(x-\theta(x))\ \forall\ x,\ \theta(x) > 0\\ & \text{or}\ \ G_2(x) \leq G_1(x) \quad \forall\ x \text{ and } G_2(x) < G_1(x)\\ & \text{for at least one } x \text{ s.t. } \theta(x) > 0\}\end{aligned}$$

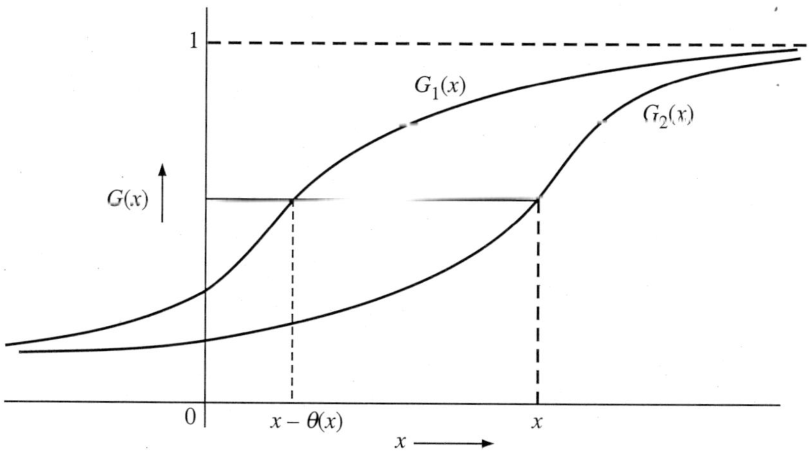


**Figure 11.2:** Sense-II.

**Example 11.2.1.** *Show that* $\Gamma_1^{(2)} \subset \Gamma_1^{(1)}$.

***Solution:*** Consider, $(G_1, G_2) \in \Gamma_1^{(2)}$, i.e. $G_2(x) = G_1(x - \theta(x))$, for $\theta(x) > 0$ let, $\theta(x) = \theta$, we have, $G_2(x) = G_1(x - \theta)$. This shows that, $(G_1, G_2) \in \Gamma_1^{(1)}$.

**Theorem 11.2.1.** *$X_2$ is stochastically larger than $X_1$ if and only if there exists a non-decreasing function $h(x)$ such that*

(a) $h(X) \geq x \quad \forall\, x \in \mathbb{R}^1$

(b) *$h(X_1)$ is distributed same as $X_2$ and*

(c) $P[h(X_1) > X_1] > 0$

*Proof.* Consider (a), which says

$$h(x) \geq x \quad \text{or} \quad h(x) = x + \theta$$

Further, consider

$$P[h(X_1) \leq x] = P[X_1 + \theta \leq x] = P[X_1 \leq x - \theta] = G_1(x - \theta)$$

Since (b) says $h(X_1)$ is distributed same as $X_2$, i.e.

$$P[h(X_1) \leq x] = P[X_2 \leq x] = G_2(x)$$

This implies

$$G_2(x) = G_1(x - \theta)$$

or $G_2$ is stochastically larger then $G_1$, or $X_2$ is stochastically larger than $X_1$.
Only if proof: Suppose $X_2$ is stochastically larger than $X_1$,

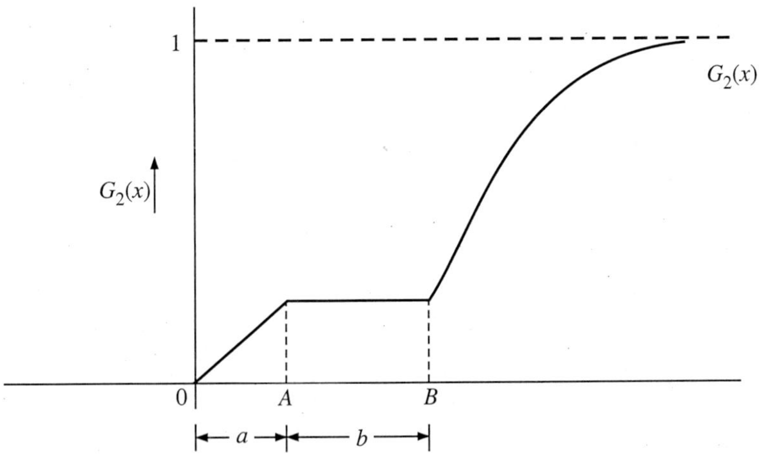


**Figure 11.3:** $X_2$ is stochastically larger than $X_1$.

Define $a$ and $b$ s.t.

$$a = G_2^{-1}(y) = \inf_{\{x: G_2(x) = y\}} x; \qquad b = G_2^{-1}(y) = \sup_{\{x: G_2(x) = y\}} x \quad \text{(refer Fig. 11.3)}$$

Let us consider a function

$$h(x) = G_2^{-1}(G_1(x))$$

Now consider, $x_1, x_2 \in \mathbb{R}^1$ so that, $x_1 \leq x_2$. Also consider

$$h(x_1) = G_2^{-1}(G_1(x_1)) \text{ or } G_2(h(x_1)) = G_1(x_1) \text{ since } x_1 \leq x_2$$

$G_1(x_1) \leq G_1(x_2)$ (by the definition of distribution function $G_1$), therefore,

$$G_2(h(x_1)) \leq G_1(x_2)$$

or

$$h(x_1) \leq G_2^{-1}(G_1(x_2)) = h(x_2)$$

This shows that $h$ is a non-decreasing function and this proves (a).
We shall now show that $h(X_1)$ is distributed like $X_2$. For this consider

$$\begin{aligned} P[h(X_1) \leq a] &= P[G_2^{-1}G_1(X_1) \leq a] \\ &= P[G_1(X_1) \leq G_2(a)] \\ &= P[X_1 \leq G_1^{-1}G_2(a)] \\ &= G_1G_1^{-1}G_2(a) = G_2(a) \\ &= P[X_2 \leq a] \end{aligned}$$

This shows that $h(X_1)$ and $X_2$ are identically distributed and this proves (b).
Let us now consider

$$\begin{aligned} P[h(X_1) > X_1] &= P[G_2^{-1}G_1(X_1) > X_1] \\ &= P[G_1(X_1) > G_2(X_1)] \\ &> 0 \text{ (since } G_2 \text{ is stochastically larger than } G_1) \end{aligned}$$

This proves (c). □

**Theorem 11.2.2.** *If $G_1$ and $G_2$ are the two univariate continuous distribution functions which are members of $\Gamma_1^{(2)}$, then there exists an open interval $(a, b)$, finite or infinite, for which*

$$G_2(x) < G_1(x) \;\; \forall\, x \in (a, b) \;\; \textit{and} \;\; P[a < X_1 < b] \;\; \textit{and} \;\; P[a < X_2 < b]$$

*are positive.*

*Proof.* It is given that $(G_1, G_2) \in \Gamma_1^{(2)}$, by its definition there exists at least one point

$$X = x_1$$

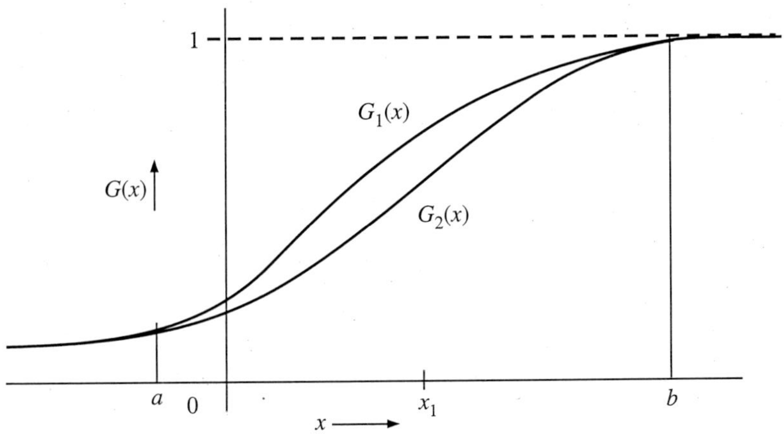


**Figure 11.4:** Distributions of $G_1$ and $G_2$ (Theorem 11.2.2).

at which

$$G_2(x_1) < G_1(x_1)$$

or

$$G_1(x_1) - G_2(x_1) > 0$$

Since both the distributions are continuous, therefore, we must have a neighbourhood around $x_1, (a, b)$ say, s.t.

$$G_2(x) < G_1(x) \ \ \forall \ x \ \in (a, b)$$

$a$ and $b$ would be defined as

$$a = \begin{cases} \sup_{\{x : G_2(x) = G_1(x), \ x < x_1\}} x & \text{if } \{x : G_2(x) = G_1(x), \ x < x_1\} \\ & \text{is non-empty} \\ -\infty & \text{if this class is empty} \end{cases}$$

$$b = \begin{cases} \inf_{\{x : G_2(x) = G_1(x), \ x > x_1\}} x & \text{if } \{x : G_2(x) = G_1(x), x > x_1\} \\ & \text{is non-empty} \\ +\infty & \text{otherwise} \end{cases}$$

To show $P[a < X_1 < b]$ and $P[a < X_2 < b]$ is positive it is enough to show that the interval $(a, b)$ is non-empty. But the definition of $a$ and $b$ shows that $(a, b)$ is non-empty (Fig. 11.4). This proves the theorem. □

**Sense-III:** In this sense, $G_2$ is said to be located to the right of $G_1$ when

$$P[X_1 < X_2] \ > \ P[X_1 > X_2] \quad (X_2 \text{ is stochastically larger than } X_1) \quad (11.3)$$

Since $X_1$ and $X_2$ are continuous random variables

$$P(X_1 = X_2) = 0$$

Therefore, on adding $P[X_1 < X_2]$ on both sides of Eq. (11.3), we get

$$P[X_1 < X_2] + P[X_1 < X_2] > P[X_1 > X_2] + P[X_1 < X_2]$$

or

$$2P[X_1 < X_2] > 1 \quad \text{or} \quad P[X_1 < X_2] > 1/2$$

Now, consider

$$\begin{aligned} P[X_1 < X_2] &= \int_{-\infty}^{\infty} P[X_1 < x | X_2 = x] \cdot P[X_2 = x]\, dx \\ &= \int_{-\infty}^{\infty} P[X_1 < x | X_2 = x]\, dG_2(x) \\ &= \int_{-\infty}^{\infty} G_1(x)\, dG_2(x) > 1/2 \end{aligned}$$

or

$$\int_{-\infty}^{\infty} 2G_1(x)\, dG_2(x) > 1 \quad \text{or} \quad \int_{-\infty}^{\infty} [2G_1(x) - 1]\, dG_2(x) > 0$$

Denoting $\int_{-\infty}^{\infty} [2G_1(x) - 1]\, dG_2(x) = \Delta_W(G_1, G_2)$, we have, $\Delta_W(G_1, G_2) > 0$. But under $H_0 : G_2(x) = G_1(x) \ \ \forall\ x$, we have

$$\Delta_W(G_1, G_2) = \int_{-\infty}^{\infty} [2G_1(x) - 1]\, dG_1(x)$$

Let

$$2\, G_1(x) - 1 = y \quad \text{or} \quad 2\, dG_1(x) = dy$$

Therefore,

$$\Delta_W(G_1, G_2) = \frac{1}{2} \int_{-1}^{1} y\, dy = \frac{1}{2} \frac{y^2}{2} \bigg|_{-1}^{1} = \frac{1}{4}[1 - 1] = 0$$

Hence, $H_0$ can we written as

$$H_0 : \Delta_W(G_1, G_2) = 0$$

We shall now denote the set of alternatives under this sense as $\Gamma_1^{(3)}$

$$\Gamma_1^{(3)} = \{(G_1, G_2) \,:\, \Delta_W(G_1, G_2) > 0\}$$

The set of alternatives $\Gamma_1^{(3)}$ shall be used while discussing Wilcoxon Mann Whitney test later in this chapter.

**Example 11.2.2.** *Show* $\Gamma_1^{(2)} \subset \Gamma_1^{(3)}$.

***Solution:*** Let $(G_1, G_2) \in \Gamma_1^{(2)}$

i.e. $G_2(x) \le G_1(x)\ \forall\ x$ and $G_2(x) < G_1(x)$ for at least one $x$

Consider now
$$\Delta_W(G_1, G_2) = \int_{-\infty}^{\infty} (2G_1(x) - 1)\, dG_2(x)$$
$$> \int_{-\infty}^{\infty} (2G_2(x) - 1)\, dG_2(x) = 0$$

This implies
$$(G_1, G_2) \in \Gamma_1^{(3)}.$$

**Sense-IV:** We have already discussed the sequences $\{n_{1(k)}\}$ and $\{n_{2(k)}\}$ of individual sample sizes from the first and the second populations, respectively, at the beginning of this chapter. We have also discussed the conditions

$$f_1 = \lim_{k\to\infty} \frac{n_{1(k)}}{n_{(k)}} \quad \text{and} \quad f_2 = \lim_{k\to\infty} \frac{n_{2(k)}}{n_{(k)}}$$

and that, $0 < f_1,\ f_2 < 1$ so that $f_1 + f_2 = 1$. Let $X$ be a normal random variable. The ordinates may be expressed as $N^{-1}(y)$, for some $0 < y < 1$, $N^{-1}$ being the inverse of the cdf of $N(0, 1)$ (Fig. 11.5).

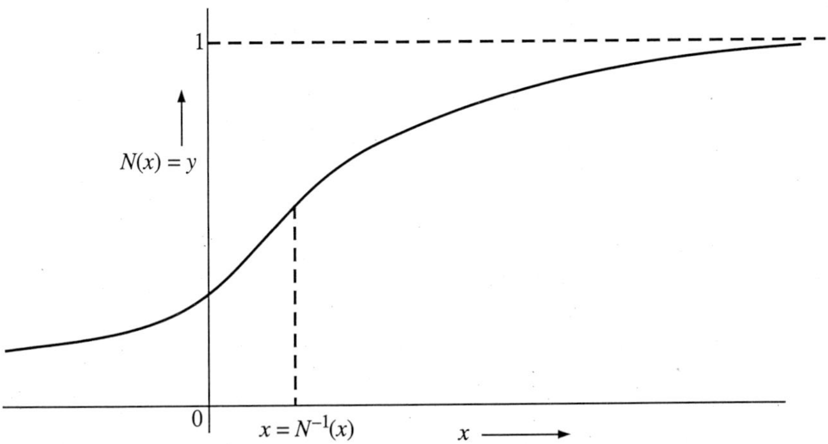


**Figure 11.5:** Sense-IV.

Let us consider

$$\Delta_N(G_1, G_2) = \int_{-\infty}^{\infty} N^{-1}[f_1 G_1(x) + f_2 G_2(x)]\, dG_2(x)$$

Under $H_0$ it takes the value

$$\Delta_N(G_1, G_2) = \int_{-\infty}^{\infty} N^{-1}[(f_1 + f_2)\, G_2(x)]\, dG_2(x)$$

Let $G_2(x) = z$ then, we have $\Delta_N(G_1, G_2) = \int_{z=0}^{z=1} N^{-1}(z)\, dz$

$$N^{-1}(z) = u; \quad z = N(u); \quad dz = dN(u)$$

We have, now

$$\Delta_N(G_1, G_2) = \int_{-\infty}^{\infty} u\, dN(u) = 0$$

The set of alternatives for which $\Delta_N(G_1, G_2) > 0$ denoted by

$$\Gamma_1^{(4)} = \{(G_1, G_2) : \Delta_N(G_1, G_2) > 0\}$$

**Example 11.2.3.** *Show that* $\Gamma_1^{(2)} \subset \Gamma_1^{(4)}$.

***Solution:*** Let

$$(G_1, G_2) \in \Gamma_1^{(2)}$$

$$G_2(x) \leq G_1(x) \quad \forall\, x$$

and $G_2(x) < G_1(x)$ for at least one $x$ Let us consider

$$\Delta_N(G_1, G_2) = \int_{-\infty}^{\infty} N^{-1}(f_1 G_1(x) + f_2 G_2(x))\, dG_2(x)$$

$$> \int_{-\infty}^{\infty} N^{-1}(f_1 G_2(x) + f_2 G_2(x))\, dG_2(x)$$

$$= \int_{-\infty}^{\infty} N^{-1}(G_2(x))\, dG_2(x) = 0$$

or

$$\Delta_N(G_1, G_2) > 0 \text{ this implies } \Gamma_1^{(2)} \subset \Gamma_1^{(4)}.$$

**Sense-V:** Let

$$m(G_i) = \inf x_{\{x:G_i(x)=\frac{1}{2}\}} = A_i; \quad M(G_i) = \sup x_{\{x:G_i(x)=\frac{1}{2}\}} = B_i$$

The set of alternatives of fifth sense is defined as

$$\Gamma_1^{(5)} = \{(G_1, G_2) : m(G_2) > M(G_1)\}$$

We shall see that the set of alternatives $\Gamma_1^{(5)}$ arises in connection with the Median test and also with the Mood's median test.

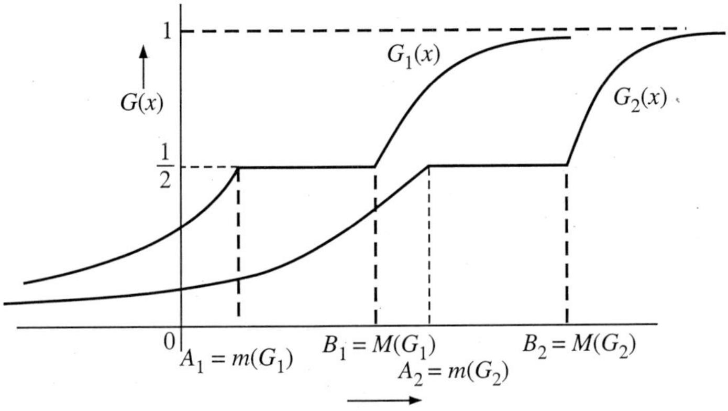


**Figure 11.6:** Sense-V.

We are now prepared to test the equality of the two populations $G_1$ and $G_2$ in terms of location, but the null hypotheses we had actually formulated were in regard to test whether two populations are completely identical. This is an apparent limitation of the above two sample location problem. The literature suggests that this is not a very serious limitation since tests which are consistent only for certain alternatives are insensitive against other alternatives, and secondly, location tests are applied only when there is a possibility of location difference.

## 11.3 DATA SUMMARIZATION THROUGH INVARIANCE PRINCIPLE

We refer Fraser (1953)[63], 1965 [65] for the following developments. In the beginning of the Section 11.2, we noted that if $X_1$ and $X_2$ are two independent random variables with continuous cdf's $G_1(x)$ and $G_2(x)$, the cdf of the difference $X_2 - X_1$ shall be given by

$$P\{X_2 - X_1 \le z\} = \int_{-\infty}^{\infty} G_2(z + x)\, dG_1(x)$$

(Section 11.2) which is continuous in $z$ since $G_2$, on the right hand side, is continuous in $z$. This gives

$$P\{X_2 - X_1 = 0\} = 0,$$

i.e. the probability of there being one or more than one ties in their values is zero. As a consequence, we shall now exclude those points from combined ordered sample space in which the coordinates are not all distinct, since the probability measure of such points is zero for all $G \in \Gamma$.

Let the two samples $X_{11}, X_{12}, \ldots, X_{1n_1}$, and $X_{21}, X_{22}, \ldots, X_{2n_2}$ be combined. Arrange the values in increasing order by assigning the rank 1 to the least value, the rank 2 to the next higher value, and so on, the rank $n$ being assigned to the largest value. There shall be no difficulty in assigning rank to these observations since probability of ties is zero. Let the ranks assigned to first sample observations be denoted by $R_{11}, R_{12}, \ldots, R_{1n_1}$ and corresponding to the second sample by $R_{21}, R_{22}, \ldots, R_{2n_2}$. We shall use pooled ranks to define the statistic for the two sample testing problem. There are two considerations by which rank tests are preferred, first, the practical consideration of finite sample space so that computations become easier. Such tests are not sensitive to outlying observations which may come from bad data where a particular variable is difficult to measure but easy to rank by. Secondly, the theoretical considerations suggest the use of rank tests as these come out to be the invariant tests by applying the principle of invariance.

We shall now show that the invariance consideration lead us to a special kind of test based on combined sample ranks when applied to the two sample problem.

Let us consider the testing problem $H_0 : G_1(x) = G_2(x) \;\; \forall\; x$ against the alternative $G = (G_1, G_2) \in \Gamma_1^{(i)}$, $i = 2, 3, 4$ or $5$. Let $f$ be a continuous and strictly increasing function applied on the two sets of sample observations $X_{1i_1}, X_{1i_2}, \ldots, X_{1i_n}$ and $X_{2j_1}, X_{2j_2}, \ldots, X_{2j_n}$ where, $(i_1, i_2, \ldots, i_{n_1})$ and $(j_1, j_2, \ldots, j_{n_2})$ are some permutation of digits $(1, 2, \ldots, n_1)$ and $(1, 2, \ldots, n_2)$, respectively.

The transformed random variables we have $Y_{11}, Y_{12}, \ldots, Y_{1n_1}$ with $Y_{1k} = f(X_{1i_k}), k = 1, 2, \ldots, n_1$ and $Y_{21}, Y_{22}, \ldots, Y_{2n_2}$ with $Y_{2k} = f(X_{2j_k}), k = 1, 2, \ldots, n_2$. The independence of $X's$ now passes on to transformed random variables $Y's$. Here, $Y_{11}, \ldots, Y_{1n_1}$ have the common cdf $H_1(y) = P(Y \leq y) = P(h(X_{1i}) \leq y) = P(X_{1i} \leq h^{-1}(y)) = G_1\{h^{-1}(y)\}$ and $Y_{21}, \ldots, Y_{2n_2}$ have $H_2(y) = G_2\{h^{-1}(y)\}$ (since $h^{-1}(y)$ is well defined and continuous by the definition of $h$). Also, $H = (H_1, H_2)$ are continuous so as $G_1$ and $G_2$.

Further, if

$$G_1 = G_2$$

or

$$P(X_1 \leq x) = P(X_2 \leq x)$$

or

$$P(h(X_1) \leq h(x)) = P(h(X_2) \leq h(x))$$

(since $h$ is continuous and is strictly increasing)

implies $P(Y_1 \leq y) = P(Y_2 \leq y)$ or $H_1(y) = H_2(y)$ and conversely, $H_1 = H_2$ implies $G_1 = G_2$ that could easily be shown.

This proves $\overline{f}(\gamma) = \gamma$, i.e. the testing problem remains invariant under the above transformation over the null space $\gamma$.

We shall further show the same for the alternatives $\Gamma_1^{(i)}, i = 2, 3, 4, 5$ in other words, we shall show $\overline{f}(\Gamma_1^{(i)}) = \Gamma_1^{(i)}$. For this it is enough to show that

$$G = (G_1, G_2) \in \Gamma_1^{(i)} \;\text{ iff }\; H = (H_1, H_2) \in \Gamma_1^{(i)},\; i = 2, 3, 4, 5.$$

Let $(G_1, G_2) \in \Gamma_1^{(2)}$, we know that

$$H_1(y) = G_1(h^{-1}(y)) \quad \text{and} \quad H_2(y) = G_2(h^{-1}(y))$$

We have

$$G_2(x) \le G_1(x) \quad \forall\, x$$

iff

$$G_2(h^{-1}(y)) \le G_1(h^{-1}(y)) \quad \text{or} \quad H_2(y) \le H_1(y)$$

Which implies that

$$H = (H_1, H_2) \in \Gamma_1^{(2)}$$

Let us now consider

$$G = (G_1, G_2) \in \Gamma_1^{(3)} \quad \text{so that} \quad \Delta_W(G_1, G_2) > 0$$

or

$$\int_{-\infty}^{\infty} (2G_1(x) - 1)\, dG_2(x) > 0$$

iff

$$\int_{-\infty}^{\infty} (2G_1(h^{-1}(y)) - 1)\, dG_2(h^{-1}(y)) > 0$$

iff

$$\int_{-\infty}^{\infty} (2H_1(y) - 1)\, dH_2(y) > 0,$$

i.e. $\Delta_W(H_1, H_2) > 0$ which implies that $H : (H_1, H_2) \in \Gamma_1^{(3)}$.
Further, consider

$$(G_1, G_2) \in \Gamma_1^{(4)} \quad \text{so that } \Delta_N(G_1, G_2) > 0$$

or

$$\int_{-\infty}^{\infty} N^{-1}[f_1 G_1(x) + f_2 G_2(x)]\, dG_2(x) > 0$$

iff

$$\int_{-\infty}^{\infty} N^{-1}[f_1 G_1(h^{-1}(y)) + f_2 G_2(h^{-1}(y))]\, dG_2(h^{-1}(y)) > 0$$

or

$$\int_{-\infty}^{\infty} N^{-1}[f_1 H_1(y) + f_2 H_2(y)]\, dH_2(y) > 0$$

or

$$\Delta_N(H_1, H_2) \in \Gamma_1^{(4)}$$

Which implies that $H : (H_1, H_2) \in \Gamma_1^{(4)}$
Now, consider $(G_1, G_2) \in \Gamma_1^{(5)}$. By definition

$$m(G_i) = \inf_{\{x | G_i(x) = 1/2\}} (x) \quad \text{and} \quad M(G_i) = \sup_{\{x | G_i(x) = 1/2\}} (x)$$

By definition, we have

$$m(G_2) > M(G_1)$$

or

$$\inf_{\{x|G_2(x)=1/2\}}(x) > \sup_{\{x|G_1(x)=1/2\}}(x)$$

iff

$$\inf_{\{y|G_2(h^{-1}(y))=1/2\}}(y) > \sup_{\{y|G_1(h^{-1}(y))=1/2\}}(y)$$

or

$$\inf_{\{y|H_2(y)=1/2\}}(y) > \sup_{\{y|H_1(y)=1/2\}}(y)$$

which implies $H : (H_1, H_2) \in \Gamma_1^{(5)}$.

This clearly shows that the testing problem $H_0 : G_1(x) = G_2(x) \forall x$ against the alternative $G = (G_1, G_2) \in \Gamma_1^{(i)}, i = 2, 3, 4,$ or 5 is invariant under the above transformation $f$, i.e. $\overline{f}(\gamma) = \gamma$ and $\overline{f}(\Gamma_1^{(i)}) = \Gamma_1^{(i)}$, $i = 2, 3, 4, 5$. In other words, the problem remains same whether it is stated in terms of original variables or in terms of transformed variables. Therefore, test for original problem and for the changeover problem must satisfy

$$\phi(x_{11}, \ldots, x_{1n_1}; x_{21}, \ldots, x_{2n_2}) = \phi(y_{11}, \ldots, y_{1n_1}; y_{21}, \ldots, y_{2n_2})$$

Whenever

$$y_{1k} = h(x_{1i_k}); k = 1, 2, \ldots, n_1; \quad y_{2k} = h(x_{2j_k}); k = 1, 2, \ldots, n_2$$

whatever $f(x)$ be the strictly increasing and continuous function, the permutations $(i_1, \ldots, i_{n_1})$ and $(j_1, \ldots, j_{n_2})$ and whatever point $(\mathbf{x}_1, \mathbf{x}_2)$. But the two points $(\mathbf{x}_1, \mathbf{x}_2)$ and $(\mathbf{y}_1, \mathbf{y}_2)$ are connected by a transformation of the type $f(x)$, if and only if, the unordered set of ranks $\{R_{21}, \ldots R_{2n_2}\}$ assumed by the last $n_2$ observations is same for both. Thus, the statistic $\{R_{21}, \ldots, R_{2n_2}\}$ is maximal invariant for the transformation $f$. Let $S_1, \ldots, S_{n_2}$ be the ranks $R_{21}, \ldots, R_{2n_2}$ arranged in increasing order. Then $(S_1, \ldots, S_{n_2})$ represents the maximal invariant statistic for the transformation $f(x)$. Further, if we define $n$ new variables, $Z_1, Z_2, \ldots, Z_n$ where

$$Z_i = \begin{cases} 1 & \text{if the pooled rank i in the combined ordered} \\ & \text{sample comes from the second sample} \\ 0 & \text{otherwise} \end{cases}$$

Then clearly, $(S_1, \ldots, S_{n_2})$ and $(Z_1, \ldots, Z_n)$ are equivalent representations and they represent each other. Therefore, $(Z_1, \ldots, Z_n)$ is maximal invariant.

Therefore, a test $\phi$ which is invariant under all the transformations of the type $f(x)$, must be the function of the maximal invariant statistic $(S_1, \ldots, S_{n_2})$ or equivalently of $(Z_1, \ldots, Z_n)$.

It seems reasonable to define a test

$$T = \sum_{i=1}^{n_2} l(S_i) = \sum_{i=1}^{n} Z_i l(i)$$

for some non-decreasing function $l$ defined at least at points $x = 1, 2 \ldots, n$.

It is clear that large values of $T$ indicates the large values of $S_1, \ldots, S_{n_2}$, showing that the second sample comes from the population having a higher location relative to the first if $l(x)$ is non-decreasing.
Let us consider

$$l(x) = x \quad \text{which gives}$$

$$T_W = \sum_{i=1}^{n_2} S_i = \sum_{i=1}^{n} Z_i . i.$$

This gives rise to the famous Wilcoxon-Mann-Whitney test which was originally proposed for the equal sample case by Wilcoxon (1945)[212] and later developed by Mann and Whitney (1947)[137]. Next consider

$$l(i) = d_n(i) = E(V_{(i)}), \quad i = 1, 2, \ldots, n$$

where, $V_1, \ldots, V_n$ is a sample of size $n$ from $N(0, 1)$. Let $V_{(1)} \leq V_{(2)} \leq \cdots \leq V_{(n)}$ be the corresponding order statistics, $E(V_{(i)}) = d_n(i)$, $i = 1, 2, \ldots, n$ are called the normal scores and the test based on the corresponding statistic

$$T_N = \sum_{i=1}^{n_2} d_n(i) = \sum_{i=1}^{n} Z_i \, d_n(i)$$

is called the normal scores test. This was originally proposed by Fisher and Yates (1958) in their tables and later developed by Hoeffding (1951)[88], (1952)[91], Terry (1952)[202] and Cherroff and Savage (1958)[32].
Further, consider

$$l(i) = \begin{cases} 0 & \text{if } i \leq \left[\frac{n}{2}\right] \\ 1 & \text{if } i > \left[\frac{n}{2}\right] \end{cases}$$

where, $\left[\frac{n}{2}\right]$ is the largest integer not excluding $\frac{n}{2}$. This gives rise to the statistic

$$T_M = \sum_{i=\left[\frac{n}{2}\right]+1}^{n} Z_i : \text{ Number of second sample ranks more than} \left[\frac{n}{2}\right]$$

This test was originally proposed by Mood (1950)[143] and is known as *Median test.*

We shall see that the three tests described above are sensitive against the classes of alternatives $\Gamma_1^{(3)}$, $\Gamma_1^{(4)}$, $\Gamma_1^{(5)}$.

## 11.4 THE WILCOXON-MANN-WHITNEY TEST $T_W$

In this section we shall discuss the testing problem $H_0 : G_1 = G_2$ against the class of alternatives $\Gamma_1^{(3)}$. Wilcoxon-Mann-Whitney test, for testing this problem, is defined as

$$T_W = \sum_{i=1}^{n_2} S_i = \sum_{i=1}^{n_2} R_{2i} = \sum_{i=1}^{n} iZ_i$$

where, $R_{21}, R_{22}, \ldots, R_{2n_2}$ are the ranks of the second sample observations and $S_1, S_2, \ldots, S_{n_2}$ are the corresponding ordered values, and $Z_i's$ are defined by

$$Z_i = \begin{cases} 1 & \text{if the pooled rank } i \text{ in the combined ordered} \\ & \text{sample comes from the second sample} \\ 0 & \text{otherwise} \end{cases}$$

Large values of $T_W$ lead to the rejection of $H_0$. $T_W$ sometimes referred to as rank sum test, the name arising by way it is defined.

For many purposes, however, an alternative description of the test is more convenient.

Let $u(x_1, x_2)$ be a bivariate function defined by

$$u(x_1, x_2) = \begin{cases} 1 & \text{if } x_1 < x_2 \\ 0 & \text{otherwise} \end{cases}$$

Consider the sum

$$U = \sum_{i=1}^{n_1} \sum_{j=1}^{n_2} u(x_{1i}, x_{2j})$$

It is clear that $u$ is the number of pairs among $n_1 \cdot n_2$ pairs $(x_{1i}, x_{2j})$ for which $x_{2j} > x_{1i}$ and could be called as the number of times second sample observations exceed first sample observations.

It can be easily noted that $u$ is unaffected if $u(x_{1i}, x_{2j})$ is replaced by $u(R_{1i}, R_{2j})$, i.e.

$$U = \sum_{i=1}^{n_1} \sum_{j=1}^{n_2} u(x_{1i}, x_{2j}) = \sum_{i=1}^{n_1} \sum_{j=1}^{n_2} u(R_{1i}, R_{2j}) = \sum_{j=1}^{n_2} \sum_{i=1}^{n_1} u(R_{1i}, S_j)$$

$$= \sum_{j=1}^{n_2} \{S_j - j\} = T_W - \frac{n_2(n_2 + 1)}{2} \tag{11.4}$$

So, the relationship in Eq. (11.4) shows the statistics $U$ and $T_w$ are equivalent for testing $H_0 : G_1 = G_2$ against the alternatives in $\Gamma_1^{(3)}$. Forms of critical regions based on $T_W$ for testing different-types of testing problems are summarized in Table 11.1 as follows:

**Table 11.1:** Testing Problems

| *Null hypothesis* | *Alternative hypothesis* | *Critical region* | *p-value ($t_W$ is the observed value of $T_W$)* |
|---|---|---|---|
| $G_1 = G_2$ | $G_1 \neq G_2$ | $T_W \leq t_W^{(1)}$ or $T_W \geq t_W^{(2)}$ | $2P(T_W \geq t_W; H_0)$ |
| $G_1 = G_2$ | $G_1 \geq G_2$ | $T_W \geq t_W^{(1)}$ | $P(T_W \geq t_W; H_0)$ |
| $G_1 = G_2$ | $G_1 \leq G_2$ | $T_W \leq t_W^{(2)}$ | $P(T_W \leq t_W; H_0)$ |

The constants $t_W^{(1)}, t_W^{(2)}$ are calculated from the size conditions. The calculations of these involve the distribution of $T_W | H_0$, which are readily available in the form of standard tables for $n_1, n_2 \leq 10$ so that $n_2 \leq n_1$. Also, using these distributions, the $p$-values could easily be calculated. We can equivalently define these critical regions based on $U$ since $T_W$ and $U$ are related by Eq. (11.4).

We shall note here that

$$\overline{U} = \frac{1}{n_1 n_2} \cdot U = \frac{1}{n_1 n_2} \sum_{i=1}^{n_1} \sum_{j=1}^{n_2} u(x_{1i}, x_{2j})$$

where $U$ is a two sample statistic with kernel $u(x_{1i}, x_{2j})$.

### 11.4.1 Expected Value and Variance of $T_W$ (or $U$)

The mean and variance of $T_W$ under the null hypothesis $H_0$ are found by noting that for the set of digits $\{1, 2, \ldots, n\}$, the mean is $\frac{n+1}{2}$ and the variance is $\frac{n^2-1}{12}$ and then applying the formula for mean and variance of sample mean of $n_2$ digits, taken without replacement.

We know that $n_1 + n_2 = n$. The population mean is given by

$$\frac{1}{n} \sum_{i=1}^{n} i = \frac{1}{n} \cdot \frac{n(n+1)}{2} = \frac{n+1}{2}$$

and the population variance

$$= \frac{1}{n-1} \left[ \sum_{i=1}^{n} i^2 - n \cdot \left( \frac{\sum i}{n} \right)^2 \right]$$

$$= \frac{1}{n-1} \left[ \frac{n(n+1)(2n+1)}{6} - n \cdot \frac{(n+1)^2}{4} \right]$$

$$= \frac{1}{n-1} \left[ \frac{4(2n^3 + n^2 + 2n^2 + n) - 6(n^3 + 2n^2 + n)}{24} \right]$$

$$= \frac{1}{n-1} \left[ \frac{2n^3 - 2n}{24} \right] = \frac{1}{n-1} \frac{2n(n^2-1)}{24} = \frac{n(n+1)}{12}$$

But in case of simple random sampling without replacement (srswor)

$$E\{\text{ sample mean}\} = \text{population mean}$$

$$E\left\{\frac{\sum_{i=1}^{n_2} R_{2i}}{n_2}\right\} = \frac{n+1}{2}$$

or

$$E\{T_W \mid H_0\} = n_2 \cdot \frac{(n+1)}{2}$$

Further

$$\begin{aligned} V(\text{ sample mean}) &= \Big(\frac{1}{n_2} - \frac{1}{n}\Big) \cdot V(\text{population mean}) \\ &= \frac{n - n_2}{nn_2} \cdot V(\text{population mean}) \\ &= \frac{(n - n_2)}{nn_2} \cdot \frac{n(n+1)}{12} \\ V\Big(\frac{T_W}{n_2}\Big| H_0\Big) &= \frac{n_1(n+1)}{12n_2} \\ V(T_W|H_0) &= \frac{n_1 n_2(n+1)}{12} \end{aligned}$$

Hence, under the null hypothesis, the first two moments of $U$ would be given by

$$E(U|H_0) = \frac{n_1 n_2}{2}, \; V(U|H_0) = \frac{n_1 n_2(n+1)}{12}$$

## 11.4.2 Some Properties of Distribution of $T_W$

Two facts about the null distribution of $U$ are noteworthy:

(a) *The distribution of $U$ is unaltered by interchanging $n_1$ and $n_2$:* To see this for any ordered sequence of random variables $Y_1, Y_2, \ldots, Y_m$, we write

$$Q(Y_1, Y_2, \ldots, Y_m) = \sum_{i<j}{}' u(Y_i, Y_j)$$

As $Q(Y_1, \ldots, Y_m)$ is unaffected by replacing $Y_1, \ldots, Y_m$ by the corresponding ranks, if $Y_1, \ldots, Y_m$ are iid, distribution of $Q$ is distribution-free and depends only on $m$. Let us write $\psi_m(t)$ for the characteristic function of $Q(Y_1, \ldots, Y_m)$ when $Y_1, \ldots, Y_m$ are identically distributed. Now for our samples

$$\begin{aligned} Q(X_{11}, \ldots, X_{1n_1}, X_{21}, \ldots, X_{2n_2}) = {} & Q(X_{11}, \ldots, X_{1n_1}) \\ & + Q(X_{21}, \ldots, X_{2n_2}) + U \end{aligned}$$

The terms on the right hand side are distributed independently of each other. Hence under $H_0$, we have

$$\psi_n(t) = \psi_{n_1}(t) \cdot \psi_{n_2}(t) \cdot \psi_U(t)$$

We have

$$\psi_U(t) = \frac{\psi_n(t)}{\psi_{n_1}(t) \cdot \psi_{n_2}(t)}$$

where, we write $\psi_U(t)$ as the characteristic function of $U$. Hence, $\psi_U(t)$ is unaffected by an interchange of $n_1$ and $n_2$. The characteristic function $\psi_U(t)$ of $U$ can be found explicitly as

$$\psi_U(t) = \frac{\psi_n(t)}{\psi_{n_1}(t) \cdot \psi_{n_2}(t)}$$

(b) *The distribution of $U|H_0$ is symmetric about the mean point $n_1n_2/2$:*

We have already defined

$$\begin{aligned} U &= \sum_{i=1}^{n_1}\sum_{j=1}^{n_2} u(X_{1i}, X_{2j}) \\ &= \sum_{i=1}^{n_1}\sum_{j=1}^{n_2}(1 - u(X_{2j}, X_{1j})) \end{aligned}$$

or

$$U - \frac{n_1n_2}{2} = -\{\sum_{j=1}^{n_2}\sum_{i=1}^{n_1} u(X_{2j}, X_{1i}) - \frac{n_1n_2}{2}\}$$

or

$$U - \frac{n_1n_2}{2} = -\left\{U' - \frac{n_1n_2}{2}\right\}$$

as $\sum_{j=1}^{n_2}\sum_{i=1}^{n_1} u(x_{2j}, x_{1i})$ under $H_0$ has the distribution of $U$ with $n_1$ interchanged with $n_2$, by the proceeding result, $U - \frac{n_1n_2}{2}$ and $-\{U - \frac{n_1n_2}{2}\}$ are identically distributed which proves the symmetry of the $U$-distribution.

### 11.4.3 The Exact Null Distribution of $U$

Under $H_0$, all the $n$ observations $X_{11}, \ldots, X_{1n_1}; X_{2_1}, \ldots, X_{2n_2}$ are iid so that $R_{21}, \ldots, R_{2n_2}$ can be considered as a random sample of size $n_2$ taken without replacement out of the set of digits $\{1, 2, \ldots, n\}$. Hence, the distribution of $T_W$ and $U$ will strictly be distribution-free.

The null distribution of $T_W$ or $U$ is easy to construct for small values of $n$ by considering all possible $\binom{n}{n_2}$ samples of size $n_2$ from $\{1, 2, \ldots, n\}$ and getting the value of statistic for each. For large $n$, however, labour in this becomes prohibitive. Writing $f_{n_1,n_2}(u)$ for the frequency function of $U$ for sample sizes $n_1, n_2$ the following recursion relation is easily seen to hold

$$f_{n_1,\, n_2}(u) = f_{n_1-1,\, n_2}(u) + f_{n_1,\, n_2-1}(u - n_1)$$

By writing

$$p_{n_1,n_2} = \frac{f_{n_1,n_2}(u)}{\binom{n}{n_1}}$$

We have

$$p_{n_1,n_2}(u) = \frac{n_1}{n} p_{n_1-1,n_2}(u) + \frac{n_2}{n} p_{n_1,n_2-1}(u - n_1)$$

Using this recursion formula Whitney [137] tabulated the null distribution of $U$ for $n_1, n_2 \leq 8$. Extensive tables are available in D.B. Qwen's (1962)[158].

### 11.4.4 Asymptotic Null Distribution of $T_W$ or $U$

Suppose $n \to \infty$ so that

$$\frac{n_1}{n} \to f_1;\ \frac{n_2}{n} \to f_2; 0 < f_1, f_2 < 1,\ s.t.\ f_1 + f_2 = 1$$

where, $f_1$ and $f_2$ are being fixed numbers. Then under $H_0$

$$\frac{U - E(U|H_0)}{\sqrt{V(U|H_0)}} = \frac{T - E(T|H_0)}{\sqrt{V(T|H_0)}}$$

is distributed asymptotically as $N(0, 1)$. The result can be proved either in terms of $U$ or in terms of $T$. We shall indicate both the approaches here as they illustrate the application of two central limit theorems which are of great importance in non-parametric theory.

To prove the result in terms of $U$ we require to apply a theorem on the asymptotic distribution of two-sample $U$ statistics which was obtained by Lehmann (1951)[117] by extending an earlier theorem of Hoeffding (1948)[90] on single sample $U$-statistic. We state the theorem below:

Let $X_{11}, X_{12}, \ldots, X_{1n_1}$ and $X_{21}, X_{22}, \ldots, X_{2n_2}$ be two independent samples from the cdfs as $G_1(x)$ and $G_2(x)$. Also let

$$f(x_1, \ldots, x_{m_1}; y_1, \ldots, y_{m_2})$$

where, $m_1, m_2$ are two fixed positive integers, be a $(m_1+m_2)$ -variate function which is invariant under all permutations of $x_1, x_2, \ldots, x_{m_1}$ and all permutations of $y_1, y_2, \ldots, y_{m_2}$. On the basis of this sample we define the two sample $U$-statistic with kernel $f(x_1, \ldots, x_{m_1}; y_1, \ldots, y_{m_2})$ as

$$\overline{U}_{n_1,n_2} = \frac{1}{\binom{n_1}{m_1}\binom{n_2}{m_2}} \sum f(x_{1\alpha_1}, \ldots, x_{1\alpha_{m_1}}; x_{2\beta_1}, \ldots, x_{2\beta_{m_2}})$$

where the summation is over all the $\binom{n_1}{m_1}$ possible choices of $\alpha_1, \ldots, \alpha_{m_1}$ out of $1, 2, \ldots, n_1$ and over all the possible choices $\binom{n}{m_2}$ of $\beta_1, \ldots, \beta_{m_2}$ out of $1, 2, \ldots, n_2$.

The following theorem has been given by Hoeffding and Lehmann (1951) [90, 116] on the asymptotic null distribution of $U$-statistic:

**Theorem 11.4.1. (Hoeffding-Lehmann Central Limit Theorem)** *If* $n = n_1 + n_2 \to \infty$ *so that* $\frac{n_1}{n} \to f_1, \frac{n_2}{n} \to f_2$, *where* $0 < f_1, f_2 < 1$, *then*

$$\frac{\overline{U}_{n_1,n_2} - E(\overline{U}_{n_1,n_2})}{\sqrt{V(\overline{U}_{n_1,n_2})}} \xrightarrow{\mathcal{L}} N(0,1)$$

*provided* $V(f(X_{11}, \ldots, X_{1m_1}, X_{21}, \ldots, X_{2m_2}))$ *exists. Also as* $n \to \infty$

$$V(\overline{U}_{n_1,n_2}) = o(1/n)$$

**Corollary 11.4.1.** *As* $n \to \infty$

$$\overline{U}_{n_1,n_2} \xrightarrow{p} E\{f(X_{11}, \ldots, X_{1m_1}; X_{21}, \ldots, X_{2m_2})\}$$

This follows clearly from the last part of the theorem and the fact:

$$E(\overline{U}_{n_1,n_2}) = E\{f(X_{11}, \ldots, X_{1m_1}; X_{21}, \ldots, X_{2m_2})\}$$

To apply the theorem in the present instance we see that $\overline{U}$ as given by

$$\overline{U} = \frac{1}{n_1 n_2} \sum_i \sum_j u(X_{1i}, X_{2j})$$

is a two-sample $U$-statistic with bounded kernel $u(X_1, X_2)$. Hence, as $n \to \infty$ subject to

$$\frac{n_1}{n} \to f_1 \text{ and } \frac{n_2}{n} \to f_2 \text{ so that } f_1 + f_2 = 1$$

$$\frac{\overline{U} - E(\overline{U}|G_1, G_2)}{\sqrt{V(\overline{U}|G_1, G_2)}} \xrightarrow{\mathcal{L}} N(0,1)$$

for whatever $G_1, G_2$. As this holds in general for any $(G_1, G_2)$, it is true under $H_0 : G_1 = G_2$ also. This shows that asymptotically $\overline{U}$ is distributed as $N(E(\overline{U}|H_0), V(\overline{U}|H_0))$ under $H_0$. For the use in future, we note here from the Corollary 11.4.1 to Hoeffding-Lehmann theorem that for given $(G_1, G_2)$

$$\begin{aligned}\overline{U} &\xrightarrow{p} E\{u(X_{1i}, X_{2j})|(G_1, G_2)\} \\ &= 1.P\{X_{1i} < X_{2j}|(G_1, G_2)\} + 0.P\{X_{1i} \geq X_{2j}|(G_1, G_2)\} \\ &= \int_{-\infty}^{\infty} G_1(x)\, dG_2(x)\end{aligned}$$

or

$$\overline{U} = \frac{1}{2}(\Delta_W(G_1, G_2) + 1)$$

where, $\Delta_W(G_1, G_2)$ is defined as had been defined while discussing the five standard senses of alternatives.

### 11.4.5 Permutation Central Limit Theorem

To prove the asymptotic normality of $T$ under $H_0$ we shall apply a permutation central limit theorem originally established by Wald and Wolfovitz (1944)[217, 218] and later generalized by Noether (1949) [157] and Hoeffding (1948) [90] (see Fraser Section 6.6). We shall now state the theorem.

Suppose for each $n$, two $n$-vectors $(a_{n1}, a_{n2}, \ldots, a_{nn})$ and $(b_{n1}, b_{n2}, \ldots, b_{nn})$ are defined, and let $T_n$ by

$$T_n = a_{n\alpha_1} b_{n1} + \cdots + a_{n\alpha_n} b_{nn}$$

where $(\alpha_1, \alpha_2, \ldots, \alpha_n)$ is a random permutation of digits $(1, 2, \ldots, n)$.

**Theorem 11.4.2.** *If as* $n \to \infty$

$$\frac{\max_{1 \le i \le n}(a_{ni} - \bar{a}_n)^2}{\sum_{i=1}^{n}(a_{ni} - \bar{a}_n)^2} \to 0$$

*and*

$$\frac{\sum_{i=1}^{n}(b_{ni} - \bar{b}_n)^r}{[\sum_{i=1}^{n}(b_{ni} - \bar{b}_n)^2]^{r/2}} = o(n^{1-r/2})$$

*for every* $r > 2$

*where*

$$\bar{a}_n = \frac{1}{n}\sum_{i=1}^{n} a_{ni}; \quad \bar{b}_n = \frac{1}{n}\sum_{i=1}^{n} b_{ni}$$

*then*

$$\frac{T_n - E(T_n)}{\sqrt{V(T_n)}} \xrightarrow{\mathcal{L}} N(0, 1)$$

To apply this theorem on Mann-Whitney Test statistic, $T_W = \sum_{i=1}^{n} Z_i \cdot i$, where under $H_0$, $(Z_1, \ldots, Z_n)$ is a random permutation of $n_1$ $0's$ and $n_2$ $1's$. Thus, here we have

$$(a_{n1}, \ldots, a_{nn}) = (\underbrace{0, \ldots, 0}_{n_1}, \underbrace{1, \ldots, 1}_{n_2})$$

$$(b_{n1}, \ldots, b_{nn}) = (1, 2, \ldots, n)$$

where

$$\bar{a}_n = n_2/n$$

We now have

$$\frac{\max_{1\le i\le n}(a_{ni}-\bar{a}_n)^2}{\sum_{i=1}^{n}(a_{ni}-\bar{a}_n)^2}$$

$$=\frac{\max\{(-n_2/n)^2,\ldots,(-n_2/n)^2,(1-n_2/n)^2,\ldots,(n_1/n)^2\}}{n_1\cdot(n_2/n)^2+n_2\cdot(n_1/n)^2}$$

$$=\frac{\max\{(n_2/n)^2,(n_1/n)^2\}}{n_1n_2/n}=\frac{(n_2/n)^2}{n_1n_2/n}\text{ or }\frac{(n_1/n)^2}{n_1n_2/n}$$

$$=\frac{1}{n}\cdot\frac{n_2/n}{n_1/n}\text{ or }\frac{1}{n}\cdot\frac{n_1/n}{n_2/n}\to 0\cdot\frac{f_2}{f_1}\text{ or }0\cdot\frac{f_1}{f_2}\text{ or }\to 0$$

in both the cases. Now the second condition, for every $r>2$

$$\frac{\sum(b_{ni}-\bar{b}_n)^r}{[\sum(b_{ni}-\bar{b}_n)^2]^{r/2}}=0 \qquad \text{if } r \text{ is odd}$$

$$\le\frac{n(n-\frac{n+1}{2})^r}{\{\frac{n(n^2-1)}{12}\}^{r/2}}=o(n^{1-r/2}) \qquad \text{if } r \text{ is even}$$

Thus, the second condition is also satisfied. Therefore, asymptotic normality of $T$ under $H_0$ follows directly as a consequence of the Theorem 11.4.2.

It has been observed that the convergence of $\frac{T-E(T|H_0)}{\sqrt{V(T|H_0)}}$ to normality is very rapid. In fact, it has been found that for $n_1, n_2 \ge 8$, the normal approximation works very well for most practical purposes.

### 11.4.6 Consistency of $T_W$ (or $U$-statistic)

Under this we show that the Wilcoxon Mann-Whitney test is consistent against the class of alternatives $\Gamma_1^{(3)}$, as defined earlier.

Let us consider the test in terms of $U$. Writing $U_\alpha$ for the upper $\alpha$-point of the null distribution of $U$. The power of $U$ for any alternative $(G_1, G_2)$ is given by

$$P\{U>U_\alpha|(G_1,G_2)\}=P\Big\{\frac{1}{n_1n_2}(U)-\frac{1}{2}>\frac{1}{n_1n_2}(U_\alpha)-\frac{1}{2}|(G_1,G_2)\Big\}$$

But, as $n\to\infty$ subject to the conditions described under $(G_1, G_2)$, we have seen that

$$\frac{1}{n_1n_2}U-\frac{1}{2}\xrightarrow{p}\frac{1}{2}\Delta_W(G_1,G_2)$$

where, $\Delta_W(G_1, G_2)$ is defined as we did in the discussion of five senses of alternative.

Also, as $U_\alpha$ is the upper $\alpha$-point of the null distribution of $U$ and under $H_0$

$$E(U|H_0)=\frac{n_1n_2}{2};\ V(U|H_0)=\frac{n_1n_2(n+1)}{12}$$

And by Hoeffding-Lehmann theorem

$$\left.\frac{\overline{U}_{n_1,n_2} - E(\overline{U}_{n_1,n_2})}{\sqrt{V(\overline{U}_{n_1,n_2})}}\right|_{H_0} \xrightarrow{\mathcal{L}} N(0,1)$$

$$\frac{\frac{1}{n_1n_2}U - \frac{1}{n_1n_2}E(U)}{\sqrt{\left(\frac{1}{n_1n_2}\right)^2 V(U)}} \xrightarrow{\mathcal{L}} N(0,1)$$

or

$$\frac{U - \frac{n_1n_2}{2}}{\sqrt{\frac{n_1n_2(n+1)}{12}}} \xrightarrow{\mathcal{L}} N(0,1)$$

Therefore,

$$\frac{U_\alpha - \frac{n_1n_2}{2}}{\sqrt{\frac{n_1n_2(n+1)}{12}}} \rightarrow Z_\alpha \text{ (the upper } \alpha\text{-point of } N(0,1) \text{ distribution)}$$

$$n_1n_2\left\{\frac{U_\alpha}{n_1n_2} - \frac{1}{2}\right\} \rightarrow \sqrt{\frac{n_1n_2(n+1)}{12}} \cdot Z_\alpha$$

$$\frac{U_\alpha}{n_1n_2} - \frac{1}{2} \rightarrow \sqrt{\frac{(n+1)}{12\, n_1n_2}} \cdot Z_\alpha$$

$$= \sqrt{\frac{(1+1/n)}{12\,(n_1/n)\cdot(n_2/n)\cdot n}} \cdot Z_\alpha$$

$$\rightarrow 0$$

Hence, $\frac{1}{n_1n_2}U_\alpha - \frac{1}{2} \rightarrow 0$. From these results, it follows that for any $(G_1, G_2)$ For which

$$\Delta_W(G_1, G_2) > 0$$

$$P\left\{\frac{1}{n_1n_2}U - \frac{1}{2} > \frac{1}{n_1n_2}U_\alpha - \frac{1}{2}\,\middle|\,(G_1,G_2)\right\}$$

$$= P\left\{\frac{1}{2}\Delta_W(G_1,G_2) > 0\,\middle|\,(G_1,G_2)\right\}$$

$$= P\{\Delta_W(G_1,G_2) > 0 | (G_1,G_2)\} \text{ as } n \rightarrow \infty$$

$= 1$ (as $n \rightarrow \infty$) by the definition of $3^{rd}$ sense of defining alternatives.

It shows that the Wilcoxon-Mann Whitney test is consistent against the alternatives $\Gamma_1^{(3)}$.

### 11.4.7 Asymptotic Relative Efficiency of $T_W$

Let us consider Wilcoxon test based on $U$. Take any absolute continuous cdf $G_0(x) \in \Gamma$ with a continuous density $g_0(x)$ and consider the subset of $\Gamma$ represented by all elements $(G_0(x), G_0(x-\theta))$, $\theta \geq 0$. Within this subset $H_0$ corresponds to $\theta = 0$. We shall confine ourselves to this subset and have

$$E(U|\theta) = n_1 n_2 \int_{-\infty}^{\infty} G_0(x+\theta)\, dG_0(x) = \mathcal{T}_n(\theta) \text{ say}$$

and

$$V(U|\theta) = \delta_n^2(\theta) \quad \text{(say)}$$

In the subsection 11.4.6 we have seen that

$$\delta_n^2(0) = \frac{n_1 n_2 (n+1)}{12}$$

and that under $H_0$

$$\frac{U - \mathcal{T}_n(0)}{\delta_n(0)} \xrightarrow{\mathcal{L}} N(0,1)$$

So, for any sequence of alternatives $\theta_n = \lambda/\sqrt{n}$ sequence of statistics $U_n$, which is based on a sample of $n$ observations from $\{G_0(x),\, G_0(x-\theta)\}$, is asymptotically distributed as $N(\mathcal{T}_n(\theta_n), \delta_n(\theta_n))$.

This follows from the well known fact that asymptotically the $U$-statistic, $\overline{U}$ is equivalent to a sum of independent random variables on which the Berry-Essen theorem is applicable. This shows that the first two conditions, i.e. regularity conditions under which ARE is determined as a limiting ratio of efficacies are satisfied here. The other conditions may be easily verified. The efficacy of $U$ shall be given by

$$\text{Efficacy of } U = \frac{\left[\frac{d}{d\theta} E(U)|H_0\right]^2}{V(U|H_0)} = \frac{[\mathcal{T}_n'(0)]^2}{\delta_n^2(0)}$$

$$= \frac{[n_1 n_2 \int_{-\infty}^{\infty} [g_0(x)]^2\, dx]^2}{\frac{n_1 n_2 (n+1)}{12}}$$

$$= \frac{12 n_1 n_2 (\int_{-\infty}^{\infty} [g_0(x)]^2\, dx)^2}{n+1}$$

To determine the Pitman efficiency of Wilcoxon-Mann-Whitney test relative to the large sample test based on the differences of the two sample means $\overline{X}_1$ and $\overline{X}_2$, we set up the test statistic as

$$Z = \left.\frac{\overline{X}_2 - \overline{X}_1}{\sqrt{\frac{s_1^2}{n_1} + \frac{s_2^2}{n_2}}}\right|_{H_0} \xrightarrow{\mathcal{L}} N(0,1)$$

Generally, for the elements $(G_0(x), G_0(x-\theta))Z$ has asymptotic mean and variance

$$\mathcal{T}_n^*(\theta) = \frac{\sqrt{n_1 n_2}\,\theta}{\sqrt{n}\,\sigma(G_0)}\ ;\ \ \delta_n^{*2}(\theta) = 1$$

where, $\sigma(G_0)$ is standard deviation of $G_0(x)$ for which we now assume that the second moment exists. (All the regularity conditions are satisfied here). Hence

$$\text{Efficacy of } Z = \frac{[\mathcal{T}_n^{*\prime}(\theta)|H_0]^2}{\delta_n^{*2}(\theta)|H_0} = \frac{\dfrac{n_1 n_2}{n\sigma^2(G_0)}}{1} = \frac{n_1 n_2}{n\sigma^2(G_0)}$$

Taking the limits of the two efficacies, we get

ARE (Wilcoxon-Mann-Whitney, differences of mean test)

$$\lim_{n\to\infty} \frac{e(U)}{e(Z)} = \frac{\dfrac{12 n_1 n_2}{n+1}(\int_{-\infty}^{\infty}[g_0(x)]^2 dx)^2}{\dfrac{n_1 n_2}{n\sigma^2_{(G_0)}}}$$

$$= 12\sigma^2(G_0)\left[\int_{-\infty}^{\infty}\{g_0(x)\}^2 dx\right]^2$$

Incidentally the expression obtained here is identical with the expression obtained for the ARE of the Single sample Wilcoxon Signed-Rank Test relative to the mean test.

ARE expression obtained here has values $3/\pi (= 95\%), 100\%$ and $150\%$ respectively for normal, rectangular and Laplac populations. For population for which $\sigma(G_0)$ does not exist, the difference of means test is not applicable and there we can interpret by saying that the efficiency becomes $\infty$. Hodges (1958)[87] and Lehman (1951)[117] have shown that whatever be the population, ARE can never fall below 86.4%.

This fact is very reassuring for this shows that whatever be the population by using Wilcoxon-Mann-Whitney test instead of the difference of means test, we can not loose more than 13.6 per cent in terms of asymptotic efficiency, whereas we can make considerable gain.

# 11.5 THE NORMAL SCORE TEST

In this section we consider the population of testing

$$H_0 : G_1 = G_2$$

against the class of alternatives $\Gamma_1^{(4)}$.

## 11.5.1 The Test Statistic and its Null Distribution

Writing $V_1, V_2, \ldots, V_n$ for a sample of size $n$ from $N(0,1), V_{(1)} < V_{(2)} < \cdots < V_{(n)}$ for the corresponding order statistics we have the normal scores

$$E(V_{(i)}) = d_n(i); \qquad i = 1, 2, \ldots, n.$$

These have been tabulated in Fisher-Yates and Biometrika tables up to $n = 50$. These clearly satisfy (as the distribution $N(0,1)$ is symmetric about 0).

$$d_n(i) = -d_n(n-i+1) \tag{11.5}$$

and

$$\sum_{i=1}^{n} d_n(i) = 0$$

The test statistic for the normal score test

$$T = T_N = \sum_{i=1}^{n_2} d_n(S_i) = \sum_{i=1}^{n} Z_i\, d_n(i) \tag{11.6}$$

As, under $H_0, S_1, S_2, \ldots, S_{n_2}$ represents a random sample taken without replacement out of a set of digits $\{1, 2, \ldots, n\}$, the null distribution of $T$ is clearly distribution free. From this fact and Eq. (11.6) we get that the null distribution is symmetric about the origin. Also by Eq. (11.6) we get

$$\sum_{i=1}^{n_2} d_n(S_i) = \sum_{i=S_1, S_2, \ldots, S_{n_2}} d_n(i)$$

But

$$\sum_{i=1}^{n} d_n(i) = 0$$

$$\sum_{i=S_1, S_2, \ldots, S_{n_2}} d_n(i) + \sum_{i \neq S_1, \ldots, S_{n_2}} d_n(i) = 0$$

Therefore,

$$\sum_{i=1}^{n_2} d_n(S_i) = \sum_{i=S_1, \ldots, S_{n_2}} d_n(i) = - \sum_{i \neq S_1, \ldots, S_{n_2}} d_n(i)$$

so that $T$ for sample sizes $n_1, n_2$ is distributed as -$T$ for sample sizes $n_2, n_1$. This, by virtue of the symmetry of the $F$-distribution, implies that the null distribution of $T$ remains unchanged by interchanging $n_1, n_2$.

From the known results for random sampling without replacement, we get that

$$\begin{aligned} E(T|H_0) &= 0 \\ V\Big(\frac{T}{n_2}\Big|H_0\Big) &= \Big(\frac{1}{n_2}-\frac{1}{n}\Big)V(d_n(1),\ldots,d_n(n)) \\ &= \frac{n_1}{n_2 n}\cdot\frac{1}{n-1}\Big[\sum d_n^2(i) - n\Big(\frac{\sum d_n(i)}{n}\Big)^2\Big] \\ V(T|H_0) &= \frac{n_1 n_2^2}{n_2 n}\cdot\frac{1}{n-1}\Big[\sum d_n^2(i)\Big] \\ &= \frac{n_1 n_2}{n(n-1)}\sum d_n^2(i) \end{aligned}$$

Hoeffding (1951)[88, 91, 92] has proved that as $n \to \infty$ the distribution represented by the $n$ points $d_n(i), i = 1, \ldots, n$ approaches the distribution $N(0,1)$ and that every moment of the former approaches every moment of the latter. Hence

$$\frac{1}{n}\sum_{i=1}^{n}\{d_n(i)\}^2 \to 1$$

Thus, for large $n$ we have

$$V(T|H_0) \approx \frac{n_1 n_2}{n}$$

Starting from the normal scores $d_n(i),\ i = 1, 2, \ldots, n$, it is conceptually positive to construct the null distribution of $T$ considering all $\binom{n}{n_2}$ possible choices of $\{S_1, \ldots, S_{n_2}\}$. The labour however becomes prohibitive unless $n_1, n_2$ are small.

Terrey (1952)[202] has tabulated the distribution for $n \leq 10$, $n_1 \leq n_2$.

As $n \to \infty$, under $H_0$

$$\frac{T - E(T|H_0)}{\sqrt{V(T|H_0)}} \overset{\alpha}{\sim} N(0,1)$$

This follows from the representation $T = \sum_{i=1}^{n} Z_i d_n(i)$ by an application of the permutation central limit theorem discussed earlier. As, under $H_0$, $Z_1$, $Z_2, \ldots, Z_n$ is a random permutation of $n_1$ $0's$ and $n_2$ $1's$. Condition

$$\frac{\max\limits_{1\leq i\leq n}(a_{ni}-\bar{a}_n)^2}{\sum_{i=1}^{n}(a_{ni}-\bar{a}_n)^2} \to 0 \quad \text{as } n \to \infty \tag{11.7}$$

is seen to be satisfied. As for the other condition

$$L = \frac{\sum_{i=1}^{n}(b_{ni}-\bar{b}_n)^r}{[\sum_{i=1}^{n}(b_{ni}-\bar{b}_n)^2]^{r/2}} = o(n^{1-r/2}) \quad \text{for every } r > 2 \tag{11.8}$$

We have here

$$(b_{n1}, \ldots, b_{nn}) = (d_n(1), d_n(2), \ldots, d_n(n))$$

$$\bar{b}_n = \frac{1}{n}\sum b_{ni} = \frac{1}{n}\sum_{i=1}^{n} d_n(i) = \frac{1}{n}\cdot 0 = 0$$

By the result of Hoeffding (1952)[92] referred in the present sub-sectin 11.5.1

$$\frac{1}{n}\sum_{i=1}^{n}\{d_n(i)\}^2 \to 1$$

$$\frac{1}{n}\sum_{i=1}^{n}\{d_n(i)\}^r = 0 \qquad \text{for } r \text{ odd}$$

$$\frac{1}{n}\sum_{i=1}^{n}\{d_n(i)\}^r \to \int_{-\infty}^{\infty} x^r dN(x) \qquad \text{for } r \text{ even}$$

$$\sum_{i=1}^{n}(b_{ni} - \bar{b}_n)^2 \to n$$

$$\Rightarrow [\sum_{i=1}^{n}(b_{ni} - \bar{b}_n)^2]^{r/2} \to n^{r/2} \quad \text{for } r \text{ odd or even}$$

$$L \to 0 \qquad \text{if } r \text{ is odd}$$

$$L \to n^{1-r/2} \qquad \text{if } r \text{ is even}$$

$N(x)$ representing the cdf of the distribution. These together imply the validity of the Eq. (11.6).

Presumably here the normal approximation to the null distribution of $T$ would be close for values of $n$ of the order 20 or even less. For still lower values of $n$ close approximation is available. Consider

$$r = \frac{T}{\sqrt{(n-1)V(T|H_0)}} = \frac{\sum_{i=1}^{n} Z_i d_n(i)}{\sqrt{\frac{n_1 n_2}{n}\sum\{d_n(i)\}^2}}$$

$$\sum d_n(i) = 0,\ \overline{Z} = \frac{1}{n}\sum Z_i = \frac{n_2}{n},\ \sum_{i=1}^{n}(Z_i - \overline{Z})^2 = \frac{n_1 n_2}{n}$$

has the structure of the correlation coefficient based on the pairs $((z_1, d_n(1)), \ldots, (z_n, d_n(n)))$ and hence $-1 < r < 1$. Thus, distribution for $r$ under $H_0$ is symmetric about 0, all odd-order moments of $r$ are zero. Also $E(r^2|H_0) = \frac{1}{n-1}$, and as Terry (1952)[202] have shown, if for the common parent distribution under $H_0$ the fourth moment exists, $E(r^4|H_0) \backsimeq 3/n^2 - 1$ for large $n$. These properties all agree with those of the distribution

$$\text{const} \cdot (1 - r^2)\frac{n-4}{2}, \quad -1 < r < 1$$

Hence, for $n$ not too small, the distribution of $r$ would follow closely the distribution of the correlation of a sample of size $n$ taken from an uncorrelated bivariate normal distribution. With stronger reason, the distribution of $r\sqrt{n-2}/\sqrt{1-r^2}$ under $H_0$, is approximately the students $t$ distribution with $(n-2)$ degrees of freedom. It has been found that the approximation is excellent even for $n$ as low as 10.

### 11.5.2 Consistency and Asymptotic Efficiency of Normal Score Test

For studying the asymptotic properties of the normal score test, it is convenient to write the test statistic in an alternative form:

For $x > 0$, let us define the function $d_n(x)$ by

$$\begin{aligned} d_n(x) &= 0 \quad \text{for} \quad x < 1 \\ &= d_n(i) \quad \text{for} \quad i \le x \le i+1, \; i = 1, 2, \ldots, n-1. \end{aligned}$$

Also let

$$c_n(y) = d_n(ny), \quad \text{for} \quad 0 < y \le 1 \tag{11.9}$$

Then, we can write

$$T = T_N = \sum_{i=1}^{n} Z_i \, d_n(i) = \sum_{i=1}^{n} Z_i \, c_n\left(\frac{i}{n}\right) \tag{11.10}$$

The power of the test for any alternative $(G_1, G_2)$

$$P\{T > T_\alpha | (G_1, G_2)\} = P\left\{\frac{1}{n_2} T > \frac{1}{n_2} T_\alpha | (G_1, G_2)\right\} \tag{11.11}$$

where $T_\alpha$ is the cut off point of the null distribution corresponding to level $\alpha$.

As the null distribution of $T$ is asymptotically $N(0, \frac{n_1 \cdot n_2}{n})$, as $n \to \infty$ subject to

$$\frac{n_i}{n} \to f_i, \; i = 1, 2 \text{ and } f_1 + f_2 = n \quad 0 < f_i < 1 \tag{11.12}$$

$\sqrt{\frac{n}{n_1 n_2}} T_\alpha \to z_\alpha$, the upper $\alpha$-point of the distribution $N(0, 1)$. Hence

$$\begin{aligned} \lim_{n \to \infty} \frac{1}{n_2} T_\alpha &= \lim_{n \to \infty} \frac{1}{n_2} \cdot \sqrt{\frac{n_1 n_2}{n}} \cdot \sqrt{\frac{n}{n_1 n_2}} T_\alpha \\ &= \lim_{n \to \infty} \sqrt{\frac{n}{n_1 n_2}} T_\alpha \cdot \lim_{n \to \infty} \cdot \sqrt{\frac{n_1}{n n_2}} \\ &= z_\alpha \cdot 0 = 0 \end{aligned}$$

We now show that as $n \to \infty$ subject to Eq. (11.8) for $(G_1, G_2) \in \Gamma_1^{(4)}$, $1/n_2 T \xrightarrow{P} (a)$, positive quantity. This would prove that the probability approaches 1 asymptotically. For this we make use of certain results proved by

Chernoff ans Savage (1958)[32]. These authors had considered a sequence of functions $J_n(y)$ defined for $0 < y \leq 1$ such that $\lim_{n\to\infty} J_n(y) = J(y)$ exists and certain regularity conditions on $\{J_n(y)\}$, $J(y)$ are satisfied and for the distributions $G_1(x), G_2(x)$, Theorem 11.4.1 implies that

$$\frac{1}{n_2}\sum_{i=1}^{n} Z_i\, J_n(i/n) \xrightarrow{p} \int_{-\infty}^{+\infty} J[\overline{G}(x)]\, dG_2(x)$$

as $n \to \infty$ subject to Eq. (11.8) where

$$\overline{G}(x) = f_1 G_1(x) + f_2 G_2(x)$$

In this case from the result of Hoeffding (1951)[91](1952)[92] referred to in the preceding subsection, it follows that $C_n(y)$, the quantile of order $y$ for the distribution represented by the points $d_n(i)$, $i = 1, \ldots, n$, converges to $N^{-1}(y)$, the quantile of order $y$ for the distribution $N(x)$. Also, all the required regularity conditions are satisfied by these functions (Chernoff and Savage (1958)[32]. Hence as $n \to \infty$ subject to Eq. (11.12)

$$\frac{1}{n_2} T_2 \xrightarrow{P} \int_{-\infty}^{+\infty} N^{-1}(\overline{G}(x))\, dG_2(x) = \Delta_N(G_1, G_2)$$

In the five standard senses of alternatives we have defined $\Gamma_1^{(4)}$ as

$$\Gamma_1^{(4)} = \{(G_1, G_2) \,|\, \Delta_N(G_1, G_2) > 0\}$$

Hence, the consistency of the normal scores test against the alternatives $\Gamma_1^{(4)}$ follows.

To study the asymptotic efficiency of the normal score test we confine ourself to a subclass of the class of translation alternatives $\Gamma_1^{(1)}$ in which $G_1(x) = G_0(x)$, $G_2(x) = G_0(x-\theta)$, $G_0$ being any fixed cdf and $\theta$ assuming any positive value. We have seen that within this class

$$T|H_0 \sim N\left(0, \frac{n_1 n_2}{n}\right)$$

From the Chernoff and Savage theorem it follows further that asymptotically $T_n$ is normally distributed when $T_n$ is based on a pooled sample of size $n$ from $G_0(x)$, $G_0(x-\theta_n)$ and $\theta_n = \lambda/\sqrt{n}$. The asymptotic mean of $T_n$ here is

$$\begin{aligned} \mathcal{T}_n(\theta) &= n_2 \int_{-\infty}^{+\infty} N^{-1}\{f_1\, G_0(x) + f_2\, G_0(x-\theta)\}\, dG_0(x-\theta) \\ &= n_2 \int_{-\infty}^{\infty} N^{-1}\{f_1\, G_0(x+\theta) + f_2\, G_0(x)\}\, dG_0(x) \end{aligned}$$

The other regularity conditions under which ARE calculations work are satisfied. Thus efficacy of $T$ can be defined as

$$\text{Efficacy of } T = \frac{\left[\frac{d}{d\theta}\mathcal{T}_n(\theta)|H_0\right]^2}{V(T|H_0)} = \frac{\{\mathcal{T}_n'(0)\}^2}{\frac{n_1 n_2}{n}}$$

Where

$$\mathcal{T}_n(\theta) = n_2 \int_{-\infty}^{+\infty} N^{-1}\{f_1\, G_0(x+\theta) + f_2\, G_0(x)\}\, dG_0(x)$$

$$\mathcal{T}_n'(\theta) = n_2 \int_{-\infty}^{\infty} \frac{d}{d\theta} N^{-1}\{f_1\, G_0(x+\theta) + f_2\, G_0(x)\}\, dG_0(x)$$

$$= \frac{n\, n_2}{n_1} f_1^2 \Big[\int_{-\infty}^{\infty} q\{G_0(x)\}\{g_0(x)\}^2\, dx\Big]^2$$

where we write

$$q(y) = \frac{d}{dy} N^{-1}(y)$$

and assume that $g_0(x) = G_0'(x)$ exist and is continuous everywhere. As

$$N\{N^{-1}(y)\} = y$$

$$\frac{d}{dy} N\{N^{-1}(y)\} = \Big[\frac{e^{-x^2/2}}{\sqrt{2\pi}}\Big]_{x=N^{-1}(y)} \frac{d}{dy} N^{-1}(y) = 1$$

We have

$$q(y) = \big[\sqrt{2\pi} e^{+x^2/2}\big]_{x=N^{-1}(y)}$$

Hence, efficacy of the $T$-statistic

$$= \frac{n\, n_2 f_1^2}{n_1} 2\pi \Big[\int_{-\infty}^{\infty} \{e^{x^2/2}\}_{x=N^{-1}(G_0(x))} \{g_0(x)\}^2 dx\Big]^2$$

If for $G_0(x)$, the second moment exists, then the difference of mean test is also usable for the problem and that we have already discussed. The efficacy of the difference of mean test is equal to

$$\frac{n_1 n_2}{n\, \sigma^2(G_0)}$$

Taking the limit of the ratio of efficacy of normal score test to the efficacy of difference of means test, we get asymptotic relative efficiency as

$$2\pi\sigma^2(G_0)\Big[\int_{-\infty}^{+\infty} \{e^{x^2/2}\}_{x=N^{-1}(G_0(x))} \{g_0(x)\}^2 dx\Big]^2$$

Taking $G_0(x) = N(x)$ we see that the above expression reduces to 1. Chernoff and Savage (1958)[32] have shown that for any other $G_0(x)$ the expression has values exceeding 1. Whereas, for the normal population the efficiency is 100%, for any other population it is more than 100%. Thus, at least for large samples, there is no point in using the difference of means test in preference to normal score test.

## 11.6 MEDIAN TEST

We have already introduced the test statistic of the median test as

$$T = T_M = \text{number of second sample ranks exceeding } [n/2]$$

If we agree to call the $[n/2]$th smallest value in the pooled sample as the pooled sample median, we can also describe $T$ as the number of second sample values exceeding the pooled sample median. The null distribution of $T$ has a simple form. Writing $n' = n/2$, the totality of pooled ranks $\{1, 2, \ldots, n\}$ gets comprised of two subsets one consisting of digits $1, 2, \ldots, n'$, the other consisting of $n' + 1, \ldots, n$. Under $H_0$ the second sample ranks represent a random sample of size $n_2$ from the entire set. So, the probability that these would be just $t$ members from the second subset in the random sample is given by hypergeometric law. Explicitly

$$P[T = t|H_0] = \frac{\binom{n-n'}{t}\binom{n'}{n_2-t}}{\binom{n}{n_2}} \tag{11.13}$$

Thus, the cut-off point of the test may be found with reference to the hypergeometric distribution. From Eq. (11.13) we have

$$E(T|H_0) = n_2\frac{(n-n')}{n} \backsimeq \frac{n_2}{n} \quad \text{for large } n.$$

$$V(T|H_0) = \frac{n_1 n_2 n'(n-n')}{n^2(n-1)} \backsimeq \frac{1}{4}\frac{n_1 n_2}{n} \quad \text{for large } n. \tag{11.14}$$

By writing $T = \sum_{i=1}^{n} Z_i f(i)$ where, $f(x) = 0$ or $1$ according as $x \leq n/2$ or $x > n/2$ and then appealing the permutation central limit theorem, we show that under $H_0$, as $n \to \infty$ subject to Eq. (11.12)

$$\frac{T - E(T|H_0)}{\sqrt{V(T|H_0)}} \xrightarrow{\mathcal{L}} N(0,1) \tag{11.15}$$

### 11.6.1 Consistency of Median Test

The median test is consistent against the class of alternatives $\Gamma_1^{(5)}$ discussed in the early sections. Writing as before $m(G_i)$ and $M(G_i)$ for the lower and upper bounds of the median interval for univariate cdf $G_i$ for any $(G_1, G_2) \in \Gamma_1^{(5)}$ we have $M(G_1) < m(G_2)$. Hence, for $\overline{G} = f_1G_1 + f_2G_2$, we will have

$$M(G_1) < m(\overline{G}) < M(\overline{G}) < m(G_2) \tag{11.16}$$

Now the power of the test for any $(G_1, G_2)$

$$P[T > T_\alpha|G_1, G_2] = P\Big[\frac{T}{n_2} - \frac{1}{2} > \frac{1}{n_2}(T_\alpha - \frac{1}{2}n_2)|G_1, G_2\Big] \tag{11.17}$$

By Eq. (11.15), as $n \to \infty$ subject to Eq. (11.12), $\frac{1}{n_2}(T_\alpha - \frac{1}{2}n_2) \to 0$. Also, by an application of Glivenko-Cantelli Lemma, we get from Eq. (11.16) that for any arbitrary $\epsilon > 0$

$$P\Big[\frac{1}{n_2}T > 1 - G_2(M(\overline{G})) - \epsilon\Big] \to 1$$

or

$$P\Big[\frac{1}{n_2}T > \frac{1}{2} + \eta\Big] \to 1$$

where, $\eta > 0$ is some fixed number. Hence the probability Eq. (11.17) approaches to 1 as $n \to \infty$.

### 11.6.2 Asymptotic Relative Efficiency

The asymptotic efficiency of the median test has been studied by Mood (1940)[142]. Considering the joint distribution of the pooled sample median and $T$, he showed that the conditions for the applicability of Pitman's theorem are satisfied here for the subclass of alternatives $(G_0(x),\ G_0(x-\theta)), \theta > 0$, where $G_0(x)$ is assumed to be strictly increasing.

This means that the median of $G_0(x)$ is unique, say, $\mu$. Also for any $f_1, f_2$ the median of $f_1 G_0(x) + f_2\, G_0(x-\theta)$ is unique, say, $m(\theta)$, where, of course $x = m(\theta)$ is the solution of

$$f_1\, G_0(x) + f_2\, G_0(x-\theta) = 1/2 \tag{11.18}$$

and where, $m(0) = \mu$. The asymptotic mean of $T$ is

$$\tau_n(\theta) = n_2\{1 - G_2(m(\theta))\} = n_2\{1 - G_0(m(\theta) - \theta)\}$$

Hence we get

$$\begin{aligned}\tau_n'(0) &= -n_2[g_0(m(\theta)-\theta) \times \{m'(\theta) - 1\}]_{\theta=0}\\ &= -n_2\, g_0(\mu)\{m'(0) - 1\}\end{aligned}$$

where $g_0(x)$ is $G_0'(x)$. We assume $g_0(\mu) > 0$. Then, if we differentiate Eq. (11.18), taking $x = m(\theta)$ as an implicit function of $\theta$, we get

$$\{f_1 g_0(x) + f_2 g_0(x-\theta)\} \cdot \frac{dx}{d\theta} - f_2 g_0(x-\theta) = 0$$

Hence, for $\theta = 0$

$$\begin{aligned}\{g_0(x)\} \cdot m'(0) - f_2 g_0(x) &= 0\\ m'(0) &= f_2\end{aligned}$$

So,

$$\tau_n'(0) = -n_2\, g_0(\mu).\{f_2 - 1\} = n_2\, f_1 g_0(\mu)$$

Hence, for efficacy of $T$

$$= 4\,\frac{n_2^2 f_1^2\{g_0(\mu)\}^2}{\frac{n_1 n_2}{n}} = 4\,\frac{n_2^2 f_1^2\{g_0(\mu)\}^2}{f_1 f_2 \cdot n}$$

$$= \frac{4n_2^2 f_1}{n f_2}\{g_0(\mu)\}^2$$

We have already found that the efficiency of difference of mean test which is usable if moments up to the second order exist for $G_0(x)$. Hence, the ARE of the median test relative to the difference of means test is

$$= \lim_{n\to\infty} \frac{\frac{4n_2^2 f_1}{n f_2}\{g_0(\mu)\}^2}{\frac{n_1 n_2}{n\sigma^2_{(G_0)}}} = 4\,\sigma^2_{(G_0)}\,[g_0(\mu)]^2$$

This expression is identical with that for the efficiency of the sign test, relative to the mean test derived earlier. As was noted there, this has value $2/\pi(\approx 64\%), 33.3\%$ and $200\%$, respectively for the normal, rectangular and double exponential populations.

## 11.7 KOLMOGOROV-SMIRNOV TEST

Kolmogorov-Smirnov is another two-sample test for testing the hypothesis

$$H_0 : \mathbf{G} = (G_1, G_2) \in \nu \;\text{ against }\; H_1 : \mathbf{G} = (G_1, G_2) \in \Gamma_1$$

where

$$\Gamma_1 = \{(G_1, G_2) | G_1(x) \neq G_2(x) \quad \text{for some } x\}$$

or, it could be

$$\Gamma_1 = \{(G_1, G_2) | G_2(x) \leq G_1(x) \;\; \forall\, x$$

and

$$G_2(x) < G_1(x) \;\text{ for some } x\}$$

Let $X_{11}, X_{12}, \ldots, X_{1_{n_1}}$ and $X_{21}, X_{22}, \ldots, X_{2_{n_2}}$ be two independent samples of size $n_1$ and $n_2$ drawn from $G_1$ and $G_2$, respectively. Let the order statistics be

$$X_{1(1)}, X_{1(2)}, \ldots, X_{1(n_1)} \;\text{ and }\; X_{2(1)}, X_{2(2)}, \ldots, X_{2(n_2)}$$

Let us write the empirical df's

$$G^*_{1n_1} = \begin{cases} 0 & \text{if } x < X_{1(1)} \\ \frac{k}{n_1} & \text{if } X_{1(k)} \leq x < X_{1(k+1)},\; k = 1, 2, \ldots, n_1 - 1 \\ 1 & \text{if } x \geq X_{1(n_1)} \end{cases}$$

and

$$G^*_{2n_2} = \begin{cases} 0 & \text{if } x < X_{2(1)} \\ \frac{k}{n_2} & \text{if } X_{2(k)} \leq x < X_{2(k+1)},\ k = 1, 2, \ldots, n_2 - 1 \\ 1 & \text{if } x \geq X_{2(n_2)} \end{cases}$$

We have seen that $G^*_{1n_1}$ and $G^*_{2n_2}$ represent the proportions of $X_1$ and $X_2$ values that do not exceed $x$ in the combined ordered arrangement of $n_1$ $X_1's$ and $n_2$ $X_2's$. The empirical distributions $G^*_{1n_1}$ and $G^*_{2n_2}$ are usually taken as estimates of $G_1$ and $G_2$ respectively.

If the null hypothesis is true, i.e. the populations $G_1$ and $G_2$ are identical, $X_1$ and $X_2$ samples could be treated as if these are drawn from the same population. Therefore, allowing the sample variations, the empirical distributions $G^*_{1n_1}$ and $G^*_{2n_2}$ would expectedly agree with each other. Kolmogorov-Smirnov had suggested the maximum absolute difference between the two empirical distributions as the test criterion, defined as

$$D_{n_1,n_2} = \sup_x |G^*_{1n_1}(x) - G^*_{2n_2}(x)| \tag{11.19}$$

Since the test statistic in Eq. (11.19), measures the magnitude of disagreement between the two populations but not the directions, it is appropriate for testing

$$H_1 : G_1(x) \neq G_2(x) \quad \text{for some} \quad x$$

The corresponding test shall be given by

$$\phi(D_{n_1,n_2}) = \begin{cases} 1 & \text{if } D_{n_1,n_2} \geq D_{n_1,n_2,\alpha} \\ 0 & \text{otherwise} \end{cases}$$

where, $D_{n_1,n_2,\alpha}$ is obtained by

$$P_{H_0}\{D_{n_1,n_2} \geq D_{n_1,n_2,\alpha}\} \leq \alpha$$

If we consider the hypothesis testing problem with alternative hypothesis that $X_1$ is stochastically larger than $X_2$, i.e.

$$P(X_1 > x) > P(X_2 > x)$$

or

$$1 - P(X_1 >) \leq 1 - P(X_2 > x)$$

or

$$P(X_1 \leq x) \leq P(X_2 \leq x)$$

$$G_1(x) \leq G_2(x) \quad \forall\ x$$

and

$$G_1(x) < G_2(x) \quad \text{for some } x$$

We define

$$D^+_{n_1,n_2} = \max_x [G^*_{2n_2}(x) - G^*_{1n_1}(x)]$$

and the test is given by

$$\phi(D^+_{n_1,n_2}) = \begin{cases} 1 & \text{if } D^+_{n_1,n_2} \geq D^+_{n_1,n_2,\alpha} \\ 0 & \text{otherwise} \end{cases}$$

where, $D^+_{n_1,n_2,\alpha}$ is determined by

$$P_{H_0}(D^+_{n_1,n_2} \geq D^+_{n_1,n_2,\alpha}) \leq \alpha$$

If the alternative hypothesis is that $X_2$ is stochastically larger than $X_1$, i.e.

$$P(X_2 > x) > P(X_1 > x)$$

or

$$1 - P(X_2 > x) \leq 1 - P(X_1 > x)$$

or

$$P(X_2 \leq x) \leq P(X_1 \leq x)$$

or

$$G_2(x) \leq G_1(x) \quad \forall\, x$$

or

$$G_2(x) < G_1(x) \;\text{ for some }\; x$$

We define

$$D^-_{n_1,n_2} = \sup_x [G^*_{1n_1}(x) - G^*_{2n_2}(x)]$$

and the appropriate test shall be given by

$$\phi(D^-_{n_1,n_2}) = \begin{cases} 1 & \text{if } D^-_{n_1,n_2} \geq D^-_{n_1,n_2,\alpha} \\ 0 & \text{otherwise} \end{cases}$$

where, $D^-_{n_1,n_2,\alpha}$ is obtained by

$$P_{H_0}\{D^-_{n_1,n_2} \geq D^-_{n_1,n_2,\alpha}\} \leq \alpha$$

Tables for the null distribution of $D_{n_1,n_2}$ for both equal and unequal sample sizes are given in Massy (1951). And tables for null distribution of $D^+_{n_1,n_2}$ are available in Goodman (1954)[74] for $n_1 = n_2$.

Smirnov (1939)[195] has derived the asymptotic null distribution of $D_{n_1,n_2}$ when $n_1$ and $n_2$ approach infinity in such a way that $n_1/n_2$ remains constant

$$\lim_{n_1,n_2 \to \infty} P\left(\sqrt{\frac{n_1 n_2}{n_1 + n_2}}\, D_{n_1,n_2} \leq z\right) = L(z)$$

where

$$L(z) = 1 - 2\sum_{i=1}^{\infty}(-1)^{i-1}e^{-2i^2z^2}$$

Further, the asymptotic distribution of $D^+_{n_1,n_2}$ shall be given by

$$\lim_{n_1,n_2\to\infty} P\left(\sqrt{\frac{n_1 n_2}{n_1+n_2}}D^+_{n_1,n_2} \le z\right) = 1 - e^{-2z^2}$$

## 11.8 TWO-SAMPLE PROBLEM OF SCALE

In the Section 11.7 we have considered tests for alternatives where two populations $G_1$ and $G_2$ were taken to be different in terms of their location from each other. In the present section we shall consider the alternative

$$H_1 : \mathbf{G} = (G_1, G_2) \in \Gamma_1^{(s)} \tag{11.20}$$

where

$$\Gamma_1^{(s)} = \{(G_1, G_2) : G_2(x) = G_1(\theta x)\ \forall\ x \text{ and some } \theta > 0,\ \theta \neq 1\}$$

$\Gamma_1^{(s)}$ is known as the *scale alternative.* $G_2$ is same as $G_1$, but with a compressed scale when $\theta > 1$ or enlarged scale when $\theta < 1$.

If we decide to base our test criterion on the combined ordered sample, the characteristics of respective locations and dispersions may be inextricably mixed in this, and possible location differences may mask the dispersions differences present in the combined ordered sample. If we want the ranks on the combined ordered sample only to be used towards detecting the differences in dispersion, we must ensure that the location parameter of the two populations (may it be mean or median) must be the same though it may be unknown if not known. In such a case both the sample observations can be adjusted by their location parameter, i.e. $X_{1i} - Md_1(= \mu_1),\ i = 1, 2, \ldots, n_1,\ X_{2i} - Md_2(= \mu_2)$ by subtracting the respective location parameters from each set. Under these assumptions, we shall use linear rank statistic as a test criterion for testing prolem in Eq. (11.20). In this process we shall use appropriate weights which would provide linear rank test, sensitive to scale differences only. If $X_1$ observations are spread approximately symmetrically towards both extreme values of $X_2$, in the combined ordered sample, then $G_1$ population has larger dispersion as compared to $G_2$. This situation suggests that the weights must be symmetric and shall be small in the middle and large at the extremes. There are several such test prevalent in the related literature among these are Mood test, Freund-Ansari-Bradley-David-Barton test, Klotz normal-scores test and Siegal-Tukey test, etc. We shall consider the Mood's test only for the purpose of brevity.

### 11.8.1 Moods Test

Mood (1954)[144] defined the test as the sum of squares of deviations of second sample ranks from the average combined rank

$$T_M = \sum_{i=1}^{n} \Big(i - \frac{n+1}{2}\Big)^2 Z_i$$

where $n = n_1 + n_2$

$$\text{average combined rank} = \sum_{i=1}^{n} i/n = \frac{n+1}{2}$$

and

$$Z_i = \begin{cases} 1 & \text{if the rank i in the combined ordered sample comes from the second sample.} \\ 0 & \text{otherwise} \end{cases}$$

Large values of $T_M$ would indicate that $X_2$ are more widely dispersed, i.e. $\sigma(G_2) > \sigma(G_1)$. or, in $G_2(x) = G_1(\theta x)$, $\theta = \frac{\sigma(G_1)}{\sigma(G_2)} < 1$. And, similarly, small values of $T_M$ suggest that $\theta > 1$. Therefore, for the hypothesis testing problem

$$H_0 : \theta = 1 \text{ against } H_1 : \theta < 1$$

One-sided test would be given by

$$\phi(T_M) = \begin{cases} 1 & \text{if } T_M \geq t_{m,\alpha} \\ 0 & \text{otherwise} \end{cases}$$

where, $t_{m,\alpha}$ are obtained by

$$P_{H_0}\{T_M \geq t_{m,\alpha}\} \leq \alpha$$

The weight used in the Mood's test are shown in Table 11.2 given for $n$ even and $n$ odd respectively. Table 11.1 indicates that one uses large weights for low and high ranks.
We see from these arrangements that median in the combined ordered sample receives 0 weight, but this is necessary for weights to be symmetric around median.

Let us consider the null moments of $T_M$ which are found as follows:

$$E(T_M) = \sum_{i=1}^{n} \Big(i - \frac{n+1}{2}\Big)^2 E(Z_i)$$

Where

$$E(Z_i) = \frac{n_2}{n}$$

**Table 11.2:** Weight Table in Mood's test

| $N$: even | | | | | | |
|---|---|---|---|---|---|---|
| i | 1 | 2 | 3 | $\cdots$ | $\frac{n}{2}-1$ | $\frac{n}{2}$ |
| $w_i$ | $(\frac{n-1}{2})^2$ | $(\frac{n-3}{2})^2$ | $(\frac{n-5}{2})^2$ | $\cdots$ | $(\frac{3}{2})^2$ | $(\frac{1}{2})^2$ |
| i | $\frac{n}{2}+1$ | $\frac{n}{2}+2$ | $\cdots$ | $n-2$ | $n-1$ | $n$ |
| $w_i$ | $(\frac{1}{2})^2$ | $(\frac{3}{2})^2$ | $\cdots$ | $(\frac{n-5}{2})^2$ | $(\frac{n-2}{2})^2$ | $(\frac{n-1}{2})^2$ |
| $N$: odd | | | | | | |
| i | 1 | 2 | 3 | $\cdots$ | $\frac{n-1}{2}$ | $\frac{n+1}{2}$ |
| $w_i$ | $(\frac{n-1}{2})^2$ | $(\frac{n-3}{2})^2$ | $(\frac{n-5}{2})^2$ | $\cdots$ | $1^2$ | 0 |
| i | $\frac{n+3}{2}$ | $\cdots$ | $n-2$ | $n-1$ | $n$ | |
| $w_i$ | $1^2$ | $\cdots$ | $(\frac{n-5}{2}\;^2$ | $(\frac{n-3}{2})^2$ | $(\frac{n-1}{2})^2$ | |

We have

$$E(T_M) = \frac{n_2}{n}\sum_{i=1}^{n}\Big(i - \frac{n+1}{2}\Big)^2$$

$$= \frac{n_2}{n}\Big[\sum i^2 - (n+1)\sum i + \frac{n(n+1)^2}{4}\Big]$$

$$= \frac{n_2}{n}\Big[\frac{n(n+1)(2n+1)}{2} - \frac{n(n+1)^2}{2} + \frac{n(n+1)^2}{4}\Big]$$

$$= \frac{n_2}{n}\,\frac{n(n+1)(n-1)}{12}$$

$$E(T_M) = \frac{n_2(n^2-1)}{12}$$

And

$$V(T_M) = \sum\Big(i - \frac{n+1}{2}\Big)^2 V(z_i) + \sum_{i\neq j}{}'\Big(i - \frac{n+1}{2}\Big)$$

$$\cdot\Big(j - \frac{n+1}{2}\Big)\ \operatorname{cov}(Z_i, Z_j)$$

Where

$$V(Z_i) = E(Z_i^2) - (EZ_i)^2$$

$$= \frac{n_2}{n} - \Big(\frac{n_2}{n}\Big)^2 = \frac{n_2}{n}\Big(1 - \frac{n_2}{n}\Big) = \frac{n_1 n_2}{n^2}$$

Let us find out

$$E(Z_i, Z_j) = P(Z_i = 1 \cap Z_j = 1)\ \ \forall\, i \neq j$$

$$= \frac{\binom{n_2}{2}}{\binom{n}{2}} = \frac{n_2(n_2-1)}{n(n-1)}$$

So that

$$\begin{aligned}\operatorname{cov}(Z_i, Z_j) &= E(Z_i Z_j) - E(Z_i)\cdot E(Z_j) \;\; \forall\, i \neq j \\ &= \frac{n_2(n_2-1)}{n(n-1)} - \left(\frac{n_2}{n}\right)^2 \\ &= -\frac{n_1 n_2}{n^2(n-1)}\end{aligned}$$

On putting these values in $V(T_M)$, we get

$$V(T_M) = \frac{n_1 n_2}{n^2}\sum\left(i - \frac{n+1}{2}\right)^2 - \frac{n_1 n_2}{n^2(n-1)} \cdot \sum_{i\neq j}{}' \left(i - \frac{n+1}{2}\right)\left(j - \frac{n+1}{2}\right)$$

And after some simplifications, we get

$$V(T_M) = \frac{n_1 n_2}{n^2(n-1)}\left[n\sum\left(i - \frac{n+1}{2}\right)^2 - \left\{\sum\left(i - \frac{n+1}{2}\right)\right\}^2\right]$$

After algebraic simplifications, we get

$$\begin{aligned}V(T_M) = \frac{n_1 n_2}{n^2(n-1)}\bigg[n\bigg\{&\sum i^4 - 4\cdot\frac{n+1}{2}\sum i^3 + 6\frac{(n+1)^2}{4}\sum i^2 \\ &- 4\frac{(n+1)^3}{8}\sum i + \frac{n(n+1)^4}{16}\bigg\} - \left\{\frac{n(n^2-1)}{12}\right\}^2\bigg]\end{aligned}$$

By principle of induction, we have

$$\sum_{i=1}^{n} i^3 = \left[\frac{n(n+1)}{2}\right]^2$$

$$\sum i^4 = \frac{n(n+1)(2n+1)(3n^2+3n-1)}{30}$$

After some simplifications, we get

$$V(T_M) = \frac{n_1 n_2 (n+1)(n^2-4)}{180}$$

The null distribution of $T_M$ for small samples could be derived by using the properties of linear rank statistic. The null distribution gets simplified by noting $a_i = a_{n-i+1}$, i.e.

$$\left(i - \frac{n+1}{2}\right)^2 = \left(n - i + 1 - \frac{n+1}{2}\right)^2 = \left(\frac{n+1}{2} - i\right)^2$$

and one can see this null distribution is symmetric about $\dfrac{n(n^2-1)}{24}$ for $n_1 = n_2$, but this property of symmetry of the null distribution dose not hold for

$n_1 \neq n_2$. The asymptotic distribution of $T_M$ can be obtained by Chernoff and Savage(1958)[32] theorem

$$\lim_{n\to\infty} P\Big(\frac{T_M - E(T_M)}{\sigma(T_M)} \leq t\Big|_{H_0}\Big) = \Phi(t)$$

where, $\Phi$ is normal cdf. This is further to be stated that when $F$ test is used to test $\sigma(G_2) = \sigma(G_1)$, asymptotic relative efficiency of Mood's test relative to the $F$ test would be given by

$$ARE(T_M, F) = \lim_{n\to\infty} \frac{e(T_M)}{e(F)} = \frac{15}{2\pi^2} = 0.76$$

where, $e$ is the efficacy of a test. In other words, if one uses Mood's test in the place of $F$-test, one would not fall below 76% of efficiency.

## 11.9 Solved Example

**Example 11.9.1.** *Railway Board of India was receiving several complaints of breaking of power supply wires on rail tracks used for providing power supply to engines of electric trains. A company claims that it has a better option of supply wires of stronger breaking strength. Board engineers now have to decide whether to deal a contract with the company and replace the existing supply wires. The following observations were recorded:*

| *Sample on $X_1$ from population of existing wires $(G_1)$, $n_1 = 12$* | *Sample on $X_2$ from population of wires from new company $(G_2)$, $n_2 = 36$* | | |
|---|---|---|---|
| 2.1 | 11.0 | 8.1 | 18.2 |
| 19.1 | 7.9 | 16.1 | 11.3 |
| 8.9 | 6.2 | 0.8 | 5.7 |
| 5.1 | 8.7 | 7.3 | 8.6 |
| 6.2 | 16.5 | 10.2 | 14.2 |
| 9.8 | 11.2 | 8.7 | 9.6 |
| 7.2 | 18.2 | 17.3 | 14.3 |
| 4.5 | 2.3 | 18.2 | 7.2 |
| 10.9 | 9.6 | 11.2 | 6.1 |
| 11.8 | 7.8 | 8.6 | 12.8 |
| 6.4 | 9.3 | 7.5 | 5.6 |
| 18.2 | 18.5 | 13.3 | 16.2 |

*Test the hypothesis:*

$H_0 : G_1(x) = G_2(x)$ *(Breaking strengths of wires in use and of proposed are same).*

$H_1 : G_1(x) > G_2(x)$ *(Company's wire has a better breaking strength as compared to the existing supply wires)*

***Solution:*** The combined ordered sample is constructed shown in the Table 11.3.

**Table 11.3:** Combined ordered sample

| | | | | | | | |
|---|---|---|---|---|---|---|---|
| Observations: | 2.1 | 2.1 | 2.3 | 4.5 | 5.1 | 5.6 | 5.6 |
| Ranks: | 1.5 | 1.5 | 3 | 4 | 5 | 6 | 7 |
| Sample indicators: | $X_1$ | $X_2$ | $X_2$ | $X_1$ | $X_1$ | $X_2$ | $X_2$ |
| Observations: | 6.1 | 6.2 | 6.2 | 7.2 | 7.2 | 7.3 | |
| Ranks: | 8 | 9.5 | 9.5 | 11.5 | 11.5 | 13 | |
| Sample indicator: | $X_2$ | $X_2$ | $X_1$ | $X_1$ | $X_2$ | $X_2$ | |
| Observations: | 7.5 | 7.8 | 7.9 | 8.1 | 8.6 | 8.6 | 8.7 |
| Ranks: | 14 | 15 | 16 | 17 | 18.5 | 18.5 | 20.5 |
| Sample indicator: | $X_2$ | $X_2$ | $X_2$ | $X_2$ | $X_2$ | $X_2$ | $X_2$ |
| Observations: | 8.7 | 8.9 | 9.3 | 9.6 | 9.6 | 9.8 | 9.8 |
| Ranks: | 20.5 | 22 | 23 | 24.5 | 24.5 | 26.5 | 26.5 |
| Sample indicator: | $X_2$ | $X_2$ | $X_2$ | $X_2$ | $X_2$ | $X_2$ | $X_1$ |
| Observations: | 10.2 | 10.9 | 11.0 | 11.2 | 11.2 | 11.3 | 11.8 |
| Ranks: | 28 | 29 | 30 | 31.5 | 31.5 | 33 | 34 |
| Sample indicators: | $X_2$ | $X_1$ | $X_2$ | $X_2$ | $X_2$ | $X_2$ | $X_2$ |
| Observations: | 12.8 | 13.3 | 14.2 | 14.3 | 16.1 | 16.2 | 16.5 |
| Ranks: | 35 | 36 | 37 | 38 | 39 | 40 | 41 |
| Sample indicator: | $X_2$ | $X_2$ | $X_2$ | $X_2$ | $X_2$ | $X_2$ | $X_2$ |
| Observations: | 17.3 | 18.2 | 18.2 | 18.2 | 18.2 | 18.5 | 19.1 |
| Ranks: | 42 | 43 | 44.5 | 44.5 | 44.5 | 47 | 48 |
| Sample indicator: | $X_2$ | $X_1$ | $X_2$ | $X_2$ | $X_2$ | $X_2$ | $X_2$ |

Note, in the above table, tied observations are assigned average ranks. Here, $n_1 = 12, n_2 = 36, n = n_1 + n_2 = 12 + 36 = 48$. The statistic $T_W$ calculates to:

$$\begin{aligned} t_W = {} & 1.5 + 3 + 6 + 7 + 8 + 9.5 + 11.5 + 13 + 14 + 15 + 16 + 17 + 18.5 + 18.5 \\ & + 20.5 + 20.5 + 22 + 23 + 24.5 + 24.5 + 26.5 + 28 + 30 + 31.5 + 31.5 \\ & + 33 + 34 + 35 + 36 + 37 + 38 + 39 + 40 + 41 + 42 + 44.5 + 44.5 \\ & + 44.5 + 47 + 48 \\ = {} & 1044.5 \end{aligned}$$

Since each of $n_1$ and $n_2$ are larger than 10, therefore, we may conveniently assume that $T_W|H_0$ follows normal distribution. We have

$$E\left(T_W/H_0\right) = \frac{n_2(n+1)}{2} = \frac{36 \times 49}{2} = 882$$

$$V\left(T_W/H_0\right) = \frac{n_1 n_2(n+1)}{12} = \frac{12 \times 36 \times 49}{12} = 1764$$

$$T_W^0 = \frac{T_W - E\left(T_W/H_0\right)}{\sqrt{V\left(T_W/H_0\right)}};$$

$$t_W^0 = \frac{1044.5 - 882}{\sqrt{1764}} = \frac{162.5}{42} = 3.87$$

The critical region is $T_W^0 > c$, where $c$ is obtained at 5% level, so that

$$P(T_W^0 > c) = 0.05$$

we get, $C = 1.64$ from normal table. We see that $t_W^0 = 3.87$ falls in the 5% critical region $T_W^0 > 1.64$. So, the null hypothesis is rejected at 5% level of significance, and we conclude that the company's claim of better breaking strength of supply wires is true. Therefore, engineers may recommend the Railway Board for necessary replacements of wires by more stronger ones. Further, p-value is calculated by

$$P\left(T_W^0 > 3.87/H_0\right) \simeq 0$$

that too confirms that the null hypothesis is strongly rejected.

**Example 11.9.2.** *A central university has recently introduced a correspondence programme in management in addition to its regular programme. To check whether two teaching programme are equally effective, the university academicians took a sample of 15 students; taught 7 of them in classrooms and 8 through correspondence, the same part of a course. At the end of the month, all of them were given the same test with the following scores:*

| *Classroom teaching* $X_2, (n_2 = 7)$ | 61 | 82 | 26 | 75 | 82 | 77 | 73 | |
|---|---|---|---|---|---|---|---|---|
| *Teaching through correspondence* $X_1, (n_1 - 8)$ | 40 | 59 | 77 | 34 | 71 | 63 | 76 | 59 |

*Is there evidence of difference in the two modes of teaching namely, classroom teaching and corresponding teaching on learning and performance of the students.*

*(a) make conclusions on the basis of p-value.*

*(b) use Wilcoxon-Mann-Whitney test at 5% level of significance.*

***Solution:*** Note the students, within and between the categories, are selected independently for the test. The testing problem is stated by $H_0 : G_1 = G_2$ against alternatives in $\Gamma_1^{(3)}$. Since the tables of $T_W$ are given for $n_1, n_2$, $n_2 \leq n_1$, and the distribution of $T_W$ remains unchanged by interchanging $n_1$ and $n_2$ (by subsection 11.4.2(a)), we denote the test-scores of the students of the correspondence course by $X_1$ values ($n_1$ observations) and of class-room teaching by $X_2$ values ($n_2$ observations) so that $n_2 < n_1$. Next, we prepare

**Table 11.4:** Combined ordered sample

| | | | | | | | | |
|---|---|---|---|---|---|---|---|---|
| Observations: | 26 | 34 | 40 | 59 | 59 | 61 | 63 | 71 |
| Ranks: | 1 | 2 | 3 | 4.5 | 4.5 | 6 | 7 | 8 |
| | $Y$ | $X$ | $X$ | $X$ | $X$ | $Y$ | $X$ | $X$ |
| Observations: | 73 | 75 | 76 | 77 | 77 | 82 | 82 | |
| Ranks: | 9 | 10 | 11 | 12.5 | 12.5 | 14.5 | 14.5 | |
| | $Y$ | $Y$ | $X$ | $X$ | $Y$ | $Y$ | $Y$ | |

a combined ordered sample by assigning ranks to the observations along the sample indicators.

(a) Thus

$$t_W = 1 + 6 + 9 + 10 + 12.5 + 14.5 + 14.5 = 67.5$$

This value of $T_W$ falls is the right tail region of the null distribution of $t_W$ since

$$t_W = 67.5 > E(T_W|H_0) = \frac{n_2(n+1)}{2}$$
$$= \frac{7 \times 16}{2} = 56.$$

Therefore, the p-value associating to $T_W$ is $2P(T_W \geq 67.5|H_0)$

$$= 2 \cdot \frac{P(P(T_W \geq 67|H_0) + P(T_W \geq 68|H_0))}{2}$$

(since tables for $T_W$ are given for the whole numbers)

$$= 0.116 + 0.095 = 0.211$$

This shows that there is 21% chance of getting a large value of $T_W$ as 67.5 due to sampling fluctuations under a random sampling from distributions under $H_0$. Therefore, the data do not have enough evidence to show that classroom teaching and teaching through correspondence differently effect the learning of students as far as their test scores are concerned.

(b) $\alpha = 0.05$; the form of the critical region is $T_W \leq T_W^{(1)}$ or $T_W \geq t_W^{(2)}$. The distribution of $T_W|H_0$ is symmetric about $E(T_W|H_0) = \frac{n_2(n+1)}{2} = 56$, gives $t_W^{(1)} = 2 \times 56 - t_W^{(2)}$. Here, $t_W^{(2)}$ is obtained by

$$P\left(T_W \geqslant t_W^{(2)}|H_0\right) \leqslant \frac{0.05}{2} = 0.025$$

Tables for null distribution of $T_W$ gives $t_W^{(2)} = 74, t_W^{(1)} = 2 \times 56 - 74 = 38$. Since the calculated value of $T_W$ is 67.5, which is in the acceptance region, therefore, we accept the hypothesis.

**Example 11.9.3.** *In order to make Government policies on pollution campaigns on rivers, Ganga and Yamuna at different locations have been considered. The quantity of oxygen dissolved in water at each locations, as a measure of pollution, has been recorded for both the rivers:*

| Ganga ($X_1$) | 3.5 | 4.6 | 9.4 | 7.3 | 7.6 | 6.2 |
|---|---|---|---|---|---|---|
| ($n_1 = 10$) | 8.1 | 6.6 | 8.7 | 9.2 | | |
| Yamuna ($X_2$) | 8.7 | 7.4 | 4.1 | 5.3 | 6.6 | |
| ($n_2 = 9$) | 7.9 | 8.8 | 5.7 | 6.1 | | |

*Using normal score test, test the hypothesis that both the rivers are equally polluted.*

***Solution:*** The hypothesis that we wish to test is $H_0 : G_1 = G_2$ against $H_1 : G_1 \neq G_2$ where $G_1$ is the distribution of pollution levels of Ganga and $G_2$ is the distribution of pollution levels of Yamuna. The test statistic is given by

$$T_N = \sum_{i=1}^{n_2} d_n(S_i) = \sum_{i=1}^{n} d_n(i) Z_i$$

where $d_n(i) = E(V_{(i)})$.

Although $d_n(i)s$, the expected normal scores, have been tabulated by Terry (1952), Harter (1961) for $n \leq 100$, and the null distributions of $T_N$ by Terry (1952) and Klotz (1964), it is convenient to use the first approximation of $d_n(i)$ by $\phi^{-1}[i/(n+1)]$ because of ready acces to normal tables. Here, $\phi^{-1}[i/n+1]$ is the $(i/(n+1))^{st}$ quantile point of standard normal distribution. Moreover, it is not difficult to show that $d_n(i) \to \phi^{-1}[i/(n+1)]$ for large $n$, and ven der Waerden (1952, 1953) has shown that $T_N$ is asymptotically equivalent to

$$T_N = \sum_{i=1}^{n} \phi^{-1} \left[ \frac{i}{(n+1)} \right] Z_i$$

This form of Normal score test is called van der Waerden test.

**Table 11.5:** Normal scores table

| Observations | 3.5 | 4.1 | 4.6 | 5.3 | 5.7 | 6.1 |
|---|---|---|---|---|---|---|
| Ranks | 1 | 2 | 3 | 4 | 5 | 6 |
| $[i/(n+1)]$ | 0.050 | 0.100 | 0.150 | 0.200 | 0.250 | .0300 |
| $\phi^{-1}[i/(n+1)]$ | −1.6449 | −1.2816 | −1.03 64 | −0.8416 | −0.6745 | −0.5244 |
| Sample indicator | $X_1$ | $X_2$ | $X_1$ | $X_2$ | $X_2$ | $X_2$ |

*(Contd.)*

**Table 11.5:** Normal scores table (*Contd.*)

| Observations | 6.2 | 6.6 | 6.6 | 7.3 | 7.4 | 7.6 |
|---|---|---|---|---|---|---|
| Ranks | 7 | 8.5 | 8.5 | 10 | 11 | 12 |
| $[i/(n+1)]$ | 0.350 | 0.425 | 0.425 | 0.5 | 0.550 | 0.600 |
| $\phi^{-1}[i/(n+1)]$ | –0.3853 | –0.1891 | –0.1891 | 0 | 0.1257 | 0.2533 |
| Sample indicator | $X_1$ | $X_2$ | $X_1$ | $X_1$ | $X_2$ | $X_1$ |

| Observations | 7.9 | 8.1 | 8.7 | 8.7 | 8.8 | 9.2 | 9.4 |
|---|---|---|---|---|---|---|---|
| Ranks | 13 | 14 | 15.5 | 15.5 | 17 | 18 | 19 |
| $[i/(n+1)]$ | 0.650 | 0.700 | 0.775 | 0.775 | 0.850 | 0.900 | 0.950 |
| $\phi^{-1}[i/(n+1)]$ | 0.3853 | 0.5244 | 0.7388 | 0.7388 | 1.0364 | 1.2816 | 1.6449 |
| Sample indicator | $X_2$ | $X_1$ | $X_1$ | $X_2$ | $X_2$ | $X_1$ | $X_1$ |

Though van der Waerden et. al. (1956) have tabulated critical values for the test $T_N$ for $n \leq 50$, but these tables are not conveniently available. Further, $n = 19$ is sufficiently large, we consider here normal approximations,

$$E\left(T_N|H_0\right) = 0$$

and

$$V\left(T_N|H_0\right) = n_1 n_2 \frac{\sum\limits_{1=1}^{n}\left[\phi^{-1}\left(\frac{i}{n+1}\right)\right]^2}{n(n-1)}$$

so that

$$Z = \frac{T_N - E\left(T_N|H_0\right)}{\sqrt{V\left(T_N|H_0\right)}} \xrightarrow{\mathcal{L}} N(0,1)$$

$$T_N = -1.225, V\left(T_N|H_0\right) = 3.709977$$

gives

$$z = -0.636$$

The critical region at 5% level of significance is $|z| \leq 1.96$. Since tabulated value of $z$ does not fall in the critical region, therefore, the hypothesis that both the rivers are equally polluted is accepted at 5% level. Further, $p$-value is calculated by

$$P\left(|z| > 1.225|H_0\right) = 2p\left(Z \leqslant -1.225|H_0\right) = 2 \times 0.22$$
$$= 0.22 >> 0.05$$

$p$-value 0.22 also confirms the null hypothesis is accepted.

**Example 11.9.4.** *To study whether amount of aggression is same in male and female students, 24 students were given two play session of 20-minutes. These students were observed for incidence and amount of aggression in them during the play*

| *Boys:* | 45 | 118 | 113 | 41 | 86 | 50 | 141 | 104 | 72 | 69 | 65 | 65 |
|---|---|---|---|---|---|---|---|---|---|---|---|---|
| *Girls:* | 20 | 55 | 15 | 7 | 40 | 22 | 36 | 16 | 26 | 16 | 9 | 58 |

*Use median test to test the hypothesis, $H_0$: There is no gender difference in terms of amount of aggression shown by them against $H_1$: Boys show higher incidence and amount of aggression as compared to girls.*

***Solution:*** Assume the incidence and aggression scores for boys follow the distribution $G_1$ and for girls follow $G_2$. The hypothesis that we wish to test can be stated as,

$$H_0 : G_1 = G_2$$

against

$$H_1 : G_1 < G_2$$

where $G_1 < G_2$ implies $P(X_1 > x) > P(X_2 > x)$. Too small values of $T$ indicates this situations. In other words, if $T_M \leq c$, we reject $H_0$ and infer that the incidence and amount of aggression is higher in boys as compared to girls. The combined ordered sample is given by:

| Observations | 7 | 9 | 15 | 16 | 16 | 20 | 22 | 26 |
|---|---|---|---|---|---|---|---|---|
| Sample indicators | $X_2$ | $X_2$ | $X_2$ | $X_2$ | $X_2$ | $X_2$ | $X_2$ | $X_2$ |
| Observations: | 36 | 40 | 41 | 45 | 50 | 55 | 58 | 65 |
| Sample indicators: | $X_2$ | $X_2$ | $X_1$ | $X_1$ | $X_1$ | $X_2$ | $X_2$ | $X_1$ |
| Observation: | 65 | 69 | 72 | 86 | 104 | 113 | 118 | 141 |
| Sample indicators: | $X_1$ | $X_1$ | $X_1$ | $X_1$ | $X_1$ | $X_1$ | $X_1$ | $X_1$ |

Since $n_1 + n_2 = 24$ is even, median in the combined ordered sample i.e. [12]th smallest value in the pooled ordered sample is any number between 45 and 50. Here, $T_M = 2$, the corresponding $p$-value calculates to

$$p\text{-value} = P\left(T_M \leqslant 2|H_0\right)$$

$$= \sum_{k=0}^{2} \frac{\binom{n-n'}{k}\binom{n'}{n_2-k}}{\binom{n}{n_2}}$$

For, $n = 24, n' = 12, n_1 = n_2 = 12$, we have,

$$p\text{-value} = \sum_{k=0}^{2} \frac{\binom{12}{k}\binom{12}{12-k}}{\binom{24}{12}}$$

$$= \frac{1}{\binom{24}{12}}\left[\binom{12}{0}\binom{12}{12} + \binom{12}{1}\binom{12}{11} + \binom{12}{2}\binom{12}{10}\right]$$

$$= 0.0017$$

Since $P(T_M \leq 2|H_0) = 0.002 < 0.05$, we reject the null hypothesis. In other words, we say that in random sampling there is 0.2 per cent chance of getting $T_M$ as small as 2 under $H_0$, therefore, data has enough evidence to reject $H_0$. So, we conclude that boys show higher incidence and amount of aggression as compared to girls.

**Example 11.9.5.** *Two brands of automobile batteries namely Exide and Bosch are to be compared to see which of them has a better life. Independent samples of batteries were draw from Exide and Bosch, and batteries were put to a test under the similar conditions. The following observations on lengths of life (in days) were recorded:*

| *Exide:* | *463* | *658* | *804* | *783* | *721* | *688* | *529* | *871* |
|---|---|---|---|---|---|---|---|---|
| *Bosch:* | *504* | *550* | *688* | *371* | *429* | *467* | *408* | |

*Use Kolmogorov-Smirnov test to check whether the data support the claim that Exide batteries have better life as compared to Bosch.*

***Solution:*** Since the quantiles of Kolmogorov-Smirnov test are available due to Massey for $n_1 < n_2$, therefore, we consider battery lives of Bosch by $X_1, n_1 = 7$ and Exide by $X_2, n_2 = 8$. We wish to test the hypothesis:

$$H_0 : G_1 = G_2 \quad \text{against} \quad H_1 : G_1(x) \geq G_2(x) \text{ for all } x$$

and

$$G_1(x) > G_2(x) \qquad \text{for atleast one } x$$

Since we suspect that $X_1$'s might be situated to left of $X_2$ or $X_1$'s tends to be stochastically smaller than $X_2$. The critical region in this case is given by

$$D^+_{7,\,8} \geq D^+_{7,\,8,\,\alpha}$$

The following table helps in calculating the test statistic $D^+_{7,\,8}$.

**Table 11.6:** Test-statistic-calculation table

| $x$ | $G^*_{1,7}$ | $G^*_{2,8}$ | $(G^*_{1,7} - G^*_{2,8})$ |
|---|---|---|---|
| 371 | 1/7 | 0 | 1/7 |
| 408 | 2/7 | 0 | 2/7 |
| 429 | 3/7 | 0 | 3/7 |
| 463 | 3/7 | 1/8 | 17/56 |
| 467 | 4/7 | 1/8 | 25/56 |
| 504 | 5/7 | 1/8 | 33/56 |
| 529 | 5/7 | 2/8 | 26/56 |
| 550 | 6/7 | 2/8 | 34/56 |
| 658 | 6/7 | 3/8 | 27/56 |
| 688 | 1 | 4/8 | 4/8 |
| 721 | 1 | 5/8 | 3/8 |
| 783 | 1 | 6/8 | 2/8 |
| 804 | 1 | 7/8 | 1/8 |
| 871 | 1 | 1 | 0 |

$$\begin{aligned} D^+_{7,\,8} &= \sup_x [G^*_{1,\,7}(x) - G^*_{2,\,8}(x)] \\ &= \frac{34}{56} \end{aligned}$$

$\alpha$th quantile of $D^+_{7,8}$ is obtained by the tables due to Massey, which are also available in other textbooks. For $n_1 = 7, n_2 = 8$ at level $\alpha = 0.05$, the critical value is $D^+_{7,\,8,\,0.05} = 33/56$. Since $D^+_{7,\,8} > D^+_{7,\,8,\,0.05}$, we reject $H_0$, and we conclude that Exide automobile batteries have longer life as compared to Bosch batteries. $p$-value is

$$\begin{aligned} p\text{-value} &= P\left(D^+_{7,8} \geqslant \frac{34}{56} | H_0\right) \\ &= 0.0375 < 0.05 \end{aligned}$$

In random sampling, there is a 3.75 per cent chance of observing a value of $D^+_{7,8}$ as large as 34/56. This shows that the data has some evidence, though not very strong, against the null hypothesis, therefore, we accept the alternative hypothesis and conclude that Exide Batteries are superior to Bosch batteries in terms of their life.

*Remark* 11.9.1. (1) If $n_1 \nless n_2$, we must interchange samples from $G_1$ and $G_2$, since quantile tables, for the statistics $D_{n_1,n_2}$ and $D^+_{n_1,n_2}$, are given for $n_1 < n_2$.

(2) The critical values $D^-_{n_1,n_2,\alpha}$ corresponding to the critical region $D^-_{n_1,n_2} \geq D^-_{n_1,n_2,\alpha}$ of testing,

$$H_0 : G_1(x) = G_2(x) \qquad \forall\ x \text{ against}$$

$$H_1 : G_1(x) \leq G_2(x) \qquad \forall\ x \text{ and } G_1(x) < G_2(x) \text{ for some } x$$

are read from quantile tables of null distribution of $D^+_{n_1,n_2}$ since null distributions of $D^+_{n_1,n_2}$ and $D^-_{n_1,n_2}$ are identical.

## *Review Questions*

**11.1** Explain the advantages of non-parametric tests over parametric tests. Derive a non-parametric test which is used in a situation similar to where two sample $t$-test is applied. State some optimal properties of the test.

**11.2** Define the shift alternatives and the alternatives of stochastic dominance; prove that the former are contained in latter. Establish that Terry Heoffding Normal Scores test is unbiased against the alternatives of stochastic dominance. State the alternatives against which this test is consistent. Prove that these alternatives are more general than the alternatives of stochastic dominance.

**11.3** Establish the two-sample rank sum test statistic for location as function of a suitably defined kernel of U-statistic. Calling this function as Mann-Whitney U, prove that a test based on M-W U is invariant. State the model for the test.

**11.4** What do you mean by non-parametric inference? What are its main features? What are the various non-parametric tests available for comparision of two populations. Describe in detail any two of them with illustrations.

**11.5** Define a two-sample problem of location and a linear rank statistic. Let $T = \sum_i^n a_i Z_i$ where $a_i$ denotes the given weight and $Z_i$ the indicator function of the first sample observation in the ordered pooled sample, $i = 1, 2, \ldots, N$. Determine $E(T)$ and $V(T)$ under the null hypothesis of identity of the two populations, and hence evaluate the same for

(a) The Mann-Whitney test

(b) The Median test.

**11.6** Describe clearly (i) Wilcoxon-Mann-Whitney test and (ii) Kolmogorov-Smirnov test for the two-sample problem. Consider both one-sided and two-sided alternatives.

**11.7** Obtain distribution-free confidence bands for distribution functions.

**11.8** Describe the Mann-Whitney U-test for two independent samples. Derive the relationship between the Wilcoxon statistic W and U-statistic and the expressions for the mean and variance of U under the null hypothesis.

**11.9** Describe Mann-Whitney U-statistic for non-parametric hypothesis testing.

$$H_0 : F(x) = G(x) \;\; \forall\, x \;\text{ against }\; H_1 : F(x) \neq G(x)$$

for at least one $x$. Also, calculate $E_{H_0}(U)$ and $V_{H_0}(U)$. Show that the probability of $U = u$ under $H_0$ are calculated by the recursion relation:

$$p_{m,n}(u) = \frac{m}{m+n}\, p_{m-1,\,n}(u) + \frac{n}{m+n}\, p_{m,\,n-1}(u-m)$$

where, $x_1, \ldots, x_m$ and $y_1, \ldots, y_n$ be two independent samples from $F$ and $G$ respectively.

**11.10** Define $U$-statistic and prove that it is conditional expectation of a symmetric kernel.

Express sample variance $s_x^2 = \frac{1}{n-1}\sum(x_i - \bar{x})^2$ as $U$-statistic. Hence, drive the asymptotic distribution of sample variance.

**11.11** Let $X_1, \ldots, X_m$ and $Y_1, \ldots, Y_n$ be independent random samples and let $\mu$ and $\gamma$ denote the location parameters of the distributions of $X_1$ and $Y_1$ respectively. Discuss the problem of testing the null hypothesis $H_0 : \mu = \gamma$ against the alternative $H_1 : \mu \neq \gamma$, (a) $X$ and $Y$ r.v.'s are normally distributed and (b) the $X$ and $Y$ r.v.'s have continuous distributions.

**11.12** Let $(X_1, X_2, \ldots, X_m)$ and $(Y_1, Y_2, \ldots, Y_n)$ be independent random samples from the continuous distribution function $F(x)$ and $F(x - \theta)$, respectively, where $F$ is unknown. It is required to test $H_0 : \theta = 0$. Write down the median test statistic $T$ and its asymptotic distribution under $H_0$.

**11.13** Explain the main difference between the parametric and non-parametric approaches to the theory of statistical inference. Specify the underlying assumptions and the null hypothesis in median, sign and U tests.

**11.14** Write short notes on any two of the following:

(a) U-statistics.
(b) Test for association based on Kendall's tau.
(c) Mood's test for randomness.

**11.15** (a) State the (one-sided) alternatives for which M-W U test is consistent and establish the consistency for such alternatives.

(b) Determine the efficacy of student's t-test. State the model. Assuming the efficacy of M-W U test is

$$\frac{12 n_1 n_2}{n+1}\left[\int_{-\infty}^{\infty} g_0^2(x)dx\right]^2$$

determine the Pitman efficiency of M-W U test relative to Student's t-test. Comment on the result.
[$n_1$ is the sample size from population I and $n_2$ from II. $n = n_1 + n_2$ and $g_0$ is the common pdf of the two populations under $H_0$ ].

**11.16** Two sleep inducing drugs were administered to two batches of 6 patients each and the patients were kept under identical circumstances. The hours of sleep (rounded off) induced by the drugs are given below:

| Drug 1 | 4 | 5 | 6 | 7 | 10 | 14 |
|---|---|---|---|---|---|---|
| Drug 2 | 8 | 9 | 11 | 12 | 13 | 15 |

Using Mann-Whitney test decide whether the median effects of the two drugs are equal.
(Table values of U-statistic at 5% level of signifieance are:

$U_{5,5} = 2,\ U_{5,6} = 3,\ U_{6,6} = 5$)

**11.17** Describe the Wilcoxon Signed-Rank test. The following are the weight gains (in kg) of two samples of young calves fed two different diets but otherwise kept under identical conditions:

| Diet 1 | 16.3 | 10.1 | 10.7 | 13.5 | 14.9 | 11.8 | 14.3 | 10.2 |
|---|---|---|---|---|---|---|---|---|
| | 12.0 | 14.7 | 23.6 | 15.1 | 14.5 | 18.4 | 13.2 | 14.0 |
| Diet 2 | 21.3 | 23.8 | 15.4 | 19.6 | 12.0 | 13.9 | 18.8 | 19.2 |
| | 15.3 | 20.1 | 14.8 | 18.9 | 20.7 | 21.1 | 15.8 | 16.2 |

Apply Mann-Whitney test (U-test) to test the null hypothesis at 1% level of signifiance that the populations sampled are indentical against the alternative hypothesis that on the average the second diet produces a greater gain in weight.

**11.18** (a) Describe Wilcoxon Signed-Rank Test. Explain how to obtain the exact null distribution of the test statistic.

(b) The life in (000) kms. of samples of two brand of tyres were found as follows:

| Brand A | 8.3 | 7.9 | 9.5 | 7.1 | 7.8 | 8.4 | 8.2 | 7.1 | 7.5 | | |
|---|---|---|---|---|---|---|---|---|---|---|---|
| Brand B | 9.2 | 8.5 | 8.1 | 6.8 | 8.2 | 7.4 | 7.2 | 9.1 | 8.1 | 8.4 | 8.2 |

Apply

(a) Median Test

(b) Mann-Whitney test to test the null hypothesis that the samples come from the same population.

**11.19** Consider the following data giving the blood cholesterol levels of men in two different socio-economic groups.

| Socio-Economic Group | Blood cholesterol |
|---|---|
| High | 403 301 269 336 259 423 244 383 235 319 260 |
| Low | 312 222 302 400 340 350 353 210 286 290 |

Using the normal approximation to the Wilcoxon-Mann Whitney test at level 0.05, can you conclude that the two populations of blood cholesterol level are identical against the alternative that they differ in location only?

**11.20** (a) State the Chernoff-Savage theorem regarding the asymptotic distribution of linear rank statistic.

(b) Using the theorem in (a) calculate the null and non-null means and variances of the Wilcoxon statistic in the asymptotic case.

(c) Prove that the exact null distribution of the Wilcoxon statistic is symmetric.

**11.21** State Hoeffding-Lehmann theorem for the asymptotic distribution of two sample U-statistic. Apply this theorem to determine the asymptotic null-distribution of M-W U.

**11.22** (a) State Hoeffding version of the Wald-Wolfowitz central limit theorem.
(b) Give two examples of statistics whose asymptotic distributions may be obtained by applying the above central limit theorem.

**11.23** Write an essay on any one of the following topics:

(a) Properties of null distribution of general linear rank test statistic.

(b) Problem of ties in two-samples problem.

(c) Wald-Walfowitz-Noether-Hoeffding Permutation Central Limit Theorem (Statement only) and its application in establishing asymptotic distribution of Mann-Whitney rank sum test and Terry-Hoeffding Normal Scores test under the null hypothesis.

**11.24** Describe the concepts of Asymptotic power and Pitman Efficiency in a two-sample problem. State and prove the theorems which determine their values under suitable assumptions. Apply the above theorems to derive the Pitman Efficiency of Terry-Hoeffding Normal Scores test relative to the classical difference of means test for the two-sample univariate problem of location against the class of shift alternatives when the population were normal. Prove that the Van Der Warden Normal Scores test is asymptotically equivalent to the Terry-Hoeffding test.

**11.25** State the test statistic of Terry-Hoeffding's test and Van Der Warden's Test. Prove that one is asymptotically equivalent to other. Derive the Pitman efficiency of one of these tests against the classical difference of means test when the populations were normal and alternatives were $\Gamma_1^{(2)}$.

**11.26** Explain how to construct the Kolmogorov-Smirnov two-sample test statistic $T$. Suppose $X_1$, $X_2$, $X_3$; $Y_1$, $Y_2$ are the samples from the two continuous populations. Obtain the exact distribution of $T$ if the null hypothesis in the two-sided test is true.

**11.27** What do you mean by two sample problem? Discuss Kolmogorov-Smirnov test and Chi-square test for homogeneity for two sample problems.

# Chapter 12

# Measures of Association for Bivariate Samples

## 12.1 INTRODUCTION

Let $(X_1, Y_1), \ldots, (X_n, Y_n)$ be a random sample from a bivariate population $F(x, y)$ to detect some general relationship between the two dependent random variables. For this we may consider the population of differences $(X - Y)$ and its one parameter i.e. variance, which contains information on this relationship as shown by the following expression,

$$V(X - Y) = V(X) + V(Y) - 2\ \text{cov}(X, Y)$$

It is this covariance in the above expression that measures (a) the direction and (b) the amount of the relationship between $X$ and $Y$. The positive and large value of this indicates large values of $X$ associated with large values of $Y$ and small values of $X$ with small values of $Y$. The negative and large value of this indicates the large values of $X$ combined with small values of $Y$ or small values of $X$ with large values of $Y$. This association is termed as *concordance (agreement)*. But covariance as a measure of association suffers from two drawbacks, first that its value depends on the order of magnitude and second, units of random variables $X$ and $Y$. It is in this connection that Pearson defined a product moment correlation coefficient which overcomes the above drawback

$$\rho = \frac{\text{cov}(X, Y)}{\sigma_X \cdot \sigma_Y}$$

$\rho$ is invariant under location and scale transformations on $X$ and $Y$, $-1 \leq \rho \leq 1$ and has been accepted as reasonable measure of association in a bivariate population. Independence of r.v.s $X$ and $Y$ implies $\rho = 0$ conversely, if $\rho = 0$ the r.v.s $X$ and $Y$ are not necessarily independent unless the underlying population is bivariate normal. $\rho$ in general for other bivariate populations, is not a good description of relationship since dependence is reflected in a wide variety of relationships. Therefore, $\rho$ cannot be accepted as a good measure of association between $X$ and $Y$ in non-parametric situations, where no distributional assumptions are required on the parent population.

In non-parametric statistics we would prefer such a measure which is distribution free. This can happen only when the measure is determined by relative magnitude as opposed to absolute magnitude of variables under study. In other words, a reasonable measure in nonparametric statistic must be invariant under all order-preserving transformations, however, $\rho$ is invariant under positive linear transformations of random variables but not invariant to all order-preserving transformations. It is further noted for a resonable measure that the probabilities involving the events, $X < Y$, of two random variables must be invariant under all order preserving transformations. The perfect direct and indirect association between $X$ and $Y$ are given by *perfect concordance* and *perfect discordance* respectively. Therefore, a reasonable measure of association between $X$ and $Y$ in a nonparametric situation would be an appropriate combination of probabilities of concordance and discordance between the variables under study.

In the first section we shall discuss Kendall's tau coefficient (1962)[104] and in the next the independence of two variables $X$ and $Y$ in contingency tables, popularly known as chi-square test of independence.

## 12.2 KENDALL'S TAU

Let $(X_i, Y_i)$ and $(X_j, Y_j)$ be two independent pairs of random variables—drawn from $F(x, y)$. The relationship between these pairs is said to be in perfect concordance if

$$X_i < X_j \ \cap \ Y_i < Y_j \quad \text{or} \quad X_i > X_j \ \cap \ Y_i > Y_j$$

and perfect discordance (disagreement) if

$$X_i < X_j \ \cap \ Y_i > Y_j \quad \text{or} \quad X_i > X_j \ \cap \ Y_i < Y_j$$

We shall write $\pi_c$ and $\pi_d$ as probability of perfect concordance and perfect discordance respectively, defined as

$$\begin{aligned}
\pi_c &= P[\{(X_i < X_j) \cap (Y_i < Y_j)\} \cup \{(X_i > X_j) \cap (Y_i > Y_j)\}] \\
&= P[(X_i < X_j) \cap (Y_i < Y_j)] + P[(X_i > X_j) \cap (Y_i > Y_j)] \\
&= P[(X_j - X_i)(Y_j - Y_i) > 0]
\end{aligned}$$

and

$$\begin{aligned}
\pi_d &= P[\{(X_i < X_j) \cap (Y_i > Y_j)\} \cup \{(X_i > X_j) \cap (Y_i < Y_j)\}] \\
&= P[(X_i < X_j) \cap (Y_i > Y_j)] + P[(X_i > X_j) \cap (Y_i < Y_j)] \\
&= P[(X_j - X_i)(Y_j - Y_i) < 0]
\end{aligned}$$

If we assume the marginal distributions of $X$ and $Y$ are continuous, i.e.

$$P(X_i = X_j) = P(Y_i = Y_j) = 0$$

We have

$$\begin{aligned}\pi_c &= [P(Y_i < Y_j) - P\{(X_i > X_j) \cap (Y_i < Y_j)\}] \\ &\quad + [P(Y_i > Y_j) - P\{(X_i < X_j) \cap (Y_i > Y_j)\}] \\ &= P(Y_i < Y_j) + P(Y_i > Y_j) - \pi_d = 1 - \pi_d\end{aligned}$$

or

$$\pi_c + \pi_d = 1$$

Kendall has defined a measure of association between two random variables from any bivariate population $F(x, y)$ as

$$\tau = \pi_c - \pi_d = 2\pi_c - 1 = 1 - 2\pi_d$$

If $X$ and $Y$ are independent and continuous random variables, i.e.

(a) $P(X_i < X_j) = P(X_i > X_j)$

(b) $P\{(X_i < X_j) \cap (Y_i < Y_j)\}$
$$= P(X_i < X_j) \cdot (Y_i < Y_j)$$

We have

$$\begin{aligned}\pi_c &= P(X_i < X_j) \cdot P(Y_i < Y_j) + P(X_i > X_j) \cdot P(Y_i > Y_j) \\ &= P(X_i > X_j) \cdot P(Y_i < Y_j) + P(X_i < X_j) \cdot P(Y_i > Y_j) \\ &= \pi_d\end{aligned}$$

This implies $\tau = 0$. But, conversely if $\tau = 0$ it does not necessarily implies $X$ and $Y$ are independent. But this disadvantage we have also observed in case of $\rho$ as well. $\tau$ has been considered as a measure of association since its distribution is distribution-free. However, $\tau = 0$ iff $\rho = 0$, i.e. if and only if, $X$ and $Y$ are independent.

### 12.2.1 An Estimate of $\tau$

Let $(X_1, Y_1), (X_2, Y_2), \ldots, (X_n, Y_n)$ be a random sample of size $n$ drawn from a bivariate population $F(x, y)$. Let us define the indicator variables,

$$A_{ij} = \text{sgn}(X_i - X_j) \cdot \text{sgn}(Y_j - Y_i)$$

where

$$sgn(u) = \begin{cases} -1 & \text{if } u < 0 \\ 0 & \text{if } u = 0 \\ 1 & \text{if } u > 0 \end{cases}$$

Then the values taken by $A_{ij}$ would be $a_{ij}$ where

$$a_{ij} = \begin{cases} 1 & \text{if } i \text{ and } j \text{ pairs are concordant} \\ 0 & \text{if } i \text{ and } j \text{ pairs are neither concordant nor discordant} \\ -1 & \text{if } i \text{ and } j \text{ pairs are discordant} \end{cases}$$

The marginal distribution of these indicator variables would be given by:

$$P\{A_{ij} = a_{ij}\} = \begin{cases} \pi_c & \text{if } a_{ij} = 1 \\ \pi_d & \text{if } a_{ij} = -1 \\ 1 - \pi_c - \pi_d & \text{if } a_{ij} = 0 \end{cases}$$

and expected value of $A_{ij}$ would be given by

$$\begin{aligned} E(A_{ij}) &= 1.\pi_c + (-1) \cdot \pi_d + 0 \cdot (1 - \pi_c - \pi_d) \\ &= \pi_c - \pi_d = \tau \end{aligned}$$

where, $a_{ij} = a_{ji}$ and $a_{ii} = 0$, only $\binom{n}{2}$ pairs would be considered here. An unbiased estimate of $\tau$ would be given by

$$T = \sum_{1 \le i} \sum_{\le j \le n} \frac{A_{ij}}{\binom{n}{2}}$$

This measure of association is known as *Kendall's sample tau coefficient.*

### 12.2.2 An Alternative Form of $T$ (an Estimator of $\tau$)

Kendall(1962)[104] suggested an alternative expression for putting $T$, so that it becomes more convenient for computation. For a situation when one or both the variables $X$ and $Y$ are not continuous, i.e. $X$ (or, and) $Y$ pairs are with ties, the total of pairs $\begin{pmatrix} n \\ 2 \end{pmatrix}$ may be categorized into concordant pairs $P(A_{ij} = +1)$, discordant pairs, $Q(A_{ij} = -1)$ and neither concordant nor discordant pairs $O(A_{ij} = 0)$ so that $1 \le i \le j \le n$ and $P + Q + O = \begin{pmatrix} n \\ 2 \end{pmatrix}$. Let the total sum is $S = P - Q$. Then we have

$$T = \frac{P - Q}{\binom{n}{2}} = \frac{S}{\binom{n}{2}}$$

If $X$ and $Y$ are continuous, i.e. there are no ties between $X$ and $Y$ variables, i.e. $A_{ij} \neq 0$ for $i \neq j$, $P + Q = \binom{n}{2}$, we can write $T$ as

$$T = \frac{2P}{\binom{n}{2}} - 1 = 1 - \frac{2Q}{\binom{n}{2}}$$

Note the analogous expression for $\tau$

$$\tau = 2\pi_c - 1 = 1 - 2\pi_d$$

This shows $P/\binom{n}{2}$ and $Q/\binom{n}{2}$ are the unbiased estimators of $\pi_c$ and $\pi_d$ respectively. The calculation of $P$ is simple for a given sample of $n$ pairs. For this we arrange the pairs according to the smallest value of $X$ to largest, $P$ is the count of pairs for which $Y_i - Y_j > 0,\ 1 \le i < j \le n$, since only then, we have $a_{ij} = 1$.

## 12.3 TEST FOR INDEPENDENCE

Let us consider the hypothesis

$$H_0 : \text{The random variables X and Y are independent}$$

$$\text{against} \quad H_1 : X \text{ and } Y \text{ are dependent.}$$

Intuitively, large values of $|T|$ would lead to rejection of $H_0$, therefore, the test on the basis of $T$ is defined as

$$\phi(T) = \begin{cases} 1 & \text{if } |T| \ge c \\ 0 & \text{if } |T| < c \end{cases}$$

so that

$$P_{H_0}(|T| \ge c) \le \alpha$$

We shall note that the test $\phi(|T|)$ is non-randomized. Under the null hypothesis, $\tau = 0$

$$\tau_c = \tau_d$$

$$P(A_{ij} = -1) = P(A_{ij} = 1)$$

showing that $P = Q$, or, $T = 0$

Therefore, under the null hypothesis $\tau = 0$ the distribution is symmetric about the origin. From this

$$P_{H_0}(T \le -c) + P_{H_0}(T \ge c) \le \alpha$$

or

$$2P_{H_0}(T \ge c) \le \alpha$$

or

$$P_{H_0}(T \ge c) \le \alpha/2$$

which gives $c = t_{\alpha/2}$ (upper-$\alpha/2^{\text{th}}$ quantile of the distribution of $T$) This gives rise to the appropriate test as

$$\phi(|T|) = \begin{cases} 1 & \text{if } |T| \ge t_{\alpha/2} \\ 0 & \text{if } |T| < t_{\alpha/2} \end{cases}$$

In order to calculate $t_{\alpha/2}$, it is necessary to determine the null distribution of $T$. For small values of $n$ the null distribution could directly be calculated. Kendall (1962) had tabulated these values for $4 \leq n \leq 10$. In these tables $S_\alpha$ are given for which

$$P\{S > S_\alpha\} \leq \alpha \text{ where } S = \binom{n}{2} T, \text{ for selected values of } n \text{ and } \alpha.$$

For testing $H_0$ against $H_1$ : direct association, the critical region is given by $T \geq c$, and for testing. $H_0$ against $H_1$: inverse association, the critical region is given by $T \leq c$. The critical values $c$ are obtained by tables given by Kendall, which are readily available in standard textbooks.

Kendall has shown for large $n(\geq 8)$

$$T \sim AN\Big(0, \frac{2(2n+5)}{9n(n-1)}\Big)$$

Therefore,

$$Z = \frac{3\sqrt{n(n-1)}}{\sqrt{2(2n+5)}} \cdot T \sim N(0,1)$$

This result could be used for testing the hypothesis of independence for large $n$.

### 12.3.1 The Null Distribution of $T$

To determine the test of independence of $X$ and $Y$ we must know the complete null distribution of $T$ or $S$. By the definition of $T$ it is clear that it is invariant under all order-preserving transformations. The value of $T$ depends on the relative magnitudes of the observations and is the same whether $T$ has been calculated by using the variate values or ranks. It is with this reason that we assign integer ranks to $X$ and $Y$ values. The data then consist of $n$ sets of pairs of ranks. We have already seen that the samples have no ties, then under the null hypothesis all $n!$ distinguishable pairs of ranks are equally likely. Values of $T$ are completely determined by $P$ or $S$ because of relations we have outlined earlier. The null distribution of $P$ shall be given by

$$P(P = p|\, H_0) = \frac{u(n,p)}{n!}$$

where, $u(n,p)$ is number of pairs of $n$ ranks which have resulted into exactly $p$ $a_{ij}$ such that $a_{ij} = 1;\ 1 \leq i < j \leq n$. And

$$P(T = t|\, H_0) = P\Big[P = \binom{n}{2}\frac{t+1}{2}\Big|\, H_0\Big]$$

and

$$P(T = t|\, H_0) = P\Big[S = \binom{n}{2} t \Big|\, H_0\Big]$$

### 12.3.2 A Recursive Relation to Find $P[T = t|H_0]$

We know that the null distribution of $T$ can directly be obtained from the null distribution of $P$ or of $S$. We shall now develop a recursive relation to general $u(n+1,\, p)$ having $u(n, p)$ known for all $p$. We shall assume that $n$ observations, i.e. pairs are arranged in the increasing order of magnitude of $X$ component. The value of $P$ depends on the resulting permutation of the $Y$ ranks. The $n$ observations now would look like $(1, s_1), (2, s_2), \ldots, (i, s_i), \ldots, (n, s_n)$, $s_i$ being the rank of $Y$ observation with the rank $i$ in the $X$ samples. Here

$$\begin{aligned} P = {} & \text{no. of integers greater than } s_1 \\ & + \text{no. of integers greater than } s_2 \text{ excluding } s_1 \\ & + \text{no. of integers greater than } s_3 \text{ excluding } s_1 \text{ and } s_2 \\ & + \text{etc.} \end{aligned}$$

So, for $n$ we have the permutation $(s_1, s_2, \ldots, s_n)$ that gives $P = p$. For $n+1$, we shall consider the insertion of the number $n + 1$ in any of $n + 1$ possible positions of the permutation $(s_1, s_2, \ldots, s_n)$ does to the value of $p$. If $n + 1$ is at the first position, $p$ is unchanged, if it is at the second position, there is one additional integer greater than $s_1$, so that $p$ is increased by 1. If $n + 1$ is at the third position, there is one additional integer greater than both $s_1$ and $s_2$ so that $p$ is increased by 2. Therefore, if $n + 1$ is at the $k^{th}$ position, $p$ is increased by $k - 1$ for all $k = 1, 2, \ldots, n + 1$. Therefore, the desired recursive relation is

$$u(n + 1,\, p) = u(n,\, p) + u(n,\, p - 1) + u(n,\, p - 2) + \cdots + u(n,\, p - n)$$

But we know that

$$T = \frac{2P}{\binom{n}{2}} - 1 = \frac{S}{\binom{n}{2}} \quad \text{or} \quad S = 2P - \binom{n}{2} = 2P - \frac{n(n-1)}{2}$$

Let the new value of $S'$ for $n + 1$ pairs be,

$$S' = 2P' - \frac{n(n+1)}{2}$$

if $n + 1$ is inserted at the $k$th position, we know that $p$ is increased by $k - 1$, i.e.

$$P' = P + k - 1$$

This gives

$$\begin{aligned} S' &= 2(P+k-1) - \frac{n(n+1)}{2} \\ &= 2P - \left[\frac{n(n+1)}{2} - n\right] + 2(k-1) - n \\ &= 2P - \frac{n(n-1)}{2} + 2(k-1) - n \\ &= S + 2(k-1) - n \end{aligned}$$

This shows that $S$ is increased by $2(k-1)-n$ for $k = 1, 2, \ldots, n+1$, therefore, the recursive relation for $S$ we have

$$\begin{aligned} u(n+1, s) = u(n,\, s+n) + u(n,\, s+n-2) + u(n,\, s+n-4) \\ + \cdots + u(n,\, s-n+2) + u(n,\, s-n) \end{aligned}$$

The null distribution of $S$ is symmetric about 0.

The values of $S$ would be odd or even depending on whether $\binom{n}{2}$ is odd or even. It is with this reason the tables of $S$ or of $T$ are most easily constructed instead for $T$ or $Q$. The tables of null distribution of $S$ has been given by Kendall (1962)[104] for $4 \le n \le 10$.

The following example helps us to understand the above calculations. Let us consider, $n = 3$, we have 3! permutations of $Y$ ranks. We now have corresponding values of $P$, $S$ and $T$ as:

| Permutations of $Y$ ranks | (1,2,3) | (1,3,2) | (2,1,3) | (2,3,1) | (3,1,2) | (3,2,1) |
|---|---|---|---|---|---|---|
| P | 3 | 2 | 2 | 1 | 1 | 0 |
| S | 3 | 1 | 1 | –1 | –1 | –3 |
| T | 1 | 0.33 | 0.33 | –0.33 | –0.33 | –1 |

We have

$$S = 2P - \binom{n}{2} = 2P - 3 \;\text{ and }\; T = \frac{S}{\binom{n}{2}} = \frac{S}{3}$$

The frequencies and null distribution of $T$ then given by

| $P$ | 0 | 1 | 2 | 3 |
|---|---|---|---|---|
| $S$ | –3 | –1 | 1 | 3 |
| $T$ | –1 | –0.33 | 0.33 | 1 |
| u(3,P) or u(3,T) | 1 | 2 | 2 | 1 |
| $P_{H_0}\{T = t\}$ | 1/6 | 2/6 | 2/6 | 1/6 |

We note that the null distribution is symmetric about 0, therefore, only half of the distribution about 0 need to be calculated and the rest comes from symmetry.

We shall not obtain the distribution for $S$ or $T$ for $n+1$ by making use of recursive relations that we have developed earlier. We have, $n = 3 + 1 = 4$.

$$u(4, P) = \sum_{i=0}^{3} u(3, P - i)$$

We then have

$$u(4, 0) = u(3, 0) = 1 \text{ (assume that } u(n, x) = 0 \text{ for } x < 0 \text{ and } u(n, x) = 0 \text{ for } x > n)\cdot$$

$$u(4, 1) = u(3, 1) + u(3, 0) = 2 + 1 = 3$$

$$u(4, 2) = u(3, 2) + u(3, 1) + u(3, 0) = 2 + 2 + 1 = 5$$

$$u(4, 3) = u(3, 3) + u(3, 2) + u(3, 1) + u(3, 0) = 1 + 2 + 2 + 1 = 6$$

$$u(4, 4) = u(3, 3) + u(3, 2) + u(3, 1) = 1 + 2 + 2 = 5$$

$$u(4, 5) = u(3, 3) + u(3, 2) = 1 + 2 = 3$$

$$u(4, 6) = u(3, 3) = 1$$

Frequency calculations for $S$ at $n = 4$ would be done by recursive relation

$$u(4, 5) = \sum_{i=0}^{3} u(3, S + 3 - 2i)$$

Note that since $P$ ranges from 0 to 6, $S$ would range from $-6$ to $+6$ at even integer numbers. We now have

$$u(4, -6) = u(3, -3) = 1$$

$$u(4, -4) = u(3, -1) + u(3, -3) = 2 + 1 = 3$$

$$u(4, -2) = u(3, 1) + u(3, -1) + u(3, -3) = 2 + 2 + 1 = 5$$

$$u(4, 0) = u(3, 3) + u(3, +1) + u(3, -1) + u(3, -3) = 1 + 2 + 2 + 1 = 6$$

$$u(4, 2) = u(3, 3) + u(3, 1) + u(3, -1) = 1 + 2 + 2 = 5$$

$$u(4, 4) = u(3, 3) + u(3, 1) = 1 + 2 = 3$$

$$u(4, 6) = u(3, 3) = 1$$

Therefore, the null distribution of $T$ for $n = 4$ would be given by:

| P | 0 | 1 | 2 | 3 | 4 | 5 | 6 |
|---|---|---|---|---|---|---|---|
| S | -6 | -4 | -2 | 0 | 2 | 4 | 6 |
| T | -1 | -2/3 | -1/3 | 0 | 1/3 | 2/3 | 1 |
| $P_{H_0}\{T = t\}$ | 1/24 | 3/24 | 5/24 | 6/24 | 5/24 | 3/24 | 1/24 |

Note that

$$T = \frac{S}{\binom{n}{2}} = \frac{S}{\binom{4}{2}} = \frac{S}{6}$$

## 12.4 TEST OF INDEPENDENCE IN CONTINGENCY TABLES

The non-parametric situations in this section, remains the same as has been considered in Section 12.2, i.e. $(X_1, Y_1), (X_2, Y_2), \ldots, (X_n, Y_n)$ be a random sample of size $n$ drawn from a bivariate population $F(x, y)$. Except that $X$ and $Y$ are termed here as *sets or families of attributes*, each of which has two or more *categories*, say $A_1, A_2, \ldots, A_r$ for $X$ and $B_1, B_2, \ldots, B_c$ for $Y$. Each of $n$ observations, which were measured on interval scale, is classified in some category of each family as a count to cross-category cell. Note here that the data available on the interval scale, loses information when categorized into cells as a count. Such a layout is called *contingency table* of order $r \times c$, etc. We are interested in this section in a measure of association between the families, or in testing the null hypothesis of independence of families or that one particular family is independent of the others. In general, families $X$ and $Y$ of events are defined to be completely independent if

$$P(A_i \cap B_j) = P(A_i) \cdot P(B_j) \quad \forall\ A_i \subset A \text{ and } B_j \subset B.$$

In a $r \times c$ layout, the entry in the $(i, j)$th cell shall be the number of $n$ data points $(X_i, X_j)$ belonging to the cross-classification $A_i \cap B_j$ and denoted by $O_{ij}$. The contingency table is written as follows:

| | $B_1$ | $B_2$ | $\cdots$ | $B_c$ | *Row total* |
|---|---|---|---|---|---|
| $A_1$ | $O_{11}$ | $O_{12}$ | $\cdots$ | $O_{1c}$ | $O_{1\cdot}$ |
| $A_2$ | $O_{21}$ | $O_{22}$ | $\cdots$ | $O_{2c}$ | $O_{2\cdot}$ |
| $\cdot$ | $\cdot$ | $\cdot$ | $\cdots$ | $\cdot$ | $\cdot$ |
| $\cdot$ | $\cdot$ | $\cdot$ | $\cdots$ | $\cdot$ | $\cdot$ |
| $A_r$ | $O_{r1}$ | $O_{r2}$ | $\cdots$ | $O_{rc}$ | $O_{r\cdot}$ |
| | $O_{\cdot 1}$ | $O_{\cdot 2}$ | $\cdots$ | $O_{\cdot c}$ | $O_{\cdot\cdot} = n$ |

Row and column totals are given by

$$O_{i\cdot} = \sum_{j=1}^{c} O_{ij} \quad \text{for} \quad i = 1, 2, \ldots, r$$

and

$$O_{\cdot j} = \sum_{i=1}^{r} O_{ij} \quad \text{for} \quad j = 1, 2, \ldots, c, \text{respectively.}$$

$$\sum_{i=1}^{r} O_{i\cdot} = \sum_{j=1}^{c} O_{\cdot j} = n$$

We know that $rc$ random variables $O_{11}, O_{12}, \ldots, O_{rc}$ follows multinomial probability distribution with parameters

$$\theta_{ij} = P(A_i \cap B_j)$$

So that

$$\sum_{i=1}^{r}\sum_{j=1}^{c} \theta_{ij} = 1$$

We are interested in testing the hypothesis

$$\begin{aligned} H_0 &: \text{ families X and Y are independent or X and Y} \\ &\quad \text{classifications are independent.} \qquad (12.1) \\ H_1 &: \text{ that there is some kind of dependence between} \\ &\quad \text{these families.} \end{aligned}$$

In other words

$$H_0 : P(A_i \cap B_j) = P(A_i) \cdot P(B_j)$$

or

$$H_0 : \theta_{ij} = \theta_{i.} \cdot \theta_{.j} \tag{12.2}$$

Where

$$\theta_{i.} = \sum_{j=1}^{c} \theta_{ij} \quad \text{and} \quad \theta_{.j} = \sum_{i=1}^{r} \theta_{ij}$$

Likelihood function for the parameter $\theta_{ij}$ is given by

$$L(\theta_{11}, \theta_{12}, \ldots, \theta_{rc}) = \prod_{i=1}^{r}\prod_{j=1}^{c} (\theta_{ij})^{O_{ij}}$$

$L$ under $H_0$ takes the form

$$L(\theta_{1\cdot}, \theta_{2\cdot}, \cdots, \theta_{r\cdot}, \theta_{\cdot 1}, \theta_{\cdot 2}, \cdots, \theta_{\cdot c}) = \prod_{i=1}^{r}\prod_{j=1}^{c} (\theta_{i.}\ \theta_{.j})^{O_{ij}}$$

If $\theta_{ij}$ were specified under $H_0$ say, $\theta_{ij} = \theta_{ij}^{(0)}$, we would have been using goodness-of-fit test for this hypothesis testing problem. But in the present case, the underlying multinomial distribution is not specified, instead only a particular relation between the parameters $\theta_{ij} = \theta_{i.} \cdot \theta_{.j}$ is mentioned under the null hypothesis. This is a situation where the null hypothesis is composite. Let the expected frequencies $E_{ij}$ be estimated from the data as $n\hat{\theta}_{ij}^{0}$, $i = 1, \ldots, r,\ j = 1, \ldots, c$, goodness-of-fit statistic in this case is given by

$$Q = \sum_{i=1}^{r}\sum_{j=1}^{c} \frac{(O_{ij} - n\widehat{\theta}_{ij})^2}{n\widehat{\theta}_{ij}}$$

or under $H_0$

$$Q = \sum_{i=1}^{r}\sum_{j=1}^{c} \frac{(O_{ij} - n\widehat{\theta}_{i.}^{0}\,\widehat{\theta}_{.j}^{0})^2}{n\,\widehat{\theta}_{i.}^{0}\,\widehat{\theta}_{.j}^{0}}$$

where, $\widehat{\theta}_{i.}, \widehat{\theta}_{.j}$ are the estimator of the independent parameters $\theta_{i.}, \theta_{.j}$ which are obtained subject to the maximization of likelihood function under $H_0$ with respect to these parameters. MLE's of $\theta_{i.}$ and $\theta_{.j}$ are obtained by maximizing $L$ subject to the restrictions

$$\sum_{i=1}^{r} \theta_{i.} = 1 = \sum_{j=1}^{c} \theta_{.j}$$

By Lagrange's multipliers method, we get

$$\widehat{\theta}_{i.} = \frac{O_{i.}}{n} \quad \text{and} \quad \widehat{\theta}_{.j} = \frac{O_{.j}}{n} \quad \text{for } i = 1, 2, \ldots, r; \quad j = 1, 2, \ldots, c.$$

so that the ML estimates of the expected cell frequencies under $H_0$ are

$$n\widehat{\theta}_{ij}^{0} = n\widehat{\theta}_{i.}^{0}\widehat{\theta}_{.j}^{0} = \frac{O_{i.}O_{.j}}{n}$$

On putting these values in $Q$ under $H_0$, we have

$$Q = \sum_{i=1}^{r}\sum_{j=1}^{c} \frac{\left(O_{ij} - \frac{O_{i.}O_{.j}}{n}\right)^2}{O_{i.}O_{.j}/n}$$

or

$$Q = \sum_{i=1}^{r}\sum_{j=1}^{c} \frac{(nO_{ij} - O_{i.}O_{.j})^2}{nO_{i.}O_{.j}}$$

The likelihood ratio test for the testing problem in Eqs. (12.1) and (12.2) is given by

$$T = \frac{\sup_{\theta_{ij} \subset H_0} L(\theta_{11}, \ldots, \theta_{rc})}{\sup_{\theta_{ij} \in \Theta} L(\theta_{11}, \ldots, \theta_{rc})} = \frac{L(\hat{\theta}_{1.}^{0}, \ldots, \hat{\theta}_{r.}^{0}\ \hat{\theta}_{.1}^{0}\hat{\theta}_{.2}^{0} \ldots, \hat{\theta}_{.c}^{0})}{L(\hat{\theta}_{11}, \ldots, \hat{\theta}_{rc})}$$

$$= \prod_{i=1}^{r}\prod_{j=1}^{c} \left(\frac{\hat{\theta}_{ij}^{0}}{\hat{\theta}_{ij}}\right)^{O_{ij}}$$

where, $\hat{\theta}_{i.}$ and $\hat{\theta}_{.j}$ are MLE's of $\theta_{i.}$ and $\theta_{.j}$ respectively and $\hat{\theta}_{ij} = O_{ij}/n$. Let us consider the quantity

$$-2\log T = -2\sum_{i=1}^{r}\sum_{j=1}^{c} O_{ij}(\log\hat{\theta}_{ij}^{0} - \log\hat{\theta}_{ij})$$

$$= -2\sum_{i=1}^{r}\sum_{j=1}^{c} O_{ij}(\log\hat{\theta}_{i.}^{0}\hat{\theta}_{.j}^{0} - \log\frac{O_{ij}}{n})$$

By using Taylor's expansion one can show that $-2\log T$ and $Q$ are asymptotically equivalent. But from the theory of likelihood ratio test we know that asymptotically $-2\log T \sim \chi^2_f$, $f$ being the number of independent parameters in the parameter space $\Theta$ of $\theta_{ij}$'s. Therefore, $f$ is calculated as

$$f = (rc-1) \text{ due to the restriction } \sum_{i=1}^{r}\sum_{j=1}^{c}\theta_{ij} = 1$$

$$-\,(r-1) \text{ and } (c-1) \text{ parameters were estimated by noting the restriction } \textstyle\sum_{i=1}^{r}\theta_{i\cdot} = 1 \text{ and } \sum_{j=1}^{r}\theta_{\cdot j} = 1$$

Which gives

$$\begin{aligned} d &= (rc-1) - \{(r-1)+(c-1)\} = rc - r - c + 1 \\ &= r(c-1) - 1(c-1) = (r-1)(c-1) \end{aligned}$$

Therefore, $Q|H_0 \sim \chi^2_{(r-1)(c-1)}$ asymptotically. The test would be given by

$$\phi(Q) = \begin{cases} 1 & \text{if } Q \geq q_0 \\ 0 & \text{otherwise} \end{cases}$$

since non-independence between $X$ and $Y$ results into lack of agreement between observed and expected cell frequencies and that results into large values of $Q$ giving rise to greater than type critical region $Q \geq q_0$, where $q_0$ is obtained by

$$P_{H_0}\{Q \geq q_0\} = \alpha$$

or

$$P_{H_0}\{\chi^2_{(r-1)(c-1)} \geq q_0\} = \alpha$$

### 12.4.1 Pearson's Contingency Coefficient

If the null hypothesis of independence of two families $X$ and $Y$, is rejected one may be interested in knowing as to how strong is the relationship. To measure this Pearson (1904) had proposed the contingency coefficient as

$$c = \left(\frac{Q}{Q+n}\right)^{1/2}$$

where, $Q$ is the $\chi^2$ statistic defined in Section 12.4. The values of $c$ would lie between 0 and 1, large value of $c$ would indicate the strength of relationship. But only disadvantage with using $c$ is that it can not attain the value 1.

## 12.5 SOLVED EXAMPLES

**Example 12.5.1.** *In a flower show the judges agreed that five exhibits were outstanding and these were numbered arbitrarily from* 1 *to* 5. *Three judges*

| Judge A | 5 | 3 | 1 | 2 | 4 |
|---|---|---|---|---|---|
| Judge B | 3 | 1 | 5 | 4 | 2 |
| Judge C | 5 | 2 | 3 | 1 | 4 |

*each arranged these five exhibits in order of merit, giving the following rankings:*
*Compute Kandall's sample tau coefficient $T$ from the three possible pairs of rankings. Also, test the null hypothesis that rankings of judge A and judge C are independent on the basis of Kendall's tau.*

***Solution:*** Let us consider the rankings of judges A and B and arrange them in the increasing order of rankings of Judge A. Then we have

| Judge A | 1 | 2 | 3 | 5 | 5 |
|---|---|---|---|---|---|
| Judge B | 5 | 4 | 1 | 2 | 3 |

$$\begin{aligned} P &= \text{ number of pairs of rankings for judge B such that } Y_j - Y_i > 0 \text{ for all } j > i \\ &= 2(\text{the pairs (1,2) and (1,3)}) \end{aligned}$$

This gives $$T = \frac{2P}{\binom{n}{2}} - 1 = \frac{2 \cdot 2}{\binom{5}{2}} - 1 = \frac{4}{10} - 1 = -\frac{6}{10} = -0.6$$

Similarly, for Judge A and C, arranging them in the increasing order of rankings of Judge A, we have

| Judge A | 1 | 2 | 3 | 4 | 5 |
|---|---|---|---|---|---|
| Judge C | 3 | 1 | 2 | 4 | 5 |

$$\begin{aligned} P &= \text{number of pairs}(3,4),\ (3,5),\ (1,2),\ (1,4),\ (1,5),\ (2,4),\ (2,5),\ (4,5) \\ &= 8 \end{aligned}$$

This gives
$$T = \frac{2 \cdot 8}{10} - 1 = \frac{16}{10} - 1 = 0.6$$

Now consider the judges B and C and arrange the data in the increasing order of ranks due to judge B, we have

| Judge B | 1 | 2 | 3 | 4 | 5 |
|---|---|---|---|---|---|
| Judge C | 2 | 4 | 5 | 1 | 3 |

$$\begin{aligned} P &= \text{number of pairs}(2,4), (2,5), (2,3), (4,5), (1,3) \\ &= 5 \end{aligned}$$

We then have
$$T = \frac{2 \cdot 5}{10} - 1 = 0$$

We would now test the hypothesis

$$H_0: \text{ Judge A and Judge C are independent}$$
$$H_1: \text{ They are not independent.}$$

We shall now find out

$$P_{H_0}\{|T| \geq 0.6\}$$

For $n = 5$, values of $P$ would be $0, 1, 2, \ldots, 10$ and therefore, $S$ would range from $-10, -8, -6, \ldots, 0, \ldots, 6, 8, 10$ and $T = S/\binom{n}{2} = S/10$ would range from $-1, -0.8, -0.6, \ldots, 0, \ldots, 0.6, 0.8, 1$. Event $|T| \geq 0.6$ indicates $T = -1, -0.8, -0.6, 0.6, 0.8, 1$ or $S = -10, -8, -6, 6, 8, 10$. We shall calculate this probability by the recursive relation

$$u(5, S) = \sum_{i=0}^{4} u(4, S + 4 - 2i)$$

and null-table obtained for $n = 4$ in the subsection 12.3.2, we have

$$u(5, -10) = u(4, -6) = 1$$
$$u(5, -8) = u(4, -4) + u(4, -6) = 3 + 1 = 4$$
$$u(5, -6) = u(4, -2) + u(4, -4) + u(4, -6)$$
$$= 5 + 3 + 1 = 9$$

From the symmetry of the null distribution of $S$, we have

$$P_{H_0}[|T| \geq 0.6] = P_{H_0}[S = -10, -8, -6, 6, 8, 10]$$
$$= \frac{2(1 + 4 + 9)}{5!} = \frac{28}{120} = 0.23 > 0.05 (= \alpha)$$

Therefore, we accept the null hypothesis at 5% level of significance. Alternatively, we find $t_{\alpha/2}$ s.t.

$$P[T > t_{\alpha/2}] \leq \alpha/2$$

or

$$P\left[\binom{n}{2} T > \binom{n}{2} t_{\alpha/2} = \right] \leq \alpha/2$$

When

$$\alpha = 0.05, \ n = 5$$
$$P[S > 10 \cdot t_{\alpha/2}] \leq 0.025$$

We have

$$10 \cdot t_{\alpha/2} = 8 \quad \text{[from tables given in Kendall(1962)]}$$
$$t_{\alpha/2} = 0.8$$

Since, calculated value of $t$ is 0.6 which is less than the tabulated value, i.e. 0.8, therefore, we accept the null hypothesis at 5% level of significance.

**Example 12.5.2.** *Two separate groups of coaches and sports writers have ranked eight international football teams, as a preseason poll exiercise, as follows:*

**Team**

| | $A$ | $B$ | $C$ | $D$ | $E$ | $F$ | $G$ | $H$ |
|---|---|---|---|---|---|---|---|---|
| Coaches | 3.5 | 2 | 3.5 | 8 | 6 | 7 | 1 | 5 |
| Sports writers | 2 | 3 | 8 | 7 | 5.5 | 4 | 1 | 5.5 |

*Test the hypothesis that there is a direct association between the two polls.*

***Solution:*** The hypothesis that we wish to test is, i.e. $H_0$ : No association between the two polls, against $H_1$: There is a direct association between the two polls.

Scores given by coaches and sports writers are not continuous random variables since we observe ties on their rank scores. The following tables lists all $\binom{n}{2} = \binom{8}{2} = 28$ pairs by labelling them into concordant (+1), discordant (–1), and neither concordant nor discordant (0) categories.

**Table 12.1:** Computation of $P, Q$ and $O$

| $(X_i, X_j)$ | $(Y_i, Y_j)$ | labels | $(X_i, X_j)$ | $(Y_i, Y_j)$ | labels |
|---|---|---|---|---|---|
| (3.5, 2) | (2,3) | –1 | (3.5, 6) | (8, 5.5) | –1 |
| (3.5, 3.5) | (2,8) | 0 | (3.5, 7) | (8, 4) | –1 |
| (3.5, 8) | (2, 7) | +1 | (3.5, 1) | (8, 1) | +1 |
| (3.5, 6) | (2, 5.5) | +1 | (3.5, 5) | (8, 5.5) | –1 |
| (3.5, 7) | (2, 4) | +1 | (8, 6) | (7, 5.5) | +1 |
| (3.5, 1) | (2, 1) | +1 | (8, 7) | (7, 4) | +1 |
| (3.5, 5) | (2, 5.5) | +1 | (8, 1) | (7, 1) | +1 |
| (2, 3.5) | (3, 8) | + 1 | (8, 5) | (7, 5.5) | +1 |
| (2, 8) | (3, 7) | +1 | (6, 7) | (5.5, 4) | –1 |
| (2, 6) | (3, 5.5) | +1 | (6, 1) | (5.5, 1) | +1 |
| (2, 7) | (3, 4) | +1 | (6, 5) | (5.5, 5.5) | 0 |
| (2, 1) | (3, 1) | +1 | (7, 1) | (4, 1) | +1 |
| (2, 5) | (3, 5.5) | +1 | (7, 5) | (4, 5.5) | –1 |
| (3.5, 8) | (8, 7) | –1 | (1, 5) | (1, 5.5) | +1 |

We have

$$T = \frac{P - Q}{\binom{n}{2}} = \frac{19 - 7}{28} = \frac{12}{28} = 0.43$$

The critical region is of the form $T \geq c$ ($T$ is too large) (note if the alternative hypothesis had of an inverse association, the critical region would have $T \leq c$). This gives,

$$P(T \geqslant c | H_0) \leqslant 0.05$$

We have from tables:

$$P\,(T \geqslant 0.571|H_0) = 0.031$$

and

$$P\,(T \geqslant 0.500|H_0) = 0.054;$$

$$C \approx \frac{0.571 + 0.500}{2} = 0.535$$

Since calculated value of $T(= 0.43)$ is smaller than its tabulated value 0.535 at 5%, therefore, we state that the data has not enough evidence to reject. $H_0$. Further, $p$-value is calculated by:

$$P\,(T \geqslant 0.43|H_0) = 0.089 > 0.05$$

This also indicates acceptance of $H_0$, but it is a weak acceptance.

**Example 12.5.3.** *A random sample of 500 individuals was taken to investigate whether smoking and alcohol drinking habits are related. The following results were obtained:*

| | *Heavy smoker* | *Moderate smoker* | *Non-smoker* | *Total* |
|---|---|---|---|---|
| Heavy drinker | 20 | 62 | 6 | 88 |
| Moderate drinker | 40 | 8 | 159 | 207 |
| Non-drinker | 10 | 20 | 175 | 205 |
| Total | 70 | 90 | 340 | 500 |

*Test the hypothesis that alcohol drinking and smoking habits are independent.*

***Solution:*** We wish to test the following hypothesis:

$H_0$: Drinking and smoking habits are independent

against $H_1$: Drinking and smoking habits are not independent.

Under the hypothesis $H_0$ we expect $\dfrac{O_{i\cdot} \times O_{\cdot j}}{n}$ observations in the $(i, j)$th cell. These expected frequencies are calculated in the following table:

| Expected Frequencies | Heavy smoker | Moderate smoker | Non-smoker | Total |
|---|---|---|---|---|
| Heavy drinker | 12.32 | 15.84 | 59.84 | 88 |
| Moderate drinker | 28.98 | 37.26 | 140.76 | 207 |
| Non-drinker | 28.70 | 36.90 | 139.40 | 205 |
| Total | 70 | 90 | 340 | 500 |

$$Q = \frac{(20 - 12.32)^2}{12.32} + \frac{(62 - 15.84)^2}{15.84} + \cdots + \frac{(175 - 139.40)^2}{139.40}$$

$$= 246.0061$$

Thus $p$-value for $(3-1)(3-1) = 4$ d.f. is $P(Q \geq 246.0061|H_0) < .001$ which indicates that the data has strong evidence against the null hypothesis, therefore, we conclude that drinking and smoking habits of individuals are some way related.

**Example 12.5.4.** *The following table gives data, relating to 36 deceased Presidents of USA, on the age at their first inauguration and the age at death:*

| *President* | *Age at first Inauguration* | *Age at Death* |
|---|---|---|
| Washington | 57 | 67 |
| J. Adams | 61 | 90 |
| Jefferson | 57 | 83 |
| Madison | 57 | 85 |
| Monroe | 58 | 73 |
| J.Q. Adams | 57 | 80 |
| Jackson | 61 | 78 |
| Van Buren | 54 | 79 |
| Harrison | 68 | 68 |
| Tyler | 51 | 71 |
| Polk | 49 | 53 |
| Taylor | 64 | 65 |
| Filmore | 50 | 74 |
| Pierce | 48 | 64 |
| Buchanan | 65 | 77 |
| Lincoln | 52 | 56 |
| A. Johnson | 56 | 66 |
| Grant | 46 | 63 |
| Hayes | 54 | 70 |
| Garfield | 49 | 49 |
| Arthur | 50 | 56 |
| Cleveland | 57 | 71 |
| Harrison | 55 | 67 |
| Me Kinley | 54 | 58 |
| T. Roosevelt | 42 | 60 |
| Taft | 51 | 72 |
| Wilson | 56 | 67 |
| Harding | 55 | 57 |
| Coolidge | 51 | 60 |
| Hoover | 54 | 90 |
| F. Roosevelt | 51 | 63 |
| Truman | 60 | 88 |
| Eisenhover | 62 | 78 |
| Kennedy | 43 | 46 |
| L. Johnson | 55 | 64 |
| Nixon | 56 | 81 |

*Test whether the age at inauguration and age at death of U.S. Presidents are dependent.*

***Solution:*** The null hypothesis that we wish to test is stated as follows:

$H_0$ : The age of U.S. Presidents at first inauguration and age at which they die are independent.

against $H_1$ : The age at first inauguration and age at death are dependent.

Age at Inauguration may be categorized into $C_1 = (41, 50]$; $C_2 = (50, 60]$ and $C_3 = (60, 70]$ and age at death may be categorized into $D_1 = (45, 60]$; $D_2 = (60, 75]$; $D_3 = (75, 90]$. Summarizing the data under these categories gives the following $3 \times 3$ contingency table:

| *Age at inauguration* | *Age at death* | | | *Total* |
|---|---|---|---|---|
| | $D_1\,(45, 60]$ | $D_2\,(60, 75]$ | $D_3\,(75, 90]$ | |
| $C_1\,(41, 50]$ | [2.0] | [3.56] | [2.44] | 8 |
| $C_2\,(50, 60]$ | [5.5] | [9.78] | [6.72] | 22 |
| $C_2\,(60, 70]$ | [1.5] | [2.67] | [1.83] | 6 |
| Total | 9 | 16 | 11 | 36 |

The values in table within the [ ] indicate expected frequencies. Thus test statistic

$$Q = 11.84$$

The corresponding $p$-value for $(3-1)(3-1) = 4$ d.f. is:

$$0.01 < P\,(Q > 11.84|H_0) < 0.025$$

We, therefore, reject $H_0$ at 2.5% but accept at 1%.

## *Review Questions*

**12.1** A random sample of 200 retired men was classified according to education and the number of children they had:

| *Number of children*→ *Education* ↓ | 0 *or* 1 | 2 *or* 3 | *more than* 3 |
|---|---|---|---|
| *Elementary* | 14 | 37 | 32 |
| *Secondary* | 19 | 42 | 17 |
| *College* | 12 | 17 | 10 |

Test the hypothesis that the size of the family is independent of the level of education of the father. (Given $\chi^2_{0.05,\,9} = 16.919$, $\chi^2_{0.05,\,4} = 9.488$, $\chi^2_{0.05,\,5} = 11.07$).

**12.2** A random sample of 10 couples was taken. The heights of these couples were recorded:

| | Heights of married couples (inches) | | | | | | | | | |
|---|---|---|---|---|---|---|---|---|---|---|
| | Couple | | | | | | | | | |
| | 1 | 2 | 3 | 4 | 5 | 6 | 7 | 8 | 9 | 10 |
| Husband | 62 | 73 | 68 | 70 | 74 | 69 | 67 | 78 | 70 | 67 |
| Wife | 63 | 61 | 66 | 68 | 68 | 65 | 64 | 72 | 67 | 61 |

Test whether heights of husband and wife are directly associated.

**12.3** Consider the data of solved example 12.5.4. Test the hypothesis that there is direct association between the age at inauguration and the age at death of U.S. Presidents.

**12.4** In a manufacturing company a technician is appointed temporarily on the terms that he will be observed for 13 days. If, however, he shows improvement over time, he will be given 2 years appointment in the company. Each day a random sample was selected from the items produced by him and percentage of defective items were recorded:

| *Day* | *percentage of defective items* | *Day* | *Percentage of defective items* |
|---|---|---|---|
| 1 | 7.8 | 8 | 6.1 |
| 2 | 7.5 | 9 | 5.3 |
| 3 | 7.7 | 10 | 4.6 |
| 4 | 6.9 | 11 | 3.2 |
| 5 | 6.1 | 12 | 4.0 |
| 6 | 5.8 | 13 | 3.5 |
| 7 | 5.2 | | |

On the basis of the above data should the company offer the job to the technician? (Hint: use Kandell's Tau).

**12.5** In order to study whether there is a direct association between heights and weights of athletes, heights and weights of eight athletes were recorded

| | Athlete | | | | | | | |
|---|---|---|---|---|---|---|---|---|
| | 1 | 2 | 3 | 4 | 5 | 6 | 7 | 8 |
| Height (inches) | 68 | 72 | 65 | 70 | 69 | 72 | 71 | 74 |
| Weight (pounds) | 190 | 194 | 181 | 198 | 186 | 208 | 196 | 208 |

Test the hypothesis of evidence of direct association between the heights and weights of athletes.

**12.6** A random sample of 3013 Indian citizens of different ethnic groups was taken, their blood types were recorded:

| | *Blood types* | | | |
|---|---|---|---|---|
| *Ethnic groups* | 0 | A | B | AB |
| Bodo | 190 | 160 | 140 | 96 |
| Parsis | 177 | 148 | 128 | 39 |
| Naga | 531 | 441 | 292 | 219 |
| Mizo | 47 | 49 | 22 | 10 |
| Santhal | 102 | 120 | 70 | 32 |

Test the hypothesis that the blood types of Indian ethnic citizens are independent of their ethnic groups.

**12.7** In a public opinion poll of 720 Indian nationals all across the country were asked the question "Do you agree with policy of the present Government on the privatization of public sectors such as Railways, Electricity and so on." Choices were yes, no or no opinion. The responses were categorized according to the political affiliations of the respondents and tabulated as follows:

| | *Response* | | | |
|---|---|---|---|---|
| *Political affiliation* | *Yes* | *No* | *No opinion* | *Total* |
| Congress | 164 | 55 | 45 | 264 |
| BJP | 100 | 190 | 60 | 350 |
| BSP | 70 | 20 | 16 | 106 |
| | 334 | 265 | 121 | 720 |

Test the hypothesis that attitude towards privatization of public sector is independent of political party affiliation.

**12.8** A market survey is conducted to assess if the magazine a reader likes the most is related to his or her annual income. The following table gives results of a sample of 800 readers:

| *Magazine liked the most* | *Annual income* | | | *Total* |
|---|---|---|---|---|
| | < Rs. 36000 | Rs. 36000 –Rs. 1,00,000 | above Rs. 1,00,000 | |
| Business Today | 4 | 170 | 130 | 304 |
| Frontline | 10 | 70 | 66 | 146 |
| India Today | 25 | 86 | 84 | 195 |
| Outlook | 15 | 70 | 70 | 155 |
| | 54 | 396 | 350 | 800 |

Test the hypothesis that the annual income of a reader and the magazine he likes most are independent.

# References


[1] Ansari, A.R. and Bradley, R.A. (1960), Rank sum tests for dispersion, *Ann. Math. stat.*, **31**, pp. 1174–1189.

[2] Arrow, K. (1960), Decision theory and the choice of a level of significance for the t-test, In *contributions to probability and statistics* (*Olkin et al., eds.*), Stanford U.P., Stanford, Calif.

[3] Auble, J.D. (1953), Extended tables for the Mann-Whitney statistic, *Bull. Inst. Educ. Res.*, I: i–iii, and pp. 1–39.

[4] Bahadur, R.R. (1954), Sufficiency and statistical decision functions, *Ann. Math. Statist.*, **25**, pp. 423–462.

[5] ——— (1979), A note on UMV estimates and ancillary statistics, In *contribution to statistics*, J. Hajek Memorial Volume (Jureckova, ed.), Academia, Prague.

[6] ——— and Lehmann, E.L. (1955), Two comments on sufficiency and statistical decision functions, *Ann. Math. Statist.*, **26**, pp. 139–142.

[7] Barankin, E.W. and Maitra, A.P. (1963), Generalization of the Fisher-Darmois-Koopman-Pitman theorem on sufficient statistics, *Sankhya*, A25, pp. 217–244.

[8] Barndorff-Nielsen, O. (1978), *Information and exponential families instatistics theory*, Wiley, New York.

[9] ——— and Pedersen, K. (1968), Sufficient data reduction and exponential families, *Math. Scand.*, **2**, pp. 197–202.

[10] Barnett, M.S. (1957), A comment on D.V. Lindley's statistical paradox. *Biometrika.*, **44**, pp. 533–534.

[11] Bartlett, M.S. (1937), Properties of sufficiency and statistical tests. *Proc. Roy. Soc. Ser.*, A160, pp. 268–282.
[Points out that exact (that is, similar) tests can be obtained by combining the conditional tests given the different values of sufficient statisticapplications.]

[12] Basu, D. (1955), On statistics independent of a complete sufficient statistic, *Sankhya*, **15**, pp. 377–380.

[13] Basu, D. (1958), On statistics independent of a sufficient statistic. *Sankhya*, **20**, pp. 223–226.

[14] ——— (1978), On partial sufficiency: A review. *J. Statist. Planning and Inference*, **2**, pp. 1–13.

[15] Bateman, G. (1948), On the power function of the longest run as a test for randomness in a sequence of alternatives, *Biometrika*, **35**, pp. 97–112.

[16] Berger, J.O. (1985), *Statistical Decision Theory and Bayesian Analysis*, 2nd ed., Springer, New York.

[17] ——— and Sellke, T. (1984), Testing a point null hypothesis: The irreconci-lability of significance levels and evidence. Tech. report: (no. 84–27), Purdue University.

[18] Berkson, J. (1955), Maximum likelihood and minimum $\chi^2$-estimates of the logistic function. *J. Amer. Statist., Assoc.*, **50**, pp. 130–162.

[19] Birnbaum, Z.W. (1952), Numerical tabulation of the distribution of Kolmogorov's statistic for finite sample size, *J. Am. Statist. Assoc.*, **47**, pp. 425–441.

[20] Birnbaum, Z.W. and Tingey, F.H. (1952), One-sided confidence contours for probability distribution functions, *Ann. Math. Stat.*, **22**, pp. 592–596.

[21] Billingsley, P. (1979), *Probability and Measure*, Wiley, New York.

[22] Blackwell, D. and Dubins, L.E. (1975), On existence and non-existence of proper, regular conditional distributions, *Ann. probab.*, **3**, pp. 741–752.

[23] ——— and Ryll-Nardzwski, C. (1963), Non-existence of everywhere proper conditional distributions. *Ann. Math.Statist.*, **34**, pp. 223–225.

[24] Blackwell, D. and Girshick, M.A. (1954), *Theory of Games and Statistical Decisions.* Wiley, New York.

[25] Bradley, J.V. (1968), *Distribution Free Statistical Tests*, Prentice-Hall Inc., Englewood Cliffs, N.J.

[26] Brown, L. (1964), Sufficient statistics in the case of independent random variables, *Ann. Math. Statist.*, **35**, pp. 1456–1474.

[27] Brown, L.D., Cohen, A. and Strawderman, W.E. (1976), A complete class theorem for strict monotone likelihood ratio with applications. *Ann. Math. Statist.*, **4**, pp. 712-722.

[28] Burkholder, D.L. (1961), Sufficiency in the undominated case. *Ann. Math. Statist.*, **32**, pp. 1191–1200.

[29] Chapman, J.W. (1976), A comparison of $\chi^2$; $-2 \log R$, and multinomial probability criteria for significance tests when expected frequencies are small. *J. Amer. Statist. Assoc.*, **71**, pp. 854–863.

[30] Chernoff, H. and Moses, L.E. (1959), *Elementary Decision Theory.* Wiley, New York.

[31] Chernoff, H. and Lehmann, E.L. (1954), The use of maximum likelihood estimate in $\hat{A}2$ tests for goodness of fit, *Ann. Math. Stat.*, **25**, pp. 579–586.

[32] —— and Savage, I.R. (1958), Asymptotic normality and efficiency of certain nonparametric test statistics, *Ann. Math. Stat.*, **29**, pp. 972–994.

[33] Chernoff, H. and Scheffe, H. (1952), A generalization of the Neyman-Pearson fundamental lemma. *Ann. Math. Stat.*, **23**, pp. 213–225.

[34] Cochran, W.G. (1952), The $\chi^2$ Test of goodness of fit, *Ann. Math. Stat.*, **23**, 315–345.

[35] Cox, D. (1977), The role of significance tests. *Scand. J. Statist.*, **4**, pp. 49–62.

[36] Cramér, H. (1946), *Mathematical Methods of Statistics.* Princeton University Press, Princeton N.J.

[37] ——— (1937), *Random Variables and Probability Distributions*, Cambridge Univ. Press.

[38] Dantzig, G.B. and Wald, A. (1951), On the fundamental lemma of Neyman and Pearson. *Ann. Math. Stat.*, **22**, pp. 87–93.

[39] Darling, D.A. (1957), The Kolmogorov-Smirnov, Cramer-Von Mises tests, *Ann. Math. Stat.*, **28**, pp. 823–838.

[40] David, F.N. (1947), A power function for tests for randomness in a sequence of alternatives, *Biometrika*, **34**, pp. 335–339.

[41] David, H.T. (1952), Discrete populations and the Kolmogorov-Smirnov tests, *Univ. Chicago Statist. Res. Center. Rept.*, SRC 21103D27.

[42] Dawid, A.P. (1975), On the concepts of sufficiency and ancillarity in the presence of nuisance parameters. *J. Roy. Statist. Soc.*, B37, pp. 248–258.

[43] Drion, E.F. (1952), Some distribution free tests for the difference between two empirical cumulative distributions, *Ann. Math. Stat.*, **23**, pp. 563–574.

[44] Dvoretzky, A., Kiefer, J. and Wolfowitz, J. (1953), Sequential decision problems for processes with continuous time parameter in testing hypotheses. *Ann. Math. Stat.*, **24**, pp. 254–264.

[45] Dvoretzky, A., Wald, A. and Wolfowitz, J. (1951), Elimination of randomization in certain statistical decision procedures and zero-sum two-person games. *Ann. Math. Stat.*, **22**, pp. 1–21.

[46] Edgeworth, F.Y. (1885), *Methods of Statistics*, Jubilee volume of the statist. Soc. Stanford, London.

[47] Engelhardt, M. and Bain, L.J. (1977), Uniformly most powerful unbiased tests on the scale parameter of a gamma distribution with a nuisance shape parameter. *Technometrics.*, **19**, pp. 77–81.

[48] ——— (1978), Construction of optimal unbiased inference procedures for the parameters of the gamma distribution. *Technometrics.*, **20**, pp. 485–489.

[49] Falk, M. and Kohne, W. (1984), A robustification of the sign test under mixing conditions. *Ann. Math. Stat.*, **12**, pp. 716–729.

[50] Feller, W. (1950), *Introduction to Probability Theory*, John Wiley and Sons.

[51] ——— (1957), *An Introduction to Probability Theory and Its Applications*, **1**, 2nd ed., Wiley, New York.

[52] ——— (1968), *An Introduction to Probability Theory and Its Applications*, **1**, 3rd ed., John Wiley, New York.

[53] ——— (1971), *An Introduction to Probability Theory and Its Applications*, **2**, 2nd ed., John Wiley, New York.

[54] Ferguson, T.S. (1967), *Mathematical Statistics: A Decision Theoretic Approach*, Academic Press, New York.

[55] Fisher, R.A. (1920), A mathematical examination of the methods of determining the accuracy of an observation by the mean error and by the mean square error. *Monthly Notices Roy. Astron. Soc.*, **80**, pp. 758–770.

[56] ——— (1922), On the mathematical foundations of theoretical statistics, *Phil. Trans. Roy. Soc. Ser.*, A 222, pp. 309–368.

[57] ——— (1925), Theory of statistical estimation. *Proc. Cambridge Phil. Soc.*, **22**, pp. 700–725.

[58] ——— (1925), *Statistical Methods for Research Workers*, (14th ed. 1970), Oliver and Boyd, Edinburgh.

[59] ——— (1930), Inverse Probability. *Proc. Cambridge Phil. Soc.*, **26**, pp. 528–535.

[60] ——— (1934), *Statistical Methods for Research Workers*, 5th and subsequent eds., Oliver and Boyd, Edinburgh.

[61] ——— (1956), *Statistical Methods and Scientific Inference.*, Oliver and Boyd, Edinburgh, (3rd ed. 1973), Hafner, New York.

[62] Fisz, M. (1963), *Probability Theory and Mathematical Statistics*, 3rd ed., John Wiley, New York.

[63] Fraser, D.A.S. (1953), Non-parametric theory: Scale and Location parameters. *Canad. J. Math.*, **6**, pp. 46–48.

[64] Fraser, D.A.S. (1956), Sufficient statistics with nuisance parameters, *Ann. Math. Statist.*, **27**, pp. 838–842.

[65] ——— (1965), *Non-parametric Methods of Statistics*, John Wiley, New York.

[66] ——— (1957), *Non-parametric Methods in Statistics* , John Wiley, New York.

[67] ——— (1978), Fiducial inference. In internat, *Encycl. of statistics*, **1**, Free Press, New York.

[68] Ghosh, B.K. (1970), *Sequential Tests of Statistical Hypotheses*, Addison-Wesley, Reading, Mass.

[69] Ghosh, J.K., Morimoto, H. and Yamada, S. (1981), Neyman factorization and minimality of pairwise sufficient subfields. *Ann. Math. Statist.*, **9**, pp. 514–530.

[70] Ghosh, M.N. (1948), On the problems of similar regions.*Sankhya*, **8**, pp. 329–338.

[71] Gibbons, J.D. (1971), *Nonparametric Inference*, McGraw-Hill, New York.

[72] ——— and Pratt, J.W. (1975), P-values: Interpretation and methodology. *Amer. Statist.*, **29**, pp. 20–24.

[73] Godambe, V.P. (1980), On sufficiency and ancillarity in the presence of a nuisance parameter. *Biometrika.*, **67**, pp. 155–162.

[74] Goodman, L.A. (1954), Kolmogorov-Smirnov tests for psychological research. *Pychological Bill.*, **51**, pp. 160–168.

[75] Greenwald, A.G. (1975), Consequences of prejudice against the null hypothesis. *Psych.Bull.*, **82**, pp. 1–20.

[76] Guenther, W.C. (1969), Shortest Confidence Interval *Ann. Stat.*, **23**, No. 1, pp. 22–25.

[77] ——— (1971), Unbiased Confidence Interval *Ann. Stat.*, **25**, No. 1, pp. 51–53.

[78] Gupta, G., Gupta, D. and Goon, A.M. (1985), *An Outline of Statistical theory*, The world Press Pvt. Ltd., Calcutta.

[79] Hall, I.J. and Kudo, A. (1968), On slippage tests-(I) A generalization of Neyman-Pearson's lemma, *Ann. Math. Statist.*, **39**, pp. 2029–2039.

[80] Hall, P. (1982), Improving the normal approximation when constructing one-sided confidence intervals for binomial or poisson parameters. *Biometrika*, **69**, pp. 647–652.

[81] Hall, W.J., Wijsman, R.A. and Ghosh J.K. (1965), The relationship between sufficiency and invariance with applications in sequential analysis, *Ann. Math. Statist.*, **36**, pp. 575–614.

[82] Halmos, P.R. and Savage, L.J. (1948), Application of the Radon-Nikodym theorem to the theory of sufficient statistics, *Ann. Math. Statist*, **20**, pp. 225–241.

[83] Halmos, P.R. (1950), *Measure Theory*, D. Van Nostrand Co, New York.

[84] Halmos, P. (1974), *Measure Theory*, Springer, New York.

[85] Harris, B. and Soms, A.P. (1973), On testing for sufficiency, *Ann. Stat.*, **27**, p. 192.

[86] Hipp, C. (1974), Sufficient statistics and exponential families. *Ann. Stat.*, **2**, pp. 1283–1292.

[87] Hodges, J.L., Jr (1958), The significance probability of Smirnov two-sample test, *Arkiv Mat.*, **3**, pp. 469–486.

[88] Hoeffding, W. (1951), Optimum non-parametric tests. *Proc. 2nd Berkeley Symp. on Math. Statist. and Prob.*, 83–92. University of California Press, Berkeley.

[89] Hoeffding, W. and Robbins, H. (1948), The central limit theorem for dependent random variables, *Duke Math. J.*, **15**, p. 773.

[90] Hoeffding, W. (1948), A class of statistics with asymptotically normal distribution, *Ann. Math. Stat.*, **19**, p. 293.

[91] ——— (1951), A combinatorial central limit theorem, *Ann. Math. Stat.*, **22**, p. 558.

[92] ——— (1952), The large sample power of tests based on permutations of observations, *Ann. Math. Stat.*, **23**, pp. 169–192.

[93] Hoel, P.G. (1945), Testing the homogeneity of Poisson frequencies.*Ann. Math. Statist.* **16**, pp. 362–368.

[94] Johnson, N.L. and Kotz, S. (1969), *Distributions in statistics: Discrete Distributions*, Houghton Mi²in, New York.

[95] ——— (1970), *Distributions in Statistics: Continuous Univariate Distributiions,* **1**, Houghton Mifflin, Boston.

[96] Johansen, S. (1979), *Introduction to Theory of Regular Exponential Families*, Lecture Notes, No. 3, Inst. of Math. Stat., Univ. of Copenhagen.

[97] Karlin, S. (1955), Decision Theory for Polya type distributions, case of two actions. I. In Proc. Third *Berkeley Symposium on Mathematical Statistics and Probability*, 1, Univ. of Calif. Press, Berkeley, pp. 115–129.

[98] Karlin, S. (1957), Polya type distributions II. *Ann. Math. Statist.*, **28**, 281–308. [Properties of TP distributions.

[99] ——— (1968), *Total Positivity.* I, Stanford U.P. Stanford, Calif.

[100] Karlin, S. (1957b), Polya type distributions III: Admissibility for multiaction problems, *Ann. Math. Statist.*, **28**, pp. 839–860.

[101] ——— (1959), *Mathematical Methods and Theory in Games, Programming and Economics*, Vols. 1 and 2. Addison-Wesley, Reading, Mass.

[102] ——— and Rubbin, H. (1956), The theory of decision procedures for distributions with monotone likelihood ratio, *Ann. Math. Statist.*, **27**, pp. 272–299.
[General theory of families with monotone likelihood ratio. For further developments of this theory, see Brown, Cohen and Strawderman (1976).]

[103] ——— and Truax D.R. (1960), Slippage problems, *Ann. Math. Statist.*, **31**, pp. 296–323.

[104] Kendall, M.G. (1962), *Rank Correlation Methods*, 3rd ed., Griffin, London.

[105] Kolmogorov, A. (1933), Sulla determinazione empiria di una leggc di distribuzione, Giorn. Inst. Ital. Attuari., **4**, pp. 83–91.

[106] Kolmogorov, A.N. and Fomin, S.V. (1961), *Elements of the Theory of Functions and Functional Analysis*, **2**, Graylock Press, Albany, N.Y.

[107] Kruskal, W.H. (1978), *Tests of Significance,* In International Encyclopedia of statistics, Free Press and Macmillan, New York and London.

[108] Kulldorf, G. (1957), On the conditions for consistency and asymptotic efficiency of maximum likelihood estimates, *Skand. Aktuarietidskr*, **40**, pp. 129-144.

[109] Lambert, D. and Hall, W.J. (1982), Asymptotic lognormality of P-values. *Ann. Statist.*, **10**, pp. 44–64.

[110] LeCam, L. (1964), Sufficiency and approximate sufficiency. *Ann. Math. Stat.*, **35**, pp. 1419–1455.

[111] Lehmann, E.L. (1947), On families of admissible tests. *Ann. Math. Stat.*, **18**, pp. 97–104.
[Introduction of the complete class concept in connection with a special class of testing problems.]

[112] ——— (1947), On optimum tests of composite hypotheses with one constrains. *Ann. Math. Stat.*, **18**, pp. 473–494.
[Determines best similar regions for a number of problems.]

[113] Lehmann, E.L. and Stein, C. (1948), Most powerful tests of composite hypotheses. *Ann. Math. Stat.*, **19**, pp. 495–516.

[114] Lehmann, E.L. and Stein, C. (1949), On the theory of some non-parametric hypotheses. constraint, *Ann. Math. Stat.*, **20**, pp. 28–45.
[Develops the theory of optimum permutation tests.]

[115] Lehmann, E.L. (1950), Some principles of the theory of testing hypothesis. *Ann. Math. Stat.*, **21**, pp. 1–26.

[116] ——— (1951), A general concept of unbiasedness. *Ann. Math. Stat.*, **22**, pp. 587–597.

[117] ——— (1951), Consistency and unbiasedness of certain nonparametric tests, *Ann. Math. Stat.*, **22**, p. 165.

[118] ——— (1952), Testing multiparameter hypotheses. *Ann. Math. Stat.*, **23**, pp. 541–552.

[119] ——— (1952), On the existence of least favorable distributions. *Ann. Math. Stat.*, **23**, pp. 408–416.

[120] ——— (1955), Ordered families of distributions. *Ann. Math. Stat.*, **26**, pp. 399–419.

[121] ——— (1957), A Theory of some multiple decision procedures. *Ann. Math. Stat.*, **28**, pp. 1–25, pp. 547–572.

[122] ——— (1958), Significance level and power. *Ann. Math. Stat.*, **29**, pp. 1167–1176.

[123] ——— (1959), *Testing Statistical Hypotheses.* Wiley, New York.

[124] ——— (1961), Some model I problems of section. *Ann. Math. Stat.*, **32**, pp. 990–1012.

[125] ——— (1966), Some concepts of dependence. *Ann. Math. Stat.*, **37**, pp. 1137–1153.

[126] ——— (1975), *Nonparametrics: Statistical Methods Based on Ranks*, Holden-Day, San Francisco.

[127] ——— (1980), An interpretation of completeness and Basu's theorem. *J. Amer. Statist. Assoc.*, **76**, pp. 335–340.

[128] ——— (1984), Specification Problems in The Neymann-Pearson-Wald Theory. In Statistics: An Appraisal (David and David, eds.), Iowa State Univ. Press, Ames.

[129] ——— (1985), *The Neyman-Pearson Theory after 50 years.* In proc. Neymann-Keifer Confrence (LeCam and Olshen, eds.), Wadsworth, Belmont, Cal.

[130] ——— (1986), *Testing Statistical Hypotheses.* Wiley, New York, pp. 58–59.

[131] ——— and C. Stein (1950), Completeness in the sequential case. *Ann. Math. Statist.*, **21**, pp. 376–385.

[132] ——— and Scheffe, H. (1950, 1955), Completeness, similar regions and unbiased estimation, *Sankhya.* **10**, pp. 305-340, and **15**, pp. 219–236.

[133] Lindley, D.V. (1957), A statistical paradox. *Biometrika.*, **44**, pp. 187–192.

[134] Loéve, M. (1963), *Probability Theory*, 3rd ed. Van Nostrand, Princeton, N.J.

[135] ——— (1977–78), *Probability Theory*, 4th ed. (2 vols.), Springer, Berlin.

[136] Mann, H.B. (1945), Nonparametric tests against trend, *Econometrica*, **13**, p. 245.

[137] ——— and Whitney, D.R. (1947), On a test whether one of the two random variables is stochastically larger than other. *Ann. Math. Statist.*, **18**, pp. 50–60.

[138] Massy, I.J. (1951), The distribution of the maximum deviation between two sample cummulative slip function, *Ann. Math.Statist.*, **22**, pp. 125–128.

[139] ——— (1952), Distribution table for the deviation between two-sample derivatives, *Ann. Math. Statist.*, **23**, pp. 435–441.

[140] Michel, R. (1979), On the asymptotic efficiency of conditional tests for exponential families. *Ann. Math. Stat.*, **7**, pp. 1256–1263.

[141] Monroe, M.V.E., *Introduction to Measure and Integration*, Addison and Wesley.

[142] Mood, A.M. (1940), The distribution theory of runs. *Ann. Math. Stat.*, **11**, p. 367.

[143] ——— (1950), Introduction to the Theory of Statistics, McGraw-Hill Book company, New York, pp. 394–406.

[144] ——— (1954), On the asymptotic efficiency of certain nonparametric two sample tests. *Ann. Math. Statist.*, **25**, pp. 514–522.

[145] Nair, U.S. (1936), The standard error of Gini's mean difference, *Biometrika*, **28**, p. 428.

[146] Neyman, J. and Pearson, E.S. (1933), On the problem of the most efficient tests of statistical hypotheses, *Phil. Trans. Roy. Soc.*, A231, pp. 289–337. [Introduces the concept of similarity and develops a methods for determining the totality of similar regions.]

[147] ——— (1936, 1938). Contributions to the theory of testing statistical hypotheses.*Statist. Res. Mem.*, **1**, pp. 1–37; **2**, pp. 25–57.
[Defines unbiased and determines both locally and UMP unbiased tests of certain classes of simple hypotheses.]

[148] Neyman, J. (1937), Outline of a theory of statistical estimation based on the classical theory of probability. *Phil. Trans. Roy. Soc. Ser.* A236, pp. 333–380.
[Develops the theory of optimum confidence sets so that it reduces to the determination of optimum tests of associated classes of hypotheses.]

[149] Neyman, J. (1938), L'estimation statistique traitee comme un probleme classique de probabilite, *Actualites Sci. et. Ind.*, **739**, pp. 25–57.

[150] ——— (1941), Fiducial argument and the theory of confidence intervals. *Biometrika.*, **32**, pp. 128–150.

[151] ——— (1952), *Lectures and Conference on Mathematical Statistics*, 2nd ed. Washington Graduate School, U.S. Dept. of Agriculture, **43–66**. [An account of various approaches to the problem of hypothesis testing.]

[152] Neyman, J. and Pearson, E.S. (1928), On the use and interpretation of certain test criteria, *Biometrika*, A20, pp. 175–240, pp. 263–294.

[153] ——— (1933), On the problem of the most efficient tests of the statistical hypotheses. *Phil. Trans. Roy. Soc. Ser.* A231, pp. 289–337. [The basic paper on the theory of hypothesis testing. Formulates the problem in terms if the two kinds of errors, and develops a body of theory including the fundamental lemma.]

[154] ——— (1936a), Contributions to the theory of testing statistical hypotheses I. Unbiased Critical Regions of Type A and Type $A1$. *Statist. Res. Mem.*, **1**, pp. 1–37.
[Generalization of the fundamental lemma to more than one side condition.]

[155] ——— (1936b), Sufficient statistics and uniformly most powerful test of statistical hypotheses. *statist. Res. Mem.*, **1**, pp. 113–137.

[156] Noether, G.E. (1967), *Elements of Nonparametric Statistics*, John Wiley & Sons, Inc., New york.

[157] ——— (1949), On a theorem by Wald and Wolfowitz, *Ann. Math. Stat.*, **20**, p. 455.

[158] Owen, D.B. (1962), *Handbook of Statistical Tables*, Addison-Wesley Publishing Copmany, Inc., Reading, Mass.

[159] Pachares, J. (1961), Tables for unbiased tests on the variance of a normal population. *Ann. Math. Statist.*, **32**, pp. 84–87.

[160] Pfanzagl, J. (1967), A technical lemma for monotone likelihood ratio families. *Ann. Math. Statist.*, **38**, pp. 611–613.

[161] ——— (1968). A characterization of the one parameter exponential family by existence of uniformly most powerful tests. *Sankhya*, A30, pp. 147–156.

[162] Pitman, E.J.G. (1939), The estimation of location and scale parameters of a continuous population of any given form. *Biometrika.*, **30**, pp. 391–421.

[163] Pratt, J.W. (1961), Length of confidence intervals, *J. Am. Stat. Assoc.*, **56**, pp. 260–272.

[164] Pratt, J.W. (1962), A note on unbiased tests. *Ann. Math. Statist.*, **33**, pp. 292–294.

[165] Pearson, K. (1900), On the criterion that a given system of deviations from the probable in the case of a correlated system of variables is such that it can reasonably be supposed to have arisen in random sampling, *Phil. Mag.*, **50**, pp. 157–175.

[166] Pearson, E.S. (1966), The Neyman-Pearson story: 1926-1934. In *research papers in statistics: Festschrift for J. Neyman* (F. N. David, Ed.), Wiley, New York.

[167] Pratt, J.W. and Gibbons, J.D. (1981), *Concepts of Nonparametric Theory*, Springer, New York.

[168] Przyborowski, J. and Wilenski, H. (1939), Homogeneity of results in testing samples from Poisson series.*Biometrika.*, **31**, pp. 313–323.

[169] Putter, J. (1955), The treatment of tie in some nonparametric tests.*Ann. Math. Statist.*, **26**, pp. 368–386.
[Discusses the treatment of ties in the sign test.]

[170] Raiffa, H. and Schlaifer R. (1961), *Applied Statistical Decision Theory.* Graduate School of Business Administration, Harvard.

[171] Rao, C.R. (1965), *Linear Statistical Inference and Its Applications*, John Wiley, New York.

[172] ——— (1945), Information and accuracy attainable in estimation of statistical parameters. *Bull. Calcutta Math. Soc.*, **37**, pp. 81–91.

[173] Reid, C. (1982), *Neyman from Life*, Springer, New York.

[174] Robinson, G.K. (1976), Properties of student's t and of the Behrens-Fisher solution to the two means problem.*Ann. Math. Statist.*, **4**, pp. 963–971.

[175] Rojo, J. (1983), *On Lehmann's General Concept of Unbiasedness and Some of Its Applications*, Ph.D. Thesis, Univ. California, Berkeley.

[176] Royden, H.L. (1963), *Real Analysis*, Macmillan, New York.

[177] Ruben, H. (1954), On the moments of order statistics in samples from normal populations, *Biometrika*, **41**, pp. 200–227.

[178] Rudin, W.C. (1976), *Principle of Mathematical Analysis*,3rd ed., McGraw-Hill, Kogakusha Ltd., Tokyo.

[179] Sanathanan, L. (1974), Critical power function decision making. *J. Amer. Statist. Assoc.*, **69**, pp. 398–402.

[180] Sarhan, A.E. and Greenberg, B.G. (1962), *Contributions to Order Statistics*, John Wiley and Sons, Inc.; New york.

[181] Savage, L.J. (1954), *The Foundations of Statistics.* Wiley, New York.

[182] Savage, L.J. (1962), *The Foundations of Statistical Inference*, Methuen, London.

[183] ——— (1976), On Rereading R.A. Fisher (with discussion). *Ann. Math. Statist.*, **4**, pp. 441–500.

[184] Savage, I.R. (1962), *Bibliography of Nonparametric Statistics*, Harvard University Press, Cambridge, Mass.

[185] Schafer, G. (1982), Lindley's paradox(with discussions) *J. Amer. Statist. Assoc.*, **77**, pp. 325–351.

[186] Scheffé, H. (1943), On a measure problem arising in the theory of non-parametric tests.*Ann. Math. Statist.*, **14**, pp. 227–233. [Proves the completeness of order statistics.]

[187] ——— (1947), A useful convergence theorem for probability distributions, *Ann. Math. Stat.*, **18**, pp. 434–438.

[188] ——— (1959), *The Analysis of Variance.* Wiley, New York.

[189] ——— (1970), Practical solutions of the Behrens-Fisher problem. *J. Amer. Statist. Assoc.*, **65**, pp. 1501–1508.

[190] Scholz, F.W. (1982), Combining independent P-values .In A *Festschrift for Erich*L. Lehmann (Bickel, Doksum, and Hodges, eds.) Wadsworth, Belmont, Calif.

[191] Serffing, R.J. (1980), *Approximation Theorems of Mathematical Statistics*, Wiley, New York.

[192] Siegel, S. (1956), *Nonparametric Statistics for the Behavioral Sciences*, McGraw-Hill Book Company, New York.

[193] Smirnov, N.V. (1935), Uber die verteilung des allgemeinen gliedes in der variationsreihe, *Metron*, **12**, pp. 59–81.

[194] ——— (1936), Sur la distribution de–2, *Compt. Rend.*, **202**, pp. 449–452.

[195] ——— (1939), On the estimation of the discrepancy between empirical curves of distributions for two independent samples (in Russian), *Bull. Moscow Univ.*, **2**, pp. 3–16.

[196] ——— (1939), Estimate of deviation between empirical distribution functions in two independent samples (In Russian). *Bull. Moscow Univ.*, **2**, pp. 3–16.

[197] ——— (1948), Table for estimating the goodness of fit of empirical distributions, *Ann. Math. Stat.*, **19**, pp. 279–281.

[198] Sterling, T.D. (1959), Publication decision and thier possible effects on inference drawn from tests of significance-or vice versa. *J. Amer. Statist. Assoc.*, **54**, pp. 30–34.

[199] Sverdrup, E. (1953), Similarity, unbiasedness, minimaxibility and admissibility of statistical test procedures.*Skand. Aktuar. Tidskrift.*, **36**, 64–86.

[200] Tate, R.F. and Klett, G.W. (1959), Optimum confidence intervals for the variance of a normal distribution, *J. Am. Stat. Assoc.*, **54**, pp. 674–682.

[201] Tate, M.W. and Clelland, R.C. (1957), *Nonparametric and Shortcut Statistics*, The Interstate Publishers and Printers, Danville, III.

[202] Terry, M.E. (1952), Some rank order tests which are most powerful against specific parametric alternatives, *Ann. Math. Stat.*, **23**, pp. 346–366.

[203] Tucker, H.G. (1962), *An Introduction to Probability and Mathematical Statistics.* Academic Press, New York.

[204] Uspensky, J.V. (1937), *Introduction to Mathematical Probability*, McGraw-Hill Book Co., New York.

[205] Waerden, B.L. Van der (1952, 1953), Order test for the two sample problem and their power. ,I, II, III *Indagationes Math.*, 14, [*Proc. Koninkl. Ned. Akad. Wetenschap.* 55]: 453–458; *Indag.* 15 [*Proc.* 56]: 303–310, 311–316; correction, *Indag.* 15 [*Proc.* 56] : 80.

[206] Wald, A. (1950), *Statistical Decision Functions.* Wiley, New York.

[207] ——— and Wolfowitz, J. (1940), On a test whether two samples are from the same population, *Ann. Math. Stat.*, **11**, pp. 147–162.

[208] ——— (1944), Statistical tests based on permutations of the observations, *Ann. Math. Stat.*, **15**, p. 358.

[209] ——— (1948), Optimum character of the Sequencial Probability Ratio Test., *Ann. Math. Stat.*, **19**, pp. 326–339.

[210] Walsh, J.E. (1949), Some significance tests for the median which are valid under very general conditions, *Ann. Math. stat.*, **20**, pp. 64–81.

[211] Wolfowitz, J. (1943), On the theory of runs with some applications to quality control, *Ann. Math. Stat.*, **14**, pp. 280 288.

[212] Wilcoxon, F. (1945), Individual comparisons by ranking methods, *Biomctrics*, **1**, pp. 80 83.

[213] ——— (1947), Probability tables for individual comparisons by ranking methods, *Biometrics*, **3**, pp. 119–122.

[214] ——— (1949), *Some Rapid Approximate Statistical Procedures*, American Cyanamid Company, Stanford Research Laboratories, Standford, Calif.

[215] Wilks, S.S. (1962), *Mathematical Statistics.* Wiley, New York.

[216] Wolfowitz, J. (1942), Additive partition functions and a class of statistical hypotheses, *Ann. Math. Stat.*, **13**, p. 247.

[217] ——— (1944a), Asymptotic distribution of runs up and down, *Ann. Math. Stat.*, **15**, pp. 163–172.

[218] Wolfowitz, J. (1944b), Note on runs of consecutive elements, *Ann. Math. Stat.*, **15**, pp. 97–98.

[219] ——— (1949), *Non-parametric Statistical Inference*, in J. Neyman (ed.), *Proc. Berkeley Symp. Math. Statistics Probability,* pp. 93–113.

[220] Zacks, S. (1971), *The Theory of Statistical Inference*, John Wiley, New York.

[221] ——— and Savage I.R. (1958), Asymptotic normality efficiency of certain nonparametric test statistics, *Ann. Math. Stat.*, **29**, pp. 972–994.

# STATISTICAL INFERENCE
# Testing of Hypotheses

**Manoj Kr. Srivastava**
Associate Professor, Department of Statistics
Institute of Social Sciences
Dr. B.R. Ambedkar University
Agra

**Namita Srivastava**
Associate Professor, Department of Statistics
St. John's College
Agra

**PHI Learning Private Limited**
Delhi-110092
2025

*In fond memory of* ***Shri Asoke K. Ghosh*** *(October 1942 – February 2024), Founder Chairman and Managing Director of PHI Learning, whose vision endlessly inspires.*

*The Legacy Continues....*

Published by Pushpita Ghosh, PHI Learning Private Limited, Rimjhim House, 111, Patparganj Industrial Estate, Delhi-110092 and Printed by Syndicate Binders, A-20, Hosiery Complex, Noida, Phase-II Extension, Noida-201305 (N.C.R. Delhi).

**₹850.00**

**STATISTICAL INFERENCE: TESTING OF HYPOTHESES**
Manoj Kumar Srivastava and Namita Srivastava

© 2025 by PHI Learning Private Limited, Delhi.

All right reserved. This publication is protected by copyright and may not be reproduced, in whole or in part, in any form or by any electronic, mechanical, or other means, now known or hereafter invented, including photocopying, recording, or any information storage and retrieval system, OR to train artificial intelligence systems without permission in writing from the publisher.

**ISBN-978-81-203-3728-2 (Print Book)**
**ISBN-978-93-5443-785-4 (e-Book)**

The export rights of the book are vested solely with the publisher.

Note in the theorem, the set functions $\nu_c$ and $\nu_s$ on $\mathcal{C}$ have been defined as

$$\nu_c(E) = \int_E f\, d\mu, \quad \nu_s(E) = \nu(E) - \nu_c(E)$$

**Definition 1.2.8.** (**Radon-Nikodym Derivative**) The integrand $f$ in $\nu(E) = \int_E f d\mu$ defined in $\nu_c$ is called the derivative of $\nu$ with respect $\mu$, and is denoted by $f = d\nu/d\mu$. In this, the finite measurable function $f$ is called the Radon-Nikodym derivative of $\nu$ with respect to $\mu$, and written as $f = d\nu/d\mu$.

We shall now state the famous Radon-Nikodym Theorem.

**Theorem 1.2.5.** (**Radon-Nikodym Theorem**) *Let us consider the measure space* $(\mathcal{L}, \mathcal{C}, \mu)$ *with* $\mu$ *as a* $\sigma$*-finite measure and* $\nu$ *a completely additive* $\sigma$*-finite set function on* $\mathcal{C}$. *If* $\nu$ *is* $\mu$*-continuous then* $\nu$ *is indefinite integral with respect to* $\mu$ *of a finite measurable function determined up to* $\mu$*-equivalence.*

Complete characterization of indefinite integral of a finite measurable function $f$ with respect to a $\sigma$-finite measure $\mu$ on the measure space $(\mathcal{L}, \mathcal{C}, \mu)$ is given in Theorem 1.2.6.

**Theorem 1.2.6.** *Given a measure space* $(\mathcal{L}, \mathcal{C}, \mu)$ *and a* $\sigma$*-finite measure* $\mu$ *on* $\mathcal{C}$, *a set function* $\nu$ *on* $\mathcal{C}$ *is the indefinite integral of a finite measurable function* $f$ *(determined upto* $\mu$*-equivalence), if and only if* $\nu$ *is* $\sigma$*-finite,* $\sigma$*-additive and* $\mu$*-continuous.*

Another important result is given as follows:

**Theorem 1.2.7.** *Let* $\mu$ *and* $\nu$ *be two* $\sigma$*-finite measures on the measure space* $(\mathcal{L}, \mathcal{C}, \mu)$ *and* $\nu$ *has been given to be* $\mu$*-continuous. If* $f$ *is a measurable function for which* $\int f d\mu$ *exists almost everywhere on* $\mathcal{C}$, *then*

$$\int_A f\, d\nu = \int_A (f \cdot \frac{d\nu}{d\mu})\, d\mu$$

### 1.2.3 Lebesgue-Stieltjes Integral

Let us consider a class of intervals on the real line,

$$\mathcal{I} = \{(a, b] \ : \ -\infty < a < b < \infty\}$$

and $F$ as a distribution function defined as $F : \mathbb{R}^1 \to \mathbb{R}^1$. Let $\mathcal{H}$ be a field generated by the class $\mathcal{I}$. Define a set function $\psi$ on $\mathcal{I}$ by

$$\psi(a, b] = F(b) - F(a)$$

Every set $A$ in $\mathcal{H}$ can be expressed as disjoint countable union of intervals in $\mathcal{I}$, $A = \cup_{n=1}^{\infty} E_n$ where $\{E_n\}$ is a disjoint sequence in $\mathcal{I}$. Define a set function $\mu$ on $\mathcal{H}$ by

$$\mu(A) = \sum_{n=1}^{\infty} \psi(E_n)$$

It can easily be seen that $\mu$ is a measure on $\mathcal{H}$ and agrees with $\psi$ (i.e. $\mu = \psi$) on $\mathcal{I}$. By definition of $\psi$, the measure $\mu$, by the extension theorem, could be extended to a unique measure $\mu_0$ on the $\sigma$-field (the Borel field $\mathcal{B}$ in $\mathbb{R}^1$) generated by $\mathcal{H}$. This measure is called induced measure by distribution function $F$. Let the Borel field $\mathcal{B}$ be completed by the measure $\mu_0$, the completion field be denoted by $\mathcal{B}_{\mu_0}$, then $\mathcal{B}_{\mu_0}$ is called *Lebesgue-Stieltjes field in* $\mathbb{R}^1$, and the complete measure on the completion $\mathcal{B}_{\mu_0}$ denoted by $\mu^*$ is called *Lebesgue-Stieltjes measure.* The measure space may now be denoted by $(\mathcal{H}, \mathcal{B}_{\mu_0}, \mu^*)$. Consider a measurable function $f$ over sets in $\mathcal{B}_{\mu_0}$. Consider a set $E$ in $\mathcal{B}_{\mu_0}$; $E$ is called as *Lebesgue-Stieltjes set.* Such a set $E$ may be an interval $(a, b)$ with division points $x_1, x_2, \ldots, x_{n-1}$ such that $a < x_1 < x_2 \cdots < x_{n-1} < b$. Define the sum

$$\begin{aligned} J_n &= \sum_{i=1}^{n} f(y_i)\, \mu^*(x_{i-1}, x_i) \\ &= \sum_{i=1}^{n} f(y_i)\, [F(x_i) - F(x_{i-1}] \end{aligned}$$

for any arbitrary point $y_i \in (x_{i-1}, x_i)$, $x_0 = a$, $x_n = b$. If lengths of each subdivision tends to 0 as $n \to \infty$

$$\int_E f\, dF = \lim_{n\to\infty} J_n$$

is called *Lebesgue-Stieltjes integral of f* over a Lebesgue-Stieltjes set $E$ in $\mathcal{B}_{\mu_0}$. The improper integral is defined as

$$\int f\, dF = \lim_{\substack{a\to-\infty,\\ b\to+\infty}} \int_{E\equiv(a,b)} f\, dF$$

### Riemann integral as a special case

We know that the Lebesgue-Stieltjes measure induced by the distribution function $F(x) = x$ is called *Lebesgue measure.* The corresponding measure space is denoted by $(\mathcal{H}, \mathcal{B}_{\mu_0}, \mu^*)$, where $\mu^*$ is the complete measure on the completion $\mathcal{B}_{\mu_0}$. Consider a measurable function $f$ which is bounded and continuous almost everywhere with respect to the Lebesgue measure $\mu^*$. Define the sum

$$\begin{aligned} J_n &= \sum_{i=1}^{n} f(y_i)\, \mu^*(x_{i-1}, x_i) \\ &= \sum_{i=1}^{n} f(y_i)\, (x_i - x_{i-1}) \end{aligned}$$

Then $$\int_a^b f(x)\, dx = \lim_{n\to\infty} J_n$$

# Index